P9-BJU-412

Operating Systems
Principles and Practice

Second Edition

Thomas Anderson

University of Washington

Michael Dahlin

University of Texas at Austin and Google

Recursive Books

recursivebooks.com

Operating Systems: Principles and Practice (Second Edition) by Thomas Anderson and Michael Dahlin

Copyright ©Thomas Anderson and Michael Dahlin, 2011-2014.

ISBN 978-0-9856735-2-9

Publisher:	Recursive Books, Ltd.
	http://recursivebooks.com/
Cover:	Reflection Lake, Mt. Ranier
Cover design:	Cameron Neat
Illustrations:	Cameron Neat
Copy editors:	Sandy Kaplan, Whitney Schmidt
Printer:	CreateSpace

SUGGESTIONS, COMMENTS, and ERRORS. We welcome suggestions, comments and error reports, by email to suggestions@recursivebooks.com

To Robin, Sandra, Katya, and Adam

Tom Anderson

To Marla, Kelly, and Keith

Mike Dahlin

Contents

7   Scheduling   313

Part III   Memory Management

8   Address Translation   371

9   Caching and Virtual Memory   421

10   Advanced Memory Management   465

Part IV   Persistent Storage

Preface

Why We Wrote This Book

Many of our students tell us that operating systems was the best course they took as an undergraduate and also the most important for their careers. We are not alone — many of our colleagues report receiving similar feedback from their students.

Part of the excitement is that the core ideas in a modern operating system — protection, concurrency, virtualization, resource allocation, and reliable storage — have become widely applied throughout computer science, not just operating system kernels. Whether you get a job at Facebook, Google, Microsoft, or any other leading-edge technology company, it is impossible to build resilient, secure, and flexible computer systems without the ability to apply operating systems concepts in a variety of settings. In a modern world, nearly everything a user does is distributed, nearly every computer is multi-core, security threats abound, and many applications such as web browsers have become mini-operating systems in their own right.

It should be no surprise that for many computer science students, an undergraduate operating systems class has become a *de facto* requirement: a ticket to an internship and eventually to a full-time position.

Unfortunately, many operating systems textbooks are still stuck in the past, failing to keep pace with rapid technological change. Several widely-used books were initially written in the mid-1980's, and they often act as if technology stopped at that point. Even when new topics are added, they are treated as an afterthought, without pruning material that has become less important. The result are textbooks that are very long, very expensive, and yet fail to provide students more than a superficial understanding of the material.

Our view is that operating systems have changed dramatically over the past twenty years, and that justifies a fresh look at both *how* the material is taught and *what* is taught. The pace of innovation in operating systems has, if anything, increased over the past few years, with the introduction of the iOS and Android operating systems for smartphones, the shift to multicore computers, and the advent of cloud computing.

To prepare students for this new world, we believe students need three things to succeed at understanding operating systems at a deep level:

- **Concepts and code.** We believe it is important to teach students both *principles* and *practice*, concepts and implementation, rather than either alone. This textbook takes concepts all the way down to the level of working code, e.g., how a context switch works in assembly code. In our experience, this is the only way students will really understand and master the material. All of the code in this book is available from the author's web site, www.cs.uw.edu/homes/tom/code.

- **Extensive worked examples.** In our view, students need to be able to apply concepts in practice. To that end, we have integrated a large number of example exercises, along with solutions, throughout the text. We uses these exercises extensively in our own lectures, and we have found them essential to challenging students to go beyond a superficial understanding.

- **Industry practice.** To show students how to apply operating systems concepts in a variety of settings, we use detailed, concrete examples from Facebook, Google, Microsoft, Apple, and other leading-edge technology companies throughout the textbook. Because operating systems concepts are important in a wide range of computer systems, we take these examples not only from traditional operating systems like Linux, Windows, and OS X but also from other systems that need to solve problems of protection, concurrency, virtualization, resource allocation, and reliable storage like databases, web browsers, web servers, mobile applications, and search engines.

Taking a fresh perspective on what students need to know to apply operating systems concepts in practice has led us to innovate in every major topic covered in an undergraduate-level course:

- **Kernels and Processes.** The safe execution of untrusted code has become central to many types of computer systems, from web browsers to virtual machines to operating systems. Yet existing textbooks treat protection as a side effect of UNIX processes, as if they are synonyms. Instead, we start from first principles: what are the minimum requirements for process isolation, how can systems implement process isolation efficiently, and what do students need to know to implement functions correctly when the caller is potentially malicious?

- **Concurrency.** With the advent of multi-core architectures, most students today will spend much of their careers writing concurrent code. Existing textbooks provide a blizzard of concurrency alternatives, most of which were abandoned decades ago as impractical. Instead, we focus on providing students a *single* methodology based on Mesa monitors that will enable students to write correct concurrent programs — a methodology that is by far the dominant approach used in industry.

- **Memory Management.** Even as demand-paging has become less important, virtualization has become even more important to modern computer systems. We provide a deep treatment of address translation hardware, sparse address spaces, TLBs, and on-chip caches. We then use those concepts as a springboard for describing virtual machines and related concepts such as checkpointing and copy-on-write.

- **Persistent Storage.** Reliable storage in the presence of failures is central to the design of most computer systems. Existing textbooks survey the history of file systems, spending most of their time ad hoc approaches to failure recovery and de-fragmentation. Yet no modern file systems still use those ad hoc approaches. Instead, our focus is on how file systems use extents, journaling, copy-on-write, and RAID to achieve both high performance and high reliability.

Intended Audience

Operating Systems: Principles and Practice is a textbook for a first course in undergraduate operating systems. We believe operating systems should be taken as early as possible in an undergraduate's course of study; many students use the course as a springboard to an internship and a career. To that end, we have designed the textbook to assume minimal pre-requisites: specifically, students should have taken a data structures course and one on computer organization. The code examples are written in a combination of x86 assembly, C, and C++. In particular, we have designed the book to interface well with the Bryant and O'Halloran textbook. We review and cover in much more depth the material from the second half of that book.

We should note what this textbook is *not*: it is not intended to teach the API or internals of any specific operating system, such as Linux, Android, Windows 8, OS X, or iOS. We use many concrete examples from these systems, but our focus is on the shared problems these systems face and the technologies these systems use to solve those problems.

A Guide to Instructors

One of our goals is enable instructors to choose an appropriate level of depth for each course topic. Each chapter begins at a conceptual level, with implementation details and the more advanced material towards the end. The more advanced material can be omitted without compromising the ability of students to follow later material. No single-quarter or single-semester course is likely to be able to cover every topic we have included, but we think it is a good thing for students to come away from an operating systems course with an appreciation that there is *always* more to learn.

For each topic, we attempt to convey it at three levels:

- **How to reason about systems.** We describe core systems concepts, such as protection, concurrency, resource scheduling, virtualization, and storage, and we provide practice applying these concepts in various situations. In our view, this provides the biggest long-term payoff to students, as they are likely to need to apply these concepts in their work throughout their career, almost regardless of what project they end up working on.

- **Power tools.** We introduce students to a number of abstractions that they can apply in their work in industry immediately after graduation, and that we expect will continue to be useful for decades such as sandboxing, protected procedure calls, threads, locks, condition variables, caching, checkpointing, and transactions.

- **Details of specific operating systems.** We include numerous examples of how different operating systems work in practice. However, this material changes rapidly, and there is an order of magnitude more material than can be covered in a single semester-length course. The purpose of these examples is to illustrate how to use the operating systems principles and power tools to solve concrete problems. We do not attempt to provide a comprehensive description of Linux, OS X, or any other particular operating system.

The book is divided into five parts: an introduction (Chapter 1), kernels and processes (Chapters 2-3), concurrency, synchronization, and scheduling (Chapters 4-7), memory management (Chapters 8-10), and persistent storage (Chapters 11-14).

- **Introduction.** The goal of Chapter 1 is to introduce the recurring themes found in the later chapters. We define some common terms, and we provide a bit of the history of the development of operating systems.

- **The Kernel Abstraction.** Chapter 2 covers kernel-based process protection—the concept and implementation of executing a user program with restricted privileges. Given the increasing importance of computer security issues, we believe protected execution and safe transfer across privilege levels are worth treating in depth. We have broken the description into sections, to allow instructors to choose either a quick introduction to the concepts (up through Section 2.3), or a full treatment of the kernel implementation details down to the level of interrupt handlers. Some instructors start with concurrency, and cover kernels and kernel protection afterwards. While our textbook can be used that way, we have found that students benefit from a basic understanding of the role of operating systems in executing user programs, before introducing concurrency.

- **The Programming Interface.** Chapter 3 is intended as an impedance match for students of differing backgrounds. Depending on student background, it can be skipped or covered in depth. The chapter covers the operating system from a programmer's perspective: process creation and management, device-independent input/output, interprocess communication, and network sockets. Our goal is that students should understand at a detailed level what happens when a user clicks a link in a web browser, as the request is transferred through operating system kernels and user space processes at the client, server, and back again. This chapter also covers the organization of the operating system itself: how device drivers and the hardware abstraction layer work in a modern operating system; the difference between a monolithic and a microkernel operating system; and how policy and mechanism are separated in modern operating systems.

- **Concurrency and Threads.** Chapter 4 motivates and explains the concept of threads. Because of the increasing importance of concurrent programming, and its integration with modern programming languages like Java, many students have been introduced to multi-threaded programming in an earlier class. This is a bit dangerous, as students at this stage are prone to writing programs with race conditions, problems that may or may not be discovered with testing. Thus, the goal of this chapter is to provide a solid conceptual framework for understanding the semantics of concurrency, as well as how concurrent threads are implemented in both the operating system kernel and in user-level libraries. Instructors needing to go more quickly can omit these implementation details.

- **Synchronization.** Chapter 5 discusses the synchronization of multi-threaded programs, a central part of all operating systems and increasingly important in many other contexts. Our approach is to describe one effective method for structuring concurrent programs (based on Mesa monitors), rather than to attempt to cover several different approaches. In our view, it is more important for students to master one methodology. Monitors are a particularly robust and simple one, capable of implementing most concurrent programs efficiently. The implementation of synchronization primitives should be included if there is time, so students see that there is no magic.

- **Multi-Object Synchronization.** Chapter 6 discusses advanced topics in concurrency — specifically, the twin challenges of multiprocessor lock contention and deadlock. This material is increasingly important for students working on multicore systems, but some courses may not have time to cover it in detail.

- **Scheduling.** This chapter covers the concepts of resource allocation in the specific context of processor scheduling. With the advent of data center computing and multicore architectures, the principles and practice of resource allocation have renewed importance. After a quick tour through the tradeoffs between response time and throughput for uniprocessor scheduling, the chapter covers a set of more advanced topics in affinity and multiprocessor scheduling, power-aware and deadline scheduling, as well as basic queueing theory and overload management. We conclude these topics by walking students through a case study of server-side load management.

- **Address Translation.** Chapter 8 explains mechanisms for hardware and software address translation. The first part of the chapter covers how hardware and operating systems cooperate to provide flexible, sparse address spaces through multi-level segmentation and paging. We then describe how to make memory management efficient with translation lookaside buffers (TLBs) and virtually addressed caches. We consider how to keep TLBs consistent when the operating system makes changes to its page tables. We conclude with a discussion of modern software-based protection mechanisms such as those found in the Microsoft Common Language Runtime and Google's Native Client.

- **Caching and Virtual Memory.** Caches are central to many different types of computer systems. Most students will have seen the concept of a cache in an earlier class on machine structures. Thus, our goal is to cover the theory and implementation of caches: when they work and when they do not, as well as how they are implemented in hardware and software. We then show how these ideas are applied in the context of memory-mapped files and demand-paged virtual memory.

- **Advanced Memory Management.** Address translation is a powerful tool in system design, and we show how it can be used for zero copy I/O, virtual machines, process checkpointing, and recoverable virtual memory. As this is more advanced material, it can be skipped by those classes pressed for time.

- **File Systems: Introduction and Overview.** Chapter 11 frames the file system portion of the book, starting top down with the challenges of providing a useful file abstraction to users. We then discuss the UNIX file system interface, the major internal elements inside a file system, and how disk device drivers are structured.

- **Storage Devices.** Chapter 12 surveys block storage hardware, specifically magnetic disks and flash memory. The last two decades have seen rapid change in storage technology affecting both application programmers and operating systems designers; this chapter provides a snapshot for students, as a building block for the next two chapters. If students have previously seen this material, this chapter can be skipped.

- **Files and Directories.** Chapter 13 discusses file system layout on disk. Rather than survey all possible file layouts — something that changes rapidly over time — we use file systems as a concrete example of mapping complex data structures onto block storage devices.

- **Reliable Storage.** Chapter 14 explains the concept and implementation of reliable storage, using file systems as a concrete example. Starting with the ad hoc techniques used in early file systems, the chapter explains checkpointing and write ahead logging as alternate implementation strategies for building reliable storage, and it discusses how redundancy such as checksums and replication are used to improve reliability and availability.

We welcome and encourage suggestions for how to improve the presentation of the material; please send any comments to the publisher's website, suggestions@recursivebooks.com.

Acknowledgements

We have been incredibly fortunate to have the help of a large number of people in the conception, writing, editing, and production of this book.

We started on the journey of writing this book over dinner at the USENIX NSDI conference in 2010. At the time, we thought perhaps it would take us the summer to complete the first version and perhaps a year before we could declare ourselves done. We were very wrong! It is no exaggeration to say that it would have taken us a lot longer without the help we have received from the people we mention below.

Perhaps most important have been our early adopters, who have given us enormously useful feedback as we have put together this edition:

Carnegie-Mellon	David Eckhardt and Garth Gibson
Clarkson	Jeanna Matthews
Cornell	Gun Sirer
ETH Zurich	Mothy Roscoe
New York University	Laskshmi Subramanian
Princeton University	Kai Li
Saarland University	Peter Druschel
Stanford University	John Ousterhout
University of California Riverside	Harsha Madhyastha
University of California Santa Barbara	Ben Zhao
University of Maryland	Neil Spring
University of Michigan	Pete Chen
University of Southern California	Ramesh Govindan
University of Texas-Austin	Lorenzo Alvisi
Universtiy of Toronto	Ding Yuan
University of Washington	Gary Kimura and Ed Lazowska

In developing our approach to teaching operating systems, both before we started writing and afterwards as we tried to put our thoughts to paper, we made extensive use of lecture notes and slides developed by other faculty. Of particular help were the materials created by Pete Chen, Peter Druschel, Steve Gribble, Eddie Kohler, John Ousterhout, Mothy Roscoe, and Geoff Voelker. We thank them all.

Our illustrator for the second edition, Cameron Neat, has been a joy to work with.

We are also grateful to Lorenzo Alvisi, Adam Anderson, Pete Chen, Steve Gribble, Sam Hopkins, Ed Lazowska, Harsha Madhyastha, John Ousterhout,

Mark Rich, Mothy Roscoe, Will Scott, Gun Sirer, Ion Stoica, Lakshmi Subramanian, and John Zahorjan for their helpful comments and suggestions as to how to improve the book.

We thank Josh Berlin, Marla Dahlin, Sandy Kaplan, John Ousterhout, Whitney Schmidt, and Mike Walfish for helping us identify and correct grammatical or technical bugs in the text.

We thank Jeff Dean, Garth Gibson, Mark Oskin, Simon Peter, Dave Probert, Amin Vahdat, and Mark Zbikowski for their help in explaining the internal workings of some of the commercial systems mentioned in this book.

We would like to thank Dave Wetherall, Dan Weld, Mike Walfish, Dave Patterson, Olav Kvern, Dan Halperin, Armando Fox, Robin Briggs, Katya Anderson, Sandra Anderson, Lorenzo Alvisi, and William Adams for their help and advice on textbook economics and production.

The Helen Riaboff Whiteley Center as well as Don and Jeanne Dahlin were kind enough to lend us a place to escape when we needed to get chapters written.

Finally, we thank our families, our colleagues, and our students for supporting us in this larger-than-expected effort.

All I really need to know I learned in kindergarten.

Robert Fulgham

1 Introduction

How do we construct reliable, portable, efficient, and secure computer systems? An essential component is the computer's *operating system* — the software that manages a computer's resources.

First, the bad news: operating systems concepts are among the most complex in computer science. A modern, general-purpose operating system can exceed 50 million lines of code, or in other words, more than a thousand times longer than this textbook. New operating systems are being written all the time: if you use an e-book reader, tablet, or smartphone, an operating system is managing your device. Given this inherent complexity, we limit our focus to the essential concepts that every computer scientist should know.

Now the good news: operating systems concepts are also among the most accessible in computer science. Many topics in this book will seem familiar to you — if you have ever tried to do two things at once, or picked the "wrong" line at a grocery store, or tried to keep a roommate or sibling from messing with your things, or succeeded at pulling off an April Fool's joke. Each of these activities has an analogue in operating systems. It is this familiarity that gives us hope that we can explain how operating systems work in a single textbook. All we assume of the reader is a basic understanding of the operation of a computer and the ability to read pseudo-code.

Why is studying operating systems useful? We believe that understanding how operating systems work is essential for any student interested in building modern computer systems. Of course, everyone who uses a computer or a smartphone — or even a modern toaster — uses an operating system, so understanding the function of an operating system is useful to most computer scientists. This book aims to go much deeper than that, to explain operating system internals that we rely on every

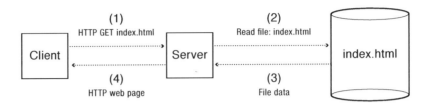

Figure 1.1: The operation of a web server. The client machine sends an HTTP GET request to the web server. The server decodes the packet, reads the file, and sends the contents back to the client.

day without realizing it.

Software engineers use many of the same technologies and design patterns as those used in operating systems to build other complex systems. Whether your goal is to work on the internals of an operating system kernel—or to build the next generation of software for cloud computing, secure web browsers, game consoles, graphical user interfaces, media players, databases, or multicore software—the concepts and abstractions needed for reliable, portable, efficient and secure software are much the same. In our experience, the best way to learn these concepts is to study how they are used in operating systems, but we hope you will apply them to a much broader range of computer systems.

To get started, consider the web server in Figure 1.1. Its behavior is amazingly simple: it receives a packet containing the name of the web page from the network, as an HTTP GET request. The web server decodes the packet, reads the file from disk, and sends the contents of the file back over the network to the user's machine.

What challenges does a web client or web server operating system face? Part of an operating system's job is to make it easy to write applications like web servers. But digging a bit deeper, this simple story quickly raises as many questions as it answers:

- Many web requests involve both data and computation. For example, the Google home page presents a simple text box, but each search query entered in that box consults data spread over many machines. To keep their software manageable, web servers often invoke helper applications, e.g., to manage the actual search function. The main web server must be able to communicate with the helper applications for this to work. How does the operating system enable multiple applications to communicate with each other?

- What if two users (or a million) request a web page from the server at the same time? A simple approach might be to handle each request

[Handwritten notes overlaying the top of the page:]

Handle each request at time.
→ multitasking (multicore)

web server

cache
↳ helps faster response
not starting each request
from scratch.

in turn. If _____ ever, every
other requ _____ re complex,
solution is _____ ests at once.
Multitaski _____ computers,
where eacl _____ same time.
How does _____ tiple things
at once?

- For better _____ copy, sometimes calle _____ if multiple
  users requ _____ sequent requests mo _____ ch request
  from scratc _____ the web server to coordinate, or *synchronize*,
  access to the cache's data structures by possibly thousands of web requests at the same time. How does the operating system synchronize
  application access to shared data?

- To customize and animate the user experience, web servers typically
  send clients scripting code along with the contents of the web page. But
  this means that clicking on a link can cause someone else's code to run
  on your computer. How does the client operating system protect itself
  from compromise by a computer virus surreptitiously embedded into
  the scripting code?

- Suppose the web site administrator uses an editor to update the web
  page. The web server must be able to read this file. How does the operating system store the bytes on disk so that the web server can find and
  read them?

- Taking this a step further, the administrator may want to make a consistent set of changes to the web site so that embedded links are not
  left dangling, even temporarily. How can the operating system let users
  make a set of changes to a web site, so that requests see either the old or
  new pages, but not a combination of the two?

- What happens when the client browser and the web server run at different speeds? If the server tries to send a web page to the client faster than
  the client can render the page on the screen, where are the contents of
  the file stored in the meantime? Can the operating system decouple the
  client and server so that each can run at its own speed without slowing
  the other down?

- As demand on the web server grows, the administrator may need to
  move to more powerful hardware, with more memory, more processors, faster network devices, and faster disks. To take advantage of new
  hardware, must the web server be re-written each time, or can it be
  written in a hardware-independent fashion? What about the operating
  system — must it be re-written for every new piece of hardware?

We could go on, but you get the idea. This book will help you understand the answers to these and many more questions.

Chapter roadmap: The rest of this chapter discusses three topics in detail:

- **Operating System Definition.** What is an operating system, and what does it do? (Section 1.1)

- **Operating System Evaluation.** What design goals should we look for in an operating system? (Section 1.2)

- **Operating Systems: Past, Present, and Future.** How have operating systems evolved, and what new functionality are we likely to see in future operating systems? (Section 1.3)

1.1 │ What Is An Operating System?

operating system

An *operating system* (OS) is the layer of software that manages a computer's resources for its users and their applications. Operating systems run in a wide range of computer systems. They may be invisible to the end user, controlling embedded devices such as toasters, gaming systems, and the many computers inside modern automobiles and airplanes. They are also essential to more general-purpose systems such as smartphones, desktop computers, and servers.

Our discussion will focus on general-purpose operating systems because the technologies they need are a superset of those needed for embedded systems. Increasingly, operating systems technologies developed for general-purpose computing are migrating into the embedded sphere. For example, early mobile phones had simple operating systems to manage their hardware and to run a handful of primitive applications. Today, smartphones — phones capable of running independent third-party applications — are the fastest growing segment of the mobile phone business. These devices require much more complete operating systems, with sophisticated resource management, multi-tasking, security and failure isolation.

Likewise, automobiles are increasingly software controlled, raising a host of operating system issues. Can anyone write software for your car? What if the software fails while you are driving down the highway? Can a car's operating system be hijacked by a computer virus? Although this might seem far-fetched, researchers recently demonstrated that they could remotely turn off a car's braking system through a computer virus introduced into the car's computers via a hacked car radio. A goal of this book is to explain how to build more reliable and secure computer systems in a variety of contexts.

For general-purpose systems, users interact with applications, applications execute in an environment provided by the operating system, and the operating system mediates access to the underlying hardware, as shown in

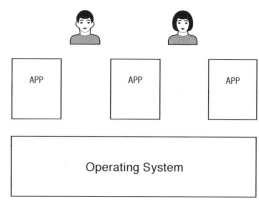

Figure 1.2: A general-purpose operating system is a layer of software that manages a computer's resources for its users and applications.

Figure 1.2 and expanded in Figure 1.3. How can an operating system run multiple applications? For this, operating systems need to play three roles:

What roles does an OS play?

1. **Referee.** Operating systems manage resources shared between different applications running on the same physical machine. For example, an operating system can stop one program and start another. Operating systems isolate applications from each other, so a bug in one application does not corrupt other applications running on the same machine. An operating system must also protect itself and other applications from malicious computer viruses. And since the applications share physical resources, the operating system needs to decide which applications get which resources and when.

2. **Illusionist.** Operating systems provide an abstraction of physical hardware to simplify application design. To write a "Hello world!" program, you do not need (or want!) to think about how much physical memory the system has, or how many other programs might be sharing the computer's resources. Instead, operating systems provide the illusion of nearly infinite memory, despite having a limited amount of physical memory. Likewise, they provide the illusion that each program has the computer's processors entirely to itself. Obviously, the reality is quite different! These illusions let you write applications independently of the amount of physical memory on the system or the physical number of processors. Because applications are written to a higher level of abstraction, the operating system can invisibly change the amount of resources assigned to each application.

3. **Glue.** Operating systems provide a set of common services that facilitate

Figure 1.3: This shows the structure of a general-purpose operating system, as an expansion on the simple view presented in Figure 1.2. At the lowest level, the hardware provides processors, memory, and a set of devices for storing data and communicating with the outside world. The hardware also provides primitives that the operating system can use for fault isolation and synchronization. The operating system runs as the lowest layer of software on the computer. It contains both a device-specific layer for managing the myriad hardware devices and a set of device-independent services provided to applications. Since the operating system must isolate malicious and buggy applications from other applications or the operating system itself, much of the operating system runs in a separate execution environment protected from application code. A portion of the operating system can also run as a system library linked into each application. In turn, applications run in an execution context provided by the operating system kernel. The application context is much more than a simple abstraction on top of hardware devices: applications execute in a virtual environment that is more constrained (to prevent harm), more powerful (to mask hardware limitations), and more useful (via common services) than the underlying hardware.

sharing among applications. As a result, cut and paste works uniformly across the system; a file written by one application can be read by another. Many operating systems provide common user interface routines so applications can have the same "look and feel." Perhaps most importantly, operating systems provide a layer separating applications from hardware input and output (I/O) devices so applications can be written independently of the specific keyboard, mouse, and disk drive in use on a particular computer.

We next discuss these three roles in greater detail.

1.1.1　Resource Sharing: Operating System as Referee

What happens when multiple applications share resources?

Sharing is central to most uses of computers. Right now, my laptop is running a browser, podcast library, text editor, email program, document viewer, and newspaper. The operating system must somehow keep all of these activities separate, yet allow each the full capacity of the machine if the others are not running. At a minimum, when one program stops running, the operating system should let me run another. Better still, the operating system should let multiple applications run at the same time, so I can read email while I download a security patch to the system software.

Even individual applications can do multiple tasks at once. For instance, a web server's responsiveness improves if it handles multiple requests concurrently rather than waiting for each to complete before starting the next one. The same holds for the browser—it is more responsive if it can start rendering a page while the rest of the page is transferring. On multiprocessors, the computation inside a parallel application can be split into separate units that can be run independently for faster execution. The operating system itself is an example of software written to do multiple tasks at once. As we will illustrate throughout the book, the operating system is a customer of its own abstractions.

Sharing raises several challenges for an operating system:

- **Resource allocation.** The operating system must keep all simultaneous activities separate, allocating resources to each as appropriate. A computer usually has only a few processors and a finite amount of memory, network bandwidth, and disk space. When there are multiple tasks to do at the same time, how should the operating system decide how many resources to give to each? Seemingly trivial differences in how resources are allocated can impact user-perceived performance. As we will see in Chapter 9, an operating system that allocates too little memory to a program slows down not only that particular program, but often other applications as well.

  To illustrate the difference between execution on a physical machine versus on the abstract machine provided by the operating system, what should happen if an application executes an infinite loop?

```
while (true) {
    ;
}
```

If programs ran directly on raw hardware, this code fragment would lock up the computer, making it completely non-responsive to user input. If the operating system ensures that each program gets its own slice of the computer's resources, a specific application might lock up, but other programs could proceed unimpeded. Additionally, the user could ask the operating system to force the looping program to exit.

- **Isolation.** An error in one application should not disrupt other applications, or even the operating system itself. This is called *fault isolation*. Anyone who has taken an introductory computer science class knows the value of an operating system that can protect itself and other applications from programmer bugs. Debugging would be vastly harder if an error in one program could corrupt data structures in other applications. Likewise, downloading and installing a screen saver or other application should not crash unrelated programs, provide a way for a malicious attacker to surreptitiously install a computer virus, or let one user access or change another's data without permission.

  fault isolation

  Fault isolation requires restricting the behavior of applications to less than the full power of the underlying hardware. Otherwise, any application downloaded off the web, or any script embedded in a web page, could completely control the machine. Any application could install spyware into the operating system to log every keystroke you type, or record the password to every web site you visit. Without fault isolation provided by the operating system, any bug in any program might irretrievably corrupt the disk. Error-prone or malignant applications could cause all sorts of havoc.

- **Communication.** The flip side of isolation is the need for communication between different applications and different users. For example, a web site may be implemented by a cooperating set of applications: one to select advertisements, another to cache recent results, yet another to fetch and merge data from disk, and several more to cooperatively scan the web for new content to index. For this to work, the various programs must communicate with one another. If the operating system prevents bugs and malicious users and applications from affecting other users and their applications, how does it also support communication to share results? In setting up boundaries, an operating system must also allow those boundaries to be crossed in carefully controlled ways when the need arises.

In its role as referee, an operating system is somewhat akin to that of a particularly patient kindergarten teacher. It balances needs, separates conflicts, and facilitates sharing. One user should not be allowed to monopolize system resources or to access or corrupt another user's files without permission; a buggy application should not be able to crash the operating system or other unrelated applications; and yet, applications must also work together. Enforcing and balancing these concerns is a central role of the operating system.

1.1.2　Masking Limitations: Operating System as Illusionist

What happens when applications need more resources than the hardware provides?

A second important role of an operating system is to mask the restrictions inherent in computer hardware. Physical constraints limit hardware resources — a computer has only a limited number of processors and a limited amount of physical memory, network bandwidth, and disk. Further, since the operating system must decide how to divide its fixed resources among the various applications running at each moment, a particular application can have differing amounts of resources from time to time, even when running on the same hardware. While some applications are designed to take advantage of a computer's specific hardware configuration and resource assignment, most programmers prefer to use a higher level of abstraction.

virtualization

Virtualization provides an application with the illusion of resources that are not physically present. For example, the operating system can provide the abstraction that each application has a dedicated processor, even though at a physical level there may be only a single processor shared among all the applications running on the computer.

With the right hardware and operating system support, most physical resources can be virtualized. For example, hardware provides only a small, finite amount of memory, while the operating system provides applications the illusion of a nearly infinite amount of virtual memory. Wireless networks drop or corrupt packets; the operating system masks these failures to provide the illusion of a reliable service. At a physical level, magnetic disk and flash RAM support block reads and writes, where the size of the block depends on the physical device characteristics, addressed by a device-specific block number. Most programmers prefer to work with byte-addressable files organized by name into hierarchical directories. Even the type of processor can be virtualized to allow the same, unmodified application to run on a smartphone, tablet, and laptop computer.

virtual machine

guest operating system

Pushing this one step further, some operating systems virtualize the entire computer, running the operating system as an application on top of another operating system (see Figure 1.4). This is called creating a *virtual machine*. The operating system running in the virtual machine, called the *guest operating system*, thinks it is running on a real, physical machine, but this is an illusion presented by the true operating system running underneath.

What is the purpose of a virtual machine?

One benefit of a virtual machine is application portability. If a program runs only on an old version of an operating system, it can still work on a new system running a virtual machine. The virtual machine hosts the application on the old operating system, running atop the new one. Virtual machines also

Figure 1.4: A guest operating system running inside a virtual machine.

aid debugging. If an operating system can be run as an application, then its developers can set breakpoints, stop the kernel, and single step their code just as they would when debugging an application.

Throughout the book, we discuss techniques that the operating system uses to accomplish these and other illusions. In each case, the operating system provides a more convenient and flexible programming abstraction than that provided by the underlying hardware.

1.1.3   Providing Common Services: Operating System as Glue

Can we raise the level of abstraction above bare hardware?

Operating systems play a third key role: providing a set of common, standard services to applications to simplify and standardize their design. An example is the web server described earlier in this chapter. The operating system hides the specifics of how the network and disk devices work, providing a simpler abstraction based on receiving/sending reliable streams of bytes and reading/writing named files. This lets the web server focus on its core task — decoding incoming requests and filling them — rather than on formatting data into individual network packets and disk blocks.

An important reason for the operating system to provide common services, rather than letting each application provide its own, is to facilitate sharing among applications. The web server must be able to read the file that the text editor wrote. For applications to share files, they must be stored in a standard format, with a standard system for managing file directories. Most operating systems also provide a standard way for applications to pass messages and to share memory.

The choice of which services an operating system should provide is often judgment call. For example, computers can come configured with a blizzard of different devices: different graphics co-processors and pixel formats, different network interfaces (WiFi, Ethernet, and Bluetooth), different disk drives (SCSI, IDE), different device interfaces (USB, Firewire), and different sensors (GPS, accelerometers), not to mention different versions of each. Most applications can ignore these differences, by using only a generic interface provided by the operating system. For other applications, such as a database, the specific disk drive may matter quite a bit. For applications that can operate at a higher level of abstraction, the operating system serves as an interoperability layer so that both applications and devices can evolve independently.

Another standard service in most modern operating systems is the graphical user interface library. Both Microsoft's and Apple's operating systems provide a set of standard user interface widgets. This facilitates a common "look and feel" to users so that frequent operations — such as pull down menus and "cut" and "paste" commands — are handled consistently across applications.

Most of the code in an operating system implements these common services. However, much of the complexity of operating systems is due to resource sharing and the masking of hardware limits. Because common service code uses the abstractions provided by the other two operating system roles, this book will focus primarily on the operating system as a referee and as an illusionist.

1.1.4   Operating System Design Patterns

Are the roles of referee, illusionist, and glue unique to operating systems?

The challenges that operating systems address are not unique — they apply to many different computer domains. Many complex software systems have multiple users, run programs written by third-party developers, and/or need to coordinate many simultaneous activities. These pose questions of resource allocation, fault isolation, communication, abstractions of physical hardware, and how to provide a useful set of common services for software developers. Not only are the challenges the same, but often the solutions are, as well: these systems use many of the design patterns and techniques described in this book.

We next describe some of the systems with design challenges similar to those found in operating systems:

- **Cloud computing** (Figure 1.5) is a model of computing where applications run on shared computing and storage infrastructure in large-scale data centers instead of on the user's own computers. Cloud computing must address many of the same issues as in operating systems in terms of sharing, abstraction, and common services.

    - **Referee.** How are resources allocated between competing applications running in the cloud? How are buggy or malicious applications prevented from disrupting other applications?

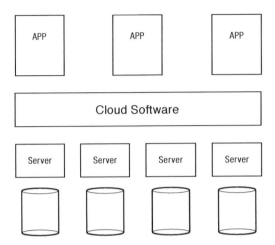

Figure 1.5: Cloud computing software provides a convenient abstraction of server resources to cloud applications.

- **Illusionist.** The computing resources in the cloud are continually evolving; what abstractions are provided to isolate application developers from changes in the underlying hardware?

- **Glue.** Cloud services often distribute their work across different machines. What abstractions should cloud software provide to help services coordinate and share data between their various activities?

• **Web browsers** (Figure 1.6), such as Chrome, Internet Explorer, Firefox, and Safari, play a role similar to an operating system. Browsers load and display web pages, but, as we mentioned earlier, many pages embed scripting programs that the browser must execute. These scripts can be buggy or malicious; hackers have used them to take over vast numbers of home computers. Like an operating system, the browser must isolate the user, other web sites, and even the browser itself from errors or malicious activity by these scripts. Similarly, most browsers have a plug-in architecture for supporting extensions, and these extensions must also be isolated to prevent them from causing harm.

- **Referee.** How can a browser ensure responsiveness when a user has multiple tabs open with each tab running a script from a different web site? How can we limit web scripts and plug-ins to prevent bugs from crashing the browser and malicious scripts from accessing sensitive user data?

- **Illusionist.** Many web services are geographically distributed to improve the user experience. Not only does this put servers closer to users, but if one server crashes or its network connection has

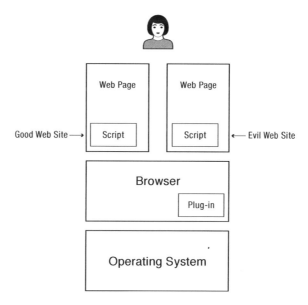

Figure 1.6: A web browser isolates scripts and plug-ins from accessing privileged resources on the host operating system.

problems, a browser can connect to a different site. The user in most cases does not notice the difference, even when updating a shopping cart or web form. How does the browser make server changes transparent to the user?

– **Glue.** How does the browser achieve a portable execution environment for scripts that works consistently across operating systems and hardware platforms?

- **Media players**, such as Flash and Silverlight, are often packaged as browser plug-ins, but they themselves provide an execution environment for scripting programs. Thus, these systems face many of the same issues as both browsers and operating systems on which they run: isolation of buggy or malicious code, concurrent background and foreground tasks, and plug-in architectures.

  – **Referee.** Media players are often in the news for being vulnerable to some new, malicious attack. How should media players sandbox malicious or buggy scripts to prevent them from corrupting the host machine?

  – **Illusionist.** Media applications are often both computationally intensive and highly interactive. How do they coordinate foreground and background activities to maintain responsiveness?

Figure 1.7: Databases perform many of the tasks of an operating system: they allocate resources among user queries to ensure responsiveness, they mask differences in the underlying operating system and hardware, and they provide a convenient programming abstraction to developers.

- **Glue.** High-performance graphics hardware rapidly evolves in response to the demands of the video game market. How do media players provide a set of standard API's for scripts to work across a diversity of graphics accelerators?

• **Multiplayer games** often have extensibility API's to allow third party software vendors to extend the game in significant ways. Often these extensions are miniature games in their own right, yet game extensions must also be prevented from breaking the overall rules of the game.

- **Referee.** Many games try to offload work to client machines to reduce server load and improve responsiveness, but this opens up games to the threat of users installing specialized extensions to gain an unfair advantage. How do game designers set limits for extensions and game players to ensure a level playing field?

- **Illusionist.** If objects in the game are spread across client and server machines, is that distinction visible to extension code or is the interface at a higher level?

- **Glue.** Most successful games have a large number of extensions; how should a game designer set up their API's to make it easier to foster a community of developers?

- **Multi-user database systems** (Figure 1.7), such as Oracle and Microsoft's SQL Server, allow large organizations to store, query, and update large data sets, such as detailed records of every purchase ever made at Amazon or Walmart. Large scale data analysis greatly optimizes business operations, but, as a consequence, databases face many of the same challenges as operating systems. They are simultaneously accessed by many different users in many different locations. They therefore must allocate resources among different user requests, isolate concurrent updates to shared data, and ensure that data is stored consistently on disk. In fact, several of the techniques we discuss in Chapter 14 were originally developed for database systems.

  - **Referee.** How should resources be allocated among the various users of a database? How does the database enforce data privacy so that only authorized users access relevant data?

  - **Illusionist.** How does the database mask machine failures so that data is always stored consistently regardless of when the failure occurs?

  - **Glue.** What common services make it easier to develop database applications?

- **Parallel applications** are programs designed to take advantage of multiple processors on a single computer. Each application divides its work onto a fixed number of processors and must ensure that accesses to shared data structures are coordinated to preserve consistency. While some parallel programs directly use the services provided by the underlying operating system, others need careful control of the assignment of work to processors to achieve good performance. These systems interpose a runtime system on top of the operating system to manage user-level parallelism, essentially building a mini-operating system on top of the underlying one.

  - **Referee.** When there are more tasks to perform than processors, how does the runtime system decide which tasks to perform first?

  - **Illusionist.** How does the runtime system hide physical details of the hardware from the programmer, such as the number of processors or the interprocessor communication latency?

  - **Glue.** Highly concurrent data structures can make it easier to write efficient parallel programs; how do we program trees, hash tables, and lists so that they can be used by multiple processors at the same time?

- **The Internet** is used everyday by a huge number of people, but at the physical layer, those users share the same underlying resources. How should the Internet handle resource contention? Because of its diverse user base, the Internet is rife with malicious behavior, such as denial-of-service attacks that flood traffic on certain links to prevent legitimate users from communicating. Various attempts are underway to design solutions that will let the Internet continue to function despite such attacks.

- **Referee.** Should the Internet treat all users identically (e.g., network neutrality) or should ISPs be able to favor some uses over others? Can the Internet be re-designed to prevent denial-of-service, spam, phishing, and other malicious behaviors?

- **Illusionist.** The Internet provides the illusion of a single worldwide network that can deliver a packet from any machine on the Internet to any other machine. However, network hardware is composed of many discrete network elements with: (i) the ability to transmit limited size packets over a limited distance, and (ii) some chance that packets will be garbled in the process. The Internet transforms the network into something more useful for applications like the web — a facility to reliably transmit data of arbitrary length, anywhere in the world.

- **Glue.** The Internet protocol suite was explicitly designed to act as an interoperability layer that lets network applications evolve independently of changes in network hardware, and vice versa. Does the success of the Internet hold any lessons for operating system design?

Many of these systems use the same techniques and design patterns as operating systems. Studying operating systems is a great way to understand how these others systems work. In a few cases, different mechanisms are used to achieve the same goals, but, even here, the boundaries are fuzzy. For example, browsers often use compile-time checks to prevent scripts from gaining control over them, while most operating systems use hardware-based protection to limit application programs from taking over the machine. More recently, however, some smartphone operating systems have begun to use the same compile-time techniques as browsers to protect against malicious mobile applications. In turn, some browsers have begun to use operating system hardware-based protection to improve the isolation they provide.

To avoid spreading our discussion too thinly, this book focuses on how operating systems work. Just as it is easier to learn a second computer programming language after you become fluent in the first, it is better to see how operating systems principles apply in one context before learning how they can be applied in other settings. We hope and expect, however, that you will be able to apply the concepts in this book more widely than just operating system design.

1.2 | Operating System Evaluation

What design goals should we look for in an operating system?

Having defined what an operating system does, how should we choose among alternative designs? We discuss several desirable criteria for operating systems:

- **Reliability and Availability.** Does the operating system do what you want?

- **Security.** Can the operating system be corrupted by an attacker?

- **Portability.** Is the operating system easy to move to new hardware platforms?

- **Performance.** Is the user interface responsive, or does the operating system impose too much overhead?

- **Adoption.** How many other users are there for this operating system?

In many cases, tradeoffs between these criteria are inevitable — improving a system along one dimension may hurt it along another. We conclude this section with some concrete examples of design tradeoffs.

1.2.1   Reliability and Availability

reliability

Perhaps the most important characteristic of an operating system is its reliability. *Reliability* means that a system does exactly what it is designed to do. As the lowest level of software running on the system, operating system errors can have devastating and hidden effects. If the operating system breaks, you may not be able to get work done, and in some cases, you may even lose previous work, e.g., if the failure corrupts files on disk. By contrast, application failures can be much more benign, precisely because operating systems provide fault isolation and a rapid and clean restart after an error.

Making an operating system reliable is challenging. Operating systems often operate in a hostile environment, one where computer viruses and other malicious code try to take control of the system by exploiting design or implementation errors in the operating system's defenses.

Unfortunately, the most common ways to improve software reliability, such as running test cases for common code paths, are less effective when applied to operating systems. Since malicious attacks can target a specific vulnerability precisely to cause execution to follow a rare code path, everything must work correctly for the operating system to be reliable. Even without intentionally malicious attacks, extremely rare corner cases can occur regularly: for an operating system with a million users, a once in a billion event will eventually occur to someone.

availability

A related concept is *availability*, the percentage of time that the system is usable. A buggy operating system that crashes frequently, losing the user's work, is both unreliable and unavailable. A buggy operating system that crashes frequently but never loses the user's work and cannot be subverted by a malicious attack is reliable but unavailable. An operating system that has been subverted but continues to appear to run normally while logging the user's keystrokes is unreliable but available.

Thus, both reliability *and* availability are desirable. Availability is affected by two factors: the frequency of failures, measured as the *mean time to failure (MTTF)*, and the time it takes to restore a system to a working state after a failure (for example, to reboot), called the *mean time to repair (MTTR)*. Availability can be improved by increasing the MTTF or reducing the MTTR.

mean time to failure

mean time to repair

Throughout this book, we will present various approaches to improving operating system reliability and availability. In many cases, the abstractions may seem at first glance overly rigid and formulaic. It is important to realize this is done on purpose! Only precise abstractions provide a basis for constructing reliable and available systems.

1.2.2   Security

security

Two concepts closely related to reliability are security and privacy. *Security* means the computer's operation cannot be compromised by a malicious attacker. *Privacy* is an aspect of security: data stored on the computer is only accessible to authorized users.

privacy

Alas, no useful computer is perfectly secure! Any complex piece of software has bugs, and seemingly innocuous bugs can be exploited by an attacker to gain control of the system. Or the computer hardware might be tampered with, to provide access to the attacker. Or the computer's administrator might be untrustworthy, using his or her credentials to steal user data. Or an OS software developer might be untrustworthy, inserting a backdoor for the attacker to gain access to the system.

Nevertheless, an operating system can be, and should be, designed to minimize its vulnerability to attack. For example, strong fault isolation can prevent third party applications from taking over the system. Downloading and installing a screen saver or other application should not provide a way for an attacker to surreptitiously install a *computer virus* on the system. A computer program that modifies an operating system or application to copy itself from computer to computer without the computer owner's permission or knowledge. Once installed on a computer, a virus often provides the attacker control over the system's resources or data. An example computer virus is a keylogger: a program that modifies the operating system to record every keystroke entered by the user and send them back to the attacker's machine. In this way, the attacker could gain access to the user's passwords, bank account numbers, and other private information. Likewise, a malicious screen saver might surreptitiously scan the disk for files containing personal information or turn the system into an email spam server.

computer virus

Even with strong fault isolation, a system can be insecure if its applications are not designed for security. For example, the Internet email standard provides no strong assurance of the sender's identity; it is possible to form an email message with anyone's email address in the "from" field, not necessarily the actual sender's. Thus, an email message can appear to be from someone (perhaps someone you trust), when in reality it is from the attacker and contains, as an attachment, a malicious virus that takes over the computer when the attachment is opened. By now, you are hopefully suspicious of clicking on any email attachment. Stepping back, the issue could be seen as a limitation of the interaction between the email system and the operating system. If the operating system provided a cheap and easy way to process an attachment in an isolated execution environment with limited capabilities, then even attachments containing viruses would do no harm.

Complicating matters is that the operating system must not only prevent unwanted access to shared data, it must also *allow* access in many cases. Users and programs must be able to interact with each other, so that it is possible to cut and paste text between different applications, and to share data written to disk or over the network. If each program were completely standalone and never needed to interact with any other program, then fault isolation by itself would be sufficient. However, we not only want to isolate programs from one another, but to easily share data between programs and between users.

enforcement

security policy

Thus, an operating system needs both an enforcement mechanism and a security policy. *Enforcement* is how the operating system ensures that only permitted actions are allowed. The *security policy* defines what is permitted — who is allowed to access what data, and who can perform what operations.

Malicious attackers can target vulnerabilities in either enforcement mechanisms or security policies. An error in enforcement can allow an attacker to evade the policy; an error in the policy can allow the attacker access when it should have been prohibited.

1.2.3   Portability

portability

All operating systems provide applications with an abstraction of the underlying computer hardware; a *portable* abstraction is one that does not change as the hardware changes. A program written for Microsoft's Windows 8 should run correctly regardless of whether a specific graphics card is being used, whether persistent storage is provided via flash memory or rotating magnetic disk, or whether the network is Bluetooth, WiFi, or gigabit Ethernet.

Portability also applies to the operating system itself. As we have noted, operating systems are among the most complex software systems ever invented, making it impractical to re-write them from scratch every time new hardware is produced or a new application is developed. Instead, new operating systems are often derived, at least in part, from old ones. As one example, iOS, the operating system for the iPhone and iPad, was derived from the MacOS X code base.

As a result, most successful operating systems have a lifetime measured in decades. Microsoft Windows 8 originally began with the development of Windows NT starting in 1988. At that time, the typical computer was 10000 times less powerful, and with 10000 times less memory and disk storage, than is the case today. Operating systems that last decades are no anomaly. Microsoft's prior operating system, MS/DOS, was introduced in 1981. It later evolved into the early versions of Microsoft Windows before finally being phased out around 2000.

This means that operating systems must be designed to support applications that have not yet been written and to run on hardware that has not yet been developed. Likewise, developers do not want to re-write applications when the operating system is ported from machine to machine. Sometimes, the importance of "future-proofing" an operating system is discovered only in retrospect. Microsoft's first operating system, MS/DOS, was designed in 1981 assuming that personal computers would never have more than 640 KB of memory. This limitation was acceptable at the time, but today, even cellphones have orders of magnitude more memory than that.

How might we design an operating system to achieve portability? As we illustrated earlier in Figure 1.3, it helps to have a simple, standard way for applications to interact with the operating system, the *abstract virtual machine (AVM)*. This is the interface provided by operating systems to applications, including: (i) the *application programming interface (API)*, the list of function calls the operating system provides to applications, (ii) the memory access model, and (iii) which instructions can be legally executed. For example, an instruction to change whether the hardware is executing trusted operating system code, or untrusted application code, must be available to the operating system but not to applications.

abstract virtual machine

application programming interface

A well-designed operating system AVM provides a fixed point across which both application code and hardware can evolve independently. This is similar to the role of the Internet Protocol (IP) standard in networking. Distributed applications such as email and the web, written using IP, are insulated from changes in the underlying network technology (Ethernet, WiFi, optical). Equally important is that changes in applications, from email to instant messaging to file sharing, do not require simultaneous changes in the underlying hardware.

This notion of a portable hardware abstraction is so powerful that operating systems use the same idea internally: the operating system itself can largely be implemented independently of the hardware specifics. The interface that makes this possible is called the *hardware abstraction layer (HAL)*. It might seem that the operating system AVM and the operating system HAL should be identical, or nearly so — after all, both are portable layers designed to hide hardware details. The AVM must do more, however. As we noted, applications execute in a restricted, virtualized context and with access to high-level common services, while the operating system itself uses a procedural abstraction much closer to the actual hardware.

hardware abstraction layer

Today, Linux is an example of a highly portable operating system. It has been used as the operating system for web servers, personal computers, tablets, netbooks, e-book readers, smartphones, set top boxes, routers, WiFi access points, and game consoles. Linux is based on an operating system called UNIX, which was originally developed in the early 1970's. UNIX was written by a small team of developers. It was designed to be compact, simple to program, and highly portable, but at some cost in performance. Over the years, UNIX's and Linux's portability and convenient programming abstractions have been keys to their success.

1.2.4   Performance

While the portability of an operating system becomes apparent over time, the performance of an operating system is often immediately visible to its users. Although we often associate performance with each individual application, the operating system's design can greatly affect the application's perceived performance. The operating system decides when an application can run, how much memory it can use, and whether its files are cached in memory or clustered efficiently on disk. The operating system also mediates application access to memory, the network, and the disk. It must avoid slowing down the critical path while still providing needed fault isolation and resource sharing between applications.

overhead

efficiency

Performance is not a single quantity. Rather, it can be measured in several different ways. One performance metric is the *overhead*, the added resource cost of implementing an abstraction presented to applications. A related concept is *efficiency*, the lack of overhead in an abstraction. One way to measure overhead (or inversely, efficiency) is the degree to which the abstraction impedes application performance. Suppose you could run the application directly on the underlying hardware without the overhead of the operating system abstraction; how much would that improve the application's performance?

fairness

Operating systems also need to allocate resources among applications, and this can affect the performance of the system as perceived by the end user. One issue is *fairness* between different users or applications running on the same machine. Should resources be divided equally between different users or applications, or should some get preferential treatment? If so, how does the operating system decide what tasks get priority?

response time

throughput

Two related concepts are response time and throughput. *Response time*, sometimes called *delay*, is how long it takes for a single task to run, from the time it starts to the time it completes. For example, a highly visible response time for desktop computers is the time from when the user moves the hardware mouse until the pointer on the screen reflects the user's action. An operating system that provides poor response time can be unusable. *Throughput* is the rate at which the system completes tasks. Throughput is a measure of efficiency for a group of tasks rather than a single one. While it might seem that designs that improve response time would also necessarily improve throughput, this is not the case, as we discuss in Chapter 7.

predictability

A related consideration is performance *predictability*: whether the system's response time or other metric is consistent over time. Predictability can often be more important than average performance. If a user operation sometimes takes an instant but sometimes much longer, the user may find it difficult to adapt. Consider, for example, two systems. In one, each keystroke is usually instantaneous, but 1% of the time, it takes 10 seconds to take effect. In the other system, a keystroke always takes exactly 0.1 seconds to appear on the screen. Average response time is the same in both systems, but the second is more predictable. Which do you think would be more user-friendly?

EXAMPLE   To illustrate the concepts of efficiency, overhead, fairness, response time, throughput, and predictability, consider a car driving to its destination. If no other cars or pedestrians were ever on the road, the car could go quite quickly, never needing to slow down for stoplights. Stop signs and stoplights enable multiple cars to share the road, at some cost in overhead and response time for each individual driver. As the system becomes more congested, predictability suffers. Throughput of the system improves with carpooling. With dedicated carpool lanes, carpooling can even reduce delay despite carpoolers needing to coordinate their pickups. Scrapping the car and building mass transit can improve predictability, throughput, and fairness.

1.2.5   Adoption

In addition to reliability, portability and performance, the success of an operating system depends on two factors outside its immediate control: the wide availability of applications ported to that operating system, and the wide availability of hardware that the operating system can support. An iPhone runs iOS, but without the pre-installed applications and the contents of the App Store, the iPhone would be just another cellphone.

network effect   The *network effect* occurs when the value of some technology depends not only on its intrinsic capabilities, but also on the number of other people who have adopted it. Application and hardware designers spend their efforts on those operating system platforms with the most users, while users favor those operating systems with the best applications or the cheapest hardware. If this sounds circular, it is! More users imply more applications and cheaper hardware; more applications and cheaper hardware imply more users, in a virtuous cycle.

Consider how you might design an operating system to take advantage of the network effect, or at least to avoid being crushed by it. An obvious step would be to design the system to make it easy to accommodate new hardware and for applications to be ported across different versions of the same operating system.

A more subtle issue is the choice of whether the operating system programming interface (API), or the operating system source code itself, is open or proprietary system   proprietary. A *proprietary* system is one under the control of a single company; it can be changed at any time by its provider to meet the needs of its customers. open system   An *open system* is one where the system's source code is public, giving anyone the ability to inspect and change the code. Often, an open system has an API that can be changed only with the agreement of a public standards body. Adherence to standards provides assurance to application developers that the API will not be changed except by general agreement; on the other hand, standards bodies can make it difficult to quickly add new, desired features.

Neither open nor proprietary systems are intrinsically better for adoption. Windows 8 and MacOS are proprietary operating systems; Linux is an open operating system. All three are widely used. Open systems are easier to adapt to a wide variety of hardware platforms, but they risk devolving into multiple versions, impairing the network effect. Purveyors of proprietary operating systems argue that their systems are more reliable and better adapted to the needs of their customers. Interoperability problems can be reduced if the same company controls both the hardware and the software, but limiting an operating system to one hardware platform impairs the network effect and risks alienating consumers.

Making it easy to port applications from existing systems to a new operating system can help a new system become established; conversely, designing an operating system API that makes it difficult to port applications away from the operating system can help prevent competition from becoming established. Thus, there are often commercial pressures for operating system interfaces to become idiosyncratic. Throughout this book, we discuss operating systems issues at a conceptual level, but remember that the details may vary considerably for any specific operating system due to important, but sometimes chaotic, commercial interests.

1.2.6   Design Tradeoffs

Most practical operating system designs strike a balance between the goals of reliability, security, portability, performance, and adoption. Design choices that improve portability — for example, preserving legacy interfaces — often make the system as a whole less reliable and less secure. Similarly, it is often possible to increase system performance by breaking an abstraction. However, such performance optimizations may add complexity and therefore potentially hurt reliability. The operating system designer must carefully weigh these competing goals.

EXAMPLE   To illustrate the tradeoff between performance and complexity, consider the following true story. A research operating system developed in the late 1980's used a type-safe language to reduce the incidence of programmer errors. For speed, the most frequently used routines at the core of the operating system were implemented in assembly code. In one of these routines, the implementation team decided to use a sequence of instructions that shaved a single instruction off a very frequently used code path, but that would sometimes break if the operating system exceeded a particular size. At the time, the operating system was nowhere near this limit. After a few years of production use, however, the system started mysteriously crashing, apparently at random, and only after many days of execution. Many weeks of painstaking investigation revealed the problem: the operating system had grown beyond the limit assumed in the assembly code implementation. The fix was easy,

	1981	1997	2014	Factor (2014/1981)
Uniprocessor speed (MIPS)	1	200	2500	2.5 K
CPUs per computer	1	1	10+	10+
Processor MIPS/$	$100K	$25	$0.20	500 K
DRAM Capacity (MiB)/$	0.002	2	1K	500 K
Disk Capacity (GiB)/$	0.003	7	25K	10 M
Home Internet	300 bps	256 Kbps	20 Mbps	100 K
Machine room network	10 Mbps (shared)	100 Mbps (switched)	10 Gbps (switched)	1000+
Ratio of users to computers	100:1	1:1	1:several	100+

Figure 1.8: Approximate computer server performance over time, reflecting widely used servers of each era: in 1981, a minicomputer; in 1997, a high-end workstation; in 2014, a rack-mounted multicore server. MIPS stands for "millions of instructions per second," a rough measure of processor performance. The VAX 11/782 was introduced in 1982; it achieved 1 MIP. DRAM prices are from Hennessey and Patterson, *Computer Architecture: A Quantitative Approach*. Disk drive prices are from John McCallum. The Hayes smartmodem, introduced in 1981, ran at 300 bps. The 10 Mbps shared Ethernet standard was also introduced in 1981. One of the authors built his first operating system in 1982, used a VAX at his first job, and owned a Hayes to work from home.

once the problem was found, but the question is: do you think the original optimization was worth the risk?

1.3 | Operating Systems: Past, Present, and Future

How have operating systems evolved, and what new functionality are we likely to see in future operating systems?

We conclude this chapter by discussing the origins of operating systems, in order to illustrate where these systems are heading in the future. As the lowest layer of software running on top of computer hardware, operating systems date back to the first computers, evolving nearly as rapidly as computer hardware.

1.3.1   Impact of Technology Trends

How has hardware changed?

Moore's Law

The most striking aspect of the last fifty years in computing technology has been the cumulative effect of Moore's Law and the comparable advances in related technologies, such as memory and disk storage. *Moore's Law* states that transistor density increases exponentially over time; similar exponential improvements have occurred in many other component technologies. Figure 1.8 provides an overview of the past three decades of technology improvements in computer hardware. The cost of processing and memory has decreased by almost six orders of magnitude over this period; the cost of disk capacity has decreased by seven orders of magnitude. Not all technologies have improved at the same rate; disk latency (not shown in the table) has improved, but at a much slower rate than disk capacity. These relative changes have radically altered both the use of computers and the tradeoffs faced by operating system designers.

It is hard to imagine how things used to be. Today, you probably carry a smartphone in your pocket, with an incredibly powerful computer inside. Thousands of server computers wait patiently for you to type in a search query; when the query arrives, they can synthesize a response in a fraction of a second. In the early years of computing, however, the computers were more expensive than the salaries of the people who used them. Users would queue up, often for days, for their turn to run a program. A similar progression from expensive to cheap devices occurred with telephones over the past hundred years. Initially, telephone lines were very expensive, with a single shared line among everyone in a neighborhood. Over time, of course, both computers and telephones have become cheap enough to sit idle until we need them.

Despite these changes, operating systems still face the same conceptual challenges as they did fifty years ago. To manage computer resources for applications and users, they must allocate resources among applications, provide fault isolation and communication services, abstract hardware limitations, and so forth. We have made tremendous progress towards improving the reliability, security, efficiency, and portability of operating systems, but much more is needed. Although we do not know precisely how computing technology or application demand will evolve over the next 10-20 years, it is highly likely that these fundamental operating system challenges will persist.

1.3.2   Early Operating Systems

Computers were expensive; users would wait.   The first operating systems were runtime libraries intended to simplify the programming of early computer systems. Rather than the tiny, inexpensive yet massively complex hardware and software systems of today, the first computers often took up an entire floor of a warehouse, cost millions of dollars, and yet were capable of being used only by a single person at a time. The user would first reset the computer, load the program by toggling it into the system one bit at a time, and hit go, producing output to be pored over during the next user's turn. If the program had a bug, the user would need to wait to try the run over again, often the next day.

It might seem like there was no need for an operating system in this setting. However, since computers were enormously expensive, reducing the likelihood of programmer error was paramount. The first operating systems were developed as a way to reduce errors by providing a standard set of common services. For example, early operating systems provided standard input/output (I/O) routines that each user could link into their programs. These services made it more likely that a user's program would produce useful output.

Although these initial operating systems were a huge step forward, the result was still extremely inefficient. It was around this time that the CEO of IBM famously predicted that we would only ever need five computers in the world. If computers today cost millions of dollars and could only run tiny applications by one person at a time, he might have been right.

1.3.3   Multi-User Operating Systems

How do we run multiple programs at the same time?

The next step forward was sharing, introducing many of the advantages, and challenges, that we see in today's operating systems. When processor time is valuable, restricting the system to one user at a time is wasteful. For example, in early systems the processor remained idle while the user loaded the program, even if there was a long line of people waiting their turn.

batch operating system

A *batch operating system* works on a queue of tasks. It runs a simple loop: load, run, and unload each job in turn. While one job was running, the operating system sets up the I/O devices to do background transfers for the next/previous job using a process called *direct memory access (DMA)*. With DMA, the I/O device transfers its data directly into memory at a location specified by the operating system. When the I/O transfer completes, the hardware interrupts the processor, transferring control to the operating system interrupt handler. The operating system starts the next DMA transfer and then resumes execution of the application. The interrupt appears to the application as if nothing had happened, except for some delay between one instruction and the next.

direct memory access

Batch operating systems were soon extended to run multiple applications at once, called *multitasking* or sometimes *multiprogramming*. Multiple programs are loaded into memory at the same time, each ready to use the processor if for any reason the previous task needed to pause, for example, to read additional input or produce output. Multitasking increases processor efficiency to nearly 100%; if the queue of tasks is long enough, and a sufficient number of I/O devices can keep feeding the processor, there is no need for the processor to wait.

multitasking

multiprogramming

However, processor sharing raises the need for program isolation, to limit a bug in one program from crashing or corrupting another. During this period, computer designers added hardware memory protection, to reduce the overhead of fault isolation.

How do we debug an operating system?

A practical challenge with batch computing, however, is how to debug the operating system itself. Unlike an application program, a batch operating system assumes it is in direct control of the hardware. New versions can only be tested by stopping every application and rebooting the system, essentially turning the computer back into a single-user system. Needless to say, this was an expensive operation, often scheduled for the dead of the night.

host operating system

Virtual machines address this limitation (see Figure 1.4). Instead of running a test operating system directly on the hardware, virtual machines run an *operating system* as an application. The *host operating system*, also called a *virtual machine monitor*, exports an abstract virtual machine (AVM) that is

Figure 1.9: Genealogy of several modern operating systems.

identical to the underlying hardware. The test operating system running on top of the virtual machine does not need to know that it is running in a virtual environment—it executes instructions, accesses hardware devices, and restores application state after an interrupt just as if it were running on real hardware.

Virtual machines are now widely used for operating system development, backward compatibility, and cross-platform support. Application software that runs only on an old version of an operating system can share hardware with entirely new applications. The virtual machine monitor runs two virtual machines—one for the new operating system for current applications and a separate one for legacy applications. As another example, MacOS users who need to run Windows or Linux applications can do so by running them inside a virtual machine.

1.3.4　Time-Sharing Operating Systems

How do we make operating systems interactive?

Eventually, the cumulative effect of Moore's Law meant that the cost of computing dropped to where systems could be optimized for users rather than for efficient use of the processor. UNIX, for example, was developed in the early 70's on a spare computer that no one was using at the time. UNIX became the basis for Apple's MacOS X, Linux, VMware (a widely used virtual machine monitor), and Google Android. Figure 1.9 traces the lineage of these operating systems.

time-sharing operating system

Time-sharing operating systems—such as Windows, MacOS, or Linux— are designed to support interactive use of the computer rather than the batch mode processing of earlier systems. With time-sharing, the user types input on a keyboard or other input device directly connected to the computer. Each keystroke or mouse action causes an interrupt to the processor signaling the event; the interrupt handler reads the event from the device and queues it inside the operating system. When the user's word processor, game, or other application resumes, it fetches the event from the operating system, processes it, and alters the display appropriately before fetching the next event. Hundreds or even thousands of such events can be processed per second, requiring both the operating system and the application to be designed for frequent, very short bursts of activity rather than the sustained execution model of batch processing.

The basic operation of a web server is similar to a time-sharing system. The web server waits for a packet to arrive, to request a web page, web search, or book purchase. The network hardware copies the arriving packet into memory using DMA. Once the transfer is complete, the hardware signals the packet's arrival by interrupting the processor. This triggers the server to perform the requested task. Likewise, the processor is interrupted as each block of a web page is read from disk into memory. Like a time-sharing system, server operating systems must be designed to handle very large numbers of short actions per second.

The earliest time-sharing systems supported many simultaneous users, but even this was just a phase. Eventually, computers became cheap enough that people could afford their own dedicated "personal" computers, which would sit patiently unused for much of the day. Access to shared data became paramount, cementing the shift to client-server computing.

1.3.5   Modern Operating Systems

Today, we have a vast diversity of computing devices, with many different operating systems running on them. The tradeoffs faced by an operating system designer depend on the physical capabilities of the hardware as well as application and user needs. Here are some examples of operating systems that you may have used recently:

- **Desktop, laptop, and netbook operating systems.** Examples include Windows 8, MacOS X, and Linux. These systems are single user, run many applications, and have various I/O devices. One might think that with only one user, there would be no need to design the system to support sharing, and indeed the initial personal computer operating systems took this approach. They had a very limited ability to isolate different parts of the system from each other. Over time, however, it became clear that stricter fault isolation was needed to improve system reliability and resilience against computer viruses. Other key design goals for these systems include adoption (to support a rich set of applications) and interactive performance.

- **Smartphone operating systems.** A smartphone is a cellphone with an embedded computer capable of running third party applications. Examples of smartphone operating systems include iOS, Android, Symbian, WebOS, Blackberry OS and Windows Phone. While smartphones have only one user, they must support many applications. Key design goals include responsiveness, support for a wide variety of applications, and efficient use of the battery. Another design goal is user privacy. Because third-party applications might surreptitiously gather private data such as the user's contact list for marketing purposes, the operating system must be designed to limit access to protected user data.

- **Server operating systems.** Search engines, web media, e-commerce sites, and email systems are hosted on computers in data centers; each of these computers runs an operating system, often an industrial strength version of one of the desktop systems described above. Usually, only a single application, such as a web server, runs per machine, but the operating system must coordinate thousands of simultaneous incoming network connections. Throughput in handling a large number of requests per second is a key design goal. At the same time, there is a premium on responsiveness: Amazon and Google both report that adding even 100 milliseconds of delay to each web request can significantly affect revenue. Servers also operate in a hostile environment, where malicious attackers may attempt to subvert or block the service; resistance to attack is an essential requirement.

- **Virtual machines.** As we noted, a virtual machine monitor is an operating system that can run another operating system as if it were an application. Examples include VMWare, Xen, and Windows Virtual PC. Virtual machine monitors face many of the same challenges as other operating systems, with the added challenge posed by coordinating a set of coordinators. A guest operating system running inside a virtual machine makes resource allocation and fault isolation decisions as if it were in complete control of its resources, even though it is sharing the system with other operating systems and applications.

  A commercially important use of virtual machines is to to allow a single server machine to run a set of independent services. Each virtual machine can be configured as needed by that particular service. For example, this allows multiple unrelated web servers to share the same physical hardware. The primary design goal for virtual machines is thus efficiency and low overhead.

- **Embedded systems.** Over time, computers have become cheap enough to integrate into any number of consumer devices, from cable TV set-top boxes, to microwave ovens, the control systems for automobiles and airplanes, LEGO robots, and medical devices, such as MRI machines and WiFi-based intravenous titration systems. Embedded devices typically run a customized operating system bundled with the task-specific software that controls the device. Although you might think these systems as too simple to merit much attention, software errors in them can have devastating effects. One example is the Therac-25, an early computer-controlled radiology device. Programming errors in the operating system code caused the system to malfunction, leading to several patient deaths.

- **Server clusters.** For fault tolerance, scale, and responsiveness, web sites are increasingly implemented on distributed clusters of computers housed in one or more geographically distributed data centers located close to users. If one computer fails due to a hardware fault, software crash, or power failure, another computer can take over its role. If demand for the web site exceeds what a single computer can accommodate, web requests can be partitioned among multiple machines. As with normal operating systems, server cluster applications run on top of an abstract cluster interface to isolate the application from hardware changes and to isolate faults in one application from affecting other applications in the same data center. Likewise, resources can be shared between: (1) various applications on the same web site (such as Google Search, Google Earth, and Gmail), and (2) multiple web sites hosted on the same cluster hardware (such as with Amazon's Elastic Compute Cloud or Google's Compute Engine).

1.3.6   Future Operating Systems

Where are operating systems heading from here over the next decade? Operating systems have become dramatically better at resisting malicious attacks, but they still have quite a ways to go. Provided security and reliability challenges can be met, huge potential benefits would result from having computers tightly control and coordinate physical infrastructure, such as the power grid, the telephone network, and a hospital's medical devices and medical record systems. Thousands of lives are lost annually through traffic accidents that could potentially be prevented through computer control of automobiles. If we are to rely on computers for these critical systems, we need greater assurance that operating systems are up to the task.

Second, underlying hardware changes will often trigger new work in operating system design. The future of operating systems is also the future of hardware:

- **Very large scale data centers.** Operating systems will need to coordinate the hundreds of thousands or even millions of computers in data centers to support essential online services.

- **Very large scale multicore systems.** Computer architectures already contain several processors per chip; this trend will continue, yielding systems with hundreds or possibly even thousands of processors per machine.

- **Ubiquitous portable computing devices.** With the advent of smartphones, tablets, and e-book readers, computers and their operating systems will become untethered from the keyboard and the screen, responding to voice, gestures, and perhaps even brain waves.

- **Very heterogeneous systems.** As every device becomes programmable, operating systems will be needed for a huge variety of devices, from supercomputers to refrigerators to individual light switches.

- **Very large scale storage.** All data that can be stored, will be; the operating system will need to store enormous amounts of data reliably, so that it can be retrieved at any point, even decades later.

Managing all this is the job of the operating system.

Exercises

1. What is an example of an operating system as:

   a) Referee?

   b) Illusionist?

   c) Glue?

2. What is the difference, if any, between the following terms:

   a) Reliability vs. availability?

   b) Security vs. privacy?

   c) Security enforcement vs. security policy?

   d) Throughput vs. response time?

   e) Efficiency vs. overhead?

   f) Application programming interface (API) vs. abstract virtual machine (AVM)?

   g) Abstract virtual machine (AVM) vs. hardware abstraction layer (HAL)?

   h) Proprietary vs. open operating system?

   i) Batch vs. interactive operating system?

   j) Host vs. guest operating system?

3. Define the term, direct memory access (DMA).

For the following questions, take a moment to speculate. We provide answers to these questions throughout the book, but, given what you know now, how would you answer them? Before there were operating systems, someone needed to develop solutions without being able to look them up! How would you have designed the first operating system?

4. Suppose a computer system and all of its applications were completely bug free. Suppose further that everyone in the world were completely honest and trustworthy. In other words, we need not consider fault isolation.

   a) How should an operating system allocate time on the processor? Should it give the entire processor to each application until it no longer needs it? If there were multiple tasks ready to go at the same time, should it schedule first the task with the least amount of work to do or the one with the most? Justify your answer.

   b) How should the operating system allocate physical memory to applications? What should happen if the set of applications does not fit in memory at the same time?

   c) How should the operating system allocate its disk space? Should the first user to ask acquire all of the free space? What would the likely outcome be for that policy?

5. Now suppose the computer system needs to support fault isolation. What hardware and/or operating support do you think would be needed to do the following?

   a) Protect an application's data structures in memory from being corrupted by other applications.

   b) Protecting one user's disk files from being accessed or corrupted by another user.

   c) Protecting the network from a virus trying to use your computer to send spam.

6. How should an operating system support communication between applications? Explain your reasoning.

   a) Through the file system?

   b) Through messages passed between applications?

   c) Through regions of memory shared between the applications?

   d) All of the above?

   e) None of the above?

7. How would you design combined hardware and software support to provide the illusion of a nearly infinite virtual memory on a limited amount of physical memory?

8. How would you design a system to run an entire operating system as an application on top of another operating system?

9. How would you design a system to update complex data structures on disk in a consistent fashion despite machine crashes?

10. Society itself must grapple with managing resources. What ways do governments use to allocate resources, isolate misuse, and foster sharing in real life?

11. Suppose you were tasked with designing and implementing an ultra-reliable and ultra-available operating system. What techniques would you use? What tests, if any, might be sufficient to convince you of the system's reliability, short of handing your operating system to millions of users to serve as beta testers?

12. MTTR, and therefore availability, can be improved by reducing the time to reboot a system after a failure. What techniques might you use to speed up booting? Would your techniques always work after a failure?

13. For the computer you are currently using, how should the operating system designers prioritize among reliability, security, portability, performance, and adoption? Explain why.

Part I

Kernels and Processes

Good fences make good neighbors.

17th century proverb

2 The Kernel Abstraction

protection

A central role of operating systems is *protection* — the isolation of potentially misbehaving applications and users so that they do not corrupt other applications or the operating system itself. Protection is essential to achieving several of the operating systems goals noted in the previous chapter:

Why does an operating system have a kernel?

- **Reliability.** Protection prevents bugs in one program from causing crashes in other programs or in the operating system. To the user, a system crash appears to be the operating system's fault, even if the root cause of the problem is some unexpected behavior by an application or user. Thus, for high system reliability, an operating system must bullet proof itself to operate correctly regardless of what an application or user might do.

- **Security.** Some users or applications on a system may be less than completely trustworthy; therefore, the operating system must limit the scope of what they can do. Without protection, a malicious user might surreptitiously change application files or even the operating system itself, leaving the user none the wiser. For example, if a malicious application can write directly to the disk, it could modify the file containing the operating system's code; the next time the system starts, the modified operating system would boot instead, installing spyware and disabling virus protection. For security, an operating system must prevent untrusted code from modifying system state.

- **Privacy.** On a multi-user system, each user must be limited to only the data that she is permitted to access. Without protection provided by the operating system, any user or application running on a system could access anyone's data, without the knowledge or approval of the data's

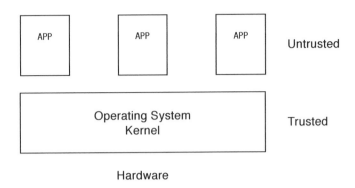

Figure 2.1: User-level and kernel-level operation. The operating system kernel is trusted to arbitrate between untrusted applications and users.

owner. For example, hackers often use popular applications—such as games or screen savers—as a way to gain access to personal email, telephone numbers, and credit card data stored on a smartphone or laptop. For privacy, an operating system must prevent untrusted code from accessing unauthorized data.

- **Fair resource allocation.** Protection is also needed for effective resource allocation. Without protection, an application could gather any amount of processing time, memory, or disk space that it wants. On a single-user system, a buggy application could prevent other applications from running or make them run so slowly that they appear to stall. On a multi-user system, one user could grab all of the system's resources. Thus, for efficiency and fairness, an operating system must be able to limit the amount of resources assigned to each application or user.

operating system kernel

Implementing protection is the job of the *operating system kernel*. The kernel, the lowest level of software running on the system, has full access to all of the machine hardware. The kernel is necessarily *trusted* to do anything with the hardware. Everything else—that is, the untrusted software running on the system— is run in a restricted environment with less than complete access to the full power of the hardware. Figure 2.1 illustrates this difference between kernel-level and user-level execution.

Do applications need to implement protection?

In turn, applications themselves often need to safely execute untrusted third party code. An example is a web browser executing embedded Javascript to draw a web page. Without protection, a script with an embedded virus can take control of the browser, making users think they are interacting directly with the web when in fact their web passwords are being forwarded to an attacker.

This design pattern—extensible applications running third-party scripts— occurs in many different domains. Applications become more powerful and widely used if third party developers and users can customize them, but doing so raises the issue of how to protect the application itself from rogue extensions. This chapter focuses on how the operating system protects the kernel from untrusted applications, but the principles also apply at the application level.

process

A *process* is the execution of an application program with restricted rights; the process is the abstraction for protected execution provided by the operating system kernel. A process needs permission from the operating system kernel before accessing the memory of any other process, before reading or writing to the disk, before changing hardware settings, and so forth. In other words, the operating system kernel mediates and checks each process's access to hardware. This chapter explains the process concept and how the kernel implements process isolation.

Does protection compromise performance?

A key consideration is the need to provide protection while still running application code at high speed. The operating system kernel runs directly on the processor with unlimited rights. The kernel can perform any operation available on the hardware. What about applications? They need to run on the processor with all potentially dangerous operations disabled. To make this work, hardware needs to provide a bit of assistance, which we will describe shortly. Throughout the book, there are similar examples of how small amounts of carefully designed hardware can help make it much easier for the operating system to provide what users want.

Of course, both the operating system kernel and application processes running with restricted rights are in fact sharing the same machine — the same processor, the same memory, and the same disk. When reading this chapter, keep these two perspectives in mind: when we are running the operating system kernel, it can do anything; when we are running an application process on behalf of a user, the process's behavior is restricted.

Thus, a processor running an operating system is somewhat akin to someone with a split personality. When running the operating system kernel, the processor is like a warden in charge on an insane asylum with complete access to everything. At other times, the processor runs application code in a process — the processor becomes an inmate, wearing a straightjacket locked in a padded cell by the warden, protected from harming anyone else. Of course, it is the same processor in both cases, sometimes completely trustworthy and at other times completely untrusted.

Chapter roadmap: Protection raises several important questions that we will answer in the rest of the chapter:

- **The Process Abstraction.** What is a process and how does it differ from a program? (Section 2.1)

- **Dual-Mode Operation.** What hardware enables the operating system to efficiently implement the process abstraction? (Section 2.2)

- **Types of Mode Transfer.** What causes the processor to switch control from a user-level program to the kernel? (Section 2.3)

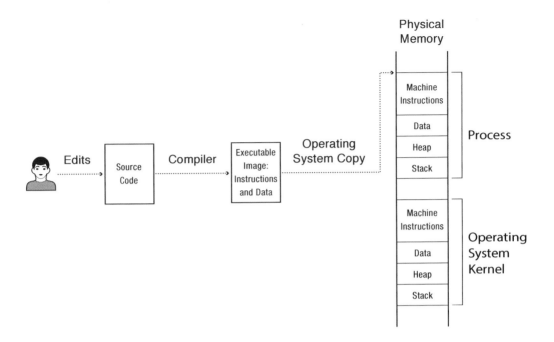

Figure 2.2: A user edits, compiles, and runs a user program. Other programs can also be stored in physical memory, including the operating system itself.

- **Implementing Safe Mode Transfer.** How do we safely switch between user level and the kernel? (Section 2.4)

- **Putting It All Together: x86 Mode Transfer.** What happens on an x86 mode switch? (Section 2.5)

- **Implementing Secure System Calls.** How do library code and the kernel work together to implement protected procedure calls from the application into the kernel? (Section 2.6)

- **Starting a New Process.** How does the operating system kernel start a new process? (Section 2.7)

- **Implementing Upcalls.** How does the operating system kernel deliver an asynchronous event to a user process? (Section 2.8)

- **Case Study: Booting an OS Kernel.** What steps are needed to start running an operating system kernel, to the point where it can create a process? (Section 2.9)

- **Case Study: Virtual Machines.** Can an operating system run inside a process? (Section 2.10)

2.1 | The Process Abstraction

What is a process?   In the model you are likely familiar with, illustrated in Figure 2.2, a programmer types code in some high-level language. A compiler converts that code into a sequence of machine instructions and stores those instructions in a file,

executable image   called the program's *executable image*. The compiler also defines any static data the program needs, along with its initial values, and includes them in the executable image.

To run the program, the operating system copies the instructions and data from the executable image into physical memory. The operating system sets

execution stack   aside a memory region, the *execution stack*, to hold the state of local variables during procedure calls. The operating system also sets aside a memory region,

heap   called the *heap*, for any dynamically allocated data structures the program might need. Of course, to copy the program into memory, the operating system itself must already be loaded into memory, with its own stack and heap.

Ignoring protection, once a program is loaded into memory, the operating system can start it running by setting the stack pointer and jumping to the program's first instruction. The compiler itself is just another program: the operating system starts the compiler by copying its executable image into memory and jumping to its first instruction.

To run multiple copies of the same program, the operating system can make multiple copies of the program's instructions, static data, heap, and stack in memory. As we describe in Chapter 8, most operating systems reuse memory wherever possible: they store only a single copy of a program's instructions when multiple copies of the program are executed at the same time. Even so, a separate copy of the program's data, heap, and stack are needed. For now, we will keep things simple and assume the operating system makes a separate copy of the entire program for each process.

What is the difference between a process and a program?   Thus, a process is an *instance* of a program, in much the same way that an object is an instance of a class in object-oriented programming. Each program can have zero, one or more processes executing it. For each instance of a program, there is a process with its own copy of the program in memory.

The operating system keeps track of the various processes on the computer

process control block   using a data structure called the *process control block*, or PCB. The PCB stores all the information the operating system needs about a particular process: where it is stored in memory, where its executable image resides on disk, which user asked it to execute, what privileges the process has, and so forth.

A process combines execution and protection.   Earlier, we defined a process as an instance of a program executing with restricted rights. Each of these roles — execution and protection — is important enough to merit several chapters.

This chapter focuses on protection, and so we limit our discussion to simple processes, each with one program counter, code, data, heap, and stack.

Some programs consist of multiple concurrent activities, or threads. A web browser, for example, might need to receive user input at the same time it is drawing the screen or receiving network input. Each of these separate

Processes, lightweight processes, and threads

The word "process", like many terms in computer science, has evolved over time. The evolution of words can sometimes trip up the unwary — systems built at different times will use the same word in significantly different ways.

A "process" was originally coined to mean what is now called a "thread" — a logical sequence of instructions that executes either operating system or application code. The concept of a process was developed as a way of simplifying the correct construction of early operating systems that provided no protection between application programs.

Organizing the operating system as a cooperating set of processes proved immensely successful, and soon almost every new operating system was built this way, including systems that also provided protection against malicious or buggy user programs. At the time, almost all user programs were simple, single-threaded programs with only one program counter and one stack, so there was no confusion. A process was needed to run a program, that is, a single sequential execution stream with a protection boundary.

As parallel computers became more popular, though, we once again needed a word for a logical sequence of instructions. A multiprocessor program can have multiple instruction sequences running in parallel, each with its own program counter, but all cooperating within a single protection boundary. For a time, these were called "lightweight processes" (each a sequence of instructions cooperating inside a protection boundary), but eventually the word "thread" became more widely used.

This leads to the current naming convention used in almost all modern operating systems: a process executes a program, consisting of one or more threads running inside a protection boundary.

---

activities has its own program counter and stack but operates on the same code and data as the other threads. The operating system runs multiple threads in a process, in much the same way that it runs multiple processes in physical memory. We generalize on the process abstraction to allow multiple activities in the same protection domain in Chapter 4.

2.2 | Dual-Mode Operation

What hardware enables the OS to efficiently implement the process abstraction?

Once a program is loaded into memory and the operating system starts the process, the processor fetches each instruction in turn, then decodes and executes it. Some instructions compute values, say, by multiplying two registers and putting the result into another register. Some instructions read or write locations in memory. Still other instructions, like branches or procedure calls, change the program counter and thus determine the next instruction to execute.

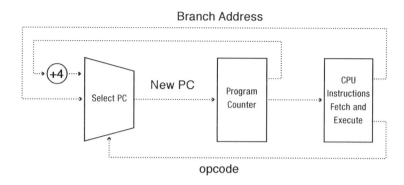

Figure 2.3: The basic operation of a CPU. Opcode, short for operation code, is the decoded instruction to be executed, e.g., branch, memory load, or arithmetic operation.

Figure 2.3 illustrates the basic operation of a processor.

How does the operating system kernel prevent a process from harming other processes or the operating system itself? After all, when multiple programs are loaded into memory at the same time, what prevents a process from overwriting another process's data structures, or even overwriting the operating system image stored on disk?

If we step back from any consideration of performance, a very simple, safe, and entirely hypothetical approach would be to have the operating system kernel simulate, step by step, every instruction in every user process. Instead of the processor directly executing instructions, a software interpreter would fetch, decode, and execute each user program instruction in turn. Before executing each instruction, the interpreter could check if the process had permission to do the operation in question: is it referencing part of its own memory, or someone else's? Is it trying to branch into someone else's code? Is it directly accessing the disk, or is it using the correct routines in the operating system to do so? The interpreter could allow all legal operations while halting any application that overstepped its bounds.

Now suppose we want to speed up our hypothetical simulator. Most instructions are perfectly safe, such as adding two registers together and storing the result in a third register. Can we modify the processor in some way to allow safe instructions to execute directly on the hardware?

dual-mode operation

user mode

kernel mode

To accomplish this, we implement the same checks as in our hypothetical interpreter, but in hardware rather than software. This is called *dual-mode operation*, represented by a single bit in the processor status register that signifies the current mode of the processor. In *user mode*, the processor checks each instruction before executing it to verify that it is permitted to be performed by that process. (We describe the specific checks next.) In *kernel mode*, the operating system executes with protection checks turned off.

Figure 2.4 shows the operation of a dual-mode processor; the program counter and the mode bit together control the processor's operation. In turn, the mode bit is modified by some instructions, just as the program counter is

The kernel vs. the rest of the operating system

The operating system kernel is a crucial piece of an operating system, but it is only a portion of the overall operating system. In most modern operating systems, a portion of the operating system runs in user mode as a library linked into each application. An example is library code that manages an application's menu buttons. To encourage a common user interface across applications, most operating systems provide a library of user interface widgets. Applications can write their own user interface routines, but most developers choose to reuse the routines provided by the operating system. This code could run in the kernel but does not need to do so. If the application crashes, it will not matter if that application's menu buttons stop working. The library code (but not the operating system kernel) *shares fate* with the rest of the application: a problem with one has the same effect as a problem with the other.

Likewise, parts of the operating system can run in their own user-level processes. A window manager is one example. The window manager directs mouse actions and keyboard input that occurs inside a window to the correct application, and the manager also ensures that each application modifies only that application's portion of the screen, and not the operating system's menu bar or any other application's window. Without this restriction, a malicious application could potentially take control of the machine. For example, a virus could present a login prompt that looked identical to the system login, potentially inducing users to disclose their passwords to the attacker.

Why not include the entire operating system — the library code and any user-level processes — in the kernel itself? While that might seem more logical, one reason is that it is often easier to debug user-level code than kernel code. The kernel can use low-level hardware to implement debugging support for breakpoints and for single stepping through application code; to single step the kernel requires an even lower-level debugger running underneath the kernel. The difficulty of debugging operating system kernels was the original motivation behind the development of virtual machines.

More importantly, the kernel must be trusted, as it has full control over the hardware. Any error in the kernel can corrupt the disk, the memory of some unrelated application, or simply crash the system. By separating out code that does not need to be in the kernel, the operating system can become more reliable — a bug in the window system is bad enough, but it would be even worse if it could corrupt the disk. This illustrates the *principle of least privilege*, that security and reliability are enhanced if each part of the system has exactly the privileges it needs to do its job, and no more.

modified by some instructions.

What hardware is needed to let the operating system kernel protect applications and users from one another, yet also let user code run directly on the processor? At a minimum, the hardware must support three things:

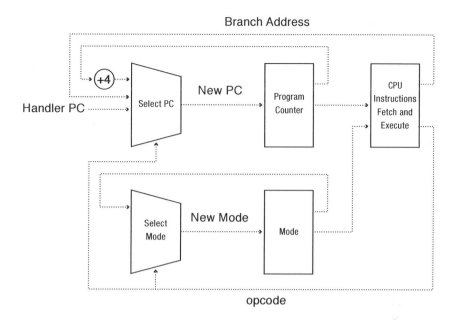

Figure 2.4: The operation of a CPU with kernel and user modes.

- **Privileged Instructions.** All potentially unsafe instructions are prohibited when executing in user mode. (Section 2.2.1)

- **Memory Protection.** All memory accesses outside of a process's valid memory region are prohibited when executing in user mode. (Section 2.2.2)

- **Timer Interrupts.** Regardless of what the process does, the kernel must have a way to periodically regain control from the current process. (Section 2.2.3)

In addition, the hardware must also provide a way to safely transfer control from user mode to kernel mode and back. As the mechanisms to do this are relatively involved, we defer the discussion of that topic to Sections 2.3 and 2.4.

2.2.1 Privileged Instructions

What instructions can't a process execute?

Process isolation is possible only if there is a way to limit programs running in user mode from directly changing their privilege level. We discuss in Section 2.3 that processes can indirectly change their privilege level by executing a special instruction, called a *system call*, to transfer control into the kernel at a fixed location defined by the operating system. Other than transferring control into the operating system kernel (that is, in effect, becoming the kernel) at these fixed locations, an application process cannot change its privilege level.

The processor status register and privilege levels

Conceptually, the kernel/user mode is a one-bit register. When set to 1, the processor is in kernel mode and can do anything. When set to 0, the processor is in user mode and is restricted. On most processors, the kernel/user mode is stored in the *processor status register*. This register contains flags that control the processor's operation and is typically not directly accessible to application code. Rather, flags are set or reset as a by-product of executing instructions. For example, the hardware automatically saves the status register to memory when an interrupt occurs because otherwise the interrupt handler code would inadvertently overwrite its contents.

The kernel/user mode bit is one flag in the processor status register, set whenever the kernel is entered and reset whenever the kernel switches back to user mode. Other flags include *condition codes*, set as a side effect of arithmetic operations, to allow a more compact encoding of conditional branch instructions. Still other flags can specify whether the processor is executing with 16-bit, 32-bit, or 64-bit addresses. The specific contents of the processor status register are processor architecture dependent.

Some processor architectures, including the Intel x86, support more than two privilege levels in the processor status register (the x86 supports four privilege levels). The original reason for this was to allow the operating system kernel to be separated into two layers: (i) a core with unlimited access to the machine, and (ii) an outer layer restricted from certain operations, but with more power than completely unprivileged application code. This way, bugs in one part of the operating system kernel might not crash the entire system. However, to our knowledge, neither MacOS, Windows, nor Linux make use of this feature.

A potential future use for multiple privilege levels would be to simplify running an operating system as an application, or virtual machine, on top of another operating system. Applications running on top of the virtual machine operating system would run at user level; the virtual machine would run at some intermediate level; and the true kernel would run in kernel mode. Of course, with only four levels, this does not work for a virtual machine running on a virtual machine running on a virtual machine. For our discussion, we assume the simpler and more universal case of two levels of hardware protection.

Other instructions are also limited to use by kernel code. The application cannot be allowed to change the set of memory locations it can access; we discuss in Section 2.2.2 how limiting an application to accessing only its own memory is essential to preventing it from either intentionally, or accidentally, corrupting or misusing the data or code from other applications or the operating system. Further, applications cannot disable processor interrupts, as we will explain in Section 2.2.3.

Instructions available in kernel mode, but not in user mode, are called

privileged instruction

privileged instructions. The operating system kernel must be able to execute these instructions to do its work — it needs to change privilege levels, adjust memory access, and disable and enable interrupts. If these instructions were available to applications, then a rogue application would in effect have the power of the operating system kernel.

Thus, while application programs can use only a subset of the full instruction set, the operating system executes in kernel mode with the full power of the hardware.

What happens if an application attempts to access restricted memory or attempts to change its privilege level? Such actions cause a *processor exception.* Unlike taking an exception in a programming language where the language runtime and user code handles the exception, a processor exception causes the processor to transfer control to an exception handler in the operating system kernel. Usually, the kernel simply halts the process after a privilege violation.

EXAMPLE

What could happen if applications were allowed to jump into kernel mode at any location in the kernel?

ANSWER

Although it might seem that the worst that could happen would be that the operating system would crash (bad enough!), this might also allow a malicious application to gain access to privileged data or possibly control over the machine. The operating system kernel implements a set of privileged services on behalf of applications. Typically, one of the first steps in a kernel routine is to verify whether the user has permission to perform the operation; for example, the file system checks if the user has permission to read a file before returning the data. If an application can jump past the permission check, it could potentially evade the kernel's security limits.   □

2.2.2 Memory Protection

How does the hardware limit a program to only accessing its own memory?

To run an application process, both the operating system and the application must be resident in memory at the same time. The application must be in memory in order to execute, while the operating system must be there to start the program and to handle any interrupts, processor exceptions, or system calls that happen while the program runs. Further, other application processes may also be stored in memory; for example, you may read email, download songs, Skype, instant message, and browse the web at the same time.

To make memory sharing safe, the operating system must be able to configure the hardware so that each application process can read and write only its own memory, not the memory of the operating system or any other application. Otherwise, an application could modify the operating system kernel's code or data to gain control over the system. For example, the application could change the login program to give the attacker full system administrator privileges. While it might seem that read-only access to memory is harmless, recall that operating systems need to provide both security and privacy. Kernel data structures — such as the file system buffer — may contain private user

MS/DOS and memory protection

As an illustration of the power of memory protection, MS/DOS was an early Microsoft operating system that did not provide it. Instead, user programs could read and modify any memory location in the system, including operating system data structures. While this was seen as acceptable for a personal computer that was only used by a single person at a time, there were a number of downsides. One obvious problem was system reliability: application bugs frequently crashed the operating system or corrupted other applications. The lack of memory protection also made the system more vulnerable to computer viruses.

Over time, some applications took advantage of the ability to change operating system data structures, for example, to change certain control parameters or to directly manipulate the frame buffer for controlling the display. As a result, changing the operating system became quite difficult; either the new version could not run the old applications, limiting its appeal, or it needed to leave these data structures in precisely the same place as they were in the old version. In other words, memory protection is not only useful for reliability and security; it also helps to enforce a well-defined interface between applications and the operating system kernel to aid future evolvability and portability.

data. Likewise, user passwords may be stored in kernel memory while they are being verified.

How does the operating system prevent a user program from accessing parts of physical memory? We discuss a wide variety of different approaches in Chapter 8, but early computers pioneered a simple mechanism to provide protection. We describe it now to illustrate the general principle.

base and bound memory protection

With this approach, a processor has two extra registers, called *base and bound*. The base specifies the start of the process's memory region in physical memory, while the bound gives its endpoint (Figure 2.5). These registers can be changed only by privileged instructions, that is, by the operating system executing in kernel mode. User-level code cannot change their values.

Every time the processor fetches an instruction, it checks the address of the program counter to see if it is between the base and the bound registers. If so, the instruction fetch is allowed to proceed; otherwise, the hardware raises an exception, suspending the program and transferring control back to the operating system kernel. Although it might seem extravagant to perform two extra comparisons for each instruction, memory protection is worth the cost. In fact, we will discuss much more sophisticated and "extravagant" memory protection schemes in Chapter 8.

Likewise, for instructions that read or write data to memory, the processor checks each memory reference against the base and bound registers, generat-

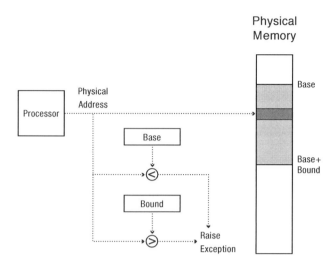

Figure 2.5: Base and bound memory protection using physical addresses. Every code and data address generated by the program is first checked to verify that its address lies within the memory region of the process.

ing a processor exception if the boundaries are violated. Complex instructions, such as a block copy instruction, must check every location touched by the instruction, to ensure that the application does not inadvertently or maliciously read or write to a buffer that starts in its own region but that extends into the kernel's region. Otherwise, applications could read or overwrite key parts of the operating system code or data and thereby gain control of the system.

The operating system kernel executes without the base and bound registers, allowing it to access any memory on the system — the kernel's memory or the memory of any application process running on the system. Because applications touch only their own memory, the kernel must explicitly copy any input or output into or out of the application's memory region. For example, a simple program might print "hello world". The kernel must copy the string out of the application's memory region into the screen buffer.

Memory allocation with base and bound registers is simple, analogous to heap memory allocation. When a program starts up, the kernel finds a free block of contiguous physical memory with enough room to store the entire program, its data, heap and execution stack. If the free block is larger than needed, the kernel returns the remainder to the heap for allocation to some other process.

Using physically addressed base and bound registers can provide protection, but this does not provide some important features:

- **Expandable heap and stack.** With a single pair of base and bound registers per process, the amount of memory allocated to a program is fixed when the program starts. Although the operating system can change the bound, most programs have two (or more) memory regions that need

Memory-mapped devices

On most computers, the operating system controls input/output devices — such as the disk, network, or keyboard — by reading and writing to special memory locations. Each device monitors the memory bus for the address assigned to it, and when it sees its address, the device triggers the desired I/O operation.

The operating system can use memory protection to prevent user-level processes from accessing these special memory locations. Thus, memory protection has the added advantage of limiting direct access to input/output devices by user code. By limiting each process to just its own memory locations, the kernel prevents processes from directly reading or writing to the disk controller or other devices. In this way, a buggy or malicious application cannot modify the operating system's image stored on disk, and a user cannot gain access to another user's files without first going through the operating system to check file permissions.

---

to independently expand depending on program behavior. The execution stack holds procedure local variables and grows with the depth of the procedure call graph; the heap holds dynamically allocated objects. Most systems today grow the heap and the stack from opposite sides of program memory; this is difficult to accommodate with a pair of base and bound registers.

- **Memory sharing.** Base and bound registers do not allow memory to be shared between different processes, as would be useful for sharing code between multiple processes running the same program or using the same library.

- **Physical memory addresses.** When a program is compiled and linked, the addresses of its procedures and global variables are set relative to the beginning of the executable file, that is, starting at zero. With the mechanism we have just described using base and bound registers, each program is loaded into physical memory at runtime and must use those physical memory addresses. Since a program may be loaded at different locations depending on what other programs are running at the same time, the kernel must change every instruction and data location that refers to a global address, each time the program is loaded into memory.

- **Memory fragmentation.** Once a program starts, it is nearly impossible to relocate it. The program might store pointers in registers or on the execution stack (for example, the program counter to use when returning from a procedure), and these pointers need to be changed to move the program to a different region of physical memory. Over time, as

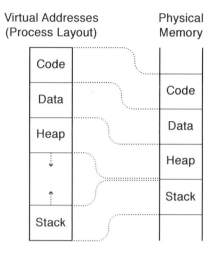

Figure 2.6: Virtual addresses allow the stack and heap regions of a process to grow independently. To grow the heap, the operating system can move the heap in physical memory without changing the heap's virtual address.

applications start and finish at irregular times, memory will become increasingly fragmented. Potentially, memory fragmentation may reach a point where there is not enough contiguous space to start a new process, despite sufficient free memory in aggregate.

virtual address

For these reasons, most modern processors introduce a level of indirection, called *virtual addresses*. With virtual addresses, every process's memory starts at the same place, e.g., zero. Each process thinks that it has the entire machine to itself, although obviously that is not the case in reality. The hardware translates these virtual addresses to physical memory locations. A simple algorithm would be to add the base register to every virtual address so that the process can use virtual addresses starting from zero.

In practice, modern systems use much more complex algorithms to translate between virtual and physical addresses. The layer of indirection provided by virtual addresses gives operating systems enormous flexibility to efficiently manage physical memory. For example, many systems with virtual addresses allocate physical memory in fixed-sized, rather than variable-sized, chunks to reduce fragmentation.

Virtual addresses can also let the heap and the stack start at separate ends of the virtual address space so they can grow according to program need (Figure 2.6). If either the stack or heap grows beyond its initially allocated region, the operating system can move it to a different larger region in physical memory but leave it at the same virtual address. The expansion is completely transparent to the user process. We discuss virtual addresses in more depth in Chapter 8.

```
int staticVar = 0;        // a static variable
main() {
    staticVar += 1;

    // sleep causes the program to wait for x seconds
    sleep(10);
    printf ("Address: %x; Value: %d\n", &staticVar, staticVar);
}

Produces:
    Address: 5328; Value: 1
```

Figure 2.7: A simple C program whose output illustrates the difference between execution in physical memory versus virtual memory. When multiple copies of this program run simultaneously, the output does not change.

How can we tell if a machine uses virtual addresses?

Figure 2.7 lists a simple test program to verify that a computer supports virtual addresses. The program has a single static variable; it updates the value of the variable, waits for a few seconds, and then prints the location of the variable and its value.

With virtual addresses, if multiple copies of this program run simultaneously, each copy of the program will print exactly the same result. This would be impossible if each copy were directly addressing physical memory locations. In other words, each instance of the program appears to run in its own complete copy of memory: when it stores a value to a memory location, it alone sees its changes to that location. Other processes change their own copies of the memory location. In this way, a process cannot alter any other process's memory, because it has no way to reference the other process's memory; only the kernel can read or write the memory of a process other than itself.

This is very much akin to a set of television shows, each occupying their own universe, even though they all appear on the same television. Events in one show do not (normally) affect the plot lines of other shows. Sitcom characters are blissfully unaware that Jack Bauer has just saved the world from nuclear Armageddon. Of course, just as television shows can from time to time share characters, processes can also communicate if the kernel allows it. We will discuss how this happens in Chapter 3.

EXAMPLE   Suppose we have a "perfect" object-oriented language and compiler in which only an object's methods can access the data inside the object. If the operating system runs only programs written in that language, would it still need hardware memory address protection?

ANSWER   In theory, no, but in practice, yes. The compiler would be responsible for ensuring that no application program read or modified data outside of its own objects. This requires, for example, the language runtime to do garbage collection: once an object is released back to the heap (and possibly reused by some other application), the application cannot continue to hold a pointer to the object.

Address randomization

Computer viruses often work by attacking hidden vulnerabilities in operating system and server code. For example, if the operating system developer forgets to check the length of a user string before copying it into a buffer, the copy can overwrite the data stored immediately after the buffer. If the buffer is stored on the stack, this might allow a malicious user to overwrite the return program counter from the procedure; the attacker can then cause the server to jump to an arbitrary point (for example, into code embedded in the string). These attacks are easier to mount when a program uses the same locations for the same variables each time it runs.

Most operating systems, such as Linux, MacOS, and Windows, combat viruses by randomizing (within a small range) the virtual addresses that a program uses each time it runs. This is called *address space layout randomization*. A common technique is to pick a slightly different start address for the heap and stack for each execution. Thus, in Figure 2.7, if instead we printed the address of a procedure local variable, the address might change from run to run, even though the value of the variable would still be 1.

Some systems have begun to randomize procedure and static variable locations each, as well as the offset between adjacent procedure records on the stack to make it harder to force the system to jump to the attacker's code. Nevertheless, each process appears to have its own copy of memory, disjoint from all other processes.

In practice, this approach means that system security depends on the correct operation of the compiler in addition to the operating system kernel. Any bug in the compiler or language runtime becomes a possible way for an attacker to gain control of the machine. Many languages have extensive runtime libraries to simplify the task of writing programs in that language; often these libraries are written for performance in a language closer to the hardware, such as C. Any bug in a library routine also becomes a possible means for an attacker to gain control.

Although it may seem redundant, many systems use both language-level protection and process-level protection. For example, Google's Chrome web browser creates a separate process (e.g., one per browser tab) to interpret the HTML, Javascript, or Java on a web page. This way, a malicious attacker must compromise both the language runtime as well as the operating system process boundary to gain control of the client machine.   □

MacOS and preemptive scheduling

Until 2002, Apple's MacOS lacked the ability to force a process to yield the processor back to the kernel. Instead, all application programmers were told to design their systems to periodically call into the operating system to check if there was other work to be done. The operating system would then save the state of the original process, switch control to another application, and return only when it again became the original process's turn. This had a drawback: if a process failed to yield, e.g., because it had a bug and entered an infinite loop, the operating system kernel had no recourse. The user needed to reboot the machine to return control to the operating system. This happened frequently enough that it was given its own name: the "spinning cursor of death."

2.2.3   Timer Interrupts

How does the kernel regain control from a runaway process?

Process isolation also requires hardware to provide a way for the operating system kernel to periodically regain control of the processor. When the operating system starts a user-level program, the process is free to execute any user-level (non-privileged) instructions it chooses, call any function in the process's memory region, load or store any value to its memory, and so forth. To the user program, it appears to have complete control of the hardware within the limits of its memory region.

However, this too is only an illusion. If the application enters an infinite loop, or if the user simply becomes impatient and wants the system to stop the application, then the operating system must be able to regain control. Of course, the operating system needs to execute instructions to decide if it should stop the application, but if the application controls the processor, the operating system by definition is not running on that processor.

The operating system also needs to regain control of the processor in normal operation. Suppose you are listening to music on your computer, downloading a file, and typing at the same time. To smoothly play the music, and to respond in a timely way to user input, the operating system must be able to regain control to switch to a new task.

hardware timer

Almost all computer systems include a device called a *hardware timer*, which can be set to interrupt the processor after a specified delay (either in time or after some number of instructions have been executed). Each timer interrupts only one processor, so a multiprocessor will usually have a separate timer for each CPU. The operating system might set each timer to expire every few milliseconds; human reaction time is a few hundred of milliseconds. Resetting the timer is a privileged operation, accessible only within the kernel, so that the user-level process cannot inadvertently or maliciously disable the timer.

When the timer interrupt occurs, the hardware transfers control from the user process to the kernel running in kernel mode. Other hardware interrupts, such as to signal the processor that an I/O device has completed its work, likewise transfer control from the user process to the kernel. A timer or other interrupt does not imply that the program has an error; in most cases, after resetting the timer, the operating system resumes execution of the process, setting the mode, program counter and registers back to the values they had immediately before the interrupt occurred. We discuss the hardware and kernel mechanisms for implementing interrupts in Section 2.4.

EXAMPLE   How does the kernel know if an application is in an infinite loop?

ANSWER   It doesn't. Typically, the operating system will terminate a process only when requested by the user or system administrator, e.g., because the application has become non-responsive to user input. The operating system needs to be able to regain control to be able to ask the user if she wants to shut down a particular process.   □

2.3 | Types of Mode Transfer

Once the kernel has placed a user process in a carefully constructed sandbox, the next question is how to safely transition from executing a user process to executing the kernel, and vice versa. These transitions are not rare events. A high-performance web server, for example, might switch between user mode and kernel mode thousands of times per second. Thus, the mechanism must be both fast and safe, leaving no room for malicious or buggy programs to corrupt the kernel, either intentionally or inadvertently.

2.3.1   User to Kernel Mode

What causes execution to switch into the kernel?

We first focus on transitions from user mode to kernel mode; as we will see, transitioning in the other direction works by "undo"-ing the transition from the user process into the kernel.

There are three reasons for the kernel to take control from a user process: interrupts, processor exceptions, and system calls. Interrupts occur asynchronously — that is, they are triggered by an external event and can cause a transfer to kernel mode after any user-mode instruction.

Processor exceptions and system calls are synchronous events triggered by process execution. We use the term *trap* to refer to any synchronous transfer of control from user mode to the kernel; some systems use the term more generically for any transfer of control from a less privileged to a more privileged level.

trap

interrupt

How does an I/O device get the processor's attention?

- **Interrupts.** An *interrupt* is an asynchronous signal to the processor that some external event has occurred that may require its attention. As the processor executes instructions, it checks for whether an interrupt has arrived. If so, it completes or stalls any instructions that are in progress. Instead of fetching the next instruction, the processor hardware saves the current execution state and starts executing at a specially designated interrupt handler in the kernel. On a multiprocessor, an interrupt is taken on only one of the processors; the others continue to execute as if nothing happened.

Each different type of interrupt requires its own handler. For timer interrupts, the handler checks if the current process is being responsive to user input to detect if the process has gone into an infinite loop. The timer handler can also switch execution to a different process to ensure that each process gets a turn. If no change is needed, the timer handler resumes execution at the interrupted instruction, transparently to the user process.

Interrupts are also used to inform the kernel of the completion of I/O requests. For example, mouse device hardware triggers an interrupt every time the user moves or clicks on the mouse. The kernel, in turn, notifies the appropriate user process — the one the user was "mousing" across. Virtually every I/O device — the Ethernet, WiFi, hard disk, thumb drive, keyboard, mouse — generates an interrupt whenever some input arrives for the processor and whenever a request completes.

polling

An alternative to interrupts is *polling*: the kernel loops, checking each input/output device to see if an event has occurred that requires handling. Needless to say, if the kernel is polling, it is not available to run user-level code.

Interprocessor interrupts are another source of interrupts. A processor can send an interrupt to any other processor. The kernel uses these interrupts to coordinate actions across the multiprocessor; for example, when a parallel program exits, the kernel sends interrupts to stop the program from continuing to run on any other processor.

processor exception

What happens when a program executes an illegal instruction?

• **Processor exceptions.** A *processor exception* is a hardware event caused by user program behavior that causes a transfer of control to the kernel. As with an interrupt, the hardware finishes all previous instructions, saves the current execution state, and starts running at a specially designated exception handler in the kernel. For example, a processor exception occurs whenever a process attempts to perform a privileged instruction or accesses memory outside of its own memory region. Other processor exceptions occur when a process divides an integer by zero, accesses a word of memory with a non-aligned address, attempts to write to read-only memory, and so forth. In these cases, the operating system simply halts the process and returns an error code to the user. On a multiprocessor, the exception only stops execution on the processor triggering the exception; the kernel then needs to send interprocessor interrupts to stop execution of the parallel program on other processors.

Buffer descriptors and high-performance I/O

In early computer systems, the key to good performance was to keep the processor busy; particularly for servers, the key to good performance today is keeping I/O devices, such as the network and disk device, busy. Neither Internet nor disk bandwidth has kept pace with the rapid improvement in processor performance over the past four decades, leaving them relatively more important than the CPU to system performance.

A simple, but inefficient, approach to designing the operating system software to manage an I/O device is to allow only one I/O operation to the device at any one time. In this case, interrupt handling can be a limiting factor to performance. When the device completes a request, it raises an interrupt, causing the device interrupt handler to run. The handler can then issue the next pending request to the hardware. In the meantime, while the processor is handling the interrupt, the device is idle.

For higher performance, the operating system sets up a circular queue of requests for each device to handle. (A network interface will have two queues: one for incoming packets and one for outgoing packets.) Each entry in the queue, called a *buffer descriptor*, specifies one I/O operation: the requested operation (e.g., disk read or write) and the location of the buffer to contain the data. The device hardware reads the buffer descriptor to determine what operations to perform. Provided the queue of buffer descriptors is full, the device can start working on the next operation while the operating system handles with the previous one.

Buffer descriptors are stored in memory, accessed by the device using DMA (direct memory access). An implication is that each logical I/O operation can involve several DMA requests: one to download the buffer descriptor from memory into the device, then to copy the data in or out, and then to store the success/failure of the operation back into buffer descriptor.

Processor exceptions are also caused by more benign program events. For example, to set a breakpoint in a program, the kernel replaces the machine instruction in memory with a special instruction that invokes a trap. When the program reaches that point in its execution, the hardware switches into the kernel. The kernel restores the old instruction and transfers control to the debugger. The debugger can then examine the program's variables, set a new breakpoint, and resume the program at the instruction causing the exception.

system call

How does a user program ask the kernel to do something?

- **System calls.** User processes can also transition into the operating system kernel voluntarily to request that the kernel perform an operation on the user's behalf. A *system call* is any procedure provided by the kernel that can be called from user level. Most processors implement system calls with a special trap or syscall instruction. However, a special instruction is

Processor exceptions and virtualization

Processor exceptions are a particularly powerful tool for virtualization — the emulation of hardware that does not actually exist. As one example, it is common for different versions of a processor architecture family to support some parts of the instruction set and not others, such as when an inexpensive, low-power processor does not support floating point operations. At some cost in performance, the operating system can use processor exceptions to make the difference completely transparent to the user process. When the program issues a floating point instruction, an exception is raised, trapping into the operating system kernel. Instead of halting the process, the operating system can *emulate* the missing instruction, and, on completion, return to the user process at the instruction immediately after the one that caused the exception. In this way, the same program binary can run on different versions of the processor.

More generally, processor exceptions are used to transparently emulate a virtual machine. When a guest operating system is running as a user-level process on top of an operating system, it will attempt to execute privileged instructions as if it were running on physical hardware. These instructions will cause processor exceptions, trapping into the host operating system kernel. To maintain the illusion of physical hardware, the host kernel then performs the requested instruction of behalf of the user-level virtual machine and restarts the guest operating system at the instruction immediately following the one that caused the exception.

As a final example, processor exceptions are a key building block for memory management. With most types of virtual addressing, the processor can be set up to take an exception whenever it reads or writes inside a particular virtual address range. This allows the kernel to treat memory as *virtual* — a portion of the program memory may be stored on disk instead on in physical memory. When the program touches a missing address, the operating system exception handler fills in the data from disk before resuming the program. In this way, the operating system can execute programs that require more memory than can fit on the machine at the same time.

---

not strictly required; on some systems, a process triggers a system call by executing an instruction with a specific invalid opcode.

As with an interrupt or a processor exception, the trap instruction changes the processor mode from user to kernel and starts executing in the kernel at a pre-defined handler. To protect the kernel from misbehaving user programs, it is essential that the hardware transfers control on a system call to a pre-defined address — user processes *cannot* be allowed to jump to arbitrary places in the kernel.

Operating systems can provide any number of system calls. Examples include system calls to establish a connection to a web server, to send or receive packets over the network, to create or delete files, to read or write data into files, and to create a new user process. To the user program, these are called like normal procedures, with parameters and return values. The caller needs to be concerned only with the interface; it does not need to know that the routine is actually being implemented by the kernel. The kernel handles the details of checking and copying arguments, performing the operation, and copying return values back into the process's memory. When the kernel completes the system call, it resumes user-level execution at the instruction immediately after the trap.

2.3.2   Kernel to User Mode

What causes execution to switch back to user mode?

Just as there are several different types of transitions from user to kernel mode, there are several types of transitions from kernel to user mode:

- **New process.** To start a new process, the kernel copies the program into memory, sets the program counter to the first instruction of the process, sets the stack pointer to the base of the user stack, and switches to user mode.

- **Resume after an interrupt, processor exception, or system call.** When the kernel finishes handling the request, it resumes execution of the interrupted process by restoring its program counter (in the case of a system call, the instruction after the trap), restoring its registers, and changing the mode back to user level.

- **Switch to a different process.** In some cases, such as on a timer interrupt, the kernel switches to a different process than the one that had been running before the interrupt. Since the kernel will eventually resume the old process, the kernel needs to save the process state — its program counter, registers, and so forth — in the process's control block. The kernel can then resume a different process by loading its state — its program counter, registers, and so forth — from the process's control block into the processor and then switching to user mode.

- **User-level upcall.** Many operating systems provide user programs with the ability to receive asynchronous notification of events. The mechanism, which we describe in Section 2.8, is similar to kernel interrupt handling, except at user level.

2.4 | Implementing Safe Mode Transfer

How do we safely switch between user and kernel modes?

Whether transitioning from user to kernel mode or in the opposite direction, care must be taken to ensure that a buggy or malicious user program cannot corrupt the kernel. Although the basic idea is simple, the low-level implementation can be a bit complex: the processor must save its state and switch what it is doing, *while* executing instructions that might alter the state that it is in the process of saving. This is akin to rebuilding a car's transmission while it barrels down the road at 60 mph.

The context switch code must be carefully crafted, and it relies on hardware support. To avoid confusion and reduce the possibility of error, most operating systems have a common sequence of instructions both for entering the kernel — whether due to interrupts, processor exceptions or system calls — and for returning to user level, again regardless of the cause.

At a minimum, this common sequence must provide:

- **Limited entry into the kernel.** To transfer control to the operating system kernel, the hardware must ensure that the entry point into the kernel is one set up by the kernel. User programs cannot be allowed to jump to arbitrary locations in the kernel. For example, the kernel code for handling the read file system call first checks whether the user program has permission to do so. If not, the kernel should return an error. Without limited entry points into the kernel, a malicious program could jump immediately after the code to perform the check, allowing the program to access to anyone's file.

- **Atomic changes to processor state.** In user mode, the program counter and stack point to memory locations in the user process; memory protection prevents the user process from accessing any memory outside of its region. In kernel mode, the program counter and stack point to memory locations in the kernel; memory protection is changed to allow the kernel to access both its own data and that of the user process. Transitioning between the two is atomic — the mode, program counter, stack, and memory protection are all changed at the same time.

- **Transparent, restartable execution.** An event may interrupt a user-level process at any point, between any instruction and the next one. For example, the processor could have calculated a memory address, loaded it into a register, and be about to store a value to that address. The operating system must be able to restore the state of the user program exactly as it was before the interrupt occurred. To the user process, an interrupt is invisible, except that the program temporarily slows down. A "hello world" program is not written to understand interrupts, but an interrupt might still occur while the program is running.

  On an interrupt, the processor saves its current state to memory, temporarily defers further events, changes to kernel mode, and then jumps to the interrupt or exception handler. When the handler finishes, the steps are reversed: the processor state is restored from its saved location, with the interrupted program none the wiser.

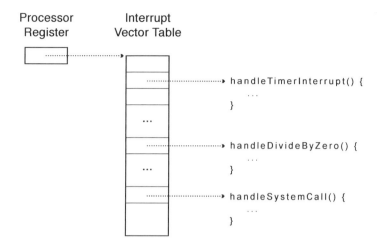

Figure 2.8: An interrupt vector table lists the kernel routines to handle various hardware interrupts, processor exceptions, and system calls.

With that context, we now describe the hardware and software mechanism for handling an interrupt, processor exception, or system call. Later, we reuse this same basic mechanism as a building block for implementing user-level signals.

2.4.1   Interrupt Vector Table

How does the hardware know which location to jump to on a trap?

interrupt vector table

interrupt handler

When an interrupt, processor exception or system call trap occurs, the operating system must take different actions depending on whether the event is a divide-by-zero exception, a file read system call, or a timer interrupt. How does the processor know what code to run?

As Figure 2.8 illustrates, the processor has a special register that points to an area of kernel memory called the *interrupt vector table*. The interrupt vector table is an array of pointers, with each entry pointing to the first instruction of a different handler procedure in the kernel. An *interrupt handler* is the term used for the procedure called by the kernel on an interrupt.

The format of the interrupt vector table is processor-specific. On the x86, for example, interrupt vector table entries 0 - 31 are for different types of processor exceptions (such as divide-by-zero); entries 32 - 255 are for different types of interrupts (timer, keyboard, and so forth); and, by convention, entry 64 points to the system call trap handler. The hardware determines which hardware device caused the interrupt, whether the trap instruction was executed, or what exception condition occurred. Thus, the hardware can select the right entry from the interrupt vector table and invoke the appropriate handler.

Some other processors have a smaller number of entry points, instead putting a code indicating the cause of the interrupt into a special hardware

Multiprocessors and interrupt routing

On a multiprocessor, which of the various processors should take an interrupt? Some early multiprocessors dedicated a single processor ("processor 0") to handle all external interrupts. If an event required a change to what one of the other processors was doing, processor 0 could send an interprocessor interrupt to trigger that processor to switch to a new process.

For systems needing to do a large amount of input and output, such as a web server, directing all I/O through a single processor can become a bottleneck. In modern systems, interrupt routing is increasingly programmable, under control of the kernel. Each processor usually has its own hardware timer. Likewise, disk I/O events can be sent directly to the processor that requested the I/O operation rather than to a random processor. Modern processors can run substantially faster if their data is already loaded into the processor cache, versus if their code and data are in some other processor's cache.

Efficient delivery of network I/O packets is even more challenging. A high performance server might send and receive tens of thousands of packets per second, representing thousands of different connections. From a processing perspective, it is best to deliver incoming packets to the processor responsible for handling that connection; this requires the network interface hardware to re-direct the incoming packet based on the contents of its header (e.g., the IP address and port number of the client). Recent network controllers accomplish this by supporting multiple buffer descriptor rings for the same device, choosing which ring to use, and therefore which processor to interrupt, based on the header of the arriving packet.

---

register. In that case, the operating system software uses the code to index into the interrupt vector table.

EXAMPLE   Why is the interrupt vector table stored in kernel rather than user memory?

ANSWER   If the interrupt vector table could be modified by application code, the application could potentially hijack the network by directing all network interrupts to its own code. Similarly, the hardware register that points to the interrupt vector table must be a protected register that can be set only when in kernel mode.   □

2.4.2   Interrupt Stack

Where should the interrupted process's state be saved, and what stack should the kernel's code use?

interrupt stack   On most processors, a special, privileged hardware register points to a region of kernel memory called the *interrupt stack*. When an interrupt, processor exception, or system call trap causes a context switch into the kernel, the hardware changes the stack pointer to point to the base of the kernel's interrupt stack. The hardware automatically saves some of the interrupted process's registers by pushing them onto the interrupt stack before calling the kernel's handler.

When the kernel handler runs, it pushes any remaining registers onto the stack before performing its work. When returning from the interrupt, processor exception or system call trap, the reverse occurs: first, the handler pops the saved registers, and then, the hardware restores the registers it saved, returning to the point where the process was interrupted. When returning from a system call, the value of the saved program counter must be incremented so that the hardware returns to the instruction immediately *after* the one that caused the trap.

Why do interrupt handlers need to run on a kernel stack? You might think you could use the process's user-level stack to store its state. However, a separate, kernel-level interrupt stack is needed for two reasons.

- **Reliability.** The process's user-level stack pointer might not be a valid memory address (e.g., if the program has a bug), but the kernel handler must continue to work properly.

- **Security.** On a multiprocessor, other threads running in the same process can modify user memory during the system call. If the kernel handler stores its local variables on the user-level stack, the user program might be able to modify the kernel's return address, potentially causing the kernel to jump to arbitrary code.

On a multiprocessor, each processor needs to have its own interrupt stack so that, for example, the kernel can handle simultaneous system calls and exceptions across multiple processors. For each processor, the kernel allocates a separate region of memory as that processor's interrupt stack.

2.4.3   Two Stacks per Process

Most operating system kernels go one step farther and allocate a kernel interrupt stack for every user-level process (and as we discuss in Chapter 4, every thread that executes user code). When a user-level process is running, the hardware interrupt stack points to that process's kernel stack. Note that when a process is running at user level, it is not running in the kernel so its kernel stack is empty.

Allocating a kernel stack per process makes it easier to switch to a new process inside an interrupt or system call handler. For example, a timer interrupt handler might decide to give the processor to a different process. Likewise, a system call might need to wait for an I/O operation to complete; in the meantime, some other process should run. With per-process stacks, to suspend a process, we store a pointer to its kernel stack in the process control block, and

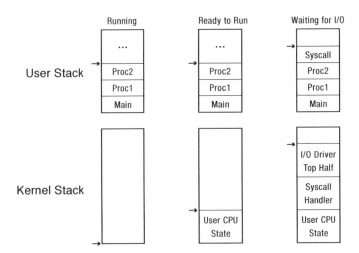

Figure 2.9: In most operating systems, a process has two stacks: on for executing user code and one for kernel code. The Figure shows the kernel and user stacks for various states of a process. When a process is running in user mode, its kernel stack is empty. When a process has been preempted (ready but not running), its kernel stack will contain the user-level processor state at the point when the user process was interrupted. When a process is inside a system call waiting for I/O, the kernel stack contains the context to be resumed when the I/O completes, and the user stack contains the context to be resumed when the system call returns.

switch to the stack of the new process. We describe this mechanism in more detail in Chapter 4.

Figure 2.9 summarizes the various states of a process's user and kernel stacks:

- If the process is running on the processor in user mode, its kernel stack is empty, ready to be used for an interrupt, processor exception, or system call.

- If the process is running on the processor in kernel mode — due to an interrupt, processor exception or system call — its kernel stack is in use, containing the saved registers from the suspended user-level computation as well as the current state of the kernel handler.

- If the process is available to run but is waiting for its turn on the processor, its kernel stack contains the registers and state to be restored when the process is resumed.

- If the process is waiting for an I/O event to complete, its kernel stack contains the suspended computation to be resumed when the I/O finishes.

UNIX and kernel stacks

In the original implementation of UNIX, kernel memory was at a premium; main memory was roughly one million times more expensive per byte than it is today. The initial system could run with only 50KB of main memory. Instead of allocating an entire interrupt stack per process, UNIX allocated just enough memory in the process control block to store the user-level registers saved on a mode switch. In this way, UNIX could suspend a user-level process with the minimal amount of memory. UNIX still needed a few kernel stacks: one to run the interrupt handler and one for every system call waiting for an I/O event to complete, but that is much less than one for every process.

Of course, now that memory is much cheaper, most systems keep things simple and allocate a kernel stack per process or thread.

2.4.4   Interrupt Masking

Can an interrupt occur while the kernel is in the middle of handling an interrupt?

Interrupts arrive asynchronously; the processor could be executing either user or kernel code when an interrupt arrives. In certain regions of the kernel—such as inside interrupt handlers themselves, or inside the CPU scheduler—taking an interrupt could cause confusion. If an interrupt handler is interrupted, we cannot set the stack pointer to point to the base of the kernel's interrupt stack—doing so would obliterate the state of the first handler.

interrupt disable

interrupt enable

To simplify the kernel design, the hardware provides a privileged instruction to temporarily defer delivery of an interrupt until it is safe to do so. On the x86 and several other processors, this instruction is called *disable interrupts*. However, this is a misnomer: the interrupt is only deferred (masked), and not ignored. Once a corresponding *enable interrupt* instruction is executed, any pending interrupts are delivered to the processor. The instructions to mask and unmask interrupts must be privileged; otherwise, user code could inadvertently or maliciously disable the hardware timer, allowing the machine to freeze.

If multiple interrupts arrive while interrupts are disabled, the hardware delivers them in turn when interrupts are re-enabled. However, since the hardware has limited buffering for pending interrupts, some interrupts may be lost if interrupts are disabled for too long a period of time. Generally, the hardware will buffer one interrupt of each type; the interrupt handler is responsible for checking the device hardware to see if multiple pending I/O events need to be processed.

If the processor takes an interrupt in kernel mode with interrupts enabled, it is safe to use the current stack pointer rather than resetting it to the base of the interrupt stack. This approach can recursively push a series of handlers' states onto the stack; then, as each one completes, its state is popped from the stack, and the earlier handler is resumed where it left off.

Interrupt handlers: top and bottom halves

When a machine invokes an interrupt handler because some hardware event occurred (e.g., a timer expired, a key was pressed, a network packet arrived, or a disk I/O completed), the processor hardware typically masks interrupts while the interrupt handler executes. While interrupts are disabled, another hardware event will not trigger another invocation of the interrupt handler until the interrupt is re-enabled.

Some interrupts can trigger a large amount of processing, and it is undesirable to leave interrupts masked for too long. Hardware I/O devices have a limited amount of buffering, which can lead to dropped events if interrupts are not processed in a timely fashion. For example, keyboard hardware can drop keystrokes if the keyboard buffer is full. Interrupt handlers are therefore divided into a *top half* and a *bottom half*. Unfortunately, this terminology can differ a bit from system to system; in Linux, the sense of top and bottom are reversed. In this book, we adopt the more common (non-Linux) usage.

The interrupt handler's bottom half is invoked by the hardware and executes with interrupts masked. It is designed to complete quickly. The bottom half typically saves the state of the hardware device, resets it so that it can receive a new event, and notifies the scheduler that the top half needs to run. At this point, the bottom half is done, and it can re-enable interrupts and return to the interrupted task or (if the event is high priority) switch to the top half but with interrupts enabled. When the top half runs, it can do more general kernel tasks, such as parsing the arriving packet, delivering it to the correct user-level process, sending an acknowledgment, and so forth. The top half can also do operations that require the kernel to wait for exclusive access to shared kernel data structures, the topic of Chapter 5.

2.4.5   Hardware Support for Saving and Restoring Registers

How do we save and restore the current state of the user process?

An interrupted process's registers must be saved so that the process can be restarted exactly where it left off. Because the handler might change the values in those registers as it executes, the state must be saved *before* the handler runs. Because most instructions modify the contents of registers, the hardware typically provides special instructions to make it easier to save and restore user state.

To make this concrete, consider the x86 architecture. Rather than relying on handler software to do all the work, when an interrupt or trap occurs:

- If the processor is in user mode, the x86 pushes the interrupted process's stack pointer onto the kernel's interrupt stack and switches to the kernel stack.

- The x86 pushes the interrupted process's instruction pointer.

- The x86 pushes the x86 *processor status word*. The processor status word includes control bits, such as whether the most recent arithmetic operation in the interrupted code resulted in a positive, negative, or zero value. This needs to be saved and restored for the correct behavior of any subsequent conditional branch instruction.

The hardware saves the values for the stack pointer, program counter, and processor status word *before* jumping through the interrupt vector table to the interrupt handler. Once the handler starts running, these values will be those of the handler, not those of the interrupted process.

Once the handler starts running, it can use the pushad ("push all double") instruction to save the remaining registers onto the stack. This instruction saves all 32-bit x86 integer registers. On a 16-bit x86, pusha is used instead. Because the kernel does not typically perform floating point operations, those do not need to be saved unless the kernel switches to a different process.

The x86 architecture has complementary features for restoring state: a popad instruction to pop an array of integer register values off the stack into the registers and an iret (return from interrupt) instruction that loads a stack pointer, instruction pointer, and processor status word off of the stack into the appropriate processor registers.

2.5 | Putting It All Together: x86 Mode Transfer

The high level steps needed to handle an interrupt, processor exception, or system call are simple, but the details require some care.

To give a concrete example of how such "carefully crafted" code works, we now describe one way to implement an interrupt-triggered mode switch on the x86 architecture. Different operating systems on the x86 follow this basic approach, though details differ. Similarly, different architectures handle the same types of issues, but they may do so with different hardware support.

First, we provide some background on the x86 architecture. The x86 is segmented, so pointers come in two parts: (i) a segment, a region of memory such as code, data, or stack, and (ii) an offset within that segment. The current user-level instruction is a combination of the code segment (cs register) plus the instruction pointer (eip register). Likewise, the current stack position is the combination of the stack segment (ss) and the stack pointer within the stack segment (esp). The current privilege level is stored as the low-order bits of the cs register rather than in the processor status word (eflags register). The eflags register has condition codes that are modified as a by-product of executing instructions; the eflags register also has other flags that control the processor's behavior, such as whether interrupts are masked or not.

When a user-level process is running, the current state of the processor, stack, kernel interrupt vector table, and kernel stack is illustrated in Figure 2.10. When a processor exception or system call trap occurs, the hardware carefully

Architectural support for fast mode switches

Some processor architectures are able to execute user- and kernel-mode switches very efficiently, while other architectures are much slower at performing these switches.

The SPARC architecture is in the first camp. SPARC defines a set of *register windows* that operate like a hardware stack. Each register window includes a full set of the registers defined by the SPARC instruction set. When the processor performs a procedure call, it shifts to a new window, so the compiler never needs to save and restore registers across procedure calls, making them quite fast. (At a deep enough level of recursion, the SPARC will run out of its register windows; it then takes an exception that saves half the windows and resumes execution. Another exception occurs when the processor pops its last window, allowing the kernel to reload the saved windows.)

Mode switches can be quite fast on the SPARC. On a mode switch, the processor switches to a different register window. The kernel handler can then run, using the registers from the new window and not disturbing the values stored in the interrupted process's copy of its registers. Unfortunately, this comes at a cost: switching between different processes is quite expensive on the SPARC, as the kernel needs to save and restore the entire register set of every active window.

The Motorola 88000 was in the second camp. The 88000 was an early pipelined architecture; now, almost all modern computers are pipelined. For improved performance, pipelined architectures execute multiple instructions at the same time. For example, one instruction is being fetched while another is being decoded, a third is completing a floating point operation, and a fourth is finishing a store to memory. When an interrupt or processor exception occurred on the 88000, the pipeline operation was suspended, and the operating system kernel was required to save and restore the entire state of the pipeline to preserve transparency to user code.

Most modern processors with deep execution pipelines, such as the x86, instead provide *precise interrupts*: the hardware first completes all instructions that occur, in program order, before the interrupted instruction. The hardware annuls any instruction that occurs, in program order, after the interrupt or trap, even if the instruction is in progress when the processor detects the interrupt.

---

saves a small amount of the interrupted thread state, leaving the system as shown in Figure 2.11:

1. **Mask interrupts.** The hardware starts by preventing any interrupts from occurring while the processor is in the middle of switching from user mode to kernel mode.

2. **Save three key values.** The hardware saves the values of the stack pointer (the x86 esp and ss registers), the execution flags (the x86 eflags register),

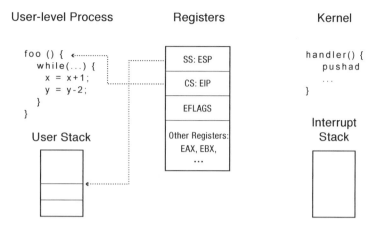

Figure 2.10: State of the system before an interrupt handler is invoked on the x86 architecture. SS is the stack segment, ESP is the stack pointer, CS is the code segment, and EIP is the program counter. The program counter and stack pointer refer to locations in the user process, and the interrupt stack is empty.

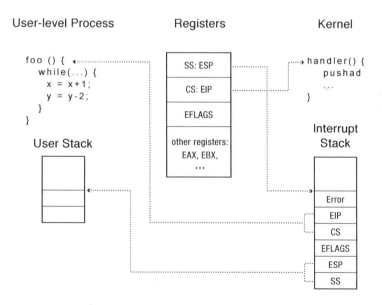

Figure 2.11: State of the system after the x86 hardware has jumped to the interrupt handler. The hardware saves the user context on the kernel interrupt stack and changes the program counter/stack to locations in kernel memory.

and the instruction pointer (the x86 eip and cs registers) to internal, temporary hardware registers.

3. **Switch onto the kernel interrupt stack.** The hardware then switches the stack segment/stack pointer to the base of the kernel interrupt stack, as specified in a special hardware register.

4. **Push the three key values onto the new stack.** Next, the hardware stores the internally saved values onto the stack.

5. **Optionally save an error code.** Certain types of exceptions, such as page faults, generate an error code to provide more information about the event; for these exceptions, the hardware pushes this code, making it the top item on the stack. For other types of events, the software interrupt handler pushes a dummy value onto the stack so that the stack format is identical in both cases.

6. **Invoke the interrupt handler.** Finally, the hardware changes the code segment/program counter to the address of the interrupt handler procedure. A special register in the processor contains the location of the interrupt vector table in kernel memory. This register can only be modified by the kernel. The type of interrupt is mapped to an index in this array, and the code segment/program counter is set to the value at this index.

This starts the handler software.

The handler must first save the rest of the interrupted process's state — it needs to save the other registers before it changes them! The handler pushes the rest of the registers, including the current stack pointer, onto the stack using the x86 pushad instruction.

As Figure 2.12 shows, at this point the kernel's interrupt stack holds (1) the stack pointer, execution flags, and program counter saved by the hardware, (2) an error code or dummy value, and (3) a copy of all of the general registers (including the stack pointer but not the instruction pointer or eflags register).

Once the handler has saved the interrupted thread's state to the stack, it can use the registers as it pleases, and it can push additional items onto the stack. So, the handler can now do whatever work it needs to do.

When the handler completes, it can resume the interrupted process. To do this, the handler pops the registers it saved on the stack. This restores all registers except the execution flags, program counter, and stack pointer. For the x86 instruction set, the popad instruction is commonly used. The handler also pops the error value off the stack.

Finally, the handler executes the x86 iret instruction to restore the code segment, program counter, execution flags, stack segment, and stack pointer from the kernel's interrupt stack.

This restores the process state to exactly what it was before the interrupt. The process continues execution as if nothing happened.

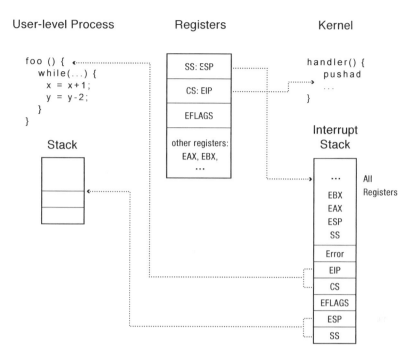

Figure 2.12: State of the system after the interrupt handler has started executing on the x86 architecture. The handler first saves the current state of the processor registers, since it may overwrite them. Note that this saves the stack pointer twice: first, the user stack pointer then the kernel stack pointer.

A small but important detail occurs when the hardware takes an exception to emulate an instruction in the kernel, e.g., for missing floating point hardware. If the handler returns back to the instruction that caused the exception, another exception would instantly recur! To prevent an infinite loop, the exception handler modifies the program counter stored at the base on the stack to point to the instruction immediately after the one causing the mode switch. The iret instruction can then return to the user process at the correct location.

For a system call trap, the Intel x86 hardware does the increment when it saves the user-level state. The program counter for the instruction after the trap is saved on the kernel's interrupt stack.

EXAMPLE   A trapframe is the data stored by the hardware and interrupt handler at the base of the interrupt stack, describing the state of the user-level execution context. Typically, a pointer to the trapframe is passed as an argument to the handler, e.g., to allow system calls to access arguments passed in registers.

How large is the 32-bit x86 trapframe in the example given above?

ANSWER   The hardware saves six registers; the interrupt handler saves another eight general-purpose registers. In all, **56 bytes** are saved in the trapframe.   □

2.6 | Implementing Secure System Calls

How do library code and the kernel work together to implement protected procedure calls from the application into the kernel?

The operating system kernel constructs a restricted environment for process execution to limit the impact of erroneous and malicious programs on system reliability. Any time a process needs to perform an action outside of its protection domain — to create a new process, read from the keyboard, or write a disk block — it must ask the operating system to perform the action on its behalf, via a system call.

System calls provide the illusion that the operating system kernel is simply a set of library routines available to user programs. To the user program, the kernel provides a set of system call procedures, each with its own arguments and return values, that can be called like any other routine. The user program need not concern itself with how the kernel implements these calls.

Implementing system calls requires the operating system to define a *calling convention* — how to name system calls, pass arguments, and receive return values across the user/kernel boundary. Typically, the operating system uses the same convention as the compiler uses for normal procedures — some combination of passing arguments in registers and on the execution stack.

Once the arguments are in the correct format, the user-level program can issue a system call by executing the trap instruction to transfer control to the kernel. System calls, like interrupts and processor exceptions, share the same mechanism for switching between user and kernel mode. In fact, the x86 instruction to trap into the kernel on a system call is called int, for "software interrupt."

Inside the kernel, a procedure implements each system call. This procedure behaves exactly as if the call was made from within the kernel but with one notable difference: the kernel must implement its system calls in a way that protects itself from all errors and attacks that might be launched by the misuse of the interface. Of course, most applications will use the interface correctly! But errors in an application program must not crash the kernel, and a computer virus must not be able to use the system call interface to take control of the kernel. One can think of this as an extreme version of defensive programming: the kernel should always assume that the parameters passed to a system call are intentionally designed to be as malicious as possible.

pair of stubs   We bridge these two views — the user program calling the system call, and the kernel implementing the system call — with a pair of stubs. A *pair of stubs* is a pair of procedures that mediate between two environments, in this case between the user program and the kernel. Stubs also mediate procedure calls between computers in a distributed system.

Figure 2.13 illustrates the sequence of steps involved in a system call:

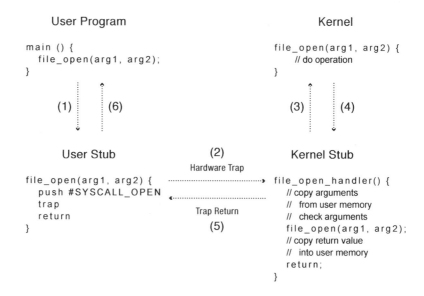

Figure 2.13: A pair of stubs mediates between the user-level caller and the kernel's implementation of system calls. The code is for the file_open system call; other calls have their own stubs. (1) The user process makes a normal procedure call to a stub linked with the process. (2) The stub executes the trap instruction. This transfers control to the kernel trap handler. The trap handler copies and checks its arguments and then (3) calls a routine to do the operation. Once the operation completes, (4) the code returns to the trap handler, which copies the return value into user memory and (5) resumes the user stub immediately after the trap. (6) The user stub returns to the user-level caller.

1. The user program calls the user stub in the normal way, oblivious to the fact the implementation of the procedure is in fact in the kernel.

2. The user stub fills in the code for the system call and executes the trap instruction.

3. The hardware transfers control to the kernel, vectoring to the system call handler. The handler acts as a stub on the kernel side, copying and checking arguments and then calling the kernel implementation of system call.

4. After the system call completes, it returns to the handler.

5. The handler returns to user level at the next instruction in the stub.

6. The stub returns to the caller.

We next describe these steps in more detail. Figure 2.14 illustrates the behavior of the user-level stub for the x86. The operating system provides a

```
// We assume that the caller put the filename onto the stack,
// using the standard calling convention for the x86.

open:
// Put the code for the system call we want into %eax.
    movl #SysCallOpen, %eax

// Trap into the kernel.
    int #TrapCode

// Return to the caller; the kernel puts the return value in %eax.
    ret
```

Figure 2.14: User-level library stub for the file system open system call for the x86 processor. SysCallOpen is the code for the specific system call to run. TrapCode is the index into the x86 interrupt vector table for the system call handler.

library routine for each system call that takes its arguments, reformats them according to the calling convention, and executes a trap instruction. When the kernel returns, the stub returns the result provided by the kernel. Of course, the user program need not use the library routine — it is free to trap directly to the kernel; in turn, the kernel must protect itself from misbehaving programs that do not format arguments correctly.

The system call calling convention is arbitrary. In Figure 2.14, the code passes its arguments on the user stack, storing the system call code in the register %eax. The return value comes back in %eax, so there is no work to do on the return.

The int instruction saves the program counter, stack pointer, and eflags on the kernel stack before jumping to the system call handler through the interrupt vector table. The kernel handler saves any additional registers that must be preserved across function calls. It then examines the system call integer code in %eax, verifies that it is a legal opcode, and calls the correct stub for that system call.

The kernel stub has four tasks:

- **Locate system call arguments.** Unlike a regular kernel procedure, the arguments to a system call are stored in user memory, typically on the user stack. Of course, the user stack pointer may be corrupted! Even if it is valid, it is a virtual, not a physical, address. If the system call has a pointer argument (e.g., a file name or buffer), the stub must check the address to verify it is a legal address within the user domain. If so, the stub converts it to a physical address that the kernel can safely use it. In Figure 2.14, the pointer to the string representing the file name is stored on the stack; therefore, the stub must check and translate both the stack address and the string pointer.

- **Validate parameters.** The kernel must also protect itself against malicious or accidental errors in the format or content of its arguments. A file name is typically be a zero-terminated string, but the kernel cannot trust the user code to always work correctly. The file name may be corrupted; it may point to memory outside the application's region; it may start inside the application's memory region but extend beyond it; the application may not have permission to access the file; the file may not exist; and so forth. If an error is detected, the kernel returns it to the user program; otherwise, the kernel performs the operation on the application's behalf.

- **Copy before check.** In most cases, the kernel copies system call parameters into kernel memory before performing the necessary checks. The reason for this is to prevent the application from modifying the parameter *after* the stub checks the value, but *before* the parameter is used in the actual implementation of the routine. This is called a *time of check vs. time of use* (TOCTOU) attack. For example, the application could call open with a valid file name but, after the check, change the contents of the string to be a different name, such as a file containing another user's private data.

  time of check vs. time of use attack

  TOCTOU is not a new attack — the first occurrence dates from the mid-1960's. While it might seem that a process necessarily stops whenever it does a system call, this is not always the case. For example, if one process shares a memory region with another process, then the two processes working together can launch a TOCTOU attack. Similarly, a parallel program running on two processors can launch a TOCTOU attack, where one processor traps into the kernel while the other modifies the string at precisely the right (or wrong) time. Note that the kernel needs to be correct in every case, while the attacker can try any number of times before succeeding.

- **Copy back any results.** For the user program to access the results of the system call, the stub must copy the result from the kernel into user memory. Again, the kernel must first check the user address and convert it to a kernel address before performing the copy.

Putting this together, Figure 2.15 shows the kernel stub for the system call open. In this case, the return value fits in a register so the stub can return directly; in other cases, such as a file read, the stub would need to copy data back into a user-level buffer.

After the system call finishes, the handler pops any saved registers (except %eax) and uses the iret instruction to return to the user stub immediately after the trap, allowing the user stub to return to the user program.

2.7 | Starting a New Process

How does the operating system kernel start a new process?

Thus far, we have described how to transfer control from a user-level process to the kernel on an interrupt, processor exception, or system call and how the kernel resumes execution at user level when done.

```
int KernelStub_Open() {
    char *localCopy[MaxFileNameSize + 1];

// Check that the stack pointer is valid and that the arguments are stored at
// valid addresses.

    if (!validUserAddressRange(userStackPointer, userStackPointer + size of arguments))
        return error_code;

// Fetch pointer to file name from user stack and convert it to a kernel pointer.

    filename = VirtualToKernel(userStackPointer);

// Make a local copy of the filename.  This prevents the application
// from changing the name surreptitiously.

// The string copy needs to check each address in the string before use to make sure
// it is valid.

// The string copy terminates after it copies MaxFileNameSize to ensure we
// do not overwrite our internal buffer.

    if (!VirtualToKernelStringCopy(filename, localCopy, MaxFileNameSize))
        return error_code;

// Make sure the local copy of the file name is null terminated.

    localCopy[MaxFileNameSize] = 0;

// Check if the user is permitted to access this file.

    if (!UserFileAccessPermitted(localCopy, current_process)
        return error_code;

// Finally, call the actual routine to open the file.  This returns a file
// handle on success, or an error code on failure.

    return Kernel_Open(localCopy);
}
```

Figure 2.15: Stub routine for the open system call inside the kernel. The kernel must validate all parameters to a system call before it uses them.

We now examine how to start running at user level in the first place. The kernel must:

- Allocate and initialize the process control block.

- Allocate memory for the process.

- Copy the program from disk into the newly allocated memory.

- Allocate a user-level stack for user-level execution.

- Allocate a kernel-level stack for handling system calls, interrupts and processor exceptions.

To start running the program, the kernel must also:

- **Copy arguments into user memory.** When starting a program, the user may give it arguments, much like calling a procedure. For example, when you click on a file icon in MacOS or Windows, the window manager asks the kernel to start the application associated with the file, passing it the file name to open. The kernel copies the file name from the memory of the window manager process to a special region of memory in the new process. By convention, arguments to a process are copied to the base of the user-level stack, and the user's stack pointer is incremented so those addresses are not overwritten when the program starts running.

- **Transfer control to user mode.** When a new process starts, there is no saved state to restore. While it would be possible to write special code for this case, most operating systems re-use the same code to exit the kernel for starting a new process and for returning from a system call. When we create the new process, we allocate a kernel stack to it, and we reserve room at the bottom of the kernel stack for the initial values of its user-space registers, program counter, stack pointer, and processor status word. To start the new program, we can then switch to the new stack and jump to the end of the interrupt handler. When the handler executes popad and iret, the processor "returns" to the start of the user program.

Finally, although you can think of a user program as starting with a call to main, in fact the compiler inserts one level of indirection. It puts a stub at the location in the process's memory where the kernel will jump when the process starts. The stub's job is to call main and then, if main returns, to call exit — the system call to terminate the process. Without the stub, a user program that returned from main would try to pop the return program counter, and since there is no such address on the stack, the processor would start executing random code.

```
start(arg1, arg2) {
    main(arg1, arg2);    // Call program main.
    exit();              // If main returns, call exit.
}
```

2.8 | Implementing Upcalls

How does the kernel deliver an asynchronous event to a user process?

We can use system calls for most of the communication between applications and the operating system kernel. When a program requests a protected operation, it can trap to ask the kernel to perform the operation on its behalf. Likewise, if the application needs data inside the kernel, a system call can retrieve it.

To allow applications to implement operating system-like functionality, we need something more. For many of the reasons that kernels need interrupt-based event delivery, applications can also benefit from being told when events occur that need their immediate attention. Throughout this book, we will see this pattern repeatedly: the need to *virtualize* some part of the kernel so that applications can behave more like operating systems. We call virtualized interrupts and exceptions *upcalls*. In UNIX, they are called *signals*; in Windows, they are *asynchronous events*.

upcall

There are several uses for immediate event delivery with upcalls:

- **Preemptive user-level threads.** Just as the operating system kernel runs multiple processes on a single processor, an application may run multiple tasks, or threads, in a process. A user-level thread package can use a periodic timer upcall as a trigger to switch tasks, to share the processor more evenly among user-level tasks or to stop a runaway task, e.g., if a web browser needs to terminate an embedded third party script.

- **Asynchronous I/O notification.** Most system calls wait until the requested operation completes and then return. What if the process has other work to do in the meantime? One approach is *asynchronous I/O*: a system call starts the request and returns immediately. Later, the application can poll the kernel for I/O completion, or a separate notification can be sent via an upcall to the application when the I/O completes.

asynchronous I/O

- **Interprocess communication.** Most interprocess communication can be handled with system calls — one process writes data, while the other reads it sometime later. A kernel upcall is needed if a process generates an event that needs the instant attention of another process. As an example, UNIX sends an upcall to notify a process when the debugger wants to suspend or resume the process. Another use is for logout — to notify applications that they should save file data and cleanly terminate.

- **User-level exception handling.** Earlier, we described a mechanism where processor exceptions, such as divide-by-zero errors, are handled by the kernel. However, many applications have their own exception handling routines, e.g., to ensure that files are saved before the application shuts down. For this, the operating system needs to inform the application when it receives a processor exception so the application runtime, rather than the kernel, handles the event.

- **User-level resource allocation.** Operating systems allocate resources — deciding which users and processes should get how much CPU time, how much memory, and so forth. In turn, many applications are resource adaptive — able to optimize their behavior to differing amounts of CPU time or memory. An example is Java garbage collection. Within limits, a Java process can adapt to different amounts of available memory by changing the frequency with which it runs its garbage collector. The more memory, the less time Java needs to run its collector, speeding

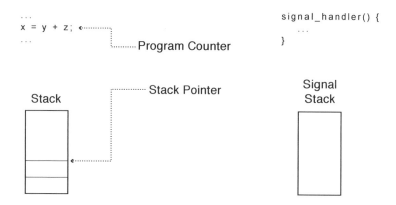

Figure 2.16: The state of the user program and signal handler before a UNIX signal. UNIX signals behave analogously to processor exceptions, but at user level.

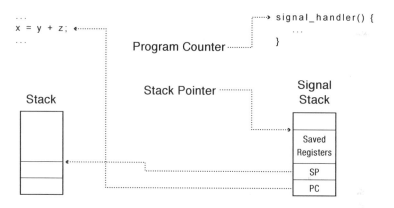

Figure 2.17: The state of the user program and signal handler during a UNIX signal. The signal stack stores the state of the hardware registers at the point where the process was interrupted, with room for the signal handler to execute on the signal stack.

execution. For this, the operating system must inform the process when its allocation changes, e.g., because some other process needs more or less memory.

Upcalls from kernels to user processes are not always needed. Many applications are more simply structured around an event loop that polls for events and then processes each event in turn. In this model, the kernel can pass data to the process by sending it events that do not need to be handled immediately. In fact, until recently, Windows lacked support for the immediate delivery of upcalls to user-level programs.

We next describe UNIX signals as a concrete example of kernel support for upcalls. As shown in Figures 2.16 and 2.17, UNIX signals share many similarities with hardware interrupts:

- **Types of signals.** In place of hardware-defined interrupts and processor exceptions, the kernel defines a limited number of signal types that a process can receive.

- **Handlers.** Each process defines its own handlers for each signal type, much as the kernel defines its own interrupt vector table. If a process does not define a handler for a specific signal, then the kernel calls a default handler instead.

- **Signal stack.** Applications have the option to run UNIX signal handlers on the process's normal execution stack or on a special signal stack allocated by the user process in user memory. Running signal handlers on the normal stack makes it more difficult for the signal handler to manipulate the stack, e.g., if the runtime needs to raise a language-level exception.

- **Signal masking.** UNIX defers signals for events that occur while the signal handler for those types of events is in progress. Instead, the signal is delivered once the handler returns to the kernel. UNIX also provides a system call for applications to mask signals as needed.

- **Processor state.** The kernel copies onto the signal stack the saved state of the program counter, stack pointer, and general-purpose registers at the point when the program stopped. Normally, when the signal handler returns, the kernel reloads the saved state into the processor to resume program execution. The signal handler can also modify the saved state, e.g., so that the kernel resumes a different user-level task when the handler returns.

The mechanism for delivering UNIX signals to user processes requires only a small modification to the techniques already described for transferring control across the kernel-user boundary. For example, on a timer interrupt, the hardware and the kernel interrupt handler save the state of the user-level computation. To deliver the timer interrupt to user level, the kernel copies that saved state to the bottom of the signal stack, resets the saved state to point to the signal handler and signal stack, and then exits the kernel handler. The reti instruction then resumes user-level execution at the signal handler. When the signal handler returns, these steps are unwound: the processor state is copied back from the signal handler into kernel memory, and the reti returns to the original computation.

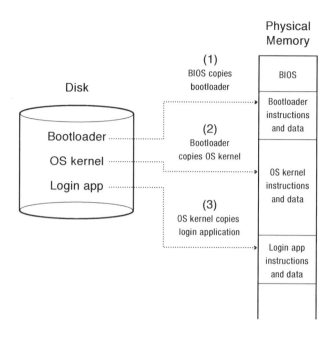

Figure 2.18: The boot ROM copies the bootloader image from disk into memory, and the bootloader copies the operating system kernel image from disk into memory.

2.9 | Case Study: Booting an Operating System Kernel

What steps are needed to start running an operating system kernel?

When a computer boots, it sets the machine's program counter to start executing at a pre-determined position in memory. Since the computer is not yet running, the initial machine instructions must be fetched and executed immediately after the power is turned on before the system has had a chance to initialize its DRAM. Instead, systems typically use a special read-only hardware memory (*Boot ROM*) to store their boot instructions. On most x86 personal computers, the boot program is called the BIOS, for "Basic Input/Output System".

Boot ROM

Why not put the kernel in ROM?

There are several drawbacks to trying to store the entire kernel in ROM. The most significant problem is that the operating system would be hard to update. ROM instructions are fixed when the computer is manufactured and (except in rare cases) are never changed. If an error occurs while the BIOS is being updated, the machine can be left in a permanently unusable state — unable to boot and unable to complete the update of the BIOS.

By contrast, operating systems need frequent updates, as bugs and security vulnerabilities are discovered and fixed. This, and the fact that ROM storage is relatively slow and expensive, argues for putting only a small amount of code in the BIOS.

Instead, the BIOS provides a level of indirection, as illustrated in Figure 2.18.

bootloader

The BIOS reads a fixed-size block of bytes from a fixed position on disk (or flash RAM) into memory. This block of bytes is called the *bootloader*. Once the BIOS has copied the bootloader into memory, it jumps to the first instruction in the block. On some newer machines, the BIOS also checks that the bootloader has not been corrupted by a computer virus. (If a virus could change the bootloader and get the BIOS to jump to it, the virus would then be in control of the machine.) As a check, the bootloader is stored with a *cryptographic signature*, a specially designed function of the bytes in a file and a private cryptographic key that allows someone with the corresponding public key to verify that an authorized entity produced the file. It is computationally intractable for an attacker without the private key to create a different file with a valid signature. The BIOS checks that the bootloader code matches the signature, verifying its authenticity.

cryptographic signature

The bootloader in turn loads the kernel into memory and jumps to it. Again, the bootloader can check the cryptographic signature of the operating system to verify that it has not been corrupted by a virus. The kernel's executable image is usually stored in the file system. Thus, to find the bootloader, the BIOS needs to read a block of raw bytes from disk; the bootloader, in turn, needs to know how to read from the file system to find and read the operating system image.

When the kernel starts running, it can initialize its data structures, including setting up the interrupt vector table to point to the various interrupt, processor exception, and system call handlers. The kernel then starts the first process, typically the user login page. To run this process, the operating system reads the code for the login program from its disk location, and jumps to the first instruction in the program, using the start process procedure described above. The login process in turn can trap into the kernel using a system call whenever it needs the kernel's services, e.g., to render the login prompt on the screen. We discuss the system calls needed for processes to do useful work in Chapter 3.

2.10 | Case Study: Virtual Machines

Can an operating system run inside a process?

Some operating system kernels provide the abstraction of an entire virtual machine at user level. How do interrupts, processor exceptions, and system calls work in this context? To avoid confusion when discussing virtual machines, we need to recap some terminology introduced in Chapter 1. The operating system providing the virtual machine abstraction is called the *host operating system*. The operating system running inside the virtual machine is called the *guest operating system*.

host operating system

guest operating system

The host operating system provides the illusion that the guest kernel is running on real hardware. For example, to provide a guest disk, the host kernel simulates a virtual disk as a file on the physical disk. To provide network access to the guest kernel, the host kernel simulates a virtual network using physical network packets. Likewise, the host kernel must manage memory to provide

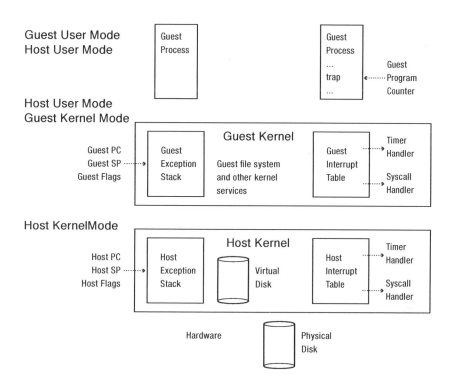

Figure 2.19: Emulation of user- and kernel-mode transfer for processes running inside a virtual machine. Both the guest kernel and the host kernel have their own copies of an interrupt vector table and interrupt stack. The guest vector table points to interrupt handlers in the guest kernel; the host vector table points to interrupt handlers in the host kernel.

the illusion that the guest kernel is managing its own memory protection even though it is running with virtual addresses. We discuss address translation for virtual machines in more detail in Chapter 10.

How does the host kernel manage mode transfer between guest processes and the guest kernel? During boot, the host kernel initializes its interrupt vector table to point to its own interrupt handlers in host kernel memory. When the host kernel starts the virtual machine, the guest kernel starts running as if it is being booted:

1. The host loads the guest bootloader from the virtual disk and starts it running.

2. The guest bootloader loads the guest kernel from the virtual disk into memory and starts it running.

3. The guest kernel then initializes its interrupt vector table to point to the guest interrupt handlers.

4. The guest kernel loads a process from the virtual disk into guest memory.

5. To start a process, the guest kernel issues instructions to resume execution at user level, e.g., using reti on the x86. Since changing the privilege level is a privileged operation, this instruction traps into the host kernel.

6. The host kernel simulates the requested mode transfer as if the processor had directly executed it. It restores the program counter, stack pointer, and processor status word exactly as the guest operating system had intended. Note that the host kernel must protect itself from bugs in the guest operating system, and so it also must check the validity of the mode transfer — to ensure that the guest kernel is not surreptitiously attempting to get the host kernel to "switch" to an arbitrary point in the kernel code.

Next, consider what happens when the guest user process does a system call, illustrated in Figure 2.19. To the hardware, there is only one kernel, the host operating system. Thus, the trap instruction traps into the host kernel's system call handler. Of course, the system call was not intended for the host! Rather, the host kernel simulates what would have happened had the system call instruction occurred on real hardware running the guest operating system:

1. The host kernel saves the instruction counter, processor status register, and user stack pointer on the interrupt stack of the guest operating system.

2. The host kernel transfers control to the guest kernel at the beginning of the interrupt handler, but with the guest kernel running with user-mode privilege.

3. The guest kernel performs the system call — saving user state and checking arguments.

4. When the guest kernel attempts to return from the system call back to user level, this causes a processor exception, dropping back into the host kernel.

5. The host kernel can then restore the state of the user process, running at user level, as if the guest OS had been able to return there directly.

The host kernel handles processor exceptions similarly, with one caveat. Some exceptions generated by the virtual machine are due to the user process; the host kernel forwards these to the guest kernel for handling. Other exceptions are generated by the guest kernel (e.g., when it tries to execute privileged instructions); the host kernel simulates these itself. Thus, the host kernel must track whether the virtual machine is executing in virtual user mode or virtual kernel mode.

The hardware vectors interrupts to the host kernel. Timer interrupts need special handling, as time can elapse in the host without elapsing in the guest.

When a timer interrupt occurs, enough virtual time may have passed that the guest kernel is due a timer interrupt. If so, the host kernel returns from the interrupt to the interrupt handler for the guest kernel. The guest kernel may in turn switch guest processes; its reti will cause a processor exception, returning to the host kernel, which can then resume the correct guest process.

Handling I/O interrupts is simpler: the simulation of the virtual device does not need to be anything like a real device. When the guest kernel makes a request to a virtual disk, the kernel writes instructions to the buffer descriptor ring for the disk device; the host kernel translates these instructions into operations on the virtual disk. The host kernel can simulate the disk request however it likes — e.g., through regular file reads and writes, copied into the guest kernel memory as if there was true DMA hardware. The guest kernel expects to receive an interrupt when the virtual disk completes its work; this can be triggered by the timer interrupt, but vectored to the guest disk interrupt handler instead of the guest timer interrupt handler.

2.11 | Summary and Future Directions

The process concept — the ability to execute arbitrary user programs with restricted rights — has been remarkably successful. With the exception of devices that run only a single application at a time (such as embedded systems and game consoles), every commercially successful operating system provides process isolation.

The reason for this success is obvious. Without process isolation, computer systems would be much more fragile and less secure. As recently as a decade ago, it was common for personal computers to crash on a daily basis. Today, laptops can remain working for weeks at a time without rebooting. This has occurred even though the operating system and application software on these systems have become more complex. While some of the improvement is due to better hardware reliability and automated bug tracking, process isolation has been a key technology in constructing more reliable system software.

Process isolation is also essential to building more secure computer systems. Without isolation, computer users would be forced to trust every application loaded onto the computer, not just the operating system code. In practice, however, complete process isolation remains more an aspiration than a reality. Most operating systems are vulnerable to malicious applications because the attacker can exploit any vulnerability in the kernel implementation. Even a single bug in the kernel can leave the system vulnerable. Keeping your system current with the latest patches provides some level of defense, but it is still inadvisable to download and install untrusted software off the web.

In the future, we are likely to see three complementary trends:

- **Operating system support for fine-grained protection.** Process isolation is becoming more flexible and fine-grained in order to reflect different levels of trust in different applications. Today, it is typical for a user

Hardware support for operating systems

We have described a number of hardware mechanisms that support operating systems:

- **Privilege levels**, user and kernel.

- **Privileged instructions**: instructions available only in kernel mode.

- **Memory translation** prevents user programs from accessing kernel data structures and aids in memory management.

- **Processor exceptions** trap to the kernel on a privilege violation or other unexpected event.

- **Timer interrupts** return control to the kernel on time expiration.

- **Device interrupts** return control to the kernel to signal I/O completion.

- **Interprocessor interrupts** cause another processor to return control to the kernel.

- **Interrupt masking** prevents interrupts from being delivered at inopportune times.

- **System calls** trap to the kernel to perform a privileged action on behalf of a user program.

- **Return from interrupt**: switch from kernel mode to user mode, to a specific location in a user process.

- **Boot ROM**: code that loads startup routines from disk into memory.

To support threads, we will need one additional mechanism, described in Chapter 5:

- **Atomic read-modify-write instructions** used to implement synchronization in multi-threaded programs.

---

application to have the permissions of that user. This allows a virus masquerading as a screen saver to steal or corrupt that user's data without needing to compromise the operating system first. Smartphone operating systems have started to add better controls to prevent certain applications without a "need to know" from accessing sensitive information, such as the smartphone's location or the list of frequently called telephone numbers.

- **Application-layer sandboxing.** Increasingly, many applications are becoming mini-operating systems in their own right, capable of safely executing third-party software to extend and improve the user experience. Sophisticated scripts customize web site behavior; web browsers must efficiently and completely isolate these scripts so that they cannot steal the user's data or corrupt the browser. Other applications — such as databases and desktop publishing systems — are also moving in the direction of needing application-layer sandboxing. Google's Native Client and Microsoft's Application Domains are two example systems that provide general-purpose, safe execution of third-party code at the user level.

- **Hardware support for virtualization.** Virtual machines provide an extra layer of protection beneath the operating system. Even if a malicious process run by a guest operating system on a virtual machine were able to corrupt the kernel, its impact would be limited to just that virtual machine. Below the virtual machine interface, the host operating system needs to provide isolation between different virtual machines; this is much easier in practice because the virtual machine interface is much simpler than the kernel's system call interface. For example, in a data center, virtual machines provide users with the flexibility to run any application without compromising data center operation.

  Computer manufacturers are re-designing processor architectures to reduce the cost of running a virtual machine. For example, on some new processors, guest operating systems can directly handle their own interrupts, processor exceptions, and system calls without those events needing to be mediated by the host operating system. Likewise, I/O device manufacturers are re-designing their interfaces to do direct transfers to and from the guest operating system without the need to go through the host kernel.

Exercises

1. When a user process is interrupted or causes a processor exception, the x86 hardware switches the stack pointer to a kernel stack, before saving the current process state. Explain why.

2. For the "Hello world" program, we mentioned that the kernel must copy the string from the user program to screen memory. Why must the screen's buffer memory be protected? Explain what might happen if a malicious application could alter any pixel on the screen, not just those within its own window.

3. For each of the three mechanisms that supports dual-mode operation—privileged instructions, memory protection, and timer interrupts—explain what might go wrong without that mechanism, assuming the system still had the other two.

4. Suppose you are tasked with designing the security system for a new web browser that supports rendering web pages with embedded web page scripts. What checks would you need to implement to ensure that executing buggy or malicious scripts could not corrupt or crash the browser?

5. Define three types of user-mode to kernel-mode transfers.

6. Define four types of kernel-mode to user-mode transfers.

7. Most hardware architectures provide an instruction to return from an interrupt, such as iret. This instruction switches the mode of operation from kernel-mode to user-mode.

   a) Explain where in the operating system this instruction would be used.

   b) Explain what happens if an application program executes this instruction.

8. A hardware designer argues that there is now enough on-chip transistors to provide 1024 integer registers and 512 floating point registers. As a result, the compiler should almost never need to store anything on the stack. As an operating system guru, give your opinion of this design.

   a) What is the effect on the operating system of having a large number of registers?

   b) What hardware features would you recommend adding to the design?

   c) What happens if the hardware designer also wants to add a 16-stage pipeline into the CPU, with precise exceptions. How would that affect the user-kernel switching overhead?

9. With virtual machines, the host kernel runs in privileged mode to create a virtual machine that runs in user mode. The virtual machine provides the illusion that the guest kernel runs on its own machine in privileged mode, even though it is actually running in user mode.

   Early versions of the x86 architecture (pre-2006) were not *completely virtualizable* — these systems could not guarantee to run unmodified guest operating systems properly. One problem was the popf "pop flags" instruction that restores the processor status word. When popf was run in privileged mode, it changed both the ALU flags (e.g., the condition codes) and the systems flags (e.g., the interrupt mask). When popf was run in unprivileged mode, it changed just the ALU flags.

   a) Why do instructions like popf prevent transparent virtualization of the (old) x86 architecture?

   b) How would you change the (old) x86 hardware to fix this problem?

10. Which of the following components is responsible for loading the initial value in the program counter for an application program before it starts running: the compiler, the linker, the kernel, or the boot ROM?

11. We described how the operating system kernel mediates access to I/O devices for safety. Some newer I/O devices are *virtualizable* — they permit safe access from user-level programs, such as a guest operating system running in a virtual machine. Explain how you might design the hardware and software to get this to work. (Hint: The device needs much of the same hardware support as the operating system kernel.)

12. System calls vs. procedure calls: How much more expensive is a system call than a procedure call? Write a simple test program to compare the cost of a simple procedure call to a simple system call (getpid() is a good candidate on UNIX; see the man page). To prevent the optimizing compiler from "optimizing out" your procedure calls, do not compile with optimization on. You should use a system call such as the UNIX gettimeofday() for time measurements. Design your code so the measurement overhead is negligible. Also, be aware that timer values in some systems have limited resolution (e.g., millisecond resolution).

   Explain the difference (if any) between the time required by your simple procedure call and simple system call by discussing what work each call must do.

13. Suppose you have to implement an operating system on hardware that supports interrupts and exceptions but does not have a trap instruction. Can you devise a satisfactory substitute for traps using interrupts and/or exceptions? If so, explain how. If not, explain why.

14. Suppose you have to implement an operating system on hardware that supports exceptions and traps but does not have interrupts. Can you devise a satisfactory substitute for interrupts using exceptions and/or traps? If so, explain how. If not, explain why.

15. Explain the steps that an operating system goes through when the CPU receives an interrupt.

16. When an operating system receives a system call from a program, a switch to operating system code occurs with the help of the hardware. The hardware sets the mode of operation to kernel mode, calls the operating system trap handler at a location specified by the operating system, and lets the operating system return to user mode after it finishes its trap handling.

    Consider the stack on which the operating system must run when it receives the system call. Should this stack be different from the one the application uses, or could it use the same stack as the application program? Assume that the application program is blocked while the system call runs.

17. Write a program to verify that the operating system on your computer correctly protects itself from rogue system calls. For a single system call—such as file system open—try all possible illegal calls: e.g., an invalid system call number, an invalid stack pointer, an invalid pointer stored on the stack, etc. What happens?

From a programmer's point of view, the user is a peripheral that types when you issue a read request.

Peter Williams

3 The Programming Interface

The previous chapter concerned the mechanisms needed in the operating system kernel to implement the process abstraction. A process is an instance of a program — the kernel provides an efficient sandbox for executing untrusted code at user-level, running user code directly on the processor.

This chapter concerns how we choose to use the process abstraction: what functionality does the operating system provide applications, and what should go where — what functionality should be put in the operating system kernel, what should be put into user-level libraries, and how should the operating system itself be organized?

There are as many answers to this as there are operating systems. Describing the full programming interface and internal organization for even a single operating system would take an entire book. Instead, in this chapter we explore a subset of the programming interface for UNIX, the foundation of Linux, MacOS, iOS, and Android. We also touch on how the same issues are addressed in Windows.

First, we need to answer "what" — what functions do we need an operating system to provide applications?

- **Process management.** Can a program create an instance of another program? Wait for it to complete? Stop or resume another running program? Send it an asynchronous event?

- **Input/output.** How do processes communicate with devices attached to the computer and through them to the physical world? Can processes communicate with each other?

- **Thread management.** Can we create multiple activities or threads that share memory or other resources within a process? Can we stop and start threads? How do we synchronize their use of shared data structures?

- **Memory management.** Can a process ask for more (or less) memory space? Can it share the same physical memory region with other processes?

- **File systems and storage.** How does a process store the user's data persistently so that it can survive machine crashes and disk failures? How does the user name and organize their data?

- **Networking and distributed systems.** How do processes communicate with processes on other computers? How do processes on different computers coordinate their actions despite machine crashes and network problems?

- **Graphics and window management.** How does a process control pixels on its portion of the screen? How does a process make use of graphics accelerators?

- **Authentication and security.** What permissions does a user or a program have, and how are these permissions kept up to date? On what basis do we know the user (or program) is who they say they are?

In this chapter, we focus on just the first two of these topics: process management and input/output. We will cover thread management, memory management, and file systems in detail in later chapters in this book.

Remarkably, we can describe a functional interface for process management and input/output with just a dozen system calls, and the rest of the system call interface with another dozen. Even more remarkably, these calls are nearly unchanged from the original UNIX design. Despite being first designed and implemented in the early 1970's, most of these calls are still in wide use in systems today!

Second, we need to answer "where"—for any bit of functionality the operating system provides to user programs, we have several options for where it lives, illustrated in Figure 3.1:

- We can put the functionality in a user-level program. In both Windows and UNIX, for example, there is a user program for managing a user's login and another for managing a user's processes.

- We can put the functionality in a user-level library linked in with each application. In Windows and MacOS, user interface widgets are part of user-level libraries, included in those applications that need them.

- We can put the functionality in the operating system kernel, accessed through a system call. In Windows and UNIX, low-level process management, the file system and the network stack are all implemented in the kernel.

Figure 3.1: Operating system functionality can be implemented in user-level programs, in user-level libraries, in the kernel itself, or in a user-level server invoked by the kernel.

- We can access the function through a system call, but implement the function in a standalone server process invoked by the kernel. In many systems, the window manager is implemented as a separate server process.

How do we make this choice? It is important to realize that the choice can be (mostly) transparent to both the user and the application programmer. The user wants a system that works; the programmer wants a clean, convenient interface that does the job. As long as the operating system provides that interface, where each function is implemented is up to the operating system, based on a tradeoff between flexibility, reliability, performance, and safety.

- **Flexibility.** It is much easier to change operating system code that lives outside of the kernel, without breaking applications using the old interface. If we create a new version of a library, we can just link that library in with new applications, and over time convert old applications to use the new interface. However, if we need to change the system call interface, we must either simultaneously change both the kernel and all applications, or we must continue to support both the old and the new versions until all old applications have been converted. Many applications are written by third party developers, outside of the control of the operating system vendor. Thus, changing the system call interface is a huge step, often requiring coordination across many companies.

  One of the key ideas in UNIX, responsible for much of its success, was to design its system call interface to be simple and powerful, so that almost all of the innovation in the system could happen in user code without changing the interface to the operating system. The UNIX system call interface is also highly portable — the operating system can be ported to new hardware without needing to rewrite application code. As shown in Figure 3.2, the kernel can be seen as a "thin waist," enabling inno-

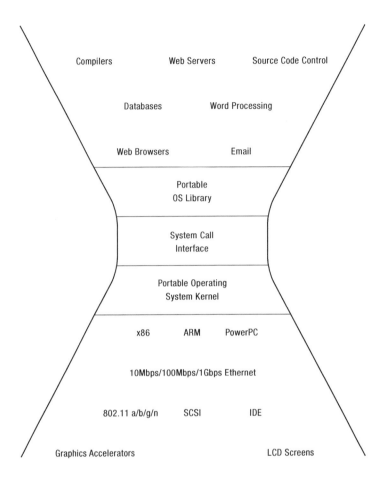

Figure 3.2: The kernel system call interface can be seen as a "thin waist," enabling independent evolution of applications and hardware.

vation at the application-level, and in the hardware, without requiring simultaneous changes in the other parts of the system.

- **Safety.** However, resource management and protection are the responsibility of the operating system kernel. As Chapter 2 explained, protection checks cannot be implemented in a user-level library because application code can skip any checks made by the library.

- **Reliability.** Improved reliability is another reason to keep the operating system kernel minimal. Kernel code needs the power to set up hardware devices, such as the disk, and to control protection boundaries between applications. However, kernel modules are typically not protected from one another, and so a bug in kernel code (whether sensitive or not) may corrupt user or kernel data. This has led some systems to use

The Internet and the "thin waist"

The Internet is another example of the benefit of designing interfaces to be simple and portable. The Internet defines a packet-level protocol that can run on top of virtually any type of network hardware and can support almost any type of network application. Creating the World Wide Web required no changes to the Internet packet delivery mechanism; likewise, the introduction of wireless networks required changes in hardware devices and in the operating system, but no changes in network applications. Although the Internet's "thin waist" can sometimes lead to inefficiencies, the upside is to foster innovation in both applications and hardware by decoupling changes in one from changes in the other.

microkernel

a philosophy of "what can be at user level, should be." An extreme version of approach is to isolate privileged, but less critical, parts of the operating system such as the file system or the window system, from the rest of the kernel. This is called a *microkernel* design. In a microkernel, the kernel itself is kept small, and instead most of the functionality of a traditional operating system kernel is put into a set of user-level processes, or servers, accessed from user applications via interprocess communication.

- **Performance.** Finally, transferring control into the kernel is more expensive than a procedure call to a library, and transferring control to a user-level file system server via the kernel is still even more costly. Hardware designers have attempted to reduce the cost of these boundary crossings, but their performance remains a problem. Microsoft Windows NT, a precursor to Windows 7, was initially designed as a microkernel, but over time, much of its functionality has been migrated back into the kernel for performance reasons.

There are no easy answers! We will investigate the question of how to design the system call interface and where to place operating system functionality through case studies of UNIX and other systems.

Chapter roadmap:

- **Process management.** What is the system call interface for process management? (Section 3.1)

- **Input/output.** What is the system call interface for performing I/O and interprocess communication? (Section 3.2)

Application-level sandboxing and operating system functionality

Applications that support executing third-party code or scripts in a restricted sandbox must address many of these same questions, with the sandbox playing the role of the operating system kernel. In terms of functionality: Can the scripting code start a new instance of itself? Can it do input/output? Can it perform work in the background? Can it store data persistently, and if it can, how does it name that data? Can it communicate data over the network? How does it authenticate actions?

For example, in web browsers, HTML5 not only allows scripts to draw on the screen, communicate with servers, and save and read cookies, it also has recently added programming interfaces for offline storage and cross-document communication. The Flash media player provides scripts with the ability to do asynchronous operations, file storage, network communication, memory management, and authentication.

Just as with system calls, these interfaces must be carefully designed to be bulletproof against malicious use. A decade ago, email viruses became widespread because scripts could be embedded in documents that were executed on opening; the programming interfaces for these scripts would allow them to discover the list of correspondents known to the current email user and to send them email, thereby propagating and expanding the virus with a single click. The more fully featured the interface, the more convenient it is for developers, and the more likely that some aspect of the interface will be abused by a hacker.

- **Case study: Implementing a shell.** We will illustrate these interfaces by using them to implement a user-level job control system called a *shell*. (Section 3.3)

- **Case study: Interprocess communication.** How does the communication between a client and server work? (Section 3.4)

- **Operating system structure.** Can we use the process abstraction to simplify the construction of the operating system itself and to make it more secure, more reliable, and more flexible? (Section 3.5)

3.1 | Process Management

On a modern computer, when a user clicks on a file or application icon, the application starts up. How does this happen and who is called? Of course, we could implement everything that needs to happen in the kernel — draw the icon for every item in the file system, map mouse positions to the intended icon, catch the mouse click, and start the process. In early batch processing systems, the kernel was in control by necessity. Users submitted jobs, and the operating system took it from there, instantiating the process when it was time to run the job.

A different approach is to allow user programs to create and manage their own processes. This has fostered a blizzard of innovation. Today, programs that create and manage processes include window managers, web servers, web browsers, shell command line interpreters, source code control systems, databases, compilers, and document preparation systems. We could go on, but you get the idea. If creating a process is something a process can do, then anyone can build a new version of any of these applications, without recompiling the kernel or forcing anyone else to use it.

An early motivation for user-level process management was to allow **shell** developers to write their own shell command line interpreters. A *shell* is a job control system; both Windows and UNIX have a shell. Many tasks involve a sequence of steps to do something, each of which can be its own program. With a shell, you can write down the sequence of steps, as a sequence of programs to run to do each step. Thus, you can view it as a very early version of a scripting system.

For example, to compile a C program from multiple source files, you might type:

```
cc −c sourcefile1.c
cc −c sourcefile2.c
In −o program sourcefile1.o sourcefile2.o
```

If we put those commands into a file, the shell reads the file and executes it, creating, in turn, a process to compile sourcefile1.c, a process to compile sourcefile2, and a process to link them together. Once a shell script is a program, we can create other programs by combining scripts together. In fact, on UNIX, the C compiler is itself a shell program! The compiler first invokes a process to expand header include files, then a separate process to parse the output, another process to generate (text) assembly code, and yet another to convert assembly into executable machine instructions.

3.1.1 Windows Process Management

One approach to process management is to just add a system call to create a process, and other system calls for other process operations. This turns out to be simple in theory and complex in practice. In Windows, there is a routine called, unsurprisingly, CreateProcess, in simplified form below:

```
boolean CreateProcess(char *prog, char *args);
```

parent process   We call the process creator the *parent* and the process being created, the **child process**   *child*.

There is an app for that

User-level process management is another way of saying "there is an app for that." Instead of a single program that does everything, we can create specialized programs for each task, and mix and match what we need. The formatting system for this textbook uses over fifty separate programs.

The web is a good example of the power of composing complex applications from more specialized services. A web page does not need to do everything itself: it can mash up the results of many different web pages, and it can invoke process creation on the local server to generate part of the page. The flexibility to create processes was extremely important early on in the development of the web. HTML was initially just a way to describe the formatting for static information, but it included a way to escape to a process, e.g., to do a lookup in a database or to authenticate a user. Over time, HTML has added support for many different features that were first prototyped via execution by a separate process. And of course, HTML can still execute a process for any format not supported by the standard.

What steps does CreateProcess take? As we explained in the previous chapter, the kernel needs to:

- Create and initialize the process control block (PCB) in the kernel.

- Create and initialize a new address space.

- Load the program prog into the address space.

- Copy arguments args into memory in the address space.

- Initialize the hardware context to start execution at "start".

- Inform the scheduler that the new process is ready to run.

Unfortunately, there are quite a few aspects of the process that the parent might like to control, such as: its privileges, where it sends its input and output, what it should store its files, what to use as a scheduling priority, and so forth. We cannot trust the child process itself to set its own privileges and priority, and it would be inconvenient to expect every application to include code for figuring out its context. So the real interface to CreateProcess is quite a bit more complicated in practice, given in Figure 3.3.

3.1.2   UNIX Process Management

UNIX takes a different approach to process management, one that is complex in theory and simple in practice. UNIX splits CreateProcess in two steps, called fork and exec, illustrated in Figure 3.4.

```
// Start the child process
if (!CreateProcess(NULL,      // No module name (use command line)
    argv[1],           // Command line
    NULL,              // Process handle not inheritable
    NULL,              // Thread handle not inheritable
    FALSE,             // Set handle inheritance to FALSE
    0,                 // No creation flags
    NULL,              // Use parent's environment block
    NULL,              // Use parent's starting directory
    &si,               // Pointer to STARTUPINFO structure
    &pi )              // Pointer to PROCESS_INFORMATION structure
)
```

Figure 3.3: Excerpt from an example of how to use the Windows CreateProcess system call. The first two arguments specify the program and its arguments; the rest concern aspects of the process runtime environment.

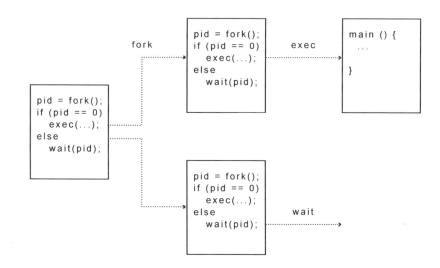

Figure 3.4: The operation of the UNIX fork and exec system calls. UNIX fork makes a copy of the parent process; UNIX exec changes the child process to run the new program.

UNIX fork   *UNIX fork* creates a complete copy of the parent process, with one key exception. (We need some way to distinguish between which copy is the parent and which is the child.) The child process sets up privileges, priorities, and I/O for the program that is about to be started, e.g., by closing some files, opening others, reducing its priority if it is to run in the background, etc. Because the child runs exactly the same code as the parent, it can be trusted to set up the context for the new program correctly.

UNIX exec   Once the context is set, the child process calls *UNIX exec*. UNIX exec brings the new executable image into memory and starts it running. It may seem wasteful to make a complete copy of the parent process, just to overwrite that copy when we bring in the new executable image into memory using exec. It turns out that fork and exec can be implemented efficiently, using a set of techniques we will describe in Chapter 8.

With this design, UNIX fork takes no arguments and returns an integer. UNIX exec takes two arguments (the name of the program to run and an array of arguments to pass to the program). This is in place of the ten parameters needed for CreateProcess. In part because of the simplicity of UNIX fork and exec, this interface has remained nearly unchanged since UNIX was designed in the early 70's. (Although the interface has not changed, the word fork is now a bit ambiguous. It is used for creating a new copy of a UNIX process, and in thread systems for creating a new thread. To disambiguate, we will always use the term "UNIX fork" to refer to UNIX's copy process system call.)

UNIX fork

The steps for implementing UNIX fork in the kernel are:

- Create and initialize the process control block (PCB) in the kernel

- Create a new address space

- Initialize the address space with a copy of the entire contents of the address space of the parent

- Inherit the execution context of the parent (e.g., any open files)

- Inform the scheduler that the new process is ready to run

A strange aspect of UNIX fork is that the system call returns *twice*: once to the parent and once to the child. To the parent, UNIX returns the process ID of the child; to the child, it returns zero indicating success. Just as if you made a clone of yourself, you would need some way to tell who was the clone and who was the original, UNIX uses the return value from fork to distinguish the two copies. Some sample code to call fork is given in Figure 3.5.

If we run the program in Figure 3.5, what happens? If you have access to a UNIX system, you can try it and see for yourself. UNIX fork returns twice, once in the child, with a return value of zero, and once in the parent with a return value of the child's process ID. However, we do not know whether the parent will run next or the child. The parent had been running, and so it is likely that it will reach its print statement first. However, a timer interrupt could intervene between when the parent forks the process and when it reaches the print statement, so that the processor is reassigned to the child. Or we could be running on a multicore system, where both the parent and child are running simultaneously. In either case, the child could print its output before the parent. We will talk in much more depth about the implications of different orderings of concurrent execution in the next chapter.

```
int child_pid = fork();

if (child_pid == 0) {              // I'm the child process.
    printf("I am process #%d\n", getpid());
    return 0;
} else {                          // I'm the parent process.
    printf("I am the parent of process #%d\n", child_pid);
    return 0;
}
```

```
Possible output:
    I am the parent of process 495
    I am process 495

Another less likely but still possible output:
    I am process 456
    I am the parent of process 456
```

Figure 3.5: Example UNIX code to fork a process, and some possible outputs of running the code. getpid is a system call to get the current process's ID.

UNIX fork and the Chrome Web browser

Although UNIX fork is normally paired with a call to exec, in some cases UNIX fork is useful on its own. A particularly interesting example is in Google's Chrome web browser. When the user clicks on a link, Chrome forks a process to fetch and render the web page at the link, in a new tab on the browser. The parent process continues to display the original referring web page, while the child process runs the same browser, but in its own address space and protection boundary. The motivation for this design is to isolate the new link, so that if the web site is infected with a virus, it will not infect the rest of the browser. Closing the infected browser tab will then remove the link and the virus from the system.

Some security researchers take this a step further. They set up their browsers and email systems to create a new *virtual machine* for every new link, running a copy of the browser in each virtual machine; even if the web site has a virus that corrupts the guest operating system running in the virtual machine, the rest of the system will remain unaffected. In this case, closing the virtual machine cleans the system of the virus.

Interestingly, on Windows, Google Chrome does not use CreateProcess to fork new copies of the browser on demand. The difficulty is that if Chrome is updated while Chrome is running, CreateProcess will create a copy of the new version, and that may not interoperate correctly with the old version. Instead, they create a pool of helper processes that wait in the background for new links to render.

UNIX exec and wait

The UNIX system call exec completes the steps needed to start running a new program. The child process typically calls UNIX exec once it has returned from UNIX fork and configured the execution environment for the new process. We will describe more about how this works when after we discuss UNIX pipes in the next section.

UNIX exec does the following steps:

- Load the program prog into the current address space.

- Copy arguments args into memory in the address space.

- Initialize the hardware context to start execution at "start."

Note that exec does not create a new process!

On the other side, often the parent process needs to pause until the child process completes, e.g., if the next step depends on the output of the previous step. In the shell example we started the chapter with, we need to wait for the two compilations to finish before it is safe to start the linker.

UNIX wait   UNIX has a system call, naturally enough called *wait*, that pauses the parent until the child finishes, crashes, or is terminated. Since the parent could have created many child processes, wait is parameterized with the process ID of the child. With wait, a shell can create a new process to perform some step of its instructions, and then pause for that step to complete before proceeding to the next step. It would be hard to build a usable shell without wait.

However, the call to wait is optional in UNIX. For example, the Chrome browser does not need to wait for its forked clones to finish. Likewise, most UNIX shells have an option to run operations in the background, signified by appending '&' to the command line. (As with fork, the word wait is now a bit ambiguous. It is used for pausing the current UNIX process to wait for another process to complete; it is also used in thread synchronization, for waiting on a condition variable. To disambiguate, we will always use the term "UNIX wait" to refer to UNIX's wait system call. Oddly, waiting for a thread to complete is called "thread join", even though it is most analogous to UNIX wait. Windows is simpler, with a single function called "WaitForSingleObject" that can wait for process completion, thread completion, or on a condition variable.)

UNIX signal   Finally, as we outlined in the previous chapter, UNIX provides a facility for one process to send another an instant notification, or upcall. In UNIX, the notification is sent by calling *signal*. Signals are used for terminating an application, suspending it temporarily for debugging, resuming after a suspension, timer expiration, and a host of other reasons. In the default case, where the receiving application did not specify a signal handler, the kernel implements a standard one on its behalf.

Kernel handles and garbage collection

As we discussed in the previous chapter, when a UNIX process finishes, it calls the system call exit. Exit can release various resources associated with the process, such as the user stack, heap, and code segments. It must be careful, however, in how it garbage collects the process control block (PCB). Even though the child process has finished, if it deletes the PCB, then the parent process will be left with a dangling pointer if later on it calls UNIX wait. Of course, we don't know for sure if the parent will ever call wait, so to be safe, the PCB can only be reclaimed when both the parent and the child have finished or crashed.

Generalizing, both Windows and UNIX have various system calls that return a handle to some kernel object; these handles are used in later calls as an ID. The process ID returned by UNIX fork is used in later calls to UNIX wait; we will see below that UNIX open returns a file descriptor that is used in other system calls. It is important to realize that these handles are *not* pointers to kernel data structures; otherwise, an erroneous user program could cause havoc in the kernel by making system calls with fake handles. Rather, they are specific to the process and checked for validity on each use.

Further, in both Windows and UNIX, handles are reference counted. Whenever the kernel returns a handle, it bumps a reference counter, and whenever the process releases a handle (or exits), the reference counter is decremented. UNIX fork sets the process ID reference count to two, one for the parent and one for the child. The underlying data structure, the PCB, is reclaimed only when the reference count goes to zero, that is, when both the parent and child terminate.

3.2 | Input/Output

Computer systems have a wide diversity of input and output devices: keyboard, mouse, disk, USB port, Ethernet, WiFi, display, hardware timer, microphone, camera, accelerometer, and GPS, to name a few.

To deal with this diversity, we could specialize the application programming interface for each device, customizing it to the device's specific characteristics. After all, a disk device is quite different from a network and both are quite different from a keyboard: a disk is addressed in fixed sized chunks, while a network sends and receives a stream of variable sized packets, and the keyboard returns individual characters as keys are pressed. While the disk only returns data when asked, the network and keyboard provide data unprompted. Early computer systems took the approach of specializing the interface to the device, but it had a significant downside: every time a new type of hardware device is invented, the system call interface has to be upgraded to handle that device.

One of the primary innovations in UNIX was to regularize all device input and output behind a single common interface. In fact, UNIX took this one giant step further: it uses this same interface for reading and writing files and for interprocess communication. This approach was so successful that it is almost universally followed in systems today. We will sketch the interface in this section, and then in the next section, show how to use it to build a shell.

The basic ideas in the UNIX I/O interface are:

- **Uniformity.** All device I/O, file operations, and interprocess communication use the same set of system calls: open, close, read and write.

- **Open before use.** Before an application does I/O, it must first call open on the device, file, or communication channel. This gives the operating system a chance to check access permissions and to set up any internal bookkeeping. Some devices, such as a printer, only allow one application access at a time — the open call can return an error if the device is in use.

  Open returns a handle to be used in later calls to read, write and close to identify the file, device or channel; this handle is somewhat misleadingly called a *file descriptor*, even when it refers to a device or channel so there is no file involved. For convenience, the UNIX shell starts applications with open file descriptors for reading and writing to the terminal.

- **Byte-oriented.** All devices, even those that transfer fixed-size blocks of data, are accessed with byte arrays. Similarly, file and communication channel access is in terms of bytes, even though we store data structures in files and send data structures across channels.

- **Kernel-buffered reads.** Stream data, such as from the network or keyboard, is stored in a kernel buffer and returned to the application on request. This allows the UNIX system call read interface to be the same for devices with streaming reads as those with block reads, such as disks and Flash memory. In both cases, if no data is available to be returned immediately, the read call blocks until it arrives, potentially giving up the processor to some other task with work to do.

- **Kernel-buffered writes.** Likewise, outgoing data is stored in a kernel buffer for transmission when the device becomes available. In the normal case, the system call write copies the data into the kernel buffer and returns immediately. This decouples the application from the device, allowing each to go at its own speed. If the application generates data faster than the device can receive it (as is common when spooling data to a printer), the write system call blocks in the kernel until there is enough room to store the new data in the buffer.

- **Explicit close.** When an application is done with the device or file, it calls close. This signals to the operating system that it can decrement the reference-count on the device, and garbage collect any unused kernel data structures.

UNIX file descriptor

Open vs. creat vs. stat

By default, the UNIX open system call returns an error if the application tries to open a file that does not exist; as an option (not shown above), a parameter can tell the kernel to instead create the file if it does not exist. Since UNIX also has system calls for creating a file (creat) and for testing whether a file exists (stat), it might seem as if open could be simplified to always assume that the file already exists.

However, UNIX often runs in a multi-user, multi-application environment, and in that setting the issue of system call design can become more subtle. Suppose instead of the UNIX interface, we had completely separate functions for testing if a file exists, creating a file, and opening the file. Assuming that the user has permission to test, open, or create the file, does this code work?

```
if (!exists(file)) {     // If the file doesn't exist create it.
// Are we guaranteed the file doesn't exist?
    create(file);
}
// Are we guaranteed the file does exist?
open(file);
```

The problem is that on a multi-user system, some other user might have created the file in between the call to test for its existence, and the call to create the file. Thus, call to create must also test the existence of the file. Likewise, some other user might have deleted the file between the call to create and the call to open. So open also needs the ability to test if the file is there, and if not to create the file (if that is the user's intent).

UNIX addresses this with an all-purpose, atomic open: test if the file exists, optionally create it if it does not, and then open it. Because system calls are implemented in the kernel, the operating system can make open (and all other I/O systems calls) non-interruptible with respect to other system calls. If another user tries to delete a file while the kernel is executing an open system call on the same file, the delete will be delayed until the open completes. The open will return a file descriptor that will continue to work until the application closes the file. The delete will remove the file from the file system, but the file system does not actually reclaim its disk blocks until the file is closed.

For interprocess communication, we need a few more concepts:

UNIX pipe

- **Pipes.** A *UNIX pipe* is a kernel buffer with two file descriptors, one for writing (to put data into the pipe) and one for reading (to pull data out of the pipe), as illustrated in Figure 3.6. Data is read in exactly the same sequence it is written, but since the data is buffered, the execution of the producer and consumer can be decoupled, reducing waiting in the

Figure 3.6: A pipe is a temporary kernel buffer connecting a process producing data with a process consuming the data.

common case. The pipe terminates when either endpoint closes the pipe or exits.

The Internet has a similar facility to UNIX pipes called TCP (Transmission Control Protocol). Where UNIX pipes connect processes on the same machine, TCP provides a bi-directional pipe between two processes running on different machines. In TCP, data is written as a sequence of bytes on one machine and read out as the same sequence on the other machine.

- **Replace file descriptor.** By manipulating the file descriptors of the child process, the shell can cause the child to read its input from, or send its output to, a file or a pipe instead of from a keyboard or to the screen. This way, the child process does not need to be aware of who is providing or consuming its I/O. The shell does this redirection using a special system call named dup2(from, to) that replaces the to file descriptor with a copy of the from file descriptor.

- **Wait for multiple reads.** For client-server computing, a server may have a pipe open to multiple client processes. Normally, read will block if there is no data to be read, and it would be inefficient for the server to poll each pipe in turn to check if there is work for it to do. The UNIX system call select(fd[], number) addresses this. Select allows the server to wait for input from any of a set of file descriptors; it returns the file descriptor that has data, but it does not read the data. Windows has an equivalent function, called WaitForMultipleObjects.

Figure 3.7 summarizes the dozen UNIX system calls discussed in this section.

3.3 | Case Study: Implementing a Shell

The dozen UNIX system calls listed above are enough to build a flexible and powerful command line shell, one that runs entirely at user-level with no special permissions. As we mentioned, the process that creates the shell is responsible for providing it an open file descriptor for reading commands for its input (e.g., from the keyboard), called *stdin* and for writing output (e.g., to

UNIX stdin

Creating and managing processes	
fork()	Create a child process as a clone of the current process. The fork call returns to both the parent and child.
exec(prog, args)	Run the application prog in the current process.
exit()	Tell the kernel the current process is complete, and its data structures should be garbage collected.
wait(processID)	Pause until the child process has exited.
signal(processID, type)	Send an interrupt of a specified type to a process.
I/O operations	
fileDesc open(name)	Open a file, channel, or hardware device, specified by name; returns a file descriptor that can be used by other calls.
pipe(fileDesc[2])	Create a one-directional pipe for communication between two processes. Pipe returns two file descriptors, one for reading and one for writing.
dup2(fromFileDesc, toFileDesc)	Replace the toFileDesc file descriptor with a copy of fromFileDesc. Used for replacing stdin or stdout or both in a child process before calling exec.
int read(fileDesc, buffer, size)	Read up to size bytes into buffer, from the file, channel, or device. Read returns the number of bytes actually read. For streaming devices this will often be less than size. For example, a read from the keyboard device will (normally) return all of its queued bytes.
int write(fileDesc, buffer, size)	Analogous to read, write up to size bytes into kernel output buffer for a file, channel, or device. Write normally returns immediately but may stall if there is no space in the kernel buffer.
fileDesc select(fileDesc[], arraySize)	Return when any of the file descriptors in the array fileDesc[] have data available to be read. Returns the file descriptor that has data pending.
close(fileDescriptor)	Tell the kernel the process is done with this file, channel, or device.

Figure 3.7: List of UNIX system calls discussed in this section.

UNIX stdout the display), called *stdout*.

Figure 3.8 illustrates the code for the basic operation of a shell. The shell reads a command line from the input, and it forks a process to execute that command. UNIX fork automatically duplicates all open file descriptors in the parent, incrementing the kernel's reference counts for those descriptors, so the input and output of the child is the same as the parent. The parent waits for the child to finish before it reads the next command to execute.

Because the commands to read and write to an open file descriptor are the same whether the file descriptor represents a keyboard, screen, file, device, or pipe, UNIX programs do not need to be aware of where their input is coming from, or where their output is going. This is helpful in a number of ways:

- **A program can be a file of commands.** Programs are normally a set of machine instructions, but on UNIX a program can be a file containing a

```
main() {
    char *prog = NULL;
    char **args = NULL;

    // Read the input a line at a time, and parse each line into the program
    // name and its arguments. End loop if we've reached the end of the input.
    while (readAndParseCmdLine(&prog, &args)) {

        // Create a child process to run the command.
        int child_pid = fork();

        if (child_pid == 0) {
            // I'm the child process.
            // Run program with the parent's input and output.
            exec(prog, args);
            // NOT REACHED
        } else {
            // I'm the parent; wait for the child to complete.
            wait(child_pid);
            return 0;
        }
    }
}
```

Figure 3.8: Example code for a simple UNIX shell.

list of commands for a shell to interpret. To disambiguate, shell programs signified in UNIX by putting "#! interpreter" as the first line of the file, where "interpreter" is the name of the shell executable.

The UNIX C compiler works this way. When it is exec'ed, the kernel recognizes it as a shell file and starts the interpreter, passing it the file as input. The shell reads the file as a list of commands to invoke the pre-processor, parser, code generator and assembler in turn, exactly as if it was reading text input from the keyboard. When the last command completes, the shell interpreter calls exit to inform the kernel that the program is done.

- **A program can send its output to a file.** By changing the stdout file descriptor in the child, the shell can redirect the child's output to a file. In the standard UNIX shell, this is signified with a "greater than" symbol. Thus, "ls > tmp" lists the contents of the current directory into the file "tmp." After the fork and before the exec, the shell can replace the stdout file descriptor for the child using dup2. Because the parent has been cloned, changing stdout for the child has no effect on the parent.

- **A program can read its input from a file.** Likewise, by using dup2 to change the stdin file descriptor, the shell can cause the child to read its input from a file. In the standard UNIX shell, this is signified with a "less than" symbol. Thus, "zork < solution" plays the game "zork" with a list of instructions stored in the file "solution."

- **The output of one program can be the input to another program.** The shell can use a pipe to connect two programs together, so that the output of one is the input of another. This is called a *producer-consumer* relationship. For example, in the C-compiler, the output of the preprocessor is sent to the parser, and the output of the parser is sent to the code-generator and then to the assembler. In the standard UNIX shell, a pipe connecting two programs is signified by a " | " symbol, as in: "cpp file.c | cparse | cgen | as > file.o". In this case the shell creates four separate child processes, each connected by pipes to its predecessor and successor. Each of the phases can run in parallel, with the parent waiting for all of them to finish.

3.4 | Case Study: Interprocess Communication

For many of the same reasons it makes sense to construct complex applications from simpler modules, it often makes sense to create applications that can specialize on a specific task, and then combine those applications into more complex structures. We gave an example above with the C compiler, but many parts of the operating system are structured this way. For example, instead of every program needing to know how to coordinate access to a printer, UNIX has a printer server, a specialized program for managing the printer queue.

For this to work, we need a way for processes to communicate with each other. Three widely used forms of interprocess communication are:

- **Producer-consumer.** In this model, programs are structured to accept as input the output of other programs. Communication is one-way: the producer only writes, and the consumer only reads. As we explained above, this allows chaining: a consumer can be, in turn, a producer for a different process. Much of the success of UNIX was due to its ability to easily compose many different programs together in this fashion.

- **Client-server.** An alternative model is to allow two-way communication between processes, as in client-server computing. The server implements some specialized task, such as managing the printer queue or managing the display. Clients send requests to the server to do some task, and when the operation is complete, the server replies back to the client.

- **File system.** Another way programs can be connected together is through reading and writing files. A text editor can import an image created by a drawing program, and the editor can in turn write an HTML file that a web server can read to know how to display a web page. A key distinction is that, unlike the first two modes, communication through the file system can be separated in *time*: the writer of the file does not need to be running at the same time as the file reader. Therefore, data needs to be stored persistently on disk or other stable storage, and the

Figure 3.9: Interprocess communication between a producer application and a consumer. The producer uses the write system call to put data into the buffer; the consumer uses the read system call to take data out of the buffer.

data needs to be named so that you can find the file when needed later on.

All three models are widely used both on a single system and over a network. For example, the Google MapReduce utility operates over a network in a producer-consumer fashion: the output of the map function is sent to the machines running the reduce function. The web is an example of client-server computing, and many enterprises and universities run centralized file servers to connect a text editor on one computer with a compiler running on another.

As persistent storage, file naming, and distributed computing are each complex topics in their own right, we defer the discussions of those topics to later chapters. Here we focus on interprocess communication, where both processes are running simultaneously on the same machine.

3.4.1   Producer-Consumer Communication

Figure 3.9 illustrates how two processes communicate through the operating system in a producer-consumer relationship. Via the shell, we establish a pipe between the producer and the consumer. As one process computes and produces a stream of output data, it issues a sequence of write system calls on the pipe into the kernel. Each write can be of variable size. Assuming there is room in the kernel buffer, the kernel copies the data into the buffer, and returns immediately back to the producer.

At some point later, the operating system will schedule the consumer process to run. (On a multicore system, the producer and consumer could be running at the same time.) The consumer issues a sequence of read calls. Because the pipe is just a stream of bytes, the consumer can read the data out in any convenient chunking — the consumer can read chunks in 1 KB chunks, while the producer wrote its data in 4 KB chunks, or vice versa. Each system call read made by the consumer returns the next successive chunk of data out of the kernel buffer. The consumer process can then compute on its input, sending its output to the display, a file, or onto the next consumer.

The kernel buffer allows each process to run at its own pace. There is no requirement that each process have equivalent amounts of work to do. If the producer is faster than the consumer, the kernel buffer fills up, and when the producer tries to write to a full buffer, the kernel stalls the process until there is room to store the data. Equivalently, if the consumer is faster than the producer, the buffer will empty and the next read request will stall until the producer creates more data.

In UNIX, when the producer finishes, it closes its side of the pipe, but there may still be data queued in the kernel for the consumer. Eventually, the consumer reads the last of the data, and the read system call will return an "end of file" marker. Thus, to the consumer, there is no difference between reading from a pipe and reading from a file.

Using kernel buffers to decouple the execution of the producer and consumer reduces the number and cost of context switches. Modern computers make extensive use of hardware caches to improve performance, but caches are ineffective if a program only runs for a short period of time before it must yield the processor to another task. The kernel buffer allows the operating system to run each process long enough to benefit from reuse, rather than alternating between the producer and consumer on each system call.

3.4.2   Client-Server Communication

We can generalize the above to illustrate client-server communication, shown in Figure 3.10. Instead of a single pipe, we create two, one for each direction. To make a request, the client writes the data into one pipe, and reads the response from the other. The server does the opposite: it reads requests from the first pipe, performs whatever is requested (provided the client has permission to make the request), and writes the response onto the second pipe.

The client and server code are shown in Figure 3.11. To simplify the code, we assume that the requests and responses are fixed-size.

Frequently, we want to allow many clients to talk to the same server. For example, there is one server to manage the print queue, although there can be many processes that want to be able to print. For this, the server uses the select system call to identify the pipe containing the request, as shown in Figure 3.12. The client code is unchanged.

3.5 | Operating System Structure

We started this chapter with a list of functionality that users and applications need from the operating system. We have shown that by careful design of the

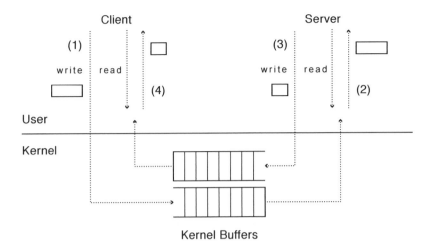

Figure 3.10: Interprocess communication between a client process and a server process. Once the client and server are connected, the client sends requests to the server by writing them into a kernel buffer. The server reads the requests out of the buffer, and returns the results by writing them into a separate buffer read by the client.

system call interface, we can offload some of the work of the operating system to user programs, such as to a shell or to a print server.

In the rest of this chapter, we ask how should we organize the remaining parts of the operating system. There are many dependencies among the modules inside the operating system, and there is often quite frequent interaction between these modules:

- Many parts of the operating system depend on synchronization primitives for coordinating access to shared data structures with the kernel.

- The virtual memory system depends on low-level hardware support for address translation, support that is specific to a particular processor architecture.

- Both the file system and the virtual memory system share a common pool of blocks of physical memory. They also both depend on the disk device driver.

- The file system can depend on the network protocol stack if the disk is physically located on a different machine.

This has led operating system designers to wrestle with a fundamental tradeoff: by centralizing functionality in the kernel, performance is improved and it makes it easier to arrange tight integration between kernel modules. However, the resulting systems are less flexible, less easy to change, and less adaptive to user or application needs. We discuss these tradeoffs by describing several options for the operating system architecture.

```
Client:
    char request[RequestSize];
    char reply[ReplySize]

    // ..compute..

    // Put the request into the buffer.

    // Send the buffer to the server.
    write(output, request, RequestSize);

    // Wait for response.
    read(input, reply, ReplySize);

    // ..compute..

Server:
    char request[RequestSize];
    char reply[ReplySize];

    // Loop waiting for requests.
    while (1) {
        // Read incoming command.
        read(input, request, RequestSize);

        // Do operation.

        // Send result.
        write(output, reply, ReplySize);
    }
```

Figure 3.11: Example code for client-server interaction.

3.5.1   Monolithic Kernels

monolithic kernel

Almost all widely used commercial operating systems, such as Windows, MacOS, and Linux, take a similar approach to the architecture of the kernel—a monolithic design. As shown in Figure 3.13, with a *monolithic kernel*, most of the operating system functionality runs inside the operating system kernel. In truth, the term is a bit of a misnomer, because even in so-called monolithic systems, there are often large segments of what users consider the operating system that runs outside the kernel, either as utilities like the shell, or in system libraries, such as libraries to manage the user interface.

Internal to a monolithic kernel, the operating system designer is free to develop whatever interfaces between modules that make sense, and so there is quite a bit of variation from operating system to operating system in those internal structures. However, two common themes emerge across systems: to improve portability, almost all modern operating systems have both a hardware abstraction layer and dynamically loaded device drivers.

Streamlining client-server communication

Client-server communication is a common pattern in many systems, and so one can ask: how can we improve its performance? One step is to recognize that both the client and the server issue a write immediately followed by a read, to wait for the other side to reply; at the cost of adding a system call, these can be combined to eliminate two kernel crossings per round trip. Further, the client will always need to wait for the server, so it makes sense for it to donate its processor to run the server code, reducing delay. Microsoft added support for this optimization to Windows in the early 1990's when it converted to a microkernel design (explained a bit later in this chapter). However, as we noted earlier, modern computer architectures make extensive use of caches, so for this to work we need code and data for both the client and the server to be able to be in cache simultaneously. We will talk about mechanisms to accomplish that in a later chapter.

We can take this streamlining even further. On a multicore system, it is possible or even likely that both the client and server each have their own processor. If the kernel sets up a shared memory region accessible to both the client and the server and no other processes, then the client and server can (safely) pass requests and replies back and forth, as fast as the memory system will allow, without ever traversing into the kernel or relinquishing their processors.

```
Server:
    char request[RequestSize];
    char reply[ReplySize];
    FileDescriptor clientInput[NumClients];
    FileDescriptor clientOutput[NumClients];

    // Loop waiting for a request from any client.
    while (fd = select(clientInput, NumClients) {

        // Read incoming command from a specific client.
        read(clientInput[fd], request, RequestSize);

        // Do operation.

        // Send result.
        write(clientOutput[fd], reply, ReplySize);
    }
```

Figure 3.12: Server code for communicating with multiple clients.

Hardware Abstraction Layer

A key goal of operating systems is to be portable across a wide variety of hardware platforms. To accomplish this, especially within a monolithic sys-

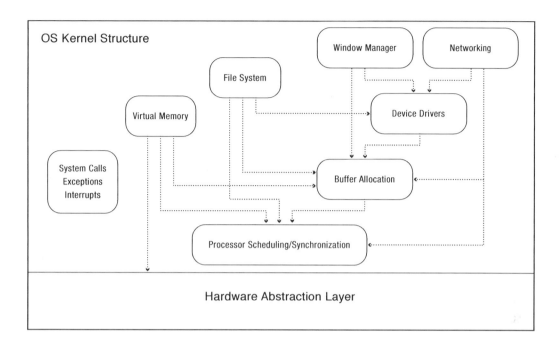

Figure 3.13: In a monolithic operating system kernel, most of the operating system functionality is linked together inside the kernel. Kernel modules directly call into other kernel modules to perform needed functions. For example, the virtual memory system uses buffer management, synchronization, and the hardware abstraction layer.

hardware abstraction layer tem, requires careful design of the *hardware abstraction layer*. The hardware abstraction layer (HAL) is a portable interface to machine configuration and processor-specific operations within the kernel. For example, within the same processor family, such as an Intel x86, different computer manufacturers will require different machine-specific code to configure and manage interrupts and hardware timers.

Operating systems that are portable across processor families, say between an ARM and an x86 or between a 32-bit and a 64-bit x86, will need processor-specific code for process and thread context switches. The interrupt, processor exception, and system call trap handling is also processor-specific; all systems have those functions, but the specific implementation will vary. As we will see in Chapter 8, machines differ quite a bit in their architecture for managing virtual address spaces; most kernels provide portable abstractions on top of the machine-dependent routines, such as to translate virtual addresses to physical addresses or to copy memory from applications to kernel memory and vice versa.

With a well-defined hardware abstraction layer in place, most of the operating system is machine- and processor-independent. Thus, porting an operating

The Hardware Abstraction Layer in Windows

As a concrete example, Windows has a two-pronged strategy for portability. To allow the same Windows kernel binary to be used across personal computers manufactured by different vendors, the kernel is dynamically linked at boot time with a set of library routines specifically written for each hardware configuration. This isolates the kernel from the specifics of the motherboard hardware.

Windows also runs across a number of different processor architectures. Typically, a different kernel binary is produced for each type of processor, with any needed processor-specific code; sometimes, conditional execution is used to allow a kernel binary to be shared across closely related processor designs.

system to a new computer is just a matter of creating new implementations of these low-level HAL routines and re-linking.

Dynamically Installed Device Drivers

A similar consideration leads to operating systems that can easily accommodate a wide variety of physical I/O devices. Although there are only a handful of different instruction set architectures in wide use today, there are a huge number of different types of physical I/O devices, manufactured by a large number of companies. There is diversity in the hardware interfaces to devices as well as in the hardware chip sets for managing the devices. A recent survey found that approximately 70% of the code in the Linux kernel was in device-specific software.

To keep the rest of the operating system kernel portable, we want to decouple the operating system source code from the specifics of each device. For instance, suppose a manufacturer creates a new printer — what steps does the operating system manufacturer need to take to accommodate that change?

dynamically loadable device driver

The key innovation, widely adopted today, is a *dynamically loadable device driver*. A dynamically loadable device driver is software to manage a specific device, interface, or chipset, added to the operating system kernel after the kernel starts running, to handle the devices that are present on a particular machine. The device manufacturer typically provides the driver code, using a standard interface supported by the kernel. The operating system kernel calls into the driver whenever it needs to read or write data to the device.

The operating system boots with a small number of device drivers — e.g., for the disk (to read the operating system binary into memory). For the devices physically attached to the computer, the computer manufacturer bundles those drivers into a file it stores along with the bootloader. When the operating system starts up, it queries the I/O bus for which devices are attached to the computer and then loads those drivers from the file on disk. Finally, for any network-attached devices, such as a network printer, the operating system can load those drivers over the Internet.

While dynamically loadable device drivers solve one problem, they pose a different one. Errors in a device driver can corrupt the operating system kernel and application data structures; just as with a regular program, errors may not be caught immediately, so that user may be unaware that their data is being silently modified. Even worse, a malicious attacker can use device drivers to introduce a computer virus into the operating system kernel, and thereby silently gain control over the entire computer. Recent studies have found that 90% of all system crashes were due to bugs in device drivers, rather than in the operating system itself.

Operating system developers have taken five approaches to dealing with this issue:

- **Code inspection.** Operating system vendors typically require all device driver code to be submitted in advance for inspection and testing, before being allowed into the kernel.

- **Bug tracking.** After every system crash, the operating system can collect information about the system configuration and the current kernel stack, and sends this information back to a central database for analysis. Microsoft does this on a wide scale. With hundreds of millions of installed computers, even a low rate of failure can yield millions of bug reports per day. Many crashes happen inside the device driver itself, but even those that do not can sometimes be tracked down. For example, if failures are correlated with the presence of a particular device driver, or increase after the release of a new version of the driver, that can indicate the source of a problem.

- **User-level device drivers.** Both Apple and Microsoft strongly encourage new device drivers to run at user-level rather than in the kernel. Each device driver runs in a separate user-level process, using system calls to manipulate the physical device. This way, a buggy driver can only affect its own internal data structures and not the rest of the operating system kernel; if the device driver crashes, the kernel can restart it easily.

  Although user-level device drivers are becoming more common, it can be time-consuming to port existing device drivers to run at user-level. Unfortunately, there is a huge amount of existing device driver code that directly addresses internal kernel data structures; drawing a boundary around these drivers has proven difficult. Of course, supporting legacy drivers is less of a problem as completely new hardware and operating system platforms, such as smartphones and tablets, are developed.

- **Virtual machine device drivers.** To handle legacy device drivers, one approach that has gained some traction is to run device driver code inside a guest operating system running on a virtual machine, as shown in Figure 3.14. The guest operating system loads the device drivers as if

Hardware

Figure 3.14: Legacy device drivers can run inside a guest operating system on top of a virtual machine in order to isolate the effect of implementation errors in driver code.

it was running directly on the real hardware, but when the devices attempt to access the physical hardware, the underlying virtual machine monitor regains control to ensure safety. Device drivers can still have bugs, but they can only corrupt the guest operating system and not other applications running on the underlying virtual machine monitor.

- **Driver sandboxing.** A further challenge for both user-level device drivers and virtual machine drivers is performance. Some device drivers need frequent interaction with hardware and the rest of the kernel. Some researchers have proposed running device drivers in their own restricted execution environment inside the kernel. This requires lightweight sandboxing techniques, a topic we will return to at the end of Chapter 8.

3.5.2   Microkernel

An alternative to the monolithic kernel approach is to run as much of the operating system as possible in one or more user-level servers. The window manager on most operating systems works this way: individual applications draw items on their portion of the screen by sending requests to the window manager. The window manager adjudicates which application window is in front or in back for each pixel on the screen, and then renders the result. If the system has a hardware graphics accelerator present, the window manager can use it to render items more quickly. Some systems have moved other parts of the operating system into user-level servers: the network stack, the file system, device drivers, and so forth.

The difference between a monolithic and a microkernel design is often transparent to the application programmer. The location of the service can be hidden in a user-level library — calls go to the library, which casts the requests either as system calls or as reads and writes to the server through a pipe. The location of the server can also be hidden inside the kernel — the application calls the kernel as if the kernel implements the service, but instead the kernel reformats the request into a pipe that the server can read.

A microkernel design offers considerable benefit to the operating system developer, as it easier to modularize and debug user-level services than kernel code. Aside from a potential reliability improvement, however, microkernels offer little in the way of visible benefit to end users and can slow down overall performance by inserting extra steps between the application and the services it needs. Thus, in practice, most systems adopt a hybrid model where some operating system services are run at user-level and some are in the kernel, depending on the specific tradeoff between code complexity and performance.

3.6 | Summary and Future Directions

In this chapter, we have seen how system calls can be used by applications to create and manage processes, perform I/O, and communicate with other processes. Every operating system has its own unique system call interface; describing even a single interface in depth would be beyond the scope of this book. In this chapter, we focused parts of the UNIX interface because it is both compact and powerful. A key aspect of the UNIX interface are that creating a process (with fork) is separate from starting to run a program in that process (with exec); another key feature is the use of kernel buffers to decouple reading and writing data through the kernel.

Operating systems use the system call interface to provide services to applications and to aid in the internal structuring of the operating system itself. Almost all general-purpose computer systems today have a user-level shell and/or a window manager that can start and manage applications on behalf of the user. Many systems also implement parts of the operating system as user-level services accessed through kernel pipes.

As we noted, a trend is for applications to become mini-operating systems in their own right, with multiple users, resource sharing and allocation, untrusted third-party code, processor and memory management, and so forth. The system call interfaces for Windows and UNIX were not designed with this in mind, and an interesting question is how they will change to accommodate this future of powerful meta-applications.

In addition to the fine-grained sandboxing and process creation we described at the end of the last chapter, a trend is to re-structure the system call interface to make resource allocation decisions explicit and visible to applications. Traditionally, operating systems make resource allocation decisions — when to schedule a process or a thread, how much memory to give a particular application, where and when to store its disk blocks, when to send its network packets — transparently to the application, with a goal of improving end user and overall system performance. Applications are unaware of how many resources they have, appearing to run by themselves, isolated on their own (virtual) machine.

Of course, the reality is often quite different. An alternate model is for operating systems to divide resources among applications and then allow each application to decide for itself how best to use those resources. One can think of this as a type of federalism. If both the operating system and applications are governments doing their own resource allocation, they are likely to get in each other's way if they are not careful. As a simple example, consider how a garbage collector works; it assumes it has a fixed amount of memory to manage. However, as other applications start or stop, it can gain or lose memory, and if the operating system does this reallocation transparently, the garbage collector has no hope of adapting. We will see examples of this same design pattern in many different areas of operating system design.

Exercises

A manual page (or "man page") is a standard way of documenting Unix system calls and utility programs. On a Unix machine, you can access a manual page by running the man command (e.g., "man fork"). Another way to find manual pages is via web search (e.g., search for "man fork" and many of the top results will be manual pages for the fork system call).

1. Can UNIX fork return an error? Why or why not?
   Note: You can answer this question by looking at the manual page for fork, but before you do that, think about what the fork system call does. If you were designing this call, would you need to allow fork to return an error?

2. Can UNIX exec return an error? Why or why not?
   Note: You can answer this question by looking at the manual page for exec, but before you do that, think about what the exec system call does. If you were designing this call, would you need to allow it to return an error?

3. What happens if we run the following program on UNIX?
   ```
   main() {
       while (fork() >= 0)
           ;
   }
   ```

4. Explain what must happen for UNIX wait to return (successfully and) immediately.

5. Suppose you were the instructor of a very large introductory programming class. Explain (in English) how you would use UNIX system calls to automate testing of submitted homework assignments.

6. What happens if you run "exec csh" in a UNIX shell? Why?

7. What happens if you run "exec ls" in a UNIX shell? Why?

8. How many processes are created if the following program is run?

```
main(int argc, char ** argv) {
    forkthem(5)
}
void forkthem(int n) {
    if (n > 0) {
        fork ();
        forkthem(n-1);
    }
}
```

9. Consider the following program:

```
main (int argc, char ** argv) {
    int child = fork ();
    int x = 5;

    if (child == 0) {
        x += 5;
    } else {
        child = fork ();
        x += 10;
        if(child) {
            x += 5;
        }
    }
}
```

How many different copies of the variable x are there? What are their values when their process finishes?

10. What is the output of the following programs? (Please try to solve the problem without compiling and running the programs.)

```
// Program 1
main() {
    int val = 5;
    int pid;

    if (pid = fork ())
        wait(pid);
    val++;
    printf("%d\n", val);
    return val;
}
```

```
// Program 2:
main() {
    int val = 5;
    int pid;
    if (pid = fork ())
        wait(pid);
    else
        exit(val);
    val++;
    printf("%d\n", val);
    return val;
}
```

11. Implement a simple Linux shell in C capable of executing a sequence of programs that communicate through a pipe. For example, if the user types ls | wc, your program should fork off the two programs, which together will calculate the number of files in the directory. For this, you will need to use several of the Linux system calls described in this chapter: fork, exec, open, close, pipe, dup2, and wait. **Note:** You will to replace stdin and stdout in the child process with the pipe file descriptors; that is the role of dup2.

12. Extend the shell implemented above to support foreground and background tasks, as well as job control: suspend, resume, and kill.

Part II

Concurrency

Many hands make light work.

John Heywood (1546)

4 Concurrency and Threads

How does an operating system manage multiple simultaneous activities?

In the real world — outside of computers — different activities often proceed at the same time. Five jazz musicians play their instruments while reacting to each other; one car drives north while another drives south; one part of a drug molecule is attracted to a cell's receptor, while another part is repelled; a humanoid robot walks, raises its arms, and turns its head; you fetch one article from the *New York Times* website while someone else fetches another; or millions of people make long distance phone calls on Mother's Day.

concurrency

We use the word *concurrency* to refer to multiple activities that can happen at the same time. The real world is concurrent, and internally, modern computers are also concurrent. For example, a high-end server might have more than a dozen processors, 10 disks, and 4 network interfaces; a workstation might have a dozen active I/O devices including a screen, keyboard, mouse, camera, microphone, speaker, wireless network interface, wired network interface, printer, scanner, and disk drive. Today, even mobile phones often have multi-core processors.

Correctly managing concurrency is a key challenge for operating system developers. To manage hardware resources, to provide responsiveness to users, and to run multiple applications simultaneously, the operating system needs a structured way of keeping track of the various actions it needs to perform. Over the next several chapters, we will present a set of abstractions for expressing and managing concurrency. These abstractions are in widespread use in commercial operating systems because they reduce implementation complexity, improve system reliability, and improve performance.

Concurrency is also a concern for many application developers. Although the abstractions we discuss were originally developed to make it easier to write

Figure 4.1: The operating system provides the illusion that programmers can create as many threads as they need, and each thread runs on its own dedicated virtual processor. In reality, of course, a machine only has a finite number of processors, and it is the operating system's job to transparently multiplex threads onto the actual processors.

correct operating system code, they have become widely used in applications:

- Network services need to be able to handle multiple requests from their clients; a Google that could handle only one search request at a time, or an Amazon that could only allow one book to be bought at a time, would be much less useful.

- Most applications today have user interfaces; providing good responsiveness to users while simultaneously executing application logic is much easier with a structured approach to concurrency.

- Parallel programs need to be able to map work onto multiple processors to get the performance benefits of multicore architectures.

- Data management systems need concurrency to mask the latency of disk and network operations.

Why threads?   From the programmer's perspective, it is much easier to think sequentially than to keep track of many simultaneous activities. For example, when reading or writing the code for a procedure, you can identify an initial state and a set of pre-conditions, think through how each successive statement changes the state, and from that determine the post-conditions. How can you write a correct program with dozens of events happening at once?

The key idea is to write a concurrent program—one with many simultaneous activities—as a set of sequential streams of execution, or *threads*, that interact and share results in very precise ways. Threads let us define a set of tasks that run concurrently while the code for each task is sequential. Each thread behaves as if it has its own dedicated processor, as illustrated in Figure 4.1. As we will see later, using the thread abstraction often requires the programmer to write additional code for coordinating multiple threads accessing shared data structures; we will discuss this topic in much more detail in Chapter 5.

The thread abstraction lets the programmer create as many threads as needed without worrying about the exact number of physical processors, or exactly which processor is doing what at each instant. Of course, threads are only an abstraction: the physical hardware has a limited number of processors (and potentially only one!). The operating system's job is to provide the illusion of a nearly infinite number of virtual processors even while the physical hardware is more limited. It sustains this illusion by transparently suspending and resuming threads so that at any given time only a subset of the threads are actively running.

This chapter will define the thread abstraction, illustrate how a programmer can use the abstraction, and explain how the operating system can implement threads on top of a limited number of processors. Chapter 5 explains how to coordinate threads when they operate on shared data, and Chapter 6 covers advanced issues when programming with threads. Chapter 7 discusses the policy question: how should the operating system choose *which* thread to run next when there are more things to run than processors on which to run them.

Chapter roadmap: The rest of this chapter discusses these topics in detail:

- **Thread Use Cases.** What are threads useful for? (Section 4.1)

- **Thread Abstraction.** What is the thread abstraction as seen by a programmer? (Section 4.2)

- **Simple Thread API.** How can programmers use threads? (Section 4.3)

- **Thread Data Structures.** What data structures does the operating system use to manage threads? (Section 4.4)

- **Thread Life Cycle.** What states does a thread go through between initialization and completion? (Section 4.5)

- **Implementing Kernel Threads.** How do we implement the thread abstraction inside the operating system kernel? (Section 4.6)

- **Combining Kernel Threads and Single-Threaded User Processes.** How do we extend the implementation of kernel threads to support simple single-threaded processes? (Section 4.7)

- **Implementing Multi-threaded Processes.** How do we implement the thread abstraction for multi-threaded applications? (Section 4.8)

- **Alternative Abstractions.** What other abstractions can we use to express and implement concurrency? (Section 4.9)

Deja vu all over again?

Threads are widely used, and several modern programming languages directly support writing programs with multiple threads. You may have programmed with threads before or have taken classes that talk about using threads. What is new here?

The discussion in this book is designed to make sense even if you have never seen threads before. If you have seen threads before, great! But we still think you will find the discussion useful.

Beyond describing the basic thread abstraction, we emphasize two points in this chapter and the following ones.

- **Implementation.** We will describe how operating systems implement threads both for their own use and for use by user-level applications. It is important to understand how threads really work so that you can understand their costs and performance characteristics and can use them effectively.

- **Practice.** We will present a methodology for writing correct multi-threaded programs. Concurrency is increasingly important in many programming tasks, but writing correct multi-threaded programs requires much more care and discipline than writing correct single-threaded programs. That said, following a few simple rules that we will describe can greatly simplify the process of writing robust multi-threaded code.

Multithreaded programming has a well-deserved reputation for being difficult, but we believe the ideas in this chapter and the subsequent ones can help almost anyone become better at programming with threads.

4.1 | Thread Use Cases

What are threads useful for?

The intuition behind the thread abstraction is simple: in a program, we can represent each concurrent task as a *thread*. Each thread provides the abstraction of sequential execution similar to the traditional programming model. In fact, we can think of a traditional program as *single-threaded* with one logical sequence of steps as each instruction follows the previous one. The program executes statements, iterates through loops, and calls/returns from procedures one after another.

single-threaded program

multi-threaded program

A *multi-threaded program* is a generalization of the same basic programming model. Each individual thread follows a single sequence of steps as it executes statements, iterates through loops, calls/returns from procedures, etc. However, a program can now have several such threads executing at the same time.

Figure 4.2: In the Earth Visualizer example, two threads each draw part of the scene, a third thread manages the user interface widgets, and a fourth thread fetches new data from a remote server. Satellite Image Credit: NASA Earth Observatory.

When is it appropriate to use multiple threads within the same program? Threads have become widely used in both operating system and application code, and based on that experience, we can identify several common themes. We illustrate these themes by describing one application in some detail, to show how and why it leverages threads.

EXAMPLE   Consider an Earth Visualizer application similar to Google Earth (http://earth.google.com/). This application lets a user virtually fly anywhere in the world, see aerial images at different resolutions, and view other information associated with each location. A key part of the design is that the user's controls are always operable: when the user moves the mouse to a new location, the image is redrawn in the background at successively better resolutions while the program continues to let the user adjust the view, select additional information about the location for display, or enter search terms.

To implement this application, as Figure 4.2 illustrates, the programmer might write code to draw a portion of the screen, display user interface (UI) widgets, process user inputs, and fetch higher resolution images for newly visible areas. In a sequential program, these functions would run in turn. With threads, they can run concurrently so that the user interface is responsive even while new data is being fetched and the screen being redrawn.

4.1.1   Four Reasons to Use Threads

Using threads to express and manage concurrency has several advantages:

How do we keep track of multiple activities?

- **Program structure: expressing logically concurrent tasks.** Programs often interact with or simulate real-world applications that have concurrent activities. Threads let you express an application's natural concurrency by writing each concurrent task as a separate thread.

  In the Earth Visualizer application, threads let different activities—updating the screen, fetching additional data, and receiving new user inputs—run at the same time. For example, to get mouse input while also re-drawing the screen and sending and receiving packets off the network, the physical processors need to split their time among these tasks.

  Although one could imagine manually writing a program that inter-leaves these activities (e.g., draw a few pixels on the screen, then check to see if the user has moved the mouse, then check to see if new image data have arrived on the network, . . .), using threads greatly simplifies concurrent code.

  Another example is on the server side of the Earth Visualizer. The server needs to manage the requests of a large number of clients, each focused on a different point on the planet. Since the clients are likely behind a wide variety of access link technologies (e.g., from dialup to gigabit Ethernet), it would slow everyone down if each request needed to be completely handled before the server could start on the next one. By creating a separate thread for each client, the computation and network-ing needed for that client can be intermixed with other clients, without affecting the logical structure of the program. This design pattern—one server thread per client—is common; for example, the popular Apache web server assigns each client its own thread when it first connects to the server.

How do we make sure the user interface is responsive?

- **Responsiveness: shifting work to run in the background.** To improve user responsiveness and performance, a common design pattern is to create threads to perform work that in the background, without the user wait-ing for the result. This way, the user interface can remain responsive to further commands, regardless of the complexity of the user request. In a web browser, for example, the cancel button should continue to work even (or especially!) if the downloaded page is gigantic or a script on the page takes a long time to execute.

  How does this work? Many applications have a loop: get a user com-mand, then execute the command, then get the next command. If some commands take a long time to perform, however, an application that executes everything sequentially will not be able to check for the next operation until the previous one completes. To keep the interface responsive, we can use threads to split each command into two parts: anything that can be done instantly can be done in the main event loop, and a separate thread can perform the rest of the task in the background. In the Earth Visualizer example, we used threads to move the computationally difficult parts of the application logic — rendering the display — out of the main loop.

Operating system kernels make extensive use of threads to preserve responsiveness. Many operating systems are designed so that the common case is fast. For example, when writing a file, the operating system stores the modified data in a kernel buffer, and returns immediately to the application. In the background, the operating system kernel runs a separate thread to flush the modified data out to disk. Another example is on file reads: the kernel can have a thread which attempts to anticipate which blocks are likely to be read next (e.g., if the application is reading a large file from beginning to end), and to bring those blocks from disk before the application asks for them.

How do we write parallel code?

- **Performance: exploiting multiple processors.** Programs can use threads on a multiprocessor to do work in parallel; they can do the same work in less time or more work in the same elapsed time. Today, a server might have more than a dozen processors; a desktop or laptop may include eight processor cores; even most smartphones are multicore machines. Looking forward, Moore's law makes it likely that the number of processors per system will continue to increase. An advantage to using threads for parallelism is that the number of threads need not exactly match the number of processors in the hardware on which it is running. The operating system transparently switches which threads run on which processors.

  For an 8-processor machine, you could parallelize the Earth Visualizer application by splitting the demanding job of rendering different portions of the image on the screen across six threads. Then, the operating system could run those six rendering threads on six processors and run the various other threads on the two remaining processors to update the on-screen navigation widgets, construct the network messages needed to fetch additional images from the distant servers, and parse reply messages.

How do we hide I/O latency?

- **Performance: managing I/O devices.** To do useful work, computers must interact with the outside world via I/O devices. By running tasks as separate threads, when one task is waiting for I/O, the processor can make progress on a different task.

  The benefit of concurrency between the processor and the I/O is two-fold: First, processors are often much faster than the I/O systems with which they interact, so keeping the processor idle during I/O would waste much of its capacity. For example, the latency to read from disk can be tens of milliseconds, enough to execute more than 10 million instructions on a modern processor. After requesting a block from disk, the operating system can switch to another program, or another thread within the same program, until the disk completes and the original thread is ready to resume.

Second, I/O provides a way for the computer to interact with external entities, such as users pressing keys on a keyboard or a remote computer sending network packets. The arrival of this type of I/O event is unpredictable, so the processor must be able to work on other tasks while still responding quickly to these external events.

In the Earth Visualizer application, a snappy user interface is essential, but much of the imagery is stored on remote servers and fetched by the application only when needed. The application provides a responsive experience when a user changes location by first downloading a small, low-resolution view of the new location. While rendering those images with one thread, another thread simultaneously fetches progressively higher-resolution images, allowing the rendering thread to update the view as the higher-resolution images arrive.

4.2 | Thread Abstraction

What is the thread abstraction as seen by a programmer?

Thus far, we have described what a thread is and why it is useful. Before we go farther, we must define the thread abstraction and its properties more precisely.

thread

A *thread* is *a single execution sequence* that represents *a separately schedulable task*.

- **Single execution sequence.** Each thread executes a sequence of instructions — assignments, conditionals, loops, procedures, and so on — just as in the familiar sequential programming model.

- **Separately schedulable task.** The operating system can run, suspend, or resume a thread at any time.

4.2.1 Running, Suspending, and Resuming Threads

Threads provide the illusion of an infinite number of processors. How does the operating system implement this illusion? It must execute instructions from each thread so that each thread makes progress, but the underlying hardware has only a limited number of processors, and perhaps only one!

thread scheduler

To map an arbitrary set of threads to a fixed set of processors, operating systems include a *thread scheduler* that can switch between threads that are

Threads vs. processes

In Chapter 2, we described a process as the execution of a program with restricted rights. A thread is an independent sequence of instructions running within a program. Perhaps the best way to see how these concepts are related, is to see how different operating systems combine them in different ways:

- **One thread per process.** A simple single-threaded application has one sequence of instructions, executing from beginning to end. The operating system kernel runs those instructions in user mode to restrict access to privileged operations or system memory. The process performs system calls to ask the kernel to perform privileged operations on its behalf.

- **Many threads per process.** Alternately, a program may be structured as several concurrent threads, each executing within the restricted rights of the process. At any given time, a subset of the process's threads may be running, while the rest are suspended. Any thread running in a process can make system calls into the kernel, blocking that thread until the call returns but allowing other threads to continue to run. Likewise, when the processor gets an I/O interrupt, it preempts one of the running threads so the kernel can run the interrupt handler; when the handler finishes, the kernel resumes that thread.

- **Many single-threaded processes.** As recently as twenty years ago, many operating systems supported multiple processes but only one thread per process. To the kernel, however, each process looks like a thread: a separate sequence of instructions, executing sometimes in the kernel and sometimes at user level. For example, on a multiprocessor, if multiple processes perform system calls at the same time, the kernel, in effect, has multiple threads executing concurrently in kernel mode.

- **Many kernel threads.** To manage complexity, shift work to the background, exploit parallelism, and hide I/O latency, the operating system kernel itself can benefit from using multiple threads. In this case, each kernel thread runs with the privileges of the kernel: it can execute privileged instructions, access system memory, and issue commands directly to I/O devices. The operating system kernel itself implements the thread abstraction for its own use.

Because of the usefulness of threads, almost all modern operating systems support both multiple threads per process and multiple kernel threads.

Programmer's View	Possible Execution #1	Possible Execution #2	Possible Execution #3
.	.	.	.
.	.	.	.
.	.	.	.
x = x + 1;	x = x + 1;	x = x + 1;	x = x + 1;
y = y + x;	y = y + x;	. . . .	y = y + x;
z = x + 5y;	z = x + 5y;	Thread is suspended.	. . . .
.	.	Other thread(s) run.	Thread is suspended.
.	.	Thread is resumed.	Other thread(s) run.
.	.	. . . .	Thread is resumed.
		y = y + x;	. . . .
		z = x + 5y;	z = x + 5y;

Figure 4.3: Three possible ways that a thread might execute, all of which are equivalent to the programmer.

running and those that are ready but not running. For example, in the previous Figure 4.1, a scheduler might suspend thread 1 from processor 1, move it to the list of ready threads, and then resume thread 5 by moving it from the ready list to run on processor 1.

Switching between threads is transparent to the code being executed within each thread. The abstraction makes each thread appear to be a single stream of execution; this means the programmer can pay attention to the sequence of instruction within a thread and not whether or when that sequence may be (temporarily) suspended to let another thread run.

Threads thus provide an execution model in which *each thread runs on a dedicated virtual processor with unpredictable and variable speed.* From the point of view of a thread's code, each instruction appears to execute immediately after the preceding one. However, the scheduler may suspend a thread between one instruction and the next and resume running it later. It is as if the thread were running on a processor that sometimes becomes very slow.

Figure 4.3 illustrates a programmer's view of a simple program and three (of many) possible ways the program might be executed, depending on what the scheduler does. From the thread's point of view, other than the speed of execution, the alternatives are equivalent. Indeed, the thread would typically be unaware of which of these (or other) executions actually occurs.

How threads are scheduled affects a thread's interleavings with other threads. Figure 4.4 shows some of the many possible interleavings of a program with three threads. Thread programmers should therefore not make any assumptions about the relative speed with which different threads execute.

4.2.2   Why "Unpredictable Speed"?

It may seem strange to require programmers to assume that a thread's virtual processor runs at an unpredictable speed and that any interleaving with other

One Execution   Another Execution

Thread 1

Thread 2

Thread 3

Another Execution

Thread 1

Thread 2

Thread 3

Figure 4.4: Some of the many possible ways that three threads might be interleaved at runtime.

Cooperative vs. preemptive multi-threading

Although most thread systems include a scheduler that can — at least in principle — run any thread at any time, some systems provide the abstraction of *cooperative threads*. In these systems, a thread runs without interruption until it explicitly relinquishes control of the processor to another thread. An advantage of cooperative multi-threading is increased control over the interleavings among threads. For example, in most cooperative multi-threading systems, only one thread runs at a time, so while a thread is running, no other thread can run and affect the system's state.

Unfortunately, cooperative multi-threading has significant disadvantages. For example, a long-running thread can monopolize the processor, starving other threads and making the system's user interface sluggish or nonresponsive. Additionally, modern multiprocessor machines run multiple threads at a time, so one would still have to reason about the possible interactions between threads even if cooperative multi-threading were used. Thus, although cooperative multi-threading was used in some significant systems in the past, including early versions of Apple's MacOS operating system, it is less often used today.

The alternative we describe in this book is sometimes called *preemptive multi-threading* since running threads can be switched at any time. Whenever the book uses the term "multi-threading," it means preemptive multi-threading unless we explicitly state otherwise.

threads is possible. Surely, the programmer should be able to take advantage of the fact that some interleavings are more likely than others?

The thread programming model adopts this assumption as a way to guide programmers when reasoning about correctness. Rather than assuming that one thread runs at the same speed as another (or faster or slower) and trying to write programs that coordinate threads based on their relative speed of execution, multi-threaded programs should make no assumptions about the behavior of the thread scheduler. In turn, the kernel's scheduling decisions—when to assign a thread to a processor, and when to preempt it for a different thread—can be made without worrying whether they might affect program correctness.

If threads are completely independent of each other, sharing no memory or other resources, then the order of execution will not matter—any schedule will produce the same output as any other. Most multi-threaded programs share data structures, however. In this case, as Chapter 5 describes, the programmer must use explicit synchronization to ensure program correctness regardless of the possible interleaving of instructions of different threads.

Even if we could ignore the issue of scheduling—e.g., if there are more processors than threads so that each thread is assigned its own physical processor—the physical reality is that the relative execution speed of different threads can be significantly affected by factors outside their control. An extreme example is that the programmer may be debugging one thread by single-stepping it, while other threads run at full speed on other processors. If the programmer is to have any hope of understanding concurrent program behavior, the program's correctness cannot depend on which threads are being observed.

Variability in execution speed occurs during normal operation as well. Accessing memory can stall a processor for hundreds or thousands of cycles if a cache miss occurs. Other factors include how frequently the scheduler preempts the thread, how many physical processors are present on a machine, how large the caches are, how fast the memory is, how the energy-saving firmware adjusts the processors' clock speeds, what network messages arrive, or what input is received from the user. Execution speeds for the different threads of a program are hard to predict, can vary on different hardware, and can even vary from run to run on the same hardware. As a result, we must coordinate thread actions through explicit synchronization rather than by trying to reason about their relative speed.

EXAMPLE   Is a kernel interrupt handler a thread?

ANSWER   **No, an interrupt handler is not a thread.** A kernel interrupt handler shares some resemblance to a thread: it is a single sequence of instructions that executes from beginning to end. However, an interrupt handler is not independently schedulable: it is triggered by a hardware I/O event, rather than a decision by the thread scheduler in the kernel. Once started, the interrupt

Simple Threads API	
void thread_create(thread, func, arg)	Create a new thread, storing information about it in thread. Concurrently with the calling thread, thread executes the function func with the argument arg.
void thread_yield()	The calling thread voluntarily gives up the processor to let some other thread(s) run. The scheduler can resume running the calling thread whenever it chooses to do so.
int thread_join(thread)	Wait for thread to finish if it has not already done so; then return the value passed to thread_exit by that thread. Note that thread_join may be called only once for each thread.
void thread_exit(ret)	Finish the current thread. Store the value ret in the current thread's data structure. If another thread is already waiting in a call to thread_join, resume it.

Figure 4.5: Simplified API for using threads.

handler runs to completion, unless preempted by another (higher priority) interrupt.   □

4.3 | Simple Thread API

How can programmers use threads?

Figure 4.5 shows a simple API for using threads. This simplified API is based on the POSIX standard pthreads API, but it omits some POSIX options and error handling for simplicity. Most other thread packages are quite similar; if you understand how to program with this API, you will find it easy to write code with most standard thread APIs.

asynchronous procedure call

A good way to understand the simple threads API is that it provides a way to invoke an *asynchronous procedure call*. A normal procedure call passes a set of arguments to a function, runs the function immediately on the caller's stack, and when the function is completed, returns control back to the caller with the result. An asynchronous procedure call separates the call from the return: with thread_create, the caller starts the function, but unlike a normal procedure call, the caller continues execution concurrently with the called function. Later, the caller can wait for the function completion (with thread_join).

In Chapter 3, we saw similar concepts in the UNIX process abstraction. thread_create is analogous to UNIX process fork and exec, while thread_join is analogous to UNIX process wait. UNIX fork creates a new process that runs concurrently with the process calling fork; UNIX exec causes that process to run a specific program. UNIX wait allows the calling process to suspend execution until the completion of the new process.

```
#include <stdio.h>
#include "thread.h"

static void go(int n);

#define NTHREADS 10
static thread_t threads[NTHREADS];

int main(int argc, char **argv) {
    int i;
    long exitValue;

    for (i = 0; i < NTHREADS; i++){
        thread_create(&(threads[i]), &go, i);
    }
    for (i = 0; i < NTHREADS; i++){
        exitValue = thread_join(threads[i]);
        printf("Thread %d returned with %ld\n",
                    i, exitValue);
    }
    printf("Main thread done.\n");
    return 0;
}

void go(int n) {
    printf("Hello from thread %d\n", n);
    thread_exit(100 + n);
    // Not reached
}
```

```
% ./threadHello
Hello from thread 0
Hello from thread 1
Thread 0 returned 100
Hello from thread 3
Hello from thread 4
Thread 1 returned 101
Hello from thread 5
Hello from thread 2
Hello from thread 6
Hello from thread 8
Hello from thread 7
Hello from thread 9
Thread 2 returned 102
Thread 3 returned 103
Thread 4 returned 104
Thread 5 returned 105
Thread 6 returned 106
Thread 7 returned 107
Thread 8 returned 108
Thread 9 returned 109
```

Figure 4.6: Example multi-threaded program using the simple threads API that prints "Hello" ten times. The right side shows the output of one possible run of this program.

4.3.1   A Multi-Threaded Hello World

To illustrate how to use the simple threads API, Figure 4.6 shows a very simple multi-threaded program written in 'C'. The main function uses thread_create to create 10 threads. The interesting arguments are the second and third.

- The second argument, go, is a function pointer— where the newly created thread should begin execution.

- The third argument, i, is passed to that function.

Thus, thread_create initializes the i'th thread's state so that it is prepared to call the function go with the argument i.

When the scheduler runs the i'th thread, that thread runs the function go with the value i as an argument and prints Hello from thread i. The thread then returns the value (i + 100) by calling thread_exit. This call stores the specified value in a field in the thread_t object so that thread_join can retrieve it.

The main function uses thread_join to wait for each of the threads it created. As each thread finishes, code in main reads the thread's exit value and prints it.

EXAMPLE   Why might the "Hello" message from thread 2 print *after* the "Hello" message for thread 5, even though thread 2 was created before thread 5?

ANSWER   **Creating and scheduling threads are separate operations.** Although threads are usually scheduled in the order that they are created, there is no guarantee. Further, even if thread 2 started running before thread 5, it might be preempted before it reaches the printf call.

Rather, the only assumption the programmer can make is that each of the threads runs on its own virtual processor with unpredictable speed. Any interleaving is possible.   □

EXAMPLE   Why must the "Thread returned" message from thread 2 print *before* the Thread returned message from thread 5?

ANSWER   Since the threads run on virtual processors with unpredictable speeds, the order in which the threads finish is indeterminate. However, **the main thread checks for thread completion in the order they were created.** It calls thread_join for thread i +1 only after thread_join for thread i has returned.   □

EXAMPLE   What is the *minimum* and *maximum* number of threads that could exist when thread 5 prints "Hello?"

ANSWER   When the program starts, a main thread begins running main. That thread creates NTHREADS = 10 threads. All of those could run and complete before thread 5 prints "Hello." Thus, **the minimum is two threads** — the main thread and thread 5. On the other hand, all 10 threads could have been created, while 5 was the first to run. Thus, **the maximum is 11 threads.**   □

4.3.2   Fork-Join Parallelism

Although the interface in Figure 4.5 is simple, it is remarkably powerful. Many multi-threaded applications can be designed using only these thread

fork-join parallelism   operations and no additional synchronization. With *fork-join parallelism*, a thread can create child threads to perform work ("fork", or thread_create), and it can wait for their results ("join"). Data may be safely shared between threads, provided it is (a) written by the parent before the child thread starts or (b) written by the child and read by the parent after the join.

If these sharing restrictions are followed, each thread executes independently and in a deterministic fashion, unaffected by the behavior of any other concurrently executing thread. The multiplexing of threads onto processors has no effect other than performance.

EXAMPLE   **Parallel block zero.** A simple example of fork-join parallelism in operating systems is the procedure to zero a contiguous block of memory. To prevent unintentional data leakage, whenever a process exits, the operating system must

```
// To pass two arguments, we need a struct to hold them.
typedef struct bzeroparams {
    unsigned char *buffer;
    int length;
};

#define NTHREADS 10

// Zero a block of memory using multiple threads.
void blockzero (unsigned char *p, int length) {
    int i, j;
    thread_t threads[NTHREADS];
    struct bzeroparams params[NTHREADS];

// For simplicity, assumes length is divisible by NTHREADS.
    assert((length % NTHREADS) == 0);
    for (i = 0, j = 0; i < NTHREADS; i++, j += length/NTHREADS) {
        params[i].buffer = p + i * length/NTHREADS;
        params[i].length = length/NTHREADS;
        thread_create_p(&(threads[i]), &go, &params[i]);
    }
    for (i = 0; i < NTHREADS; i++) {
        thread_join(threads[i]);
    }
}
```

Figure 4.7: Routine to zero a contiguous region of memory in parallel using multiple threads. To pass two arguments (the pointer to the buffer and the length of the buffer) to the child thread, the program passes a pointer to a struct holding the two parameters.

zero the memory that had been allocated to the exiting process. Otherwise, a new process may be re-assigned the memory, enabling it to read potentially sensitive data. For example, an operating system's remote login program might temporarily store a user's password in memory, but the next process to use the same physical memory might be a memory-scanning program launched by a different, malicious user.

For a large process, parallelizing the zeroing function can make sense. Zeroing 1 GB of memory takes about 50 milliseconds on a modern computer; by contrast, creating and starting a new thread takes a few tens of microseconds.

Figure 4.7 illustrates the code for a parallel zero function using fork-join parallelism. The multi-threaded blockzero creates a set of threads and assigns each a disjoint portion of the memory region; the region is empty when all threads have completed their work.

In practice, the operating system will often create a thread to run blockzero in the background. The memory of an exiting process does not need to be cleared until the memory is needed — that is, when the next process is created.

To exploit this flexibility, the operating system can create a set of low priority threads to run blockzero. The kernel can then return immediately and resume running application code. Later on, when the memory is needed, the

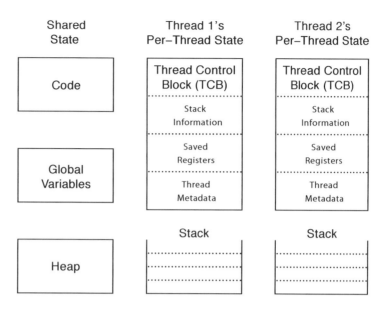

Shared State	Thread 1's Per–Thread State	Thread 2's Per–Thread State

Figure 4.8: A multi-threaded process or operating system kernel has both *per-thread state* and *shared state*. The thread control block stores the per-thread state: the current state of the thread's computation (e.g., saved processor registers and a pointer to the stack) and metadata needed to manage the thread (e.g., the thread's ID, scheduling priority, owner, and resource consumption). Shared state includes the program's code, global static variables, and the heap.

kernel can call thread_join. If the zero is complete by that point, the join will return immediately; otherwise, it will wait until the memory is safe to use.

4.4 | Thread Data Structures and Life Cycle

What data structures does the operating system use to manage threads?

As we have seen, each thread represents a sequential stream of execution. The operating system provides the illusion that each thread runs on its own virtual processor by transparently suspending and resuming threads. For the illusion to work, the operating system must precisely save and restore the state of a thread. However, because threads run either in a process or in the kernel, there is also *shared* state that is not saved or restored when switching the processor between threads.

Thus, to understand how the operating system implements the thread abstraction, we must define both the per-thread state and the state that is shared among threads. Then we can describe a thread's life cycle — how the operating system can create, start, stop, and delete threads to provide the abstraction.

4.4.1   Per-Thread State and Thread Control Block (TCB)

The operating system needs a data structure to represent a thread's state; a thread is like any other object in this regard. This data structure is called the *thread control block (TCB)*. For every thread the operating system creates, it creates one TCB.

thread control block (TCB)

The thread control block holds two types of per-thread information:

1. The state of the computation being performed by the thread.

2. Metadata about the thread that is used to manage the thread.

What are the contents of the TCB?

Per-thread Computation State   To create multiple threads and to be able to start and stop each thread as needed, the operating system must allocate space in the TCB for the current state of each thread's computation: a pointer to the thread's stack and a copy of its processor registers.

- **Stack.** A thread's stack is the same as the stack for a single-threaded computation—it stores information needed by the nested procedures the thread is currently running. For example, if a thread calls foo(), foo() calls bar(), and bar() calls bas(), then the stack would contain a *stack frame* for each of these three procedures; each stack frame contains the local variables used by the procedure, the parameters the procedure was called with, and the return address to jump to when the procedure completes.

stack frame

  Because at any given time different threads can be in different states in their sequential computations—each can be in a different place in a different procedure called with different arguments from a different nesting of enclosing procedures—each thread needs its own stack. When a new thread is created, the operating system allocates it a new stack and stores a pointer to that stack in the thread's TCB.

- **Copy of processor registers.** A processor's registers include not only its general-purpose registers for storing intermediate values for ongoing computations, but they also include special-purpose registers, such as the instruction pointer and stack pointer.

  To be able to suspend a thread, run another thread, and later resume the original thread, the operating system needs a place to store a thread's registers when that thread is not actively running. In some systems, the general-purpose registers for a stopped thread are stored on the top of the stack, and the TCB contains only a pointer to the stack. In other systems, the TCB contains space for a copy of all processor registers.

Per-thread Metadata   The TCB also includes *per-thread metadata*—information for managing the thread. For example, each thread might have a thread ID, scheduling priority, and status (e.g., whether the thread is waiting for an event or is ready to be placed onto a processor).

How big a stack?

An implementation question for thread systems is: how large a stack should be allocated for each thread? A stack grows and shrinks as procedure calls are made and those calls return. The size of the stack must be large enough to accommodate the deepest nesting level needed during in the thread's lifetime. With hundreds or thousands of threads, it can be wasteful to allocate more than the minimum needed.

Most modern operating systems allocate kernel stacks in physical memory, putting space at a premium. However, the maximum procedure nesting depth in the kernel is usually small. Thus, kernels typically allocate a very small fixed sized region for each thread stack, e.g., 8 KB by default in Linux on an Intel x86. The kernel stays within this bound due to an important kernel coding convention: buffers and data structures are always allocated on the heap and never as procedure local variables. Although most programming languages allow arbitrary data structures to be defined as procedure local or "automatic" — allocated when a procedure starts and de-allocated when the procedure exits — that can cause problems when the stack is of limited size.

User-level stacks are allocated in virtual memory and so there is less need for a tight space constraint. In a single threaded process, the stack is located at the top end of the address space, where it can grow nearly without bound. To catch program errors, most operating systems will trigger an error if the user program stack grows too large too quickly, as that is usually an indication of unbounded recursion, rather than something that was the programmer's intent.

In a multi-threaded user application, it is not possible to have each stack grow without constraint. Although some programming languages, such as Google's Go, will automatically grow the stack as needed, this is still uncommon. POSIX allows the default stack size to be library dependent (e.g., larger on a desktop machine, smaller on a smartphone). As one POSIX thread tutorial put it dryly, "Exceeding the default stack limit is often very easy to do, with the usual results: program termination and/or corrupted data." [10]. Most implementations try to detect when programs exceed the default stack limit by placing a known value at the very top and bottom of the stack to serve as a guard. The guard values can be checked on every context switch; if the value changes, it is likely the thread exceeded its stack.

To support application portability, the POSIX thread standard allows the user to redefine the default stack size to whatever is needed for the correct execution of a particular program. The thread library provided with the textbook sets the default stack size to 1 MB. This is almost certainly large enough provided you adopt the kernel approach of never putting large data objects on the stack.

4.4.2   Shared State

As opposed to per-thread state that is allocated for each thread, some state is *shared* between threads running in the same process or within the operating system kernel (Figure 4.8). In particular, program *code* is shared by all threads in a process, although each thread may be executing at a different place within that code. Additionally, statically allocated *global variables* and dynamically allocated *heap variables* can store information that is accessible to all threads.

WARNING   Although there is an important logical division between per-thread state and shared state, the operating system typically does not enforce this division. Nothing prevents one buggy thread from accessing another thread's (conceptually private) per-thread state. Writing to a bad pointer in one thread can corrupt the stack of another. Or a careless programmer might pass a pointer to a local variable on one thread's stack to another thread, giving the second thread a pointer to a stack location whose contents may change as the first thread calls and returns from various procedures. Or the first thread can exit after handing out a pointer to a variable on its stack; the heap will reassign that memory to an unrelated purpose. Because these bugs can depend on the specific interleavings of the threads' executions, they can be extremely hard to locate and correct.

To avoid unexpected behaviors, it is therefore important when writing multi-threaded programs to know which variables are designed to be shared across threads (global variables, objects on the heap) and which are designed to be private (local/automatic variables).

4.5 | Thread Life Cycle

It is useful to consider the progression of states as a thread goes from being created, to being scheduled and de-scheduled onto and off of a processor, and then to exiting. Figure 4.9 shows the states of a thread during its lifetime.

INIT.   Thread creation puts a thread into its INIT state and allocates and initializes per-thread data structures. Once that is done, thread creation code puts

ready list   the thread into the READY state by adding the thread to the *ready list*. The ready list is the set of runnable threads that are waiting their turn to use a processor. In practice, as discussed in Chapter 7, the ready list is not in fact a "list"; the operating system typically uses a more sophisticated data structure to keep track of runnable threads, such as a priority queue. Nevertheless, following convention, we will continue to refer to it as the ready list.

READY.   A thread in the READY state is available to be run but is not currently running. Its TCB is on the ready list, and the values of its registers are stored in its TCB. At any time, the scheduler can cause a thread to transition from READY

Other per-thread state: Thread-local variables

In addition to the per-thread state that corresponds to execution state in the single-threaded case, some systems include additional *thread-local variables*. These variables are similar to global variables in that their scope spans different procedures, but they differ in that each thread has its own copy of these variables.

Consider these examples:

- **Errno.** In UNIX, the return value of system calls is intentionally kept simple. For example, the UNIX read system call returns either the number of bytes read (if successful) or -1 (if there was a problem). Often, an application needs additional information about the cause of the error (e.g., permission error, disk offline, etc.). To provide this, the kernel sets a variable in the application memory, the errno, with a diagnostic code for the most recent system call. As UNIX originally had only one thread per process, there was no confusion: the errno referred to the most recent system call of that process.

  In a multi-threaded program, however, multiple threads can perform system calls concurrently. Rather than redefine the entire UNIX system call interface for a multi-threaded environment, errno is now a macro that maps to a thread-local variable containing the error code for that thread's most recent system call.

- **Heap internals.** Although a program's heap is logically shared — it is acceptable for one thread to allocate an object on the heap and then pass a pointer to that object to another thread — for performance reasons heaps may internally subdivide their space into per-thread regions. The advantage of subdividing the heap is that multiple threads can each allocate objects at the same time without interfering with one another. Further, by allocating objects used by the same thread from the same memory region, cache hit rates may improve. To implement these optimizations, each subdivision of the heap has thread-local variables that track what parts of the thread-local heap are in use, what parts are free, and so on. Then, the code that allocates new memory (e.g., malloc and new) is written to use these thread-local data structures and only take memory from the shared heap if the local heap is empty.

Thread-local variables are often useful, but, for simplicity, the rest of our discussion focuses only on the TCB, registers, and stack as the core pieces of per-thread state.

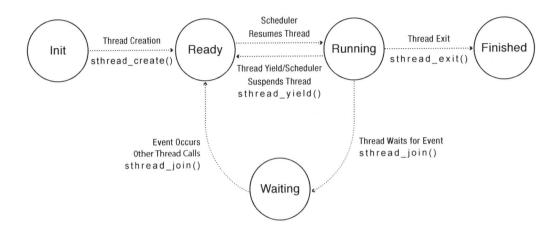

Figure 4.9: The states of a thread during its lifetime.

to RUNNING by copying its register values from its TCB to a processor's registers.

What causes a thread to transition from READY *to* RUNNING? **RUNNING.**   A thread in the RUNNING state is running on a processor. At this time, its register values are stored on the processor rather than in the TCB. A RUNNING thread can transition to the READY state in two ways:

- The scheduler can preempt a running thread and move it to the READY state by: (1) saving the thread's registers to its TCB and (2) switching the processor to run the next thread on the ready list.

- A running thread can voluntarily relinquish the processor and go from RUNNING to READY by calling yield (e.g., thread_yield in the thread library).

Notice that a thread can transition from READY to RUNNING and back many times. Since the operating system saves and restores the thread's registers exactly, only the speed of the thread's execution is affected by these transitions.

WARNING   By convention in this book, a thread that is RUNNING is not on the ready list; the ready list is for READY and not RUNNING threads. However, some operating systems, such as Linux, use a different convention, where the RUNNING thread is whichever thread is at the front of the ready list. Either convention is equivalent as long as it used consistently.

The idle thread

If a system has k processors, most operating systems ensure that there are exactly k RUNNING threads, by keeping a low priority *idle thread* per processor for when there is nothing else to run.

On old machines, the idle thread would spin in a tight loop doing nothing.

Today, the idle thread still spins in a loop, but to save power, on each iteration it puts the processor into a low-power sleep mode. In sleep mode, the processor stops executing instructions until a hardware interrupt occurs. Then, the processor wakes up and handles the interrupt in the normal way — saving the state of the currently running thread (the idle thread) and running the handler. After running the handler, a thread waiting for that I/O event may now be READY. If so, the scheduler runs that thread next; otherwise, the idle thread resumes execution, putting the processor to sleep again.

Having a low-power idle thread also helps when running the operating system inside a virtual machine. Obviously, it would be inefficient for an idle operating system to consume processing cycles that could be better used by another virtual machine on the same system. Putting the processor into sleep mode is a privileged instruction, so if the operating system is running inside a virtual machine, the hardware will trap to the host kernel. The host kernel can then switch to a different virtual machine.

What causes a thread to enter the WAITING state?

WAITING. A thread in the WAITING state is waiting for some event. Whereas the scheduler can move a thread in the READY state to the RUNNING state, a thread in the WAITING state cannot run until some action by another thread moves it from WAITING to READY.

The threadHello program in Figure 4.6 provides an example of a WAITING thread. After creating its children threads, the main thread must wait for them to complete, by calling thread_join once for each child. If the specific child thread is not yet done at the time of the join, the main thread goes from RUNNING to WAITING until the child thread exits.

waiting list

While a thread waits for an event, it cannot make progress; therefore, it is not useful to run it. Rather than continuing to run the thread or storing the TCB on the scheduler's ready list, the TCB is stored on the *waiting list* of some *synchronization variable* associated with the event. When the required event occurs, the operating system moves the TCB from the synchronization variable's waiting list to the scheduler's ready list, transitioning the thread from WAITING to READY. We describe synchronization variables in Chapter 5.

finished list

FINISHED. A thread in the FINISHED state never runs again. The system can free some or all of its state for other uses, though it may keep some remnants of the thread in the FINISHED state for a time by putting the TCB on a *finished list*. For example, the thread_exit call lets a thread pass its exit value to its parent

State of Thread	Location of Thread Control Block (TCB)	Location of Registers
INIT	Being Created	TCB
READY	Ready List	TCB
RUNNING	Running List	Processor
WAITING	Synchronization Variable's Waiting List	TCB
FINISHED	Finished List then Deleted	TCB or Deleted

Figure 4.10: Location of thread's per-thread state for different life cycle stages.

thread via thread_join. Eventually, when a thread's state is no longer needed (e.g., after its exit value has been read by the join call), the system can delete and reclaim the thread's state.

One way to understand these states is to consider where a thread's TCB and registers are stored, as shown in Figure 4.10. For example, all threads in the READY state have their TCBs on the ready list and their registers in the TCB. All threads in the RUNNING state have their TCBs on the running list and their register values in hardware registers. And all threads in the WAITING state have their TCBs on various synchronization variables' waiting lists.

EXAMPLE   For the threadHello program in Figure 4.6, when thread_join returns for thread i, what is thread i's thread state?

ANSWER   When join returns, thread i has finished running and exited. The runtime system saved the exit value in the TCB and moved the TCB to the finished list (so that its exit value can be found by the parent thread). **The thread is thus in the FINISHED state.**   □

EXAMPLE   For the threadHello program, what is the minimum and maximum number of times that the main thread enters the READY state on a *uniprocessor*?

ANSWER   The main thread must go into the READY state when it is first created; otherwise, it would never be scheduled. On a uniprocessor, it must also give up the processor (e.g., due to a time slice or in thread_join) in order for its children threads to run. The children threads could then completely run before the main thread is re-scheduled. Once the children have finished, the main thread can run to completion. Thus, **the minimum number of times is two.**

The **maximum number of times is (near) infinite.** A running thread can be preempted and re-scheduled many times, without affecting the correctness of the execution. In the limit, the thread could conceivably be preempted after each instruction!   □

Where is my TCB?

A remarkably tricky implementation question is how to find the current thread's TCB. The thread library needs access to the current TCB for a number of reasons, e.g., to change its priority or to access thread-local variables.

One might think finding the TCB would be simple: just store a pointer to the TCB in a global variable. However, recall that every thread running in the same process uses exactly the same code, and therefore each thread would look in exactly the same place for the TCB. On a uniprocessor, this works: the global variable can hold the value of the current TCB, and the library can change the value whenever it switches between threads.

This does not work on a multiprocessor, however. Some systems, such as the Intel x86, have hardware support for fetching the ID of the current processor. In these systems, the thread library can maintain a global array of pointers, with the i'th entry pointing to the TCB of the thread running on the i'th processor. A running thread can then find its TCB by looking up its processor ID and then finding the corresponding entry in the array.

For systems without this feature, however, there is another approach: the stack pointer is always unique to each thread. The thread library can store a pointer to the thread TCB at the very bottom of the stack, underneath the procedure frames. (Some systems take this one step farther, and put the entire TCB at the bottom of the stack.) As long as thread stacks are aligned to start at a fixed block boundary, the low order bits of the current stack pointer can be masked to locate the pointer to the current TCB.

4.6 | Implementing Kernel Threads

How do we implement the thread abstraction in the OS kernel?

So far, we have described the basic data structures and operation of threads. We now describe how to implement them. The specifics of the implementation vary depending on the context:

kernel thread

- **Kernel threads.** The simplest case is implementing threads inside the operating system kernel, sharing one or more physical processors. A *kernel thread* executes kernel code and modifies kernel data structures. Almost all commercial operating systems today support kernel threads.

- **Kernel threads and single-threaded processes.** An operating system with kernel threads might also run some single-threaded user processes. As shown in Figure 4.11, these processes can invoke system calls that run concurrently with kernel threads inside the kernel.

- **Multi-threaded processes using kernel threads.** Most operating systems provide a set of library routines and system calls to allow applications to use multiple threads within a single user-level process. Figure 4.12

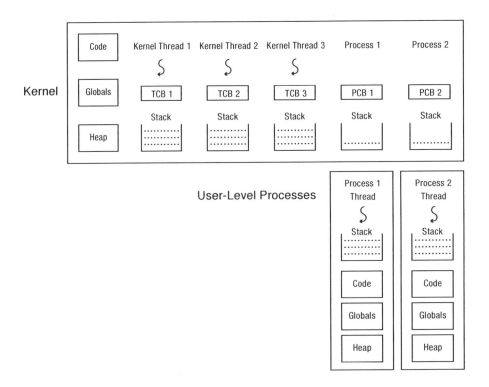

Figure 4.11: A multi-threaded kernel with three kernel threads and two single-threaded user-level processes. Each kernel thread has its own TCB and its own stack. Each user process has a stack at user-level for executing user code and a kernel interrupt stack for executing interrupts and system calls.

illustrates this case. These threads execute user code and access user-level data structures. They also make system calls into the operating system kernel. For that, they need a kernel interrupt stack just like a normal single-threaded process.

- **User-level threads.** To avoid having to make a system call for every thread operation, some systems support a model where user-level thread operations — create, yield, join, exit, and the synchronization routines described in Chapter 5 — are implemented entirely in a user-level library, without invoking the kernel.

We first describe the implementation for the baseline case of kernel threads. In Section 4.8, we explain how to extend the model to support application multi-threading implemented with kernel threads or with a user-level library.

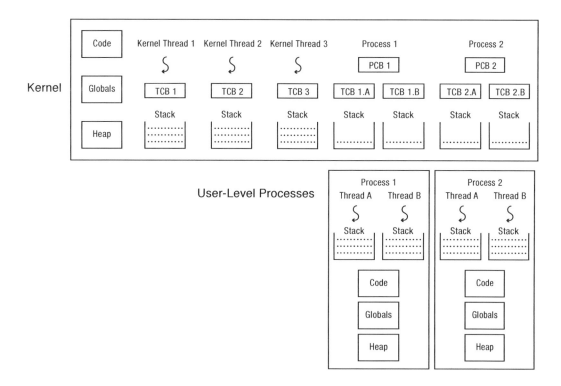

Figure 4.12: A multi-threaded kernel with three kernel threads and two user-level processes, each with two threads. Each user-level thread has a user-level stack and an interrupt stack in the kernel for executing interrupts and system calls.

4.6.1   Creating a Thread

Figure 4.13 shows the pseudo-code to allocate a new thread. The goal of thread_create is to perform an asynchronous procedure call to func with arg as the argument to that procedure. When the thread runs, it will execute func(arg) concurrently with the calling thread.

There are three steps to creating a thread:

1. **Allocate per-thread state.** The first step in the thread constructor is to allocate space for the thread's per-thread state: the TCB and stack. As we have mentioned, the TCB is the data structure the thread system uses to manage the thread. The stack is an area of memory for storing data about in-progress procedures; it is allocated in memory like any other data structure.

2. **Initialize per-thread state.** To initialize the TCB, the thread constructor sets the new thread's registers to what they need to be when the thread starts RUNNING. When the thread is assigned a processor, we want it to

```
// func is a pointer to a procedure the thread will run.
// arg is the argument to be passed to that procedure.
void
thread_create(thread_t *thread, void (*func)(int), int arg) {
    // Allocate TCB and stack
    TCB *tcb = new TCB();

    thread->tcb = tcb;
    tcb->stack_size = INITIAL_STACK_SIZE;
    tcb->stack = new Stack(INITIAL_STACK_SIZE);

    // Initialize registers so that when thread is resumed, it will start running at
    // stub. The stack starts at the top of the allocated region and grows down.
    tcb->sp = tcb->stack + INITIAL_STACK_SIZE;
    tcb->pc = stub;

    // Create a stack frame by pushing stub's arguments and start address
    // onto the stack: func, arg
    *(tcb->sp) = arg;
    tcb->sp--;
    *(tcb->sp) = func;
    tcb->sp--;

    // Create another stack frame so that thread_switch works correctly.
    // This routine is explained later in the chapter.
    thread_dummySwitchFrame(tcb);

    tcb->state = READY;
    readyList.add(tcb);      // Put tcb on ready list
}

void
stub(void (*func)(int), int arg) {
    (*func)(arg);            // Execute the function func()
    thread_exit(0);          // If func() does not call exit, call it here.
}
```

Figure 4.13: Pseudo-code for thread creation. The specifics of initializing the stack and the conventions for passing arguments to the initial function are machine-dependent. On the Intel x86 architecture, the stack starts at high addresses and grows down, while arguments are passed on the stack. On other systems, the stack can grow upwards and/or arguments can be passed in registers. Figure 4.14 provides pseudo-code for thread_dummySwitchFrame.

start running func(arg). However, instead of having the thread start in func, the constructor starts the thread in a dummy function, stub, which in turn calls func.

We need this extra step in case the func procedure returns instead of calling thread_exit. Without the stub, func would return to whatever random location is stored at the top of the stack! Instead, func returns to stub and stub calls thread_exit to finish the thread.

To start at the beginning of stub, the thread constructor sets up the stack as if stub was just called by normal code; the specifics will depend on the calling convention of the machine. In the pseudo-code, we push stub's two arguments onto the stack: func and arg. When the thread starts running, the code in stub will access its arguments just like a normal procedure.

In addition, we also push a dummy stack frame for thread_switch onto the stack; we defer an explanation of this detail until we discuss the implementation of thread switching.

3. **Put TCB on ready list.** The last step in creating a thread is to set its state to READY and put the new TCB on the ready list, enabling the thread to be scheduled.

4.6.2 Deleting a Thread

Why is it hard for a thread to delete its own state?

When a thread calls thread_exit, there are two steps to deleting the thread:

- Remove the thread from the ready list so that it will never run again.

- Free the per-thread state allocated for the thread.

Although this seems easy, there is an important subtlety: if a thread removes itself from the ready list and frees its own per-thread state, then the program may break. For example, if a thread removes itself from the ready list but an interrupt occurs before the thread finishes de-allocating its state, there is a memory leak: that thread will never resume to de-allocate its state.

Worse, suppose that a thread frees its own state? Can the thread finish running the code in thread_exit if it does not have a stack? What happens if an interrupt occurs just after the running thread's stack has been de-allocated? If the context switch code tries to save the current thread's state, it will be writing to de-allocated memory, possibly to storage that another processor has re-allocated for some other data structure. The result could be corrupted memory, where the specific behavior depends on the precise sequence of events. Needless to say, such a bug would be very difficult to locate.

Fortunately, there is a simple fix: a thread never deletes its own state. Instead, some other thread must do it. On exit, the thread transitions to the FINISHED state, moves its TCB from the ready list to a list of *finished* threads the scheduler should never run. The thread can then safely switch to the next thread on the ready list. Once the finished thread is no longer running, it is safe for some *other* thread to free the state of the thread.

4.6.3 Thread Context Switch

How does the OS run a different thread?

To support multiple threads, we also need a mechanism to switch which threads are RUNNING and which are READY.

thread context switch

A *thread context switch* suspends execution of a currently running thread and resumes execution of some other thread. The switch saves the currently running thread's registers to the thread's TCB and stack, and then it restores the new thread's registers from that thread's TCB and stack into the processor.

We need to answer several questions:

Separating mechanism from policy

Separating mechanism from policy is a useful and widely applied principle in operating system design. When mechanism and policy are cleanly separated, it is easier to introduce new policies to optimize a system for a new workload or new technology.

For example, the thread context switch abstraction cleanly separates mechanism (how to switch between threads) from policy (which thread to run) so that the mechanism works no matter what policy is used. Some systems can elect to do something simple (e.g., FIFO scheduling); other systems can optimize scheduling to meet their goals (e.g., a periodic scheduler to smoothly run real-time multimedia streams for a media device, a round-robin scheduler to balance responsiveness and throughput for a server, or a priority scheduler that devotes most resources to the visible application on a smartphone).

We will see this principle many times in this book. For example, thread synchronization mechanisms work regardless of the scheduling policy; file metadata mechanisms for locating a file's blocks work regardless of the policy for where to place the file's blocks on disk; and page translation mechanisms for mapping virtual to physical addresses work regardless of which physical pages the operating system assigns to each process.

- What triggers a context switch?

- How does a voluntary context switch (e.g., a call to thread_yield) work?

- How does an involuntary context switch differ from a voluntary one?

- What thread should the scheduler choose to run next?

We discuss these in turn, but we defer the last question to Chapter 7. The *mechanisms* we discuss in this Chapter work regardless of the *policy* the scheduler uses when choosing threads.

What Triggers a Kernel Thread Context Switch?   A thread context switch can be triggered by either a voluntary call into the thread library, or an involuntary interrupt or processor exception.

- **Voluntary.** The thread could call a thread library function that triggers a context switch. For example, most thread libraries provide a thread_yield call that lets the currently running thread voluntarily give up the processor to the next thread on the ready list. Similarly, the thread_join and thread_exit calls suspend execution of the current thread and start running a different one.

- **Involuntary.** An *interrupt* or *processor exception* could invoke an interrupt handler. The interrupt hardware saves the state of the running thread and executes the handler's code. The handler can decide that some other thread should run, and then switch to it. Alternatively, if the current thread should continue running, the handler restores the state of the interrupted thread and resumes execution.

  For example, many thread systems are designed to ensure that no thread can monopolize the processor. To accomplish this, they set a hardware timer to interrupt the processor periodically (e.g., every few milliseconds). The timer interrupt handler saves the state of the running thread, chooses another thread to run, and runs that thread by restoring its state to the processor.

  Other I/O hardware events (e.g., a keyboard key is pressed, a network packet arrives, or a disk operation completes) also invoke interrupt handlers. In these cases as well, the handlers save the state of the currently running thread so that it can be restored later. They then execute the handler code, and when the handler is done, they either restore the state of the current thread, or switch to a new thread. A new thread will be run if the I/O event moves a thread onto the ready list with a higher priority than the previously running thread.

Regardless, the thread system must save the current processor state, so that when the current thread resumes execution, it appears *to the thread* as if the event never occurred except for some time having elapsed. This provides the abstraction of thread execution on a virtual processor with unpredictable and variable speed.

To keep things simple, we do not want to do an involuntary context switch while we are in the middle of a voluntary one. When switching between two threads, we need to temporarily defer interrupts until the switch is complete, to avoid confusion. Processors contain privileged instructions to defer and re-enable interrupts; we make use of these in our implementation below.

How does thread_yield work?

Voluntary Kernel Thread Context Switch   Because a voluntary switch is simpler to understand, we start there. Figure 4.14 shows pseudo-code for a simple implementation of thread_yield for the Intel x86 hardware architecture. A thread calls thread_yield to voluntarily relinquish the processor to another thread. The calling thread's registers are copied to its TCB and stack, and it resumes running later, when the scheduler chooses it.

The pseudo-code for thread_yield first turns off interrupts to prevent the thread system from attempting to make two context switches at the same time. The pseudo-code then pulls the next thread to run off the ready list (if any), and switches to it.

The thread_switch code may seem tricky, since it is called in the context of the old thread and finishes in the context of the new thread. To make this work, thread_switch saves the state of the registers to the stack and saves the stack

Why is it necessary to turn off interrupts during thread switch?

Our implementation of thread_yield defers any interrupts that might occur during the procedure, until the yield is complete. This might seem unnecessary: after all, even if the thread context switch is interrupted, the state of the switch will be saved onto the stack. Eventually the kernel will re-schedule the thread, restore its state, and complete the thread switch.

However, a subtle inconsistency might arise. Suppose a low priority thread (e.g., the idle thread) is about to voluntarily switch to a high priority thread. It pulls the high priority thread off the ready list, and at that precise moment, an interrupt occurs. Supppose the interrupt moves a medium priority thread from WAITINGto READY. Since it appears that the processor is still running the low priority thread, the interrupt handler immediately switches to the new thread. The high priority thread is in limbo! It is ready to run, but unable to do so until the low priority thread is re-scheduled. And that may not happen for a long time.

Of course, this sequence of events would not occur very often, but when it does, it would be difficult to locate or debug.

---

pointer to the TCB. It then switches to the stack of the new thread, restores the new thread's state from the new thread's stack, and returns to whatever program counter is stored on the new stack.

A twist is that the return location may not be to thread_yield! The return is to whatever the new thread was doing beforehand. For example, the new thread might have been WAITING in thread_join and is now READY to run. The thread might have called thread_yield. Or it might be a newly created thread just starting to run.

It is essential that any routine that causes the thread to yield or block call thread_switch in the same way. Equally, to create a new thread, thread_create must set up the stack of the new thread to be as if it had suspended execution just before performing its first instruction. Then, if the newly created thread is the next thread to run, a thread can call thread_yield, switch to the newly created thread, switch to its stack pointer, pop the register values off the stack, and "return" to the new thread, even though it had never called switch in the first place.

EXAMPLE   Suppose two threads each loop, calling thread_yield on each iteration.

```
go() {
    while(1) {
        thread_yield();
    }
}
```

```
// We enter as oldThread, but we return as newThread.
// Returns with newThread's registers and stack.
void thread_switch(oldThreadTCB, newThreadTCB) {
    pushad;                       // Push general register values onto the old stack.
    oldThreadTCB->sp = %esp;      // Save the old thread's stack pointer.
    %esp = newThreadTCB->sp;      // Switch to the new stack.
    popad;                        // Pop register values from the new stack.
    return;
}

void thread_yield() {
    TCB *chosenTCB, *finishedTCB;

    // Prevent an interrupt from stopping us in the middle of a switch.
    disableInterrupts();

    // Choose another TCB from the ready list.
    chosenTCB = readyList.getNextThread();
    if (chosenTCB == NULL) {
        // Nothing else to run, so go back to running the original thread.
    } else {
        // Move running thread onto the ready list.
        runningThread->state = READY;
        readyList.add(runningThread);
        thread_switch(runningThread, chosenTCB); // Switch to the new thread.
        runningThread->state = RUNNING;
    }

    // Delete any threads on the finished list.
    while ((finishedTCB = finishedList->getNextThread()) != NULL) {
        delete finishedTCB->stack;
        delete finishedTCB;
    }
    enableInterrupts();
}

// thread_create must put a dummy frame at the top of its stack:
// the return PC and space for pushad to have stored a copy of the registers.
// This way, when someone switches to a newly created thread,
// the last two lines of thread_switch work correctly.
void thread_dummySwitchFrame(newThread) {
    *(tcb->sp) = stub;         // Return to the beginning of stub.
    tcb->sp--;
    tcb->sp -= SizeOfPopad;
}
```

Figure 4.14: Pseudo-code for thread_switch and thread_yield on the Intel x86 architecture. Note that thread_yield is a no-op if there are no other threads to run. Otherwise, it saves the old thread state and restores the new thread state. When the old thread is re-scheduled, it returns from thread_switch as the running thread.

What is the sequence of steps as seen by the physical processor and by each thread?

ANSWER   From the processor's point of view, one instruction follows the next, but now the instructions from different threads are interleaved (as they must be if they are multiplexed).

Figure 4.15 shows the interleaving: thread_yield is called by one thread but

Logical View	
Thread 1	Thread 2
go(){	go(){
while(1){	while(1){
thread_yield();	thread_yield();
}	}
}	}

Physical Reality		
Thread 1's instructions	Thread 2's instructions	**Processor's instructions**
"return" from thread_switch		"return" from thread_switch
into stub		into stub
call go		call go
call thread_yield		call thread_yield
choose another thread		choose another thread
call thread_switch		call thread_switch
save thread 1 state to TCB		save thread 1 state to TCB
load thread 2 state		load thread 2 state
	"return" from thread_switch	"return" from thread_switch
	into stub	into stub
	call go	call go
	call thread_yield	call thread_yield
	choose another thread	choose another thread
	call thread_switch	call thread_switch
	save thread 2 state to TCB	save thread 2 state to TCB
	load thread 1 state	load thread 1 state
return from thread_switch		return from thread_switch
return from thread_yield		return from thread_yield
call thread_yield		call thread_yield
choose another thread		choose another thread
call thread_switch		call thread_switch
save thread 1 state to TCB		save thread 1 state to TCB
load thread 2 state		load thread 2 state
	return from thread_switch	return from thread_switch
	return from thread_yield	return from thread_yield
	call thread_yield	call thread_yield
	choose another thread	choose another thread
	call thread_switch	call thread_switch
	save thread 2 state to TCB	save thread 2 state to TCB
	load thread 1 state	load thread 1 state
return from thread_switch		return from thread_switch
return from thread_yield		return from thread_yield
...	...	...

Figure 4.15: Interleaving of instructions when two threads loop and call thread_yield().

A zero-thread kernel

Not only can we have a single-threaded kernel or a multi-threaded kernel, it is actually possible to have a kernel with no threads of its own — a zero-threaded kernel! In fact, this used to be quite common [107].

Consider the simple picture of the operating system described in Chapter 2. Once the system has booted, initialized its device drivers, and started some user-level processes like a login shell, everything else the kernel does is event-driven, i.e., done in response to an interrupt, processor exception, or system call.

In a simple operating system like this, there is no need for a "kernel thread" or "kernel thread control block" to keep track of an ongoing computation. Instead, when an interrupt, trap, or exception occurs, the stack pointer gets set to the base of the interrupt stack, and the instruction pointer gets set to the address of the handler. Then, the handler executes and either returns immediately to the interrupted user-level process or suspends the user-level process and "returns" to some other user-level process. In either case, the next event (interrupt, processor exception, or system call) starts this process anew.

---

returns in a different thread. thread_yield deliberately violates the procedure call conventions compilers normally follow by manipulating the stack and program counter to switch between threads.

However, the threads themselves can ignore this complexity. From their point of view, they each run this loop on their own (variable-speed) virtual processor.   □

What happens when an interrupt triggers a kernel thread context switch?

Involuntary Kernel Thread Context Switch   Chapter 2 explained what happens when an interrupt, exception, or trap interrupts a running user-level process: hardware and software work together to save the state of the interrupted process, run the kernel's handler, and restore the state of the interrupted process.

The mechanism is almost identical when an interrupt or trap triggers a thread switch between threads in the kernel. The three steps described in Chapter 2 are slightly modified (*changes are written in italics*):

1. **Save the state.** Save the currently running *thread's* registers so that the handler can run code without disrupting the interrupted *thread*.

   Hardware saves some state when the interrupt or exception occurs, and software saves the rest of the state when the handler runs.

2. **Run the kernel's handler.** Run the kernel's handler code to handle the interrupt or exception. *Since we are already in kernel mode, we do not need to change from user to kernel mode in this step. We also do not need to change*

the stack pointer to the base of the kernel's interrupt stack. Instead, we can just push saved state or handler variables onto the current stack, starting from the current stack pointer.

3. **Restore the state.** Restore the *next ready thread's* registers so that the thread can resume running where it left off.

In short, comparing a switch between kernel threads to what happens on a user-mode transfer: (1) there is no need to switch modes (and therefore no need to switch stacks) and (2) the handler can resume any thread on the ready list rather than always resuming the thread or process that was just suspended.

Implementation Details On most processor architectures, a simple (but inefficient) way to swap to the next thread from within an interrupt handler is to call thread_switch just before the handler returns. As we have already seen, thread_switch saves the state of the current thread (that is, the state of the interrupt handler) and switches to the new kernel thread. When the original thread resumes, it will return from thread_switch, and immediately pop the interrupt context off the stack, resuming execution at the point where it was interrupted.

Most systems, such as Linux, make a small optimization to improve interrupt handling performance. The state of the interrupted thread is already saved on the stack, albeit in the format specified by the interrupt hardware. If we modify thread_switch to save and restore registers exactly as the interrupt hardware does, then returning from an interrupt and resuming a thread are the same action: they both pop the interrupt frame off the stack to resume the next thread to run.

For example, to be compatible with x86 interrupt hardware, the software implementation of thread_switch would simulate the hardware case, saving the return instruction pointer and eflags register before calling pushad to save the general-purpose registers. After switching to the new stack, it would call iret to resume the new thread, whether the new thread was suspended by a hardware event or a software call.

4.7 | Combining Kernel Threads and Single-Threaded User Processes

How do we extend the implementation of kernel threads to support single-threaded processes?

Previously, Figure 4.11 illustrated a system with both kernel threads and single-threaded user processes. A process is a sequential execution of instructions, so each user-level process includes the process's thread. However, a process is more than just a thread because it has its own address space. Process 1 has its own view of memory, its own code, its own heap, and its own global variables that differ from those of process 2 (and from the kernel's).

Because a process contains more than just a thread, each process's process control block (PCB) needs more information than a thread control block (TCB) for a kernel thread. Like a TCB, a PCB for a single-threaded process must store the processor registers when the process's thread is not running. In addition, the PCB has information about the process's address space; when a context switch occurs from one process to another, the operating system must change the virtual memory mappings as well as the register state.

Since the PCB and TCB each represent one thread, the kernel's ready list can contain a mix of PCBs for processes and TCBs for kernel threads. When the scheduler chooses the next thread to run, it can pick either kind. A thread switch is nearly identical whether switching between kernel threads or switching between a process's thread and a kernel thread. In both cases, the switch saves the state of the currently running thread and restores the state of the next thread to run.

As we mentioned in Chapter 2, most operating systems dedicate a kernel interrupt stack for each process. This way, when the process needs to perform a system call, or on an interrupt or processor exception, the hardware traps to the kernel, saves the user-level processor state, and starts running at a specific handler in the kernel. Once inside the kernel, the process thread behaves exactly like a kernel thread — it can create threads (or other processes), block (e.g., in UNIX process wait or on I/O), and even exit. While inside the kernel, the process can be pre-empted by a timer interrupt or I/O event, and a higher priority process or kernel thread can run in its place. The PCB and kernel stack for the preempted process stores both its current kernel state, as well as the user-level state saved when the process initiated the system call.

We can resume a process in the kernel using thread_switch. However, when we resume execution of the user-level process after the completion of a system call or interrupt, we must restore its state precisely as it was beforehand: with the correct value in its registers, executing in user mode, with the appropriate virtual memory mappings, and so forth.

An important detail is that many processor architectures have extra co-processor state, e.g., floating point registers, for user-level code. Typically, the operating system kernel does not make use of floating point operations. Therefore, the kernel does not need to save those registers when switching between kernel threads, but it does save saved and restore them when switching between processes.

4.8 | Implementing Multi-Threaded Processes

What are the different ways to implement the thread abstraction for use by applications?

multi-threaded process

So far, we have described how to implement multiple threads that run inside the operating system kernel. Of course, we also want to be able to run user programs as well. Since many user programs are single-threaded, we start with the simple case of how to integrate kernel threads and single-threaded processes. We then turn to various ways of implementing *multi-threaded processes*, processes with multiple threads. All widely used modern operating systems support both kernel threads and multi-threaded processes. Both programming languages, such as Java, and standard library interfaces such as

You may notice that a mode switch in Chapter 2 caused the x86 hardware to save not just the instruction pointer and eflags register but also the *stack pointer* of the interrupted process before starting the handler. For mode switching, the hardware changes the stack pointer to the kernel's interrupt stack, so it must save the original user-level stack pointer.

In contrast, when switching from a kernel thread to a kernel handler, the hardware does not switch stacks. Instead, the handler runs on the current stack, not on a separate interrupt stack. Therefore, the hardware does not need to save the original stack pointer; the handler just saves the stack pointer with the other registers as part of the pushad instruction.

Thus, x86 hardware works slightly differently when switching between a kernel thread and a kernel handler than when doing a mode switch:

- **Entering the handler.** When an interrupt or exception occurs, if the processor detects that it is already in kernel mode (by inspecting the eflags register), it just pushes the instruction pointer and eflags registers (but not the stack pointer) onto the existing stack. On the other hand, if the hardware detects that it is switching from user-mode to kernel-mode, then the processor also changes the stack pointer to the base of the interrupt stack and pushes the original stack pointer along with the instruction pointer and eflags registers onto the new stack.

- **Returning from the handler.** When the iret instruction is called, it inspects both the current eflags register and the value on the stack that it will use to restore the earlier eflags register. If the mode bit is identical, then iret just pops the instruction pointer and eflags register and continues to use the current stack. On the other hand, if the mode bit differs, then the iret instruction pops not only the instruction pointer and eflags register, but also the saved stack pointer, thus switching the processor's stack pointer to the saved one.

POSIX and simple threads, use this operating system support to provide the thread abstraction to the programmer.

4.8.1 Implementing Multi-Threaded Processes Using Kernel Threads

The simplest way to support multiple threads per process is to use the kernel thread implementation we have already described. When a kernel thread creates, deletes, suspends, or resumes a thread, it can use a simple procedure call. When a user-level thread accesses the thread library to do the same things, it uses a system call to ask the kernel to do the operation on its behalf.

As shown earlier in Figure 4.12, a thread in a process has:

- A user-level stack for executing user code.

- A kernel interrupt stack for when this thread makes system calls, causes a processor exception, or is interrupted.

- A kernel TCB for saving and restoring the per-thread state.

To create a thread, the user library allocates a user-level stack for the thread and then does a system call into the kernel. The kernel allocates a TCB and interrupt stack, and arranges the state of the thread to start execution on the user-level stack at the beginning of the requested procedure. The kernel needs to store a pointer to the TCB in the process control block; if the process exits, the kernel must terminate any other threads running in the process.

After creating the thread, the kernel puts the new thread on the ready list, to be scheduled like any other thread, and returns unique identifier for the user program to use when referring to the newly created thread (e.g., for join).

Thread join, yield, and exit work the same way: by calling into the kernel to perform the requested function.

4.8.2 Implementing User-Level Threads Without Kernel Support

What are the positives and negatives to implementing user-level threads entirely in a user-level library?

It is also possible to implement threads as a library completely at user level, without any operating system support. Early thread libraries took this pure user-level approach for the simple reason that few operating systems supported multi-threaded processes. Even once operating system support for threads became widespread, pure user-level threads were sometimes used to minimize dependencies on specific operating systems and to maximize portability; for example, the earliest implementations of Sun's Java Virtual Machine (JVM) implemented what were called *green threads*, a pure user-level implementation of threads.

green threads

How are green threads implemented?

The basic idea is simple. The thread library instantiates all of its data structures within the process: TCBs, the ready list, the finished list, and the waiting lists all are just data structures in the process's address space. Then, calls to the thread library are just procedure calls, akin to how the same functions are implemented within a multi-threaded kernel.

To the operating system kernel, a multi-threaded application using green threads appears to be a normal, single-threaded process. The process as a whole can make system calls, be time-sliced, etc. Unlike with kernel threads, when a process using green threads is time-sliced, the entire process, including all of its threads, is suspended.

A limitation of green threads is that the operating system kernel is unaware of the state of the user-level ready list. If the application performs a system call that blocks waiting for I/O, the kernel is unable to run a different user-level thread. Likewise, on a multiprocessor, the kernel is unable to run the different threads running within a single process on different processors.

Preemptive User-level Threads   However, it is possible on most operating systems to implement preemption among user-level threads executing within a process. As we discussed in Chapter 2, most operating systems provide an upcall mechanism to deliver asynchronous event notification to a process; on UNIX these are called signal handlers. Typical events or signals include the user hitting "Escape" or on UNIX "Control-C"; this informs the application to attempt to cleanly exit. Another common event is a timer interrupt to signal elapsed real time. To deliver an event, the kernel suspends the process execution and then resumes it running at a handler specified by the user code, typically on a separate upcall or signal stack.

To implement preemptive multi-threading for some process P:

1. The user-level thread library makes a system call to register a timer signal handler and signal stack with the kernel.

2. When a hardware timer interrupt occurs, the hardware saves P's register state and runs the kernel's handler.

3. Instead of restoring P's register state and resuming P where it was interrupted, the kernel's handler copies P's saved registers onto P's signal stack.

4. The kernel resumes execution in P at the registered signal handler on the signal stack.

5. The signal handler copies the processor state of the preempted user-level thread from the signal stack to that thread's TCB.

6. The signal handler chooses the next thread to run, re-enables the signal handler (the equivalent of re-enabling interrupts), and restores the new thread's state from its TCB into the processor. execution with the state (newly) stored on the signal stack.

This approach virtualizes interrupts and processor exceptions, providing a user-level process with a very similar picture to the one the kernel gets when these events occur.

4.8.3   Implementing User-Level Threads With Kernel Support

Can we combine the benefits of user-level and kernel threads?

Today, most programs use kernel-supported threads rather than pure user-level threads. Major operating systems support threads using standard abstractions, so the issue of portability is less of an issue than it once was.

However, various systems take more of a hybrid model, attempting to combine the lightweight performance and application control over scheduling found in user-level threads, while keeping many of the advantages of kernel threads.

Hybrid Thread Join   Thread libraries can avoid transitioning to the kernel in certain cases. For example, rather than always making a system call for thread_join to wait for the target thread to finish, thread_exit can store its exit value in a data structure in the process's address space. Then, if the call to thread_join happens after the targeted thread has exited, it can immediately return the value without having to make a system call. However, if the call to thread_join precedes the call to thread_exit, then a system call is needed to transition to the WAITING state and let some other thread run. As a further optimization, on a multiprocessor it can sometimes make sense for thread_join to spin for a few microseconds before entering the kernel, in the hope that the other thread will finish in the meantime.

Per-Processor Kernel Threads   It is possible to adapt the green threads approach to work on a multiprocessor. For many parallel scientific applications, the cost of creating and synchronizing threads is paramount, and so an approach that requires a kernel call for most thread operations would be prohibitive. Instead, the library multiplexes user-level threads on top of kernel threads, in exactly the same way that the kernel multiplexes kernel threads on top of physical processors.

When the application starts up, the user-level thread library creates one kernel thread for each processor on the host machine. As long as there is no other activity on the system, the kernel will assign each of these threads a processor. Each kernel thread executes the user-level scheduler in parallel: pull the next thread off the user-level ready list, and run it. Because thread scheduling decisions occur at user level, they can be flexible and application-specific; for example, in a parallel graph algorithm, the programmer might adjust the priority of various threads based on the results of the computation on other parts of the graph.

Of course, most of the downsides of green threads are still present in these systems:

- Any time a user-level thread calls into the kernel, its host kernel thread blocks. This prevents the thread library from running a different user-level thread on that processor in the meantime.

- Any time the kernel time-slices a kernel thread, the user-level thread it was running is also suspended. The library cannot resume that thread until the kernel thread resumes.

Scheduler Activations   To address these issues, some operating systems have added explicit support for user-level threads. One such model, implemented most recently in Windows, is called *scheduler activations*. In this approach, the user-level thread scheduler is notified (or activated) for every kernel event that might affect the user-level thread system. For example, if one thread blocks in a system call, the activation informs the user-level scheduler that it should choose another thread to run on that processor. Scheduler activations are like

scheduler activations

upcalls or signals, except that they do not return to the kernel; instead, they directly perform user-level thread suspend and resume.

Various operations trigger a scheduler activation upcall:

1. **Increasing the number of virtual processors.** When a program starts, it receives an activation to inform the program that it has been assigned a virtual processor: that activation runs the main thread and any other threads that might be created. To assign another virtual processor to the program, the kernel makes another activation upcall on the new processor; the user-level scheduler can pull a waiting thread off the ready list and run it.

2. **Decreasing the number of virtual processors.** When the kernel preempts a virtual processor (e.g., to give the processor to a different process), the kernel makes an upcall on one of the other processors assigned to the parallel program. The thread system can then move the preempted user-level thread onto the ready list, so that a different processor can run it.

3. **Transition to WAITING.** When a user-level thread blocks in the kernel waiting for I/O, the kernel similarly makes an upcall to notify the user-level scheduler that it needs to take action, e.g., to choose another thread to run while waiting for the I/O to complete.

4. **Transition from WAITING to READY.** When the I/O completes, the kernel makes an upcall to notify the scheduler that the suspended thread can be resumed.

5. **Transition from RUNNING to idle.** When a user-level activation finds an empty ready list (i.e., it has no more work to do), it can make a system call into the kernel to return the virtual processor for use by some other process.

As a result, most thread management functions — thread_create, thread_yield, thread_exit, and thread_join, as well as the synchronization functions described in Chapter 5 — are implemented as procedure calls within the process. Yet the user-level thread system always knows exactly how many virtual processors it has been assigned and is in complete control of what runs on those processors.

4.9 | Alternative Abstractions

What other abstractions can we use to express and implement concurrency?

Although threads are a common way to express and manage concurrency, they are not the only way. In this section, we describe two popular alternatives, each targeted at a different application domain:

- **Asynchronous I/O and event-driven programming.** Asynchronous I/O and events allow a single-threaded program to cope with high-latency I/O devices by overlapping I/O with processing and other I/O.

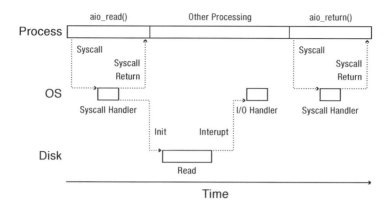

Figure 4.16: An asynchronous file read on Linux. The application calls aio_read to start the read; this system call returns immediately after the disk read is initialized. The application may then do other processing while the disk is completing the requested operation. The disk interrupts the processor when the operation is complete; this causes the kernel disk interrupt handler to run. The application at any time may ask the kernel if the results of the disk read are available, and then retrieve them with aio_return.

- **Data parallel programming.** With data parallel programming, all processors perform the same instructions in parallel on different parts of a data set.

In each case, the goal is similar: to replace the complexities of multi-threading with a deterministic, sequential model that is easier for the programmer to understand and debug.

4.9.1 Asynchronous I/O and Event-Driven Programming

asynchronous I/O

Asynchronous I/O is a way to allow a single-threaded process to issue multiple concurrent I/O requests at the same time. The process makes a system call to issue an I/O request but the call returns immediately, without waiting for the result. At a later time, the operating system provides the result to the process by either: (1) calling a signal handler, (2) placing the result in a queue in the process's memory, or (3) storing the result in kernel memory until the process makes another system call to retrieve it.

Can we overlap computation and I/O without using threads?

An example use of asynchronous I/O is to overlap reading from disk with other computation in the same process. Reading from disk can take tens of milliseconds. In Linux, rather than issuing a read system call that blocks until the requested data has been read from disk, a process can issue an aio_read (asynchronous I/O read) system call; this call tells the operating system to initiate the read from disk and then to immediately return. Later, the process can call aio_error to determine if the disk read has finished and aio_return to retrieve the read's results, as shown in Figure 4.16.

One common design pattern lets a single thread interleave different I/O-bound tasks by waiting for different I/O events. Consider a web server with

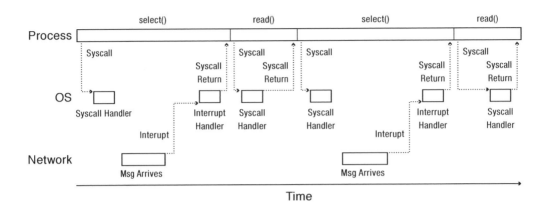

Figure 4.17: A server managing multiple concurrent connections using select. The server calls select to wait for data to arrive on any connection. The server then reads all available data, before returning to select.

10 active clients. Rather than creating one thread per client and having each thread do a blocking read on the network connection, an alternative is for the server to have one thread that processes, in turn, the next message to arrive from *any* client.

For this, the server does a select call that blocks until *any* of the 10 network connections has data available to read. When the select call returns, it provides a list of connection with available data. The thread can then read from those connections, knowing that the read will always return immediately. After processing the data, the thread then calls select again to wait for the next data to arrive. Figure 4.17 illustrates this design pattern.

event-driven programming pattern

continuation

Asynchronous I/O allows progress by many concurrent operating system requests. This approach gives rise to an *event-driven programming pattern* where a thread spins in a loop; each iteration gets and processes the next I/O event. To process each event, the thread typically maintains for each task a *continuation*, a data structure that keeps track of a task's current state and next step.

For example, handling a web request can involve a series of I/O steps: (a) make a network connection, (b) read a request from the network connection, (c) read the requested data from disk, and (d) write the requested data to the network connection. If a single thread is handling requests from multiple different clients at once, it must keep track of where it is in that sequence for each client.

Further, the network may divide a client's request into several packets so that the server needs to make several read calls to assemble the full packet. The server may be doing this request assembly for multiple clients at once. Therefore, it needs to keep several per-client variables (e.g., a request buffer, the number of bytes expected, and the number of bytes received so far). When a new message arrives, the thread uses the network connection's port number to identify which client sent the request and retrieves the appropriate client's variables using this port number/client ID. It can then process the data.

Event-Driven Programming vs. Threads

Although superficially different, overlapping I/O is fundamentally the same whether using asynchronous I/O and event-driven programming or synchronous I/O and threads. In either case, the program blocks until the next task can proceed, restores the state of that task, executes the next step of that task, and saves the task's state until it can take its next step. The differences are: (1) whether the state is stored in a continuation or TCB and (2) whether the state save/restore is done explicitly by the application or automatically by the thread system.

Consider a simple server that collects incoming data from several clients into a set of per-client buffers. The pseudo-code for the event-driven and thread-per-client cases is similar:

```
// Event-driven
Hashtable<Buffer*> *hash;

while(1) {
    connection = use select() to find a
                    readable connection ID
    buffer = hash.remove(connection);
    got = read(connection, tmpBuf,
                    TMP_SIZE);
    buffer->append(tmpBuf, got);
    buffer = hash.put(connection,
                    buffer);
}
```

```
// Thread-per-client
Buffer *b;

while(1) {
    got = read(connection, tmpBuf,
                    TMP_SIZE);
    buffer->append(tmpBuf, got);
}
```

When these programs execute, the system performs nearly the same work, as shown in Figure 4.18. With events, the code uses select to determine which connection's packet to retrieve next. With threads, the kernel transparently schedules each thread when data has arrived for it.

The state in both cases is also similar. In the event-driven case, the application maintains a hash table containing the buffer state for each client. The server must do a lookup to find the buffer each time a packet arrives for a particular client. In the thread-per-client case, each thread has just one buffer, and the operating system keeps track of the different threads' states.

To compare the two approaches, consider again the various use cases for threads from Section 4.1:

- **Performance: Coping with high-latency I/O devices.** Either approach — event-driven or threads — can overlap I/O and processing. Which provides better performance?

  The common wisdom has been that the event-driven approach was significantly faster for two reasons. First, the space and context switch overheads of this approach could be lower because a thread system must use generic code that allocates a stack for each thread's state and that saves and restores all registers on each context switch, while the

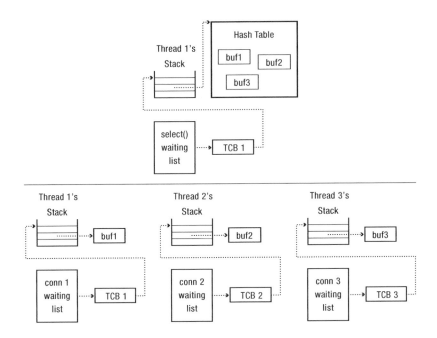

Figure 4.18: Two alternate implementations of a server. In the upper picture, a single thread uses a hash table to keep track of connection state. In the lower picture, each thread keeps a pointer to the state for one connection.

event-driven approach lets programmers allocate and save/restore just the state needed for each task. Second, some past operating systems had inefficient or unscalable implementations of their thread systems, making it important not to create too many threads for each process.

Today, the comparison is less clear cut. Many systems now have large memories, so the cost of allocating a thread stack for each task is less critical. For example, allocating 1000 threads with an 8 KB stack per thread on a machine with 1 GB of memory would consume less than 1% of the machine's memory. Also, most operating systems now have efficient and scalable threads libraries. For example, while the Linux 2.4 kernel had poor performance when processes had many threads, Linux 2.6 revamped the thread system, improving its scalability and absolute performance.

Anecdotal evidence suggests that the performance gap between the two approaches has greatly narrowed. For some applications, highly optimized thread management code and synchronous I/O paths can outperform less-optimized application code and asynchronous I/O paths. In most cases, the performance difference is small enough that other factors (e.g., code simplicity and ease of maintenance) are more important than raw performance. If performance is crucial for a particular application, then, as is often the case, there is no substitute for careful benchmarking before making your decision.

- **Performance: Exploiting multiple processors.** By itself, the event-driven approach does not help a program exploit multiple processors. In practice, event-driven and thread approaches are often combined: a program that uses n processors can have n threads, each of which uses the event-driven pattern to multiplex multiple I/O-bound tasks on each processor.

- **Responsiveness: Shifting work to run in the background.** While event-driven programming can be effective when tasks are usually short-lived, threads can be more convenient when there is a mixture of foreground and background tasks. At some cost in coding complexity, the event-driven model can be adapted to this case, e.g., by cutting long tasks into smaller chunks whose state can be explicitly saved when higher priority work is pending.

- **Program structure: Expressing logically concurrent tasks.** Whenever there are two viable programming styles, there are strong advocates for each approach. The situation is no different here, with some advocates of event-driven programming arguing that the synchronization required when threads share data makes threads more complex than events. Advocates for threads argue that they provide a more natural way to express the control flow of a program than having to explicitly store a computation's state in a continuation.

In our opinion, there remain cases where both styles are appropriate, and we use both styles in our own programs. That said, for most I/O-intensive programs, threads are preferable: they are often more natural, reasonably efficient, and simpler when running on multiple processors.

4.9.2 Data Parallel Programming

Another important application area is parallel computing, and there is an ongoing debate as to the effectiveness of threads versus other models for expressing and managing parallelism.

data parallel programming

SIMD (single instruction multiple data) programming

bulk synchronous parallel programming

One popular model is *data parallel programming*, also known as *SIMD (single instruction multiple data) programming* or *bulk synchronous parallel programming*. In this model, the programmer describes a computation to apply in parallel across an entire data set at the same time, operating on independent data elements. The work on every data item must complete before moving onto the next step; one processor can use the results of a different processor only in some later step. As a result, the behavior of the program is deterministic. Rather than having programmers divide work among threads, the runtime system decides how to map the parallel work across the hardware's processors.

For example, taking the earlier example of zeroing a buffer in parallel in Figure 4.7, a data parallel program to zero an N item array can be as simple as:

```
forall i in 0:N-1
   array[i] = 0;
```

The runtime system would divide the array among processors to execute the computation in parallel. Of course, the runtime system itself might be implemented using threads, but this is invisible to the programmer.

Large data-analysis tasks often use data parallel programming. For example, Hadoop is an open source system that can process and analyze terabytes of data spread across hundreds or thousands of servers. It applies an arbitrary computation to each data element, such as to update the popularity of a web page based on a previous estimate of the popularity of the pages that refer to it. Hadoop applies the computation in parallel across all web pages, repeatedly, until the popularity of every page has converged. A search engine can then use the results to decide which pages should be returned in response to a search query.

Another example is SQL (Structured Query Language). SQL is a standard language for accessing databases in which programmers specify the database query to perform, and the database maps the query to lower-level thread and disk operations.

Multimedia streams (e.g., audio, video, and graphics) often have large amounts of data on which similar operations are repeatedly performed, so data parallel programming is frequently used for media processing; specialized hardware to support this type of parallel processing is common. Because they are optimized for highly structured data parallel programs, GPUs (Graphical Processing Units) can provide significantly higher rates of data processing. For example, in 2013 a mid-range Radeon 7850 GPU was capable of 1.69 TFLOPS (Trillion FLoating point Operations Per Second (double-precision)); for comparison, an Intel i7 3960 CPU (a high-end, six core general-purpose processor) was capable of 0.19 double-precision TFLOPS.

Considerable effort is currently going towards developing and using General Purpose GPUs (GPGPUs) — GPUs that better support a wider-range of programs. It is still not clear which classes of programs can work well with GPGPUs and which require more traditional CPU architectures, but for those programs that can be ported to the more restrictive GPGPU programming model, performance gains could be dramatic.

4.10 | Summary and Future Directions

Concurrency is ubiquitous — not only do most smartphones, servers, desktops, laptops, and tablets have multiple cores, but users have come to expect a responsive interface at all times, I/O latencies have become gigantic compared to computer instruction cycle times, and servers must be able to process large numbers of simultaneous requests.

Although threads are not the only possible solution to these issues, they are a general-purpose technique that can be applied to a wide range of concurrency issues. In our view, multi-threaded programming is a skill that every professional programmer must master.

In this chapter, we have discussed:

- **The thread abstraction.** Threads are a set of concurrent activities, each of which executes sequentially at unpredictable speed.

- **A simple thread API.** Thread libraries, whether for use in the operating system kernel or in application code, provide the ability to perform an asynchronous procedure call.

- **Thread implementations.** The core of any implementation of preemptive multi-threading is the ability to save one thread's state and restore another's. The thread system keeps track of the saved state of all threads not currently running; it switches threads between READY and RUN-NING as needed. The implementation of multi-threading can be in the kernel or at user-level, depending on the goals of the system. In our view, most systems in the future will have both a kernel-level thread system for managing concurrency in the operating system, and a lightweight thread system for expressing parallelism at the application level.

- **Alternative abstractions.** Practical alternatives to threads exist for two important domains: event-driven programming for servers as well as data parallel programming for multiprocessors.

Technology trends suggest that concurrent programming will only increase in importance over time. After several decades in which computer architects were able to make individual processor cores run faster and faster, we have reached a point where the performance of individual cores is leveling off and where further speedups will have to come from parallel processing.

The best programming model for expressing and managing parallelism is still an active area of research, but it seems likely that threads will remain an important option for decades to come.

4.10.1 Historical Notes

The extreme engineering complexity and bugginess of commercial operating systems in the 1960's led researchers to investigate alternatives. One direct result of this experience was modern software engineering: the systematic management of complex implementation tasks through the careful control of feature lists, module testing, assertions, and so forth.

Another consequence was the use of threads for managing concurrency. One of the most influential papers in computer science history is Dijkstra's description of his THE system [48]. Dijkstra argued for constructing operating systems as a series of layered abstractions, with communicating threads implementing each layer. Within a decade, the research community was convinced. When Xerox PARC built the Alto in the late 1970's, the Alto's operating system was built from the ground up using threads. The Alto demonstrated most of the technology we now take for granted with personal computers: bit-mapped display, menus, windowing, mice, Ethernet, and email. We base much of our description of thread programming on the experiences from that project [98].

Widespread commercial adoption of threads took much longer, however. By the early 1990's, the widespread adoption of client-server computing led to several commercially important operating systems written from scratch using threads, including Microsoft's Windows NT, SUN Microsystems Solaris, and Linux. Client operating systems followed, and by the late 1990's, with Apple's introduction of OS X, all major commercial operating systems were based on threads. At about the same time, the interface to thread libraries became standardized, starting with POSIX in 1995. Likewise, modern programming languages such as Java were designed with constructs for creating and synchronizing threads.

The increasing importance of parallel processing led to the development of very lightweight user-level thread implementations, as there is little point to parallelizing an application unless it improves performance. By the early 90's, scheduler activations were developed to integrate user-level and kernel threads [2].

Even so, the topic of whether threads are a better programming model than the alternatives remains an active one [159]. Several prominent operating systems researchers have argued that normal programmers should almost never use threads because (a) it is just too hard to write multi-threaded programs that are correct and (b) most things that threads are commonly used for can be accomplished in other, safer ways [129, 160]. These are important arguments to understand—even if you disagree with them, they point out pitfalls with using threads that are important to avoid.

Exercises

For some of the following problems, you will need to download the thread library from cs.uw.edu/homes/tom/code/thread.h and cs.uw.edu/homes/tom/code/thread.c. The comment at the top of threadHello.c explains how to compile and run a program that uses this library.

1. Download the example code cs.uw.edu/homes/tom/code/threadHello.c, compile it, and run it several times. What happens when you run it? Do you get the same result if you run it multiple times? What if you are also running some other demanding processes (e.g., compiling a big program, playing a Flash game on a website, or watching streaming video) when you run this program?

2. For the threadHello program in Figure 4.6, suppose that we delete the second for loop so that the main routine simply creates NTHREADS threads and then prints "Main thread done." What are the possible outputs of

Figure 4.19: Matrix multiplication.

the program now. **Hint:** Fewer than NTHREADS+1 lines may be printed in some runs. Why?

3. How expensive are threads? Write a program that times how long it takes to create and then join 1000 threads, where each thread simply calls thread_exit(0) as soon as it starts running.

4. Write a program that has two threads. Make the first thread a simple loop that continuously increments a counter and prints a period (".") whenever the value of that counter is divisible by 10,000,000. Make the second thread repeatedly wait for the user to input a line of text and then print "Thank you for your input." On your system, does the first thread makes rapid progress? Does the second thread respond quickly?

5. Write a program that uses threads to perform a parallel matrix multiply. To multiply two matrices, $C = A * B$, the result entry $C_{(i,j)}$ is computed by taking the dot product of the ith row of A and the jth column of B: $C_{i,j} = \Sigma_{k=0}^{N-1} A_{(i,k)} B_{(k,j)}$. We can divide the work by creating one thread to compute each value (or each row) in C, and then executing those threads on different processors in parallel, as shown in Figure 4.19.

6. Write a program that uses threads to perform a parallel merge sort.

7. For the threadHello program in Figure 4.6, the procedure go() has the parameter np and the local variable n. Are these variables *per-thread* or *shared* state? Where does the compiler store these variables' states?

8. For the threadHello program in Figure 4.6, the procedure main() has local variables such as i and exitValue. Are these variables *per-thread* or *shared* state? Where does the compiler store these variables?

9. In the *thread-local variables* sidebar, we described how many thread systems have this type of per-thread state.

   Describe how you would implement thread-local variables. Each thread should have an array of 1024 pointers to its thread-local variables.

   a) What would you add to the TCB?

b) How would you change the thread creation procedure? (For simplicity, assume that when a thread is created, all 1024 entries should be initialized to NULL.)

c) How would a running thread allocate a new thread-local variable?

d) In your design, how would a running thread access a particular thread-local variable?

10. For the threadHello program, what is the minimum and maximum number of times that the main thread enters the WAITING state?

11. Using simple threads, write a program that creates several threads and then determines whether the threads package on your system allocates a fixed-size stack for each thread or whether each thread's stack starts at some small size and dynamically grows as needed.

Hints: You probably want to write a recursive procedure that you can use to consume a large amount of stack memory. You may also want to examine the addresses of variables allocated to different threads' stacks. Finally, you may want to be able to determine how much memory has been allocated to your process; most operating systems have a command or utility that can show the resource consumption of currently running processes (e.g., top in Linux, Activity Monitor in OSX, or Task Manager in Windows).

It is not enough to be industrious. So are the ants. The question is: What are we industrious about?

Henry David Thoreau

5 Synchronizing Access to Shared Objects

How should we manage concurrent access to shared state?

independent threads

cooperating threads

Multi-threaded programs extend the traditional, single-threaded programming model so that each thread provides a single sequential stream of execution composed of familiar instructions. If a program has *independent threads* that operate on completely separate subsets of memory, we can reason about each thread separately. In this case, reasoning about independent threads differs little from reasoning about a series of independent, single-threaded programs.

However, most multi-threaded programs have both *per-thread state* (e.g., a thread's stack and registers) and *shared state* (e.g., shared variables on the heap). *Cooperating threads* read and write shared state.

Sharing state is useful because it lets threads communicate, coordinate work, and share information. For example, in the Earth Visualizer example in Chapter 4, once one thread finishes downloading a detailed image from the network, it shares that image data with a rendering thread that draws the new image on the screen.

Unfortunately, when cooperating threads share state, writing correct multi-threaded programs becomes much more difficult. Most programmers are used to thinking "sequentially" when reasoning about programs. For example, we often reason about the series of states traversed by a program as a sequence of instructions is executed. However, this sequential model of reasoning does not work in programs with cooperating threads, for three reasons:

1. **Program execution depends on the possible interleavings of threads' access to shared state.** For example, if two threads write a shared variable, one thread with the value 1 and the other with the value 2, the final

value of the variable depends on which of the threads' writes finishes last.

Although this example is simple, the problem is severe because programs need to work for *any possible interleaving*. In particular, recall that thread programmers should not make any assumptions about the relative speed at which their threads operate.

Worse, as programs grow, there is a combinatorial explosion in the number of possible interleavings.

How can we reason about all possible interleavings of threads' actions in a multi-million line program?

2. **Program execution can be nondeterministic.** Different runs of the same program may produce different results. For example, the scheduler may make different scheduling decisions, the processor may run at a different frequency, or another concurrently running program may affect the cache hit rate. Even common debugging techniques — such as running a program under a debugger, recompiling with the -g option instead of -O, or adding a printf — can change how a program behaves.

Heisenbugs

Jim Gray, the 1998 ACM Turing Award winner, coined the term *Heisenbugs* for bugs that disappear or change behavior when you try to examine them. Multi-threaded programming is a common source of Heisenbugs.

Bohr bugs

In contrast, *Bohr bugs* are deterministic and generally much easier to diagnose.

How can we debug programs with behaviors that change across runs?

3. **Compilers and processor hardware can reorder instructions.** Modern compilers and hardware reorder instructions to improve performance. This reordering is generally invisible to single-threaded programs; compilers and processors take care to ensure that dependencies within a single sequence of instructions — that is, within a thread — are preserved. However, reordering can become visible when multiple threads interact through accessing shared variables.

For example, consider the following code to compute q as a function of p:

Thread 1

```
p = someComputation();
pInitialized = true;
```

Thread 2

```
while (!pInitialized)
    ;
q = anotherComputation(p);
```

Although it seems that p is always initialized before anotherComputation(p) is called, this is not the case. To maximize instruction level parallelism, the hardware or compiler may set pInitialized = true before the computation to compute p has completed, and anotherComputation(p) may be computed using an unexpected value.

How can we reason about thread interleavings when compilers and processor hardware may reorder a thread's operations?

structured synchronization

Given these challenges, multi-threaded code can introduce subtle, non-deterministic, and non-reproducible bugs. This chapter describes a *structured synchronization* approach to sharing state in multi-threaded programs. Rather than scattering access to shared state throughout the program and attempting *ad hoc* reasoning about what happens when the threads' accesses are interleaved in various ways, a better approach is to: (1) structure the program to facilitate reasoning about concurrency, and (2) use a set of standard synchronization primitives to control access to shared state. This approach gives up some freedom, but if you consistently follow the rules we describe in this chapter, then reasoning about programs with shared state becomes much simpler.

The first part of this chapter elaborates on the challenges faced by multi-threaded programmers and on why it is dangerous to try to reason about all possible thread interleavings in the general, unstructured case. The rest of the chapter describes how to structure shared objects in multi-threaded programs so that we can reason about them. First, we structure a multi-threaded program's shared state as a set of *shared objects* that encapsulate the shared state as well as define and limit how the state can be accessed. Second, to avoid *ad hoc* reasoning about the possible interleavings of access to the state variables within a shared object, we describe how shared objects can use a small set of *synchronization primitives* — locks and condition variables — to coordinate access to their state by different threads. Third, to simplify reasoning about the code in shared objects, we describe a set of *best practices* for writing the code that implements each shared object. Finally, we dive into the details of how to implement synchronization primitives.

Multi-threaded programming has a reputation for being difficult. We agree that it takes care, but this chapter provides a set of simple rules that anyone can follow to implement objects that can be safely shared by multiple threads.

Chapter roadmap:

- **Challenges.** Why is it difficult to reason about multi-threaded programs with unstructured use of shared state? (Section 5.1)

- **Structuring Shared Objects.** How should we structure access to shared state by multiple threads? (Section 5.2)

Why do compilers and processor hardware reorder operations?

We often find that students are puzzled by the notion that a compiler might produce code, or a processor might execute code, in a way that is correct for a single thread but unpredictable for a multi-threaded program without synchronization.

For compilers, the issue is simple. Modern processors have deep pipelines; they execute many instructions simultaneously by overlapping the instruction fetch, instruction decode, data fetch, arithmetic operation, and conditional branch of a sequence of instructions. The processor stalls when necessary — e.g., if the result of one instruction is needed by the next. Modern compilers will reorder instructions to reduce these stalls as much as possible, provided the reordering does not change the behavior of the program.

The difficulty arises in what assumptions the compiler can make about the code. If the code is single-threaded, it is much easier to analyze possible dependencies between adjacent instructions, allowing more optimization. By contrast, variables in (unsynchronized) multi-threaded code can potentially be read or written by another thread at any point. As the example in the text demonstrated, the precise sequence of seemingly unrelated instructions can potentially affect the behavior of the program. To preserve semantics, instruction re-ordering may no longer be feasible, resulting in more processor stalls and slower code execution.

As long as the programmer uses structured synchronization for protecting shared data, the compiler can reorder instructions as needed without changing program behavior, provided that the compiler does not reorder across synchronization operations. A compiler making the more conservative assumption that all memory is shared would produce slow code even when it was not necessary.

For processor architectures, the issue is also performance. Certain optimizations are possible if the programmer is using structured synchronization but not otherwise. For example, modern processors buffer memory writes to allow instruction execution to continue while the memory is written in the background. If two adjacent instructions issue memory writes to different memory locations, they can occur in parallel and complete out of order. This optimization is safe on a single processor, but potentially unsafe if multiple processors are simultaneously reading and writing the same locations without intervening synchronization. Some processor architectures make the conservative assumption that optimizations should never change program behavior regardless of the programming style — in this case, they stall to prevent reordering. Others make a more optimistic assumption that the programmer is using structured synchronization. For your code to be portable, you should assume that the compiler and the hardware can reorder instructions except across synchronization operations.

- **Locks: Mutual Exclusion.** How can we enforce a logical sequence of operations on shared state? (Section 5.3)

- **Condition Variables: Waiting for a Change.** How does a thread wait for a change in shared state? (Section 5.4)

- **Designing and Implementing Shared Objects.** Given locks and condition variables, what is a good way to write and reason about the code for shared objects? (Section 5.5)

- **Three Case Studies.** We illustrate our methodology by using it to develop solutions to three concurrent programming challenges. (Section 5.6)

- **Implementing Synchronization Primitives.** How are locks and condition variables implemented? (Section 5.7)

- **Semaphores Considered Harmful.** What other synchronization primitives are possible, and how do they relate to locks and condition variables? (Section 5.8)

5.1 | Challenges

Why are multi-threaded programs with unstructured use of shared state difficult to reason about?

We began this chapter with the core challenge of multi-threaded programming: a multi-threaded program's execution depends on the interleavings of different threads' access to shared memory, which can make it difficult to reason about or debug these programs. In particular, cooperating threads' execution may be affected by *race conditions*.

5.1.1 Race Conditions

race condition

A *race condition* occurs when the behavior of a program depends on the interleaving of operations of different threads. In effect, the threads run a race between their operations, and the results of the program execution depends on who wins the race.

Reasoning about even simple programs with race conditions can be difficult. To appreciate this, we now look at three extremely simple multi-threaded programs.

The world's simplest cooperating-threads program. Suppose we run a program with two threads that do the following:

Thread A	Thread B
x = 1;	x = 2;

EXAMPLE   What are the possible final values of x?

ANSWER   The result can be **x = 1 or x = 2** depending on which thread wins or loses the "race" to set x.   ☐

That was easy, so let's try one that is a bit more interesting.

The world's second-simplest cooperating-threads program. Suppose that initially y = 12, and we run a program with two threads that do the following:

Thread A	Thread B
x = y + 1;	y = y * 2;

EXAMPLE   What are the possible final values of x?

ANSWER   The result is **x = 13 if Thread A executes first or x = 25 if Thread B executes first.** More precisely, we get x = 13 if Thread A reads y before Thread B updates y, or we get x = 25 if Thread B updates y before Thread A reads y.   ☐

The world's third-simplest cooperating-threads program. Suppose that initially x = 0 and we run a program with two threads that do the following:

Thread A	Thread B
x = x + 1;	x = x + 2;

EXAMPLE   What are the possible final values of x?

ANSWER   Obviously, **one possible outcome is x = 3.** For example, Thread A runs to completion and then Thread B starts and runs to completion. However, **we can also get x = 2 or x = 1.** In particular, when we write a single statement like x = x + 1, compilers on many processors produce multiple instructions, such as: (1) load memory location x into a register, (2) add 1 to that register, and (3) store the result to memory location x. If we disassemble the above program into simple pseudo-assembly-code, we can see some of the possibilities.

One Interleaving		Another Interleaving		Yet Another Interleaving	
load r1, x		load r1, x		load r1, x	
add r2, r1, 1			load r1, x		load r1, x
store x, r2		add r2, r1, 1		add r2, r1, 1	
	load r1, x		add r2, r1, 2		add r2, r1, 2
	add r2, r1, 2	store x, r2			store x, r2
	store x, r2		store x, r2	store x, r2	
final: x == 3		final: x == 2		final: x == 1	

☐

The Case of the Therac-25

The Therac-25 was a cancer therapy device, designed to deliver very high doses of radiation to a targeted region of the body in an attempt to eliminate cancer cells before they had a chance to spread. Over a several year period in the mid-1980's, a computer malfunction caused six separate patients to receive an estimated 100 times the intended dose of radiation. Three of the patients later died as a result; the others sustained serious but non-fatal injuries.

Although there were many contributing factors to the malfunction, a race condition was at the heart of both the overdose and the delay in recognizing and repairing the problem. The Therac-25 was designed to check in software that the entered dosage was medically safe before using it to configure the radiation beam. However, the software was also concurrent: the operator interface code could run at the same time that the dosage was being checked and used, with no locking or other synchronization. In rare cases, the dosage could be changed after the check and before the use, and due to a separate user interface bug, the operator could enter an overdose without either intending or realizing it.

Because the problem required a rare sequence of events, the machine appeared to work successfully for almost all patients. Years elapsed between the first incident and the final one, and during this period, the manufacturer repeatedly insisted that no overdose was possible and that the patient injuries must be due to some other factor. It took the second occurrence of the race condition at the same hospital to help reveal the system's design flaw.

Even for this 2-line program, the complexity of reasoning about race conditions and interleavings is beginning to grow. Not only would one have to reason about all possible interleavings of statements, but one would also have to disassemble the program and reason about all possible interleavings of assembly instructions. (And if the compiler and hardware can reorder instructions, there are even more possibilities to consider.)

5.1.2   Atomic Operations

atomic operations   When we disassembled the code in last example, we could reason about *atomic operations*, indivisible operations that cannot be interleaved with or split by other operations.

On most modern architectures, a load or store of a 32-bit word from or to memory is an atomic operation. So, the previous analysis reasoned about interleaving of atomic loads and stores to memory.

Conversely, a load or store is not always an atomic operation. Depending on the hardware implementation, if two threads store the value of a 64-bit floating point register to a memory address, the final result might be the first value, the second value, or a mix of the two.

5.1.3   Too Much Milk

Can we coordinate access to shared memory by multiple threads using only loads and stores?

Although one could, in principle, reason carefully about the possible interleavings of different threads' atomic loads and stores, doing so is tricky and error-prone. Later, we present a higher level abstraction for synchronizing threads, but first we illustrate the problems with using atomic loads and stores using a simple problem called, "Too Much Milk." The example is intentionally simple; real-world concurrent programs are often much more complex. Even so, the example shows the difficulty of reasoning about interleaved access to shared state.

The Too Much Milk problem models two roommates who share a refrigerator and who — as good roommates — make sure the refrigerator is always well stocked with milk. With such responsible roommates, the following scenario is possible:

	Roommate 1's actions	Roommate 2's actions
3:00	Look in fridge; out of milk.	
3:05	Leave for store.	
3:10	Arrive at store.	Look in fridge; out of milk.
3:15	Buy milk.	Leave for store.
3:20	Arrive home; put milk away.	Arrive at store.
3:25		Buy milk.
3:30		Arrive home; put milk away.
3:35		Oh no!

We can model each roommate as a thread and the number of bottles of milk in the fridge with a variable in memory. If the only atomic operations on shared state are atomic loads and stores to memory, is there a solution to the Too Much Milk problem that ensures both *safety* (the program never enters a bad state) and *liveness* (the program eventually enters a good state)? Here, we strive for the following properties:

safety property

liveness property

- **Safety:** Never more than one person buys milk.

- **Liveness:** If milk is needed, someone eventually buys it.

WARNING

Simplifying Assumption. Throughout the analysis in this section, we assume that the instructions are executed in exactly the order written, i.e., neither the compiler nor the architecture reorders instructions. This assumption is crucial for reasoning about the order of atomic load and store operations, but many modern compilers and architectures violate it, so be extremely careful applying the style of analysis we present here to your own programs.

*Two more solutions
are coming. Be
suspicious.*

Solution 1. The basic idea is for a roommate to leave a note on the fridge before going to the store. The simplest way to leave this note — given our programming model that we have shared memory on which we can perform atomic loads and stores — is to set a flag when going to buy milk and to check this flag before going to buy milk. Each thread might run the following code:

```
if (milk==0) {          // if no milk
    if (note==0) {      // if no note
        note = 1;       // leave note
        milk++;         // buy milk
        note = 0;       // remove note
    }
}
```

Unfortunately, this implementation can violate safety. For example, the first thread could execute everything up to and including the check of the milk value and then get context switched. Then, the second thread could run through all of this code and buy milk. Finally, the first thread could be re-scheduled, see that note is zero, leave the note, buy more milk, and remove the note, leaving the system with milk == 2.

```
if (milk==0) {
                                        if (milk==0) {
                                            if (note==0) {
                                                note = 1;
                                                milk++;
                                                note = 0;
                                            }
                                        }

    if (note==0) {
        note = 1;
        milk++;
        note = 0;
    }
}
```

Oh no!

This "solution" makes the problem worse! The preceding code usually works, but it may fail occasionally when the scheduler does just the right (or wrong) thing. We have created a Heisenbug that causes the program to occasionally fail in ways that may be very difficult to reproduce (e.g., probably only when the grader is looking at it or when the CEO is demonstrating a new product at a trade show).

*Another solution is
coming, so the odds
that this one will work
seem low, don't they?*

Solution 2. In solution 1, the roommate checks the note before setting it. This opens up the possibility that one roommate has already made a decision to buy milk before notifying the other roommate of that decision. If we use two variables for the notes, a roommate can create a note before checking the other note and the milk and making a decision to buy. For example, we can do the following:

Path A

```
noteA = 1;          // leave note
if (noteB==0) {     // if no note     A1
    if (milk==0) {  // if no milk     A2
        milk++;     // buy milk       A3
    }
}
noteA = 0;          // remove note A
```

Path B

```
noteB = 1;          // leave note
if (noteA==0) {     // if no note     B1
    if (milk==0) {  // if no milk     B2
        milk++;     // buy milk       B3
    }               //                B4
}                   //                B5
noteB = 0;          // remove note
```

If the first thread executes the Path A code and the second thread executes the Path B code, this protocol is safe; by having each thread write a note ("I might buy milk") before deciding to buy milk, we ensure the safety property: at most one thread buys milk.

Although this intuition is solid, proving the safety property without enumerating all possible interleavings requires care.

Safety Proof. Assume for the sake of contradiction that the algorithm is *not* safe — both A and B buy milk. Consider the state of the two variables (noteB, milk) when thread A is at the line marked **A1**, at the precise moment when the atomic load of noteB from shared memory to A's register occurs. There are three cases to consider:

- **Case 1:** (noteB = 1, milk = any value). This state contradicts the assumption that thread A buys milk and reaches **A3**.

stable property
- **Case 2:** (noteB = 0, milk > 0). In this simple program, the property milk > 0 is a *stable property* — once it becomes true, it remains true forever. Thus, if milk > 0 is true when A is at **A1**, A's test at line **A2** will fail, and A will not buy milk, contradicting our assumption.

- **Case 3:** (noteB = 0, milk = 0). We know that thread B must not currently be executing any of the lines marked **B1-B5**. We also know that either noteA == 1 or milk > 0 will be true from this time forward (noteA OR milk is also a stable property). This means that B cannot buy milk in the future (either the test at B1 or B2 must fail), which contradicts our assumption that both A and B buy milk.

Since every case contradicts the assumption, the algorithm is safe.   □

Liveness. Unfortunately, Solution 2 does not ensure liveness. In particular, it is possible for both threads to set their respective notes, for each thread to check the other thread's note, and for both threads to decide not to buy milk. This brings us to Solution 3.

This one will work, but we will give an even better answer shortly.

Solution 3. Solution 2 was safe because a thread would avoid buying milk if there were any chance that the other thread *might* buy milk. For Solution 3, we ensure that at least one of the threads determines whether the other thread has bought milk or not before deciding whether or not to buy. In particular, we do the following:

Path A

```
noteA = 1;              // leave note A
while (noteB==1) {      // wait for no note B
    ;                   // spin
}
if (milk==0) {          // if no milk M
    milk++;             // buy milk
}
noteA = 0;              // remove note A
```

Path B

```
noteB = 1;              // leave note B
if (noteA==0) {         // if no note A
    if (milk==0) {      // if no milk
        milk++;         // buy milk
    }                   //
}                       //
noteB = 0;              // remove note B
```

We can show that Solution 3 is safe using an argument similar to the one we used for Solution 2.

To show that Solution 3 is live, observe that code path B has no loops, so eventually thread B must finish executing the listed code. Eventually, noteB == 0 becomes true and remains true. Therefore, thread A must eventually reach line **M** and decide whether to buy milk. If it finds M == 1, then milk has been bought. If it finds M == 0, then it will buy milk. Either way, the liveness property — that if needed, some milk is bought — is met.

5.1.4 Discussion

Assuming that the compiler and processor execute instructions in program order, the preceding proof shows that it is possible to devise a solution to Too Much Milk that is both safe and live using nothing but atomic load and store operations on shared memory. Although the solution we presented only works for two roommates, there is a generalization, called Peterson's algorithm, which works with any fixed number of n threads. More details on Peterson's algorithm can be found elsewhere (e.g., http://en.wikipedia.org/wiki/Peterson's_algorithm).

However, our solution for Too Much Milk (and likewise Peterson's algorithm) is not terribly satisfying:

- The solution is complex and requires careful reasoning to be convinced that it works.

busy-waiting

- The solution is *inefficient*. In Too Much Milk, while thread A is waiting, it is *busy-waiting* and consuming CPU resources. In Peterson's generalized solution, *all* n threads can busy-wait. Busy-waiting is particularly problematic on modern systems with preemptive multi-threading, as the spinning thread may be holding the processor waiting for an event that cannot occur until some preempted thread is re-scheduled to run.

Memory barriers

Suppose you are writing low-level code that must reason about the ordering of memory operations. How can this be done on modern hardware and with modern compilers?

A *memory barrier* instruction prevents the compiler and hardware from reordering memory accesses across the barrier — no accesses before the barrier are moved after the barrier and no accesses after the barrier are moved before the barrier. One can add memory barriers to the Too Much Milk solution or to Peterson's algorithm to get code that works on modern machines with modern compilers. Of course, this makes the code even more complex.

Details of how to issue a memory barrier instruction depend on hardware and compiler details. However, a good example is gcc's __sync_synchronize() builtin, which tells the compiler not to reorder memory accesses across the barrier and to issue processor-specific instructions that the underlying hardware treats as a memory barrier.

memory barrier

- The solution *may* fail if the compiler or hardware reorders instructions. This limitation can be addressed by using *memory barriers* (see sidebar). Adding memory barriers would further increase the implementation complexity of the algorithm; barriers do not address the other limitations just mentioned.

5.1.5   A Better Solution

The next section describes a better approach to writing programs in which multiple threads access shared state. We write *shared objects* that use *synchronization objects* to coordinate different threads' access to shared state.

Suppose, for example, we had a primitive called a *lock* that only one thread at a time can own. Then, we can solve the Too Much Milk problem by defining the class for a Kitchen object with the following method:

```
Kitchen :: buyIfNeeded () {
    lock . acquire ();
    if (milk == 0) {      // if no milk
        milk++;           // buy milk
    }
    lock . release ();
}
```

After outlining a strategy for managing synchronization in the next section, we define locks and condition variables (another type of synchronization object) in Sections 5.3 and 5.4.

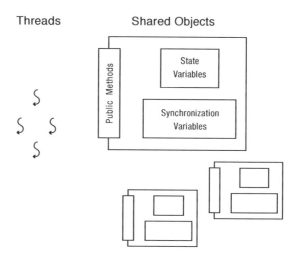

Figure 5.1: In a multi-threaded program, threads are separate from and operate concurrently on shared objects. Shared objects contain both shared state and synchronization variables, used for controlling concurrent access to shared state.

5.2 | Structuring Shared Objects

Decades of work have developed a much simpler approach to writing multi-threaded programs than using just atomic loads and stores. This approach extends the modularity of object-oriented programming to multi-threaded programs. As Figure 5.1 illustrates, a multi-threaded program is built using *shared objects* and a set of threads that operate on them.

shared object   *Shared objects* are objects that can be accessed safely by multiple threads. All shared state in a program — including variables allocated on the heap (e.g., objects allocated with malloc or new) and static, global variables — should be encapsulated in one or more shared objects.

Programming with shared objects extends traditional object-oriented programming, in which objects hide their implementation details behind a clean interface. In the same way, shared objects hide the details of synchronizing the actions of multiple threads behind a clean interface. The threads using shared objects need only understand the interface; they do not need to know how the shared object internally handles synchronization.

Like regular objects, programmers can design shared objects for whatever modules, interfaces, and semantics an application needs. Each shared object's class defines a set of public methods on which threads operate. To assemble the overall program from these shared objects, each thread executes a "main loop" written in terms of actions on public methods of shared objects.

Since shared objects encapsulate the program's shared state, the main loop code that defines a thread's high-level actions need not concern itself with

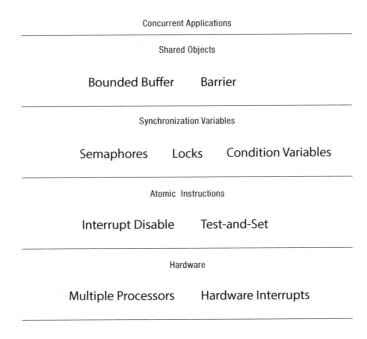

Figure 5.2: Multi-threaded programs are built with shared objects. Shared objects are built using synchronization variables and state variables. Synchronization variables are implemented using specialized processor instructions to manage interrupt delivery and to atomically read-modify-write memory locations.

synchronization details. The programming model thus looks very similar to that for single-threaded code.

5.2.1 Implementing Shared Objects

Of course, internally the shared objects must handle the details of synchronization. As Figure 5.2 shows, shared objects are implemented in three layers.

- **Shared object layer.** As in standard object-oriented programming, shared objects define application-specific logic and hide internal implementation details. Externally, they appear to have the same interface as you would define for a single-threaded program.

- **Synchronization variable layer.** Rather than implementing shared objects directly with carefully interleaved atomic loads and stores, shared objects include *synchronization variables* as member variables. Synchronization variables, stored in memory just like any other object, can be included in any data structure.

synchronization variable   A *synchronization variable* is a data structure used for coordinating concurrent access to shared state. Both the interface and the implementation of synchronization variables must be carefully designed. In particular, we

Shared objects, monitors, and syntactic sugar

We focus on *shared objects* because object-oriented programming provides a good way to think about shared state: hide shared state behind public methods that provide a clean interface to threads and that handle the details of synchronization.

Although we use object-oriented terminology in our discussion, the ideas are equally applicable to non-object-oriented languages. For example, where a C++ program might define a class of shared objects with public methods, a C program might define a struct with synchronization variables and state variables as fields. Rather than scattering the code that accesses the struct's fields, a well-designed C program will have a fixed set of functions that operate on the struct's fields.

Conversely, some programming languages build in even more support for shared objects than we describe here. When a programming language includes support for shared objects, a shared object is often called a *monitor*. Early languages with monitors include Brinch Hansen's Concurrent Pascal and Xerox PARC's Mesa; today, Java supports monitors via the synchronized keyword.

We regard the distinctions between procedural languages, object-oriented languages, and languages with built-in support for monitors as relatively unimportant syntactic sugar — they are just a different way of writing the same thing. We use the terms "shared objects" or "monitors" broadly to refer to a conceptual approach that can and should be used to manage concurrency regardless of the particular programming language.

In this book, our code and pseudo-code are based on C++'s syntax. We believe provides the right level of detail for teaching the shared objects or monitors approach. We prefer teaching with C++ to Java because we want to explicitly show where locks and condition variables are allocated and accessed rather than relying on operations hidden by a language's built in monitor syntax. Conversely, we prefer C++ to C because we think C++'s support for object-oriented programming may help you internalize the underlying philosophy of the shared object approach.

---

build shared objects using two types of synchronization variables: *locks* and *condition variables.* We define these and describe how to construct them in Sections 5.3 and 5.4.

state variable   Synchronization variables coordinate access to *state variables*, which are just the normal member variables of an object that you are familiar with from single-threaded programming (e.g., integers, strings, arrays, and pointers).

Using synchronization variables simplifies implementing shared objects. In fact, not only do shared objects externally resemble traditional single-threaded objects, but, by implementing them with synchronization variables, their internal implementations are quite similar to those of single-threaded programs.

- **Atomic instruction layer.** Although the layers above benefit from a simpler programming model, it is not turtles all the way down. Internally, synchronization variables must manage the interleavings of different threads' actions.

atomic
read-modify-write
instructions

Rather than implementing synchronization variables, such as locks and condition variables, using atomic loads and stores as we tried to do for the Too Much Milk problem, modern implementations build synchronization variables using *atomic read-modify-write instructions*. These processor-specific instructions let one thread have temporarily exclusive and atomic access to a memory location while the instruction executes. Typically, the instruction atomically reads a memory location, does some simple arithmetic operation to the value, and stores the result. The hardware guarantees that any other thread's instructions accessing the same memory location will occur either entirely before, or entirely after, the atomic read-modify-write instruction.

5.2.2   Scope and Roadmap

As Figure 5.2 indicates, concurrent programs are built on top of shared objects. The rest of this chapter focuses on the three bottom layers of the figure — how to build shared objects using synchronization objects and how to build synchronization objects out of atomic read-modify-write instructions. Chapter 6 discusses issues that arise when composing multiple shared objects into a larger program.

5.3 | Locks: Mutual Exclusion

lock

mutual exclusion

*How can we enforce a
logical sequence of
operations on shared
state?*

A *lock* is a synchronization variable that provides *mutual exclusion* — when one thread holds a lock, no other thread can hold it (i.e., other threads are *excluded*). A program associates each lock with some subset of shared state and requires a thread to hold the lock when accessing that state. Then, only one thread can access the shared state at a time.

Mutual exclusion greatly simplifies reasoning about programs because a thread can perform an arbitrary set of operations while holding a lock, and those operations *appear to be atomic* to other threads. In particular, because a lock enforces mutual exclusion and threads must hold the lock to access shared state, no other thread can observe an intermediate state. Other threads can only observe the state left after the lock release.

EXAMPLE

Locking to group multiple operations. Consider, for example, a bank account object that includes a list of transactions and a total balance. To add a new transaction, we acquire the account's lock, append the new transaction to the list, read the old balance, modify it, write the new balance, and release the lock. To query the balance and list of recent transactions, we acquire the account's lock, read the recent transactions from the list, read the balance, and release the lock. Using locks in this way guarantees that one update or query completes before the next one starts. Every query always reflects the complete set of recent transactions.

Another example of grouping is when printing output. Without locking, if two threads called printf at the same time, the individual characters of the two messages could be interleaved, garbling their meaning. Instead, on modern multi-threaded operating systems, printf uses a lock to ensure that the group of characters in each message prints as a unit.

It is much easier to reason about interleavings of atomic groups of operations rather than interleavings of individual operations for two reasons. First, there are (obviously) fewer interleavings to consider. Reasoning about interleavings on a coarser-grained basis reduces the sheer number of cases to consider. Second, and more important, we can make each atomic group of operations correspond to the logical structure of the program, which allows us to reason about *invariants* not specific *interleavings*.

In particular, shared objects usually have one lock guarding all of an object's state. Each public method acquires the lock on entry and releases the lock on exit. Thus, reasoning about a shared class's code is similar to reasoning about a traditional class's code: we assume a set of invariants when a public method is called and re-establish those invariants before a public method returns. If we define our invariants well, we can then reason about each method independently.

5.3.1 Locks: API and Properties

A lock enables mutual exclusion by providing two methods: Lock::acquire() and Lock::release(). These methods are defined as follows:

- A lock can be in one of two states: BUSY or FREE.

- A lock is initially in the FREE state.

- Lock::acquire waits until the lock is FREE and then atomically makes the lock BUSY.

  Checking the state to see if it is FREE and setting the state to BUSY are together an *atomic operation*. Even if multiple threads try to acquire the lock, at most one thread will succeed. One thread observes that the lock is FREE and sets it to BUSY; the other threads just see that the lock is BUSY and wait.

- Lock::release makes the lock FREE. If there are pending acquire operations, this state change causes one of them to proceed.

We describe how to implement locks with these properties in Section 5.7. Using locks makes solving the Too Much Milk problem trivial. Both threads run the following code:

```
lock.acquire();
if (milk == 0) {      // if no milk
    milk++;           // buy milk
}
lock.release();
```

EXAMPLE   Many routines in an operating system kernel need to allocate and de-allocate memory blocks. Assuming you are given the code for a single-threaded kernel memory allocator, explain how to implement a thread-safe memory allocator.

ANSWER   Using C malloc and free as an example, we can convert them to be thread-safe by acquiring a lock before accessing the heap, and releasing it after the block has been allocated or freed. Since malloc and free read and modify the same data structures, it is essential to use the *same* lock in both procedures, heaplock.

```
char *malloc (int n) {              void free (char *p) {
    char *p;

    heaplock.acquire();                 heaplock.acquire();
 // Code for single-threaded malloc()   // Code for single-threaded free()
 // p = allocate block of memory        // Put p back on free list.
 //     of size n.                      heaplock.release();
    heaplock.release();
    return p;                       }
}
```

□

Formal properties.   A lock can be defined more precisely as follows. A thread *holds a lock* if it has returned from a lock's acquire method more often than it has returned from a lock's release method. A thread *is attempting to acquire* a lock if it has called but not yet returned from a call to acquire on the lock.

A lock should ensure the following three properties:

1. **Mutual Exclusion.** At most one thread holds the lock.

2. **Progress.** If no thread holds the lock and any thread attempts to acquire the lock, then eventually some thread succeeds in acquiring the lock.

3. **Bounded waiting.** If thread T attempts to acquire a lock, then there exists a bound on the number of times other threads can successfully acquire the lock before T does.

Mutual exclusion is a safety property because locks prevent more than one thread from accessing shared state.

Progress and bounded waiting are liveness properties. If a lock is FREE, *some* thread must be able to acquire it. Further, any *particular* thread that wants to acquire the lock must eventually succeed in doing so.

If these definitions sound stilted, it is because we have carefully crafted them to avoid introducing subtle corner cases. For example, if a thread holding a lock never releases it, other threads cannot make progress, so we define the *bounded waiting* condition in terms of successful acquire operations.

WARNING

Non-property: Thread ordering. The *bounded waiting* property defined above guarantees that a thread will eventually get a chance to acquire the lock. However, it does not promise that waiting threads acquire the lock in FIFO order. Most implementations of locks that you will encounter — for example with POSIX threads — do not provide FIFO ordering.

5.3.2 Case Study: Thread-Safe Bounded Queue

How should we implement a thread-safe bounded queue?

As in standard object-oriented programming, each shared object is an instance of a class that defines the class's state and the methods that operate on that state.

The class's state includes both state variables (e.g., ints, floats, strings, arrays, and pointers) and synchronization variables (e.g., locks). Every time a class constructor produces another instance of a shared object, it allocates both a new lock and new instances of the state protected by that lock.

bounded queue

A *bounded queue* is a queue with a fixed size limit on the number of items stored in the queue. Operating system kernels use bounded queues for managing interprocess communication, TCP and UDP sockets, and I/O requests. Because the kernel runs in a finite physical memory, the kernel must be designed to work properly with finite resources. For example, instead of a simple, infinite buffer between a producer and a consumer thread, the kernel will instead use a limited size buffer, or bounded queue.

thread-safe bounded queue

A *thread-safe bounded queue* is a type of a bounded queue that is safe to call from multiple concurrent threads. Figure 5.3 gives an implementation; it lets any number of threads safely insert and remove items from the queue. As Figure 5.4 illustrates, a program can allocate multiple such queues (e.g., queue1, queue2, and queue3), each of which includes its own lock and state variables.

The queue stores only a fixed number, MAX, of items. When the queue is full, an insert request returns an error. Similarly, when the queue is empty, a remove request returns an error. Section 5.4 shows how *condition variables* let the calling thread *wait* instead of returning an error. On insert, the thread waits until the queue has space to store the item and, on remove, it waits until the queue has at least one item queued before returning it.

```
// Thread—safe queue interface

const int MAX = 10;

class TSQueue {
   // Synchronization variables
   Lock lock;

   // State variables
   int items[MAX];
   int front;
   int nextEmpty;

  public:
   TSQueue();
   ~TSQueue(){};
   bool tryInsert(int item);
   bool tryRemove(int *item);
};

// Initialize the queue to empty
// and the lock to free.
TSQueue::TSQueue() {
   front = nextEmpty = 0;
}
```

```
// Try to insert an item. If the queue is
// full, return false; otherwise return true.
bool
TSQueue::tryInsert(int item) {
   bool success = false;

   lock.acquire();
   if ((nextEmpty − front) < MAX) {
      items[nextEmpty % MAX] = item;
      nextEmpty++;
      success = true;
   }
   lock.release();
   return success;
}

// Try to remove an item. If the queue is
// empty, return false; otherwise return true.
bool
TSQueue::tryRemove(int *item) {
   bool success = false;

   lock.acquire();
   if (front < nextEmpty) {
      *item = items[front % MAX];
      front++;
      success = true;
   }
   lock.release();
   return success;
}
```

Figure 5.3: A thread-safe bounded queue. For implementation simplicity, we assume the queue stores integers (rather than arbitrary objects) and the total number of items stored is modest.

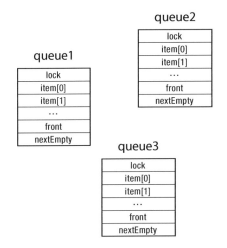

Figure 5.4: Three shared objects, each an instance of class TSQueue.

The TSQueue implementation defines a circular queue that stores data in a fixed size array, items[MAX]. The state variable, front is the next item in the queue to be removed, if any; nextEmpty is the next location for a new item, if any. To keep the example as simple as possible, only items of type int can be stored in and removed from the queue, and we assume the total number of items stored fits within a 64 bit integer.

All of these variables are as they would be for a single-threaded version of this object. The lock allows tryInsert and tryRemove to atomically read and write multiple variables just as a single-threaded version would.

EXAMPLE
What constraints are true of TSQueue at the moment immediately after the lock is acquired? What constraints hold immediately before the lock is released?

ANSWER
Because the lock enforces mutual exclusion and is always held whenever a thread modifies a state variable, when the lock is acquired the object's state variables must be either: (i) in the initial state or (ii) in the state left by a previous thread when it released the lock. These constraints are the same as for single-threaded code using a bounded queue:

- The total number of items ever inserted in the queue is nextEmpty.

- The total number of items ever removed from the queue is front.

- front $<=$ nextEmpty

- The current number of items in the queue is nextEmpty $-$ front.

- nextEmpty $-$ front $<=$ MAX

The lock holder always re-establishes these constraints before releasing the lock. □

EXAMPLE
Are these constraints also true if the lock is not held?

ANSWER
No. While it seems intuitive that if the constraints hold immediately before the lock is released, that they must also hold immediately after the lock is released. However, this is not the case. In the meantime, some other thread may have acquired the lock and may be in the process of modifying the state variables. In general, if the lock is not held, one cannot say *anything* about the object's state variables. □

Critical Sections

critical section
A *critical section* is a sequence of code that atomically accesses shared state. By ensuring that a thread holds the object's lock while executing any of its critical sections, we ensure that each critical section appears to execute atomically on its shared state. There is a critical section in each of the methods tryInsert and tryRemove.

Notice two things:

```
// TSQueueMain.cc
//   Test code for TSQueue.

int main(int argc, char **argv) {
    TSQueue *queues[3];
    sthread_t workers[3];
    int i, j;

    // Start worker threads to insert.
    for (i = 0; i < 3; i++) {
        queues[i] = new TSQueue();
        thread_create_p(&workers[i],
                putSome, queues[i]);
    }

    // Wait for some items to be put.
    thread_join(workers[0]);

    // Remove 20 items from each queue.
    for (i = 0; i < 3; i++) {
        printf("Queue %d:\n", i);
        testRemoval(&queues[i]);
    }
}
```

```
// Insert 50 items into a queue.
void *putSome(void *p) {
    TSQueue *queue = (TSQueue *)p;
    int i;

    for (i = 0; i < 50; i++) {
        queue->tryInsert(i);
    }
    return NULL;
}

// Remove 20 items from a queue.
void testRemoval(TSQueue *queue) {
    int i, item;

    for (i = 0; i < 20; j++) {
        if (queue->tryRemove(&item))
            printf("Removed %d\n", item);
        else
            printf("Nothing there.\n");
    }
}
```

Figure 5.5: This code creates three TSQueue objects and then adds and removes some items from these queues. We use thread_create_p instead of thread_create so that we can pass to the newly created thread a pointer to the queue it should use.

- Each class can define multiple methods that operate on the shared state defined by the class, so there may be *multiple critical sections per class.* However, for each instance of the class (i.e., for each object), only one thread holds the object's lock at a time, so *only one thread actively executes any of the critical sections per shared object instance.* For the TSQueue class, if one thread calls queue1.tryInsert and another calls queue1.tryRemove, the insert occurs either before the remove or vice versa.

- A program can create *multiple instances of a class.* Each instance is a shared object, and each shared object has its own lock. Thus, different threads may be active in the critical sections for different shared object instances. For the TSQueue class, if one thread calls queue1.tryInsert, another thread calls queue2.tryRemove, and a third thread calls queue3.tryInsert, all three threads may be simultaneously executing critical section code operating on *different instances* of the TSQueue class.

Using Shared Objects

Shared objects are allocated in the same way as other objects. They can be dynamically allocated from the heap using malloc and new, or they can be statically allocated in global memory by declaring static variables in the program.

Multiple threads must be able to access shared objects. If shared objects are global variables, then a thread's code can refer to an object's global name to reference it; the compiler computes the corresponding address. If shared objects are dynamically allocated, then each thread that uses an object needs a pointer or reference to it.

Two common ways to provide a thread a pointer to a shared object are: (1) provide a pointer to the shared object when the thread is created, and (2) store references to shared objects in other shared objects (e.g., containers). For example, a program might have a global, shared (and synchronized!) hash table that threads can use to store and retrieve references to other shared objects.

Figure 5.5 shows a simple program that creates three queues and then creates some threads that insert into these queues. It then removes 20 items from each queue and prints the values it removes. The initial main thread allocates the shared queues on the heap using new, and provides each worker thread a pointer to one of the shared queues.

WARNING **Put shared objects on the heap, not the stack.**While nothing prevents you from writing a program that allocates a shared object as an automatic variable in a procedure or method, you should not write programs that do this. The compiler allocates automatic variables (sometimes called "local variables", with good reason) on the stack during procedure invocation. If one thread passes a pointer or reference to one of its automatic variables to another thread and later returns from the procedure where the automatic variable was allocated, then that second thread now has a pointer into a region of the first thread's stack that may be used for other purposes. To prevent this error, a few garbage-collected languages, such as Google's Go, automatically convert all automatic data to being heap-allocated if the data can be referenced outside of the procedure.

You might be tempted to argue that, for a particular program, you know that the procedure will never return until all of the threads with which it is sharing an object are done using that object, and that therefore sharing one of the procedure's local variables is safe. The problem with this argument is that the code may change over time, introducing a dangerous and subtle bug. When sharing dynamically allocated variables, it is best to stay in the habit of sharing variables only from the heap — and never sharing variables from the stack — across threads.

5.4 | Condition Variables: Waiting for a Change

How does a thread wait for a change in shared state?

Condition variables provide a way for one thread to wait for another thread to take some action. For example, in the thread-safe queue example in Figure 5.3, rather than returning an error when we try to remove an item from an empty queue, we might wait until the queue is non-empty, and then always return an item.

```
int
TSQueue::remove() {
    int item;
    bool success;

    do {
        success = tryRemove(&item);
    } until(success);
    return item;
}
```

Figure 5.6: A polling-based implementation of TSQueue::remove. The code retries in a loop until it succeeds in removing an item.

Similarly, a web server might wait until a new request arrives; a word processor might wait for a key to be pressed; a weather simulator's coordinator thread might wait for the worker threads calculating temperatures in each region to finish; or, in our Earth Visualizer example, a thread in charge of rendering part of the screen might wait for a user command or for new data to update the view.

In all of these cases, we want a thread to wait for some action to change the system state so that the thread can make progress.

poll   One way for a thread to wait would be to *poll*—to repeatedly check the shared state to see if it has changed. As shown in Figure 5.6, a polling implementation of remove would have a simple wrapper that repeatedly calls tryRemove until it returns success. Unfortunately, this approach is inefficient: the waiting thread continually loops, or busy-waits, consuming processor cycles without making useful progress. Worse, busy-waiting can delay the scheduling of other threads—perhaps exactly the thread for which the looping thread is waiting.

5.4.1   Condition Variable Definition

condition variable   A *condition variable* is a synchronization object that lets a thread efficiently wait for a change to shared state that is protected by a lock. A condition variable has three methods:

- **CV::wait(Lock *lock).** This call atomically *releases the lock* and *suspends execution of the calling thread*, placing the calling thread on the condition variable's waiting list. Later, when the calling thread is re-enabled, it *re-acquires the lock* before returning from the wait call.

- **CV::signal().** This call takes one thread off the condition variable's waiting list and marks it as eligible to run (i.e., it puts the thread on the scheduler's ready list). If no threads are on the waiting list, signal has no effect.

The sleep fix?

We often find that students want to "fix" the polling-based approach by adding a delay. For example, in Figure 5.6, we could add a call to sleep to yield the processor for (say) 100 ms after each unsuccessful tryRemove call. This would allow some other thread to run while the waiting thread is waiting.

This approach has two problems. First, although it reduces the inefficiency of polling, it does not eliminate it. Suspending and scheduling a thread imposes non-trivial overheads, and a program with many polling threads would still waste significant resources. Second, periodic polling adds latency. In our Earth Visualizer example, if the thread waiting for keyboard input waited 100 ms between each check, the application might become noticeably more sluggish.

As an extreme example, one of the authors once had an employee implement a network server that provided several layers of processing, where each layer had a thread that received work from the layer above and sent the work to the layer below. Measurements of the server showed surprisingly bad performance; we expected each request to take a few milliseconds, but instead each took just over half a second. Fortunately, the performance was so poor that it was easy to track down the problem: layers passed work to each other through bounded queues much like TSQueue, but the queue remove method was implemented as a polling loop with a 100 ms delay. With five such layers of processing, the server became unusable. Fortunately, the fix was simple: use condition variables instead.

- **CV::broadcast().** This call takes all threads off the condition variable's waiting list and marks them as eligible to run. If no threads are on the waiting list, broadcast has no effect.

WARNING   Note that condition variable wait and signal are different from the UNIX system calls wait and signal. The nomenclature is unfortunate but longstanding. In this book, we always use the terms, UNIX wait and UNIX signal, to refer to the UNIX variants, and simple wait and signal to refer to condition variable operations.

A condition variable is used to wait for a change to shared state, and a lock must always protect updates to shared state. Thus, the condition variable API is designed to work in concert with locks. All three methods (wait, signal, and broadcast) should only be called while the associated lock is held.

The standard design pattern for a shared object is a lock and zero or more condition variables. A method that waits using a condition variable works as shown on the left in Figure 5.7. In this code, the calling thread first acquires the lock and can then read and write the shared object's state variables. To wait until testOnSharedState succeeds, the thread calls wait on the shared object's

```
SharedObject :: someMethodThatWaits ( ) {          SharedObject :: someMethodThatSignals ( ) {
    lock . acquire ( ) ;                                lock . acquire ( ) ;

// Read and/ or write shared state here .          // Read and/ or write shared state here .

    while (!testOnSharedState ( ) ) {              // If state has changed in a way that
        cv . wait (& lock ) ;                       // could allow another thread to make
    }                                              // progress , signal ( or broadcast ) .
    assert ( testOnSharedState ( ) ) ;
                                                       cv . signal ( ) ;
// Read and/ or write shared state here .
                                                       lock . release ( ) ;
    lock . release ( ) ;                           }
}
```

Figure 5.7: Design patterns for waiting using a condition variable (left) and for waking up a waiter (right). Since many critical sections need to both wait and signal, these two design patterns are often combined in one method.

condition variable cv. This atomically puts the thread on the waiting list and releases the lock, allowing other threads to enter the critical section. Once the waiting thread is signaled, it re-acquires the lock and returns from wait. The monitor can then safely test the state variables to see if testOnSharedState succeeds. If so, the monitor performs its tasks, releases the lock, and returns.

The right hand side of Figure 5.7 shows the complementary code that causes a waiting thread to wake up. Whenever a thread changes the shared object's state in a way that enables a waiting thread to make progress, the thread must signal the waiting thread using the condition variable.

A thread waiting on a condition variable must inspect the object's state in a loop. The condition variable's wait method releases the lock (to let other threads change the state of interest) and then re-acquires the lock (to check that state again).

Similarly, the only reason for a thread to signal (or broadcast) is that it has just changed the shared state in a way that may be of interest to a waiting thread. To make a change to shared state, the thread must hold the lock on the state variables, so signal and broadcast are also always called while holding a lock.

Discussion. Condition variables have been carefully designed to work in tandem with locks and shared state. The precise definition of condition variables includes three properties worth additional comment:

Is the order of wait and signal significant?

- A condition variable is *memoryless*.

    The condition variable, itself, has no internal state other than a queue of waiting threads. Condition variables do not need their own state because they are always used inside shared objects that have their own state.

    If no threads are currently on the condition variable's waiting list, a signal or broadcast has no effect. No thread calls wait unless it holds the lock, checks the state variables, and finds that it needs to wait. Thus, the condition variable has no "memory" of earlier calls to signal or broadcast. After signal is called, if sometime later another thread calls wait, it will block until the *next* signal (or broadcast) is called, regardless of how many times signal has been called in the past.

Does the waiter release the lock, then put itself on the waiting list, or vice versa?

- *CV::wait atomically releases the lock.*

  A thread always calls wait while holding a lock. The call to wait *atomically* releases the lock and puts the thread on the condition variable's waiting list. Atomicity ensures that there is no separation between checking the shared object's state, deciding to wait, adding the waiting thread to the condition variable's queue, and releasing the lock so that some other thread can access the shared object.

  If threads released the lock before calling wait, they could miss a signal or broadcast and wait forever. Consider the case where thread T_1 checks an object's state and decides to wait, so it releases the lock in anticipation of putting itself on the condition variable's waiting list. At that precise moment, T_2 preempts T_1. T_2 acquires the lock, changes the object's state to what T_1 wants, and calls signal, but the waiting list is empty so the call to signal has no effect. Finally, T_1 runs again, puts itself on the waiting list, and suspends execution. The lack of atomicity means that T_1 missed the signal and is now waiting, potentially forever.

  Once wait releases the lock, any number of threads might run before wait re-acquires the lock after a signal. In the meantime, the state variables might have changed — in fact, they are almost *certain* to have changed. Code must not assume just because something was true before wait was called, it remains true when wait returns. The only assumption you should make on return from wait is that the lock is held, and the normal invariants that hold at the start of the critical section are true.

Is the shared state when signal is called exactly the same as when wait returns?

- When a waiting thread is re-enabled via signal or broadcast, *it may not run immediately.*

  When a waiting thread is re-enabled, it is moved to the scheduler's ready queue with no special priority, and the scheduler may run it at some later time. Furthermore, when the thread finally does run, it must re-acquire the lock, which means that other threads may have acquired and released the lock in the meantime, between when the signal occurs and when the waiter re-acquires the lock. Therefore, even if the desired predicate were true when signal or broadcast was called, it may no longer be true when wait returns.

  This may seem like a small window of vulnerability, but concurrent programs must work with all possible schedules. Otherwise, programs may fail sometimes, but not always, making debugging very difficult. See the sidebar on Mesa vs. Hoare semantics for a discussion of the history behind this property.

WARNING   The points above have an important implication for programmers: wait *must always be called from within a loop.*

Because wait releases the lock, and because there is no guarantee of atomicity between signal or broadcast and the return of a call to wait, there is no guarantee that the checked-for state still holds. Therefore, a waiting thread must always wait in a loop, rechecking the state until the desired predicate holds. Thus, the design pattern is:

```
...
while (predicateOnStateVariables(...)) {
  wait(&lock);
}
...
```

and not:

```
...
if (predicateOnStateVariables(...)) {
  wait(&lock);
}
...
```

There are two fundamental reasons why condition variables impose this requirement: to simplify the implementation and to improve modularity.

- **Simplifying the implementation.** When a waiting thread is re-enabled, it may not run immediately. Other threads may access the shared state before it runs, and the desired predicate on the shared state may no longer hold when wait finally does return.

  This behavior simplifies the implementation of condition variables without increasing the complexity of the code that uses them. No special code is needed for scheduling; signal puts the signaled thread onto the ready list and lets the scheduler choose when to run it. Similarly, no special code is needed to re-acquire the lock at the end of wait. The woken thread calls acquire when it is re-scheduled. As with any attempt to acquire a lock, it may succeed immediately, or it may wait if some other thread acquired the lock first.

  Some implementations go even further and warn that a call to wait may return even if no thread has called signal or broadcast. So, not only is it possible that the desired predicate on the state *is no longer true*, it is possible that the desired predicate on the state *was never true*. For example, the Java definition of condition variables allows for "spurious wakeups":

  > When waiting upon a Condition, a "spurious wakeup" is permitted to occur, in general, as a concession to the underlying

platform semantics. This has little practical impact on most application programs as a Condition should always be waited upon in a loop, testing the state predicate that is being waited for. An implementation is free to remove the possibility of spurious wakeups but it is recommended that applications programmers always assume that they can occur and so always wait in a loop.
(From http://download.oracle.com/docs/cd/E17476_01/javase/1.5.0/docs/api/index.html)

- **Improving modularity.** Waiting in a loop that checks the shared state makes shared objects' code more modular because we can reason about when the thread will continue by looking only at the wait loop. In particular, we do not need to examine the rest of the shared object's code to understand where and why calls to signal and broadcast are made to know the post-condition for the wait loop. For example, in Figure 5.7, we know the assert call will never fail without having to look at any other code.

  Not only does waiting in a loop simplify writing and reasoning about the code that waits, it simplifies writing and reasoning about the code that signals or broadcasts. Signaling at the wrong time will never cause a waiting thread to proceed when it should not. Signal and broadcast can be regarded as *hints* that it *might* be a good time to proceed; if the hints prove to be wrong, no damage is done. You can always convert a signal to a broadcast, or add any number of signal or broadcast calls, without changing the semantics of a shared object. Avoiding extra signal and broadcast calls may matter for performance, but not for correctness.

Bottom line: Given the range of possible implementations and the modularity benefits, wait must always be done from within a loop that tests the desired predicate.

5.4.2 Thread Life Cycle Revisited

Chapter 4 discussed how a thread can switch between the READY, WAITING, and RUNNING states. We now explain the WAITING state in more detail.

A RUNNING thread that calls wait is put in the WAITING state. This is typically implemented by moving the thread control block (TCB) from the ready list to the condition variable's list of waiting threads. Later, when some RUNNING thread calls signal or broadcast on that condition variable, one (if signal) or all (if broadcast) of the TCBs on that condition variable's waiting list are moved to the ready list. This changes those threads from the WAITING state to the READY state. At some later time, the scheduler selects a READY thread and runs it by moving it to the RUNNING state. Eventually, the signaled thread runs.

Mesa vs. Hoare semantics

In modern condition variables, signal or broadcast calls take waiting threads from a condition variable's waiting list and put them on the ready list. Later, when these threads are scheduled, they may block for some time while they try to re-acquire the lock. Thus, modern condition variables implement what are often called *Mesa Semantics* (for Mesa, an early programming language at Xerox PARC that implemented these semantics). Despite the name, Mesa was not the first system to use "Mesa" semantics; Brinch Hansen had proposed their use five years earlier. However, PARC was the first to use Mesa semantics extensively in a very large operating system, and the name stuck.

C.A.R. "Tony" Hoare proposed a different definition for condition variables. Under *Hoare semantics*, when a thread calls signal, execution of the signaling thread is suspended, the ownership of the lock is immediately transferred to one of the waiting threads, and execution of that thread is immediately resumed. Later, when the resumed thread releases the lock, ownership of the lock reverts to the signaling thread, whose execution continues.

Under Hoare semantics, signaling is atomic with the resumption of a waiting thread, and a signaled thread may assume that the state has not changed since the signal that woke it up was issued. Under Mesa semantics, waiting is always done in a loop: while (predicate()) {cv.wait(&lock);}. Under Hoare semantics, waiting can be done with a simple conditional: if (predicate()) {cv.wait(&lock);}.

Mesa semantics are much more widely used, but some argue that the atomicity of signaling and resuming a waiting process makes it easier to prove liveness properties of programs under Hoare semantics. If we know that one thread is waiting on a condition, and we do a signal, we know that the waiting thread (and not some other late-arriving thread) will resume and make progress.

The authors of this book come down strongly on the side of Mesa semantics. The modularity advantages of Mesa greatly simplify reasoning about an object's core safety properties. For the properties we care most about (i.e., the safety properties that threads proceed only when they are supposed to) and for large programs where modularity matters, Mesa semantics seem vastly preferable. Later in this chapter, we will explain how to implement FIFO queueing with Mesa semantics, for where liveness concerns are paramount.

As a practical matter the debate has been settled: essentially all systems, including both Java and POSIX, use Mesa semantics. We know of no widely used system that implements Hoare semantics. Programmers that assume the weaker Mesa semantics — always writing while (predicate()) — will write programs that work under either definition. The overhead of the "extra" check of the predicate upon return from wait in a while loop is unlikely to be significant compared to the signaling and scheduling overheads. As a programmer, you will not go wrong if you write your code assuming Mesa semantics.

```
// Thread-safe blocking queue.

const int MAX = 10;

class BBQ{
  // Synchronization variables
    Lock lock;
    CV itemAdded;
    CV itemRemoved;

  // State variables
    int items[MAX];
    int front;
    int nextEmpty;

  public:
    BBQ();
    ~BBQ() {};
    void insert(int item);
    int remove();
};


// Initialize the queue to empty,
// the lock to free, and the
// condition variables to empty.
BBQ::BBQ() {
    front = nextEmpty = 0;
}
```

```
// Wait until there is room and
// then insert an item.
void
BBQ::insert(int item) {
    lock.acquire();
    while ((nextEmpty - front) == MAX) {
        itemRemoved.wait(&lock);
    }
    items[nextEmpty % MAX] = item;
    nextEmpty++;
    itemAdded.signal();
    lock.release();
}

// Wait until there is an item and
// then remove an item.
int
BBQ::remove() {
    int item;

    lock.acquire();
    while (front == nextEmpty) {
        itemAdded.wait(&lock);
    }
    item = items[front % MAX];
    front++;
    itemRemoved.signal();
    lock.release();
    return item;
}
```

Figure 5.8: A thread-safe blocking bounded queue using Mesa-style condition variables.

Locks are similar. A lock acquire on a busy lock puts the caller into the WAITING state, with the caller's TCB on a list of waiting TCBs associated with the lock. Later, when the lock owner calls release, one waiting TCB is moved to the ready list, and that thread transitions to the READY state.

Notice that threads that are RUNNING or READY have their state located at a pre-defined, "global" location: the CPU (for a RUNNING thread) or the scheduler's list of ready threads (for a READY thread). However, threads that are WAITING typically have their state located on some per-lock or per-condition-variable queue of waiting threads. Then, a signal, broadcast, or release call can easily find and re-enable a waiting thread for that particular condition variable or lock.

5.4.3   Case Study: Blocking Bounded Queue

blocking bounded queue

We can use condition variables to implement a *blocking bounded queue,* one where a thread trying to remove an item from an empty queue will wait until an item is available, and a thread trying to put an item into a full queue will wait until there is room. Figure 5.8 defines the blocking bounded queue's interface and implementation.

As in TSQueue, we acquire and release the lock at the beginning and end of the public methods (e.g., insert and remove). Now, however, we can atomically release the lock and wait if there is no room in insert or no item in remove. Before returning, insert signals on itemAdded since a thread waiting in remove may now be able to proceed; similarly, remove signals on itemRemoved before it returns.

We signal rather than broadcast because each insert allows at most one remove to proceed, and vice versa.

EXAMPLE   What invariants hold when wait returns in BBQ:remove? Is an item guaranteed to be in the queue? Why or why not?

ANSWER   **Exactly the same invariants hold when wait returns as when the thread first acquired the lock.** These are the same constraints as listed earlier for the thread-safe (non-blocking) bounded queue TSQueue.

In particular, although there is always an item in the queue when insert calls signal, there is *no* guarantee that the item is still in the queue when wait returns. Even if the language runtime avoids spurious wakeups, some other thread may have run between the signal and the return from wait. That thread may perform a remove, acquire the BBQ::lock, find the item, and empty the queue, all before wait returns.   □

5.5 | Designing and Implementing Shared Objects

Given locks and condition variables, what is a good way to write and reason about the code for shared objects?

Although multi-threaded programming has a reputation for being difficult, shared objects provide a basis for writing simple, safe code for multi-threaded programs. In this section, we provide a methodology for writing correct multi-threaded code using shared objects.

- We first define a high-level approach to designing shared objects. Given a concurrent problem, where do you start? (Section 5.5.1)

- We provide six specific rules, or best practices, that you should always follow when writing multi-threaded shared objects. (Section 5.5.2)

- We describe three common pitfalls to multi-threading in C, C++, and Java code. (Section 5.5.3)

Our experience is that following this approach and these rules makes it much more likely that you will write code that is not only correct but also easy for others to read, understand, and maintain.

Of course, writing individual shared objects is not enough. Most programs have multiple shared objects, and new issues arise when combining them. But, before trying to compose multiple shared objects, we must make sure that each individual object works. Chapter 6 discusses the issues that arise when programs use multiple shared objects.

On simplicity

One of the themes running through this textbook is the importance of simple abstractions in building robust, reliable operating systems. Operating systems place a premium on reliability; if the operating system breaks, the computer becomes temporarily unusable, or worse. And yet, it is nearly impossible to fully test whether some piece of multi-threaded operating system code works under all possible conditions and all possible schedule interleavings. This places a premium on designing solutions that work the first time they are run, by keeping code simple.

Particularly with concurrent code, it is not enough for the code to work. It also needs to be simple enough to understand. We often find students write intricate concurrent code in solutions to our homework assignments and exams. Perhaps the difficulty of the topic suggests to students that their solutions must also be difficult to understand! Sometimes these solutions work; more often the complexity hides a design flaw.

Even if your code is literally correct, we would like to encourage you to not stop there. Is it easy to understand *why* your code works? If not, try again. Even if you can get the code to work this time, someone else may need to come along later and change it. For concurrent code to be maintainable over time, it is essential that the next developer to work on the code be able to understand it.

Yet, often in technology circles, simplicity is considered an insult. Someone might say, "Anyone could have done that!", meaning it as a put down. We take the other side: a simple design should be seen as a complement. Complexity should be introduced only where it is absolutely necessary. Consider three possible states for one of your designs (hat tip to John Ousterhout for this list):

- The code is simple enough that anyone can understand it. If someone says this to you, the appropriate response is to take it as a complement and reply, "Thank you."

- The code is so complicated that only the author can understand it. While this might be useful in the short-term as a strategy to keep the author employed (after all, no one else can fix or improve code without understanding it first), it is not such a good idea over the long term. Eventually, you will want to work on something new!

- The code is so complicated not even the author can understand it. Concurrent code often lands in this category, unnecessarily in our view. Using the rules we introduce in this section will help put your code in the first and not the last bucket.

5.5.1   High Level Methodology

Given a concurrent problem, where do you start?

A shared object has public methods, private methods, state variables, and synchronization variables; its synchronization variables include a lock and one or more condition variables. At this level, shared object programming resembles standard object-oriented programming, except that we have added synchronization variables to each shared object. This similarity is deliberate: the interfaces to locks and condition variables have been carefully defined so that we can continue to apply familiar techniques for programming and reasoning about objects.

Therefore, most high-level design challenges for a shared object's class are the same as for class design in single-threaded programming:

- Decompose the problem into objects.

- For each object:

    - Define a clean interface.

    - Identify the right internal state and invariants to support that interface.

    - Implement methods with appropriate algorithms to manipulate that state.

These steps require creativity and sound engineering judgment and intuition. Going from single-threaded to multi-threaded programming does not make these steps much more difficult.

Compared to how you implement a class in a single-threaded program, the new steps needed for the multi-threaded case for shared objects are straightforward:

1. Add a lock.

2. Add code to acquire and release the lock.

3. Identify and add condition variables.

4. Add loops to wait using the condition variables.

5. Add signal and broadcast calls.

We discuss each of these steps in turn.

Other than these fairly mechanical changes, writing the rest of your code proceeds as in the single-threaded case.

1. **Add a lock.** Each shared object needs a lock as a member variable to enforce mutually exclusive access to the object's shared state.

    This chapter focuses on the simple case where each shared object includes exactly one lock. In Chapter 6, we will talk about more advanced variations, such as an ownership design pattern where higher-level program structure enforces mutual exclusion by ensuring that at most one thread at a time owns and can access an object.

2. **Add code to acquire and release the lock.** All code accessing the object's shared state—any state shared across more than one thread—must hold the object's lock. Typically, all of an object's member variables are shared state.

   The simplest and most common approach is to acquire the lock at the start of each public method and release it at the end of each public method. Doing so makes it easy to inspect your code to verify that a lock is always held when needed. It also means that the lock is already held when each private method is called, and you do not need to re-acquire it.

WARNING   You may be tempted to try to avoid acquiring the lock in some methods or parts of some methods. Do not be tempted by this "optimization" until you are an experienced programmer and have done sufficient profiling of the code to verify that the optimization will significantly speed up your program, *and* you fully understand the hazards posed by compiler and architecture instruction re-ordering.

Acquiring an uncontended lock is a relatively inexpensive operation. By contrast, reasoning about memory interleavings can be quite difficult—and the instruction reordering done by modern compilers and processors makes it even harder. Later in this section, we discuss one commonly used (and abused) "optimization," double-checked locking, that is outright dangerous to use.

3. **Identify and add condition variables.** How do you decide what condition variables a shared object needs?

   A systematic way to approach this problem is to consider each method and ask, *"When can this method wait?"* Then, you can map each situation in which a method can wait to a condition variable.

   You have considerable freedom in deciding how many condition variables a class should have and what each should represent. A good option is to add a condition variable for each situation in which the method must wait.

EXAMPLE   **Blocking bounded queue with two condition variables.** In our blocking bounded queue example, if the queue is full, insert must wait until another thread removes an item, so we created a condition variable itemRemoved. Similarly, if the queue is empty, remove must wait until another thread inserts an item, so we created a condition variable itemAdded. It is natural in this case to create two condition variables, itemAdded to wait until the queue has items, and itemRemoved to wait until the queue has space.

Alternatively, a single condition variable can often suffice. In fact, early versions of Java defined a single condition variable per object and did not let programmers allocate additional ones. Using this approach, any thread that waits for any reason uses that condition variable; if the condition variable is used by different threads waiting for different reasons, then any thread that wakes up a thread must broadcast on the condition variable.

EXAMPLE **Blocking bounded queue with one condition variable.** It is also possible to implement the blocking bounded queue with a single condition variable, i.e., somethingChanged, on which threads in both insert or threads in remove can wait. With this approach, both insert and remove need to broadcast rather than signal to ensure that the right threads get a chance to run.

Programs that are more complex make these trade-offs more interesting. For example, imagine a ResourceManager class that allows a calling thread to request exclusive access to any subset of n distinct resources. One could imagine creating 2^n condition variables; this would let a requesting thread wait on a condition variable representing exactly its desired combination. However, it would be simpler to have a single condition variable on which requesting threads wait and to broadcast on that condition whenever a resource is freed. Depending on the number of resources and the expected number of waiting threads, this simpler approach may even be more efficient.

The bottom line is that there is no hard and fast rule for how many condition variables to use in a shared object. Selecting condition variables requires thought, and different designers may use different numbers of condition variables for a given class. Like many other design decisions, this is a matter of programmer taste, judgment, and experience. Asking "When can this method wait?" will help you identify what is for you a natural way of thinking about a shared object's condition variables.

4. **Add loops to wait using the condition variables.** Add a while(...) {cv.wait()} loop into each method that you identified as potentially needing to wait before returning.

   Remember that every call to wait must be enclosed in a while loop that tests an appropriate predicate. Modern implementations almost invariably provide Mesa semantics and often allow for spurious wakeups (i.e., a thread can return from wait even if no thread called signal or broadcast). Therefore, a thread must always check the condition before proceeding. Even if the condition was true when the signal or broadcast call occurred, it may no longer be true when the waiting thread resumes execution.

Modularity benefits. If you always wait in a while loop, your code becomes highly modular. You can look at the code that waits, and when it proceeds, know *without* examining any other code that the condition holds. Even erroneous calls to signal or broadcast will not change how the waiting code behaves.

For example, consider the assertion in the following code:

```
...
while (!workAvailable()) {
    cond.wait(&lock);
}
assert(workAvailable());
...
```

We know that the assertion holds by local inspection *without knowing anything about the code that calls signal or broadcast.*

Waiting in a while loop also makes the signal and broadcast code more robust. Adding an extra signal, or changing a signal to a broadcast, will not introduce bugs.

HINT **Top-down design.** As you start writing your code, you may know that a method needs to include a wait loop, but you may not know exactly what the predicate should be. In this situation, it is often useful to name a private method function that will perform the test (e.g., workAvailable in the preceding example) and write the code that defines the function later.

5. **Add signal and broadcast calls.** Just as you must decide when methods can wait, you must decide when methods can let other waiting threads proceed. It is usually easy to ask, "Can a call to this method allow another thread to proceed?" and then add a signal or broadcast call if the answer is yes. But which call should you use?

CV::signal is appropriate when: (1) at most one waiting thread can make progress, and (2) any thread waiting on the condition variable can make progress. In contrast, broadcast is needed when: (1) multiple waiting threads may all be able to make progress, or (2) different threads are using the same condition variable to wait for different predicates, so some of the waiting threads can make progress but others cannot.

EXAMPLE Consider the n-resource ResourceManager problem described earlier. For the solution with a single condition variable, we must broadcast on the condition variable whenever a resource is freed. We do not know which thread(s) can make progress, so we tell them all to check. If, instead, we used signal, then the "wrong" thread might receive the signal, and a thread that could make progress might remain blocked.

It is always safe to use broadcast. Even in cases where signal would suffice, at worst, all of the waiting threads would run and check the condition in the while loop, but only one would continue out of the loop. Compared to signal, this would consume some additional resources, but it would not introduce any bugs.

5.5.2   Implementation Best Practices

What rules should we follow to write simple, safe code with shared objects?

Above, we described the basic thought process you should follow when designing a shared object. To make things more concrete, we next give a set of six simple rules that we strongly advocate you follow; these are a set of "best practices" for writing code for shared objects.

1. **Consistent structure.** The first rule is a meta-rule that underlies the other five rules: *follow a consistent structure.* Although programming with a clean, consistent structure is always useful, it is particularly important to strictly follow tried-and-true design patterns for shared objects.

   At a minimum, even if one way is not inherently better than another, following the same strategy every time: (1) frees you to focus on the core problem because the details of the standard approach become a habit, and (2) makes it easier for those who follow to review, maintain, and debug your code. (And it will make it easier for *you* to maintain and debug your code.)

   As an analogy, electricians follow standards for the colors of wire they use for different tasks. White is neutral. Black or red is hot. Copper is ground. An electrician does not have to decide "Hm. I have a bit more white on my belt today than black, should I use white or black for my grounds?" When an electrician walks into a room she wired last month, she does not have to spend time trying to remember which color is which. If an electrician walks into a room she has never seen before, she can immediately determine what the wiring is doing, without having to trace it back into the switchboard. Similar advantages apply to coding standards.

   However, for concurrent programs, the evidence is that the abstractions we describe *are* better than almost all others. Until you become a *very* experienced concurrent programmer, take advantage of the hard-won experience of those that have come before you. Once you are a concurrency guru, you are welcome to invent a better mousetrap.

   Sure, you can cut corners and occasionally save a line or two of typing by departing from the standards. However, you will have to spend a few minutes thinking to convince yourself that you are right on a case-by-case basis (and another few minutes typing comments to convince the next person to look at the code that you are right), and a few hours or weeks tracking down bugs when you are wrong. It is just not worth it.

Coding standards, soapboxes, and preaching

Some programmers rebel against coding standards. We do not understand their logic. For concurrent programming in particular, a few good design patterns have stood the test of time (and many unhappy people who have departed from those patterns). For concurrent programming, *debugging does not work*. You must rely on: (a) writing correct code, and (b) writing code that you and others can read and understand — not just for now, but also over time as the code changes. Following the rules we provide will help you write correct, readable code.

When we teach multi-threaded programming, we treat the six rules described in this section as *required coding standards* for all multi-threaded code that students write in our course. We say, "We cannot control what you do when you leave this class, but while you are in this class, any solution that violates these standards is, by definition, *wrong*."

In fact, we feel so strongly about these rules that one of us actually presents them in class by standing on a table and pronouncing them as the Six Commandments of multi-threaded programming:

1. Thou shalt always do things the same way

and so on.

The particular formulation (and presentation) of these rules evolved from our experience teaching multi-threaded programming dozens of times to hundreds of students and identifying common mistakes. We have found that when we insist that students follow these rules, the vast majority find it easy to write clear and correct code for shared objects. Conversely, in earlier versions of the course, when we phrased these items as "strong suggestions," many students found themselves adrift, unable to write code for even the simplest shared objects.

Our advice to those learning multi-threaded programming is to treat these rules as a given and follow them strictly for a semester or so, until writing shared objects is easy. At that point, you most likely will understand concurrent programming well enough to decide whether to continue to follow the rules.

We also believe that experienced programmers benefit from adhering closely to these rules. Since we began teaching them, we have also disciplined ourselves to follow them unless there is a very good reason not to. We have found exceptions to be rare. Conversely, when we catch ourselves being tempted to deviate from the rules, the vast majority of the time our code improves if we force ourselves to rewrite the code to follow the rules.

Although the rules may come across as opinionated (and they are), they are far from novel. Over three decades ago, Lampson and Redell's paper, "Experience with Processes and Monitors in Mesa," provided similar advice (in a more measured tone).

2. **Always synchronize with locks and condition variables.**

Many operating systems, such as Linux, Windows, and MacOS, provide a diversity of synchronization primitives. At the end of this chapter, we will describe one such primitive, semaphores, which is particularly widely used in operating system kernel implementations. Compared to locks and condition variables, semaphores are equally powerful: you can build condition variables using semaphores and vice versa. If so, why pick one over the other?

We recommend that you be able to read and understand semaphores so you can understand legacy code, but that you only write new code using locks and condition variables. Almost always, code using locks and condition variables is clearer than the equivalent code using semaphores because it is more "self-documenting." If the code is well structured, what each synchronization action is doing should be obvious. Admittedly, semaphores sometimes seem to fit what you are doing perfectly because you can map the object's invariants exactly onto the internal state of the semaphore; for example, you can write an extremely concise version of our blocking bounded queue using semaphores. But what happens when the code changes next month? Will the fit remain as good? For consistency and simplicity, choose one of the two styles and stick with it. In our opinion, the right one is to use locks and condition variables.

3. **Always acquire the lock at the beginning of a method and release it right before the return.**

This extends the principle of consistent structure: pick one way to do things and always follow it. The benefit here is that it is easy to read code and see where the lock is or is not held because synchronization is structured on a method-by-method basis. Conversely, if acquire and release calls are buried in the middle of a method, it is harder to quickly inspect and understand the code.

Taking a step back, if there is a logical chunk of code that you can identify as a set of actions that require a lock, then that section should probably be its own procedure: it is a set of logically related actions. If you find yourself wanting to acquire a lock in the middle of a procedure, that is usually a red flag that you should break the piece you are considering into a separate procedure. We are all sometimes lazy about creating new procedures when we should. Take advantage of this signal, and the result will be clearer code.

There are two corollaries to this rule. First, if your code is well structured, all shared data will be encapsulated in an object, and therefore all accesses to shared data will be protected by a lock. Since compilers and processors *never* re-order instructions across lock operations, this rule guarantees instruction re-ordering is not a concern for your code.

Second, from time to time, we see students attempting to acquire a lock in one procedure, and release it in another procedure, or worse, in a completely different thread. (One popular idea is to acquire a lock in a parent thread, pass it in thread_fork to a child, and have the child release the lock after it has started.) *Do not do this.* For one, it can make it very difficult for someone reading your code to determine which shared variables are protected by which lock; by acquiring at the beginning of the procedure and releasing at the end, which variables go with which locks is obvious.

While some early thread systems allowed lock passing, most recently designed systems prohibit it. For example, in POSIX, lock release is "undefined" when called by a different thread than the thread that acquired the lock. In other words, it might work on some systems, but it is not portable. In Java, it is completely prohibited.

4. **Always hold the lock when operating on a condition variable.**

   The reason you signal on a condition variable — after manipulating shared state — is that another thread is waiting in a loop for some test on shared state to become true. Condition variables are useless without shared state, and shared state should only be accessed while holding a lock.

   Many libraries enforce this rule — that you cannot call condition variable methods unless you hold the corresponding lock. However, some run-time systems and libraries allow sloppiness, so take care.

5. **Always wait in a while() loop**

   The pattern should always be:

   ```
   while (predicateOnStateVariables (...)) {
       condition ->wait(&lock);
   }
   ```

   and never:

   ```
   if (predicateOnStateVariables (...)) {
       condition ->wait(&lock);
   }
   ```

   Here, predicateOnStateVariables(...) is code that looks at the state variables of the current object to decide if the thread should proceed.

   You may be tempted to guard a wait call with an if conditional rather than a while loop when you can deduce from the global structure of the program that, despite Mesa semantics, any time a thread returns from wait, it can proceed. Avoid this temptation.

While works any time if does, and it works in situations when if does not. By the principle of consistent structure, do things the same way every time. But there are three additional issues.

- Using if breaks modularity. In the preceding example, to know whether using if will work, you must consider the global structure of the program: what threads there are, where signal is called, etc. The problem is that a change in code in one method (say, adding a signal) can then cause a bug in another method (where the wait is). Using while is self-documenting; anyone can look at the wait and see exactly when a thread may proceed.

- Always using while gives you incredible freedom about where to put a signal. In fact, signal becomes a hint — you can add a signal to an arbitrary place in a correct program and have it remain correct.

- Using if breaks portability. Some implementations of condition variables allow spurious wakeups, while others do not. For example, implementations of condition variables in both Java and the POSIX pthreads library are allowed to return from wait even though no thread called signal or broadcast.

6. **(Almost) never use thread_sleep.**

   Many thread libraries have a thread_sleep function that suspends execution of the calling thread for some period of wall clock time. Once that time passes, the thread is returned to the scheduler's ready queue and can run again.

   Never use thread_sleep to have one thread wait for another thread to perform a task. The correct way to wait for a condition to become true is to wait on a condition variable.

   In general, thread_sleep is appropriate only when there is a particular real-time moment when you want to perform some action, such as a timeout for when to declare a remote server non-responsive. If you catch yourself writing while(testOnObjectState() {thread_sleep();}, treat this as a red flag that you are probably making a mistake.

   Similarly, if a thread must wait for an object's state to change, it should wait on a condition variable, and not just call thread_yield. Use thread_yield only when a low-priority thread *that can still make progress* wants to let a higher-priority thread to run.

5.5.3   Three Pitfalls

We next describe three common pitfalls. The first, double-checked locking, is a problem in many different programming languages, including C, C++ and Java. The second and third pitfalls are specific to Java. Java is a modern type-safe language that included support for threads from its inception. This built-in support makes multi-threaded programming in Java convenient. However, some aspects of the language are *too* flexible and can encourage bad practices. We highlight those pitfalls here.

1. **Double-Checked Locking.**

We strongly advise holding a shared object's lock across any method that accesses the object's member variables. Programmers are often tempted to avoid some of these lock acquire and release operations. Unfortunately, such efforts often result in code that is complex, wrong, or both.

**double-checked
locking**

*This example and
analysis is taken from
Meyers and
Alexandrescu, "C++
and the Perils of
Double-Checked
Locking."*

To illustrate the challenges, consider the *double-checked locking* design pattern. The canonical example is an object that is allocated and initialized lazily the first time it is needed by any thread. Being good programmers, we can hide the lazy allocation inside an object, Singleton, which returns a pointer to the object, creating it if needed.

The "optimization" is to acquire the lock if the object has not already been allocated, but to avoid acquiring the lock if the object already exists. Because there can be a race condition between the first check and acquiring the lock, the check must be made again inside the lock.

```
class Singleton {                        // BUG!  DON'T DO THIS!
  public:                                Singleton*
    static Singleton* instance();        Singleton::instance() {
    Lock lock;                             if (pInstance == NULL) {
    ...                                        lock.acquire();
  private:                                     if (pInstance == NULL){
    static Singleton* pInstance;                   pInstance = new Instance();
};                                             }
                                               lock.release();
Singleton* Singleton::pInstance = NULL;    }
                                           return pInstance;
                                         }
```

Although the intuition is appealing, **this code does not work.** The problem is that the statement pInstance = new Instance() is not an atomic operation; in fact, it comprises at least three steps:

a) Allocate memory for a Singleton object.

b) Initialize the Singleton object's memory by running the constructor.

c) Make pInstance point to this newly constructed object.

The problem is that modern compilers and hardware architectures can reorder these events. Thus, it is possible for thread 1 to execute the first step and then the third step; then thread 2 can call instance, see that pInstance is non-null, return it, and begin using this object before thread 1 finishes initializing it.

Discussion.   This is just an example of dangers that lurk when you try to elide locks; the lesson applies more broadly. This example is extremely simple — fewer than 10 lines of code with very simple logic — yet a number of published solutions have been wrong. As Meyers and Alexandrescu note, some tempting solutions using temporary variables and the volatile keyword do not work. Bacon et al.'s "The 'Double-Checked Locking is Broken' Declaration" discusses a range of non-solutions in Java.

There are (non-portable) solutions in C/C++, but we do not present them here. To try these advanced techniques, first read the literature for more in-depth discussions so that you deeply understand the issues and why various appealing "solutions" fail.

This type of optimization is risky and often does not provide significant performance gains in practice. Most programmers should not consider them. Even expert programmers should habitually stick to simpler programming patterns, like the ones we have discussed, and only consider optimizations like double-checked locking when performance measurements and profiling indicate that the optimizations would significantly improve overall performance.

2. **Avoid defining a synchronized block in the middle of a method.**

Java provides built in language support for shared objects. The base Object class, from which all classes inherit, includes a lock and a condition variable as members. Any method declaration can include the keyword synchronized to indicate that the object's lock is to be automatically acquired on entry to the method and automatically released on any return from the method. For example:

```
public synchronized foo() {
    // Do something; lock is automatically acquired/released.
}
```

This syntax is useful — it follows rule #2 above, and it frees the programmer from having to worry about details, like making sure the lock is released before every possible return point including exceptions. The pitfall is that Java also allows a *synchronized block* in the middle of a method. For example:

```
public bar() {
    // Do something without holding the lock
    synchronized {
        // Do something while holding the lock
    }
    // Do something without holding the lock
}
```

This construct violates rule #2 from Section 5.5.2 and suffers from the disadvantages listed there. The solution is the same as discussed above: when you find yourself tempted to write a synchronized block in the middle of a Java method, treat that as a strong hint that you should define a separate method to more clearly encapsulate the logical chunk you have identified.

3. **Keep shared state classes separate from thread classes.**

   Java defines a class called Thread that implements an interface called Runnable that other classes can implement in order to be treated as threads by the runtime system. To write the code that represents a thread's "main loop," you typically extend the Thread class or implement a class that implements Runnable.

   The pitfall is that, when extending the Thread class (or writing a new class that implements Runnable), you may be tempted to include not only the thread's main loop but also state to be shared across multiple threads, blurring the lines between the threads and the shared objects. This is almost always confusing.

   For example, for a blocking bounded queue, rather than defining two classes, BBQ for the shared queue and WorkerThread for the threads, you may be tempted to combine the two into a single class — for example, a queue with an associated worker thread. If this sounds confusing, it is, but it is a pitfall that we frequently see in student code.

   The solution is simple. Always make sure threads and shared objects are defined in separate classes. State that can be accessed by multiple threads, locks, and condition variables should never appear in any Java class that extends Thread or implements Runnable.

5.6 | Three Case Studies

Can we use the methodology described above to solve real-life concurrency problems?

The best way to learn how to program concurrently is to practice. Multi-threaded programming is an important skill, and we anticipate that almost everyone reading this book will over time need to write many multi-threaded programs. To help get you started, this section walks through several examples.

5.6.1 Readers/Writers Lock

readers/writers lock

Can we allow multiple threads simultaneous read-only access to shared data?

First, we implement a *readers/writers lock*. Like a normal mutual exclusion lock, a readers/writers lock (RWLock) protects shared data. However, it makes the following optimization. To maximize performance, an RWLock allows multiple "reader" threads to simultaneously access the shared data. Any number of threads can safely read shared data at the same time, as long as no thread is modifying the data. However, only one "writer" thread may hold the RWLock at any one time. (While a "reader" thread is restricted to only read access, a "writer" thread may read *and* write the data structure.) When a writer thread holds the RWLock, it may safely modify the data, as the lock guarantees that no other thread (whether reader or writer) may simultaneously hold the

Optimizing for the common case

Reader/writer locks are an example of an important principle in the design of computer systems: optimizing for the common case. Performance optimizations often have the side effect of making the code more complex to understand and reason about. Code that is more complex is more likely to be buggy, and more likely to have new bugs introduced as features are added. How do we decide when an optimization is worth the cost?

One approach is to profile your code. Then, *and only then*, optimize the code paths that are frequently used.

In the case of locks, it is obviously simpler to use a regular mutual exclusion lock. Replacing a mutual exclusion lock with a reader-writer lock is appropriate when both of the following are true: (i) there is substantial contention for the mutual exclusion lock and (ii) a substantial majority of the accesses are read-only. In other words, it is only appropriate to use if it would make a significant difference.

---

lock. The mutual exclusion is thus between any writer and any other writer, and between any writer and *the set* of readers.

Reader-writer locks are very commonly used in databases, where they are used to support faster search queries over the database, while also supporting less frequent database updates. Another common use is inside the operating system kernel, where core data structures are often read by many threads and only infrequently updated.

To generalize our mutual exclusion lock into a readers/writers lock, we implement a new kind of a new kind of shared object, RWLock, to guard access to the shared data and to enforce these rules. The RWLock is implemented using our standard synchronization building blocks: mutual exclusion locks and condition variables.

A thread that wants to (atomically) read the shared data proceeds as follows:

```
rwLock->startRead();
// Read shared data
rwLock->doneRead();
```

Similarly, a thread that wants to (atomically) write the shared data does the following:

```
rwLock->startWrite();
// Read and write shared data
rwLock->doneWrite();
```

```
class RWLock{                                    public:
   private:                                         RWLock();
      // Synchronization variables                  ~RWLock() {};
      Lock lock;                                    void startRead();
      CV readGo;                                    void doneRead();
      CV writeGo;                                   void startWrite();
                                                    void doneWrite();
      // State variables
      int activeReaders;                        private:
      int activeWriters;                           bool readShouldWait();
      int waitingReaders;                          bool writeShouldWait();
      int waitingWriters;                    };
```

Figure 5.9: The interface and member variables for our readers/writers lock.

To design the RWLock class, we begin by defining its interface (already done in this case) and its shared state. For the state, it is useful to keep enough data to allow a precise characterization of the object; especially when debugging, having too much state is better than having too little. Here, the object's behavior is fully characterized by the number of threads reading or writing and the number of threads waiting to read or write, so we have chosen to keep four integers to track these values. Figure 5.9 shows the members of and interface to the RWLock class.

Next, we add synchronization variables by asking, "When can methods wait?" First, we add a mutual exclusion lock: the RWLock methods must wait whenever another thread is accessing the RWLock state variables. Next, we observe that startRead or startWrite may have to wait, so we add a condition variable for each case: readGo and writeGo.

RWLock::doneRead and doneWrite do not wait (other than to acquire the mutual exclusion lock). Therefore, these methods do not need any additional condition variables.

We can now implement RWLock. Figure 5.10 shows the complete solution, which we develop in a few simple steps. Much of what we need to do is almost automatic.

- Since we always acquire/release mutual exclusion locks at the beginning/end of a method (and never in the middle), we can write calls to acquire and release the mutual exclusion lock at the start and end of each public method before even thinking in detail about what these methods do.

At this point, startRead and doneRead look like this:

```
void RWLock::startRead() {          void RWLock::doneRead() {
   lock.acquire();                     lock.acquire();



   lock.release()                      lock.release()
}                                   }
```

RWLock::startWrite and RWLock::doneWrite are similar.

- Since we know startRead and startWrite may have to wait, we can write a while(...){wait(...);} loop in the middle of each. In fact, we can defer thinking about the details by inserting a private method to be defined later, as the predicate for the while loop (e.g., readShouldWait and writeShouldWait).

At this point, startRead looks like this:

```
void RWLock::startRead() {
    lock.acquire();

    while (readShouldWait()) {
        readGo.Wait(&lock);
    }

    lock.release();
}
```

RWLock::StartWrite() looks similar.

Now things get a bit more complex. We can add code to track activeReaders, activeWriters, waitingReaders, and waitingWriters. Since we hold mutual exclusion locks in all of the public methods, this is easy to do. For example, a call to startRead initially increments the number of waiting readers; when the thread gets past the while loop, the number of waiting readers is decremented, but the number of active readers is incremented.

When reads or writes finish, it may become possible for waiting threads to proceed. We therefore need to add signal or broadcast calls to doneRead and doneWrite. The simplest solution would be to broadcast on both readGo and writeGo in each method, but that would be both inefficient and (to our taste) less clear about how the class actually works.

Instead, we observe that in doneRead, when a read completes, there are two interesting cases: (a) no writes are pending, and nothing needs to be done since this read cannot prevent other reads from proceeding, or (b) a write is pending, and this is the last active read, so one write can proceed. In case (b), we use signal since at most one write can proceed, and any write waiting on the condition variable can proceed.

Our code for startRead and doneRead is now done:

```
void RWLock::startRead() {          void RWLock::doneRead() {
    lock.acquire();                     lock.acquire();
    waitingReaders++;                   activeReaders--;
    while (readShouldWait()) {          if (activeReaders == 0
        readGo.Wait(&lock);                 && waitingWriters > 0) {
    }                                       writeGo.signal();
    waitingReaders--;                   }
    activeReaders++;                    lock.release();
    lock.release();                 }
}
```

Code for startWrite and doneWrite is similar. For doneWrite, if there are any pending writes, we signal on writeGo. Otherwise, we broadcast on readGo.

Finally, we need to define the readShouldWait and writeShouldWait predicates. Here, we implement a *writers preferred* solution: reads should wait if there are any active or pending writers, while writes wait only while there are active readers or active writers. Otherwise, a continuous stream of new readers could starve a write request and prevent if from ever being serviced.

```
bool
RWLock::readShouldWait() {
    return (activeWriters > 0 || waitingWriters > 0);
}
```

The code for writeShouldWait is similar.

Since readShouldWait and writeShouldWait are private methods that are always called from public methods that hold the mutual exclusion lock, they do not need to acquire the lock.

Figure 5.10 gives the full code. This solution may not be to your taste. You may decide to use more or fewer condition variables, use different state variables to implement different invariants, or change when to call signal or broadcast. The shared object approach allows designers freedom in these dimensions.

5.6.2 Synchronization Barriers

Can we keep threads operating on the same step of a data parallel algorithm?

With data parallel programming, as we explained in Chapter 4, the computation executes in parallel across a data set, with each thread operating on a different partition of the data. Once all threads have completed their work, they can safely use each other's results in the next (data parallel) step in the algorithm. MapReduce is an example of data parallel programming, but there are many other systems with the same structure.

synchronization barrier

For this to work, we need an efficient way to check whether all n threads have finished their work. This is called a *synchronization barrier*. It has one operation, checkin. A thread calls checkin when it has completed its work; no thread may return from checkin until *all* n threads have checked in. Once all threads have checked in, it is safe to use the results of the previous step.

Note that a synchronization barrier is different from a memory barrier, defined earlier in the chapter. A synchronization barrier is called concurrently by many threads; the barrier prevents any thread from proceeding until all threads reach the barrier. A memory barrier is called by one thread, to prevent the thread from proceeding until all memory operations that occur before the barrier have completed and are visible to other threads.

An implementation of MapReduce using a synchronization barrier might look like the code in Figure 5.11.

An alternative to using a synchronization barrier would be to create n threads at each step; the main thread could then call thread_join on each thread

```
// Wait until no active or waiting          // Wait until no active read or
// writes, then proceed.                    // write then proceed.
void RWLock::startRead() {                  void RWLock::startWrite() {
    lock.acquire();                             lock.acquire();
    waitingReaders++;                           waitingWriters++;
    while (readShouldWait()) {                  while (writeShouldWait()) {
        readGo.Wait(&lock);                         writeGo.Wait(&lock);
    }                                           }
    waitingReaders--;                           waitingWriters--;
    activeReaders++;                            activeWriters++;
    lock.release();                             lock.release();
}                                           }

// Done reading. If no other active         // Done writing. A waiting write or
// reads, a write may proceed.              // read may proceed.
void RWLock::doneRead() {                    void
    lock.acquire();                         RWLock::doneWrite() {
    activeReaders--;                            lock.acquire();
    if (activeReaders == 0                      activeWriters--;
          && waitingWriters > 0) {              assert(activeWriters == 0);
        writeGo.signal();                       if (waitingWriters > 0) {
    }                                               writeGo.signal();
    lock.release();                             }
}                                               else {
                                                    readGo.broadcast();
// Read waits if any active or waiting           }
// write ("writers preferred").                 lock.release();
bool                                        }
RWLock::readShouldWait() {
    return (activeWriters > 0               // Write waits for active read or write.
              || waitingWriters > 0);       bool
}                                           RWLock::writeShouldWait() {
                                                return (activeWriters > 0
                                                          || activeReaders > 0);
                                            }
```

Figure 5.10: An implementation of a readers/writers lock.

to ensure its completion. While this would be correct, it might be inefficient. Not only would n new threads need to be started at each step, the partitioning of work among threads would also need to be redone each time. Frequently, each thread in a data parallel computation can work on the same data repeatedly over many steps, maximizing the efficiency of the hardware processor cache.

We can derive an implementation for a synchronization barrier in the same way as we described above for the readers/writers lock.

- We create a Barrier class, with a lock to protect its internal state variables: how many have checked in so far (count), and how many we are expecting (numThreads).

- We acquire the lock at the beginning of checkin, and we release it at the end.

Single stepping and model checking your code

Suppose you have written some concurrent code, and you would like to verify that the solution behaves as you expect. One thing you should *always* do — whether for sequential or concurrent code — is to use a debugger to single step through the code on various inputs, to verify that the program logic is doing what you expect it to do, and do the variables have the values you expect.

This is especially useful for concurrent programs. Since the program must work for any possible thread schedule, you can use the debugger to consider what happens when threads are interleaved in different ways. Does your program logic still do what you expect?

For example, for the RWLock class, you can:

- Start a single reader. Does it go all the way through? Obviously, it should not wait, since no one has the lock and there are no writers. When it finishes readDone, are the state variables back to their initial state?

- Start a writer, and after it acquires the mutual exclusion lock, start a reader. Does it wait for the lock? When the writer finishes startWrite, does the reader proceed and then wait for the writer to call doneWrite? Does the reader proceed after that?

- Start a reader, followed by a writer, followed by another reader. And so forth.

We encourage you to do this for the examples in this section. The examples are short enough that you can execute them by hand, but we also provide code if you want to try this in a debugger.

A more systematic approach is called model checking. To fully verify that a concurrent program does what it was designed to do, a model checker enumerates all possible sequences of operations, and tries each one in turn. Since this could result in a nearly infinite number of possible tests even for a fairly simple program, to be practical model checking needs to reduce the search space. For code that follows our guidelines — with locks to protect shared data — the exact ordering of instructions is no longer important. For example, preempting a thread that holds a lock is immaterial to the behavior of the program.

Rather, the behavior of the program depends on the sequence of synchronization instructions: which thread is first to acquire the lock, which thread waits on a condition variable, and so forth. Thus, a model checker can proceed in two steps: first verify that there are no unlocked accesses to shared data, and then enumerate various sequences of synchronization operations. Even with this, the number of possibilities can be prohibitively large, and so typically the model checker will verify however many different interleavings it can within some time limit.

```
Create n threads.
Create barrier.

Each thread executes map operation in parallel.
barrier.checkin();

Each thread sends data in parallel to reducers.
barrier.checkin();

Each thread executes reduce operation in parallel.
barrier.checkin();
```

Figure 5.11: An implementation of MapReduce using synchronization barriers.

```
// A single use synch barrier.          // No one returns until all threads
class Barrier{                          // have called checkin.
  private:                              void
    // Synchronization variables        checkin() {
    Lock lock;                              lock.acquire();
    CV allCheckedIn;                        numEntered++;
                                            if (numEntered < numThreads) {
    // State variables                          while (numEntered < numThreads)
    int numEntered;                                 allCheckedIn.wait(&lock);
    int numThreads;                         } else { // last thread to checkin
                                                allCheckedIn.broadcast();
  public:                                   }
    Barrier(int n);                         lock.release();
    ~Barrier();                         }
    void checkin();
};

Barrier::Barrier(int n) {
    numEntered = 0;
    numThreads = n;
}
```

Figure 5.12: Candidate implementation of a synchronization barrier. With this implementation, each instance of a barrier can be safely used only one time.

- Since threads may have to wait in checkin, we need a condition variable, allCheckedIn.

- We put the wait in a while loop, checking if all n threads have checked in yet.

- The last thread to checkin does a broadcast to wake up all of the waiters.

Figure 5.12 gives the full implementation. Note that we still use a while loop, even though the signal means that the thread can safely exit checkin. There is no harm in using a while statement, and it protects against the possibility of the runtime library issuing spurious wakeups.

Can we implement a re-usable synchronization barrier?   The design is straightforward, but a problem is that the barrier can only be

```
// A re-usable synch barrier.
class Barrier{
  private:
    // Synchronization variables
    Lock lock;
    CV allCheckedIn;
    CV allLeaving;

    // State variables
    int numEntered;
    int numLeaving;
    int numThreads;

  public:
    Barrier(int n);
    ~Barrier();
    void checkin();
};

Barrier::Barrier(int n) {
    numEntered = 0;
    numLeaving = 0;
    numThreads = n;
}
```

```
// No one returns until all threads
// have called checkin.
void
checkin() {
    lock.acquire();
    numEntered++;
    if (numEntered < numThreads) {
        while (numEntered < numThreads)
        allCheckedIn.wait(&lock);
    } else {
    // no threads in allLeaving.wait
        numLeaving = 0;
        allCheckedIn.broadcast();
    }
    numLeaving++;
    if (numLeaving < numThreads) {
        while (numLeaving < numThreads)
        allLeaving.wait(&lock);
    } else {
    // no threads in allCheckedIn.wait
        numEntered = 0;
        allLeaving.broadcast();
    }
    lock.release();
}
```

Figure 5.13: Implementation of a re-usable synchronization barrier.

used once. One way to see this is that the state of the barrier does not revert to the same state it had when it was created. Implementing a reusable barrier is a bit more subtle.

- The *first* thread to leave (the one that wakes up the other threads) cannot reset the state, because until the other threads have woken up, the state is needed so that they know to exit the while loop.

- The *last* thread to leave the barrier cannot reset the state for the next iteration, because there is a possible race condition. Suppose a thread finishes checkin and calls checkin on the next barrier *before* the last thread wakes up and leaves the previous barrier. In that case, the thread would find that n threads have already checked in (because the state hasn't been reset), and so it would think it is "ok to proceed!"

A simple way to implement a re-usable barrier is to use two single-use barriers. The first barrier ensures that all threads are checked in, and the second ensures that all threads have woken up from allCheckedIn.wait. The nth thread to leave can safely reset numCheckedIn; the nth thread to call checkin can safely reset numLeaving. Figure 5.13 gives the result.

5.6.3   FIFO Blocking Bounded Queue

How can we implement FIFO queues using Mesa semantics?

Assuming Mesa semantics for condition variables, our implementation of the thread-safe blocking bounded queue in Figure 5.8 does not guarantee freedom from starvation. For example, a thread may call remove and wait in the while loop because the queue is empty. Starvation would occur if every time another thread inserts an item into the queue, a *different* thread calls remove, acquires the lock, sees that the queue is full, and removes the item before the waiting thread resumes.

Often, starvation is not a concern. For example, if we have one thread putting items into the queue, and n equivalent worker threads removing items from the queue, it may not matter which of the worker threads goes first. Even if starvation is a concern, as long as calls to insert and remove are infrequent, or the buffer is rarely empty or full, every thread is highly likely to make progress.

Suppose, however, we do need a thread-safe bounded buffer that does guarantee progress to all threads. We can more formally define the liveness constraint as:

- **Starvation-freedom.** If a thread waits in insert, then it is guaranteed to proceed after a bounded number of remove calls complete, and vice versa.

- **First-in-first-out (FIFO).** A stronger constraint is that the queue is first-in-first-out, or FIFO. The nth thread to acquire the lock in remove retrieves the item inserted by the nth thread to acquire the lock in insert.

Under Hoare semantics, the implementation in Figure 5.8 is FIFO, and therefore also starvation-free, provided that signal wakes up the thread waiting the longest.

Here we consider a related question: can we implement a starvation-free or FIFO bounded buffer using Mesa semantics? We need to ensure that when one thread signals a waiter, the waiting thread (and not any other) removes the item.

The easiest way to do this is to create a condition variable for each separate waiting thread. Then, you can be precise as to which thread to wake up! Although you might be worried that this would be space inefficient, on modern computer systems a condition variable (or lock) takes up just a few words of DRAM; it is small compared to the rest of the storage needed per thread.

The outline of the solution is as follows:

- Create a condition variable for every waiter.

- Put condition variables on a queue in FIFO order.

- Signal wakes up the thread at the front of the queue.

- Be CAREFUL about spurious wakeups!

```
ConditionQueue insertQueue;
ConditionQueue removeQueue;
int numRemoveCalled = 0; // # of times remove has been called
int numInsertCalled = 0; // # of times insert has been called

int
FIFOBBQ::remove() {
    int item;
    int myPosition;
    CV *myCV, *nextWaiter;

    lock.acquire();

    myPosition = numRemoveCalled++;
    mycv = new CV;   // Create a new condition variable to wait on.
    removeQueue.append(myCV);

// Even if I am woken up, wait until it is my turn.
    while (front < myPosition || front == nextEmpty) {
        mycv->Wait(&lock);
    }

    delete self;     // The condition variable is no longer needed.
    item = items[front % size];
    front++;

// Wake up the next thread waiting in insert, if any.
    nextWaiter = insertQueue.removeFromFront();
    if (nextWaiter != NULL)
        nextWaiter->Signal(&lock);
    lock.release();
    return item;
}
```

Figure 5.14: An implementation of FIFO Blocking Bounded Buffer using Mesa semantics. ConditionQueue is a linked list of condition variables.

We give an implementation of FIFOBBQ::remove in Figure 5.14; insert is similar.

The implementation easily extends to the case where we want the queue to be last in first out (LIFO) rather than FIFO, or if want it to wake up threads in some priority order. With Hoare semantics, this is not as easy; we would need to have a different implementation of CV for each different queueing discipline, rather than leaving it to those few applications where the specific order matters.

5.7 | Implementing Synchronization Objects

How are locks and condition variables implemented?

Now that we have described locks and condition variables and shown how to use them in shared objects, we turn to how to implement these important building blocks.

Recall from Chapter 4 that threads can be implemented in the kernel or at user level. We start by describing how to implement synchronization for kernel threads; at the end of this section we discuss the changes needed to support these abstractions for user-level threads.

Both locks and condition variables have state. For locks, this is the state of the lock (FREE or BUSY) and a queue of zero or more threads waiting for the lock to become FREE. For condition variables, the state is the queue of threads waiting to be signaled. Either way, the challenge is to atomically modify those data structures.

The Too Much Milk discussion showed that it is both complex and costly to implement atomic actions with just memory reads and writes. Therefore, modern implementations use more powerful hardware primitives that let us atomically read, modify, and write pieces of state. We use two hardware primitives:

- **Disabling interrupts.** On a single processor, we can make a sequence of instructions atomic by disabling interrupts on that single processor.

- **Atomic read-modify-write instructions.** On a multiprocessor, disabling interrupts is insufficient to provide atomicity. Instead, architectures provide special instructions to atomically read and update a word of memory. These instructions are globally atomic with respect to the instructions on every processor.

Each of these primitives also serves as a memory barrier; they inform the compiler and hardware that all prior instructions must complete before the atomic instruction is executed.

5.7.1   Implementing Uniprocessor Locks by Disabling Interrupts

On a uniprocessor, any sequence of instructions by one thread appears atomic to other threads if no context switch occurs in the middle of the sequence. So, on a uniprocessor, a thread can make a sequence of actions atomic by disabling interrupts (and refraining from calling thread library functions that can trigger a context switch) during the sequence.

This observation suggests a trivial — but seriously limited — approach to implementing locks on a uniprocessor:

```
Lock :: acquire () {  disableInterrupts ();  }

Lock :: release () {  enableInterrupts ();  }
```

This implementation does provide the mutual exclusion property we need from locks. Some uniprocessor kernels use this simple approach, but it does not suffice as a general implementation for locks. If the code sequence the lock protects runs for a long time, interrupts will be disabled for that long. This will prevent other threads from running, and it will make the system unresponsive to handling user inputs or other real-time tasks. Furthermore, although this

```
class Lock {                                    Lock :: release () {
  private :                                     // next thread to hold lock
    int value = FREE;                              TCB *next;
    Queue waiting;
  public :                                         disableInterrupts ();
    void acquire ();                               if (waiting.notEmpty ()) {
    void release ();                               // move one TCB from waiting
}                                                  // to ready
                                                       next = waiting.remove ();
Lock :: acquire () {                                   next->state = READY;
  TCB *chosenTCB;                                      readyList.add (next);
                                                   } else {
  disableInterrupts ();                               value = FREE;
  if (value == BUSY) {                             }
      waiting.add (runningThread);               enableInterrupts ();
      runningThread->state = WAITING;         }
      next = readyList.remove ();
      thread_switch (runningThread,
                 chosenTCB);
      runningThread->state = RUNNING;
  } else {
      value = BUSY;
  }
  enableInterrupts ();
}
```

Figure 5.15: Pseudo-code for a uniprocessor queueing lock. Temporarily disabling interrupts provides atomic access to the data structures implementing the lock. suspend(oldTCB, newTCB) switches from the current thread to the next to be run. It returns only after some other thread calls release and moves it to the ready list.

approach can work in the kernel where all code is (presumably) carefully crafted and trusted to release the lock quickly, we cannot let untrusted user-level code run with interrupts turned off since a malicious or buggy program could then monopolize the processor.

5.7.2 Implementing Uniprocessor Queueing Locks

Can we suspend the current thread until the lock is free?

A more general solution is based on the observation that if the lock is BUSY, there is no point in running the acquiring thread until the lock is free. Instead, we should context switch to the next ready thread.

The implementation briefly disables interrupts to protect the lock's data structures, but re-enables them once a thread has acquired the lock or determined that the lock is BUSY. The Lock implementation shown in Figure 5.15 illustrates this approach. If a lock is BUSY when a thread tries to acquire it, the thread moves its TCB onto the lock's waiting list. The thread then suspends itself and switches to the next runnable thread. The call to suspend does not return until the thread is put back on the ready list, e.g., until some thread calls Lock::release.

In our implementation, if a thread is waiting for the lock, a call to release does not set value to FREE. Instead, it leaves value as BUSY. The woken thread is guaranteed to be the next that executes the critical section. This arrangement ensures freedom from starvation.

WARNING   This optimization is specific to this implementation. Users of locks should not make assumptions about the order in which waiting threads acquire a lock.

EXAMPLE   In Lock::acquire, suspend is called with interrupts turned off. Who turns them back on?

ANSWER   **The next thread to run re-enables interrupts.** In particular, most implementations of thread systems enforce the invariant that a thread always disables interrupts before performing a context switch. As a result, interrupts are always disabled when the thread runs again after a context switch. Thus, whenever a thread returns from a context switch, it must re-enable interrupts. For example, the Lock::acquire code in Figure 5.15 re-enables interrupts before returning; the yield implementation in Chapter 4 disables interrupts before the context switch and then re-enables them afterwards.   □

5.7.3   Implementing Multiprocessor Spinlocks

On a multiprocessor, however, disabling interrupts is insufficient. Even when interrupts are turned off on one processor, other threads are running concurrently. Operations by a thread on one processor are interleaved with operations by other threads on other processors.

atomic read-modify-write

Since turning off interrupts is insufficient, most processor architectures provide *atomic read-modify-write* instructions to support synchronization. These instructions can read a value from a memory location to a register, modify the value, and write the modified value to memory atomically with respect to all instructions on other processors.

As an example, some architectures provide a *test-and-set* instruction, which atomically reads a value from memory to a register and writes the value 1 to that memory location.

spinlock

Figure 5.16 implements a lock using test_and_set. This lock is called a *spinlock* because a thread waiting for a BUSY lock "spins" (busy-waits) in a tight loop until some other lock releases the lock. This approach is inefficient if locks are held for long periods. However, for locks that are only held for short periods (i.e., less time than a context switch would take), spinlocks make sense.

5.7.4   Implementing Multiprocessor Queueing Locks

On a multiprocessor, can we suspend the current thread until the lock is free?

Often, we need to support critical sections of varying length. For example, we may want a general solution that does not make assumptions about the running time of methods that hold locks.

We cannot completely eliminate busy-waiting on a multiprocessor, but we can minimize it. As we mentioned, the scheduler ready list needs a spinlock.

Implementing read-modify-write instructions

Students often ask at this point how the processor hardware implements atomic instructions such as test-and-set. If each processor has its own cache, what is to keep two processors from reading and updating the same location at the same time? Although a complete explanation is beyond the scope of this textbook, the hardware uses the same mechanism as it uses for cache coherence.

Every entry in a processor cache has a state, either *exclusive* or *read-only*. If any other processors have a cached copy of the data, it must be *read-only* everywhere. To modify a shared memory location, the processor must have an *exclusive* copy of the data; no other cache is allowed to have a copy. Otherwise, one processor could read an out-of-date value for some location that another processor has already updated. To read or write a location that is stored *exclusive* in some other cache, the processor needs to fetch the latest value from that cache.

Read-modify-write instructions piggyback on this mechanism. To execute one of these instructions, the hardware acquires an *exclusive* copy of the memory, removing copies from all other caches. Then the instruction executes on the local copy; after the instruction completes, other processors are allowed to read the result by fetching the latest value.

```
class SpinLock {
  private:
    int value = 0; // 0 = FREE; 1 = BUSY

  public:
    void acquire() {
        while (test_and_set(&value)) // while BUSY
            ; // spin
    }

    void release() {
        value = 0;
        memory_barrier();
    }
}
```

Figure 5.16: A multiprocessor spinlock implementation using test-and-set.

The scheduler holds this spinlock for only a few instructions; further, if the ready list spinlock is BUSY, there is no point in trying to switch to a different thread, as that would require access to the ready list.

To reduce contention on the ready list spinlock, we use a *separate* spinlock to guard access to each lock's internal state. Once a thread holds the lock's spinlock, the thread can inspect and update the lock's state. If the lock is FREE,

Interrupt handlers and spinlocks

Whenever an interrupt handler accesses shared data, that data must be protected by a spinlock instead of a queueing lock. As we explained in Chapter 2 and Chapter 4, interrupt handlers are not threads: they must run to completion without blocking so that the hardware can deliver the next interrupt. With a queueing lock, the lock might be held when the interrupt handler starts, making it impossible for the interrupt handler to work correctly.

Whenever any thread acquires a spinlock used within an interrupt handler, the thread *must* disable interrupts first. Otherwise, deadlock can result if the interrupt arrives at an inopportune moment. The handler could spin forever waiting for a lock held by the thread it interrupted. Most likely, the system would need to be rebooted to clear the problem.

To avoid these types of errors, most operating systems keep interrupt handlers extremely simple. For example, many interrupt handlers simply wake up a thread to do the heavy lifting of managing the I/O device. Waking up a thread requires mutually exclusive access to the ready list, protected by a spinlock that is never used without first disabling interrupts.

the thread sets the value and releases its spinlock. If the lock is BUSY, more work is needed: we need to put the current thread on the waiting list for the lock, suspend the current thread, and switch to a new thread.

Careful sequencing is needed, however, as shown in Figure 5.17. To suspend a thread on a multiprocessor, we need to first disable interrupts to ensure the thread is not preempted while holding the ready list spinlock. We then acquire the ready list spinlock, and *only then* is it safe to release the lock's spinlock and switch to a new thread. The ready list spinlock is released by the next thread to run. Otherwise, a different thread on another processor might put the waiting thread back on the ready list (and start it running) before the waiting thread has completed its context switch.

Later, when the lock is released, if any threads are waiting for the lock, one of them is moved off the lock's waiting list to the scheduler's ready list.

EXAMPLE   What might happen if we released the Lock's spinlock before the call to suspend?

ANSWER   The basic issue is that we want to make sure the acquiring thread finishes suspending itself before a thread releasing the lock tries to reschedule it. If we allowed makeReady to run before suspend, makeReady would mark the acquring thread READY, but suspend would then change the thread's state to WAITING. The acquiring thread would then be stuck in the WAITING state forever. Since this sequence would happen very rarely, it would be extremely difficult to locate the problem.   □

```
class Lock {                                    class Scheduler {
    private:                                        private:
        int value = FREE;                               Queue readyList;
        SpinLock spinLock;                              SpinLock schedulerSpinLock;
        Queue waiting;                              public:
    public:                                             void suspend(SpinLock *lock);
        void acquire();                                 void makeReady(Thread *thread);
        void release();                         }
}
                                                void
Lock::acquire() {                               Scheduler::suspend(SpinLock *lock) {
    spinLock.acquire();                             TCB *chosenTCB;
    if (value != FREE) {
        waiting.add(runningThread);                 disableInterrupts();
        scheduler.suspend(&spinLock);               schedulerSpinLock.acquire();
        // scheduler releases spinLock              lock->release();
    } else {                                        runningThread->state = WAITING;
        value = BUSY;                               chosenTCB = readyList.getNextThread();
        spinLock.release();                         thread_switch(runningThread,
    }                                                              chosenTCB);
}                                                   runningThread->state = RUNNING;
                                                    schedulerSpinLock.release();
void Lock::release() {                               enableInterrupts();
    TCB *next;                                   }

    spinLock.acquire();                         void
    if (waiting.notEmpty()) {                   Scheduler::makeReady(TCB *thread) {
        next = waiting.remove();                    disableInterrupts();
        scheduler.makeReady(next);                  schedulerSpinLock.acquire();
    } else {                                        readyList.add(thread);
        value = FREE;                               thread->state = READY;
    }                                               schedulerSpinLock.release();
    spinLock.release();                             enableInterrupts();
}                                               }
```

Figure 5.17: Pseudo-code for a multiprocessor queueing lock. Both the scheduler and the lock use spinlocks to protect their internal data structures. Any thread that tries to acquire the lock when it is BUSY is put on a queue for later wakeup. Care is needed to prevent the waiting thread from being put back on the ready list before it has completed the thread_switch.

NOTE   In the implementation in Figure 5.17, the single scheduler spinlock can become a bottleneck as the number of processors increases. Instead, as we explain in Chapter 6, most systems have one ready list per processor, each protected by a different spinlock. Different processors can then simultaneously add and remove threads to different lists. Typically, the WAITING thread is placed on the ready list of the same processor where it had previously been RUNNING; this improves cache performance as that processor's cache may still contain code and data from the last time the thread ran. Putting the thread back on the same ready list also prevents the thread from being run by any other processor before the thread has completed its context switch. Once it is READY, any idle processor can run the thread by acquiring the spinlock of the ready list where it is enqueued, removing the thread, and releasing the spinlock.

5.7.5   Case Study: Linux 2.6 Kernel Mutex Lock

How does the Linux kernel implement mutual exclusion?

We illustrate how locks are implemented in practice by examining the Linux 2.6 kernel. The Linux code closely follows the approach we described above, except that it is *optimized for the common case.*

In Linux, most locks are FREE most of the time. Further, even if a lock is BUSY, it is likely that no other thread is waiting for it. The alternative, that locks are often BUSY, or have long queues of threads waiting for them, means that any thread that needs the lock will usually need to wait, slowing the system down.

Throughout this example, we include excerpts of the Linux code; we omit debugging code, code for coordinating with signal handing, and compiler/linker directives.

The Linux implementation of locks takes advantage of this by providing an extremely fast path for the case when the thread does not need to wait for the lock in acquire, and when there is no thread not need to wake up a thread in release. A slow path, similar to Figure 5.17, is used for all other cases.

Further, having a fast path for acquiring a FREE lock, and releasing a lock with no waiting thread, is also a concern for user-level thread libraries, discussed below.

To optimize the common case path, Linux takes advantage of hardware-specific features of the x86. The x86 supports a large number of different read-modify-write instructions, including atomic decrement (subtract one from the memory location, returning the previous value), atomic increment, atomic exchange (swap the value of the memory location with the value stored in a register), and atomic test-and-set.

The key idea is to design the lock data structures to allow the lock to be acquired and released on the fast path *without* first acquiring the spinlock or disabling interrupts. The slowpath does require acquiring the spinlock. Instead of being binary, the lock value is an integer count with three states:

```
struct mutex {
        /* 1: unlocked, 0: locked, negative: locked, possible waiters */
        atomic_t              count;
        spinlock_t            wait_lock;
        struct list_head      wait_list;
};
```

The Linux lock acquire code is a macro (to avoid making a procedure call on the fast path) that translates to a short sequence of instructions. The x86 lock prefix before the decl instruction signifies to the processor that the instruction should be executed atomically.

```
    lock decl (%eax)    // atomic decrement of a memory location
                        // address in %eax is pointer to lock->count
    jns 1f              // jump if not signed (if value is now 0)
    call slowpath_acquire
1:
```

If the lock was FREE, the lock is acquired with only two instructions; if the lock was BUSY, the code leaves count < 0 and invokes a separate routine to handle the slow path. The slow path disables preemption, acquires the spin-lock, puts the thread on the lock wait queue, and then re-checks whether the lock has been released in the meantime. For this, it uses the atomic exchange instruction:

```
for (;;) {
    /*
     * Lets try to take the lock again — this is needed even if
     * we get here for the first time (shortly after failing to
     * acquire the lock), to make sure that we get a wakeup once
     * it's unlocked. Later on, if we sleep, this is the
     * operation that gives us the lock. We xchg it to −1, so
     * that when we release the lock, we properly wake up the
     * other waiters:
     */
    if (atomic_xchg(&lock->count, −1) == 1)
        break;

    /* didn't get the lock, go to sleep: */
    ...
}
```

If successful, the lock is acquired. If unsuccessful, the thread releases the spinlock and switches to the next ready thread. When the thread returns from suspend, unlike in Figure 5.17, the lock may not be FREE, and so the thread must try again.

Eventually, the thread breaks out of the loop, which means that it found a moment when the lock was FREE (lock->count = 1), and at that moment it set the lock to the "busy, possible waiters" state (by setting count = -1). The thread now has the lock, and it cleans up by resetting count = 0 if there are no other waiters.

```
/* set it to 0 if there are no waiters left: */
if (list_empty(&lock->wait_list))
    atomic_set(&lock->count, 0);
```

It then releases the spinlock and re-enables preemptions.

On release, the fast path is two inlined instructions if the lock value was 0 (the lock has no waiters).

```
    lock incl (%eax)      // atomic increment
    jg 1f                 // jump if new value is 1
    call slowpath_release
1:
```

On the slow path, count was negative. The increment instruction leaves the lock BUSY. Then, the thread acquires the spinlock, sets the count to be FREE, and wakes up one of the waiting threads.

```
spin_lock_mutex(&lock->wait_lock, flags);
    /*
     * Unlock lock here
     */
atomic_set(&lock->count, 1);
if (!list_empty(&lock->wait_list)) {
    struct mutex_waiter *waiter =
                list_entry(lock->wait_list.next,
                             struct mutex_waiter, list);
    wake_up_process(waiter->task);
}
spin_unlock_mutex(&lock->wait_lock, flags);
```

Notice that this function always sets count to 1, even if there are waiting threads. As a result, a new thread may swoop in and acquire the lock on its fast path, setting count = 0. In this case, the waiting thread is still woken up, and when it eventually runs, the main loop above will set count = -1.

This example demonstrates that acquiring and releasing a lock can be inexpensive. Programmers sometimes go to great lengths to avoid acquiring a lock in a particular situation. However, the reasoning in such cases can be subtle, and omitting needed locks is dangerous. In cases where there is little contention, avoiding locks is unlikely to significantly improve performance, so it is usually better just to keep things simple and rely on locks to ensure mutual exclusion when accessing shared state.

5.7.6   Implementing Condition Variables

How do we implement condition variable wait, signal and broadcast?

We can implement condition variables using a similar approach to the one used to implement locks, with one simplification: since the lock is held whenever the wait, signal, or broadcast is called, we already have mutually exclusive access to the condition wait queue. As with locks, care is needed to prevent a waiting thread from being put back on the ready list until it has completed its context switch; we can accomplish this by acquiring the scheduler spinlock *before* we release the monitor lock. Another thread may acquire the monitor lock and start to signal the waiting thread, but it will not be able to complete the signal until the scheduler lock is released immediately after the context switch.

Figure 5.18 shows an implementation with Mesa semantics — when we signal a waiting thread, that thread becomes READY, but it may not run immediately and must still re-acquire the monitor lock. It is possible for another thread to acquire the monitor lock first and to change the state guarded by the lock before the waiting thread returns from CV::wait.

5.7.7   Implementing Application-level Synchronization

How do we implement locks and condition variables for threads that run at user-level?

The preceding discussion focused on implementing locks and condition variables for kernel threads. In that case, everything (code, shared state, lock data structures, thread control blocks, and the ready list) is in kernel memory, and all threads run in kernel mode. Fortunately, although some details change, the

```
class CV {                                    // Monitor lock is held by current thread.
  private:                                    void CV::signal() {
    Queue waiting;                                if (waiting.notEmpty()) {
  public:                                             thread = waiting.remove();
    void wait(Lock *lock);                            scheduler.makeReady(thread);
    void signal();                                }
    void broadcast();                          }
}
                                              void CV::broadcast() {
// Monitor lock is held by current thread.       while (waiting.notEmpty()) {
void CV::wait(Lock *lock) {                          thread = waiting.remove();
    assert(lock.isHeld());                          scheduler.makeReady(thread);
    waiting.add(myTCB);                          }
    // Switch to new thread and release lock}   }
    scheduler.suspend(&lock);
    lock->acquire();
}
```

Figure 5.18: Pseudo-code for implementing a condition variable. suspend and makeReady are defined in Figure 5.17.

same basic approach works when we implement locks and condition variables for use by threads that run at user level.

Recall from Chapter 4 that there are two ways of supporting application-level concurrency: via system calls to access kernel thread operations or via a user-level thread scheduler.

Kernel-Managed Threads.   With kernel-managed threads, the kernel provides threads to a process and manages the thread ready list. The kernel scheduler needs to know when a thread is waiting for a lock or condition variable so that it can suspend the thread and switch to the next ready thread.

In the simplest case, we can place the lock and condition variable data structures, including the waiting lists, in the kernel's address space. Each method call on the synchronization object translates to a system call. Then, the implementations described above for kernel-level locks and condition variables can be used without significant change.

A more sophisticated approach splits the lock's state and implementation into a fast path and slow path, similar to the Linux lock described above. For example, each lock has two data structures: (i) the process's address space holds something similar to the count field and (ii) the kernel holds the spinlock and wait_list queue.

Then, acquiring a FREE lock or releasing a lock with no waiting threads takes a few instructions at user level, with no system call. The slow path still needs a system call (e.g., when a waiting thread needs to suspend execution). We leave the details of the implementation as an exercise for the reader.

User-Managed Threads.   In a thread library that operates completely at user level, the library creates multiple kernel threads to serve as virtual processors, and then multiplexes user-level threads over those virtual processors. This situation is similar to kernel threads, except operating inside the process's address space rather than in the kernel's address space. In particular, the code, shared state, lock and condition variable data structures, thread control blocks, and the ready list are in the process's address space.

The only significant change has to do with disabling interrupts. Obviously, a user-level thread package cannot disable system-level interrupts; the kernel cannot allow an untrusted process to disable interrupts and potentially run forever.

Fortunately, the thread library only needs to disable upcalls from the operating system; these are used to trigger thread preemption and other operations in the user-level scheduler, and they could cause inconsistency if they occur while the library is modifying scheduler data structures. Most modern operating systems have a way to temporarily disable upcalls, and then to deliver those upcalls once it is safe to do so. By ensuring the user-level scheduler and upcall handler cannot run at the same time, the fast path mutex implementation described above can be used here as well.

5.8 | Semaphores Considered Harmful

"During system conception it transpired that we used the semaphores in two completely different ways. The difference is so marked that, looking back, one wonders whether it was really fair to present the two ways as uses of the very same primitives. On the one hand, we have the semaphores used for mutual exclusion, on the other hand, the private semaphores."
(From Dijkstra "The structure of the 'THE'-Multiprogramming System" *Communications of the ACM* v. 11 n. 5 May 1968.)

What other synchronization primitives are possible, and how do they relate to locks and condition variables?

This book focuses on constructing shared objects using locks and condition variables for synchronization. However, over the years, many different synchronization primitives have been proposed, including communicating sequential processes, event delivery, message passing, and so forth. It is important to realize that none of these are more powerful than using locks and condition variables; a program using any of these paradigms can be mapped to monitors using straightforward transformations.

semaphore

One type of synchronization, a *semaphore*, is worth discussing in detail since it is still widely used. Semaphores were introduced by Dijkstra to provide synchronization in the THE operating system, which (among other advances) explored structured ways of using concurrency in operating system design.

Semaphores are defined as follows:

- A semaphore has a non-negative value.

- When a semaphore is created, its value can be initialized to any non-negative integer.

The names P and V are historical artifacts. They make only slightly more sense in Dutch. Sorry.

- Semaphore::P() waits until the value is positive. Then, it atomically decrements value by 1 and returns.

- Semaphore::V() atomically increments the value by 1. If any threads are waiting in P, one is enabled, so that its call to P succeeds at decrementing the value and returns.

- No other operations are allowed on a semaphore; in particular, no thread can directly read the current value of the semaphore.

Note that Semaphore::P is an atomic operation: the read that observes the positive value is atomic with the update that decrements it. As a result, semaphores can never have a negative value, even when multiple threads call P concurrently.

Likewise, if V occurs when there is a waiting thread in P, then P's increment and V's decrement of value are atomic: no other thread can observe the incremented value, and the thread in P is guaranteed to decrement the value and return.

Given this definition, semaphores can be used for either mutual exclusion (like locks) or general waiting for another thread to do something (a bit like condition variables).

To use a semaphore as a mutual exclusion lock, initialize it to 1. Then, Semaphore::P is equivalent to Lock::acquire, and Semaphore::V is equivalent to Lock::release.

Using a semaphore for more general waiting is trickier. A useful analogy for semaphores is thread_join. With thread_join, the precise order of events does not matter: if the forked thread finishes before the parent thread calls thread_join, then the call returns right away. On the other hand, if the parent calls thread_join first, then it waits until the thread finishes, and then returns.

Semaphore P and V can be set up to behave similarly. Typically (but not always), you initialize the semaphore to 0. Then, each call to Semaphore::P waits for the corresponding thread to call V. If the V is called first, then P returns immediately.

The difficulty comes when trying to coordinate shared state (needing mutual exclusion) with general waiting. From a distance, Semaphore::V is *similar to* CV::wait(&lock) and Semaphore::P is *similar to* CV::signal. However, there are important differences. First, CV::wait(&lock) atomically releases the monitor lock, so that you can safely check the shared object's state and then atomically suspend execution.

By contrast, Semaphore::P does *not* release an associated mutual exclusion lock. Typically, the lock is released before the call to P; otherwise, no other thread can access the shared state until the thread resumes. The programmer must carefully construct the program to work properly in this case. Second, whereas a condition variable is stateless, a semaphore has a value. If no threads are waiting, a call to CV::signal has no effect, while a call to Semaphore::V increments the value. This causes the next call to Semaphore::V to proceed without blocking.

Edsger Dijkstra is the author of the short note "Go To Statement Considered Harmful", Communications of the ACM, *v. 11 n. 3, March 1968, pp 147–148.*

Semaphores considered harmful.   Our view is that programming with locks and condition variables is superior to programming with semaphores. We advise you to always write your code using those synchronization variables for two reasons.

First, using separate lock and condition variable classes makes code more self-documenting and easier to read. As the quote from Dijkstra notes, two different abstractions are needed, and code is clearer when the role of each synchronization variable is made clear through explicit typing. For example, it is much easier to verify that every lock acquire is paired with a lock release, if they are not mixed with other calls to P and V for general waiting.

Second, a stateless condition variable bound to a lock is a better abstraction for generalized waiting than a semaphore. By binding a condition variable to a lock, we can conveniently wait on any arbitrary predicate on an object's state. In contrast, semaphores rely on the programmer to carefully map the object's state to the semaphore's value so that a decision to wait or proceed in P can be made entirely based on the value, without holding a lock or examining the rest of the shared object's state.

Although we do not recommend writing new code with semaphores, code based on semaphores is not uncommon, especially in operating systems. So, it is important to understand the semantics of semaphores and be able to read and understand semaphore-based code written by others.

NOTE   **Semaphores in interrupt handlers.** In one situation, semaphores are superior to condition variables and locks: synchronizing communication between an I/O device and threads waiting for I/O completion. Typically, the hardware communicates with the device driver via a shared in-memory data structure. This data structure is read and written concurrently by both hardware and the kernel, but the shared access cannot be coordinated with a software lock. Instead, the hardware and device drivers use carefully designed atomic memory operations.

If a hardware device needs attention, e.g., because a network packet has arrived that needs handling, or a disk request has completed, the hardware updates the shared data structure and starts an interrupt handler. The interrupt handler is often simple: it just wakes up a waiting thread and returns. For this, one might consider using a condition variable and calling signal without holding the lock (this is sometimes called a *naked notify*). Unfortunately, there is a corner case: suppose that the operating system thread first checks the data structure, sees that no work is currently needed, and is just about to call wait on the condition variable. At that moment, the hardware updates the data structure with the new work and triggers the interrupt handler to call signal. Because the thread has not called wait yet, the signal has no effect. Thus, when the thread calls wait, the signal has already occurred, and the thread waits — possibly for a long time.

A common solution is for device interrupts to use semaphores instead. Because semaphores are stateful, it does not matter whether the thread calls P or the interrupt handler calls V first: the result is the same, the V cannot be lost.

To help illustrate the difference between semaphores and condition variables, we consider four candidate implementations of condition variables using semaphores.

EXAMPLE

This is solution 1 out of 4; it is not likely to work, is it?

Suppose you are writing concurrent application software on an operating system that only provides semaphores. Does the following code correctly implement condition variables?

```
void CV::wait(Lock *lock) {              void CV::signal() {
    lock->release();                          semaphore.V();
    semaphore.P();                        }
    lock->acquire();
}
```

ANSWER

No. Condition variables are stateless, while semaphores have state. We can illustrate this difference with a counterexample.

What happens if a thread calls signal and no one is waiting? Nothing. What happens if another thread later calls wait? The thread waits.

By contrast, consider what happens with a semaphore. What happens if a thread calls V and no one is waiting? The value of the semaphore is incremented. What happens if a thread later calls P? The value of the semaphore is decremented, and the thread continues.

In other words, P and V are commutative. The result is the same no matter what order they occur. Condition variables are not commutative: wait does not return until the next signal. This is why condition variables must be accessed while holding a lock — code using a condition variable needs to access shared state variables to do its job.

With condition variables, if a thread calls signal a thousand times, when no one is waiting, the next wait will still go to sleep. With the above code, the next thousand threads that wait will return immediately.   □

EXAMPLE

This is solution 2 out of 4; it is still not likely to work, is it?

What about the following code?

```
void CV::wait(Lock *lock) {              void CV::signal() {
    lock->release();                          if (!semaphore.queueEmpty())
    semaphore.P();                                semaphore.V();
    lock->acquire();                      }
}
```

ANSWER

Closer, but still no. For one, the definition of a semaphore does not allow users of the semaphore to look at the contents of the semaphore queue. But more importantly, there is a race condition. Once the lock is released, some other thread can slip in, acquire the lock and call signal before the waiting thread gets to call P. In that case, the queue is empty, so the waiter never exits the while loop.

Instead, the definition of CV::wait is that the lock is released and the thread goes to sleep atomically. ☐

EXAMPLE   What about the following code?

This is solution 3 out of 4; we're getting warmer.

```
void CV::wait(Lock *lock) {
    waitQueue.append(myTCB);
    lock->release();
    semaphore.P();
    lock->acquire();
}
```

```
void CV::signal() {
    if (!waitQueue.isEmpty())
        semaphore.V();
}
```

ANSWER   **Very close but still no.** There is still a race condition. Suppose a thread calls wait, and releases the lock. Then another thread acquires the lock and calls signal. With condition variables, the waiter should wake up, but with the implementation above, a third thread could swoop in, acquire the lock, call wait, and decrement the semaphore before the first waiter has a chance to run.

For some programs, this difference would not be noticeable, but for others, it could cause problems. ☐

EXAMPLE   Is it possible to implement condition variables using semaphores?

ANSWER   **Yes, using the technique we outlined for implementing the FIFO bounded buffer: create a semaphore for each waiter and then wake up exactly the right waiter.** This solution was developed by Andrew Birrell in order to implement condition variables on top of Microsoft Windows before it supported them natively.

```
// Put thread on queue of waiting
// threads.
void CV::wait(Lock *lock) {
    semaphore = new Semaphore(0);
    waitQueue.Append(semaphore);
    lock.release();
    semaphore.P();
    lock.acquire();
}
```

```
// Wake up one waiter if any.
void CV::signal() {
    if (!waitQueue.isEmpty()) {
        semaphore = queue.Remove();
        semaphore.V();
    }
}
```

☐

5.9 | Summary and Future Directions

This chapter advocates using a systematic, structured approach to writing multi-threaded code that shares state across threads. The approach, shared objects with concurrent access managed with locks and condition variables, has stood the test of time. Using shared objects makes reasoning about multi-threaded programs vastly simpler than it would be if we tried to reason about the possible interleavings of individual loads and stores. Further, by following a systematic approach, we make it possible for others to read, understand, maintain, and change the multi-threaded code we write.

In this chapter, we have discussed:

- **Race conditions.** The fundamental challenge to writing multi-threaded code that uses shared data is that the behavior of the program may depend on the precise ordering of operations executed by each thread. This non-deterministic behavior is difficult to reason about, reproduce, and debug.

- **Locks and condition variables.** Two useful sychronization abstractions are locks, providing mutual exclusion, and condition variables, for waiting for shared state to change.

- **A methodology for writing shared objects.** Using locks and condition variables, we outlined a sequence of steps to writing correct synchronization code for coordinating access to shared objects. Following this methodology has proven enormously helpful for students in our classes by reducing the likelihood of design errors.

- **Implementations of synchronization.** Locks and condition variables can be efficiently implemented using hardware support for atomic read-modify-write instructions and, where necessary, the ability to temporarily defer hardware interrupts. In particular, we showed that the overhead of acquiring and releasing a non-contested lock can be as low as four instructions.

- **Semaphores.** Semaphores are a widely implemented alternative to locks and condition variables, with a constructive role in managing hardware I/O interrupts.

In short, this chapter defines a set of core skills that almost any programmer will use over and over again during the coming decade or longer.

That is not the whole story. As the next chapter will discuss, complex systems often include many shared objects and threads. This poses new challenges: synchronizing operations that span multiple shared objects, avoiding deadlocks in which a set of threads are all waiting for each other to do something, and maximizing performance when large numbers of threads are contending for a single object.

5.9.1   Historical Notes

Once researchers accepted the need to explicitly manage concurrency using threads, the challenge became how best to coordinate multi-threaded access to shared data. A large number of different abstractions were proposed, and it took some time to work out the different strengths and weaknesses of the various approaches.

Monitors — that is, managing shared data structures with locks and condition variables — were proposed in the early 1970's in separate papers by Tony Hoare [83] and Per Brinch Hansen [75]. One early advantage of monitors was the ability to formally prove properties about multi-threaded code; for example with Hoare-style semantics for condition variables, any statement which is true of the shared object immediately before a signal is also true of the object immediately after the return from wait. As we saw with the Too Much Milk example, without explicit synchronization, it can be quite difficult to reason about concurrent execution.

By the early 1980's, Xerox PARC had built the first personal computer, the Alto, with all of its system software written using threads (called lightweight processes at the time) and monitors. The methodology we present in this chapter originated with that project [98]. It is hard to overstate how radical an approach this was; almost all widely used operating systems of the time, including UNIX, were built using semaphores.

Perhaps needless to say, Hoare won the Turing Award.

An alternative line of work advocated completely prohibiting access by threads to shared data, as a way of eliminating race conditions. Instead of shared data, all data was private to a single thread; as a result, locks were never needed. An early example of this approach was Communicating Sequential Processes (CSP), also developed by Tony Hoare [84]. Google's Go language for concurrent web programming is a modern language that supports both monitors and the CSP style of programming. With CSP and Go, a thread that needs to perform an operation on some other thread's data sends it a message; the receiving thread can either reply with the result, or in data-flow style, forward the result onto some other thread.

While there was considerable and vigorous debate at the time as to whether message-passing or shared-memory were better models for programming concurrency, the debate was largely resolved by a simple observation made by Lauer and Needham [101]. Any program using monitors can be recast into CSP using a simple transformation, and vice versa. The execution of a procedure with a monitor lock is equivalent to processing a message in CSP; a monitor is, in effect, single-threaded while it is holding the lock. Thus, the choice of which style to use is largely a matter of taste and convention, and most programmers have chosen to use threads and monitors.

Exercises

1. True or False: If a multi-threaded program runs correctly in all cases on a single time-sliced processor, then it will run correctly if each thread is

run on a separate processor of a shared-memory multiprocessor. Justify your answer.

2. Show that solution 3 to the Too Much Milk problem is safe — that it guarantees that at most one roommate buys milk.

3. Precisely describe the set of possible outputs that could occur when the program shown in Figure 5.5 is run.

4. Suppose that you mistakenly create an automatic (local) variable v in one thread $t1$ and pass a pointer to v to another thread $t2$. Is it possible that a write by $t1$ to some variable other than v will change the state of v as observed by $t2$? If so, explain how this can happen and give an example. If not, explain why not.

5. Suppose that you mistakenly create an automatic (local) variable v in one thread $t1$ and pass a pointer to v to another thread $t2$. Is it possible that a write by $t2$ to v will cause $t2$ to execute the wrong code? If so, so, explain how. If not, explain why not.

6. Assuming Mesa semantics for condition variables, our implementation of the blocking bounded queue in Figure 5.8 does not guarantee freedom from starvation: if a continuous stream of threads makes insert (or remove) calls, a waiting thread could wait forever. For example, a thread may call insert and wait in the while loop because the queue is full. Starvation would occur if every time another thread removes an item from the queue and signals the waiting thread, a *different* thread calls insert, sees that the queue is not full, and inserts an item before the waiting thread resumes.

   Prove that under Hoare semantics and assuming that signal wakes the longest-waiting thread, our implementation of BBQ ensures freedom from starvation. More precisely, prove that if a thread waits in insert, then it is guaranteed to proceed after a bounded number of remove calls complete, and vice versa.

7. As noted in the previous problem, our implementation of the blocking bounded queue in Figure 5.8 does not guarantee freedom from starvation. Modify the code to ensure freedom from starvation so that if a thread waits in insert, it is guaranteed to proceed after a bounded number of remove() calls complete, and vice versa. **Note:** Your implementation must work under Mesa semantics for condition variables.

8. Wikipedia provides an implementation of Peterson's algorithm to provide mutual exclusion using loads and stores at http://en.wikipedia.org/wiki/Peterson's_algorithm. Unfortunately, this code is not guaranteed to work with modern compilers or hardware. Update the code to include memory barriers where necessary. (Of course, you could add a memory

barrier before and after each instruction; your solution should instead add memory barriers only where necessary for correctness.)

9. Linux provides a sys_futex() system call to assist in implementing hybrid user-level/kernel-level locks and condition variables.

   A call to long sys_futex(void *addr1, FUTEX_WAIT, int val1, NULL, NULL, 0) checks to see if the memory at address addr1 has the same value as val1. If so, the calling thread is suspended. If not, the calling thread returns immediately with the error return value EWOULDBLOCK. In addition, the system call returns with the value EINTR if the thread receives a signal.

   A call to long sys_futex(void *addr1, FUTEX_WAKE, 1, NULL, NULL, 0) causes one thread waiting on addr1 to return.

   Consider the following simple implementation of a hybrid user-level/kernel-level lock.

```
class TooSimpleFutexLock {
  private:
    int val;

  public:
    TooSimpleMutex () : val (0) { }   // Constructor

    void acquire () {
        int c;
        // atomic_inc returns *old* value
        while ((c = atomic_inc (val)) != 0) {
            futex_wait (&val, c + 1);
        }
    }

    void release () {
        val = 0;
        futex_wake (&val, 1);
    }
};
```

There are three problems with this code.

a) **Performance.** The goal of this code is to avoid making expensive system calls in the uncontested case of an acquire on a FREE lock or a release of a lock with no other waiting threads. This code fails to meet this goal. Why?

b) **Performance.** A subtle corner case occurs when multiple threads try to acquire the lock at the same time. It can show up as occasional slowdowns and bursts of CPU usage. What is the problem?

c) **Correctness.** A corner case can cause the mutual exclusion correctness condition to be violated, allowing two threads to both believe they hold the lock. What is the problem?

10. In the readers/writers lock example for the function RWLock::doneRead, why do we use writeGo.Signal rather than writeGo.Broadcast?

11. Show how to implement a semaphore by generalizing the multi-processor lock implementation shown in Figure 5.17.

12. In Section 5.1.3, we presented a solution to the Too Much Milk problem. To make the problem more interesting, we will also allow roommates to drink milk.

    Implement in C++ or Java a Kitchen class with a drinkMilkAndBuyIfNeeded(). This method should randomly (with a 20% probability) change the value of milk from 1 to 0. Then, if the value just became 0, it should buy milk (incrementing milk back to 1). The method should return 1 if the roommate bought milk and 0 otherwise.

    Your solution should use locks for synchronization and work for any number of roommates. Test your implementation by writing a program that repeatedly creates a Kitchen object and varying numbers of roommate threads; each roommate thread should call drinkMilkAndBuyIfNeeded() multiple times in a loop.

    Hint: You will probably write a main() thread that creates a Kitchen object, creates multiple roommate threads, and then waits for all of the roommates to finish their loops. If you are writing in C++ with the POSIX threads library, you can use pthread_join() to have one thread wait for another thread to finish. If you are writing in Java with the java.lang.Thread class, you can use the join() method.

13. For the solution to Too Much Milk suggested in the previous problem, each call to drinkMilkAndBuyIfNeeded() is atomic and holds the lock from the start to the end even if one roommate goes to the store. This solution is analogous to the roommate padlocking the kitchen while going to the store, which seems a bit unrealistic.

    Implement a better solution to drinkMilkAndBuyIfNeeded() using both locks and condition variables. Since a roommate now needs to release the lock to the kitchen while going to the store, you will no longer acquire the lock at the start of this function and release it at the end. Instead, this function will call two helper-functions, each of which acquires/releases the lock. For example:

```
int  Kitchen :: drinkMilkAndBuyIfNeeded ()  {
    int  iShouldBuy  =  waitThenDrink () ;

    if  (iShoudBuy)  {
        buyMilk () ;
    }
}
```

In this function, waitThenDrink() should wait if there is no milk (using a condition variable) until there is milk, drink the milk, and if the milk is now gone, return a nonzero value to flag that the caller should buy milk. BuyMilk() should buy milk and then broadcast to let the waiting threads know that they can proceed.

Again, test your code with varying numbers of threads.

14. Before entering a *priority critical section*, a thread calls PriorityLock:: enter(priority). When the thread exits the critical section, it calls PriorityLock::exit(). If several threads are waiting to enter a priority critical section, the one with the numerically highest priority should be the next one allowed in. Implement PriorityLock using monitors (locks and condition variables) and following the programming standards defined in this chapter.

   a) Define the state and synchronization variables and describe the purpose of each.

   b) Implement PriorityLock::enter(int priority).

   c) Implement PriorityLock::exit().

15. Implement a *priority condition variable*. A priority condition variable (PCV) has three public methods:

```
void PCV::wait(Lock *enclosingLock, int priority);

void PCV::signal(Lock *enclosingLock);

void PCV::broadcast(Lock *enclosingLock, int priority);
```

These methods are similar to those of a standard condition variable. The one difference is that a PCV enforces both *priority* and *ordering*.

In particular, signal(Lock *lock) causes the currently waiting thread with the highest priority to return from wait; if multiple threads with the same priority are waiting, then the one that is waiting the longest should return before any that have been waiting a shorter amount of time.

Similarly, broadcast(Lock *lock, int priority) causes all currently waiting threads whose priority equals or exceeds priority to return from wait.

For full credit, you must follow the *thread coding standards* described in this chapter.

16. A synchronous buffer is one where the thread placing an item into the buffer waits until the thread retrieving the item has gotten it, and only then returns.

Implement a synchronous buffer using Mesa-style locks and condition variables, with the following routines:

```
// Put item into the buffer and return only once the item
// has been retrieved by some thread.
SyncBuf :: put ( item );

// Wait until there is an item in the buffer, and then return it.
SyncBuf :: get ();
```

Any number of threads can concurrently call SyncBuf::get and SyncBuf::put; the module pairs off puts and gets. Each item should be returned exactly once, and there should be no unnecessary waiting. Once the item is retrieved, the thread that called put with the item should return.

17. You have been hired by a company to do climate modelling of oceans. The inner loop of the program matches atoms of different types as they form molecules. In an excessive reliance on threads, each atom is represented by a thread.

   a) Your task is to write code to form water out of two hydrogen threads and one oxygen thread (H2O). You are to write the two procedures: HArrives() and OArrives(). A water molecule forms when two H threads are present and one O thread; otherwise, the atoms must wait. Once all three are present, one of the threads calls MakeWater(), and only then, all three depart.

   b) The company wants to extend its work to handle cloud modelling. Your task is to write code to form ozone out of three oxygen threads. Each of the threads calls OArrives(), and when three are present, one calls MakeOzone(), and only then, all three depart.

   c) Extending the product line into beer production, your task is to write code to form alcohol (C2H6O) out of two carbon atoms, six hydrogens, and one oxygen.

You must use locks and Mesa-style condition variables to implement your solutions, using the best practices as defined in this chapter. Obviously, an atom that arrives *after* the molecule is made must wait for a different group of atoms to be present. There should be no busy-waiting and you should correctly handle spurious wakeups. There must also be no useless waiting: atoms should not wait if there is a sufficient number of each type.

When two trains approach each other at a crossing, both shall come to a full stop and neither shall start up again until the other has gone.
                                                      Kansas state law, early 1900s

6 Multi-Object Synchronization

How do we coordinate access to multiple shared objects?

In the previous chapter, we described a key building block for writing concurrent programs: how to design an object that can be shared between multiple threads. In this chapter, we need to go one step further: what happens as programs become more complex, with multiple shared objects and multiple locks? To answer this, we need to reason about the interactions between shared objects.

Several considerations arise in this context:

- **Multiprocessor performance.** Modern computers have increasing numbers of processors because of the difficulty of improving single CPU performance. The design of shared objects can have a large impact on multiprocessor performance. For example, a lock protecting a frequently accessed shared object can become a bottleneck, since only one thread can hold the lock at a time.

- **Correctness.** Performance considerations often cause designers to re-engineer their data structures for increased concurrency. Splitting a single shared object into a set of related objects each with their own lock can improve performance. However, it also raises issues of correctness. For programs with multiple shared objects, we face a problem similar to the one faced when reasoning about atomic loads and stores: even if each individual operation on a shared object is atomic, we must reason about interactions of sequences of operations across objects.

- **Deadlock.** One way to help reason about the behavior of operations across multiple objects is to hold multiple locks. This approach raises the possibility of deadlock, where threads are permanently stuck waiting for each other in a cycle.

No cookbook recipe always works for addressing these challenges. In particular, current techniques have two basic limitations. First, they pose engineering trade-offs. Some solutions are general but complex or expensive; others are simple but slow; still others are simple and cheap but not general. Second, many solutions are inherently *non-modular*: they require reasoning about the global structure of the system and internal implementation details of modules to understand or restrict how different modules can interact.

Chapter roadmap:

- **Multiprocessor Lock Performance.** Can we predict when a lock will become a bottleneck on a multiprocessor? (Section 6.1)

- **Lock Design Patterns.** If a lock is a bottleneck, can we restructure the program to reduce the problem? (Section 6.2)

- **Lock Contention.** If a lock is still a bottleneck after re-structuring, what then? (Section 6.3)

- **Multi-Object Atomicity.** How can we make a sequence of operations across multiple objects appear atomic to other threads? (Section 6.4)

- **Deadlock.** What causes deadlock in multi-threaded programs, and what solutions exist to prevent or break deadlocks? (Section 6.5)

- **Non-Blocking Synchronization.** Are there ways to eliminate locks in complex multi-object programs? (Section 6.6)

6.1 | Multiprocessor Lock Performance

Can we predict when a lock will become a bottleneck?

request parallelism

Client-server applications often have ample parallelism for modern multicore architectures with dozens of processors. Each separate client request can be handled by a different thread running on a different processor; this is called *request parallelism*. Likewise, server operating systems often have ample parallelism – applications with large numbers of threads can make a large number of concurrent system calls into the kernel.

Even with ample request parallelism, however, performance can often be disappointing. Once locks and condition variables are added to a server application to allow it to process requests concurrently, throughput may be only slightly faster on a fifty-way multiprocessor than on a uniprocessor. Most often, this can be due to three causes:

1. **Locking.** A lock implies mutual exclusion — only one thread at a time can hold the lock. As a result, access to a shared object can limit parallelism.

The evolution of Linux kernel locking

The first versions of Linux ran only on uniprocessor machines. To allow Linux to run on multiprocessors, version 2.0 introduced the Big Kernel Lock (BKL) — a single lock that protected all of the kernel's shared data structures. The BKL allowed the kernel to function on multiprocessor machines, but scalability and performance were limited. So, over time, different subsystems and different data structures got their own locks, allowing them to be accessed without holding the BKL.

By version 2.6, Linux has been highly optimized to run well on multiprocessor machines. It now has thousands of different locks, and researchers have demonstrated scalability for a range of benchmarks on a 48 processor machine. Still, the BKL remains in use in a few — mostly less performance-critical — parts of the Linux kernel, like the reboot system call, some older file systems, and some device drivers.

2. **Communication of shared data.** The performance of a modern processor can vary by a factor of ten (or more) depending on whether the data needed by the processor is already in its cache or not. Modern processors are designed with large caches, so that almost all of the data needed by the processor will already be stored in the cache. On a uniprocessor, it is rare that the processor needs to wait.

   However, on a multiprocessor, the situation is different. Shared data protected by a lock will often need to be copied from one cache to another. Shared data is often in the cache of the processor that last held the lock, and it is needed in the cache of the processor that is next to acquire the lock. Moving data can slow critical section performance significantly compared to a uniprocessor.

3. **False sharing.** A further complication is that the hardware keeps track of shared data at a fixed granularity, often in units of a cache entry of 32 or 64 bytes. This reduces hardware management overhead, but it can cause performance problems if multiple data structures with different sharing behavior fit in the same cache entry. This is called *false sharing*.

false sharing

Fortunately, these effects can be reduced through careful design of shared objects. We caution, however, that you should keep your shared object design simple until you have proven, through detailed measurement, that a more complex design is necessary to achieve your performance target.

To illustrate these concepts, consider a web server with an in-memory cache of recently fetched pages. It is often faster to simply return a page from memory rather than regenerating it from scratch. For example, Google might receive a large number of searches for election results on election night, and there is little reason to do all of the work of a general search in that case.

To implement caching of web pages, the server might have a shared data structure, such as a hash table on the search terms, to point to the cached page if it exists. The hash table is shared among the threads handling client requests, and therefore needs a lock. The hash table is updated whenever a thread generates a new page that is not in the cache. The code might also mark pages that have been recently fetched, to keep them in memory in preference to other requests that do not occur as frequently.

An important question in this design is whether the single lock on the hash table will significantly limit server parallelism. How can we tell if the lock on a shared object is going to be a problem?

A convenient approach is to derive a bound on the performance of a parallel program by assuming that the rest of the program is perfectly parallelizable — in other words, that the only limiting factor is that only one thread at a time can hold the shared lock.

EXAMPLE   Suppose that, on average, a web server spends 5% of each request accessing and manipulating its hash table of recently used web pages. If the hash table is protected by a single lock, what is the maximum possible throughput gain?

ANSWER   The time spent in the critical section is inherently sequential. If we assume all other parts of the server are perfectly parallelizable, then the maximum speedup is a **factor of 20** regardless of how many processors are used.   □

As we mentioned earlier, a further complication is that it can take much longer to fetch shared data on a multiprocessor because the data is unlikely to be in the processor cache. If the portion of the program holding the lock is slower on a multiprocessor than on a uniprocessor, the potential gain in throughput can be severely limited.

EXAMPLE   In the example above, what is the maximum throughput improvement if the hash table code runs four times slower on a multiprocessor due to the need to move shared data between processor caches?

ANSWER   The potential throughput improvement would be small even if a large number of processors are used.

$$\text{Throughput gain} \leq \frac{1}{4 \times 0.05} = \mathbf{5}$$

□

We can study the effect of cache behavior on multiprocessor performance with a simple experiment. The experiment is a intended only as an illustration; it is not meant a reflection of normal program behavior, but rather as a way of isolating the effect of hardware on the performance of code using shared objects.

Suppose we set up an array of a thousand shared objects, where each object is a simple integer counter protected by a spinlock. (We use a spinlock rather than a lock to avoid measuring context switch time.) The program

One thread, one array	51.2
Two threads, two arrays	52.5
Two threads, one array	197.4
Two threads, alternating	127.3

Figure 6.1: Number of CPU cycles to execute a simple critical section to increment a counter. Measurements taken on a 64-core AMD Opteron 6262, with threads assigned to processor cores that do not share a cache. The performance difference between these cases largely disappears when threads are assigned to cores that share an L2 cache.

iterates through the array. For each item, it acquires the lock, increments the counter, and releases the lock. We repeat the loop a thousand times to improve measurement precision.

Consider the following scenarios:

- **One thread, one array.** When one thread iterates through the array, incrementing each counter in turn, the test gives the time it takes to acquire and release an array of uncontended locks.

- **Two threads, two arrays.** When two threads iterate through disjoint arrays, this gives the slowdown when doing work in parallel. On most architectures, there is little to no slowdown to parallel execution.

- **Two threads, one array.** When two threads iterate through the *same* array, each lock is acquired by a thread running on one processor, and then, shortly afterwards, acquired by a different thread running on a different processor. Thus, the performance illustrates the added cost of moving the shared object data from one processor to another.

- **Two threads, alternate elements of one array.** To measure the impact of false sharing, one thread can iterate through the array acquiring the odd entries, and the other thread can iterate through the array acquiring the even entries. If there was no effect to false sharing, this would be identical to the two array case — the threads never use the same data.

Table 6.1 shows example results for a single multiprocessor, a 64-core AMD Opteron; the performance on different machines will vary. The threads were assigned to cores that do not share a cache.

On this machine, there is very little slowdown in critical section performance when threads access disjoint locks. However, critical section execution time slows down by a factor of four when multiple processors access the same data. The slowdown is also significant when false sharing occurs.

6.2 | Lock Design Patterns

If a lock is a bottleneck, can we restructure the program to reduce the problem?

We next discuss a set of approaches that can reduce the impact of locking on multiprocessor performance. Often, the best practice is to start simple, with a single lock per shared object. If an object's interface is well designed, then refactoring its implementation to increase concurrency and performance can be done once the system is built and performance measurements can identify any bottlenecks. An adage to follow is: "It is easier to go from a working system to a working, fast system than to go from a fast system to a fast, working system."

We discuss four design patterns to increase concurrency when it is necessary:

- **Fine-Grained Locking.** Partition an object's state into different subsets each protected by a different lock.

- **Per-Processor Data Structures.** Partition an object's state so that all or most accesses are performed by threads running on the same processor.

- **Ownership Design Pattern.** Remove a shared object from a shared container so that only a single thread can read or modify the object.

- **Staged Architecture.** Divide system into multiple stages, so that only those threads within each stage can access that stage's shared data.

6.2.1   Fine-Grained Locking

A simple and widely used approach to decrease contention for a shared lock is to partition the shared object's state into different subsets, each protected by its own lock. This is called *fine-grained locking*.

fine-grained locking

The web server cache discussed above provides an example. The cache can use a shared hash table to store and locate recently used web pages; because the hash table is shared, it needs a lock to provide mutual exclusion. The lock is acquired and released at the start and end of each of the hash table methods: put(key, value), value = get(key), and value = remove(key).

If the single lock limits performance, an alternative is to have one lock per hash bucket. The methods acquire the lock for bucket b before accessing any record that hashes to that bucket. Provided that the number of buckets is large enough, and no single bucket receives a large fraction of requests, then different threads can use and update the hash table in parallel.

However, there is no free lunch. Dividing an object's state into different pieces protected by different locks can significantly increase the object's complexity. Suppose we want to implement a hash table whose number of hash buckets grows as the number of objects it stores increases. If we have a single lock, this is easy to do. But, what if we use fine-grained locking? Then, the design becomes more complex because we have some methods, like put and get, that operate on one bucket and other methods, like resize, that operate across multiple buckets.

Several solutions are possible:

1. **Introduce a readers/writers lock.** Suppose we have a readers/writers lock on the overall structure of the hash table (e.g., the number of buckets and the array of buckets) and a mutual exclusion lock on each bucket. Methods that work on a single bucket at a time, such as put and get, acquire the table's readers/writers lock in read mode and also acquire the relevant bucket's mutual exclusion lock. Methods that change the table's structure, such as resize, must acquire the readers/writers lock in write mode; the readers/writers lock prevents any other threads from using the hash table while it is being resized.

2. **Acquire every lock.** Methods that change the structure of the hash table, such as resize, must first iterate through every bucket, acquiring its lock, before proceeding. Once resize has a lock on every bucket, it is guaranteed that no other thread is concurrently accessing or modifying the hash table.

3. **Divide the hash key space.** Another solution is to divide the hash key space into r regions, to have a mutual exclusion lock for each region, and to allow each region to be resized independently when it becomes heavily loaded. Then, get, put, and resizeRegion each acquire the relevant region's mutual exclusion lock.

Which solution is best? It is not obvious. The first solution is simple and appears to allow high concurrency, but acquiring the readers/writers lock even in read mode may have high overhead. For example, we gave an implementation of a readers/writers lock in Chapter 5 where acquiring a read-only lock involves acquiring a mutual exclusion lock on both entrance and exit. Access to the underlying mutual exclusion lock may become a bottleneck.

The second solution makes resize expensive, but if resize is a rare operation, that may be acceptable. The third solution balances concurrency for get/put against the cost of resize, but it is more complex and may require tuning the number of groups to get good performance.

Further, these trade-offs may change as the implementation becomes more complex. For example, to trigger resize at appropriate times, we probably need to maintain an additional nObjects count of the number of objects currently stored in the hash table, so whatever locking approach we use would need to be extended to cover this information.

EXAMPLE How might you use fine-grained locking to reduce contention for the lock protecting the shared memory heap in malloc/free or new/delete?

ANSWER **One approach would be to partition the heap into separate memory regions, each with its own lock.** For example, a fast implementation of a heap on a uniprocessor uses n buckets, where the ith bucket contains blocks of size 2^i, and serves requests of size $2^{i-1} + 1$ to 2^i. If there are no free blocks in the ith bucket, an item from the next larger bucket $i + 1$ is split in two. Using fine-grained locking, each bucket can be given its own lock.   □

6.2.2   Per-Processor Data Structures

A related technique to fine-grained locking is to partition the shared data structure based on the number of processors on the machine. For example, instead of one shared hash table of cached pages, an alternative design would have N separate hash tables, where N is the number of processors. Each thread uses the hash table based on the processor where it is currently running. Each hash table still needs its own lock in case a thread is context switched in the middle of an operation, but in the common case, only threads running on the same processor contend for the same lock.

Often, this is combined with a per-processor ready list, ensuring that each thread preferentially runs on the same processor each time it is context switched, further improving execution speed.

An advantage of this approach is better hardware cache behavior; as we saw in the previous section, shared data that must be communicated between processors can slow down the execution of critical sections. Of course, the disadvantage is that the hash tables are now partitioned, so that a web page may be cached in one processor's hash table, and needed in another. Whether this is a performance benefit depends on the relative impact of reducing communication of shared data versus the decreased effectiveness of the cache.

EXAMPLE   How might you use per-processor data structures to reduce contention for the memory heap? Under what conditions would this work well?

ANSWER   **The heap can be partitioned into N separate memory regions, one for each processor.** Calls to malloc/new would use the local heap; free/delete would return the data to the heap where it was allocated. **This would perform well provided that (i) rebalancing the heaps was rare and (ii) most allocated data is freed by the thread that acquires it.**   □

6.2.3   Ownership Design Pattern

ownership design pattern

A common synchronization technique in large, multi-threaded programs is an *ownership design pattern*. In this pattern, a thread removes an object from a container and can then access the object without holding a lock: the program structure guarantees that at most one thread owns an object at a time.

As an example, a single web page can contain multiple objects, including HTML frames, style sheets, and images. Consider a multi-threaded web browser whose processing is divided into three stages: receiving an object via the network, parsing the object, and rendering the object (see Figure 6.2).

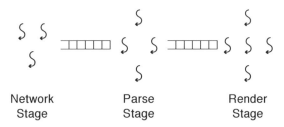

Network   Parse   Render
Stage   Stage   Stage

Figure 6.2: A multi-stage server based on the ownership pattern. In the first stage, one thread exclusively owns each network connection. In later stages, one thread parses and renders a given object at a time.

The first stage has one thread per network connection; the other stages have several worker threads, each of which processes one object at a time.

The work queues between stages coordinate object ownership. Objects in the queues are not being accessed by any thread. When a worker thread in the *parse* stage removes an object from the stage's work queue, it owns the object and has exclusive access to it. When the thread is done parsing the object, it puts it into the second queue and stops accessing it. A worker thread from the *render* stage then removes it from the second queue, gaining exclusive access to it to render it to the screen.

EXAMPLE   How might you use the ownership design pattern to reduce contention for the memory heap?

ANSWER   Ownership can be seen as an extension of per-processor data structures; instead of one heap per processor, **we can have one heap per thread.** Provided that the same thread that allocates memory also frees it, the thread can safely use its own heap without a lock and only return to the global heap when the local heap is out of space.   □

6.2.4   Staged Architecture

staged architecture   The *staged architecture* pattern, illustrated in Figure 6.3, divides a system into multiple subsystems, called stages. Each stage includes state private to the stage and a set of one or more worker threads that operate on that state. Different stages communicate by sending messages to each other via shared producer-consumer queues. Each worker thread repeatedly pulls the next message from a stage's incoming queue and then processes it, possibly producing one or more messages for other stages' queues.

Figure 6.3 shows a staged architecture for a simple web server that has a first *connect* stage that uses one thread to set up network connections and that passes each connection to a second *read and parse* stage.

The *read and parse* stage has several threads, each of which repeatedly gets a connection from the incoming queue, reads a request from the connection,

Commutative interface design

Class and interface design can often constrain implementations in ways that require locking. An example is the UNIX API. Like most operating systems, the UNIX open system call returns a file handle that is used for further operations on the file; the same system call is also used to initialize a network socket. The open call gives the operating system the ability to allocate internal data structures to track the current state of the file or network socket, and more broadly, which files and sockets are in use.

UNIX also specifies that each successive call to open returns the next integer file handle; as we saw in Chapter 3, the UNIX shell uses this feature when redirecting stdin and stdout to a file or pipe.

A consequence of the design of the UNIX API is that the implementation of open requires a lock. For early UNIX systems, this was not an issue, but modern multi-threaded web servers open extremely large numbers of network sockets and files. Because of the semantics of the API, the implementation of open cannot use fine-grained locking or a per-processor data structure.

A better choice, where possible, is to design the API to be *commutative*: the result of two calls is the same regardless of which call was made first. For example, if the implementation can return any unique integer as a file handle, rather than the next successive one, then the implementation could allocate out of a per-processor bucket of open file handles. The implementation would then need a lock only for the special case of allocating specific handles such as stdin and stdout.

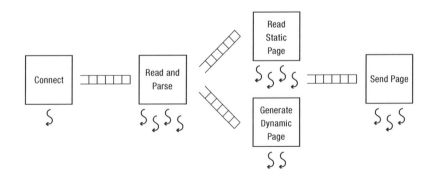

Figure 6.3: A staged architecture for a simple web server.

parses the request to determine what web page is being requested, and checks to see if the page is already cached.

Assuming the page is not already cached, if the request is for a static web page (e.g., an HTML file), the *read and parse* stage passes the request and connection to the *read static page* stage, where one of the stage's threads reads the specified page from disk. Otherwise, the *read and parse* stage passes the request and connection to the *generate dynamic page* stage, where one of the stage's threads runs a program that dynamically generates a page in response to the request.

Once the page has been fetched or generated, the page and connection are passed to the *send page* stage, where one of the threads transmits the page over the connection.

What are the benefits of staged architectures?

The key property of a staged architecture is that the state of each stage is private to that stage. This improves modularity, making it easier to reason about each stage individually and about interactions across stages.

As an example of the modularity benefits, consider a system where different stages are produced by different teams or even different companies. Each stage can be designed and tested almost independently, and the system is likely to work as expected when the stages are brought together. For example, it is common practice for a web site to use a web server from one company and a database from another company and for the two to communicate via messages.

Another benefit is improved cache locality. A thread operating on a subset of the system's state may have better cache behavior than a thread that accesses state from all stages. On the other hand, for some workloads, passing a request from stage to stage could hurt cache behavior compared to doing all of the processing for a request on one processor.

Also note that for good performance, the processing in each stage must be large enough to amortize the cost of sending and receiving messages.

The special case of exactly one thread per stage is *event-driven programming*, described in Chapter 4. With event-driven programming, there is no concurrency within a stage, so no locking is required. Each message is processed atomically with respect to that stage's state.

What are the drawbacks of staged architectures?

One challenge with staged architectures is dealing with overload. System throughput is limited by the throughput of the slowest stage. If the system is overloaded, the slowest stage will fall behind, and its work queue will grow. Depending on the system's implementation, two bad things could happen. First, the queue could grow indefinitely, consuming more and more memory until the system memory heap is exhausted. Second, if the queue is limited to a finite size, once that size is reached, earlier stages must either discard work for the overloaded stage or block until the queue has room. Notice that if they block, then the backpressure will limit the throughput of earlier stages to that of the bottleneck stage, and their queues in turn may begin to grow.

One solution is to dynamically vary the number of threads per stage. If a stage's incoming queue is growing, the program can shift processing resources to it by reducing the number of threads for a lightly-loaded stage in favor of more threads for the stage that is falling behind.

6.3 | Lock Contention

If a lock is still a bottleneck after re-structuring, what then?

Sometimes, even after applying the techniques described in the previous section, locking may remain a bottleneck to good performance on a multiprocessor. For example, with fine-grained locking of a hash table, if a bucket contains a particularly popular item, say the cached page for Justin Bieber, then the lock on that bucket can be a source of contention.

In this section, we discuss two alternate implementations of the lock abstraction that work better for locks that are bottlenecks:

- **MCS Locks.** MCS is an implementation of a spinlock optimized for the case when there are a significant number of waiting threads.

- **RCU Locks.** RCU is an implementation of a reader/writer lock, optimized for the case when there are many more readers than writers. RCU reduces the overhead for readers at a cost of increased overhead for writers. More importantly, RCU has somewhat different semantics than a normal reader/writer lock, placing a burden on the user of the lock to understand its dangers.

Although both approaches are used in modern operating system kernels, we caution that neither is a panacea. They should only be used once profiling has shown that the lock is a source of contention and no other options are available.

6.3.1 MCS Locks

Can we optimize locks for the case when many threads are waiting?

Recall that the lock implementation described in Chapter 5 was tuned for the common case where the lock was usually FREE. Is there an efficient implementation of locks when the lock is usually BUSY?

Unfortunately, the overhead of acquiring and releasing a lock can *increase* dramatically with the number of threads contending for the lock. For a contended lock, this can further increase the number of threads waiting for the lock. Consider again the example we used earlier, of a spinlock protecting a shared counter:

```
void Counter::Increment() {
    while (test_and_set(&lock)) // while BUSY
        ; // spin
    value++;
    lock = FREE;
    memory_barrier();
}
```

Even if many threads try to increment the same counter, only one thread at a time can execute the critical section; the other threads must wait their turn. As we observed earlier, because the counter value must be communicated from

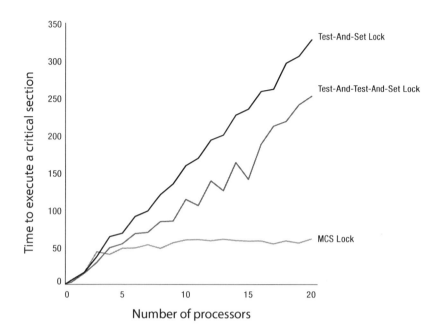

Figure 6.4: The overhead of three alternative lock implementations as a function of the number of processors contending for the lock: (a) test-and-set, (b) test and test-and-set, and (c) MCS. Measurements taken on a 64-core AMD Opteron 6262. The non-smooth curves are typical of measurements of real systems.

one lock holder to the next, the critical section will take significantly longer on a multiprocessor than on a single processor.

However, the situation with multiple waiting threads is even worse. The time to execute a critical section protected by a spinlock increases linearly with the number of spinning processors. Figure 6.4 illustrates this effect. The problem is that before a processor can execute an atomic read-modify-write instruction, the hardware must obtain exclusive access to that memory location. Any other read-modify-write instruction must occur either before or afterwards.

Thus, if a number of processors are executing a spin loop, they will all be trying to gain exclusive access to the memory location of the lock. The store instruction to clear the lock also needs exclusive access, and the hardware has no way to know that it should prioritize the lock release ahead of the competing requests to see if the lock is free.

test and test-and-set One might think that it would help to check that the lock is free before trying to acquire it with a test-and-set; this is called *test and test-and-set*:

```
void Counter :: Increment () {
    while (lock == BUSY || test_and_set(&lock)) // while BUSY
        ; // spin
    value++;
    lock = FREE;
    memory_barrier ();
}
```

However, it turns out this does not help. When the lock is released, the new value of the lock, FREE, must be communicated to the other waiting processors. On modern systems, each processor separately fetches the data into its cache. Eventually one of them gets the new value and acquires the lock. If the critical section is not very long, the other processors will still be busy fetching the new value and trying to acquire the lock, preventing the lock release from completing.

One approach is to adjust the frequency of polling to the length of time that the thread has been waiting. A more scalable solution is to assign each waiting thread a separate memory location where it can spin. To release a lock, the bit is set for *one* thread, telling it that it is the next to acquire the lock.

The most widely used implementation of this idea is known as the MCS lock, after the initials of its authors, Mellor-Crummey and Scott. The MCS lock takes advantage of an atomic read-modify-write instruction called *compare-and-swap* that is supported on most modern multiprocessor architectures. Compare-and-swap tests the value of a memory location and swaps in a new value if the old value has not changed.

compare-and-swap

Compare-and-swap can be used to build a queue of waiting threads, without a separate spinlock. A waiting thread atomically adds itself to the *tail* of the queue, and then spins on a flag in its queue entry. When a thread releases the lock, it sets the flag in the next queue entry, signaling to the thread that its turn is next. Figure 6.5 provides an implementation, and Figure 6.6 illustrates the algorithm in action.

Because each thread in the queue spins on its own queue entry, the lock can be passed efficiently from one thread to another along the queue. Of course, the overhead of setting up the queue means that an MCS lock is less efficient than a normal spinlock unless there are a large number of waiting threads.

6.3.2   Read-Copy-Update (RCU)

Read-copy-update

Read-copy-update (RCU) provides high-performance synchronization for data structures that are frequently read and occasionally updated. In particular, RCU optimizes the read path to have extremely low synchronization costs even with a large number of concurrent readers. However, writes can be delayed for a long time — tens of milliseconds in some implementations.

```
class MCSLock {                          MCSLock::acquire() {
  private:                                 Queue *oldTail = tail;
    Queue *tail = NULL;
}                                          myTCB->next = NULL;
                                           while (!compare_and_swap(&tail,
MCSLock::release() {                                              oldTail, &myTCB)) {

    if (compare_and_swap(&tail,               // Try again if someone else
                 myTCB, NULL)) {              // changed tail in the meantime.

        // If tail == myTCB, no one is        oldTail = tail;
        // waiting. MCSLock is now free.    }

    } else {                               // If oldTail == NULL, lock acquired.
        // Someone is waiting.             if (oldTail != NULL) {
        while (myTCB->next == NULL)           // Need to wait.
            ; // spin until next is set       myTCB->needToWait = TRUE;
                                              memory_barrier();
        // Tell next thread to proceed.       oldTail->next = myTCB;
        myTCB->next->needToWait = FALSE;      while (myTCB->needToWait)
    }                                             ; // spin
}                                          }
                                         }
```

Figure 6.5: Pseudo-code for an MCS queueing lock, where each waiting thread spins on a separate memory location in its thread control block (myTCB). The operation, compare-and-swap, atomically inserts the TCB at the tail of the queue.

Why Not Use a Readers/Writers Lock?

Standard readers/writers locks are a poor fit for certain types of read-dominated workloads. Recall that these locks allow an arbitrary number of concurrent active readers, but when there is an active writer, no other writer or reader can be active.

The problem occurs when there are many concurrent reads with short critical sections. Before reading, each reader must acquire a readers/writers lock in read mode and release it afterwards. On both entrance and exit, the reader must update some state in the readers/writers synchronization object. Even when there are only readers, the readers/writers synchronization object can become a bottleneck. This limits the rate at which readers can enter the critical section, because they can only acquire the lock one at a time. For critical sections of less than a few thousand cycles, and for programs with dozens of threads simultaneously reading a shared object, the standard readers/writers lock can limit performance.

While the readers/writers synchronization object could be implemented with an MCS lock and thereby reduce some of the effects of lock contention, it does not change the inherent serial access of the readers/writers control structure.

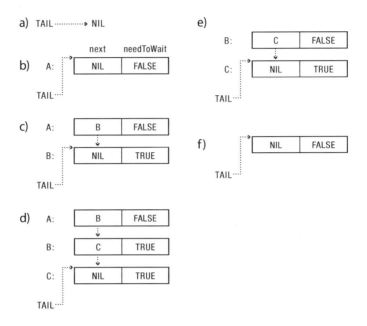

Figure 6.6: The behavior of the MCS queueing lock. Initially (a), tail is NULL indicating that the lock is FREE. To acquire the lock (b), thread A atomically sets tail to point to A's TCB. Additional threads B and C queue by adding themselves (atomically) to the tail (c) and (d); they then spin on their respective TCB's needToWait flag. Thread A hands the lock to B by clearing B's needToWait flag (e); B hands the lock to C by clearing C's needToWait fla (f). C releases the lock by setting tail back to NULL (a) iff no one else is waiting — that is, iff tail still points to C's TCB.

The RCU Approach

How can concurrent reads access a data structure — one that can also be written — without having to update the state of a synchronization variable on each read?

To meet this challenge, an RCU lock retains the basic structure of a reader/writers lock: readers (and writers) surround each critical section with calls to acquire and release the RCU lock in read-mode (or write-mode). An RCU lock makes three important changes to the standard interface:

publish
1. **Restricted update.** With RCU, the writer thread must *publish* its changes to the shared data structure with a single, atomic memory write. Typically, this is done by updating a single pointer, as we illustrate below by using RCU to update a shared list.

   Although restricted updates might seem to severely limit the types of data structure operations that are possible under RCU, this is not the case. A common pattern is for the writer thread to make a *copy* of a complex data structure (or a portion of it), update the copy, and then

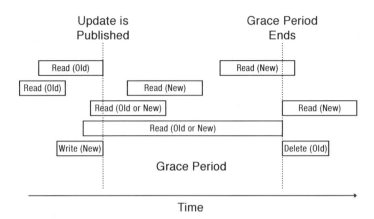

Figure 6.7: Timeline for an update concurrent with several reads for a data structure accessed with read-copy-update (RCU) synchronization.

publish a pointer to the copy into a shared location where it can be accessed by new readers.

2. **Multiple concurrent versions.** RCU allows any number of read-only critical sections to be in progress at the same time as the update. These read-only critical sections may see the old or new version of the data structure.

3. **Integration with the thread scheduler.** Because there may be readers still in progress when an update is made, the shared object must maintain multiple versions of its state, to guarantee that an old version is not freed until all readers have finished accessing it. The time from when an update is published until the last reader is done with the previous version is called the *grace period*. The RCU lock uses information provided by the thread scheduler to determine when a grace period ends.

grace period

Figure 6.7 shows the timeline for the critical sections of a writer and several reader threads under RCU. If a function that reads the data structure completes before a write is published, it sees the old version of the data structure; if a reader begins after a write is published, it sees the new version. But, if a reader begins *before* and ends *after* a write is published, it may see either the old version or the new one. If it reads the updated pointer more than once, it may see the old one and then the new one. Which version it sees depends on which version of the single, atomically-updated memory location it observes. However, the system guarantees that the old version is not deleted until the grace period expires. The deletion of the old version must be delayed until all reads that might observe the old version have completed.

	Reader API
RCU::readLock()	Enter read-only critical section.
RCU::readUnlock()	Exit read-only critical section.

	Writer API
RCU::writeLock()	Enter read-write critical section.
RCU::publish()	Atomically update shared data structure.
RCU::writeUnlock()	Exit read-write critical section.
RCU::synchronize()	Wait for all currently active readers to exit critical section, to allow for garbage collection of old versions of the object.

	Scheduler API
RCU::quiescentState()	Of the read-only threads on this processor who were active during the most recent RCU::publish, all have exited the critical section.

Figure 6.8: Sample programming interface for read-copy-update (RCU) synchronization. In Java's implementation of RCU locks, synchronize and quiescentState are not needed because the language-level garbage collector automatically detects when old versions can no longer be accessed. In the implementation of RCU in the Linux kernel, synchronize is split into two calls: one to start the grace period, and one to wait until the grace period completes.

Figure 6.9: RCU allows one write at a time, and it allows reads to overlap each other and writes. The initial version is v0, and overlapping writes update the version to v1, v2, and then v3.

RCU API and Use

RCU is a synchronization abstraction that allows concurrent access to a data structure by multiple readers and a single writer at a time. Figure 6.8 shows a typical API.

A reader calls RCU::readLock and RCU::readUnlock before and after accessing the shared data structure. A writer calls: RCU::writeLock to exclude other writers;

```
typedef struct ElementS{                    bool
  int key;                                  RCUList::search(int key, int *valuep) {
  int value;                                    bool result = FALSE;
  struct ElementS *next;                        Element *current;
} Element;
                                                rcuLock.readLock();
class RCUList {                                  current = head;
  private:                                       for (current = head; current != NULL;
    RCULock rcuLock;                                       current = current->next) {
    Element *head;                                    if (current->key == key) {
  public:                                                *valuep = current->value;
    bool search(int key, int *value);                   result = TRUE;
    void insert(Element *item, value);                   break;
    bool remove(int key);                            }
};                                              }
                                                rcuLock.readUnlock();
                                                return result;
                                            }
```

Figure 6.10: Declaration of data structures and API for a linked list that uses RCU for synchronization, and the implementation of a read-only method for searching the linked list using RCU.

RCU::publish to issue the write that atomically updates the data structure so that reads can see the updates; RCU::writeUnlock to let other writers proceed; and RCU::synchronize to wait for the grace period to expire so that the old version of the object can be freed.

As Figure 6.9 illustrates, writes are serialized — only one write can proceed at a time. However, a write can be concurrent with any number of reads. A write can also be concurrent with another write's grace period: there may be any number of versions of the object until multiple overlapping grace periods expire.

EXAMPLE   For each read in Figure 6.9, which version(s) of the shared state can the read observe?

ANSWER   If a read overlaps a publish, it can return the published value or the previous value:

$read_1$	v0 or v1	Overlaps publish v1.
$read_2$	v2	After publish v2, before publish v3.
$read_3$	v3	After publish v3.
$read_4$	v0 or v1	Overlaps publish v1.
$read_5$	v1 or v2	Overlaps publish v2.
$read_6$	v0, v1, or v2	Overlaps publish v1 and v2.
$read_7$	v3	After publish v2.

EXAMPLE   **RCU linked list.** Figures 6.10 and 6.11 show how to use RCU locks to implement a linked list that can be accessed concurrently by many readers, while also being updated by one writer.

The list data structure comprises an RCU lock and a pointer to the head of the list. Each entry in the list has two data fields — key and value — as well as a pointer to the next record on the list.

```
void                                    bool
RCUList::insert(int key,                RCUList::remove(int key) {
                int value) {                bool found = FALSE;
    Element *item;                          Element *prev, *current;

    // One write at a time.                 // One write at a time.
    rcuLock.writeLock();                    rcuLock.WriteLock();
                                            for (prev = NULL, current = head;
    // Initialize item.                          current != NULL; prev = current,
    item = (Element*)                            current = current->next) {
        malloc(sizeof(Element));            if (current->key == key) {
    item->key = key;                            found = TRUE;
    item->value = value;
    item->next = head;                              // Publish update to readers
                                                    if (prev == NULL) {
    // Atomically update list.                          rcuLock.publish(&head,
    rcuLock.publish(&head, item);                                    current->next);
                                                    } else {
    // Allow other writes                               rcuLock.publish(&(prev->next),
    // to proceed.                                                   current->next);
    rcuLock.writeUnlock();                          }
                                                    break;
    // Wait until no reader                     }
    // has old version.                     }
    rcuLock.synchronize();
}                                           // Allow other writes to proceed.
                                            rcuLock.writeUnlock();

                                            // Wait until no reader has old version.
                                            if (found) {
                                                rcuLock.synchronize();
                                                free(current);
                                            }
                                            return found;
                                        }
```

Figure 6.11: Implementation a linked list using RCU for synchronization.

The search method is read-only: after registering with readLock, it scans down the list until it finds an element with a matching key. If the element is found, the method uses the parameter to return the value field and then returns TRUE. Otherwise, the method returns FALSE to indicate that no matching record was found.

The methods to update the list are more subtle. Each of them is arranged so that a single pointer update is sufficient to publish the new version of the list to the readers. In particular, it is important that insert initialize the data structure *before* updating the head pointer to make the new element visible to readers.

Implementing RCU

When implementing RCU, the central goal is to minimize the cost of read critical sections: the system must allow an arbitrary number of concurrent

```
class RCULock{                              void RCULock::writeLock() {
  private:                                      writerSpin.acquire();
  // Global state                           }
    Spinlock globalSpin;
    long globalCounter;                     void RCULock::writeUnlock() {
  // One per processor                          writerSpin.release();
    DEFINE_PER_PROCESSOR(                    }
        static long, quiescentCount);
                                            void RCULock::publish (void **pp1,
  // Per-lock state                                                 void *p2){
    Spinlock writerSpin;                        memory_barrier();
                                                *pp1 = p2;
  // Public API omitted                         memory_barrier();
}                                           }

void RCULock::ReadLock() {                  void
    disableInterrupts();                    RCULock::synchronize() {
}                                               int p, c;

void RCULock::ReadUnlock() {                     globalSpin.acquire();
    enableInterrupts();                         c = ++globalCounter;
}                                               globalSpin.release();

// Called by scheduler                           FOREACH_PROCESSOR(p) {
void RCULock::QuiescentState(){                     while ((PER_PROC_VAR(
    memory_barrier();                               quiescentCount, p) - c) < 0) {
    PER_PROC_VAR(quiescentCount) =                    // release CPU for 10ms
                    globalCounter;                    sleep(10);
    memory_barrier();                              }
}                                               }
                                            }
```

Figure 6.12: A quiescence-based RCU implementation. The code assumes that spinlock acquire/release and interrupt enable/disable trigger a memory barrier. *Credit:* This pseudo-code is based on an implementation by Paul McKenney in "Is Parallel Programming Hard, And, If So, What Can be Done About It?"

readers. Conversely, writes can have high *latency*. In particular, grace periods can be long, with tens of milliseconds from when an update is published until the system can guarantee that no readers are still using the old version. Even so, write *overhead* — the CPU time needed per write — should be modest.

A common technique for achieving these goals is to integrate the RCU implementation with that of the thread scheduler. This is in contrast with the readers/writers lock described in the previous chapter, which makes no assumptions about the thread scheduler, but which must track exactly how many readers are active at any given time.

In particular, the implementation we present requires two things from the scheduler: (1) read-only critical sections complete without being interrupted and (2) whenever a thread on a processor is interrupted, the scheduler updates some per-processor RCU state. Then, once a write completes, RCU-Lock::Synchronize simply waits for all processors to be interrupted at least once. **quiescent** At that point, the old version of the object is known to be *quiescent* — no thread has access to the old version (other than the writer who changed it).

Figure 6.12 shows an implementation of RCU based on quiescent states. Notice first that readLock and readUnlock are inexpensive: they update no state and merely ensure that the read is not interrupted. RCU::writeLock and writeUnlock are also inexpensive. They acquire and release a spinlock to ensure that at most one write per RCULock can proceed at a time.

RCU::publish is also simple. It executes a memory barrier so that all modifications to the shared object are completed before the pointer is updated. It then updates the pointer, and then executes another memory barrier so that other processors observe the update.

RCU::synchronize and quiescentState work together to ensure that when synchronize returns, all threads are guaranteed to be done with the old version of the object. RCU::synchronize increments a global counter and then waits until all processors' match the new value of that counter. RCU::quiescentState is called by the scheduler whenever that processor is interrupted. It updates that processor's quiescentCount to match the current globalCounter. Thus, once quiescentCount is at least as large as c, on every processor, synchronize knows that no remaining readers can observe the old version.

6.4 | Multi-Object Atomicity

How can we make a sequence of operations across multiple objects appear atomic to other threads?

Once a program has multiple shared objects, it becomes both necessary and challenging to reason about interactions across objects. For example, consider a system storing a bank's accounts. A reasonable design choice might be for each customer's account to be a shared object with a lock (either a mutual exclusion lock or a readers/writers lock, as described in Chapter 5). Consider, however, transferring $100 from account A to account B, as follows:

```
A->subtract(100);
B->add(100);
```

Although each individual action is atomic, the sequence of actions is not. As a result, there may be a time where, say, A tells B that the money has been sent, but the money is not yet in B's account.

Similarly, consider a bank manager who wants to answer a question: "How much money does the bank have?" If the manager's program simply reads from each account, the calculation may exclude or double-count money "in flight" between accounts, such as in the transfer from A to B.

These examples illustrate a general problem that arises whenever a program contains multiple shared objects. Even if the object guarantees that each method operates atomically, *sequences* of operations by different threads can be interleaved. The same issues of managing multiple locks also apply to fine-grained locking within an object.

6.4.1 Careful Class Design

Sometimes it is possible to address this issue through careful class and interface design. This includes the design of individual objects (e.g., specifying clean interfaces that expose the right abstractions). It also includes the architecture of how those objects interact (e.g., structuring a system architecture in well-defined layers).

For example, you would face the same issues if you tried to solve Too Much Milk problem with a Note object that has two methods, readNote and writeNote, and a Fridge object with two methods, checkForMilk and addMilk. Atomicity of these individual operations is not sufficient to provide the desired behavior without considerable programming effort.

On the other hand, if we refactor the objects so that we have:

```
Fridge :: checkforMilkAndSetNoteIfNeeded ( );
Fridge :: addMilk ( );
```

Then, the problem becomes straightforward.

This advice may seem obvious: of course, you should strive for elegant designs for both single- and multi-threaded code. Nonetheless, we emphasize that the choices you make for your interfaces, abstractions, and software architecture can dramatically affect the complexity or feasibility of your designs.

6.4.2 Acquire-All/Release-All

Better interface design has limits, however. Sometimes, multiple locks are needed for program structure or for greater concurrency. Is there a general technique to perform a set of operations that require multiple locks, so that the group of operations appears atomic? For clarity, we will refer to a group of operations as a *request*.

acquire-all/release-all

One approach, called *acquire-all/release-all* is to acquire *every* lock that may be needed at any point while processing the entire set of operations in the request. Then, once the thread has all of the locks it might need, the thread can execute the request, and finally, release the locks.

EXAMPLE

Consider a hash table with one lock per hash bucket. To move an item from one bucket to another, the hash table supports a changeKey(item, k1, k2) operation. With acquire-all/release-all, this function could be implemented to first acquire both the locks for k1 and k2, then remove the item under k1 and insert it under k2, and finally release both locks.

Acquire-all/release-all allows significant concurrency. When individual requests touch non-overlapping subsets of state protected by different locks, they can proceed in parallel.

serializability

A key property of this approach is *serializability* across requests: the result of any program execution is equivalent to an execution in which requests are

Figure 6.13: Locking multiple objects using an acquire-all/release-all pattern results in a serializable execution that is equivalent to an execution where requests are executed sequentially in some order.

processed one at a time in some sequential order. Serializability allows one to reason about multi-step tasks *as if* each task executed alone.

As Figure 6.13 illustrates, requests that access non-overlapping data can proceed in parallel. The result is the same as if the system first executed one request and then the other (or equivalently, the reverse). On the other hand, if two requests touch the same data, then the fact that all locks are acquired at the beginning and released at the end implies that one request is completed before the other one begins.

One challenge to using this approach is knowing exactly what locks will be needed by a request before beginning to process it. A potential solution is to conservatively acquire more locks than needed (e.g., acquire any locks that *may* be needed by a particular request), but this may be difficult to determine. Without first executing the request, how can we know which locks will be needed?

6.4.3   Two-Phase Locking

two-phase locking   *Two phase locking* refines the acquire-all/release-all pattern to address this concern. Instead of acquiring all locks before processing the request, locks can be acquired as needed for each operation. However, locks are not *released* until all locks needed by the request have been acquired. Most implementations simply release all locks at the end of the request.

Two-phase locking avoids needing to know what locks to grab *a priori*. Therefore, programs can avoid acquiring locks they do not need, and they may not need to hold locks as long.

EXAMPLE   The changeKey(item, k1, k2) function for a hash table with per-bucket locks could be implemented to acquire k1's lock, remove the item using key k1, acquire k2's lock, insert the item using key k2, and release both locks.

Like acquire-all/release-all, two-phase locking is serializable. If two requests have non-overlapping data, they are commutative and therefore serializable. Otherwise, there is some overlapping data between the two requests, protected by one or more locks. Provided a request completes, it must have acquired all of those locks, and made its changes to the overlapping data, before releasing any of them. Thus, any overlapping request must have read or modified the data in the overlap either entirely before or after the other request.

Unlike acquire-all/release-all, however, two-phase locking can in some cases lead to deadlock, the topic of the next section.

EXAMPLE   Suppose one thread starts executing changeKey(item, k1, k2) and another thread simultaneously tries to move a different item in the other direction from k2 to k1. If the first thread acquires k1's lock and the second thread acquires k2's lock, neither will be able to make progress.

6.5 | Deadlock

deadlock   A challenge to constructing complex multi-threaded programs is the possibility of deadlock. A *deadlock* is a cycle of waiting among a set of threads, where each thread waits for some other thread in the cycle to take some action.

mutually recursive locking   Deadlock can occur in many different situations, but one of the simplest is *mutually recursive locking*, shown in the code fragment below:

```
// Thread A                          // Thread B

lock1 . acquire ( ) ;               lock2 . acquire ( ) ;
lock2 . acquire ( ) ;               lock1 . acquire ( ) ;
lock2 . release ( ) ;               lock1 . release ( ) ;
lock1 . release ( ) ;               lock2 . release ( ) ;
```

Suppose two shared objects with mutual exclusion locks can call into each other while holding their locks. Deadlock can occur when one thread holds the lock on the first object, and another thread holds the lock on the second object. If the first thread calls into the second object while still holding onto its lock, it will need to wait for the second object's lock. If the other thread does the same thing in reverse, neither will be able to make progress.

We can also get into deadlock with two locks and a condition variable, shown below:

```
// Thread A                          // Thread B

lock1.acquire();                     lock1.acquire();
...                                  ...
lock2.acquire();                     lock2.acquire();
while (need to wait) {               ...
    cv.wait(&lock2);                 cv.signal();
}                                    lock2.release();
...                                  ...
lock2.release();                     lock1.release();
...
lock1.release();
```

nested waiting   In *nested waiting*, one shared object calls into another shared object while holding the first object's lock, and then waits on a condition variable. CV::wait releases the lock of the second object, but not the first. Deadlock results if the thread that can signal the condition variable needs the first lock to make progress.

The problem of deadlock is much broader than just locks and condition variables. Deadlock can occur anytime a thread waits for an event that cannot happen because of a cycle of waiting for a resource held by the first thread. As in the examples above, resources can be locks, but they can also be any other scarce quantity: memory, processing time, disk blocks, or space in a buffer.

Suppose we have two bounded buffers, where one thread puts a request into one buffer, and gets a response out of the other. Deadlock can result if another thread does the reverse.

```
// Thread A                          // Thread B

buffer1.put();                       buffer2.put();
buffer1.put();                       buffer2.put();
...                                  ...
buffer2.get();                       buffer1.get();
buffer2.get();                       buffer1.get();
```

If the buffers are almost full, both threads will need to wait for there to be room, and so neither will be able to reach the point where they can pull data out of the other buffer to allow the other thread to make progress.

Deadlocks also occur in real life. We encourage you to develop your intuition about deadlocks by considering why deadlocks occur and how we might prevent them. For example, if we lived in a world without stop signs, we might see the deadlock in Figure 6.14 more often.

The scarce resource leading to deadlock can even be a chopstick. The Dining Philosophers problem is a classic illustration of both the challenges and solutions to deadlock; an example is shown in Figure 6.15. There is a round table with n plates alternating with n chopsticks around the circle. A philosopher sitting at a plate requires two chopsticks to eat. Suppose that each

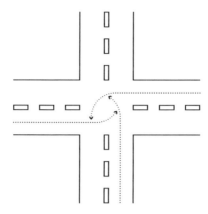

Figure 6.14: An example of deadlock where three tractor-trailer trucks enter an intersection without first checking whether they can clear the intersection.

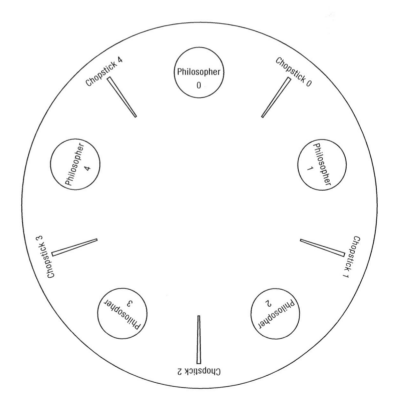

Figure 6.15: In this example of the dining philosophers problem, there are 5 philosophers, 5 plates, and 5 chopsticks.

philosopher proceeds by picking up the chopstick on the left, picking up the chopstick on the right, eating, and then putting down both chopsticks. If every philosopher follows this approach, there can be a deadlock: each philosopher takes the chopstick on the left but can be stuck waiting for the philosopher on the right to release the chopstick.

Note that mutually recursive locking is equivalent to Dining Philosophers with $n = 2$.

The rest of this section addresses the following questions:

- **Deadlock vs. Starvation.** How does deadlock relate to the concepts of liveness and starvation?

- **Necessary Conditions for Deadlock.** What conditions are required for deadlock to be possible?

- **Preventing Deadlock.** What techniques can be used to prevent deadlock?

- **The Banker's Algorithm for Avoiding Deadlock.** The Banker's Algorithm is a general-purpose mechanism for preventing deadlock by exploiting knowledge of what resources may be needed in the future.

- **Detecting and Recovering From Deadlock.** In some systems, deadlock is not prevented but repaired when it occurs. How can we detect deadlock and then recover?

6.5.1   Deadlock vs. Starvation

Deadlock and starvation are both liveness concerns. In *starvation*, a thread fails to make progress for an indefinite period of time. Deadlock is a form of starvation but with the stronger condition: a group of threads forms a cycle where none of the threads make progress because each thread is waiting for some other thread in the cycle to take action. Thus, deadlock implies starvation (literally, for the dining philosophers), but starvation does not imply deadlock.

For example, recall the readers/writers example discussed in Section 5.6.1. A writer only waits if a reader or writer is active. In the writers-preferred solution we gave, waiting readers can starve if new writers arrive sufficiently frequently; likewise, waiting writers can starve if there is an active reader, and new readers arrive and become active before the last one completes. Note that such starvation would not be deadlock because there is no cycle. The waiting readers are waiting on the active writers to finish, and the waiting writers are waiting on the active readers to finish, but no active thread is waiting on a waiting reader or writer.

Does the possibility of deadlock imply that it must happen?

Just because a system can suffer deadlock or starvation does not mean that it always will. A system is *subject to starvation* if a thread could starve in some circumstances. A system is *subject to deadlock* if a group of threads could deadlock in some circumstances. Here, the circumstances that affect whether deadlock or starvation occurs could include a broad range of factors, such as: the choices made by the scheduler, the number of threads running, the workload or sequence of requests processed by the system, which threads win races to acquire locks, and which threads are enabled in what order when signals or broadcasts occur.

A system that is subject to starvation or deadlock may be live in many or most runs and starve or deadlock only for particular workloads or "unlucky" interleavings. For example, in mutually recursive locking, the deadlock only occurs if both threads obtain the outer locks at about the same time. For the Dining Philosophers problem, philosophers may succeed in eating for a long time before hitting the unlucky sequence of events that causes them to deadlock. Similarly, in the readers/writers example, the writers-preferred solution will allow some reads to complete as long as the rate of writes stays below some threshold.

Since testing may not discover deadlock problems, it is important to construct systems that are deadlock-free by design.

6.5.2   Necessary Conditions for Deadlock

What conditions are required for deadlock to be possible?

There are four necessary conditions for deadlock to occur. Knowing these conditions is useful for designing solutions: if you can prevent any one of these conditions, then you can eliminate the possibility of deadlock.

1. **Bounded resources.** There are a finite number of threads that can simultaneously use a resource.

2. **No preemption.** Once a thread acquires a resource, its ownership cannot be revoked until the thread acts to release it.

multiple independent requests

3. **Wait while holding.** A thread holds one resource while waiting for another. This condition is sometimes called *multiple independent requests* because it occurs when a thread first acquires one resource and then tries to acquire another.

4. **Circular waiting.** There is a set of waiting threads such that each thread is waiting for a resource held by another.

EXAMPLE   Show that the Dining Philosophers meet all four conditions for deadlock.

ANSWER   To see that all four conditions are met, observe that

1. **Bounded resources.** Each chopstick can be held by a single philosopher at a time.

2. **No preemption.** Once a philosopher picks up a chopstick, she does not release it until she is done eating, even if that means no one will ever eat.

3. **Wait while holding.** When a philosopher needs to wait for a chopstick, she continues to hold onto any chopsticks she has already picked up.

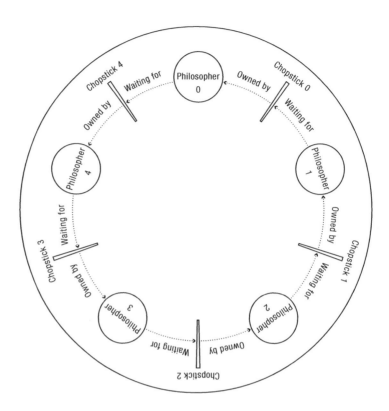

Figure 6.16: Graph representation of the state of a deadlocked Dining Philosophers system. Circles represent threads, boxes represent resources, an arrow from a box/resource to a circle/thread represents an *owned by* relationship, and an arrow from a circle/thread to a box/resource represents a *waiting for* relationship.

4. **Circular waiting.** Figure 6.16 maps the state of a deadlocked Dining Philosophers implementation to an abstract graph that shows which resources are *owned by* which threads and which threads *wait for* which resources. In this type of graph, if there is one instance of each type of resource (e.g., a particular chopstick), then a cycle implies deadlock assuming the system does not allow preemption.

□

The four conditions are necessary *but not sufficient* for deadlock. When there are multiple instances of a type of resource, there can be a cycle of waiting without deadlock because a thread not in the cycle may return resources that enable a waiting thread to proceed.

Suppose we have 5 philosophers at a table with 5 chopsticks, but the chopsticks are placed in a tray at the center of the table when not in use. We could be in the state illustrated in Figure 6.17, where philosopher 1 has two chopsticks, philosophers 2, 3, and 4 each have one chopstick and are waiting

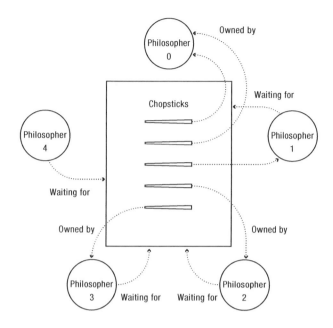

Figure 6.17: Graph representation of the state of a Dining Philosophers system that includes a cycle among waiting threads and resources but that is not deadlocked. Circles represent threads, boxes represent resources, dots within a box represent multiple instances of a resource, an arrow from a dot/resource instance to a circle/thread represents an *owned by* relationship and an arrow from a circle/thread to a box/resource represents a *waiting for* relationship.

for another chopstick, while philosopher 5 has no chopsticks. In this state, we have bounded resources (five chopsticks), no preemption (we cannot forcibly remove a chopstick from a hungry philosopher's hand), wait while holding (philosophers 2, 3 and 4 are holding a chopstick while waiting for another), and circular waiting (each of philosophers 2, 3, and 4 are waiting for a resource held by another of them). However, we do not have deadlock. Eventually, philosopher 1 will release its two chopsticks, which may, for example, allow philosophers 2 and 3 to eat and release their chopsticks. In turn, this would allow philosophers 4 and 5 to eat.

Although the system shown in Figure 6.17 is not currently deadlocked, it is still *subject to deadlock*. For example, if philosopher 1 returns two chopsticks, philosopher 5 picks up one, and philosopher 1 picks up the other, then the system would deadlock.

6.5.3 Preventing Deadlock

What techniques can be used to prevent deadlock?

Preventing deadlock can be challenging. For example, consider a system with three resources — A, B, and C — and two threads that access them. Thread 1 acquires A then C then B, and thread 2 acquires B then C then A. The following sequence can lead to deadlock:

	Thread 1	**Thread 2**
1	Acquire A	
2		Acquire B
3	Acquire C	
4		Wait for C
5	Wait for B	

How could we avoid this deadlock? The deadlock's circular waiting occurs when we reach step 5, but our fate was sealed much earlier. In particular, once we complete step 2 and thread 2 acquires B, deadlock is inevitable. To prevent the deadlock, we have to realize at step 2 that it will occur at step 5. Once step 1 completes and thread 1 acquires A, we cannot let thread 2 complete step 2 and acquire B or deadlock will follow.

This example illustrates that for an arbitrary program, preventing deadlock can take one of three approaches:

1. **Exploit or limit the behavior of the program.** Often, we can change the behavior of a program to prevent one of the four necessary conditions for deadlock, and thereby eliminate the possibility of deadlock. In the above example, we can eliminate deadlock by changing the program to never wait for B while holding C.

2. **Predict the future.** If we can know what threads may or will do, then we can avoid deadlock by having threads wait (e.g., thread 2 can wait at step 2 above) *before* they would head into a possible deadlock.

3. **Detect and recover.** Another alternative is to allow threads to recover or "undo" actions that take a system into a deadlock; in the above example, when thread 2 finds itself in deadlock, it can recover by reverting to an earlier state.

Can we restructure programs to avoid one of the four necessary conditions for deadlock?

We discuss these three options in this and the following two sub-sections. Section 6.5.2 listed four necessary conditions for deadlock. These conditions are useful because they suggest approaches for preventing deadlock: if a system is structured to prevent at least one of the conditions, then the system cannot deadlock. Considering these conditions in the context of a given system often points to a viable deadlock prevention strategy. Below, we discuss some commonly used approaches.

Bounded resources: Provide sufficient resources.   One way to ensure deadlock freedom is to arrange for sufficient resources to satisfy all threads' demands. A simple example would be to add a single chopstick to the middle of the table in Dining Philosophers; that is enough to eliminate the possibility of deadlock. As another example, thread implementations often reserve space in the TCB for the thread to be inserted into a waiting list or the ready list. While it would be theoretically possible to dynamically allocate space for the list entry only when it is needed, that could open up the chance that the system would run out of memory at exactly the wrong time, leading to deadlock.

No preemption: Preempt resources.   Another technique is to allow the run-time system to forcibly reclaim resources held by a thread. For example, an operating system can preempt a page of memory from a running process by copying it to disk in order to prevent applications from deadlocking as they acquire memory pages.

Wait while holding: Release lock when calling out of module.   For nested modules, each of which has its own lock, waiting on a condition variable in an inner module can lead to a nested waiting deadlock. One solution is to restructure a module's code so that no locks are held when calling other modules. For example, we can change the code on the left to the code on the right, provided that the program does not depend on the three steps occurring atomically:

```
Module :: foo () {                        Module :: foo () {
    lock . acquire ();                        doSomeStuff ();
    doSomeStuff ();                           otherModule –>bar ();
    otherModule –>bar ();                     doOtherStuff ();
    doOtherStuff ();                      }
    lock . release ();
}                                         Module :: doSomeStuff () {
                                              lock . acquire ();
Module :: doSomeStuff () {                     x = x + 1;
    x = x + 1;                                lock . release ();
}                                         }

Module :: doOtherStuff () {               Module :: doOtherStuff () {
    y = y – 2;                                lock . acquire ();
}                                             y = y – 2;
                                              lock . release ();
                                          }
```

In theory, one could eliminate the risk of deadlocks due to nested monitors by always releasing locks when calling code outside of a module. In practice, doing so is likely to be cumbersome, not only from the extra code needed to acquire and release locks, but also because of the extra thought needed to transform a single atomic method that holds a lock across a series of actions to a sequence of atomic methods that each acquire and release the lock. As a result, programmers often take the decidedly non-modular and admittedly unsatisfying approach of considering whether the outside module being called is likely to wait on something that depends on enclosing monitor lock. If such waiting is unlikely, the call can made with the enclosing lock held.

Circular waiting: Lock ordering.   An approach used in many systems is to identify an ordering among locks and only acquire locks in that order.

Deadlock and kernel paging

Early operating systems were often run on machines with very limited amounts of main memory. In response, going back at least as far as Multics, portions of the kernel (both code and data) could be swapped to disk in order to save space. Then, when the code and data was needed, they could be brought into main memory, swapping with some other portion of the kernel that was not currently in use.

A challenge to making this work was deadlock. The code to swap in or out portions of the kernel needed to be kept in memory, along with any code or data it might touch along any possible execution path. Without very strict module layering, it would be easy to miss a dependency that would, in rare cases, trigger a latent deadlock. Often, the only possible repair would be to reboot.

Because of the inherent complexity of this approach, most modern operating systems keep all kernel code and almost all data structures memory resident; the one exception is that some kernels still swap the page tables for application virtual memory, a topic we will discuss in Chapter 9.

For example, C printf acquires a lock to ensure printed messages appear atomic rather than mixed up with those of other threads. Because waiting for that lock does not lead to circular waiting, printf can be safely called while holding most kernel locks.

For a hash table with per-bucket locks and an operation changeKeys(item, k1, k2) to move an item from one bucket to another, we can avoid deadlock by always acquiring the lock for the lower-numbered bucket before the one for the higher-numbered bucket. This prevents circular waiting since a thread only waits for threads holding higher-numbered locks. Those threads can be waiting as well, but only for threads with even higher-numbered locks, and so forth.

Likewise, we can eliminate deadlock among the dining philosophers if — instead of always picking up the chopstick on the left and then the one on the right — the philosophers number the chopsticks from 1 to n and always pick up the lower-numbered chopstick before the higher-numbered one.

6.5.4   The Banker's Algorithm for Avoiding Deadlock

Can we prevent deadlock if we know the resources each thread might need to complete its work?

A general technique to eliminate wait-while-holding is to wait until all needed resources are available and then to acquire them atomically at the beginning of an operation, rather than incrementally as the operation proceeds. We saw this earlier with acquire-all/release-all; it cannot deadlock as long as the implementation acquires all of the locks atomically rather than one at a time. As another example, a dining philosopher might wait until the two

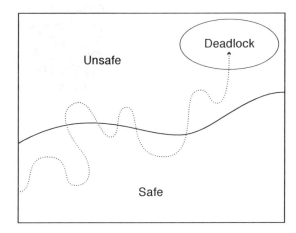

Figure 6.18: A process can be in a *safe*, *unsafe*, or *deadlocked* state. The dashed line illustrates a sequence of states visited by a thread — some are safe, some are unsafe, and the final state is a deadlock.

neighboring chopsticks are available and then simultaneously pick them both up.

Of course, a thread may not know exactly which resources it will need to complete its work, but it can still acquire all resources that it *might* need. Consider an operating system for mobile phones where memory is constrained and cannot be preempted by copying it to disk. Rather than having applications request additional memory as needed, we might instead have each application state its maximum memory needs and allocate that much memory when it starts.

Disadvantages of this approach include: the effect on program modularity, the challenge of having applications accurately estimate their worst-case needs, and the cost of allocating significantly more resources than may be necessary in the common case.

Dijkstra developed the Banker's Algorithm as a way to improve on the performance of acquire-all. Although few systems use it in its full generality, we include the discussion because simplified versions of the algorithm are common. The Banker's Algorithm also sheds light on the distinction between *safe* and *unsafe* states and how the occurrence of deadlocks often depends on a system's workload and sequence of operations.

In the Banker's Algorithm, a thread states its maximum resource requirements when it begins a task, but it then acquires and releases those resources incrementally as the task runs. The runtime system delays granting some requests to ensure that the system never deadlocks.

The insight behind the algorithm is that a system that may deadlock will not necessarily do so: for some interleavings of requests it will deadlock, but for others it will not. By delaying when some resource requests are processed, a system can avoid interleavings that could lead to deadlock.

A deadlock-prone system can be in one of three states: a *safe state*, an *unsafe state*, and a *deadlocked state* (see Figure 6.18.)

safe state

- In a *safe state*, for any possible sequence of resource requests, there is at least one *safe sequence* of processing the requests that eventually succeeds in granting all pending and future requests.

unsafe state

- In an *unsafe state*, there is at least one sequence of future resource requests that leads to deadlock no matter what processing order is tried.

deadlocked state

- In a *deadlocked state*, the system has at least one deadlock.

A system in a safe state controls its own destiny: for any workload, it can avoid deadlock by delaying the processing of some requests. In particular, the Banker's Algorithm delays any request that takes it from a safe to an unsafe state. Once the system enters an unsafe state, it may not be able to avoid deadlock.

Notice that an unsafe state does not always lead to deadlock. A system in an unsafe state may remain that way or return to a safe state, depending on the specific interleaving of resource requests and completions. However, as long as the system remains in an unsafe state, a bad workload or unlucky scheduling of requests can force it to deadlock.

The Banker's Algorithm keeps a system in a safe state. The algorithm is based on a loose analogy with a small-town banker who has a maximum amount, total, that can be loaned at one time and a set of businesses that each have a credit line, max[i], for business i. A business borrows and pays back amounts of money as various projects start and end, so that business i always has an outstanding loan amount between 0 and max[i]. If all of a business's requests within the credit line are granted, the business eventually reaches a state where all current projects are finished, and the loan balance returns to zero.

A conservative banker might issue credit lines only until the sum is at most the total funds that the banker has available. This approach is analogous to *acquire-all* or *provide sufficient resources*. It guarantees that the system remains in a safe state. All businesses with credit lines eventually complete their projects.

However, a more aggressive banker can issue more credit as long as the bank can cover its commitment to each business — i.e., to provide a loan of max[i] if business i requests it. The algorithm assumes the bank is permitted to *delay* requests to increase a loan amount. For example, the bank might lose the paperwork for a few hours, days, or weeks.

By delaying loan requests, the bank remains in a safe state — a state for which there exists at least one series of loan fulfillments by which every business i can eventually receive its maximal loan max[i], complete its projects, and pay back all of its loan. The bank can then use that repaid money to grant pending loans to other businesses.

Figure 6.20 shows pseudo-code for a version of the Banker's Algorithm that manages a set of r resources for a set of t threads. To simplify the discussion,

```
class ResourceMgr{
   private :
     Lock lock;
     CV cv;
     int r;              // Number of resources
     int t;              // Number of threads
     int avail[];        // avail[i]: instances of resource i available
     int max[][];        // max[i][j]: max of resource i needed by thread j
     int alloc[][];      // alloc[i][j]: current allocation of resource i to thread j
   ...
}
```

Figure 6.19: State maintained by the Banker Algorithm's resource manager. Resource manager code is in Figures 6.20 and 6.21.

```
// Invariant: the system is in a safe state.
ResourceMgr :: Request( int resourceID , int threadID) {
     lock . Acquire ();
     assert (isSafe ());
     while (! wouldBeSafe (resourceID , threadID )) {
         cv . Wait(& lock );
     }
     alloc [ resourceID ][ threadID ]++;
     avail [ resourceID]−−;
     assert (isSafe ());
     lock . Release ();
}
```

Figure 6.20: High-level pseudo-code for the Banker's Algorithm. The state maintained by the algorithm is defined in Figure 6.19. The methods isSafe and wouldBeSafe are defined in Figure 6.21.

threads request each unit of resource separately, but the algorithm can be extended to allow multiple resources to be requested at the same time.

The high-level idea is simple: when a request arrives, wait to grant the request until it is safe to do so. As Figure 6.19 shows, we can realize this high-level approach by tracking: (i) the current allocation of each resource to each thread, (ii) the maximum allocation possible for each thread, and (iii) the current set of available, unallocated resources.

Figure 6.21 shows how to test whether a state is safe. Recall that a state is safe if some sequence of thread executions allows each thread to obtain its maximum resource need, finish its work, and release its resources. We first see if the currently free resources suffice to allow any thread to finish. If so, then the resources held by that thread will eventually be released back to the system. Next, we see if the currently free resources plus any resources held by the thread identified in the first step suffice to allow any other thread to finish; if so, the second thread's resources will also eventually be released back to the system. We continue this process until we have identified all threads guaranteed to finish, provided we serve requests in a particular order. If that set includes all of the threads, the state is safe.

```
// A state is safe iff there exists a safe sequence of grants that are sufficient
// to allow all threads to eventually receive their maximum resource needs.

bool
ResourceMgr::isSafe() {
    int j;
    int toBeAvail[] = copy avail[];
    int need[][] = max[][] - alloc[][];  // need[i][j] is initialized to
                                          // max[i][j] - alloc[i][j]
    bool finish[] = [false, false, false, ...]; // finish[j] is true
                                                 // if thread j is guaranteed to finish

    while (true) {
        j = any threadID such that:
            (finish[j] == false) && forall i: need[i][j] <= toBeAvail[i];
        if (no such j exists) {
            if (forall j: finish[j] == true) {
                return true;
            } else {
                return false;
            }
        } else {  // Thread j will eventually finish and return its
                  // current allocation to the pool.
            finish[j] = true;
            forall i:  toBeAvail[i] = toBeAvail[i] + alloc[i][j];
        }
    }
}

// Hypothetically grant request and see if resulting state is safe.

bool
ResourceMgr::wouldBeSafe(int resourceID, int threadID) {
    bool result = false;

    avail[resourceID]--;
    alloc[resourceID][threadID]++;
    if (isSafe()) {
        result = true;
    }
    avail[resourceID]++;
    alloc[resourceID][threadID]--;
    return result;
}
```

Figure 6.21: Pseudo-code for the Banker's Algorithm test whether the next state would be safe to enter. If not, the system delays until it would be safe.

EXAMPLE **Page allocation with the Banker's Algorithm.** Suppose we have a system with 8 pages of memory and three processes: A, B, and C, which need 4, 5, and 5 pages to complete, respectively.

If they take turns requesting one page each, and the system grants requests in order, the system deadlocks, reaching a state where each process is stuck until some other process releases memory:

Process	Allocation											
A	0	1	1	1	2	2	2	3	3	3	wait	wait
B	0	0	1	1	1	2	2	2	3	3	3	wait
C	0	0	0	1	1	1	2	2	2	wait	wait	wait
Total	0	1	2	3	4	5	6	7	8	8	8	8

On the other hand, if the system follows the Banker's Algorithm, then it can delay some processes and guarantee that all processes eventually complete:

Process	Allocation																		
A	0	1	1	1	2	2	2	3	3	3	4	0	0	0	0	0	0	0	0
B	0	0	1	1	1	2	2	2	wait	wait	wait	wait	3	4	4	5	0	0	0
C	0	0	0	1	1	1	2	2	2	wait	wait	wait	3	3	wait	wait	4	5	0
Total	0	1	2	3	4	5	6	7	7	7	8	4	6	7	7	8	4	5	0

By delaying B and C in the ninth through twelfth steps, A can complete and release its resources. Then, by delaying C in the fifteenth and sixteenth steps, B can complete and release its resources.

The Banker's Algorithm is noticeably more involved than other approaches we discuss. Although it is rarely used in its entirety, understanding the distinction between *safe*, *unsafe*, and *deadlocked* states and how deadlock events depend on request ordering are key to preventing deadlock.

Additionally, understanding the Banker's Algorithm can help to design simple solutions for specific problems. For example, if we apply the Banker's Algorithm to the Dining Philosopher's problem, then it is safe for a philosopher to pick up a chopstick provided that afterwards (a) some philosopher will have two chopsticks or (b) a chopstick will remain on the table. In case (a), eventually that philosopher will finish eating and the other philosophers will be able to proceed. In case (b), the philosopher can pick up the chopstick because deadlock can still be avoided in the future.

EXAMPLE   Use the Banker's Algorithm to devise a rule for when it is safe for a thread to acquire a pair of locks, A and B, with mutually recursive locking.

ANSWER   Suppose a thread needs to acquire locks A and B, in that order, while another thread needs to acquire lock B first, then A. **A thread is always allowed to acquire its second lock. It may acquire its first lock provided the other thread does not already hold its first lock.**   □

6.5.5   Detecting and Recovering From Deadlocks

How can we detect deadlock and then recover if it occurs?

Rather than preventing deadlocks, some systems allow deadlocks to occur and recover from them when they arise.

Why allow deadlocks to occur at all? Sometimes, it is difficult or expensive to enforce sufficient structure on the system's data and workloads to guarantee that deadlock will never occur. If deadlocks are rare, why pay the overhead in the common case to prevent them?

For this approach to work, we need: (i) a way to recover from deadlock when it occurs, ideally with minimal harm to the goals of the user, and (ii) a way to detect deadlock so that we know when to invoke the recovery mechanism. We discuss recovery first because it provides context for understanding the tradeoffs in implementing detection.

Recovering From Deadlocks

Recovering from a deadlock once it has occurred is challenging. A deadlock implies that some threads hold resources while waiting for others, and that progress is impossible.

Because the resources are by definition not revocable, forcibly taking resources away from some or all of the deadlocked threads is not an ideal solution. As a simple example, if a process is part of a deadlock, some operating systems give the user the option to kill the process and release the process's resources. Although this sounds drastic, if a deadlocked process cannot make any progress, killing it does not make the user much worse off.

However, under the lock-based shared object programming abstractions we have discussed, killing all of the threads in a given process can be dangerous. If a deadlocked thread holds a lock on a shared kernel object, killing the thread and marking the lock as free could leave the kernel object in an inconsistent state.

Instead, we need some systematic way to recover when some required resource is unavailable. Two widely used approaches have been developed to deal with this issue:

- **Proceed without the resource.** Web services are often designed to be resilient to resource unavailability. A rule of thumb for the web is that a significant fraction of a web site's customers will give up and go elsewhere if the site's latency becomes too long, for whatever reason. Whether the problem is a hardware failure, software failure, or deadlock, does not really matter. The web site needs to be designed to quickly respond back to the user, regardless of the type of problem.

    Amazon's web site is a good example of this design paradigm. It is designed as an interlocking set of modules, where any individual module can be offline because of a failure. Thus, all other parts of the web site must be designed to be able to cope when some needed resource is unavailable. For example, under normal operation, Amazon's software will check the inventory to ensure that an item is in stock before completing an order. However, if a deadlock or failure causes the inventory server to delay responding beyond some threshold, the front-end web server will give up, complete the order, and then queue a background check to make sure the item was in fact in the inventory. If the item was in fact not available (e.g., because some other customer purchased it in the

Optimistic concurrency control

Transactions can also be used to avoid deadlocks. Optimistic concurrency control lets transactions execute in parallel without locking any data, but it only lets a transaction commit if none of the objects accessed by the transaction have been modified since the transaction began. Otherwise, the transaction must abort and retry.

To implement transactions with optimistic concurrency control, Each transaction keeps track of which versions of which objects it reads and updates. All updates are applied to a local copy. Then, before a transaction commits, the system verifies that no object the transaction accessed has been modified in the meantime; if there is a conflict, the transaction must abort. Of course, committing a transaction may invalidate other transactions that are in progress (ones that use data modified by this transaction). Those conflicts will be detected when the later transactions try to commit.

Optimistic concurrency control works well when different transactions most commonly use different subsets of data. In these cases, the approach not only eliminates deadlock, but it also maximizes concurrency since threads do not wait for locks. On the other hand, many conflicting, concurrent transactions increase overhead by repeatedly rolling back and re-executing transactions.

---

meantime), an apology is sent to the customer. As long as that does not happen often, it can be better than making the customer wait, especially in the case of deadlock, where the wait could be indefinite.

Because deadlocks are rare and hard to test for, this requires coding discipline to handle error conditions systematically throughout the program.

- **Transactions: rollback and retry.** A more general technique is used by *transactions*; transactions provide a safe mechanism for revoking resources assigned to a thread. We discuss transactions in detail in Chapter 14; they are widely used in both databases and file systems. For deadlock recovery, transactions provide two important services:

  1. **Thread rollback.** Transactions ensure that revoking locks from a thread does not leave the system's objects in an inconsistent state. Instead, we rollback, or undo, the deadlocked thread's actions to a clean state. To fix the deadlock, we can choose one or more victim threads, stop them, undo their actions, and let other threads proceed.

  2. **Thread restarting.** Once the deadlock is broken and other threads have completed some or all of their work, the victim thread is restarted. When these threads complete, the system behaves as if the victim threads never caused a deadlock but, instead, just had their executions delayed.

A transaction defines a safe point for rollback and restart. Each transaction has a beginTransaction and endTransaction statement; rollback undoes all changes back to beginTransaction. After a rollback, the thread can be safely restarted at the beginTransaction.

A key feature of transactions is that no other thread is allowed to see the results of a transaction until the transaction completes. That way, if the changes a transaction makes need to be rolled back due to a deadlock, only that one thread is affected. This can be accomplished with two-phase locking, provided locks are not released until after the transaction is complete. If the transaction is successful, it *commits*, the transaction's locks are released, and the transaction's changes to shared state become visible to other threads.

If, however, a transaction fails to reach its endTransaction statement (e.g., because of a deadlock or because some other exception occurred), the transaction *aborts*. The system can reset all of the state modified by the transaction to what it was when the transaction began. One way to support this is to maintain a copy of the initial values of all state modified by each transaction; this copy can be discarded when the transaction commits.

If a transactional system becomes deadlocked, the system can abort one or more of the deadlocked transactions. Aborting these transactions rolls back the system's state to what it would have been if these transactions had never started and releases the aborted transactions' locks and other resources. If aborting the chosen transactions releases sufficient resources, the deadlock is broken, and the remaining transactions can proceed. If not, the system can abort additional transactions.

How do we make sure all transactions eventually complete?

A related question that arises in transactional systems is *which* thread to abort and which threads to allow to proceed. An important consideration is liveness. Progress can be ensured, and starvation avoided, by prioritizing the oldest transactions. Then, when the system needs to abort some transaction, it can abort the *youngest*. This ensures that *some* transaction, e.g., the oldest, will eventually complete. The aborted transaction eventually becomes the oldest, and so it also will complete.

wound wait

An example of this approach is *wound wait*. With wound wait, a younger transaction may wait for a resource held by an older transaction. Eventually, the older transaction will complete and release the resource, so deadlock cannot result. However, if an older transaction needs to wait on a resource held by a younger transaction, the resource is preempted and the younger transaction is aborted and restarted.

Detecting Deadlock

How do we efficiently detect if a deadlock has occurred?

Once we have a general way to recover from a deadlock, we need a way to tell if a deadlock has occurred, so we know when to trigger the recovery. An important consideration is that the detection mechanism can be conservative:

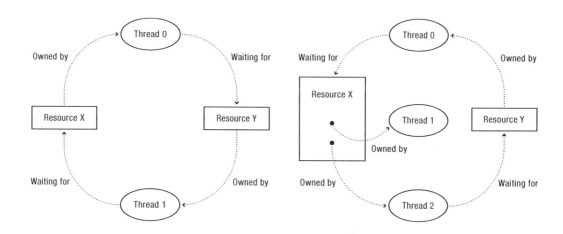

Figure 6.22: Example graphs used for deadlock detection. Left: single instance of each resource. Right: multiple instances of one resource. Threads and resources are nodes; directed edges represent the *owned by* and *waiting for* relationships among them.

it can trigger the repair if we *might* be in a deadlock state. This approach risks a false positive where a non-deadlocked thread is incorrectly classified as deadlocked. Depending on the overhead of the repair operation, it can sometimes be more efficient to use a simpler mechanism for detection even if that leads to the occasional false positive.

For example, a program can choose to wait only briefly (or not to wait at all) before declaring that recovery is needed. We saw an example earlier with how Amazon's web site is designed. As another example, in old-style, circuit-switched telephone networks, a call reserved a circuit at a series of switches along its path. If the connection setup failed to find a free circuit at any hop, rather than wait for a circuit at the next hop to become free, it cancelled the connection attempt and gave the user an error message, "All circuits are busy. Please try again later."

A modern analogue is the Internet. When a router is overloaded and runs out of packet buffers, it simply drops incoming packets. An alternative would be for each router to wait to send a packet until it knows the next router has room — an approach that could lead to deadlock. Precisely identifying whether deadlock has occurred would incur more overhead than simply dropping and resending some packets.

There are various ways to identify deadlocks more precisely.

If there are several resources and only one thread can hold each resource at a time (e.g., one printer, one keyboard, and one audio speaker or several mutual exclusion locks), then we can detect a deadlock by analyzing a simple graph. In the graph, shown on the left in Figure 6.22, each thread and each resource is represented by a node. There is a directed edge (i) from a resource to a thread if the resource is *owned by* the thread and (ii) from a thread to a

```
// A state is safe iff there exists a safe sequence of grants that would allow
// all threads to eventually receive their maximum resource needs.
//
// avail[] holds free resource count
// alloc[][] holds current allocation
// request[][] holds currently—blocked requests
bool
ResourceMgr::isDeadlocked() {
    int j;
    int toBeAvail[] = copy avail[];
    bool finish[] = [false, false, false, ...]; // finish[j] is true if thread
                                                 // j is guaranteed to finish

    while(true) {
        j = any threadID such that (finish[j] == false) &&
                                   (forall i: request[i][j] <= toBeAvail[i]);
        if (no such j exists) {
            if (forall j: finish[j] == true) {
                return false;
            } else {
                return true;
            }
        } else {
            // Thread j *may* eventually finish and
            // return its current allocation to the pool.
            finish[j] = true;
            forall i: toBeAvail[i] = toBeAvail[i] + alloc[i][j];
        }
    }
}
```

Figure 6.23: Coffman et al.'s test for deadlock. This algorithm is similar to the isSafe() test of the Banker's Algorithm shown in Figure 6.21.

resource if the thread is *waiting for* the resource. There is a deadlock if and only if there is a cycle in such a graph.

If there are multiple instances of some resources, then we represent a resource with k interchangeable instances (e.g., k equivalent printers) as a node with k connection points. This is illustrated by the right graph in Figure 6.22. Now, a cycle is a necessary but not sufficient condition for deadlock.

Another solution, described by Coffman, Elphick, and Shoshani in 1971 is a variation of Dijkstra's Banker's Algorithm. In this algorithm, we assume we no longer know max[][], so we cannot assess whether the current state is safe or whether some future sequence of requests can force deadlock. However, we can look at the current set of resources, granted requests, and pending requests and ask whether it is possible for the current set of requests to eventually be satisfied assuming no more requests come and all threads eventually complete. If so, there is no deadlock (although we may be in an unsafe state); otherwise, there is a deadlock.

Figure 6.23 shows the pseudo-code for the isDeadlocked method, a variation of the isSafe method shown in Figure 6.21 for the Banker's Algorithm.

One might hope that we could avoid deadlock by asking, "Will satisfying the current request put us in a deadlocked state?" and then blocking any request that does. The Coffman et al. algorithm highlights that deadlock is determined not just by what requests are granted but also by what requests are waiting. The request that triggers deadlock ("circular wait") will be a request that waits, not one that is granted.

6.6 | Non-Blocking Synchronization

Are there ways to eliminate locks in complex multi-object programs?

Chapter 5 described a core abstraction for synchronization — shared objects, with one lock per object. This abstraction works well for building multi-threaded programs the vast majority of the time. As concurrent programs become more complicated, however, issues of lock contention, the semantics of operations that span multiple objects, and deadlock can arise. Worse, the solutions to these issues often require us to compromise modularity; for example, whether a particular program can deadlock requires understanding in detail how the implementations of various shared objects interact.

Some researchers have posed a radical question: would it be better to write complex concurrent programs without locks? By eliminating locking, we would remove lock contention and deadlock as design considerations, fostering a more modular program structure. However, these techniques can be *much* more complex to use. To date, concurrent implementations without locks have only been used for a few carefully designed runtime library modules written by expert programmers. We sketch the ideas because there is a chance that they will become more important as the number of processors per computer continues to increase.

Today, the cases where these approaches are warranted are rare. These advanced techniques should only be considered by experienced programmers who have mastered the basic lock-based approaches. Many of you will probably never need to use these techniques. If you are tempted to do so, take extra care. Measure the performance of your system to ensure that these techniques yield significant gains, and seek out extra peer review from trusted colleagues to help ensure that the code works as intended.

Programmers often assume that acquiring a lock is an expensive operation, and therefore try to reduce locking throughout their programs. The most likely result from premature optimization is a program that is buggy, hard to maintain, no faster than a clean implementation, and, ironically, harder to tune than a cleanly architected program. On most platforms, acquiring or releasing a lock is a highly tuned primitive — acquiring an uncontended lock is often nearly free. If there is contention, you probably needed the lock!

In Section 6.3, we saw an example of synchronization without locks. RCU lets reads proceed without acquiring a lock or updating shared synchronization state, but it still requires updates to acquire locks. If the thread that holds the lock is interrupted, has a bug that causes it to stop making progress, or becomes deadlocked, other threads can be delayed for a long — perhaps unlimited — period of time.

non-blocking data structures

It is possible to build data structures that are completely *non-blocking* for both read and write operations. A non-blocking method is one where one thread is never required to wait for another thread to complete its operation. Acquiring a lock is a blocking operation: if the thread holding the lock stops, is delayed, or deadlocks, all other threads must wait for it to finish the critical section.

wait-free data structures

More formally, a *wait-free data structure* is one that guarantees progress for every thread: every method finishes in a finite number of steps, regardless of the state of other threads executing in the data structure or their rate of execution. A *lock-free data structure* is one that guarantees progress for some thread: some method will finish in a finite number of steps.

lock-free data structures

A common building block for wait-free and lock-free data structures is the atomic compare-and-swap instruction available on most modern processors. We saw a taste of this in the implementation of the MCS lock in Section 6.3. There, we used compare-and-swap to atomically append to a linked list of waiting threads *without first acquiring a lock*.

Wait-free and lock-free data structures apply this idea more generally to completely eliminate the use of locks. For example, a lock-free hash table could be built as an array of pointers to each bucket:

- **Lookup.** A lookup de-references the pointer and checks the bucket.

- **Update.** To update a bucket, the thread allocates a new copy of the bucket, and then uses compare-and-swap to atomically replace the pointer if and only if it has not been changed in the meantime. If two threads simultaneously attempt to update the bucket (for example, to add a new entry), one succeeds and the other must retry.

The logic can be much more complex for more intricate data structures, and as a result, designing efficient wait-free and lock-free data structures remains the domain of experts. Nonetheless, non-blocking algorithms exist for a wide range of data structures, including FIFO queues, double-ended queues, LIFO stacks, sets, and balanced trees. Several of these can be found in the Java Virtual Machine runtime library.

In addition, considerable effort has also gone into studying ways to automate the construction of wait-free and lock-free data structures. For example, transactions with optimistic concurrency control provide a very flexible approach to implementing lock-free applications. Recall that optimistic concurrency control lets transactions proceed without locking the data they access. Transactions abort if, at commit-time, any of their accessed data has changed in the meantime. Most modern databases use a form of optimistic concurrency control to provide atomic and fault-tolerant updates of on-disk data structures.

EXAMPLE   Is optimistic concurrency control lock-free, wait-free, or both?

ANSWER   To see that **optimistic concurrency control is lock-free,** consider two conflicting transactions executing at the same time. The first one to commit succeeds, and the second must abort and retry. **An implementation is wait-free if it uses wound wait or some other mechanism to bound the number of retries for a transaction to successfully commit.** □

software transactional memory (STM) Extending this idea, *software transactional memory (STM)* is a promising approach to support general-purpose transactions for in-memory data structures. Unfortunately, the cost of an STM transaction is often significantly higher than that of a traditional critical section; this is because of the need to maintain the state required to check dependencies and the state required either to update the object if there is no conflict or to roll back its state if a conflict is detected. It is an open question whether the overhead of STM can be reduced to where it can be used more widely. In situations where STM can be used, it provides a way to compose different modules without having to lock contention or deadlock concerns.

6.7 | Summary and Future Directions

Advanced synchronization techniques should be approached with caution. Your first goal should be to construct a program that works, even if doing so means putting "one big lock" around everything in a data structure or even in an entire program.

Resist the temptation to do anything more complicated unless you **know** that doing so is necessary. How do you know? Do not guess. Measure your system's performance. Measuring the "before" and "after" performance of a program and its subsystems not only helps you make good decisions about the program on which you are working, but it also helps you develop good intuition for the programs you write in the future.

Spend time early in the design process developing a clean structure for your program. Given that issues with multi-object synchronization often blur module boundaries, it is vital to have an overall structure that lets you reason about how the different pieces of your program will interact. Strive for a strict layering or hierarchy of modules. It is easier to make such programs deadlock-free, and it is easier to test them as well.

Although performance is important, it is usually easier to start with a clean, simple, and correct design, measure it to identify its bottlenecks, and then optimize the bottlenecks than to start with a complex design and try to tune its performance, let alone fix its bugs.

In this chapter, we have presented a set of conceptual tools and techniques for managing complex, multi-object concurrent programs. We have addressed: estimating the impact of locks on multiprocessor performance, design patterns to reduce contention for locks, implementation techniques such as MCS and RCU for high-contention locks, strategies for achieving atomicity across multiple operations on the same object or across objects, and algorithms for deadlock prevention and recovery.

Yet, writing concurrent programs remains frustratingly complex. We believe that an important area for future work will be to develop better tools for managing and reducing that complexity. The last decade has seen the development of a new generation of tools for helping programmers improve software reliability, by automatically identifying test coverage, memory leaks, reuse of de-allocated data, buffer overflows, and bad pointer arithmetic.

Extending this approach to concurrent programs is a grand challenge. A promising avenue is to use automated tools for detecting memory races; a well-written program should have no reads or writes to shared memory without holding the lock that protects that data structure. Once a program has been shown to be without races, model checking can be used to systematically test that shared objects work for all possible thread interleavings.

Exercises

1. Figure 6.13 shows the parallel execution of some requests and an equivalent sequential execution — request 1 then request 2 then request 3. Two other sequential executions are also equivalent to the parallel execution shown in the figure. What are these other equivalent sequential executions?

2. Generalize the rules for two-phase locking to include both mutual exclusion locks and readers/writers locks. What can be done in the expanding phase? What can be done in the contracting phase?

3. Consider the variation of the Dining Philosophers problem shown in Figure 6.17, where all unused chopsticks are placed in the center of the table and any philosopher can eat with any two chopsticks.

   One way to prevent deadlock in this system is to provide sufficient resources. For a system with n philosophers, what is the minimum number of chopsticks that ensures deadlock freedom? Why?

4. If the queues between stages are finite, is it possible for a staged architecture to deadlock even if each individual stage is internally deadlock free? If so, give an example. If not, prove it.

5. Suppose you build a system using a staged architecture with some fixed number of threads operating in each stage. Assuming each stage is individually deadlock free, describe two ways to guarantee that your system as a whole cannot deadlock. Each way should eliminate a different one of the 4 necessary conditions for deadlock.

6. Consider a system with four mutual exclusion locks (A, B, C, and D) and a readers/writers lock (E). Suppose the programmer follows these rules:

   a) Processing for each request is divided into two parts.

b) During the first part, no lock may be released, and, if E is held in writing mode, it cannot be downgraded to reading mode. Furthermore, lock A may not be acquired if any of locks B, C, D, or E are held in any mode. Lock B may not be acquired if any of locks C, D, or E are held in any mode. Lock C may not be acquired if any of locks D or E are held in any mode. Lock D may not be acquired if lock E is held in any mode. Lock E may always be acquired in read mode or write mode, and it can be upgraded from read to write mode but not downgraded from write to read mode.

c) During the second part, any lock may be released, and lock E may be downgraded from write mode to read mode; releases and downgrades can happen in any order; by the end of part 2, all locks must be released; and no locks may be acquired or upgraded.

Do these rules ensure serializability? Do they ensure freedom from deadlock? Why?

7. In RCUList::remove, a possible strategy to increase concurrency would be to hold a read lock while searching for the target item, and to grab the write lock once it is found. Specifically: (i) replace the writeLock and writeUnlock calls with readLock and readUnlock calls, and (ii) insert new writeLock and writeUnlock calls at the beginning and end of the code that is executed when the if conditional test succeeds. Will this work?

8. Implement a highly concurrent, multi-threaded file buffer cache. A buffer cache stores recently used disk blocks in memory for improved latency and throughput. Disk blocks have unique numbers and are fixed size. The cache provides two routines:

```
void blockread(char *x, int blocknum);

void blockwrite(char *x, int blocknum);
```

These routines read/write complete, block-aligned, fixed-size blocks. blockread reads a block of data into x; blockwrite (eventually) writes the data in x to disk. On a read, if the requested data is in the cache, the buffer will return it. Otherwise, the buffer must fetch the data from disk, making room in the cache by evicting a block as necessary. If the evicted block is modified, the cache must first write the modified data back to disk. On a write, if the block is not already in the buffer, it must make room for the new block. Modified data is stored in the cache and written back later to disk when the block is evicted.

Multiple threads can call blockread and blockwrite concurrently, and to the maximum degree possible, those operations should be allowed to complete in parallel. You should assume the disk driver has been implemented; it provides the same interface as the file buffer cache: diskblockread and diskblockwrite. The disk driver routines are synchronous (the calling thread blocks until the disk operation completes) and re-entrant (while one thread is blocked, other threads can call into the driver to queue requests).

9. Suppose we have a version of the Dining Philosopher's problem where the chopsticks are placed in the middle of the table, each Philosopher needs three chopsticks before she will start to eat, and every Philosopher will return all of their chopsticks to the shared pool when done eating. (For example, the Philosopher needs two chopsticks to eat with and one to point at the white board.)

   a) Using the Banker's Algorithm, devise a rule for when is it safe for a Philosopher to pick up a chopstick. Explain why.

   b) Now suppose each Philosopher needs k chopsticks, for $k > 3$. Generalize the rule you developed above to work for any k.

Time is money

Ben Franklin

The best performance improvement is the transition from the non-working state to the working state. That's infinite speedup.

John Ousterhout

7 | Scheduling

When there are multiple things to do, how do you choose which one to do first? In the last few chapters, we have described how to create threads, switch between them, and synchronize their access to shared data. At any point in time, some threads are running on the system's processor. Others are waiting their turn for a processor. Still other threads are blocked waiting for I/O to complete, a condition variable to be signaled, or for a lock to be released. When there are more runnable threads than processors, the *processor scheduling policy* determines which threads to run first.

processor scheduling policy

You might think the answer to this question is easy: just do the work in the order in which it arrives. After all, that seems to be the only fair thing to do. Because it is obviously fair, almost all government services work this way. When you go to your local Department of Motor Vehicles (DMV) to get a driver's license, you take a number and wait your turn. Although fair, the DMV often feels slow. There's a reason why: as we'll see later in this chapter, doing things in order of arrival is sometimes the worst thing you can do in terms of improving user-perceived response time. Advertising that your operating system uses the same scheduling algorithm as the DMV is probably not going to increase your sales!

You might think that the answer to this question is unimportant. With the million-fold improvement in processor performance over the past thirty years, it might seem that we are a million times less likely to have anything waiting for its turn on a processor. We disagree! Server operating systems in particular are often overloaded. Parallel applications can create more work than processors, and if care is not taken in the design of the scheduling policy, performance can badly degrade. There are subtle relationships between scheduling policy and energy management on battery-powered devices such as smartphones and laptops. Further, scheduling issues apply to any scarce resource, whether the source of contention is the processor, memory, disk, or network. We will revisit the issues covered in this chapter throughout the rest of the book.

Scheduling policy is not a panacea. Without enough capacity, performance may be poor regardless of which thread we run first. In this chapter, we will also discuss how to predict overload conditions and how to adapt to them.

Fortunately, you probably have quite a bit of intuition as to impact of different scheduling policies and capacity on issues like response time, fairness, and throughput. Anyone who waits in line probably wonders how we could get the line to go faster. That's true whether we're waiting in line at the supermarket, a bank, the DMV, or at a popular restaurant. Remarkably, in each of these settings, there is a different approach to how they deal with waiting. We will try to answer why.

There is no one right answer; rather, any scheduling policy poses a complex set of tradeoffs between various desirable properties. The goal of this chapter is not to enumerate all of the interesting possibilities, explore the full design space, or even to identify specific useful policies. Instead, we describe some of the trade-offs and try to illustrate how a designer can approach the problem of selecting a scheduling policy.

Consider what happens if you are running the web site for a company trying to become the next Facebook. Based on history, you'll be able to guess how much server capacity you need to be able to keep up with demand and still have reasonable response time. What happens if your site appears on Slashdot, and suddenly you have twice as many users as you had an hour ago? If you are not careful, everyone will think your site is terribly slow, and permanently go elsewhere. Google, Amazon, and Yahoo have each estimated that they lose approximately 5-10% of their customers if their response time increases by as little as 100 milliseconds. If faced with overload:

- Would quickly implementing a different scheduling policy help, or hurt?

- How much worse will your performance be if the number of users doubles again?

- Should you turn away some users so that others will get acceptable performance?

- Does it matter which users you turn away?

- If you run out to the local electronics store and buy a server, how much better will performance get?

- Do the answers change if you are under a denial-of-service attack by a competitor?

In this chapter, we will try to give you the conceptual and analytic tools to help you answer these questions.

Performance Terminology

In Chapter 1 we defined some performance-related terms we will use throughout this chapter and the rest of the book; we summarize those terms here.

- **Task.** A user request. A task is also often called a *job*. A task can be any size, from simply redrawing the screen to show the movement of the mouse cursor to computing the shape of a newly discovered protein. When discussing scheduling, we use the term task, rather than thread or process, because a single thread or process may be responsible for multiple user requests or tasks. For example, in a word processor, each character typed is an individual user request to add that character to the file and display the result on the screen.

- **Response time (or delay).** The user-perceived time to do some task.

- **Predictability.** Low variance in response times for repeated requests.

- **Throughput.** The rate at which tasks are completed.

- **Scheduling overhead.** The time to switch from one task to another.

- **Fairness.** Equality in the number and timeliness of resources given to each task.

- **Starvation.** The lack of progress for one task, due to resources given to a higher priority task.

Chapter roadmap:

- **Uniprocessor Scheduling.** How do uniprocessor scheduling policies affect fairness, response time, and throughput? (Section 7.1)

- **Multiprocessor Scheduling.** How do scheduling policies change when we have multiple processor cores per computer? (Section 7.2)

- **Energy-Aware Scheduling.** Many new computer systems can save energy by turning off portions of the computer, slowing the execution speed. How do we make this tradeoff while minimizing the impact on user perceived response time? (Section 7.3)

- **Real-Time Scheduling.** More generally, how do we make sure tasks finish in time? (Section 7.4)

- **Queueing Theory.** In a server environment, how are response time and throughput affected by the rate at which requests arrive for processing and by the scheduling policy? (Section 7.5)

- **Overload Management.** How do we keep response time reasonable when a system becomes overloaded? (Section 7.6)

- **Case Study: Servers in a Data Center.** How do we combine these technologies to manage servers a data center? (Section 7.7)

7.1 | Uniprocessor Scheduling

We start by considering one processor, generalizing to multiprocessor scheduling policies in the next section. We begin with three simple policies — first-in-first-out, shortest-job-first, and round robin — as a way of illustrating scheduling concepts. Each approach has its own the strengths and weaknesses, and most resource allocation systems (whether for processors, memory, network or disk) combine aspects of all three. At the end of the discussion, we will show how the different approaches can be synthesized into a more practical and complete processor scheduler.

workload Before proceeding, we need to define a few terms. A *workload* is a set of tasks for some system to perform, along with when each task arrives and how long each task takes to complete. In other words, the workload defines the input to a scheduling algorithm. Given a workload, a processor scheduler decides when each task is to be assigned the processor.

We are interested in scheduling algorithms that work well across a wide variety of environments, because workloads will vary quite a bit from system to system and user to user. Some tasks are *compute-bound* and only use the

compute-bound task processor. Others, such as a compiler or a web browser, mix I/O and compu-

I/O-bound task tation. Still others, such as a BitTorrent download, are *I/O-bound*, spending most of their time waiting for I/O and only brief periods computing. In the discussion, we start with very simple compute-bound workloads and then generalize to include mixtures of different types of tasks as we proceed.

Some of the policies we outline are the best possible policy on a particular metric and workload, and some are the worst possible policy. When discussing optimality and pessimality, we are only comparing to policies that are *work-*

work-conserving policy *conserving*. A scheduler is work-conserving if it never leaves the processor idle if there is work to do. Obviously, a trivially poor policy has the processor sit idle for long periods when there are tasks in the ready list.

preemption Our discussion also assumes the scheduler has the ability to *preempt* the processor and give it to some other task. Preemption can happen either because of a timer interrupt, or because some task arrives on the ready list with a higher priority than the current task, at least according to some scheduling policy. We explained how to switch the processor between tasks in Chapter 2 and Chapter 4. While much of the discussion is also relevant to non-preemptive

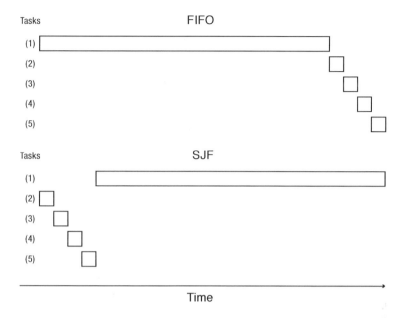

Figure 7.1: Completion times with FIFO (top) and SJF (bottom) scheduling when several short tasks (2-5) arrive immediately after a long task (1).

schedulers, there are few such systems left, so we leave that issue aside for simplicity.

7.1.1   First-In-First-Out (FIFO)

Perhaps the simplest scheduling algorithm possible is first-in-first-out (FIFO): do each task in the order in which it arrives. (FIFO is sometimes also called first-come-first-served, or FCFS.) When we start working on a task, we keep running it until it finishes. FIFO minimizes overhead, switching between tasks only when each one completes. Because it minimizes overhead, if we have a fixed number of tasks, and those tasks only need the processor, FIFO will have the best throughput: it will complete the most tasks the most quickly. And as we mentioned, FIFO appears to be the definition of fairness—every task patiently waits its turn.

Unfortunately, FIFO has a weakness. If a task with very little work to do happens to land in line behind a task that takes a very long time, then the system will seem very inefficient. Figure 7.1 illustrates a particularly bad workload for FIFO; it also shows SJF, which we will discuss in a bit. If the first task in the queue takes one second, and the next four arrive an instant later, but each only needs a millisecond of the processor, then they will all need to wait until the first one finishes. The average response time will be over a second, but the optimal average response time is much less than that. In fact,

FIFO and memcached

Although you may think that FIFO is too simple to be useful, there are some important cases where it is exactly the right choice for the workload. One such example is memcached. Many web services, such as Facebook, store their user data in a database. The database provides flexible and consistent lookups, such as, which friends need to be notified of a particular update to a user's Facebook wall. In order to improve performance, Facebook and other systems put a cache called memcached in front of the database, so that if a user posts two items to her Facebook wall, the system only needs to lookup the friend list once. The system first checks whether the information is cached, and if so uses that copy.

Because almost all requests are for small amounts of data, memcached replies to requests in FIFO order. This minimizes overhead, as there is no need to time slice between requests. For this workload where tasks are roughly equal in size, FIFO is simple, minimizes average response time, and even maximizes throughput. Win-win!

if we ignore switching overhead, there are some workloads where FIFO is literally the worst possible policy for average response time.

7.1.2 Shortest Job First (SJF)

If FIFO can be a poor choice for average response time, is there an optimal policy for minimizing average response time? The answer is yes: schedule the shortest job first (SJF).

Suppose we could know how much time each task needed at the processor. (In general, we will not know, so this is not meant as a practical policy! Rather, we use it as a thought experiment; later on, we will see how to approximate SJF in practice.) If we always schedule the task that has the least remaining work to do, that will minimize average response time. (For this reason, some call SJF shortest-remaining-time-first or SRTF.)

To see that SJF is optimal, consider a hypothetical alternative policy that is not SJF, but that we think might be optimal. Because the alternative is not SJF, at some point it will choose to run a task that is longer than something else in the queue. If we now switch the order of tasks, keeping everything the same, but doing the shorter task first, we will reduce the average response time. Thus, any alternative to SJF cannot be optimal.

Figure 7.1 illustrates SJF on the same example we used for FIFO. If a long task is the first to arrive, it will be scheduled (if we are work-conserving). When a short task arrives a bit later, the scheduler will preempt the current task, and start the shorter one. The remaining short tasks will be processed in order of arrival, followed by finishing the long task.

Starvation and Sample Bias

Systems that might suffer from starvation require extra care when being measured. Suppose you want to compare FIFO and SJF experimentally. You set up two computers, one running each scheduler, and send them the same sequence of tasks. After some period, you stop and report the average response time of completed tasks. If some tasks starve, however, the set of completed tasks will be different for the two policies. We will have excluded the longest tasks from the results for SJF, skewing the average response time even further. Put another way, if you want to manipulate statistics to "prove" a point, this is a good trick to use!

How might you redesign the experiment to provide a valid comparison between FIFO and SJF?

What counts as "shortest" is the remaining time left on the task, not its original length. If we are one nanosecond away from finishing an hour-long task, we will minimize average response time by staying with that task, rather than preempting it for a minute long task that just arrived on the ready list. Of course, if they both arrive at about the same time, doing the minute long task first will dramatically improve average response time.

Does SJF have any other downsides (other than being impossible to implement because it requires knowledge of the future)? It turns out that SJF is pessimal for variance in response time. By doing the shortest tasks as quickly as possible, SJF necessarily does longer tasks as slowly as possible (among policies that are work-conserving). In other words, there is a fundamental tradeoff between reducing average response time and reducing the variance in average response time.

Worse, SJF can suffer from starvation and frequent context switches. If enough short tasks arrive, long tasks may never complete. Whenever a new task on the ready list is shorter than the remaining time left on the currently scheduled task, the scheduler will switch to the new task. If this keeps happening indefinitely, a long task may never finish.

Suppose a supermarket manager reads a portion of this textbook and decides to implement shortest job first to reduce average waiting times. The manager tells herself: who cares about variance! A benefit is that there would no longer be any need for express lanes — if someone has only a few items, she can be immediately whisked to the front of the line, interrupting the parent shopping for eighteen kids. Of course, the wait times of the customers with full baskets skyrockets; if the supermarket is open twenty-four hours a day, customers with the largest purchases might have to wait until 3am to finally get through the line. This would probably lead their best customers to go to the supermarket down the street, not exactly what the manager had in mind!

Customers could also try to game the system: if you have a lot of items

Shortest Job First and bandwidth-constrained web service

Although SJF may seem completely impractical, there are circumstances where it is exactly the right policy. One example is in a web server for static content. Many small-scale web servers are limited by their bandwidth to the Internet, because it is often more expensive to pay for more capacity. Web pages at most sites vary in size, with most pages being relatively short, while some pages are quite large. The average response time for accessing web pages is dominated by the more frequent requests to short pages, while the bandwidth costs are dominated by the less frequent requests to large pages.

This combination is almost ideal for using SJF for managing the allocation of network bandwidth by the server. With static pages, it is possible to predict from the name of the page how much bandwidth each request will consume. By transferring short pages first, the web server can ensure that its average response time is very low. Even if most requests are to small pages, the aggregate bandwidth for small pages is low, so requests to large pages are not significantly slowed down. The only difficulty comes when the web server is overloaded, because then the large page requests can be starved. As we will see later, overload situations need their own set of solutions.

---

to purchase, simply go through the line with one item at a time — you will always be whisked to the front, at least until everyone else figures out the same dodge.

7.1.3   Round Robin

A policy that addresses starvation is to schedule tasks in a round robin fashion. With Round Robin, tasks take turns running on the processor for a limited period of time. The scheduler assigns the processor to the first task in the ready

time quantum

list, setting a timer interrupt for some delay, called the *time quantum*. At the end of the quantum, if the task has not completed, the task is preempted and the processor is given to the next task in the ready list. The preempted task is put back on the ready list where it can wait its next turn. With Round Robin, there is no possibility that a task will starve — it will eventually reach the front of the queue and get its time quantum.

Of course, we need to pick the time quantum carefully. One consideration is overhead: if we have too short a time quantum, the processor will spend all of its time switching and getting very little useful work done. If we pick too long a time quantum, tasks will have to wait a long time until they get a turn. Figure 7.2 shows the behavior of Round Robin, on the same workload as in Figure 7.1, for two different values for the time quantum.

A good analogy for Round Robin is a particularly hyperkinetic student, studying for multiple finals simultaneously. You won't get much done if you

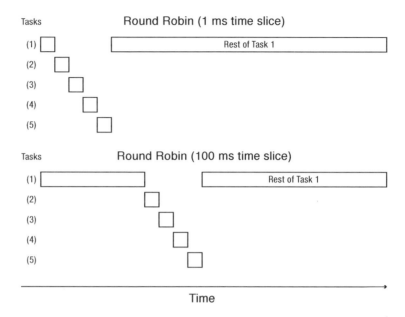

Figure 7.2: Completion times with Round Robin scheduling when short tasks arrive just after a long task, with a time quantum of 1 ms (top) and 100 ms (bottom).

read a paragraph from one textbook, then switch to reading a paragraph from the next textbook, and then switch to yet a third textbook. However, if you never switch, you may never get around to studying for some of your courses.

One way of viewing Round Robin is as a compromise between FIFO and SJF. At one extreme, if the time quantum is infinite (or at least, longer than the longest task), Round Robin behaves exactly the same as FIFO. Each task runs to completion and then yields the processor to the next in line. At the other extreme, suppose it was possible to switch between tasks with zero overhead, so we could choose a time quantum of a single instruction. With fine-grained time slicing, tasks would finish in the order of length, as with SJF, but slower: a task A will complete within a factor of n of when it would have under SJF, where n is the maximum number of other runnable tasks.

Unfortunately, Round Robin has some weaknesses. Figure 7.3 illustrates what happens for FIFO, SJF, and Round Robin when several tasks start at roughly same time and are of the same length. Round Robin will rotate through the tasks, doing a bit of each, finishing them all at roughly the same time. This is nearly the worst possible scheduling policy for this workload! FIFO does much better, picking a task and sticking with it until it finishes. Not only does FIFO reduce average response time for this workload relative to Round Robin, no task is worse off under FIFO — every task finishes at least as early as it would have under Round Robin. Time slicing added overhead without any benefit. Finally, consider what SJF does on this workload. SJF schedules tasks in exactly the same order as FIFO. The first task that arrives will be assigned

What is the overhead of a Round Robin time slice?

One might think that the cost of switching tasks after a time slice is modest: the cost of interrupting the processor, saving its registers, dispatching the timer interrupt handler, and restoring the registers of the new task. On a modern processor, all these steps can be completed in a few tens of microseconds.

However, we must also include the impact of time slices on the efficiency of the processor cache. Each newly scheduled task will need to fetch its data from memory into cache, evicting some of the data that had been stored by the previous task. Exactly how long this takes will depend on the memory hierarchy, the reference pattern of the new task, and whether any of its state is still in the cache from its previous time slice. Modern processors often have multiple levels of cache to improve performance. Reloading just the first level on-chip cache from scratch can take several milliseconds; reloading the second and third level caches takes even longer. Thus, it is typical for operating systems to set their time slice interval to be somewhere between 10 and 100 milliseconds, depending on the goals of the system: better responsiveness or reduced overhead.

---

the processor, and as soon as it executes a single instruction, it will have less time remaining than all of the other tasks, and so it will run to completion. Since we know SJF is optimal for average response time, this means that both FIFO and Round Robin are optimal for some workloads and pessimal for others, just different ones in each case.

Depending on the time quantum, Round Robin can also be quite poor when running a mixture of I/O-bound and compute-bound tasks. I/O-bound tasks often need very short periods on the processor in order to compute the next I/O operation to issue. Any delay to be scheduled onto the processor can lead to system-wide slowdowns. For example, in a text editor, it often takes only a few milliseconds to echo a keystroke to the screen, a delay much faster than human perception. However, if we are sharing the processor between a text editor and several other tasks using Round Robin, the editor must wait several time quanta to be scheduled for each keystroke — with a 100 ms time quantum, this can become annoyingly apparent to the user.

Figure 7.4 illustrates similar behavior with a disk-bound task. Suppose we have a task that computes for 1 ms and then uses the disk for 10 ms, in a loop. Running alone, the task can keep the disk almost completely busy. Suppose we also have two compute bound tasks; again, running by themselves, they can keep the processor busy. What happens when we run the disk-bound and compute-bound tasks at the same time? With Round Robin and a time quantum of 100 ms, the disk-bound task slows down by nearly a factor of twenty — each time it needs the processor, it must wait nearly 200 ms for its turn. SJF on this workload would perform well — prioritizing short tasks at

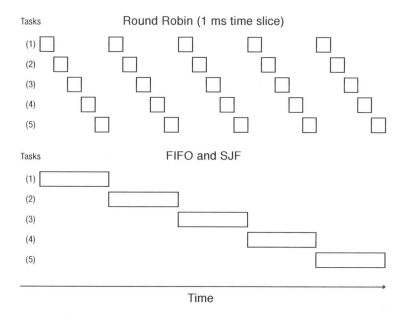

Figure 7.3: Completion times with Round Robin (top) versus FIFO and SJF (bottom) when scheduling equal length tasks.

the processor keeps the disk-bound task busy, while modestly slowing down the compute-bound tasks.

If you have ever tried to surf the web while doing a large BitTorrent download over a slow link, you can see that network operations visibly slow during the download. This is even though your browser may need to transfer only a very small amount of data to provide good responsiveness. The reason is quite similar. Browser packets get their turn, but only after being queued behind a much larger number of packets for the bulk download. Prioritizing the browser's packets would have only a minimal impact on the download speed and a large impact on the perceived responsiveness of the system.

7.1.4   Max-Min Fairness

In many settings, a fair allocation of resources is as important to the design of a scheduler as responsiveness and low overhead. On a multi-user machine or on a server, we do not want to allow a single user to be able to monopolize the resources of the machine, degrading service for other users. While it might seem that fairness has little value in single-user machines, individual applications are often written by different companies, each with an interest in making their application performance look good even if that comes at a cost of degrading responsiveness for other applications.

Another complication arises with whether we should allocate resources fairly among users, applications, processes, or threads. Some applications

Simultaneous Multi-Threading

Although zero overhead switching may seem far-fetched, most modern processors do a form of it called *simultaneous multi-threading (SMT)* or *hyper-threading*. With SMT, each processor simulates two (or more) virtual processors, alternating between them on a cycle-by-cycle basis. Since most threads need to wait for memory from time to time, another thread can use the processor during those gaps, or vice versa. In normal operation, neither thread is significantly slowed when running on an SMT.

You can test whether your computer implements SMT by testing how fast the processor operates when it has one or more tasks, each running a tight loop of arithmetic operations. (Note that on a multicore system, you will need to create enough tasks to fill up each of the cores, or physical processors, before the system will begin to use SMT.) With one task per physical processor, each task will run at the maximum rate of the processor. With a two-way SMT and two tasks per processor, each task will run at somewhat less than the maximum rate, but each task will run at approximately the same uniform speed. As you increase the number of tasks beyond the SMT level, however, the operating system will begin to use coarse-grained time slicing, so tasks will progress in spurts — alternating time on and off the processor.

Round Robin and streaming video

Round Robin is sometimes the best policy even when all tasks are roughly the same size. An example is managing the server bandwidth for streaming video. When streaming, response time is much less of a concern than achieving a predictable, stable rate of progress. For this, Round Robin is nearly ideal: all streams progress at the same rate. As long as Round Robin serves the data as fast or faster than the viewer consumes the video stream, the time to completely download the stream is unimportant.

may run inside a single process, while others may create many processes, and each process may involve multiple threads. Round robin among threads can lead to starvation if applications with only a single thread are competing with applications with hundreds of threads. We can be concerned with fair allocation at any of these levels of granularity: threads within a process, processes for a particular user, users sharing a physical machine. For example, we could be concerned with making sure that every thread within a process makes progress. For simplicity, however, our discussion will assume we are interested in providing fairness among processes — the same principles apply

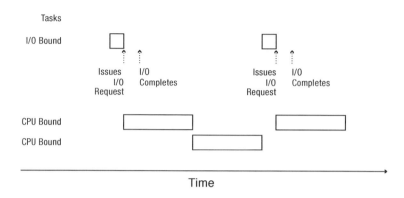

Figure 7.4: Scheduling behavior with Round Robin when running a mixture of I/O-bound and compute-bound tasks. The I/O-bound task yields the processor when it does I/O. Even though the I/O completes quickly, the I/O-bound task must wait to be reassigned the processor until the compute-bound tasks both complete their time quanta.

if the unit receiving resources is the user, application, or thread.

Fairness is easy if all processes are compute-bound: Round Robin will give each process an equal portion of the processor. In practice, however, different processes consume resources at different rates. An I/O-bound process may need only a small portion of the processor, while a compute-bound process is willing to consume all available processor time. What is a fair allocation when there is a diversity of needs?

One possible answer is to say that whatever Round Robin does is fair — after all, each process gets an equal chance at the processor. As we saw above, however, Round Robin can result in I/O-bound processes running at a much slower rate than they would if they had the processor to themselves, while compute-bound processes are barely affected at all. That hardly seems fair!

max-min fairness   While there are many possible definitions of fairness, a particularly useful one is called *max-min fairness*. Max-min fairness iteratively maximizes the minimum allocation given to a particular process (user, application or thread) until all resources are assigned.

If all processes are compute-bound, the behavior of max-min is simple: we maximize the minimum by giving each process exactly the same share of the processor — that is, by using Round Robin.

The behavior of max-min fairness is more interesting if some processes cannot use their entire share, for example, because they are short-running or I/O-bound. If so, we give those processes their entire request and redistribute the unused portion to the remaining processes. Some of the processes receiving the extra portion may not be able to use their entire revised share, and so we must iterate, redistributing any unused portion. When no remaining requests can be fully satisfied, we divide the remainder equally among all remaining processes.

Consider the example in the previous section. The disk-bound process needed only 10% of the processor to keep busy, but Round Robin only gave it 0.5% of the processor, while each of the two compute-bound processes received nearly 50%. Max-min fairness would assign 10% of the processor to the I/O-bound process, and it would split the remainder equally between the two compute-bound processes, with 45% each.

A hypothetical but completely impractical implementation of max-min would be to give the processor at each instant to whichever process has received the least portion of the processor. In the example above, the disk-bound task would always be scheduled instantly, preempting the compute-bound processes. However, we have already seen why this would not work well. With two equally long tasks, as soon as we execute one instruction in one task, it would have received more resources than the other one, so to preserve "fairness" we would need to instantly switch to the next task.

We can approximate a max-min fair allocation by relaxing this constraint — to allow a process to get ahead of its fair allocation by one time quantum. Every time the scheduler needs to make a choice, it chooses the task for the process with the least accumulated time on the processor. If a new process arrives on the queue with much less accumulated time, such as the disk-bound task, it will preempt the process, but otherwise the current process will complete its quantum. Tasks may get up to one time quantum more than their fair share, but over the long term the allocation will even out.

The algorithm we just described was originally defined for network, and not processor, scheduling. If we share a link between a browser request and a long download, we will get reasonable responsiveness for the browser if we have approximately fair allocation — the browser needs few network packets, and so under max-min its packets will always be scheduled ahead of the packets from the download.

Even this approximation, though, can be computationally expensive, since it requires tasks to be maintained on a priority queue. For some server environments, there can be tens or even hundreds of thousands of scheduling decisions to be made every second. To reduce the computational overhead of the scheduler, most commercial operating systems use a somewhat different algorithm, to the same goal, which we describe next.

7.1.5   Case Study: Multi-Level Feedback

Multi-level Feedback Queue (MFQ)

Most commercial operating systems, including Windows, MacOS, and Linux, use a scheduling algorithm called *Multi-level Feedback Queue (MFQ)*. MFQ is designed to achieve several simultaneous goals:

- **Responsiveness.** Run short tasks quickly, as in SJF.

- **Low Overhead.** Minimize the number of preemptions, as in FIFO, and minimize the time spent making scheduling decisions.

- **Starvation-Freedom.** All tasks should make progress, as in Round Robin.

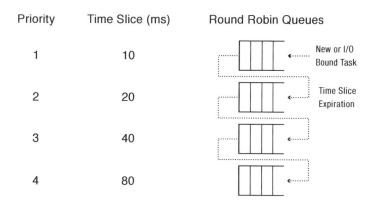

Figure 7.5: Multi-level Feedback Queue when running a mixture of I/O-bound and compute-bound tasks. New tasks enter at high priority with a short quantum; tasks that use their quantum are reduced in priority.

- **Background Tasks.** Defer system maintenance tasks, such as disk defragmentation, so they do not interfere with user work.

- **Fairness.** Assign (non-background) processes approximately their max-min fair share of the processor.

As with any real system that must balance several conflicting goals, MFQ does not perfectly achieve any of these goals. Rather, it is intended to be a reasonable compromise in most real-world cases.

MFQ is an extension of Round Robin. Instead of only a single queue, MFQ has multiple Round Robin queues, each with a different priority level and time quantum. Tasks at a higher priority level preempt lower priority tasks, while tasks at the same level are scheduled in Round Robin fashion. Further, higher priority levels have *shorter* time quanta than lower levels.

Tasks are moved between priority levels to favor short tasks over long ones. A new task enters at the top priority level. Every time the task uses up its time quantum, it drops a level; every time the task yields the processor because it is waiting on I/O, it stays at the same level (or is bumped up a level); and if the task completes it leaves the system.

Figure 7.5 illustrates the operation of an MFQ with four levels. A new compute-bound task will start as high priority, but it will quickly exhaust its time quantum and fall to the next lower priority, and then the next. Thus, an I/O-bound task needing only a modest amount of computing will almost always be scheduled quickly, keeping the disk busy. Compute-bound tasks run with a long time quantum to minimize switching overhead while still sharing the processor.

So far, the algorithm we have described does not achieve starvation freedom or max-min fairness. If there are too many I/O-bound tasks, the compute-bound tasks may receive no time on the processor. To combat this, the MFQ scheduler monitors every process to ensure it is receiving its fair share of the resources. At each level, Linux actually maintains two queues — tasks whose processes have already reached their fair share are only scheduled if all other processes at that level have also received their fair share. Periodically, any process receiving less than its fair share will have its tasks increased in priority; equally, tasks that receive more than their fair share can be reduced in priority.

Adjusting priority also addresses strategic behavior. From a purely selfish point of view, a task can attempt to keep its priority high by doing a short I/O request immediately before its time quantum expires. Eventually the system will detect this and reduce its priority to its fair-share level.

Our previously hapless supermarket manager reads a bit farther into the textbook and realizes that supermarket express lanes are a form of multi-level queue. By limiting express lanes to customers with a few items, the manager can ensure short tasks complete quickly, reducing average response time. The manager can also monitor wait times, adding extra lanes to ensure that everyone is served reasonably quickly.

7.1.6   Summary

We summarize the lessons from this section:

- FIFO is simple and minimizes overhead.

- If tasks are variable in size, then FIFO can have very poor average response time.

- If tasks are equal in size, FIFO is optimal in terms of average response time.

- Considering only the processor, SJF is optimal in terms of average response time.

- SJF is pessimal in terms of variance in response time.

- If tasks are variable in size, Round Robin approximates SJF.

- If tasks are equal in size, Round Robin will have very poor average response time.

- Tasks that intermix processor and I/O benefit from SJF and can do poorly under Round Robin.

- Max-min fairness can improve response time for I/O-bound tasks.

- Round Robin and Max-min fairness both avoid starvation.

- By manipulating the assignment of tasks to priority queues, an MFQ scheduler can achieve a balance between responsiveness, low overhead, and fairness.

In the rest of this chapter, we extend these ideas to multiprocessors, energy-constrained environments, real-time settings, and overloaded conditions.

7.2 | Multiprocessor Scheduling

Today, most general-purpose computers are multiprocessors. Physical constraints in circuit design make it easier to add computational power by adding processors, or cores, onto a single chip, rather than making individual processors faster. Many high-end desktops and servers have multiple processing chips, each with multiple cores, and each core with hyperthreading. Even smartphones have 2-4 processors. This trend is likely to accelerate, with systems of the future having dozens or perhaps hundreds of processors per computer.

This poses two questions for operating system scheduling:

- How do we make effective use of multiple cores for running sequential tasks?

- How do we adapt scheduling algorithms for parallel applications?

7.2.1 Scheduling Sequential Applications on Multiprocessors

Consider a server handling a very large number of web requests. A common software architecture for servers is to allocate a separate thread for each user connection. Each thread consults a shared data structure to see which portions of the requested data are cached, and fetches any missing elements from disk. The thread then spools the result out across the network.

How should the operating system schedule these server threads? Each thread is I/O-bound, repeatedly reading or writing data to disk and the network, and therefore makes many small trips through the processor. Some requests may require more computation; to keep average response time low, we will want to favor short tasks.

A simple approach would be to use a centralized multi-level feedback queue, with a lock to ensure only one processor at a time is reading or modifying the data structure. Each idle processor takes the next task off the MFQ and runs it. As the disk or network finishes requests, threads waiting on I/O are put back on the MFQ and executed by the network processor that becomes idle.

There are several potential performance problems with this approach:

- **Contention for the MFQ lock.** Depending on how much computation each thread does before blocking on I/O, the centralized lock may become a bottleneck, particularly as the number of processors increases.

- **Cache Coherence Overhead.** Although only a modest number of instructions are needed for each visit to the MFQ, each processor will need to fetch the current state of the MFQ from the cache of the previous processor to hold the lock. On a single processor, the scheduling data structure

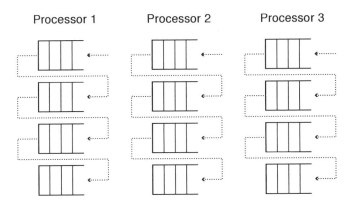

Processor 1   Processor 2   Processor 3

Figure 7.6: Per-processor scheduling data structures. Each processor has its own (multi-level) queue of ready threads.

is likely to be already loaded into the cache. On a multiprocessor, the data structure will be accessed and modified by different processors in turn, so the most recent version of the data is likely to be cached only by the processor that made the most recent update. Fetching data from a remote cache can take two to three orders of magnitude longer than accessing locally cached data. Since the cache miss delay occurs while holding the MFQ lock, the MFQ lock is held for longer periods and so can become even more of a bottleneck.

- **Limited Cache Reuse.** If threads run on the first available processor, they are likely to be assigned to a different processor each time they are scheduled. This means that any data needed by the thread is unlikely to be cached on that processor. Of course, some of the thread's data will have been displaced from the cache during the time it was blocked, but on-chip caches are so large today that much of the thread's data will remain cached. Worse, the most recent version of the thread's data is likely to be in a remote cache, requiring even more of a slowdown as the remote data is fetched into the local cache.

For these reasons, commercial operating systems such as Linux use a *per-processor* data structure: a separate copy of the multi-level feedback queue for each processor. Figure 7.6 illustrates this approach.

affinity scheduling   Each processor uses *affinity scheduling*: once a thread is scheduled on a processor, it is returned to the same processor when it is re-scheduled, maximizing cache reuse. Each processor looks at its own copy of the queue for new work to do; this can mean that some processors can idle while others have work waiting to be done. Rebalancing occurs only if the queue lengths are persistent enough to compensate for the time to reload the cache for the migrated threads. Because rebalancing is possible, the per-processor data structures must still be protected by locks, but in the common case the next processor to use the data

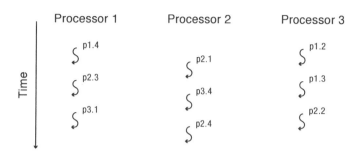

px.y = Thread y in process x

Figure 7.7: With oblivious scheduling, threads are time sliced by the multiprocessor operating system, with no attempt to ensure threads from the same process run at the same time.

will be the last one to have written it, minimizing cache coherence overhead and lock contention.

7.2.2 Scheduling Parallel Applications

A different set of challenges occurs when scheduling parallel applications onto a multiprocessor. There is often a natural decomposition of a parallel application onto a set of processors. For example, an image processing application may divide the image up into equal size chunks, assigning one to each processor. While the application could divide the image into many more chunks than processors, this comes at a cost in efficiency: less cache reuse and more communication to coordinate work at the boundary between each chunk.

If there are multiple applications running at the same time, the application may receive fewer or more processors than it expected or started with. New applications can start up, acquiring processing resources. Other applications may complete, releasing resources. Even without multiple applications, the operating system itself will have system tasks to run from time to time, disrupting the mapping of parallel work onto a fixed number of processors.

Oblivious Scheduling

One might imagine that the scheduling algorithms we have already discussed can take care of these cases. Each thread is time sliced onto the available processors; if two or more applications create more threads in aggregate than processors, multi-level feedback will ensure that each thread makes progress and receives a fair share of the processor. This is often called *oblivious scheduling*, as the operating system scheduler operates without knowledge of the intent of the parallel application — each thread is scheduled as a completely independent entity. Figure 7.7 illustrates oblivious scheduling.

oblivious
scheduling

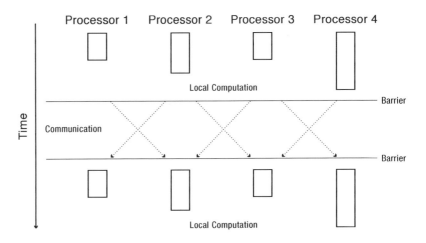

Figure 7.8: Bulk synchronous design pattern for a parallel program; each processor computes on local data and waits for every other processor to complete before proceeding to the next step. Preempting one processor can stall all processors until the preempted process is resumed.

Unfortunately, several problems can occur with oblivious scheduling on multiprocessors:

bulk synchronous

- **Bulk synchronous delay.** A common design pattern in parallel programs is to split work into roughly equal sized chunks; once all the chunks finish, the processors synchronize at a barrier before communicating their results to the next stage of the computation. This *bulk synchronous* parallelism is easy to manage—each processor works independently, sharing its results only with the next stage in the computation. Google MapReduce is a widely used bulk synchronous application.

  Figure 7.8 illustrates the problem with bulk synchronous computation under oblivious scheduling. At each step, the computation is limited by the slowest processor to complete that step. If a processor is preempted, its work will be delayed, stalling the remaining processors until the last one is scheduled. Even if one of the waiting processors picks up the preempted task, a single preemption can delay the entire computation by a factor of two, and possibly even more with cache effects. Since the application does not know that a processor was preempted, it cannot adapt its decomposition for the available number of processors, so each step is similarly delayed until the processor is returned.

- **Producer-consumer delay.** Some parallel applications use a producer-consumer design pattern, where the results of one thread are fed to the next thread, and the output of that thread is fed onward, as in Figure 7.9. Preempting a thread in the middle of a producer-consumer chain can stall all of the processors in the chain.

Processor 1   Processor 2   Processor 3   Processor 4

Figure 7.9: Producer-consumer design pattern for a parallel program. Preempting one stage can stall the remainder.

Figure 7.10: Critical path of a parallel program; delays on the critical path increase execution time.

critical path

- **Critical path delay.** More generally, parallel programs have a *critical path* — the minimum sequence of steps for the application to compute its result. Figure 7.10 illustrates the critical path for a fork-join parallel program. Work off the critical path can occur in parallel, but its precise scheduling is less important. Preempting a thread on the critical path, however, will slow down the end result. Although the application programmer may know which parts of the computation are on the critical path, with oblivious scheduling, the operating system will not; it will be equally likely to preempt a thread on the critical path as off.

- **Preemption of lock holder.** Many parallel programs use locks and condition variables for synchronizing their parallel execution. Often, to reduce the cost of acquiring locks, parallel programs will use a "spin-then-wait" strategy — if a lock is busy, the waiting thread spin-waits briefly for it to be released, and if the lock is still busy, it blocks and looks for other work to do. This can reduce overhead in the common case that the lock is held for only short periods of time. With oblivious scheduling, however, the

	Processor 1	Processor 2	Processor 3

$$\text{Time} \quad \begin{array}{ccc} \wr^{\,p1.1} & \wr^{\,p1.2} & \wr^{\,p1.3} \\[6pt] \wr^{\,p2.1} & \wr^{\,p2.2} & \wr^{\,p2.3} \\[6pt] \wr^{\,p3.1} & \wr^{\,p3.2} & \wr^{\,p3.3} \end{array}$$

px.y = Thread y in process x

Figure 7.11: With gang scheduling, threads from the same process are scheduled at exactly the same time, and they are time sliced together to provide a chance for other processes to run.

lock holder can be preempted — other tasks will spin-then-wait until the lock holder is re-scheduled, increasing overhead.

- **I/O.** Many parallel applications do I/O, and this can cause problems if the operating system scheduler is oblivious to the application decomposition into parallel work. If a read or write request blocks in the kernel, the thread blocks as well. To reuse the processor while the thread is waiting, the application program must have created more threads than processors, so that the scheduler can have an extra one to run in place of the blocked thread. However, if the thread does not block (e.g., on a file read when the file is cached in memory), that means that the scheduler has more threads than processors, and so needs to do time slicing to multiplex threads onto processors — causing all of the problems we have listed above.

Gang Scheduling

gang scheduling

One possible approach to some of these issues is to schedule all of the tasks of a program together. This is called *gang scheduling*. The application picks some decomposition of work into some number of threads, and those threads run either together or not at all. If the operating system needs to schedule a different application, if there are insufficient idle resources, it preempts all of the processors of an application to make room. Figure 7.11 illustrates an example of gang scheduling.

Because of the value of gang scheduling, commercial operating systems, such as Linux, Windows, and MacOS, have mechanisms for dedicating a set of processors to a single application. This is often appropriate on a server dedicated to a single primary use, such as a database needing precise control over thread assignment. The application can *pin* each thread to a specific processor and (with the appropriate permissions) mark it to run with high

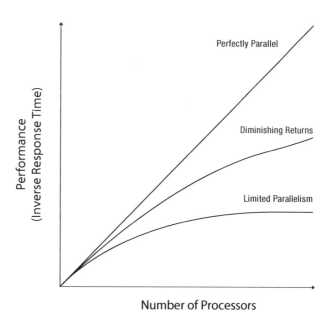

Figure 7.12: Performance as a function of the number of processors, for some typical parallel applications. Some applications scale linearly with the number of processors; others achieve diminishing returns.

priority. The system reserves a small subset of the processors to run other applications, multiplexed in the normal way but without interfering with the primary application.

For multiplexing multiple parallel applications, however, gang scheduling can be inefficient. Figure 7.12 illustrates why. It shows the performance of three example parallel programs as a function of the number of processors assigned to the application. While some applications have perfect speedup and can make efficient use of many processors, other applications reach a point of diminishing returns, and still others have a maximum parallelism. For example, if adding processors does not decrease the time spent on the program's critical path, there is no benefit to adding those resources.

An implication of Figure 7.12 is that it is usually more efficient to run two parallel programs each with half the number of processors, than to time slice the two programs, each gang scheduled onto all of the processors. Allocating

space sharing   different processors to different tasks is called *space sharing*, to differentiate it from time sharing, or time slicing—allocating a single processor among multiple tasks by alternating in time when each is scheduled onto the processor. Space sharing on a multiprocessor is also more efficient in that it minimizes processor context switches: as long as the operating system has not changed the allocation, the processors do not even need to be time sliced. Figure 7.13 illustrates an example of space sharing.

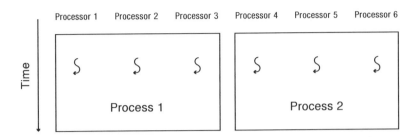

Figure 7.13: With space sharing, each process is assigned a subset of the processors.

Space sharing is straightforward if all tasks start and stop at the same time; in that case, we can just allocate evenly. However, the number of available processors is often a dynamic property in a multiprogrammed setting, because tasks start and stop at irregular intervals. How does the application know how many processors to use if the number changes over time?

Scheduler Activations

scheduler activations

A solution, recently added to Windows, is to make the assignment and re-assignment of processors to applications visible to applications. Applications are given an execution context, or *scheduler activation*, on each processor assigned to the application; the application is informed explicitly, via an upcall, whenever a processor is added to its allocation or taken away. Blocking on an I/O request also causes an upcall to allow the application to repurpose the processor while the thread is waiting for I/O.

As we noted in Chapter 4, user-level thread management is possible with scheduler activations. The operating system kernel assigns processors to applications, either evenly or according to some priority weighting. Each application then schedules its user-level threads onto the processors assigned to it, changing its allocation as the number of processors varies due to external events such as other processes starting or stopping. If no other application is running, an application can use all of the processors of the machine; with more contention, the application must remap its work onto a smaller number of processors.

multiprocessor scheduling policy

Scheduler activations defines a *mechanism* for informing an application of its processor allocation, but it leaves open the question of the *multiprocessor scheduling policy*: how many processors should we assign each process? This is an open research question. As we explained in our discussion of uniprocessor scheduling policies, there is a fundamental tradeoff between policies (such as Shortest Job First) that improve average response time and those (such as max-min fairness) that attempt to achieve fair allocation of resources among different applications. In the multiprocessor setting, average response time may be improved by giving extra resources to parallel interactive tasks provided this did not cause long-running compute intensive parallel tasks to starve for resources.

7.3 | Energy-Aware Scheduling

Another important consideration for processor scheduling is its impact on battery life and energy use. Laptops and smartphones compete on the basis of battery life, and even for servers, energy usage is a large fraction of the overall system cost. Choices that the operating system makes can have a large effect on these issues.

One might think that processor scheduling has little role to play with respect to system energy usage. After all, each application has a certain amount of computing that needs to be done, computing that requires energy whether we are running on a direct power line or off of a battery. Of course, the operating system should delay background or system maintenance tasks (such as software upgrades) for when the system is connected to power, but this is likely to be a relatively minor effect on the overall power budget.

In part because of the importance of battery life to computer users, modern architectures have developed a number of ways of trading reduced computation speed for lower energy use. In other words, the mental model of each computation taking a fixed amount of energy is no longer accurate. There is quite a bit of flux in the types of hardware support available on different systems, and systems five years from now are likely to make very different tradeoffs than those in place today. Thus, our goal in this section is not to provide a set of widely used algorithms for managing power, but rather to outline the design issues energy management poses for the operating system.

Several power optimizations are possible, provided hardware support:

- **Processor design.** There can be several orders of magnitude difference between one processor design and another with respect to power consumption. Often, making a processor faster requires extra circuitry, such as out of order execution, that itself consumes power; low power processors are slower and simpler. Likewise, processors designed for lower clock speeds can tolerate lower voltage swings at the circuit level, reducing power consumption dramatically. Some systems have begun to put this tradeoff under the control of the operating system, by including both a high power, high performance multiprocessor and a low power, lower performance uniprocessor on the same chip. High power is appropriate when response time is at a premium and low power when power consumption is more important.

- **Processor usage.** For systems with multiple processor chips, or multiple cores on a single chip, lightly used processors can be disabled to save power. Processors will typically draw much less power when they are completely idle, but as we mentioned above, many parallel programs achieve some benefit from using extra processors, yet also reach a point

Heat Dissipation

A closely related topic to energy use is heat dissipation. In laptop computers, you can save weight by not including a fan to cool the processor. However, a modern multicore chip will consume up to 150 Watts, or more than a very bright incandescent light bulb. Just as with a light bulb, the heat generated has to go somewhere. Making things significantly more complicated, the processor will also break permanently if it runs at too high a temperature. Thus, the operating system increasingly must monitor and manage the temperature of the processor to ensure it stays within its operating region. Much like a cheetah, portable computers are now capable of running at very fast speeds for short periods of time, before they need to take a break to cool down. Or they can amble at much slower speeds for a longer period of time.

The laptop one of us used to write this book illustrates this. Formatting this textbook takes about a minute when the computer is cold, but the same formatting request will stall in the middle of the build for several minutes if run immediately after a previous build request.

of diminishing returns. Thus, there is a tradeoff between somewhat faster execution (e.g., by using all available resources) and lower energy use (e.g., by turning off some processors even when using them would slightly decrease response time).

- **I/O device power.** Devices not in use can be powered off. Although this is most obvious in terms of the display, devices such as the WiFi or cell-phone network interface also consume large amounts of power. Power-constrained embedded systems such as sensors will turn on their network interface hardware periodically to send or receive data, and then go back to quiescence. For this to work, the senders and receivers need to synchronize their periods of transmission, or the hardware needs to have a low power listening mode.

At times, different power optimizations interact in subtle ways. For example, running application code quickly can sometimes improve power efficiency, by enabling the network interface hardware to be turned off more quickly once the application finishes. Because context switching consumes both time and energy to reload processor caches, affinity scheduling improves both performance and energy efficiency.

In most cases, however, there is a tradeoff: how should the operating system balance between competing demands for timeliness and energy efficiency? If the user has requested maximum responsiveness or maximum battery life, the choice is easy, but often the user wants a reasonable tradeoff between the two.

Figure 7.14: Example relationship between response time and user-perceived value. For most applications, faster response time is valuable within a range. Below some threshold, users will not be able to perceive the difference. Above some threshold, users will perform other activities while waiting for the result.

One approach would be to consider the value that the user places on fast response time for a particular application: quickly updating the display after a user interface command is probably more important than transferring files quickly in the background. We can capture the relationship between response time and value in Figure 7.14. Although the precise shape and magnitude will vary from user to user and application to application, the curve will head down and to the right — the longer something takes, the less useful it is. Often, the curve is S-shaped. Human perception is unable to tell the difference between a few tens of milliseconds, so adding a short delay will not matter that much for most tasks; likewise, if a protein folding computation has already taken a few minutes, it won't matter much if it takes a few more seconds. Not everything will be S-shaped: in high frequency stock trading, value starts high and plummets to zero within a few milliseconds.

Response time predictability affects this relationship as well. An online video that cuts out for a few seconds every minute is much less watchable than one that is lower quality on average but more predictable.

If we combine Figure 7.14 with the fact that increased energy use often provides diminishing returns in terms of improved performance, this suggests a three prong strategy to spend the system's energy budget where it will make the most difference:

Battery life and the kernel-user boundary

An emerging issue on smartphones is that application behavior can have a significant impact on battery life, e.g., by more intensive use of the network or other power-hungry features of the architecture. If a user runs a mix of applications, how can she know which was most responsible for their smartphone running out of power? Among the resources we will discuss in this book, energy is almost unique in being a *non-virtualizable* resource. When an application drains the battery, the energy lost is no longer available to any other applications.

How can we prevent a misbehaving or greedy application from using more than its share of the battery? One model is to let the user decide: for the kernel to measure and record how much energy was used by each application, so the user can determine if each application is worth it. Apple has taken a different approach with the iPhone. Because Apple controls which applications can run on the system, it can and has barred applications that (in its view) unnecessarily drain the battery. It will be interesting to see which of these models wins out over time.

- **Below the threshold of human perception.** Optimize for energy use, to the extent that tasks can be executed with greater energy efficiency without the user noticing.

- **Above the threshold of human perception.** Optimize for response time if the user will notice any slowdown.

- **Long-running or background tasks.** Balance energy use and responsiveness depending on the available battery resources.

7.4 | Real-Time Scheduling

On some systems, the operating system scheduler must account for process deadlines. For example, the sensor and control software to manage an airplane's flight path must be executed in a timely fashion, if it is to be useful at all. Similarly, the software to control anti-lock brakes or anti-skid traction control on an automobile must occur at a precise time if it is to be effective. In a less life critical domain, when playing a movie on a computer, the next frame must be rendered in time or the user will perceive the video quality as poor.

real-time constraint   These systems have *real-time constraints*: computation that must be completed by a deadline if it is to have value. Real-time constraints are a special

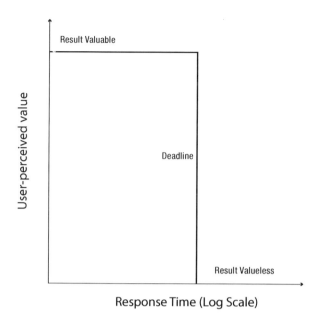

Figure 7.15: With real-time constraints, the value of completing some task drops to zero if the deadline is not met.

case of Figure 7.14, shown in Figure 7.15, where the value of completing a task is uniform up to the deadline, and then drops to zero.

How do we design a scheduler to ensure deadlines are met?

We might start by assigning real-time tasks a higher priority than any less time critical tasks. We could then run the system under a variety of different of different workloads, and see if the system continues to comfortably meet its deadlines in all cases. If not, the system may need a faster processor or other hardware resources to speed up the real-time tasks.

Unfortunately, testing alone is insufficient for guaranteeing real-time constraints. Recall that the specific ordering of execution events can sometimes lead to different execution sequences — e.g., sometimes a thread will need to wait for a lock held another thread, and other times the lock will be FREE.

One option is that, instead of threads, we should use a completely deterministic and repeatable schedule that ensures that the deadlines are met. This can work if the real-time tasks are periodic and fixed in advance. However, in dynamic systems, it is difficult to account for all possible variations affecting how long different parts of the computation will take.

There are three widely used techniques for increasing the likelihood that threads meet their deadlines. These approaches are also useful whenever timeliness matters without a strict deadline, e.g., to ensure responsiveness of a user interface.

- **Over-provisioning.** A simple step is to ensure that the real-time tasks, in aggregate, use only a fraction of the system's processing power. This way, the real-time tasks will be scheduled quickly, without having to wait for higher-priority, compute-intensive tasks. The equivalent step in college is to avoid signing up for too many hard courses in the same semester!

- **Earliest deadline first.** Careful choice of the scheduling policy can also help meet deadlines. If you have a pile of homework to do, neither shortest job first nor round robin will ensure that the assignment due tomorrow gets done in time. Instead, real-time schedulers, mimicking real life, use a policy called *earliest deadline first* (EDF). EDF sorts tasks by their deadline and performs them in that order. If it is possible to schedule the required work to meet their deadlines, and the tasks only need the processor (and not I/O, locks or other resources), EDF will ensure that all tasks are done in time.

  earliest deadline first

  For complex tasks, however, EDF can produce anomalous behavior. Consider two tasks. Task A is I/O-bound with a deadline at 12 ms, needing 1 ms of computation followed by 10 ms of I/O. Task B is compute-bound with a deadline at 10 ms, but needing 5 ms of computation. Although there is a schedule that will meet both deadlines (run task A first), EDF will run the compute-bound task first, causing the I/O-bound task to miss its deadline.

  This limitation can be addressed by breaking tasks into shorter units, each with its own deadline. In the example, the true deadline for the compute portion of the I/O-bound task is at 2 ms, because if it is not completed by then, the overall task deadline will be missed. If your homework next week needs a book from the library, you need to put that on hold first, even if that slightly delays the homework you have due tomorrow.

- **Priority donation.** Another problem can occur through the interaction of shared data structures, priorities, and deadlines. Suppose we have three tasks, each with a different priority level. The real-time task runs at the highest priority, and it has sufficient processing resources to meet its deadline, with some time to spare. However, the three tasks also access a shared data structure, protected by a lock.

  Suppose the low priority acquires the lock to modify the data structure, but it is then preempted by the medium priority task. The relative priorities imply that we should run the medium priority task first, even though the low priority task is in the middle of a critical section. Next, suppose the real-time task preempts the medium task and proceeds to access the shared data structure. It will find the lock busy and wait. Normally, the wait would be short, and the real-time task would be able to meet its deadline despite the delay. However, in this case, when the high priority task waits for the lock, the scheduler will pick the medium priority task

priority inversion

to run next, causing an indefinite delay. This is called *priority inversion*; it can occur whenever a high priority task must wait for a lower priority task to complete its work.

priority donation

A commonly used solution, implemented in most commercial operating systems, is called *priority donation*: when a high priority task waits on a shared lock, it temporarily donates its priority to the task holding the lock. This allows the low priority task to be scheduled to complete the critical section, at which point its priority reverts to its original state, and the processor is re-assigned to the high priority, waiting, task.

7.5 | Queueing Theory

Suppose you build a new web service, and the week before you are to take it live, you test it to see whether it will have reasonable response time. If your tests show that the performance is terrible, what then? Is it because the implementation is too slow? Perhaps you have the wrong scheduler? Quick, let's re-implement that linked list with a hash table! And add more levels to the multi-level feedback queue! Our advice: don't panic. In this section, we consider a third possibility, an effect that often trumps all of the others: response time depends non-linearly on the rate that tasks arrive at a system. Understanding this relationship is the topic of *queueing theory*.

Fortunately, if you have ever waited in line (and who hasn't?), you have an intuitive understanding of queueing theory. Its concepts apply whenever there is a queue waiting for a turn, whether it is tasks waiting for a processor, web requests waiting for a turn at a web server, restaurant patrons waiting for a table, cars waiting at a busy intersection, or people waiting in line at the supermarket.

While queueing theory is capable of providing precise predictions for complex systems, our interest is providing you the tools to be able to do back of the envelope calculations for where the time goes in a real system. For performance debugging, coarse estimates are often enough. For this reason, we make two simplifying assumptions for this discussion. First, we assume the system is work-conserving, so that all tasks that arrive are eventually serviced; this will normally be the case except in extreme overload conditions, a topic we will discuss in the next section of this chapter. Second, although the scheduling policy can affect a system's queueing behavior, we will keep things simple and assume FIFO scheduling.

7.5.1 Definitions

Because queueing theory is concerned with the root causes of system performance, and not just its observable effects, we need to introduce a bit more terminology. A simple abstract queueing system is illustrated by Figure 7.16. In any queueing system, tasks arrive, wait their turn, get service, and leave.

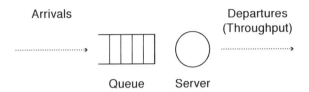

Figure 7.16: An abstract queueing system. Tasks arrive, wait their turn in the queue, get service, and leave.

If tasks arrive faster than they can be serviced, the queue grows. The queue shrinks when the service rate exceeds the arrival rate.

To begin, we will consider single-queue, single-server, work-conserving systems. Later, we will introduce more complexity such as multiple queues, multiple servers, and finite queues that can discard some requests.

- **Server.** A server is anything that performs tasks. A web server is obviously a server, performing web requests, but so is the processor on a client machine, since it executes application tasks. The cashier at a supermarket and a waiter in a restaurant are also servers.

- **Queueing delay (W) and number of tasks queued (Q).** The queueing delay, or wait time, is the total time a task must wait to be scheduled. In a time slicing system, a task might need to wait multiple times for the same server to complete its task; in this case the queueing delay includes all of the time a task spends waiting until it is completed.

- **Service time (S).** The service time S, or execution time, is the time to complete a task assuming no waiting.

- **Response time (R).** The response time is the queueing delay (how long you wait in line) plus the service time (how long it takes once you get to the front of the line).

$$R = W + S$$

In the web server example we started with, the poor performance can be due to either factor—the system could be too slow even when no one is waiting, or the system could be too slow because each request spends most of its time waiting for service.

We can improve the response time by improving either factor. We can reduce the queueing delay by buying more servers (for example, by having more processors than ready threads or more cashiers than customers), and we can reduce service time by buying a faster server or by engineering a faster implementation.

- **Arrival rate (λ) and arrival process.** The arrival rate λ is the average rate at which new tasks arrive.

  More generally, the arrival process describes when tasks arrive including both the average arrival rate and the pattern of those arrivals such as whether arrivals are bursty or spread evenly over time. As we will see, burstiness can have a large impact on queueing behavior.

- **Service rate (μ).** The service rate μ is the number of tasks the server can complete per unit of time when there is work to do. Notice that the service rate μ is the inverse of the service time S.

- **Utilization (U).** The utilization is the fraction of time the server is busy ($0 \leq U \leq 1$). In a work-conserving system, utilization is determined by the ratio of the average arrival rate to the service rate:

$$U = \begin{cases} \frac{\lambda}{\mu}, & (\lambda < \mu) \\ 1, & (\lambda \geq \mu) \end{cases}$$

  Notice that if $\lambda > \mu$, tasks arrive more quickly than they can be serviced. Such an overload condition is unstable; in a work-conserving system, the queue length and queueing delay grow without bound.

- **Throughput (X).** Throughput is the number of tasks processed by the system per unit of time. When the system is busy, the server processes tasks at the rate of μ, so we have:

$$X = U\mu$$

  Combining this equation with the previous one, we can see that when the average arrival rate λ is less than the service rate μ, the system throughput matches the arrival rate. We can also see that the throughput can never exceed μ no matter how quickly tasks arrive.

$$X = \begin{cases} \lambda, & (U < 1) \\ \mu, & (U = 1) \end{cases}$$

- **Number of tasks in the system (N).** The average number of tasks in the system is just the number queued plus the number receiving service:

$$N = Q + U$$

7.5.2 Little's Law

Little's Law

stable system

Little's Law is a theorem proved by John Little in 1961 that applies to any *stable system* where the arrival rate matches the departure rate. It defines a very general relationship between the average throughput, response time, and the number of tasks in the system:

$$N = XR$$

Although this relationship is simple and intuitive, it is powerful because the "system" can be anything with arriving and departing tasks, provided the system is stable — regardless of the arrival process, number of servers, or queueing order.

EXAMPLE   Suppose we have a queueing system like the one shown in Figure 7.16 and we observe over the course of an hour that an average of 100 requests arrive and depart each second and that the average request is completed 50 ms after it arrives. On average, how many requests are being handled by the system?

ANSWER   Since the arrival rate matches the departure rate, the system is stable and we can use Little's Law. We have a throughput X = 100 requests/second and a response time R = 50 ms = 0.05 seconds:

$$
\begin{aligned}
N &= XR \\
&= 100 \, \frac{\text{requests}}{\text{second}} \cdot 0.05 \, \text{seconds} \\
&= \mathbf{5\ requests}
\end{aligned}
$$

In this system there are, on average, 5 requests waiting in the queue or being served.   □

We can also zoom in to see what is happening at the server, ignoring the queue. The server itself is a system, and Little's Law applies there, too.

EXAMPLE   Suppose we have a server that processes one request at a time and we observe that an average of 100 requests arrive and depart each second and that the average request completes 5 ms after it arrives. What is the average utilization of the server?

ANSWER   The utilization of the server is the fraction of time the server is busy processing a request. Because the server handles one request at a time, its utilization equals the average number of requests in the server-only system. Using Little's Law:

$$
\begin{aligned}
U = N &= XR \\
&= 100 \, \frac{\text{requests}}{\text{second}} \cdot 0.005 \, \text{seconds} \\
&= \mathbf{0.5\ requests}
\end{aligned}
$$

The average utilization is 0.5 or 50%.   □

We can also look at the subsystem comprising just the queue.

EXAMPLE   For the system described in the previous two examples, how long does an average request spend in the queue, and on average how many requests are in the queue?

ANSWER   We know that an average task takes 50 ms to get through the queue and server and that it spends 5 ms at the server, so it must spend 45 ms in the queue. Similarly, we know that on average the system holds 5 tasks with 0.5 of them in the server, so the average queue length is 4.5 tasks.

We can get the same result with Little's Law. One hundred tasks pass through the queue per second and spend an average of 45 ms in the queue, so the average number of tasks in the queue is:

$$
\begin{aligned}
N &= XR \\
&= 100\,\frac{\text{requests}}{\text{second}} \cdot 0.045\,\text{seconds} \\
&= \textbf{4.5 requests}
\end{aligned}
$$

□

Although Little's Law is useful, remember that it only provides information about the system's averages over time.

EXAMPLE   One thing might puzzle you. In the previous example, if the average number of tasks in the queue is 4.5 and processing a request takes 5 ms, how can the average queueing delay for a request be 45 ms rather than $4.5 \cdot 5\,\text{ms} = 22.5\,\text{ms}$?

ANSWER   The *average* number of requests in the queue is 4.5. Sometimes there are more; sometimes there are fewer. Queues will grow during bursts of arrivals, and they will shrink when tasks are arriving slowly.

In fact, from the 0.5 server utilization rate calculated above, we know that the queue is empty half the time. To make up for the empty periods, there *must* be periods with longer-than-average queue lengths.

Unfortunately, the queues tend to be full during busy periods and they tend to be empty during idle periods, so relatively few requests enjoy short or empty queues and relatively many suffer long queues. So, the average request sees a longer queue than the average queue length over time might suggest, and the (per-request) average queueing delay exceeds the (time) average queue length times the (per-request) average service time.

□

Not only can we apply Little's Law to a simple queueing system or its subcomponents, we can apply it to more complex systems, even those whose internal structure we do not fully understand.

EXAMPLE   Suppose there is a complex web service like Google, Facebook, or Amazon, and we know that the average request takes 100 milliseconds and that the service handles an average of 10,000 queries per second. How many requests are pending in the system on average?

ANSWER   Applying Little's Law:

$$
\begin{aligned}
N &= XR \\
&= 10000 \, \frac{\text{requests}}{\text{second}} \cdot 0.1 \, \text{seconds} \\
&= \mathbf{1000 \; requests}
\end{aligned}
$$

Note that this is true regardless of the internal structure of the web service. It may have many load balancers, processors, network switches, and databases, each with separate queues, and each with different queueing policies, but in aggregate in steady state the number of requests being handled must be equal to the product of the response time and the throughput. $\square$

7.5.3   Response Time Versus Utilization

How does increasing utilization affect response time?

Because having more servers (whether processors on chip or cashiers in a supermarket) or faster servers is costly, you might think that the goal of the system designer is to maximize utilization. However, in most cases, there is no free lunch: as we will see, higher utilization normally implies higher queueing delay and higher response times.

Operating a system at high utilization also increases the risk of overload. Suppose you plan to minimize costs by operating a web site at 95% utilization, but your service turns out to be a little more popular than you expected. You can quickly find yourself operating in the unstable regime where requests are arriving faster than you can service them ($\lambda > \mu$) and where your queues and waiting times are growing without bound.

As a designer, you need to find an appropriate tradeoff between higher utilization and better response time. Fifty years ago, computer designers made the tradeoff in favor of higher utilization: when computers are wildly expensive, it is annoying but understandable to make people wait for the computer. Now that computers are much cheaper, our lives are better! We now usually make the computer do the waiting.

We can predict a queueing system's average response time from its arrival process and service time, but the relationship is more complex than the relationships discussed so far.

To provide intuition, we start with some extreme scenarios that bound the behavior of a queueing system; we will introduce more realistic scenarios as we proceed.

Broadly speaking, higher arrival rates and burstier arrival patterns tend to yield longer queue lengths and response times than lower arrival rates and smoother arrival patterns.

Evenly spaced arrivals tend to minimize queueing delay.

Best case: Evenly spaced arrivals.   Suppose we have a set of fixed-sized tasks that arrive equally spaced from one another. For As long as the rate at which tasks arrive is less than the rate at which the server completes the tasks, there will be no queueing at all. Perfection! Each server finishes the previous customer in time for the next arrival.

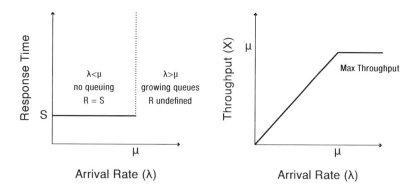

Figure 7.17: Best case response time and throughput as a function of the task arrival rate relative to the service rate. These graphs assume arrivals are evenly spaced and service times are fixed-size.

Figure 7.17 illustrates the relationship between arrival rate and response time for this best case scenario of evenly spaced arrivals. There are three regimes:

1. $\lambda < \mu$. If the arrival rate is below the service rate, there is no queueing and the response time equals the service time.

For example, suppose we have a server that can handle 1000 requests per second, and one request arrives every 1000, 100, or 10 milliseconds. The server finishes processing request $i - 1$ before request i arrives, and request i completes 1 ms after it arrives, clearing the way for request $i + 1$.

The situation remains the same if arrivals are more closely spaced at 1.1, 1.01, 1.001, and so on down to 1.0 ms, where each request arrives at the moment the previous request completes.

2. $\lambda = \mu$. If the arrival rate matches the service rate, the system is in a precarious equilibrium. If the queues are initially empty, they will stay empty, but if the queues are initially full, they will remain full.

Suppose arrivals are coming every 1.0 ms, and at some point during the day a single extra request arrives; that request must wait until the previous one completes, but the server will then be busy when the next request arrives. That single extra request produces queueing delay for every subsequent request.

3. $\lambda > \mu$. If the arrival rate exceeds the service rate, queues will grow without bound. In this case, the system is not in equilibrium, and the steady state response time is undefined.

Suppose the task arrival rate is one per 0.999 ms so that tasks arrive slightly faster than they can be processed? If a system's arrival rate exceeds its service rate, then under our simple model its queues will grow without bound, and

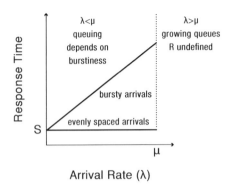

Figure 7.18: Response time for a server that can handle 10 requests per second as we vary arrival rate of fixed-size tasks in two scenarios: evenly spaced arrivals and bursty arrivals where all of a second's requests arrive in a group at the start of the second.

its queueing delay is undefined. In practice, memory is finite; once the queue's capacity is reached, he system must discard some of the arriving requests.

Figure 7.17 also shows the relationship between arrival rate and throughput. When the arrival rate is less than the service rate, increasing the arrival rate increases throughput. Once the arrival rate matches or exceeds the service rate, faster arrivals just grow the queues more quickly, they do not increase useful throughput.

Bursty arrivals tend to cause large queueing delays.

Worst case: Bursty arrivals.   Now consider the opposite case. Suppose a group of tasks arrive at exactly the same time. The average wait time increases linearly as more tasks arrive together — one task in a group can be serviced right away, but others must wait.

Figure 7.18 considers a hypothetical server with a maximum throughput of 10 tasks per second as we vary the number of tasks that arrive per second. The graph shows two cases: one where requests are evenly spaced as in Figure 7.17 and the other where requests arrive in a burst at the start of each second.

Even when the request rate is below the server's service rate, bursty arrivals suffer queueing delays. For example, when five requests arrive as a group at the start of each second, the first request is served immediately and finishes 0.1 seconds later. The server can then start processing the second request, finishing it 0.2 seconds after the start of the interval. The third, fourth, and fifth requests finish at 0.3, 0.4, and 0.5 seconds after the start of the second, giving an average response time of $(0.1 + 0.2 + 0.3 + 0.4 + 0.5)/5 = 0.3$ seconds. By the same logic, if ten requests arrive as a group, the average response time is $(0.1 + 0.2 + 0.3 + 0.4 + 0.5 + 0.6 + 0.7 + 0.8 + 0.9 + 1.0)/10 = 0.55$ seconds. If the same requests had arrived evenly spaced, their average response time would have been over five times better!

What happens if tasks arrive independently?

Exponential arrivals.   Most systems are somewhere in between this best case and worst case. Rather than being perfectly synchronized or perfectly desynchronized, task arrivals in many systems are random. For example, different customers in a supermarket do not coordinate with each other as to when they arrive.

Likewise, service times are not perfectly equal — there is randomness there as well. At a doctor's office, everyone has an appointment, so it may seem like that should be the best case scenario, and no one should ever have to wait. Even so, there is often queueing! Why? If the amount of time the doctor takes with each patient is sometimes shorter and sometimes longer than the appointment length, then random chance will cause queueing.

A particularly useful model for understanding queueing behavior is to use an exponential distribution to describe the time between tasks arriving and the time it takes to service each task. Once you get past a bit of math, the exponential provides a stunningly simple *approximate* description of most real-life queueing systems. We do not claim that all real systems always obey the exponential model in detail; in fact, most do not. However, the model is often accurate enough to provide insight on system behaviors, and as we will discuss, it is easy to understand the circumstances under which it is inaccurate.

exponential distribution

First, the math. An *exponential distribution* of a continuous random variable with a mean of $\frac{1}{\lambda}$ has the probability density function, shown in Figure 7.19:

$$f(x) = \lambda e^{-\lambda x}$$

memoryless property

Fortunately, you need not understand that equation in any detail, except for the following. A useful property of an exponential distribution is that it is *memoryless*. A memoryless distribution for the time between two events means that the likelihood of an event occurring remains the same, *no matter how long we have already waited* for the event, or what other events may have already happened. For example, on a web server, web requests from different users (usually) arrive independently. Sometimes, two requests will arrive close together in time; sometimes there will be more of a delay. For example, suppose a web server receives a request from a new user on average every 10 ms. If you want to predict how long until the next request arrives, it probably does not matter when the *last* request arrived: 0, 1, 5, or 50 ms ago. The expected time to the next request is still probably about 10 ms.

Not every distribution is memoryless. A Gaussian, or normal, distribution for the time between events is closer to the best case scenario described above — arrivals occur randomly, but they tend to occur at regular intervals, give or take a bit.

heavy-tailed distribution

Some probability distributions work the other way. With a *heavy-tailed distribution*, the longer you have waited for some event, the longer you are likely to still need to wait. This is closer to the worst case behavior above, as it means that most events are clustered together.

For example, a ticket seller's web site might see bursty workloads. For long periods of time the site might see little traffic, but when tickets for a popular

Model vs. Reality

When trying to understand a complex system, it is often useful to construct a model of its behavior. A model is a simplification that tries to capture the most important aspects of a more complex system's behavior. Models are neither true nor false, but they can be useful or not for a particular purpose. It is often the case that a more complex model will yield a closer approximation; whether the added complexity is useful or gets in the way depends on how the model is being used.

We often find it useful to use simple workload models when debugging early system implementations. Using the types of analysis described in this chapter and an understanding of the system being built, it is usually possible to predict how the system should behave under simple workloads. If measured behavior deviates from these predictions, there is a bug in our understanding or implementation of the system. Simple workloads can help us improve our understanding if it is the former and track down the bug if it is the latter.

We could, instead, evaluate early implementations by feeding them more realistic workloads. For example, if we are building a new web server, we could feed it a workload trace captured at some other server. However, this approach is often more complex. For example, to test our system under a range of conditions, we need to gather a range of traces — some with low load, some with high; some with bursty loads, some with smooth; etc.

Worst, even though this approach is more complex, it may yield less insight because it is harder to predict the expected system behavior. If we run a simulation with a trace and get worse performance than we expected, is it because we do not understand our system or because we do not understand the trace?

This is not to suggest that simple models are always superior to more complex, more realistic ones. Once we are satisfied with our new system's behavior for workloads we understand, we should test it for workloads we do not understand or control. There may be (and probably are) important behaviors not captured in our simple models. We might find, for example, that bursts of interest in particular topics create "hot spots" of load that we did not anticipate. Evaluation under more realistic models might make us realize that we need to implement more aggressive caching of recently popular pages.

Selecting the right model for system evaluation is a delicate balance between complexity and accuracy. If after abstracting away detail, we can still provide approximately correct predictions of system behavior under a variety of scenarios, then it is likely the model captures the most important aspects of the system. If the model is inaccurate in some important respect, then it means our explanation for how the system behaves is too coarse, and to improve the prediction we need to revise the model.

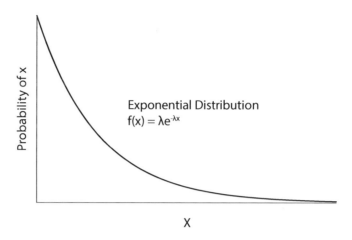

Figure 7.19: Exponential probability distribution.

concert of sporting event go on sale, the traffic may be overwhelming. Here, external factors introduce synchronization across different users' activities so that requests from different users do not arrive independently. Such a workload is unlikely to be memoryless; if you look at a ticket seller's web site at a random moment and see that it has been a long time since the last request arrived, you probably arrived during a lull, and you can predict that it will likely be a long time until the next request arrives. On the other hand, if the last request just arrived, you probably arrived during a burst, and the next request will arrive soon.

With a memoryless distribution, the behavior of queueing systems becomes simple to understand. One can think of the queue as a finite state machine: with some probability, a new task arrives, increasing the queue by one. If the queue length is non-zero, with some other probability, a task completes, decreasing the queue by one. With a memoryless distribution of arrivals and departures, the probability of each transition is constant and independent of the other transitions, as illustrated in Figure 7.20.

Assuming that $\lambda < \mu$, the system is stable Assuming stability and exponential distributions for the arrival and departure processes, we can solve the model to determine the average response time R as a function of the utilization U and service time S:

$$R = \frac{S}{1 - U}$$

Recall that the utilization, the fraction of time that the server is busy, is simply the ratio between λ and μ.

This equation is graphed in Figure 7.21. When utilization is low, there is little queueing delay and response time is close to the service time. Further-

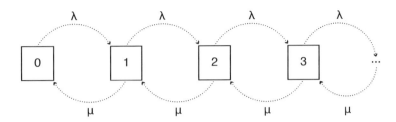

Figure 7.20: State machine representing a queue with exponentially distributed arrivals and departures. λ is the rate of arrivals; μ is the rate at which the server completes each task. With an exponential distribution, the probability of a state transition is independent of how long the system has been in any given state.

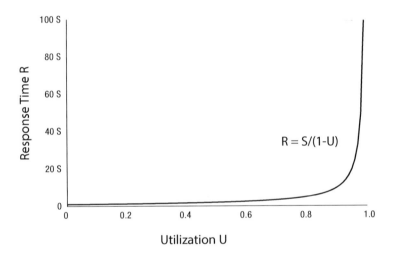

Figure 7.21: Relationship between response time and utilization, assuming exponentially distributed arrivals and departures. Average response time goes to infinity as the system approaches full utilization.

more, when utilization is low, small increases in the arrival rate result in small increases in queueing delay and response time.

As utilization increases, queueing and response time also increase, and the relationship is non-linear. At high utilizations, the queueing delay is high, and small increases in the arrival rate can drastically increase queueing delay and response time.

EXAMPLE   Suppose a queueing system with exponentially distributed arrivals and task sizes is 20% utilized and the load increases by 5%, by how much does the response time increase? How does that increase compare to the case when utilization goes from 90% to 95%?

ANSWER   At 20% utilization, the response time is:

$$R = \frac{S}{1 - U} = \frac{S}{1 - 0.2} = 1.25S$$

At 25% utilization, the response time is:

$$R = \frac{S}{1 - U} = \frac{S}{1 - 0.25} = 1.33S$$

The 5% increase in load increases response time by about 8%.

Using the same equation, at 90% utilization we have $R = 10S$ and at 95% we have $R = 20S$, **the 5% increase in load increases response time by a factor of two.**

□

The response time of a system becomes unbounded as the system approaches full utilization. Although it might seem that full utilization is an achievable goal, if there is any randomness in arrivals *or* any randomness in service times, full utilization cannot be achieved in steady state without making some tasks wait unbounded amounts of time.

In most systems, well before a system reaches full utilization, average response time will become unbearably long. In the next section, we discuss some of the steps system designers can take in response to overload.

Variance in the response time increases even faster as the system approaches full utilization, proportional to $\frac{1}{(1-U)^2}$. Even with 99% utilization, 1% of the time there is no queue at all; random chance means that while sometimes a large number of customers arrive at nearly the same time, at other times the server will be able to work through all of the backlog. If you are lucky enough to arrive at just that moment, you can receive service without waiting. If you are unlucky enough to arrive immediately after a burst of other customers, your wait will be quite long.

Exponential arrivals are burstier than the evenly spaced ones we considered in Figure 7.17 and less bursty than the ones we considered in Figure 7.18. The response time line for the exponential arrivals is higher than the one for evenly spaced arrivals, which was flat across the entire stable range form $U = 0$ to $U = 1$, and the line is lower than the one for more bursty arrivals, which rose rapidly even when utilization was low. In general burstier arrivals will produce worse response time for a given level of load.

7.5.4   "What if?" Questions

Queueing theory is particularly useful for answering "what if?" questions: what happens if we change some design parameter of the system. In this section, we consider a selection of these questions, as a way of providing you a bit more intuition.

Scheduling Policy

What happens to the response time curve for other scheduling policies? It depends on the burstiness and predictability of the workload.

If the distribution of arrivals or service times is less bursty than an exponential (e.g., evenly spaced or Gaussian), FIFO will deliver nearly optimal response times, while Round Robin will perform worse than FIFO.

If task service times are exponentially distributed but individual task times are unpredictable, the average response time is the exactly the same for Round Robin as for FIFO. With a memoryless distribution, every queued task has the same expected remaining service time, so switching among tasks has no impact other than to increase overhead.

On the other hand, if task lengths can be predicted and there is variability of service times, Shortest Job First can improve average response time, particularly if arrivals are bursty.

Many real-world systems exhibit more bursty arrivals or service times than an exponential distribution. A bursty distribution is sometimes called *heavy-tailed* because it has more very long tasks; since the mean rate is the same, this also implies that the distribution has even more very short tasks. For example, web page size is heavy-tailed; so is the processing time per web page. Process execution times on desktop computers are also heavy-tailed. For these types of systems, burstiness results in worse average response time than would be predicted by an exponential distribution. That said, for these types of systems, there is an even greater benefit to approximating SJF to avoid stalling small requests behind long ones, and Round Robin will outperform FIFO.

Using SJF (or an approximation) to improve average response time comes at a cost of an increase in response time for long tasks. At low utilization, this increase is small, but at high utilization SJF can result in a massive increase in average response time for long tasks.

To see this, note that any server alternates between periods of being idle (when the queue is empty) and periods of being busy (when the queue is non-empty). If we ignore switching overhead, the scheduling discipline has no impact on these periods—they are only affected by when tasks arrive. Scheduling can only affect which tasks the server handles first.

With SJF, a long task will only complete immediately before an idle period; it is always the last thing in the queue to complete. As utilization increases, these idle periods become increasingly rare. For example, if the server is 99% busy, the server will be idle only 1% of the time. Further, idle periods are *not* evenly distributed—a server is much more likely to be idle if it was idle a second ago. This means that the long jobs are likely to wait for a long time under SJF under high load.

Workloads That Vary With the Queueing Delay

So far, we have assumed that arrival rates and service times are independent of queueing delay. This is not always the case.

For example, suppose a system has 10 users. Each repeatedly issues one request, waits for the result, thinks about the results, and issues the next request. In such a system, the arrival rate will generally be lower during periods when many tasks are queued than during periods when few are. In the limit, during periods when 10 tasks are queued, no new tasks can arrive and the arrival rate is zero.

Or, consider an online store that becomes overloaded and sluggish during a holiday shopping season. Rather than continuing to browse, some customers may get fed up and leave, reducing the number of active browsing sessions and thereby reducing the arrival rate of requests for individual web pages.

Another example is a system with a finite queue. If there is a burst of load that fills the queue, subsequent requests will be turned away until there is space. This heavy-load behavior can be modeled as either a reduced arrival rate or a reduced average service time (some tasks are "processed" by being discarded).

Multiple Servers

Many real systems have not just one but multiple servers. Does it matter whether there is a single queue for everyone or a separate queue per server? Real systems take both approaches: supermarkets tend to have a separate queue per cashier; banks tend to have a single shared queue for bank tellers. Some systems do both: airports often have a single queue at security but have separate queues for the parking garage. Which is better for response time?

Clearly, there are often efficiency gains from having separate queues. Multiprocessor schedulers use separate queues for affinity scheduling and to reduce switching costs; in a supermarket, it may not be practical to have a single queue. On the other hand, users often consider a single (FIFO) queue to be fairer than separate queues. It often seems that we always end up in the slowest line at the supermarket, even if that cannot possibly be true for everyone.

If we focus on average response time, however, a single queue is always better than separate queues, provided that users are not allowed to jump lanes. The reason is simple: because of variations in how long each task takes to service, one server can be idle while another server has multiple queued tasks. Likewise, a single fast server is always better for response time than a large number of slower servers of equal aggregate capacity to the fast server. There is no difference when all servers are busy, but the single fast server will process requests faster when there are fewer active tasks than servers.

Secondary Bottlenecks

If a processor is 90% busy serving web requests, and we add another processor to reduce its load, how much will that improve average response time? Unfortunately, there is not enough information to say. You might like to believe that it will reduce response time by a considerable amount, from $R = \frac{S}{(1-0.9)} = 10S$ to $R = \frac{S}{(1-0.45)} = 1.8S$.

However, suppose each web request needs not only processing time, but also disk I/O and network bandwidth. If the disk was 80% busy beforehand, it will appear that the processor utilization was the primary problem. Once you add an extra processor, however, the disk becomes the new limiting factor to good performance.

In some cases, queueing theory can make a specific prediction as to the impact of improving one part of a system in isolation. For example, if arrival times are exponentially distributed and independent of the system response time, and if the service times at the processor, disk, and network are also exponentially distributed and independent of one another, then the overall response time for the system is just the sum of the response times of the components:

$$R = \sum_i \frac{S_i}{(1 - U_i)}$$

In this case, improving one part of the system will affect just its contribution to the aggregate system response time. Even though these conditions may not always hold, this is often useful as an approximation to what will occur in real life.

7.5.5 Lessons

To summarize, almost all real-world systems exhibit some randomness in their arrival process or their service times, or both. For these systems:

- Response time increases with increased load.

- System performance is predictable across a range of load factors if we can estimate the average service time per request.

- Burstiness increases average response time. It is mathematically convenient to assume an exponential distribution, but many real-world systems exhibit more burstiness and therefore worse user performance.

7.6 | Overload Management

What happens if more requests arrive than the system can handle?

Many systems operate without any direct control over their workload. In the previous section, we explained that good response time and low variance in the response time are both predicated on operating well below peak utilization. If your web service generates interest on Slashdot, however, you can suddenly receive a ton of traffic from new users. Success! Except that the new users discover your service has horrible performance. Disaster!

More sophisticated scheduling can help at low to moderate load, but if the load is more than system can handle, response time will spike, even for short tasks.

The key idea in overload management is to design your system do less work when overloaded. This will seem strange! After all, you want your system to work a particular way; how can you cripple the user's experience just when your system becomes popular? Under overload conditions, however, your system is incapable of serving all of the requests in the normal way. The only question is: do you choose what to disable, or do you let events choose for you?

An obvious step is to simply reject some requests in order to preserve reasonable response time for the remaining ones. While this can seem harsh, it is also pragmatic. Under overload, the only way to give anyone good service is to reduce or eliminate service for others.

The approach of turning away requests under overload conditions is common in streaming video applications. An overloaded movie service will reject requests to start new streams so that it can continue to provide good streaming service to users that have already started. Likewise, during the NCAA basketball tournament or during the Olympics, the broadcaster will turn requests away, rather than giving everyone poor service.

An apt analogy, perhaps, is that of a popular restaurant. Why not set out acres of tables so that everyone who shows up at the restaurant can be seated? If the waiters Round Robin among the various tables, you can be seated, but wait an hour to get a menu, then wait another hour to make an order, and so forth. That is one way of dealing with a persistent overload situation — by making the user experience so unpleasant that none of your customers will return! As absurd as this scenario is, however, it is close to how we allocate scarce space on congested highways — by making everyone wait.

A less obvious step is to somehow reduce the service time per request under overload conditions. A good example of this happened on September 11, 2001 when CNN's web page was overwhelmed with people trying to get updates about the terrorist attacks. To make the site usable, CNN shifted to a static page that was less personalized and sophisticated but that was faster to serve. As another example, when experiencing unexpected load, EBay will update its auction listings less frequently, saving work that can be used for processing other requests. Finally, an overloaded movie service can reduce the bit rate for everyone in order to serve more simultaneous requests at slightly lower quality.

Amazon has designed its web site to always return a result quickly, even when the requested data is unavailable due to overload conditions. Every backend service has both a normal interface and a fallback to use if its results are not ready in time. For example, this means a user can be told that their purchase will be shipped shortly, even when the book is actually out of stock. This is a strategic decision that it is better to give a wrong answer quickly, and apologize later, rather than to wait to give the right answer more slowly.

Unfortunately, many systems have the opposite problem: they do more work per request as load increases. A simple example of this would be using a linked list to manage a queue of requests: as more requests are queued, more processing time is used maintaining the queue and not getting useful

Figure 7.22: Measured throughput (cars per hour) versus occupancy (percentage of the road covered with vehicles). Each data point represents a separate observation. At low load, throughput increases linearly; once load passes a critical point, adding vehicles decreases average throughput. As each vehicle moves more slowly, it takes more time on the highway to complete its journey, increasing load. Data reprinted from Nagel and Schreckenberg [122].

work done. If amount of work per task increases as the load increases, then response times will soar even faster with increased utilization, and throughput can decrease as we add load. This makes overload management even more important.

A real-life example of this phenomenon is with highway traffic. Figure 7.22 provides measured data of throughput versus load for one stretch of highway. As you add cars to an empty highway, it increases the rate that cars traverse a given point on the highway. However, at very high loads, the density of cars causes a transition to stop and go traffic, where the rate of progress is much slower than when there were fewer cars. A common solution for highways is to use onramp limiters — to limit the rate that new cars can enter the highway if the system is close to overload.

Time-slicing in the presence of caches has similar behavior. When load is low, there are few time slices, and every task uses its cache efficiently. As more tasks are added to the system, there are more time slices and fewer cache hits, slowing down the processor just when we need it to be running at peak efficiency. In networks, packets are dropped when the network is overloaded. Without careful protocol design, this can cause the sender to retransmit packets, further overloading the network. TCP congestion control, now a common part of almost every Internet connection, was developed precisely to deal with this effect.

You may have even experienced this issue. Some students, as homework piles up, become less, rather than more, efficient. After all, it is hard to concentrate on one project if you know that you really ought to be also working on a different one. But if you decide to take the lessons of this textbook to heart and decide to blow off some of your homework to get the rest of your assignments done, let us suggest that you choose some class other than operating systems!

7.7 | Case Study: Servers in a Data Center

We can illustrate the application of the ideas discussed in this chapter, by considering how we should manage a collection of servers in a data center to provide responsive web service. Many web services, such as Google, Facebook, and Amazon, are organized as a set of front-end machines that redirect incoming requests to a larger set of back-end machines. We illustrate this in Figure 7.23. This architecture isolates clients from the architecture of the back-end systems, so that more capacity can be added to the back-end simply by changing the configuration of the front-end systems. Back-end servers can also be taken off-line, have their software upgraded, and so forth, completely transparently to clients.

To provide good response time to the clients of the web service:

- When clients first connect to the service, the front-end node assigns each customer to a back-end server to balance load. Customers can be spread evenly across the back-end servers or they can be assigned to a node with low current load, much as customers at a supermarket select the shortest line for a cashier.

- Additional requests from the same client can be assigned to the same back-end server, as a form of affinity scheduling. Once a server has fetched client data, it will be faster for it to handle additional requests.

- We need to prevent individual users from hogging resources, because that can disrupt performance for other users. A back-end server can favor short tasks over long ones; they can also keep track of the total resources used by each client, reducing the scheduling priority of any client consuming more than their fair share of resources.

- It is often crucial to the usability of a web service to keep response time small. This requires monitoring both the rate of arrivals and the average amount of computing, disk, and network resources consumed by each request. Back-end servers should be added before average server utilization gets too high.

- Since it often takes considerable time to bring new servers online, we need to predict future load and have a backup plan for overload conditions.

7.8 | Summary and Future Directions

Resource scheduling is an ancient topic in computer science. Almost from the moment that computers were first multiprogrammed, operating system designers have had to decide which tasks to do first and which to leave for later. This decision — the system's scheduling policy — can have a significant impact on system responsiveness and usability.

Fortunately, the cumulative effect of Moore's Law has shifted the balance towards a focus on improving response time for users, rather than on efficient utilization of resources for the computer. At the same time, the massive scale of the Internet means that many services need to be designed to provide good response time across a wide range of load conditions. Our goal in this chapter is to give you the conceptual basis for making those design choices.

Several ongoing trends pose new and interesting challenges to effective resource scheduling.

- **Multicore systems.** Although almost all new servers, desktops, laptops and smartphones are multicore systems, relatively few widely used applications have been redesigned to take full advantage of multiple processors. This is likely to change over the next few years as multicore systems become ubiquitous and as they scale to larger numbers of processors per chip. Although we have the concepts in place to manage resource sharing among multiple parallel applications, commercial systems are only just now starting to deploy these ideas. It will be interesting to see how the theory works out in practice.

- **Cache affinity.** Over the past twenty years, processor architects have radically increased both the size and number of levels of on-chip caches. There is little reason to believe that this trend will reverse. Although processor clock rates are improving slowly, transistor density is still increasing at a rapid rate. This will make it both possible and desirable to have even larger, multi-level on-chip caches to achieve good performance. Thus, it is likely that scheduling for cache affinity will be an even larger factor in the future than it is today. Balancing when to respect affinity and when to migrate is still somewhat of an open question, as is deciding how to spread or coalesce application threads across caches.

- **Energy-aware scheduling.** The number of energy-constrained computers such as smartphones, tablets, and laptops, now far outstrips powered computers such as desktops and servers. As a result, we are likely to see the development of hardware to monitor and manage energy use by applications, and the operating system will need to make use of that hardware support. We are likely to see operating systems sandbox application energy use to prevent faulty or malicious applications from running down the battery. Likewise, just as applications can adapt to

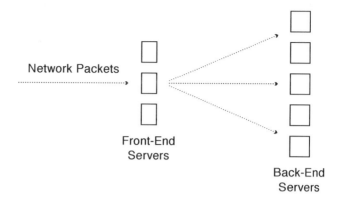

Figure 7.23: A web service often consists of a number of front-end servers who redirect incoming client requests to a larger set of back-end servers.

changing numbers of processors, we are likely to see applications that adapt their behavior to energy availability.

Exercises

1. For shortest job first, if the scheduler assigns a task to the processor, and no other task becomes schedulable in the meantime, will the scheduler ever preempt the current task? Why or why not?

2. Devise a workload where FIFO is pessimal — it does the worst possible choices — for average response time.

3. Suppose you do your homework assignments in SJF-order. After all, you feel like you are making a lot of progress! What might go wrong?

4. Given the following mix of tasks, task lengths, and arrival times, compute the completion and response time for each task, along with the average response time for the FIFO, RR, and SJF algorithms. Assume a time slice of 10 milliseconds and that all times are in milliseconds.

Task	Length	Arrival Time	Completion Time	Response Time
0	85	0		
1	30	10		
2	35	15		
3	20	80		
4	50	85		
		Average:		

5. Is it possible for an application to run slower when assigned 10 processors than when assigned 8? Why or why not?

6. Suppose your company is considering using one of two candidate scheduling algorithms. One is Round Robin, with an overhead of 1% of the processing power of the system. The second is a wizzy new system that predicts the future and so it can closely approximate SJF, but it takes an overhead of 10% of the processing power of the system.

    Assume randomized arrivals and random task lengths. Under what conditions will the simpler algorithm outperform the more complex, and vice versa?

7. Are there non-trivial workloads for which Multi-level Feedback Queue is an optimal policy? Why or why not? (A trivial workload is one with only one or a few tasks or tasks that last a single instruction.)

8. If a queueing system with one server has a workload of 1000 tasks arriving per second, and the average number of tasks waiting or getting service is 5, what is the average response time per task?

9. Is it possible for a system in equilibrium to have both bounded average response time and 100% utilization? Why or why not?

10. For a queueing system with random arrivals and service times, how does the variance in the service time affect the system response time? Briefly explain.

11. Most round-robin schedulers use a fixed size quantum. Give an argument in favor of and against a small quantum.

12. Which provides the best average response time when there are multiple servers (e.g., bank tellers, supermarket cash registers, airline ticket takers): a single FIFO queue or a FIFO queue per server? Why? Assume that you cannot predict how long any customer is going to take at the server, and that once you have picked a queue to wait in, you are stuck and cannot change queues.

13. Three tasks, A, B, and C are run concurrently on a computer system.

    - Task A arrives first at time 0, and uses the CPU for 100 ms before finishing.
    - Task B arrives shortly after A, still at time 0. Task B loops ten times; for each iteration of the loop, B uses the CPU for 2 ms and then it does I/O for 8 ms.
    - Task C is identical to B, but arrives shortly after B, still at time 0.

Assuming there is no overhead to doing a context switch, identify when A, B and C will finish for each of the following CPU scheduling disciplines:

a) FIFO

b) Round robin with a 1 ms time slice

c) Round robin with a 100 ms time slice

d) Multilevel feedback with four levels, and a time slice for the highest priority level is 1 ms.

e) Shortest job first

14. For each of the following processor scheduling policies, describe the set of workloads under which that policy is optimal in terms of minimizing average response time (does the same thing as shortest job first) and the set of workloads under which the policy is pessimal (does the same thing as longest job first). If there are no workloads under which a policy is optimal or pessimal, indicate that.

a) FIFO

b) Round robin

c) Multilevel feedback queues

15. Explain how you would set up a valid experimental comparison between two scheduling policies, one of which can starve some jobs.

16. As system administrator of a popular social networking website, you notice that usage peaks during working hours (10am – 5pm) and the evening (7 – 10pm) on the US east coast. The CEO asks you to design a system where during these peak hours there will be three levels of users. Users in level 1 are the center of the social network, and so they are to enjoy better response time than users in level 2, who in turn will enjoy better response time than users in level 3. You are to design such a system so that all users will still get some progress, but with the indicated preferences in place.

a) Will a fixed priority scheme with pre-emption and three fixed priorities work? Why, or why not?

b) Will a UNIX-style multi-feedback queue work? Why, or why not?

17. Consider the following preemptive priority-scheduling algorithm based on dynamically changing priorities. Larger numbers imply higher priority. Tasks are preempted whenever there is a higher priority task. When a task is waiting for CPU (in the ready queue, but not running), its priority changes at a rate of a:

$$P(t) = P_0 + a \times (t - t_0)$$

where t_0 is the time at which the task joins the ready queue and P_0 is its initial priority, assigned when the task enters the ready queue or is preempted. Similarly, when it is running, the task's priority changes at a rate b. The parameters a, b and P_0 can be used to obtain many different scheduling algorithms.

a) What is the algorithm that results from $P_0 = 0$ and $b > a > 0$?

b) What is the algorithm that results from $P_0 = 0$ and $a < b < 0$?

c) Suppose tasks are assigned a priority 0 when they arrive, but they retain their priority when they are preempted. What happens if two tasks arrive at nearly the same time and $a > 0 > b$?

d) How should we adjust the algorithm to eliminate this pathology?

18. For a computer with two cores and a hyperthreading level of two, draw a graph of the rate of progress of a compute-intensive task as a function of time, depending on whether it is running alone, or with 1, 2, 3, or 4 other tasks.

19. Implement a test on your computer to see if your answer to the previous problem is correct.

20. A countermeasure is a strategy by which a user (or an application) exploits the characteristics of the processor scheduling policy to get as much of the processing time as possible. For example, if the scheduler trusts users to give accurate estimates of how long each task will take, it can give higher priority to short tasks. However, a countermeasure would be for the user to tell the system that the user's tasks are short even when they are not.

Devise a countermeasure strategy for each of the following processor scheduling policies; your strategy should minimize an individual application's response time (even if it hurts overall system performance). You may assume perfect knowledge — for example, your strategy can be based on which jobs will arrive in the future, where your application is in the queue, and how long the tasks ahead of you will run before blocking. Your strategy should also be robust — it should work properly even if there are no other tasks in the system, there are only short tasks, or there are only long running tasks. If no strategy will improve your application's response time, then explain why.

a) Last in first out

b) Round robin, assuming tasks are put at the end of the ready list when they become ready to run

c) Multilevel feedback queues, where tasks are put on the highest priority queue when they become ready to run

Processor utilization	20.0%
Disk	99.7%
Network	5.0%

Figure 7.24: Measured utilizations of a computer system.

21. Consider a computer system running a general-purpose workload. Measured utilizations (in terms of time, not space) are given in Figure 7.24.

    For each of the following changes, say what its likely impact will be on processor utilization, and explain why. Is it likely to significantly increase, marginally increase, significantly decrease, marginally decrease, or have no effect on the processor utilization?

    a) Get a faster CPU

    b) Get a faster disk

    c) Increase the degree of multiprogramming

    d) Get a faster network

Part III

Memory Management

There is nothing wrong with your television set. Do not attempt to adjust the picture. We are controlling transmission. If we wish to make it louder, we will bring up the volume. If we wish to make it softer, we will tune it to a whisper. We will control the horizontal. We will control the vertical. We can roll the image, make it flutter. We can change the focus to a soft blur or sharpen it to crystal clarity. For the next hour, sit quietly and we will control all that you see and hear. We repeat: there is nothing wrong with your television set.
Opening narration, The Outer Limits

8

Address Translation

The promise of virtual reality is compelling. Who wouldn't want the ability to travel anywhere without leaving the holodeck? Of course, the promise is far from becoming a reality. In theory, by adjusting the inputs to all of your senses in response to your actions, a virtual reality system could perfectly set the scene. However, your senses are not so easily controlled. We might soon be able to provide an immersive environment for vision, but balance, hearing, taste, and smell will take a lot longer. Touch, prioperception (the sense of being near something else), and g-forces are even farther off. Get a single one of these wrong and the illusion disappears.

Can we create a virtual reality environment for computer programs? We have already seen an example of this with the UNIX I/O interface, where the program does not need to know, and sometimes cannot tell, if its inputs and outputs are files, devices, or other processes.

From the programmer's perspective, address translation occurs transparently — the program behaves correctly In the next three chapters, we take this idea a giant step further. An amazing number of advanced system features are **address translation** enabled by putting the operating system in control of *address translation*, the conversion from the memory address the program thinks it is referencing to the physical location of that memory cell. From the programmer's perspective, address translation occurs transparently — the program behaves correctly despite the fact that its memory is stored somewhere completely different from where it thinks it is stored.

You were probably taught in some early programming class that a memory address is just an address. A pointer in a linked list contains the actual memory address of what it is pointing to. A jump instruction contains the actual memory address of the next instruction to be executed. This is a useful fiction! The programmer is often better off not thinking about how each memory reference is converted into the data or instruction being referenced. In practice, there is quite a lot of activity happening beneath the covers.

Address translation is a simple concept, but it turns out to be incredibly powerful. What can an operating system do with address translation? This is only a partial list:

- **Process isolation.** As we discussed in Chapter 2, protecting the operating system kernel and other applications against buggy or malicious code requires the ability to limit memory references by applications. Likewise, address translation can be used by applications to construct safe execution sandboxes for third party extensions.

- **Interprocess communication.** Often processes need to coordinate with each other, and an efficient way to do that is to have the processes share a common memory region.

- **Shared code segments.** Instances of the same program can share the program's instructions, reducing their memory footprint and making the processor cache more efficient. Likewise, different programs can share common libraries.

- **Program initialization.** Using address translation, we can start a program running before all of its code is loaded into memory from disk.

- **Efficient dynamic memory allocation.** As a process grows its heap, or as a thread grows its stack, we can use address translation to trap to the kernel to allocate memory for those purposes only as needed.

- **Cache management.** As we will explain in the next chapter, the operating system can arrange how programs are positioned in physical memory to improve cache efficiency, through a system called page coloring.

- **Program debugging.** The operating system can use memory translation to prevent a buggy program from overwriting its own code region; by catching pointer errors earlier, it makes them much easier to debug. Debuggers also use address translation to install data breakpoints, to stop a program when it references a particular memory location.

- **Efficient I/O.** Server operating systems are often limited by the rate at which they can transfer data to and from the disk and the network. Address translation enables data to be safely transferred directly between user-mode applications and I/O devices.

- **Memory mapped files.** A convenient and efficient abstraction for many applications is to map files into the address space, so that the contents of the file can be directly referenced with program instructions.

- **Virtual memory.** The operating system can provide applications the abstraction of more memory than is physically present on a given computer.

- **Checkpointing and restart.** The state of a long-running program can be periodically checkpointed so that if the program or system crashes, it can be restarted from the saved state. The key challenge is to be able to perform an internally consistent checkpoint of the program's data while the program continues to run.

- **Persistent data structures.** The operating system can provide the abstraction of a persistent region of memory, where changes to the data structures in that region survive program and system crashes.

- **Process migration.** An executing program can be transparently moved from one server to another, for example, for load balancing.

- **Information flow control.** An extra layer of security is to verify that a program is not sending your private data to a third party; e.g., a smartphone application may need access to your phone list, but it shouldn't be allowed to transmit that data. Address translation can be the basis for managing the flow of information into and out of a system.

- **Distributed shared memory.** We can transparently turn a network of servers into a large-scale shared-memory parallel computer using address translation.

In this chapter, we focus on the mechanisms needed to implement address translation, as that is the foundation of all of these services. We discuss how the operating system and applications use the mechanisms to provide these services in the following two chapters.

For runtime efficiency, most systems have specialized hardware to do address translation; this hardware is managed by the operating system kernel. In some systems, however, the translation is provided by a trusted compiler, linker or byte-code interpreter. In other systems, the application does the pointer translation as a way of managing the state of its own data structures. In still other systems, a hybrid model is used where addresses are translated both in software and hardware. The choice is often an engineering tradeoff between performance, flexibility, and cost. However, the functionality provided is often the same regardless of the mechanism used to implement the translation. In this chapter, we will cover a range of hardware and software mechanisms.

Chapter roadmap:

- **Address Translation Concept.** We start by providing a conceptual framework for understanding both hardware and software address translation. (Section 8.1)

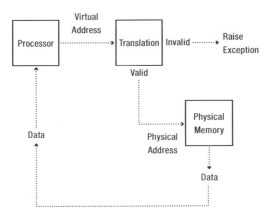

Figure 8.1: Address translation in the abstract. The translator converts (virtual) memory addresses generated by the program into physical memory addresses.

- **Flexible Address Translation.** We focus first on hardware address translation; we ask how can we design the hardware to provide maximum flexibility to the operating system kernel? (Section 8.2)

- **Efficient Address Translation.** The solutions we present will seem flexible but terribly slow. We next discuss mechanisms that make address translation much more efficient, without sacrificing flexibility. (Section 8.3)

- **Software Protection.** Increasingly, software compilers and runtime interpreters are using address translation techniques to implement operating system functionality. What changes when the translation is in software rather than in hardware? (Section 8.4)

8.1 | Address Translation Concept

Considered as a black box, address translation is a simple function, illustrated in Figure 8.1. The translator takes each instruction and data memory reference generated by a process, checks whether the address is legal, and converts it to a physical memory address that can be used to fetch or store instructions or data. The data itself — whatever is stored in memory — is returned as is; it is not transformed in any way. The translation is usually implemented in hardware, and the operating system kernel configures the hardware to accomplish its aims.

The task of this chapter is to fill in the details about how that black box works. If we asked you right now how you might implement it, your first several guesses would probably be on the mark. If you said we could use an array, a tree, or a hash table, you would be right — all of those approaches have been taken by real systems.

Given that a number of different implementations are possible, how should we evaluate the alternatives? Here are some goals we might want out of a translation box; the design we end up with will depend on how we balance among these various goals.

- **Memory protection.** We need the ability to limit the access of a process to certain regions of memory, e.g., to prevent it from accessing memory not owned by the process. Often, however, we may want to limit access of a program to its own memory, e.g., to prevent a pointer error from overwriting the code region or to cause a trap to the debugger when the program references a specific data location.

- **Memory sharing.** We want to allow multiple processes to share selected regions of memory. These shared regions can be large (e.g., if we are sharing a program's code segment among multiple processes executing the same program) or relatively small (e.g., if we are sharing a common library, a file, or a shared data structure).

- **Flexible memory placement.** We want to allow the operating system the flexibility to place a process (and each part of a process) anywhere in physical memory; this will allow us to pack physical memory more efficiently. As we will see in the next chapter, flexibility in assigning process data to physical memory locations will also enable us to make more effective use of on-chip caches.

- **Sparse addresses.** Many programs have multiple dynamic memory regions that can change in size over the course of the execution of the program: the heap for data objects, a stack for each thread, and memory mapped files. Modern processors have 64-bit address spaces, allowing each dynamic object ample room to grow as needed, but making the translation function more complex.

- **Runtime lookup efficiency.** Hardware address translation occurs on every instruction fetch and every data load and store. It would be impractical if a lookup took, on average, much longer to execute than the instruction itself. At first, many of the schemes we discuss will seem wildly impractical! We will discuss ways to make even the most convoluted translation systems efficient.

- **Compact translation tables.** We also want the space overhead of translation to be minimal; any data structures we need should be small compared to the amount of physical memory being managed.

- **Portability.** Different hardware architectures make different choices as to how they implement translation; if an operating system kernel is to be easily portable across multiple processor architectures, it needs to be able to map from its (hardware-independent) data structures to the specific capabilities of each architecture.

virtual address

physical address

We will end up with a fairly complex address translation mechanism, and so our discussion will start with the simplest possible mechanisms and add functionality only as needed. It will be helpful during the discussion for you to keep in mind the two views of memory: the process sees its own memory, using its own addresses. We will call these *virtual addresses*, because they do not necessarily correspond to any physical reality. By contrast, to the memory system, there are only *physical addresses* — real locations in memory. From the memory system perspective, it is given physical addresses and it does lookups and stores values. The translation mechanism converts between the two views: from a virtual address to a physical memory address.

8.2 | Towards Flexible Address Translation

Our discussion of hardware address translation is divided into two steps. First, we put the issue of lookup efficiency aside, and instead consider how best to achieve the other goals listed above: flexible memory assignment, space efficiency, fine-grained protection and sharing, and so forth. Once we have the features we want, we will then add mechanisms to gain back lookup efficiency.

In Chapter 2, we illustrated the notion of hardware memory protection using the simplest hardware imaginable: base and bounds. The translation box consists of two extra registers per process. The *base* register specifies the start of the process's region of physical memory; the *bound* register specifies the extent of that region. If the base register is added to every address generated by the program, then we no longer need a relocating loader — the virtual addresses of the program start from 0 and go to bound, and the physical addresses start from base and go to base + bound. Figure 8.2 shows an example of base and bounds translation. Since physical memory can contain several processes, the kernel resets the contents of the base and bounds registers on each process context switch to the appropriate values for that process.

Base and bounds translation is both simple and fast, but it lacks many of the features needed to support modern programs. Base and bounds translation supports only coarse-grained protection at the level of the entire process; it is not possible to prevent a program from overwriting its own code, for example. It is also difficult to share regions of memory between two processes. Since the memory for a process needs to be contiguous, supporting dynamic memory regions, such as for heaps, thread stacks, or memory mapped files, becomes difficult to impossible.

8.2.1 Segmented Memory

Many of the limitations of base and bounds translation can be remedied with a small change: instead of keeping only a single pair of base and bounds

Address translation in linkers and loaders

Even without the kernel-user boundary, multiprogramming requires some form of address translation. On a multiprogramming system, when a program is compiled, the compiler does not know which regions of physical memory will already in use by other applications and therefore cannot control where in physical memory the program will land. The machine instructions for a program contains both relative and absolute addresses; relative addresses, such as to branch forward or backward a certain number of instructions, continue to work regardless of where in memory the program is located. However, some instructions contain absolute addresses, such as to load a global variable or to jump to the start of a procedure. These will stop working unless the program is loaded into memory exactly where the compiler expects it to go.

Before hardware translation became commonplace, early operating systems dealt with this issue by using a *relocating loader* for copying programs into memory. Once the operating system picked an empty region of physical memory for the program, the loader would modify any instructions in the program that used an absolute address. To simplify the implementation, there was a table at the beginning of the executable image that listed all of the absolute addresses used in the program. In modern systems, this is called a *symbol table*.

Today, we still have something similar. Complex programs often have multiple files, each of which can be compiled independently and then *linked* together to form the executable image. When the compiler generates the machine instructions for a single file, it cannot know where in the executable this particular file will go. Instead, the compiler generates a symbol table at the beginning of each compiled file, indicating which values will need to be modified when the individual files are assembled together.

Most commercial operating systems today support the option of dynamic linking, taking the notion of a relocating loader one step further. With a dynamically linked library (DLL), a library is linked into a running program on demand, when the program first calls into the library. We will explain in a bit how the code for a DLL can be shared between multiple different processes, but the linking procedure is straightforward. A table of valid entry points into the DLL is kept by the compiler; the calling program indirects through this table to reach the library routine.

---

segmentation registers per process, the hardware can support an array of pairs of base and bounds registers, for each process. This is called *segmentation*. Each entry in the array controls a portion, or *segment*, of the virtual address space. The physical memory for each segment is stored contiguously, but different segments can be stored at different locations. Figure 8.3 shows segment translation in action. The high order bits of the virtual address are used to index into the array; the

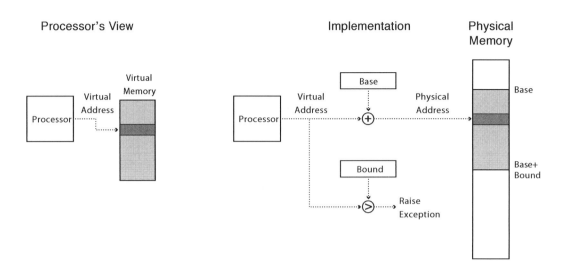

Figure 8.2: Address translation with base and bounds registers. The virtual address is added to the base to generate the physical address; the bound register is checked against the virtual address to prevent a process from reading or writing outside of its allocated memory region.

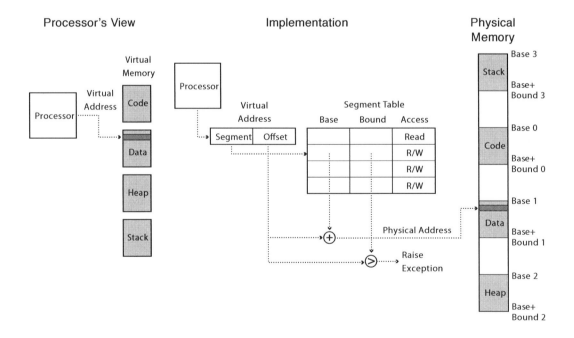

Figure 8.3: Address translation with a segment table. The virtual address has two components: a segment number and a segment offset. The segment number indexes into the segment table to locate the start of the segment in physical memory. The bound register is checked against the segment offset to prevent a process from reading or writing outside of its allocated memory region. Processes can be have restricted rights to certain segments, e.g., to prevent writes to the code segment.

rest of the address is then treated as above — added to the base and checked against the bound stored at that index. In addition, the operating system can assign different segments different permissions, e.g., to allow execute-only access to code and read-write access to data. Although only three segments are shown in the figure, in general the number of segments is determined by the number of bits for the segment number that are set aside in the virtual address.

It should seem odd to you that segmented memory has gaps; program memory is no longer a single contiguous region, but instead it is a set of regions. Each different segment starts at a new segment boundary. For example, code and data are not immediately adjacent to each other in either the virtual or physical address space.

segmentation fault

What happens if a program branches into or tries to load data from one of these gaps? The hardware will generate an exception, trapping into the operating system kernel. On UNIX systems, this is still called a *segmentation fault*, that is, a reference outside of a legal segment of memory. How does a program keep from wandering into one of these gaps? Correct programs will not generate references outside of valid memory. Put another way, trying to execute code or reading data that does not exist is probably an indication that the program has a bug in it.

Although simple to implement and manage, segmented memory is both remarkably powerful and widely used. For example, the x86 architecture is segmented (with some enhancements that we will describe later). With segments, the operating system can allow processes to share some regions of memory while keeping other regions protected. For example, two processes can share a code segment by setting up an entry in their segment tables to point to the same region of physical memory — to use the same base and bounds. The processes can share the same code while working off different data, by setting up the segment table to point to different regions of physical memory for the data segment. We illustrate this in Figure 8.4.

Likewise, shared library routines, such as a graphics library, can be placed into a segment and shared between processes. As before, the library data would be in a separate, non-shared segment. This is frequently done in modern operating systems with dynamically linked libraries. A practical issue is that different processes may load different numbers of libraries, and so may assign the same library a different segment number. Depending on the processor architecture, sharing can still work, if the library code uses *segment-local addresses*, addresses that are relative to the current segment.

segment-local address

We can also use segments for interprocess communication, if processes are given read and write permission to the same segment. Multics, an operating system from the 1960's that contained many of the ideas we now find in Microsoft's Windows 7, Apple's Mac OS X, and Linux, made extensive use of segmented memory for interprocess sharing. In Multics, a segment was allocated for every data structure, allowing fine-grained protection and sharing between processes. Of course, this made the segment table pretty large! More modern systems tend to use segments only for coarser-grained

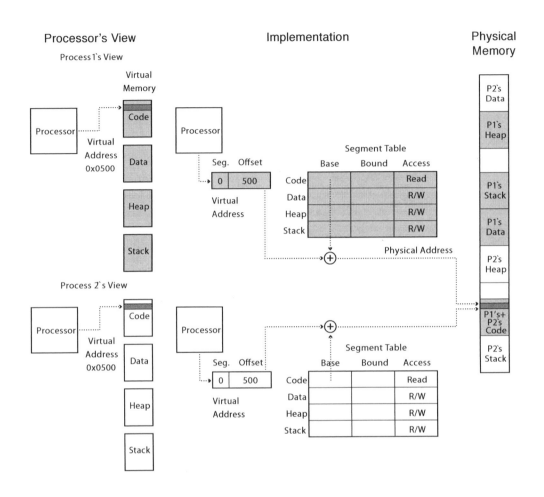

Figure 8.4: Two processes sharing a code segment, but with separate data and stack segments. In this case, each process uses the same virtual addresses, but these virtual addresses map to either the same region of physical memory (if code) or different regions of physical memory (if data).

memory regions, such as the code and data for an entire shared library, rather than for each of the data structures within the library.

As a final example of the power of segments, they enable the efficient management of dynamically allocated memory. When an operating system reuses memory or disk space that had previously been used, it must first zero out the contents of the memory or disk. Otherwise, private data from one application could inadvertently leak into another, potentially malicious, application. For example, you could enter a password into one web site, say for a bank, and then exit the browser. However, if the underlying physical memory used by the browser is then re-assigned to a new process, then the password could be leaked to a malicious web site.

Of course, we only want to pay the overhead of zeroing memory if it will

UNIX fork and copy-on-write

In Chapter 3, we described the UNIX fork system call. UNIX creates a new process by making a complete copy of the parent process; the parent process and the child process are identical except for the return value from fork. The child process can then set up its I/O and eventually use the UNIX exec system call to run a new program. We promised at the time we would explain how this can be done efficiently.

With segments, this is now possible. To fork a process, we can simply make a copy of the parent's segment table; we do not need to copy *any* of its physical memory. Of course, we want the child to have be a copy of the parent, and not just point to the same memory as the parent. If the child changes some data, it should change only its copy, and not its parent's data. On the other hand, most of the time, the child process in UNIX fork simply calls UNIX exec; the shared data is there as a programming convenience.

We can make this work efficiently by using an idea called *copy-on-write*. During the fork, all of the segments shared between the parent and child process are marked "read-only" in both segment tables. If either side modifies data in a segment, an exception is raised and a full memory copy of that segment is made at that time. In the common case, the child process modifies only its stack before calling UNIX exec, and if so, only the stack needs to be physically copied.

---

be used. This is particularly an issue for dynamically allocated memory on the heap and stack. It is not clear when the program starts how much memory it will use; the heap could be anywhere from a few kilobytes to several gigabytes, depending on the program. The operating system can address this using *zero-on-reference*. With zero-on-reference, the operating system allocates a memory region for the heap, but only zeroes the first few kilobytes. Instead, it sets the bound register in the segment table to limit the program to just the zeroed part of memory. If the program expands its heap, it will take an exception, and the operating system kernel can zero out additional memory before resuming execution.

zero-on-reference

Given all these advantages, why not stop here? The principal downside of segmentation is the overhead of managing a large number of variable size and dynamically growing memory segments. Over time, as processes are created and finish, physical memory will be divided into regions that are in use and regions that are not, that is, available to be allocated to a new process. These free regions will be of varying sizes. When we create a new segment, we will need to find a free spot for it. Should we put it in the smallest open region where it will fit? The largest open region?

However we choose to place new segments, as more memory becomes allocated, the operating system may reach a point where there is enough free

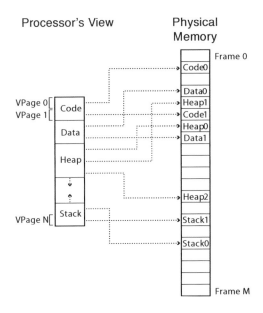

Figure 8.5: Logical view of page table address translation. Physical memory is split into page frames, with a page-size aligned block of virtual addresses assigned to each frame. Unused addresses are not assigned page frames in physical memory.

space for a new segment, but the free space is not contiguous. This is called *external fragmentation.* The operating system is free to compact memory to make room without affecting applications, because virtual addresses are unchanged when we relocate a segment in physical memory. Even so, compaction can be costly in terms of processor overhead: a typical server configuration would take roughly a second to compact its memory.

external fragmentation

All this becomes even more complex when memory segments can grow. How much memory should we set aside for a program's heap? If we put the heap segment in a part of physical memory with lots of room, then we will have wasted memory if that program turns out to need only a small heap. If we do the opposite — put the heap segment in a small chunk of physical memory — then we will need to copy it somewhere else if it changes size.

8.2.2 Paged Memory

paged memory

page frames

An alternative to segmented memory is *paged memory*. With paging, memory is allocated in fixed-sized chunks called *page frames*. Address translation is similar to how it works with segmentation. Instead of a segment table whose entries contain pointers to variable-sized segments, there is a page table for each process whose entries contain pointers to page frames. Because page frames are fixed-sized and a power of two, the page table entries only need to provide the upper bits of the page frame address, so they are more compact.

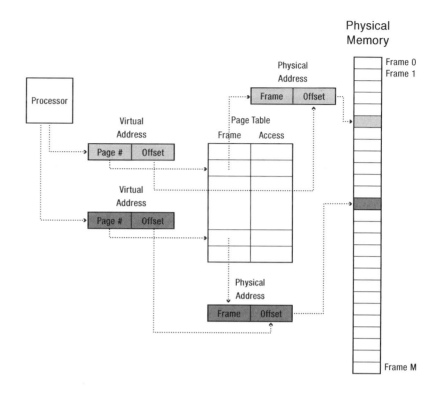

Figure 8.6: Address translation with a page table. The virtual address has two components: a virtual page number and an offset within the page. The virtual page number indexes into the page table to yield a page frame in physical memory. The physical address is the physical page frame from the page table, concatenated with the page offset from the virtual address. The operating system can restrict process access to certain pages, e.g., to prevent writes to pages containing instructions.

There is no need for a "bound" on the offset; the entire page in physical memory is allocated as a unit. Figure 8.6 illustrates address translation with paged memory.

What will seem odd, and perhaps cool, about paging is that while a program thinks of its memory as linear, in fact its memory can be, and usually is, scattered throughout physical memory in a kind of abstract mosaic. The processor will execute one instruction after another using virtual addresses; its virtual addresses are still linear. However, the instruction located at the end of a page will be located in a completely different region of physical memory from the next instruction at the start of the next page. Data structures will appear to be contiguous using virtual addresses, but a large matrix may be scattered across many physical page frames.

An apt analogy is what happens when you shuffle several decks of cards together. A single process in its virtual address space sees the cards of a single deck in order. A different process sees a completely different deck, but it will also be in order. In physical memory, however, the decks of all the processes currently running will be shuffled together, apparently at random. The page tables are the magician's assistant: able to instantly find the queen of hearts from among the shuffled decks.

Paging addresses the principal limitation of segmentation: free-space allocation is very straightforward. The operating system can represent physical memory as a bit map, with each bit representing a physical page frame that is either free or in use. Finding a free frame is just a matter of finding an empty bit.

Sharing memory between processes is also convenient: we need to set the page table entry for each process sharing a page to point to the same physical page frame. For a large shared region that spans multiple page frames, such as a shared library, this may require setting up a number of page table entries. Since we need to know when to release memory when a finishes, shared memory requires some extra bookkeeping to keep track of whether the shared **core map** page is still in use. The data structure for this is called a *core map*; it records information about each physical page frame such as which page table entries point to it.

Many of the optimizations we discussed under segmentation can also be done with paging. For copy-on-write, we need to copy the page table entries and set them to read-only; on a store to one of these pages, we can make a real copy of the underlying page frame before resuming the process. Likewise, for zero-on-reference, we can set the page table entry at the top of the stack to be invalid, causing a trap into the kernel. This allows us to extend the stack only as needed.

Page tables allow other features to be added. For example, we can start a program running before all of its code and data are loaded into memory. Initially, the operating system marks all of the page table entries for a new process as invalid; as pages are brought in from disk, it marks those pages as read-only (for code pages) or read-write (for data pages). Once the first few pages are in memory, however, the operating system can start execution of the program in user-mode, while the kernel continues to transfer the rest of the program's code in the background. As the program starts up, if it happens to jump to a location that has not been loaded yet, the hardware will cause an exception, and the kernel can stall the program until that page is available. Further, the compiler can reorganize the program executable for more efficient startup, by coalescing the initialization pages into a few pages at the start of the program, thus overlapping initialization and loading the program from disk.

data breakpoint   As another example, a *data breakpoint* is request to stop the execution of a program when it references or modifies a particular memory location. It is helpful during debugging to know when a data structure has been changed, particularly when tracking down pointer errors. Data breakpoints are sometimes implemented with special hardware support, but they can also be implemented with page tables. For this, the page table entry containing the location is marked read-only. This causes the process to trap to the operating system on every change to the page; the operating system can then check if the instruction causing the exception affected the specific location or not.

A downside of paging is that while the management of physical memory becomes simpler, the management of the virtual address space becomes more challenging. Compilers typically expects the execution stack to be contiguous (in virtual addresses) and of arbitrary size; each new procedure call assumes the memory for the stack is available. Likewise, the runtime library for dynamic memory allocation typically expects a contiguous heap. In a single-threaded process, we can place the stack and heap at opposite ends of the virtual address space, and have them grow towards each other, as shown in Figure 8.6. However, with multiple threads per process, we need multiple thread stacks, each with room to grow.

This becomes even more of an issue with 64-bit virtual address spaces. The size of the page table is proportional to the size of the virtual address space, not to the size of physical memory. The more sparse the virtual address space, the more overhead is needed for the page table. Most of the entries will be invalid, representing parts of the virtual address space that are not in use, but physical memory is still needed for all of those page table entries.

We can reduce the space taken up by the page table by choosing a larger page frame. How big should a page frame be? A larger page frame can waste space if a process does not use all of the memory inside the frame. This is called *internal fragmentation*. Fixed-size chunks are easier to allocate, but waste space if the entire chunk is not used. Unfortunately, this means that with paging, either pages are very large (wasting space due to internal fragmentation), or the page table is very large (wasting space), or both. For example, with 16 KB pages and a 64 bit virtual address space, we might need 2^{50} page table entries!

internal fragmentation

8.2.3 Multi-Level Translation

If you were to design an efficient system for doing a lookup on a sparse keyspace, you probably would not pick a simple array. A tree or a hash table are more appropriate, and indeed, modern systems use both. We focus in this subsection on trees; we discuss hash tables afterwards.

Many systems use tree-based address translation, although the details vary from system to system, and the terminology can be a bit confusing. Despite the differences, the systems we are about to describe have similar properties. They support coarse and fine-grained memory protection and memory sharing, flexible memory placement, efficient memory allocation, and efficient lookup for sparse address spaces, even for 64-bit machines.

Almost all multi-level address translation systems use paging as the lowest level of the tree. The main differences between systems are in how they reach the page table at the leaf of the tree — whether using segments plus paging, or multiple levels of paging, or segments plus multiple levels of paging. There are several reasons for this:

- **Efficient memory allocation.** By allocating physical memory in fixed-size page frames, management of free space can use a simple bitmap.

- **Efficient disk transfers.** Hardware disks are partitioned into fixed-sized regions called sectors; disk sectors must be read or written in their entirety. By making the page size a multiple of the disk sector, we simplify transfers to and from memory, for loading programs into memory, reading and writing files, and in using the disk to simulate a larger memory than is physically present on the machine.

- **Efficient lookup.** We will describe in the next section how we can use a cache called a translation lookaside buffer to make lookups fast in the common case; the translation buffer caches lookups on a page by page basis. Paging also allows the lookup tables to be more compact, especially important at the lowest level of the tree.

- **Efficient reverse lookup.** Using fixed-sized page frames also makes it easy to implement the core map, to go from a physical page frame to the set of virtual addresses that share the same frame. This will be crucial for implementing the illusion of an infinite virtual memory in the next chapter.

- **Page-granularity protection and sharing.** Typically, every table entry at every level of the tree will have its own access permissions, enabling both coarse-grained and fine-grained sharing, down to the level of the individual page frame.

Paged Segmentation

paged
segmentation
Let us start a system with only two levels of a tree. With *paged segmentation*, memory is segmented, but instead of each segment table entry pointing directly to a contiguous region of physical memory, each segment table entry points to a page table, which in turn points to the memory backing that segment. The segment table entry "bound" describes the page table length, that is, the length of the segment in pages. Because paging is used at the lowest level, all segment lengths are some multiple of the page size. Figure 8.7 illustrates translation with paged segmentation.

Although segment tables are sometimes stored in special hardware registers, the page tables for each segment are quite a bit larger in aggregate, and so they are normally stored in physical memory. To keep the memory allocator simple, the maximum segment size is usually chosen to allow the page table for each segment to be a small multiple of the page size.

For example, with 32-bit virtual addresses and 4 KB pages, we might set aside the upper ten bits for the segment number, the next ten bits for the page number, and twelve bits for the page offset. In this case, if each page table entry is four bytes, the page table for each segment would exactly fit into one physical page frame.

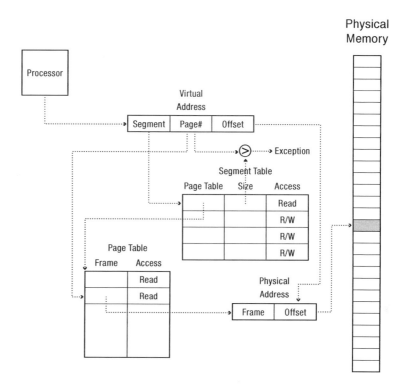

Figure 8.7: Address translation with paged segmentation. The virtual address has three components: a segment number, a virtual page number within the segment, and an offset within the page. The segment number indexes into a segment table that yields the page table for that segment. The page number from the virtual address indexes into the page table (from the segment table) to yield a page frame in physical memory. The physical address is the physical page frame from the page table, concatenated with the page offset from the virtual address. The operating system can restrict access to an entire segment, e.g., to prevent writes to the code segment, or to an individual page, e.g., to implement copy-on-write.

Multi-Level Paging

A nearly equivalent approach to paged segmentation is to use multiple levels of page tables. On the Sun Microsystems SPARC processor for example, there are three levels of page table. As shown in Figure 8.8, the top-level page table contains entries, each of which points to a second-level page table whose entries are pointers to page tables. On the SPARC, as with most other systems that use multiple levels of page tables, each level of page table is designed to fit in a physical page frame. Only the top-level page table must be filled in; the lower levels of the tree are allocated only if those portions of the virtual address space are in use by a particular process. Access permissions can be specified at each level, and so sharing between processes is possible at each level.

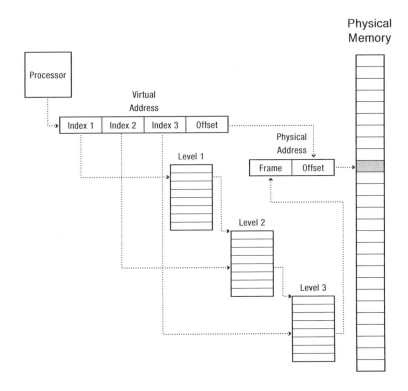

Figure 8.8: Address translation with three levels of page tables. The virtual address has four components: an index into each level of the page table and an offset within the physical page frame.

Multi-Level Paged Segmentation

We can combine these two approaches by using a segmented memory where each segment is managed by a multi-level page table. This is the approach taken by the x86, for both its 32-bit and 64-bit addressing modes.

We describe the 32-bit case first. The x86 terminology differs slightly from what we have used here. The x86 has a per-process *Global Descriptor Table* (GDT), equivalent to a segment table. The GDT is stored in memory; each entry (descriptor) points to the (multi-level) page table for that segment along with the segment length and segment access permissions. To start a process, the operating system sets up the GDT and initializes a register, the *Global Descriptor Table Register (GDTR)*, that contains the address and length of the GDT.

Because of its history, the x86 uses separate processor registers to specify the segment number (that is, the index into the GDT) and the virtual address for use by each instruction. For example, on the "32-bit" x86, there is both a segment number and 32 bits of virtual address within each segment. On the 64-bit x86, the virtual address within each segment is extended to 64 bits. Most applications only use a few segments, however, so the per-process segment

Global Descriptor Table

table is usually short. The operating system kernel has its own segment table; this is set up to enable the kernel to access, with virtual addresses, all of the per-process and shared segments on the system.

For encoding efficiency, the segment register is often implicit as part of the instruction. For example, the x86 stack instructions such as push and pop assume the stack segment (the index stored in the stack segment register), branch instructions assume the code segment (the index stored in the code segment register), and so forth. As an optimization, whenever the x86 initializes a code, stack, or data segment register it also reads the GDT entry (that is, the top-level page table pointer and access permissions) into the processor, so the processor can go directly to the page table on each reference.

Many instructions also have an option to specify the segment index explicitly. For example, the ljmp, or long jump, instruction changes the program counter to a new segment number and offset within that segment.

For the 32-bit x86, the virtual address space within a segment has a two-level page table. The first 10 bits of the virtual address index the top level page table, called the *page directory*, the next 10 bits index the second level page table, and the final 12 bits are the offset within a page. Each page table entry takes four bytes and the page size is 4 KB, so the top-level page table and each second-level page table fits in a single physical page. The number of second-level page tables needed depends on the length of the segment; they are not needed to map empty regions of virtual address space. Both the top-level and second-level page table entries have permissions, so fine-grained protection and sharing is possible within a segment.

Today, the amount of memory per computer is often well beyond what can 32 bits can address; for example, a high-end server could have two terabytes of physical memory. For the 64-bit x86, virtual addresses within a segment can be up to 64 bits. However, to simplify address translation, current processors only allow 48 bits of the virtual address to be used; this is sufficient to map 128 terabytes, using four levels of page tables. The lower levels of the page table tree are only filled in if that portion of the virtual address space is in use.

As an optimization, the 64-bit x86 has the option to eliminate one or two levels of the page table. Each physical page frame on the x86 is 4 KB. Each page of fourth level page table maps 2 MB of data, and each page of the third level page table maps 1 GB of data. If the operating system places data such that the entire 2 MB covered by the fourth level page table is allocated contiguously in physical memory, then the page table entry one layer up can be marked to point directly to this region instead of to a page table. Likewise, a page of third level page table can be omitted if the operating system allocates the process a 1 GB chunk of physical memory. In addition to saving space needed for page table mappings, this improves translation buffer efficiency, a point we will discuss in more detail in the next section.

8.2.4   Portability

The diversity of different translation mechanisms poses a challenge to the operating system designer. To be widely used, we want our operating system to be easily portable to a wide variety of different processor architectures. Even within a given processor family, such as an x86, there are a number of different variants that an operating system may need to support. Main memory density is increasing both the physical and virtual address space by almost a bit per year. In other words, for a multi-level page table to be able to map all of memory, an extra level of the page table is needed every decade just to keep up with the increasing size of main memory.

A further challenge is that the operating system often needs to keep two sets of books with respect to address translation. One set of books is the hardware view — the processor consults a set of segment and multi-level page tables to be able to correctly and securely execute instructions and load and store data. A different set of books is the operating system view of the virtual address space. To support features such as copy-on-write, zero-on-reference, and fill-on-reference, as well as other applications we will describe in later chapters, the operating system must keep track of additional information about each virtual page beyond what is stored in the hardware page table.

This software memory management data structures mirror, but are not identical to, the hardware structures, consisting of three parts:

- **List of memory objects.** Memory objects are logical segments. Whether or not the underlying hardware is segmented, the kernel memory manager needs to keep track of which memory regions represent which underlying data, such as program code, library code, shared data between two or more processes, a copy-on-write region, or a memory-mapped file. For example, when a process starts up, the kernel can check the object list to see if the code is already in memory; likewise, when a process opens a library, it can check if it has already been linked by some other process. Similarly, the kernel can keep reference counts to determine which memory regions to reclaim on process exit.

- **Virtual to physical translation.** On an exception, and during system call parameter copying, the kernel needs to be able to translate from a process's virtual addresses to its physical locations. While the kernel could use the hardware page tables for this, the kernel also needs to keep track of whether an invalid page is truly invalid, or simply not loaded yet (in the case of fill-on-reference) or if a read-only page is truly read-only or just simulating a data breakpoint or a copy-on-write page.

- **Physical to virtual translation.** We referred to this above as the *core map*. The operating system needs to keep track of the processes that map to a specific physical memory location, to ensure that when the kernel updates a page's status, it can also updated every page table entry that refers to that physical page.

The most interesting of these are the data structures used for the virtual to physical translation. For the software page table, we have all of the same options as before with respect to segmentation and multiple levels of paging, as well as some others. The software page table need not use the same structure as the underlying hardware page table; indeed, if the operating system is to be easily portable, the software data structures may be quite different from the underlying hardware.

Linux models the operating system's internal address translation data structures after the x86 architecture of segments plus multi-level page tables. This has made porting Linux to new x86 architectures relatively easy, but porting Linux to other architectures somewhat more difficult.

inverted page table

A different approach, taken first in a research system called Mach and later in Apple OS X, is to use a hash table, rather than a tree, for the software translation data. For historical reasons, the use of a hash table for paged address translation is called an *inverted page table*. Particularly as we move to deeper multi-level page tables, using a hash table for translation can speed up translation.

With an inverted page table, the virtual page number is hashed into a table of size proportional to the number of physical page frames. Each entry in the hash table contains tuples of the form (in the figure, the physical page is implicit):

```
inverted page table entry = {
    process or memory object ID,
    virtual page number,
    physical page frame number,
    access permissions
}
```

As shown in Figure 8.9, if there is a match on both the virtual page number and the process ID, then the translation is valid. Some systems do a two stage lookup: they first map the virtual address to a memory object ID, and then do the hash table lookup on the relative virtual address within the memory object. If memory is mostly shared, this can save space in the hash table without unduly slowing the translation.

An inverted page table does need some way to handle hash collisions, when two virtual addresses map to the same hash table entry. Standard techniques — such as chaining or rehashing — can be used to handle collisions.

hint

A particularly useful consequence of having a portability layer for memory management is that the contents of the hardware multi-level translation table can be treated as a *hint*. A hint is a result of some computation whose results may no longer be valid, but where using an invalid hint will trigger an exception.

With a portability layer, the software page table is the ground truth, while the hardware page table is a hint. The hardware page table can be safely used, provided that the translations and permissions are a *subset* of the translations in the software page table.

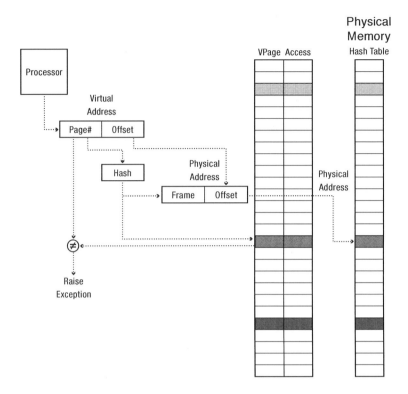

Figure 8.9: Address translation with a software hash table. The hardware page tables are omitted from the picture. The virtual page number is hashed; this yields a position in the hash table that indicates the physical page frame. The virtual page number must be checked against the contents of the hash entry to handle collisions and to check page access permissions.

8.3 | Towards Efficient Address Translation

At this point, you should be getting a bit antsy. After all, most of the hardware mechanisms we have described involve at least two and possibly as many as four memory extra references, on each instruction, before we even reach the intended physical memory location! It should seem completely impractical for a processor to do several memory lookups on every instruction fetch, and even more that for every instruction that loads or stores data.

In this section, we will discuss how to improve address translation performance without changing its logical behavior. In other words, despite the optimization, every virtual address is translated to exactly the same physical memory location, and every permission exception causes a trap, exactly as would have occurred without the performance optimization.

cache   For this, we will use a *cache*, a copy of some data that can be accessed more quickly than the original. This section concerns how we might use caches to improve translation performance. Caches are widely used in computer

Is an inverted page table enough?

The concept of an inverted page table raises an intriguing question: do we need to have a multi-level page table in hardware? Suppose, in hardware, we hash the virtual address. But instead of using the hash value to look up in a table where to find the physical page frame, suppose we just use the hash value *as* the physical page. For this to work, we need the hash table size to have exactly as many entries as physical memory page frames, so that there is a one-to-one correspondence between the hash table entry and the page frame.

We still need a table to store permissions and to indicate which virtual page is stored in each entry; if the process does not have permission to access the page, or if two virtual pages hash to the same physical page, we need to be able to detect this and trap to the operating system kernel to handle the problem. This is why a hash table for managing memory is often called called an *inverted page table*: the entries in the table are virtual page numbers, not physical page numbers. The physical page number is just the position of that virtual page in the table.

The drawback to this approach? Handling hash collisions becomes much harder. If two pages hash to the same table entry, only one can be stored in the physical page frame. The other has to be elsewhere — either in a secondary hash table entry or possibly stored on disk. Copying in the new page can take time, and if the program is unlucky enough to need to simultaneously access two virtual pages that both hash to the same physical page, the system will slow down even further. As a result, on modern systems, inverted page tables are typically used in software to improve portability, rather than in hardware, to eliminate the need for multi-level page tables.

---

architecture, operating systems, distributed systems, and many other systems; in the next chapter, we discuss more generally when caches work and when they do not. For now, however, our focus is just on the use of caches for reducing the overhead of address translation. There is a reason for this: the very first hardware caches were used to improve translation performance.

8.3.1　Translation Lookaside Buffers

If you think about how a processor executes instructions with address translation, there are some obvious ways to improve performance. After all, the processor normally executes instructions in a sequence:

```
...
add r1 , r2
mult r1 , 2
...
```

The hardware will first translate the program counter for the add instruction, walking the multi-level translation table to find the physical memory where the add instruction is stored. When the program counter is incremented, the processor must walk the multiple levels again to find the physical memory where the mult instruction is stored. If the two instructions are on the same page in the virtual address space, then they will be on the same page in physical memory. The processor will just repeat the same work — the table walk will be exactly the same, and again for the next instruction, and the next after that.

translation lookaside buffer

A *translation lookaside buffer (TLB)* is a small hardware table containing the results of recent address translations. Each entry in the TLB maps a virtual page to a physical page:

```
TLB entry = {
    virtual page number,
    physical page frame number,
    access permissions
}
```

Instead of finding the relevant entry by a multi-level lookup or by hashing, the TLB hardware (typically) checks all of the entries simultaneously against the virtual page. If there is a match, the processor uses that entry to form the physical address, skipping the rest of the steps of address translation. This is called a *TLB hit*. On a TLB hit, the hardware still needs to check permissions, in case, for example, the program attempts to write to a code-only page or the operating system needs to trap on a store instruction to a copy-on-write page.

TLB hit

TLB miss

A *TLB miss* occurs if none of the entries in the TLB match. In this case, the hardware does the full address translation in the way we described above. When the address translation completes, the physical page is used to form the physical address, and the translation is installed in an entry in the TLB, replacing one of the existing entries. Typically, the replaced entry will be one that has not been used recently.

The TLB lookup is illustrated in Figure 8.10, and Figure 8.11 shows how a TLB fits into the overall address translation system.

Although the hardware cost of a TLB might seem large, it is modest compared to the potential gain in processor performance. To be useful, the TLB lookup needs to be much more rapid than doing a full address translation; thus, the TLB table entries are implemented in very fast, on-chip static memory, situated near the processor. In fact, to keep lookups rapid, many systems now include multiple levels of TLB. In general, the smaller the memory, the faster the lookup. So, the first level TLB is small and close to the processor (and often split for engineering reasons into one for instruction lookups and a separate one for data lookups). If the first level TLB does not contain the translation, a larger second level TLB is consulted, and the full translation is only invoked if the translation misses both levels. For simplicity, our discussion will assume a single-level TLB.

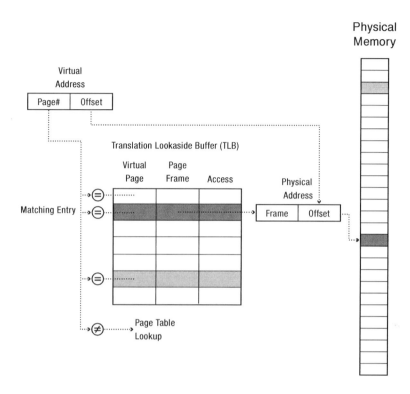

Figure 8.10: Operation of a translation lookaside buffer. In the diagram, each virtual page number is checked against all of the entries in the TLB at the same time; if there is a match, the matching table entry contains the physical page frame and permissions. If not, the hardware multi-level page table lookup is invoked; note the hardware page tables are omitted from the picture.

A TLB also requires an address comparator for each entry to check in parallel if there is a match. To reduce this cost, some TLBs are *set associative*. Compared to fully associative TLBs, set associative ones need fewer comparators, but they may have a higher miss rate. We will discuss set associativity, and its implications for operating system design, in the next chapter.

What is the cost of address translation with a TLB? There are two factors. We pay the cost of the TLB lookup regardless of whether the address is in the TLB or not; in the case of an unsuccessful TLB lookup, we also pay the cost of the full translation. If $P(hit)$ is the likelihood that the TLB has the entry cached:

$$\text{Cost(address translation)} = \begin{array}{l} \text{Cost(TLB lookup)} \\ +\text{Cost(full translation)} \times (1 - P(hit)) \end{array}$$

In other words, the processor designer needs to include a sufficiently large TLB that most addresses generated by a program will hit in the TLB, so that

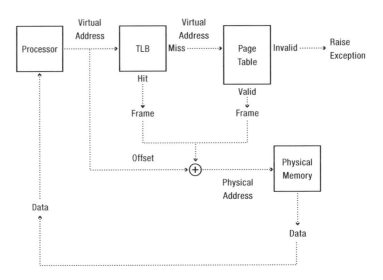

Figure 8.11: Combined operation of a translation lookaside buffer and hardware page tables.

doing the full translation is the rare event. Even so, TLB misses are a significant cost for many applications.

8.3.2 Superpages

superpage

One way to improve the TLB hit rate is using a concept called superpages. A *superpage* is a set of contiguous pages in physical memory that map a contiguous region of virtual memory, where the pages are aligned so that they share the same high-order (superpage) address. For example, an 8 KB superpage would consist of two adjacent 4 KB pages that lie on an 8 KB boundary in both virtual and physical memory. Superpages are at the discretion of the operating system — small programs or memory segments that benefit from a smaller page size can still operate with the standard, smaller page size.

Superpages complicate operating system memory allocation by requiring the system to allocate chunks of memory in different sizes. However, the upside is that a superpage can drastically reduce the number of TLB entries needed to map large, contiguous regions of memory. Each entry in the TLB has a flag, signifying whether the entry is a page or a superpage. For superpages, the TLB matches the superpage number — that is, it ignores the portion of the virtual address that is the page number within the superpage. This is illustrated in Figure 8.12.

To make this concrete, the x86 skips one or two levels of the page table when there is a 2 MB or 1 GB region of physical memory that is mapped as a

Software-loaded TLB

If the TLB is effective at amortizing the cost of doing a full address translation across many memory references, we can ask a radical question: do we need hardware multi-level page table lookup on a TLB miss? This is the concept behind a software-loaded TLB. A TLB hit works as before, as a fast path. On a TLB miss, instead of doing hardware address translation, the processor traps to the operating system kernel. In the trap handler, the kernel is responsible for doing the address lookup, loading the TLB with the new translation, and restarting the application.

This approach dramatically simplifies the design of the operating system, because it no longer needs to keep two sets of page tables, one for the hardware and one for itself. On a TLB miss, the operating system can consult its own portable data structures to determine what data should be loaded into the TLB.

Although convenient for the operating system, a software-loaded TLB is somewhat slower for executing applications, as the cost of trapping to the kernel is significantly more than the cost of doing hardware address translation. As we will see in the next chapter, the contents of page table entries can be stored in on-chip hardware caches; this means that even on a TLB miss, the hardware can often find every level of the multi-level page table already stored in an on-chip cache, but not in the TLB. For example, a TLB miss on a modern generation x86 can be completed in the best case in the equivalent of 17 instructions. By contrast, a trap to the operating system kernel will take several hundred to a few thousand instructions to process, even in the best case.

---

unit. When the processor references one of these regions, only a single entry is loaded into the TLB. When looking for a match against a superpage, the TLB only considers the most significant bits of the address, ignoring the offset within the superpage. For a 2 MB superpage, the offset is the lowest 21 bits of the virtual address. For a 1 GB superpage it is the lowest 30 bits.

A common use of superpages is to map the frame buffer for the computer display. When redrawing the screen, the processor may touch every pixel; with a high-resolution display, this can involve stepping through many megabytes of memory. If each TLB entry maps a 4 KB page, even a large on-chip TLB with 256 entries would only be able to contain mappings for 1 MB of the frame buffer at the same time. Thus, the TLB would need to repeatedly do page table lookups to pull in new TLB entries as it steps through memory. An even worse case occurs when drawing a vertical line. The frame buffer is a two-dimensional array in row-major order, so that each horizontal line of pixels is on a separate page. Thus, modifying each separate pixel in a vertical line would require loading a separate TLB entry! With superpages, the entire

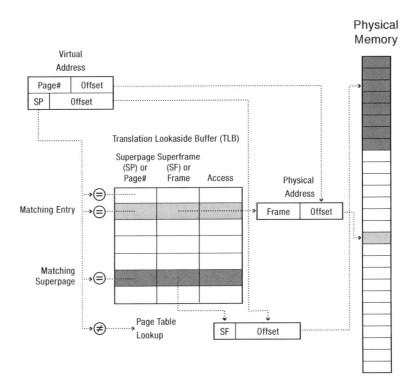

Figure 8.12: Operation of a translation lookaside buffer with superpages. In the diagram, some entries in the TLB can be superpages; these match if the virtual page is in the superpage. The superpage in the diagram covers an entire memory segment, but this need not always be the case.

frame buffer can be mapped with a single TLB entry, leaving more room for the other pages needed by the application.

Similar issues occur with large matrices in scientific code.

8.3.3   TLB Consistency

Whenever we introduce a cache into a system, we need to consider how to ensure consistency of the cache with the original data when the entries are modified. A TLB is no exception. For secure and correct program execution, the operating system must ensure that the each program sees its memory and no one else's. Any inconsistency between the TLB, the hardware multi-level translation table, and the portable operating system layer is a potential correctness and security flaw.

There are three issues to consider:

- **Process context switch.** What happens on a process context switch? The virtual addresses of the old process are no longer valid, and should no longer be valid, for the new process. Otherwise, the new process

Video Frame Buffer

Figure 8.13: Layout of a high-resolution frame buffer in physical memory. Each line of the pixel display can take up an entire page, so that adjacent pixels in the vertical dimension lie on different pages.

will be able to read the old process's data structures, either causing the new process to crash, or potentially allowing it to scavenge sensitive information such as passwords stored in memory.

On a context switch, we need to change the hardware page table register to point to the new process's page table. However, the TLB also contains copies of the old process's page translations and permissions. One approach is to *flush* the TLB — discard its contents — on every context switch. Since emptying the cache carries a performance penalty, modern processors have a *tagged TLB*, shown in Figure 8.14. Entries in a tagged TLB contain the process ID that produced each translation:

TLB flush

tagged TLB

```
tagged TLB entry = {
    process ID,
    virtual page number,
    physical page frame number,
    access permissions
}
```

With a tagged TLB, the operating system stores the current process ID in a hardware register on each context switch. When performing a lookup, the hardware ignores TLB entries from other processes, but it can reuse any TLB entries that remain from the last time the current process executed.

- **Permission reduction.** What happens when the operating system modifies an entry in a page table? For the processor's regular data cache of

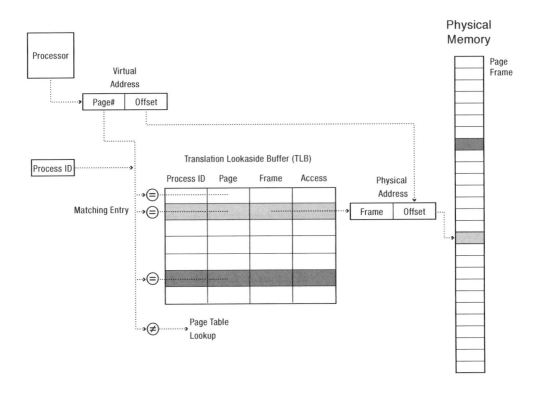

Figure 8.14: Operation of a translation lookaside buffer with process ID's. The TLB contains entries for multiple processes; only the entries for the current process are valid. The operating system kernel must change the current process ID when performing a context switch between processes.

main memory, special-purpose hardware keeps cached data consistent with the data stored in memory. However, hardware consistency is not usually provided for the TLB; keeping the TLB consistent with the page table is the responsibility of the operating system kernel.

Software involvement is needed for several reasons. First, page table entries can be shared between processes, so a single modification can affect multiple TLB entries (e.g., one for each process sharing the page). Second, the TLB contains only the virtual to physical page mapping — it does not record the address where the mapping came from, so it cannot tell if a write to memory would affect a TLB entry. Even if it did track this information, most stores to memory do not affect the page table, so repeatedly checking each memory store to see if it affects any TLB entry would involve a large amount of overhead that would rarely be needed.

Instead, whenever the operating system changes the page table, it ensures that the TLB does not contain an incorrect mapping.

Nothing needs to be done when the operating system *adds permissions* to a portion of the virtual address space. For example, the operating

	Process ID	VirtualPage	PageFrame	Access
Processor 1 TLB =	0	0x0053	0x0003	R/W
=	1	0x40FF	0x0012	R/W
Processor 2 TLB =	0	0x0053	0x0003	R/W
=	0	0x0001	0x0005	Read
Processor 3 TLB =	1	0x40FF	0x0012	R/W
=	0	0x0001	0x0005	Read

Figure 8.15: Illustration of the need for TLB shootdown to preserve correct translation behavior. In order for processor 1 to change the translation for page 0x53 in process 0 to read-only, it must remove the entry from its TLB, and it must ensure that no other processor has the old translation in its TLB. To do this, it sends an interprocessor interrupt to each processor, requesting it to remove the old translation. The operating system does not know if a particular TLB contains an entry (e.g., processor 3's TLB does not contain page 0x53), so it must remove it from all TLBs. The shootdown is complete only when all processors have verified that the old translation has been removed.

system might dynamically extend the heap or the stack by allocating physical memory and changing invalid page table entries to point to the new memory, or the operating system might change a page from read-only to read-write. In these cases, the TLB can be left alone because any references that require the new permissions will either cause the hardware load the new entries or cause an exception, allowing the operating system to load the new entries.

However, if the operating system needs to *reduce permissions* to a page, then the kernel needs to ensure the TLB does not have a copy of the old translation before resuming the process. If the page was shared, the kernel needs to ensure that the TLB does not have the copy for any of the process ID's that might have referenced the page. For example, to mark a region of memory as copy-on-write, the operating system must reduce permissions to the region to read-only, and it must remove any entries for that region from the TLB, since the old TLB entries would still be read-write.

Early computers discarded the entire contents of the TLB whenever there was a change to a page table, but more modern architectures, including the x86 and the ARM, support the removal of individual TLB entries.

- **TLB shootdown.** On a multiprocessor, there is a further complication. Any processor in the system may have a cached copy of a translation in its TLB. Thus, to be safe and correct, whenever a page table entry is modified, the corresponding entry in *every* processor's TLB has to be

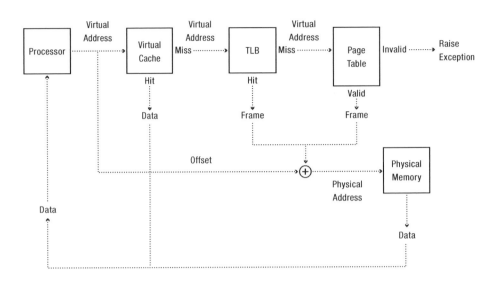

Figure 8.16: Combined operation of a virtually addressed cache, translation lookaside buffer, and hardware page table.

discarded before the change will take effect. Typically, only the current processor can invalidate its own TLB, so removing the entry from all processors on the system requires that the operating system interrupt each processor and request that it remove the entry from its TLB.

TLB shootdown

This heavyweight operation has its own name: it is a *TLB shootdown*, illustrated in Figure 8.15. The operating system first modifies the page table, then sends a TLB shootdown request to all of the other processors. Once another processor has ensured that its TLB has been cleaned of any old entries, that processor can resume. The original processor can continue only when *all* of the processors have acknowledged removing the old entry from their TLB. Since the overhead of a TLB shootdown increases linearly with the number of processors on the system, many operating systems batch TLB shootdown requests, to reduce the frequency of interprocess interrupts at some increased cost in latency to complete the shootdown.

8.3.4 Virtually Addressed Caches

Another step to improving the performance of address translation is to include a virtually addressed cache *before* the TLB is consulted, as shown in Figure 8.16. A virtually addressed cache stores a copy of the contents of physical memory, indexed by the virtual address. When there is a match, the processor can use the data immediately, without waiting for a TLB lookup or page table translation to generate a physical address, and without waiting to retrieve the data from main memory. Almost all modern multicore chips include a small, virtually addressed on-chip cache near each processor core. Often, like the TLB, the virtually addressed cache will be split in half, one for instruction lookups and one for data.

The same consistency issues that apply to TLBs also apply to virtually addressed caches:

- **Process context switch.** Entries in the virtually addressed cache must either be either with the process ID or they must be invalidated on a context switch to prevent the new process from accessing the old process's data.

- **Permission reduction and shootdown.** When the operating system changes the permission for a page in the page table, the virtual cache will not reflect that change. Invalidating the affected cache entries would require either flushing the entire cache or finding all memory locations stored in the cache on the affected page, both relatively heavyweight operations.

  Instead, most systems with virtually addressed caches use them in tandem with the TLB. Each virtual address is looked up in both the cache and the TLB at the same time; the TLB specifies the permissions to use, while the cache provides the data if the access is permitted. This way, only the TLB's permissions need to be kept up to date. The TLB and virtual cache are co-designed to take the same amount of time to perform a lookup, so the processor does not stall waiting for the TLB.

A further issue is aliasing. Many operating systems allow processes sharing memory to use different virtual addresses to refer to the same memory location. **memory address** This is called a *memory address alias*. Each process will have its own TLB entry **alias** for that memory, and the virtual cache may store a copy of the memory for each process. The problem occurs when one process modifies its copy; how does the system know to update the other copy?

The most common solution to this issue is to store the physical address along with the virtual address in the virtual cache. In parallel with the virtual cache lookup, the TLB is consulted to generate the physical address and page permissions. On a store instruction modifying data in the virtual cache, the system can do a reverse lookup to find all the entries that match the same physical address, to allow it to update those entries.

8.3.5 Physically Addressed Caches

Many processor architectures include a physically addressed cache that is consulted as a second-level cache after the virtually addressed cache and TLB, but before main memory. This is illustrated in Figure 8.17. Once the physical

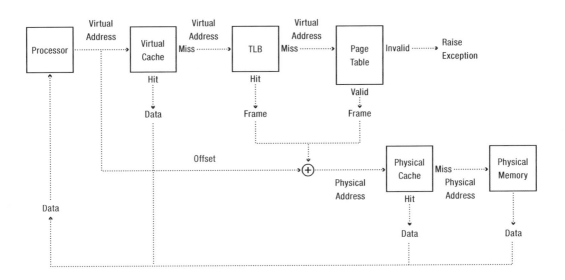

Figure 8.17: Combined operation of a virtually addressed cache, translation lookaside buffer, hardware page table, and physically addressed cache.

address of the memory location is formed from the TLB lookup, the second-level cache is consulted. If there is a match, the value stored at that location can be returned directly to the processor without the need to go to main memory.

With today's chip densities, an on-chip physically addressed cache can be quite large. In fact, many systems include both a second-level and a third-level physically addressed cache. Typically, the second-level cache is per-core and is optimized for latency; a typical size is 256 KB. The third-level cache is shared among all of the cores on the same chip and will be optimized for size; it can be as large as 2 MB on a modern chip. In other words, the entire UNIX operating system from the 70's, and all of its applications, would fit on a single modern chip, with no need to ever go to main memory.

Together, these physically addressed caches serve a dual purpose:

- **Faster memory references.** An on-chip physically addressed cache will have a lookup latency that is ten times (2nd level) or three times (3rd level) faster than main memory.

- **Faster TLB misses.** In the event of a TLB miss, the hardware will generate a sequence of lookups through its multiple levels of page tables. Because the page tables are stored in physical memory, they can be cached. Thus, even a TLB miss and page table lookup may be handled entirely on chip.

8.4 | Software Protection

An increasing number of systems complement hardware-based address translation with software-based protection mechanisms. Obviously, software-only protection is possible. A machine code interpreter, implemented in software, can simulate the exact behavior of hardware protection. The interpreter could fetch each instruction, interpret it, look each address up in a page table to determine if the instruction is permitted, and if so, execute the instruction. Of course, that would be very slow!

In this section, we ask: are there practical software techniques to execute code within a restricted domain, without relying on hardware address translation? The focus of our discussion will be on using software for providing an efficient protection boundary, as a way of improving computer security. However, the techniques we describe can also be used to provide other operating system services, such as copy-on-write, stack extensibility, recoverable memory, and user-level virtual machines. Once you have the infrastructure to reinterpret references to code and data locations, whether in software or hardware, a number of services become possible.

Hardware protection is nearly universal on modern computers, so it is reasonable to ask, why do we need to implement protection in software?

- **Simplify hardware.** One goal is simple curiosity. Do we really need hardware address translation, or is it just an engineering tradeoff? If software can provide efficient protection, we could eliminate a large amount of hardware complexity and runtime overhead from computers, with a substantial increase in flexibility.

- **Application-level protection.** Even if we need hardware address translation to protect the operating system from misbehaving applications, we often want to run untrusted code within an application. An example is inside a web browser; web pages can contain code to configure the display for a web site, but the browser needs to protect itself against malicious or buggy code provided by web sites.

- **Protection inside the kernel.** We also sometimes need to run untrusted, or at least less trusted, code inside kernel. Examples include third-party device drivers and code to customize the behavior of the operating system on behalf of applications. Because the kernel runs with the full capability of the entire machine, any user code run inside the kernel must be protected in software rather than in hardware.

- **Portable security.** The proliferation of consumer devices poses a challenge to application portability. No single operating system runs on every embedded sensor, smartphone, tablet, netbook, laptop, desktop, and server machine. Applications that want to run across a wide range of devices need a common runtime environment that isolates the application from the specifics of the underlying operating system and

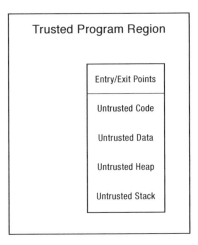

Figure 8.18: Execution of untrusted code inside a region of trusted code. The trusted region can be a process, such as a browser, executing untrusted JavaScript, or the trusted region can be the operating system kernel, executing untrusted packet filters or device drivers.

hardware device. Providing protection as part of the runtime system means that users can download and run applications without concern that the application will corrupt the underlying operating system.

The need for software protection is widespread enough that it has its own **sandbox** term: how do we provide a software *sandbox* for executing untrusted code so that it can do its work without causing harm to the rest of the system?

8.4.1   Single Language Operating Systems

A very simple approach to software protection is to restrict all applications to be written in a single, carefully designed programming language. If the language and its environment permits only safe programs to be expressed, and the compiler and runtime system are trustworthy, then no hardware protection is needed.

A practical example of this approach that is still in wide use is UNIX packet filters, shown in Figure 8.19. UNIX packet filters allow users to download code into the operating system kernel to customize kernel network processing. For example, a packet filter can be installed in the kernel to make a copy of packet headers arriving for a particular connection and to send those to a user-level debugger.

A UNIX packet filter is typically only a small amount of code, but because it needs to run in kernel-mode, the system cannot rely on hardware protection to prevent a misbehaving packet filter from causing havoc to unrelated applications. Instead, the system restricts the packet filter language to permit

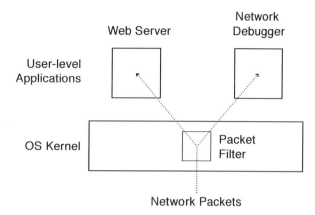

Figure 8.19: Execution of a packet filter inside the kernel. A packet filter can be installed by a network debugger to trace packets for a particular user or application. Packet headers matching the filter are copied to the debugger, while normal packet processing continues unaffected.

only safe packet filters. For example, filters may only branch on the contents of packets and no loops are allowed. Since the filters are typically short, the overhead of using an interpreted language is not prohibitive.

Another example of the same approach is the use of JavaScript in modern web browsers, illustrated in Figure 8.20. A JavaScript program customizes the user interface and presentation of a web site; it is provided by the web site, but it executes on the client machine inside the browser. As a result, the browser execution environment for JavaScript must prevent malicious JavaScript programs from taking control over the browser and possibly the rest of the client machine. Since JavaScript programs tend to be relatively short, they are often interpreted; JavaScript can also call into a predefined set of library routines. If a JavaScript program attempts to call a procedure that does not exist or reference arbitrary memory locations, the interpreter will cause a runtime exception and stop the program before any harm can be done.

Several early personal computers were single language systems with protection implemented in software rather than hardware. Most famously, the Xerox Alto research prototype used software and not hardware protection; the Alto inspired the Apple Macintosh, and the language it used, Mesa, was a forerunner of Java. Other systems included the Lisp Machine, a computer that executed only programs written in Lisp, and computers that executed only Smalltalk (a precursor to Python).

Unfortunately, language-based software protection has some practical limitations, so that on modern systems, it is often used in tandem with, rather than as a replacement for, hardware protection. Using an interpreted language seems like a safe option, but it requires trust in both the interpreter and its runtime libraries. An interpreter is a complex piece of software, and any

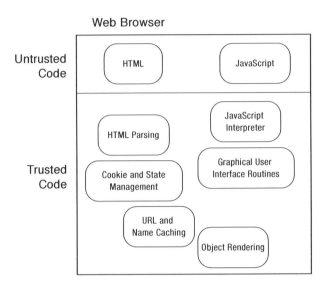

Figure 8.20: Execution of a JavaScript program inside a modern web browser. The JavaScript interpreter is responsible for containing effects of the JavaScript program to its specific page. JavaScript programs can call out to a broad set of routines in the browser, so these routines must also be protected against malicious JavaScript programs.

Language protection and garbage collection

JavaScript, Lisp, and Smalltalk all provide memory-compacting garbage collection for dynamically created data structures. One motivation for this is programmer convenience and to reduce avoidable programmer error. However, there is a close relationship between software protection and garbage collection. Garbage collection requires the runtime system to keep track of all valid pointers visible to the program, so that data structures can be relocated without affecting program behavior. Programs expressible in the language cannot point to or jump to arbitrary memory locations, as then the behavior of the program would be altered by the garbage collector. Every address generated by the program is necessarily within the region of the application's code, and every load and store instruction is to the program's data, and no one else's. In other words, this is exactly what is needed for software protection!

Cross-site scripting

Another JavaScript attack makes use of the storage interface provided to JavaScript programs. To allow JavaScript programs to communicate with each other, they can store data in cookies in the browser. For some web sites, these cookies can contain sensitive information such as the user's login authentication. A JavaScript program that can gain access to a user's cookies can potentially pretend to be the user, and therefore access the user's sensitive data stored at the server. If a web site is compromised, it can be modified to serve pages containing a JavaScript program that gathers and exploits the user's sensitive data. These are called *cross-site scripting attacks*, and they are widespread.

---

flaw in the interpreter could provide a way for a malicious program to gain control over the process, that is, to escape its protection boundary. Such attacks are common for browsers running JavaScript, although over time JavaScript interpreters have become more robust to these types of attacks.

Worse, because running interpreted code is often slow, many interpreted systems put most of their functionality into system libraries that can be compiled into machine code and run directly on the processor. For example, commercial web browsers provide JavaScript programs a huge number of user interface objects, so that the interpreted code is just a small amount of glue. Unfortunately, this raises the attack surface — any library routine that does not completely protect itself against malicious use can be a vector for the program to escape its protection. For example, a JavaScript program could attempt to cause a library routine to overwrite the end of a buffer, and depending on what was stored in memory, that might provide a way for the JavaScript program to gain control of the system. These types of attacks against JavaScript runtime libraries are widespread.

This leads most systems to use both hardware and software protection. For example, Microsoft Windows runs its web browser in a special process with restricted permissions. This way, if a system administrator visits a web site containing a malicious JavaScript program, even if the program takes over the browser, it cannot store files or do other operations that would normally be available to the system administrator. We know a computer security expert who runs each new web page in a separate virtual machine; even if the web page contains a virus that takes over the browser, and the browser is able to take over the operating system, the original, uninfected, operating system can be automatically restored by resetting the virtual machine.

A related approach is to write all the software on a system in a single, safe language, and then to compile the code into machine instructions that execute directly on the processor. Unlike interpreted languages, the libraries themselves can be written in the safe language. The Xerox Alto took this ap-

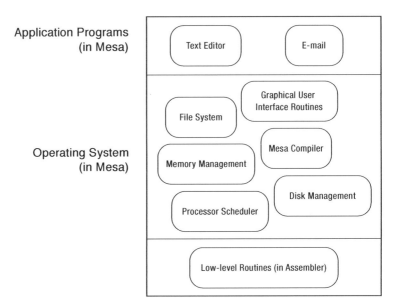

Application Programs (in Mesa)

Operating System (in Mesa)

Text Editor

E-mail

Graphical User Interface Routines

File System

Mesa Compiler

Memory Management

Disk Management

Processor Scheduler

Low-level Routines (in Assembler)

Figure 8.21: Design of the Xerox Alto operating system. Application programs and most of the operating system were implemented in a type-safe programming language called Mesa; Mesa isolated most errors to the module that caused the error.

proach: both applications and the entire operating system were written in the same language, Mesa. Like Java, Mesa had support for thread synchronization built directly into the language. Even with this, however, there are practical issues. You still need to do defensive programming at the trust boundary — between untrusted application code (written in the safe language) and trusted operating system code (written in the safe language). You also need to be able to trust the compiler to generate correct code that enforces protection; any weakness in the compiler could allow a buggy program to crash the system. The designers of the Alto built a successor system, called the Digital Equipment Firefly, which used a successor language to Mesa, called Modula-2, for implementing both applications and the operating system. However, for an extra level of protection, the Firefly also used hardware protection to isolate applications from the operating system kernel.

8.4.2 Language-Independent Software Fault Isolation

A limitation of trusting a language and its interpreter or compiler to provide safety is that many programmers value the flexibility to choose their own programming language. For example, some might use Ruby for configuring web servers, Matlab or Python for writing scientific code, or C++ for large software engineering efforts.

Since it would be impractical for the operating system to trust every compiler for every possible language, can we efficiently isolate application code, in software without hardware support, in a programming language independent fashion?

One reason for considering this is that there are many cases where systems need an extra level of protection within a process. We saw an example of this with web browsers needing to safely execute JavaScript programs, but there are many other examples. With software protection, we could give users the ability to customize the operating system by downloading code into the kernel, as with packet filters, but on a more widespread basis. Kernel device drivers have been shown to be the primary cause of operating system crashes; providing a way for the kernel to execute device drivers in a restricted environment could potentially cut down on the severity of these faults. Likewise, many complex software packages such as databases, spreadsheets, desktop publishing systems, and systems for computer-aided design, provide their users a way to download code into the system to customize and configure the system's behavior to meet the user's specific needs. If this downloaded code causes the system to crash, the user will not be able to tell who is really at fault and is likely to end up blaming the vendor.

Of course, one way to do this is to rely on the JavaScript interpreter. Tools exist to compile code written in one language, like C or C++, into JavaScript. This lets applications written in those languages to run on any browser that supports JavaScript. If executing JavaScript were safe and fast enough, then we could declare ourselves done.

In this section, we discuss an alternate approach: can we take any chunk of machine instructions and modify it to ensure that the code does not touch any memory outside of its own region of data? That way, the code could be written in any language, compiled by any compiler, and directly execute at the full speed of the processor.

Both Google and Microsoft have products that accomplish this: a sandbox that can run code written in any programming language, executed safely inside a process. Google's product is called Native Client; Microsoft's is called Application Domains. These implementations are efficient: Google reports that the runtime overhead of executing code safely inside a sandbox is less than 10%.

For simplicity of our discussion, we will assume that the memory region for the sandbox is contiguous, that is, the sandbox has a base and bound that needs to be enforced in software. Because we can disallow the execution of obviously malicious code, we can start by checking that the code in the sandbox does not use self-modifying instructions or privileged instructions.

We proceed in two steps. First, we insert machine instructions into the executable to do what hardware protection would have done, that is, to check that each address is legally within the region specified by the base and bounds, and to raise an exception if not. Second, we use control and data flow analysis to remove checks that are not strictly necessary for the sandbox to be correct. This mirrors what we did for hardware translation — first, we designed a general-purpose and flexible mechanism, and then we showed how to optimize it using TLBs so that the full translation mechanism was not needed on every instruction.

The added instructions for every load and store instruction are simple: just add a check that the address to be used by each load or store instruction is within the correct region of data. In the code, r1 is a machine register.

```
test r1, data.base
if less—than, branch to exception
test r1, data.bound
if greater—than, branch to exception
store data at r1
```

Note that the store instructions must be limited to just the data region of the sandbox; otherwise a store could modify the instruction sequence, e.g., to cause a jump out of the protected region.

We also need to check indirect branch instructions. We need to make sure the program cannot branch outside of the sandbox except for predefined entry and exit points. Relative branches and named procedure calls can be directly verified. Indirect branches and procedure returns jump to a location stored in a register or in memory; the address must be checked before use.

```
test r1, code.base
if less—than, branch to exception
test r1, code.bound
if greater—than, branch to exception
jump to r1
```

As a final detail, the above code verifies that indirect branch instructions stay within the code region. This turns out to be insufficient for protection, for two reasons. First, x86 code is byte addressable, and if you allow a jump to the middle of an instruction, you cannot be guaranteed as to what the code will do. In particular, an erroneous or malicious program might jump to the middle of an instruction, whose bytes would cause the processor to jump outside of the protected region. Although this may seem unlikely, remember that the attacker has the advantage; the attacker can try various code sequences to see if that causes an escape from the sandbox. A second issue is that an indirect branch might jump past the protection checks for a load or store instruction. We can prevent both of these by doing all indirect jumps through a table that only contains valid entry points into the code; of course, the table must also be protected from being modified by the code in the sandbox.

Now that we have logical correctness, we can run control and data flow analysis to eliminate many of the extra inserted instructions, if it can be proven that they are not needed. Examples of possible optimizations include:

- **Loop invariants.** If a loop strides through memory, the sandbox may be able to prove with a simple test at the beginning of the loop that all memory accesses in the loop will be within the protected region.

Virtual machines without kernel support

Modifying machine code to transparently change the behavior of a program, while still enforcing protection, can be used for other purposes. One application is transparently executing a guest operating system inside a user-level process without kernel support.

Normally, when we run a guest operating system in a virtual machine, the hardware catches any privileged instructions executed by the guest kernel and traps into the host kernel. The host kernel emulates the instructions and returns control back to the guest kernel at the instruction immediately after the hardware exception. This allows the host kernel to emulate privilege levels, interrupts, exceptions, and kernel management of hardware page tables.

What happens if we are running on top of an operating system that does not support a virtual machine? We can still emulate a virtual machine by modifying the machine code of the guest operating system kernel. For example, we can convert instructions to enable and disable interrupts to a no op. We can convert an instruction to start executing a user program to take the contents of the application memory, re-write those contents into a user-level sandbox, and start it executing. From the perspective of the guest kernel, the application program execution looks normal; it is the sandbox that keeps the application program from corrupting kernel's data structures and passes control to the guest kernel when the application makes a system call.

Because of the widespread use of virtual machines, some hardware architectures have begun to add support for directly executing guest operating systems in user-mode without kernel support. We will return to this issue in a later chapter, as it is closely related to the topic of stackable virtual machines: how do we manipulate page tables to handle the case where the guest operating system is itself a virtual machine monitor running a virtual machine.

- **Return values.** If static code analysis of a procedure can prove that the procedure does not modify the return program counter stored on the stack, the return can be made safely without further checks.

- **Cross-procedure checks.** If the code analysis can prove that a parameter is always checked before it is passed as an argument to a subroutine, it need not be checked when it is used inside the procedure.

8.4.3 Sandboxes Via Intermediate Code

To improve portability, both Microsoft and Google can construct their sandboxes from intermediate code generated by the compiler. This makes it easier for the system to do the code modification and data flow analysis to enforce the sandbox. Instead of generating x86 or ARM code directly, the various compilers generate their code in the intermediate language, and the sandbox runtime converts that into sandboxed code on the specific processor architecture.

The intermediate representation can be thought of as a virtual machine, with a simpler instruction set. From the compiler perspective, it is as easy to generate code for the virtual machine as it would be to go directly to x86 or ARM instructions. From the sandbox perspective though, using a virtual machine as the intermediate representation is much simpler. The intermediate code can include annotations as to which pointers can be proven to be safe and which must be checked before use. For example, pointers in a C program would require runtime checks while the memory references in a Java program may be able to be statically proven as safe from the structure of the code.

Microsoft has compilers for virtually every commercially important programming language. To avoid trusting all of these compilers with the safety of the system, the runtime is responsible for validating any of the type information needed for efficient code generation for the sandbox. Typically, verifying the correctness of static analysis is much simpler than generating it in the first place.

The Java virtual machine (JVM) is also a kind of sandbox; Java code is translated into intermediate byte code instructions that can be verified at runtime as being safely contained in the sandbox. Several languages have been compiled into Java byte code, such as Python, Ruby, and JavaScript. Thus, a JVM can also be considered a language-independent sandbox. However, because of the structure of the intermediate representation in Java, it is more difficult to generate correct Java byte code for languages such as C or Fortran.

8.5 | Summary and Future Directions

Address translation is a powerful abstraction enabling a wide variety of operating system services. It was originally designed to provide isolation between processes and to protect the operating system kernel from misbehaving applications, but it is more widely applicable. It is now used to simplify memory management, to speed interprocess communication, to provide for efficient shared libraries, to map files directly into memory, and a host of other uses.

A huge challenge to effective hardware address translation is the cumulative effect of decades of Moore's Law: both servers and desktop computers today contain vast amounts of memory. Processes are now able to map their code, data, heap, shared libraries, and files directly into memory. Each of these segments can be dynamic; they can be shared across processes or private to a single process. To handle these demands, hardware systems have converged on a two-tier structure: a multi-level segment and page table to provide very flexible but space-efficient lookup, along with a TLB to provide time-efficient lookup for repeated translations of the same page.

Much of what we can do in hardware we can also do in software; a combination of hardware and software protection has proven attractive in a number of contexts. Modern web browsers execute code embedded in web pages in a software sandbox that prevents the code from infecting the browser; the operating system uses hardware protection to provide an extra level of defense in case the browser itself is compromised.

The future trends are clear:

- **Very large memory systems.** The cost of a gigabyte of memory is likely to continue to plummet, making ever larger memory systems practical. Over the past few decades, the amount of memory per system has almost doubled each year. We are likely to look back at today's computers and wonder how we could have gotten by with as little as a gigabyte of DRAM! These massive memories will require ever deeper multi-level page tables. Fortunately, the same trends that make it possible to build gigantic memories also make it possible to design very large TLBs to hide the increasing depth of the lookup trees.

- **Multiprocessors.** On the other hand, multiprocessors will mean that maintaining TLB consistency will become increasingly expensive. A key assumption for using page table protection hardware for implementing copy-on-write and fill-on-demand is that the cost of modifying page table entries is modest. One possibility is that hardware will be added to systems to make TLB shootdown a much cheaper operation, e.g., by making TLBs cache coherent. Another possibility is to follow the trend towards software sandboxes. If TLB shootdown remains expensive, we may start to see copy-on-write and other features implemented in software rather than hardware.

- **User-level sandboxes.** Applications like browsers that run untrusted code are becoming increasingly prevalent. Operating systems have only recently begun to recognize the need to support these types of applications. Software protection has become common, both at the language level with JavaScript, and in the runtime system with Native Client and Application Domains. As these technologies become more widely used, it seems likely we may direct hardware support for application-level protection — to allow each application to set up its own protected execution environment, but enforced in hardware. If so, we may come to think of many applications as having their own embedded operating system, and the underlying operating system kernel as mediating between these operating systems.

Exercises

1. True or false. A virtual memory system that uses paging is vulnerable to external fragmentation. Why or why not?

2. For systems that use paged segmentation, what translation state does the kernel need to change on a process context switch?

3. For the three-level SPARC page table, what translation state does the kernel need to change on a process context switch?

4. Describe the advantages of an architecture that incorporates segmentation and paging over ones that are either pure paging or pure segmentation. Present your answer as separate lists of advantages over each of the pure schemes.

5. For a computer architecture with multi-level paging, a page size of 4 KB, and 64-bit physical and virtual addresses:

   a) List the required and optional fields of its page table entry, along with the number of bits per field.

   b) Assuming a compact encoding, what is the smallest possible size for a page table entry in bytes, rounded up to an even number.

   c) Assuming a requirement that each page table fits into a single page, and given your answer above, how many levels of page tables would be required to completely map the 64-bit virtual address space?

6. Consider the following piece of code which multiplies two matrices:

```
float a[1024][1024], b[1024][1024], c[1024][1024];

multiply () {
    unsigned i, j, k;

    for (i = 0; i < 1024; i++)
        for (j = 0; j < 1024; j++)
            for (k = 0; k < 1024; k++)
                c[i][j] += a[i,k] * b[k,j];
}
```

Assume that the binary for executing this function fits in one page and that the stack also fits in one page. Assume that storing a floating point number takes 4 bytes of memory. If the page size is 4 KB, the TLB has 8 entries, and the TLB always keeps the most recently used pages, compute the number of TLB misses assuming the TLB is initially empty.

7. Of the following items, which are stored in the thread control block, which are stored in the process control block, and which in neither?

   a) Page table pointer

   b) Page table

   c) Stack pointer

   d) Segment table

   e) Ready list

f) CPU registers

g) Program counter

8. Draw the segment and page table for the 32-bit Intel architecture.

9. Draw the segment and page table for the 64-bit Intel architecture.

10. For a computer architecture with multi-level paging, a page size of 4 KB, and 64-bit physical and virtual addresses:

    a) What is the smallest possible size for a page table entry, rounded up to a power of two?

    b) Using your result above, and assuming a requirement that each page table fits into a single page, how many levels of page tables would be required to completely map the 64-bit virtual address space?

11. Suppose you are designing a system with paged segmentation, and you anticipate the memory segment size will be uniformly distributed between 0 and 4 GB. The overhead of the design is the sum of the internal fragmentation and the space taken up by the page tables. If each page table entry uses four bytes per page, what page size minimizes overhead?

12. In an architecture with paged segmentation, the 32-bit virtual address is divided into fields as follows:

4 bit segment number	12 bit page number	16 bit offset

The segment and page tables are as follows (all values in hexadecimal):

Segment Table		Page Table A		Page Table B	
0	Page Table A	0	CAFE	0	F000
1	Page Table B	1	DEAD	1	D8BF
x	(rest invalid)	2	BEEF	2	3333
		3	BA11	x	(rest invalid)
		x	(rest invalid)		

Find the physical address corresponding to each of the following virtual addresses (answer "invalid virtual address" if the virtual address is invalid):

a) 00000000

b) 20022002

c) 10015555

13. Suppose a machine with 32-bit virtual addresses and 40-bit physical addresses is designed with a two-level page table, subdividing the virtual address into three pieces as follows:

| 10 bit page table number | 10 bit page number | 12 bit offset |

The first 10 bits are the index into the top-level page table, the second 10 bits are the index into the second-level page table, and the last 12 bits are the offset into the page. There are 4 protection bits per page, so each page table entry takes 4 bytes.

a) What is the page size in this system?

b) How much memory is consumed by the first and second level page tables and wasted by internal fragmentation for a process that has 64K of memory starting at address 0?

c) How much memory is consumed by the first and second level page tables and wasted by internal fragmentation for a process that has a code segment of 48K starting at address 0x1000000, a data segment of 600K starting at address 0x80000000 and a stack segment of 64K starting at address 0xf0000000 and growing upward (towards higher addresses)?

14. Write pseudo-code to convert a 32-bit virtual address to a 32-bit physical address for a two-level address translation scheme using segmentation at the first level of translation and paging at the second level. Explicitly define whatever constants and data structures you need (e.g., the format of the page table entry, the page size, and so forth).

Cash is king.

Per Gyllenhammar

9 Caching and Virtual Memory

Some may argue that we no longer need a chapter on caching and virtual memory in an operating systems textbook. After all, most students will have seen caches in an earlier machine structures class, and most desktops and laptops are configured so that they only very rarely, if ever, run out of memory. Maybe caching is no longer an operating systems topic?

We could not disagree more. Caches are central to the design of a huge number of hardware and software systems, including operating systems, Internet naming, web clients, and web servers. In particular, smartphone operating systems are often memory constrained and must manage memory carefully. Server operating systems make extensive use of remote memory and remote disk across the data center, using the local server memory as a cache. Even desktop operating systems use caching extensively in the implementation of the file system. Most importantly, understanding when caches work and when they do not is essential to every computer systems designer.

Consider a typical Facebook page. It contains information about you, your interests and privacy settings, your posts, and your photos, plus your list of friends, their interests and privacy settings, their posts, and their photos. In turn, your friends' pages contain an overlapping view of much of the same data, and in turn, their friends' pages are constructed the same way.

Now consider how Facebook organizes its data to make all of this work. How does Facebook assemble the data needed to display a page? One option would be to keep all of the data for a particular user's page in one place. However, the information that I need to draw my page overlaps with the information that my friends' friends need to draw their pages. My friends' friends' friends' friends include pretty much the entire planet. We can either

421

store everyone's data in one place or spread the data around. Either way, performance will suffer! If we store all the data in California, Facebook will be slow for everyone from Europe, and vice versa. Equally, integrating data from many different locations is also likely to be slow, especially for Facebook's more cosmopolitan users.

cache To resolve this dilemma, Facebook makes heavy use of caches; it would not be practical without them. A *cache* is a copy of a computation or data that can be accessed more quickly than the original. While any object on my page might change from moment to moment, it seldom does. In the common case, Facebook relies on a local, cached copy of the data for my page; it only goes back to the original source if the data is not stored locally or becomes out of date.

Caches work because both users and programs are predictable. You (probably!) do not change your friend list every nanosecond; if you did, Facebook could still cache your friend list, but it would be out of date before it could be used again, and so it would not help. If everyone changed their friends every nanosecond, Facebook would be out of luck! In most cases, however, what users do now is predictive of what they are likely to do soon, and what programs do now is predictive of what they will do next. This provides an opportunity for a cache to save work through reuse.

Facebook is not alone in making extensive use of caches. Almost all large computer systems rely on caches. In fact, it is hard to think of any widely used, complex hardware or software system that does *not* include a cache of some sort.

We saw three examples of hardware caches in the previous chapter:

- **TLBs.** Modern processors use a translation lookaside buffer, or TLB, to cache the recent results of multi-level page table address translation. Provided programs reference the same pages repeatedly, translating an address is as fast as a single table lookup in the common case. The full multi-level lookup is needed only in the case where the TLB does not contain the relevant address translation.

- **Virtually addressed caches.** Most modern processor designs take this idea a step farther by including a virtually addressed cache close to the processor. Each entry in the cache stores the memory value associated with a virtual address, allowing that value to be returned more quickly to the processor when needed. For example, the repeated instruction fetches inside a loop are well handled by a virtually addressed cache.

- **Physically addressed caches.** Most modern processors complement the virtually addressed cache with a second- (and sometimes third-) level physically addressed cache. Each entry in a physically addressed cache stores the memory value associated with a physical memory location. In the common case, this allows the memory value to be returned directly to the processor without the need to go to main memory.

There are many more examples of caches:

- **Internet naming.** Whenever you type in a web request or click on a link, the client computer needs to translate the name in the link (e.g., amazon.com) to an IP network address of where to send each packet. The client gets this information from a network service, called the Domain Name System (DNS), and then caches the translation so that the client can go directly to the web server in the common case.

- **Web content.** Web clients cache copies of HTML, images, JavaScript programs, and other data so that web pages can be refreshed more quickly, using less bandwidth. Web servers also keep copies of frequently requested pages in memory so that they can be transmitted more quickly.

- **Web search.** Both Google and Bing keep a cached copy of every web page they index. This allows them to provide the copy of the web page if the original is unavailable for some reason. The cached copy may be out of date — the search engines do not guarantee that the copy instantaneously reflects any change in the original web page.

- **Email clients.** Many email clients store a copy of mail messages on the client computer to improve the client performance and to allow disconnected operation. In the background, the client communicates with the server to keep the two copies in sync.

- **Incremental compilation.** If you have ever built a program from multiple source files, you have used caching. The build manager saves and reuses the individual object files instead of recompiling everything from scratch each time.

- **Just in time translation.** Some memory-constrained devices such as smartphones do not contain enough memory to store the entire executable image for some programs. Instead, systems such as the Google Android operating system and the ARM runtime store programs in a more compact intermediate representation, and convert parts of the program to machine code as needed. Repeated use of the same code is fast because of caching; if the system runs out of memory, less frequently used code may be converted each time it is needed.

- **Virtual memory.** Operating systems can run programs that do not fit in physical memory by using main memory as a cache for disk. Application pages that fit in memory have their page table entries set to valid; these pages can be accessed directly by the processor. Those pages that do not fit have their permissions set to invalid, triggering a trap to the operating system kernel. The kernel will then fetch the required page from disk and resume the application at the instruction that caused the trap.

- **File systems.** File systems also treat memory as a cache for disk. They store copies in memory of frequently used directories and files, reducing the need for disk accesses.

- **Conditional branch prediction.** Another use of caches is in predicting whether a conditional branch will be taken or not. In the common case of a correct prediction, the processor can start decoding the next instruction before the result of the branch is known for sure; if the prediction turns out to be wrong, the decoding is restarted with the correct next instruction.

In other words, caches are a central design technique to making computer systems faster. However, caches are not without their downsides. Caches can make understanding the performance of a system much harder. Something that seems like it should be fast — and even something that usually is fast — can end up being very slow if most of the data is not in the cache. Because the details of the cache are often hidden behind a level of abstraction, the user or the programmer may have little idea as to what is causing the poor performance. In other words, the abstraction of fast access to data can cause problems if the abstraction does not live up to its promise. One of our aims is to help you understand when caches do and do not work well.

In this chapter, we will focus on the caching of memory values, but the principles we discuss apply much more widely. Memory caching is common in both hardware (by the processor to improve memory latency) and in software (by the operating system to hide disk and network latency). Further, the structure and organization of processor caches requires special care by the operating system in setting up page tables; otherwise, much of the advantage of processor caches can evaporate.

Regardless of the context, all caches face three design challenges:

- **Locating the cached copy.** Because caches are designed to improve performance, a key question is often how to quickly determine whether the cache contains the needed data or not. Because the processor consults at least one hardware cache on every instruction, hardware caches in particular are organized for efficient lookup.

- **Replacement policy.** Most caches have physical limits on how many items they can store; when new data arrives in the cache, the system must decide which data is most valuable to keep in the cache and which can be replaced. Because of the high relative latency of fetching data from disk, operating systems and applications have focused more attention on the choice of replacement policy.

- **Coherence.** How do we detect, and repair, when a cached copy becomes out of date? This question, cache coherence, is central to the design of multiprocessor and distributed systems. Despite being very important, cache coherence beyond the scope of this version of the textbook. Instead, we focus on the first two of these issues.

Chapter roadmap:

- **Cache Concept.** What operations does a cache do and how can we evaluate its performance? (Section 9.1)

- **Memory Hierarchy.** What hardware building blocks do we have in constructing a cache in an application or operating system? (Section 9.2)

- **When Caches Work and When They Do Not.** Can we predict how effective a cache will be in a system we are designing? Can we know in advance when caching will *not* work? (Section 9.3)

- **Memory Cache Lookup.** What options do we have for locating whether an item is cached? How can we organize hardware caches to allow for rapid lookup, and what are the implications of cache organization for operating systems and applications? (Section 9.4)

- **Replacement Policies.** What options do we have for choosing which item to replace when there is no more room? (Section 9.5)

- **Case Study: Memory-Mapped Files.** How does the operating system provide the abstraction of file access without first reading the entire file into memory? (Section 9.6)

- **Case Study: Virtual Memory.** How does the operating system provide the illusion of a near-infinite memory that can be shared between applications? What happens if both applications and the operating system want to manage memory at the same time? (Section 9.7)

9.1 | Cache Concept

We start by defining some terms. The simplest kind of a cache is a memory cache. It stores (address, value) pairs. As shown in Figure 9.1, when we need to read value of a certain memory location, we first consult the cache, and it either replies with the value (if the cache knows it) and otherwise it forwards

cache hit   the request onward. If the cache has the value, that is called a *cache hit*. If the
cache miss   cache does not, that is called a *cache miss*.

For a memory cache to be useful, two properties need to hold. First, the cost of retrieving data out of the cache must be significantly less than fetching the data from memory. In other words, the cost of a cache hit must be less than a cache miss, or we would just skip using the cache.

Second, the likelihood of a cache hit must be high enough to make it worth
temporal locality   the effort. One source of predictability is *temporal locality*: programs tend to reference the same instructions and data that they had recently accessed. Examples include the instructions inside a loop, or a data structure that is repeatedly accessed. By caching these memory values, we can improve performance.

spatial locality   Another source of predictability is *spatial locality*. Programs tend to reference data near other data that has been recently referenced. For example, the next instruction to execute is usually near to the previous one, and different

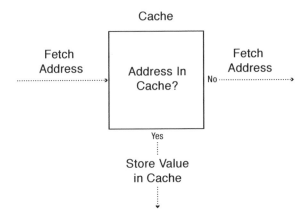

Figure 9.1: Abstract operation of a memory cache on a read request. Memory read requests are sent to the cache; the cache either returns the value stored at that memory location, or it forwards the request onward to the next level of cache.

fields in the same data structure tend to be referenced at nearly the same time. To exploit this, caches are often designed to load a block of data at the same time, instead of only a single location. Hardware memory caches often store 4-64 memory words as a unit; file caches often store data in powers of two of the hardware page size.

prefetch   A related design technique that also takes advantage of spatial locality is to *prefetch* data into the cache before it is needed. For example, if the file system observes the application reading a sequence of blocks into memory, it will read the subsequent blocks ahead of time, without waiting to be asked.

Putting these together, the latency of a read request is as follows:

$$\text{Latency(read request)} = \begin{array}{l} \text{Prob(cache hit)} \times \text{Latency(cache hit)} \\ + \text{Prob(cache miss)} \times \text{Latency(cache miss)} \end{array}$$

The behavior of a cache on a write operation is shown in Figure 9.2. The operation is a bit more complex, but the latency of a write operation is easier to understand. Most systems buffer writes. As long as there is room in the buffer, the computation can continue immediately while the data is transferred into the cache and to memory in the background. (There are certain restrictions on the use of write buffers in a multiprocessor system, so for this chapter, we are simplifying matters to some degree.) Subsequent read requests must check both the write buffer and the cache — returning data from the write buffer if it is the latest copy.

In the background, the system checks if the address is in the cache. If not, the rest of the cache block must be fetched from memory and then updated **write-through**   with the changed value. Finally, if the cache is *write-through*, all updates are **cache**   sent immediately onward to memory. If the cache is *write-back*, updates can

write-back cache

Figure 9.2: Abstract operation of a memory cache write. Memory requests are buffered and then sent to the cache in the background. Typically, the cache stores a block of data, so each write ensures that the rest of the block is in the cache before updating the cache. If the cache is write through, the data is then sent onward to the next level of cache or memory.

be stored in the cache, and only sent to memory when the cache runs out of space and needs to evict a block to make room for a new memory block.

Since write buffers allow write requests to appear to complete immediately, the rest of our discussion focuses on using caches to improve memory reads.

We first discuss the part of the equation that deals with the latency of a cache hit and a cache miss: how long does it take to access different types of memory? We caution, however, that the issues that affect the likelihood of a cache hit or miss are just as important to the overall memory latency. In particular, we will show that application characteristics are often the limiting factor to good cache performance.

9.2 Memory Hierarchy

When we are deciding whether to use a cache in the operating system or some new application, it is helpful to start with an understanding of the cost and performance of various levels of memory and disk storage.

From a hardware perspective, there is a fundamental tradeoff between the speed, size, and cost of storage. The smaller memory is, the faster it can be; the slower memory is, the cheaper it can be.

This motivates systems to have not just one cache, but a whole hierarchy of caches, from the nanosecond memory possible inside a chip to the multiple exabytes of worldwide data center storage. This hierarchy is illustrated by the table in Figure 9.3. We should caution that this list is just a snapshot; additional layers keep being added over time.

Cache	Hit Cost	Size
1st level cache/first level TLB	1 ns	64 KB
2nd level cache/second level TLB	4 ns	256 KB
3rd level cache	12 ns	2 MB
Memory (DRAM)	100 ns	10 GB
Data center memory (DRAM)	100 μs	100 TB
Local non-volatile memory	100 μs	100 GB
Local disk	10 ms	1 TB
Data center disk	10 ms	100 PB
Remote data center disk	200 ms	1 XB

Figure 9.3: Memory hierarchy, from on-chip processor caches to disk storage at a remote data center. On-chip cache size and latency is typical of a high-end processor. The entries for data center DRAM and disk latency assume the access is from one server to another in the same data center; remote data center disk latency if for access to a geographically distant data center.

- **First-level cache.** Most modern processor architectures contain a small first-level, virtually addressed, cache very close to the processor, designed to keep the processor fed with instructions and data at the clock rate of the processor.

- **Second-level cache.** Because it is impossible to build a large cache as fast as a small one, the processor will often contain a second-level, physically addressed cache to handle cache misses from the first-level cache.

- **Third-level cache.** Likewise, many processors include an even larger, slower third-level cache to catch second-level cache misses. This cache is often shared across all of the on-chip processor cores.

- **First- and second-level TLB.** The translation lookaside buffer (TLB) will also be organized with multiple levels: a small, fast first-level TLB designed to keep up with the processor, backed up by a larger, slightly slower, second-level TLB to catch first-level TLB misses.

- **Main memory (DRAM).** From a hardware perspective, the first-, second-, and third- level caches provide faster access to main memory; from a software perspective, however, main memory itself can be viewed as a cache.

- **Data center memory (DRAM).** With a high-speed local area network such as a data center, the latency to fetch a page of data from the memory of a nearby computer is much faster than fetching it from disk. In aggregate, the memory of nearby nodes will often be larger than that of the local disk. Using the memory of nearby nodes to avoid the latency of going to disk is called *cooperative caching*, as it requires the coopera-

cooperative caching

tive management of the nodes in the data center. Many large scale data center services, such as Google and Facebook, make extensive use of cooperative caching.

- **Local disk or non-volatile memory.** For client machines, local disk or non-volatile flash memory can serve as backing store when the system runs out of memory. In turn, the local disk serves as a cache for remote disk storage. For example, web browsers store recently fetched web pages in the client file system to avoid the cost of transferring the data again the next time it is used; once cached, the browser only needs to validate with the server whether the page has changed before rendering the web page for the user.

- **Data center disk.** The aggregate disks inside a data center provide enormous storage capacity compared to a computer's local disk, and even relative to the aggregate memory of the data center.

- **Remote data center disk.** Geographically remote disks in a data center are much slower because of wide-area network latencies, but they provide access to even larger storage capacity in aggregate. Many data centers also store a copy of their data on a remote robotic tape system, but since these systems have very high latency (measured in the tens of seconds), they are typically accessed only in the event of a failure.

If caching always worked perfectly, we could provide the illusion of instantaneous access to all the world's data, with the latency (on average) of a first level cache and the size and the cost (on average) of disk storage.

However, there are reasons to be skeptical. Even with temporal and spatial locality, there are thirteen orders of magnitude difference in storage capacity from the first level cache to the stored data of a typical data center; this is the equivalent of the smallest visible dot on this page versus those dots scattered across the pages of a million textbooks just like this one. How can a cache be effective if it can store only a tiny amount of the data that could be stored?

The cost of a cache miss can also be high. There are eight orders of magnitude difference between the latency of the first-level cache and a remote data center disk; that is equivalent to the difference between the shortest latency a human can perceive — roughly one hundred milliseconds — versus one year. How can a cache be effective if the cost of a cache miss is enormous compared to a cache hit?

9.3 When Caches Work and When They Do Not

How do we know whether a cache will be effective for a given workload? Even the same program will have different cache behavior depending on how it is used.

Suppose you write a program that reads and writes items into a hash table. How well does that interact with caching? It depends on the size of the hash

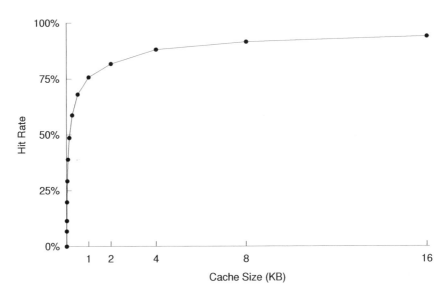

Figure 9.4: Cache hit rate as a function of cache size for a million instruction run of a C compiler. The hit rate vs. cache size graph has a similar shape for many programs. The knee of the curve is called the working set of the program.

table. If the hash table fits in the first-level cache, once the table is loaded into the cache, each access will be very rapid. If on the other hand, the hash table is too large to store in memory, each lookup may require a disk access.

Thus, neither the cache size nor the program behavior alone governs the effectiveness of caching. Rather, the interaction between the two determines cache effectiveness.

9.3.1   Working Set Model

A useful graph to consider is the cache hit rate versus the size of the cache. We give an example in Figure 9.4; of course, the precise shape of the graph will vary from program to program.

Regardless of the program, a sufficiently large cache will have a high cache hit rate. In the limit, if the cache can fit all of the program's memory and data, the miss rate will be zero once the data is loaded into the cache. At the other extreme, a sufficiently small cache will have a very low cache hit rate. Anything other than a trivial program will have multiple procedures and multiple data structures; if the cache is sufficiently small, each new instruction and data reference will push out something from the cache that will be used in the near future. For the hash table example, if the size of the cache is much smaller than the size of the hash table, each time we do a lookup, the hash bucket we need will no longer be in the cache.

Most programs will have an inflection point, or knee of the curve, where a critical mass of program data can just barely fit in the cache. This critical mass **working set**   is called the program's *working set*. As long as the working set can fit in the

Thrashing

A closely related concept to the working set is thrashing. A program thrashes if the cache is too small to hold its working set, so that most references are cache misses. Each time there is a cache miss, we need to evict a cache block to make room for the new reference. However, the new cache block may in turn be evicted before it is reused.

The word "thrash" dates from the 1960's, when disk drives were as large as washing machines. If a program's working set did not fit in memory, the system would need to shuffle memory pages back and forth to disk. This burst of activity would literally make the disk drive shake violently, making it very obvious to everyone nearby why the system was not performing well.

cache, most references will be a cache hit, and application performance will be good.

The notion of a working set can also apply to user behavior. Consider what happens when you are developing code for a homework assignment. If the files you need fit in memory, compilation will be rapid; if not, compilation will be slow as each file is brought in from disk as it is used.

Different programs, and different users, will have working sets of different sizes. Even within the same program, different phases of the program may have different size working sets. For example, the parser for a compiler needs different data in cache than the code generator. In a text editor, the working set shifts when we switch from one page to the next. Users also change their focus from time to time, as when you shift from a programming assignment to a history assignment.

phase change behavior
The result of this *phase change behavior* is that caches will often have bursty miss rates: periods of low cache misses interspersed with periods of high cache misses, as shown in Figure 9.5. Process context switches will also cause bursty cache misses, as the cache discards the working set from the old process and brings in the working set of the new process.

We can combine the graph in Figure 9.4 with the table in Figure 9.3 to see the impact of the size of the working set on computer system performance. A program whose working set fits in the first level cache will run four times faster than one whose working set fits in the second level cache. A program whose working set does not fit in main memory will run a thousand times slower than one who does, assuming it has access to data center memory. It will run a hundred thousand times slower if it needs to go to disk.

Because of the increasing depth and complexity of the memory hierarchy, an important area of work is the design of algorithms that adapt their working set to the memory hierarchy. One focus has been on algorithms that manage the gap between main memory and disk, but the same principles apply at other levels of the memory hierarchy.

Figure 9.5: Example cache hit rate over time. At a phase change within a process, or due to a context switch between processes, there will be a spike of cache misses before the system settles into a new equilibrium.

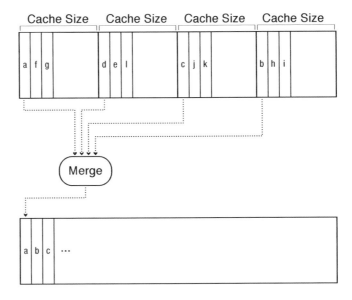

Figure 9.6: Algorithm to sort a large array that does not fit into main memory, by breaking the problem into pieces that do fit into memory.

A simple example is how to efficiently sort an array that does not fit in main memory. (Equivalently, we could consider how to sort an array that does not fit in the first level cache.) As shown in Figure 9.6, we can break the problem up into chunks each of which does fit in memory. Once we sort each chunk, we can merge the sorted chunks together efficiently. To sort a chunk that fits in main memory, we can in turn break the problem into sub-chunks that fit in the on-chip cache.

We will discuss later in this chapter what the operating system needs to do when managing memory between programs that in turn adapt their behavior to manage memory.

9.3.2 Zipf Model

web proxy cache

Although the working set model often describes program and user behavior quite well, it is not always a good fit. For example, consider a *web proxy cache*. A web proxy cache stores frequently accessed web pages to speed web access and reduce network traffic. Web access patterns cause two challenges to a cache designer:

- **New data.** New pages are being added to the web at a rapid rate, and page contents also change. Every time a user accesses a page, the system needs to check whether the page has changed in the meantime.

- **No working set.** Although some web pages are much more popular than others, there is no small subset of web pages that, if cached, give you the bulk of the benefit. Unlike with a working set, even very small caches have some value. Conversely, increasing cache size yields diminishing returns: even very large caches tend to have only modest cache hit rates, as there are an enormous group of pages that are visited from time to time.

Zipf distribution

A useful model for understanding the cache behavior of web access is the *Zipf distribution*. Zipf developed the model to describe the frequency of individual words in a text, but it also applies in a number of other settings.

Suppose we have a set of web pages (or words), and we rank them in order of popularity. Then the frequency users visit a particular web page is (approximately) inversely proportional to its rank:

$$\text{Frequency of visits to the kth most popular page} \propto \frac{1}{k^\alpha}$$

where α is value between 1 and 2. A Zipf probability distribution is illustrated in Figure 9.7.

The Zipf distribution fits a surprising number of disparate phenomena: the popularity of library books, the population of cities, the distribution of salaries, the size of friend lists in social networks, and the distribution of references in scientific papers. The exact cause of the Zipf distribution in many

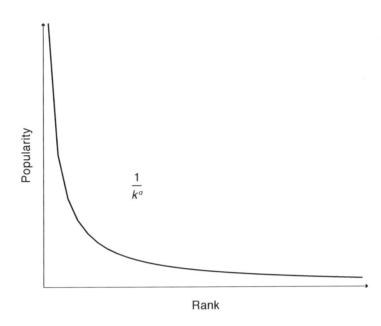

$$\frac{1}{k^a}$$

Figure 9.7: Zipf distribution

of these cases is unknown, but they share a theme of popularity in human social networks.

heavy tail   A characteristic of a Zipf curve is a *heavy tail*. Although a significant number of references will be to the most popular items, a substantial portion of references will be to less popular ones. If we redraw Figure 9.4 of the relationship between cache hit rate and cache size, but for a Zipf distribution, we get Figure 9.8. Note that we have rescaled the x-axis to be log scale. Rather than a threshold as we see in the working set model, increasing the cache size continues to improve cache hit rates, but with diminishing returns.

9.4 | Memory Cache Lookup

Now that we have outlined the available technologies for constructing caches, and the usage patterns that lend (or do not lend) themselves to effective caching, we turn to cache design. How do we find whether an item is in the cache, and what do we do when we run out of room in the cache? We answer the first question here, and we defer the second question to the next section.

A memory cache maps a sparse set of addresses to the data values stored at those addresses. You can think of a cache as a giant table with two columns: one for the address and one for the data stored at that address. To exploit spatial locality, each entry in the table will store the values for a block of memory, not just the value for a single memory word. Modern Intel processors

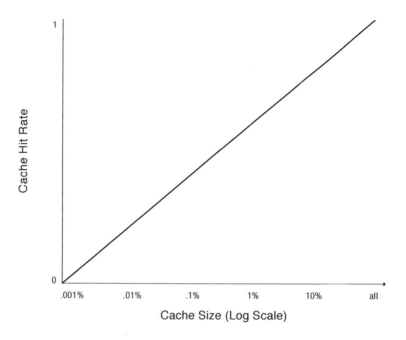

Figure 9.8: Cache hit rate as a function of the percentage of total items that can fit in the cache, on a log scale, for a Zipf distribution.

cache data in 64 byte chunks. For operating systems, the block size is typically the hardware page size, or 4 KB on an Intel processor.

We need to be able to rapidly convert an address to find the corresponding data, while minimizing storage overhead. The options we have for cache lookup are all of the same ones we explored in the previous chapter for address lookup: we can use a linked list, a multi-level tree, or a hash table. Operating systems use each of those techniques in different settings, depending on the size of the cache, its access pattern, and how important it is to have very rapid lookup.

For hardware caches, the design choices are more limited. The latency gap between cache levels is very small, so any added overhead in the lookup procedure can swamp the benefit of the cache. To make lookup faster, hardware caches often constrain where in the table we might find any specific address. This constraint means that there could be room in one part of the table, but not in another, raising the cache miss rate. There is a tradeoff here: a faster cache lookup needs to be balanced against the cost of increased cache misses.

Three common mechanisms for cache lookup are:

- **Fully associative.** With a fully associative cache, the address can be stored anywhere in the table, and so on a lookup, the system must check the address against all of the entries in the table as illustrated in Figure 9.9. There is a cache hit if any of the table entries match. Because any address

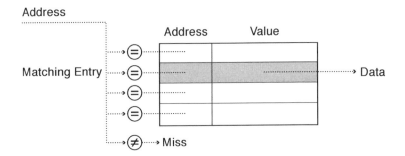

Figure 9.9: Fully associative cache lookup. The cache checks the address against every entry and returns the matching value, if any.

can be stored anywhere, this provides the system maximal flexibility when it needs to choose an entry to discard when it runs out of space.

We saw two examples of fully associative caches in the previous chapter. Until very recently, TLBs were often fully associative — the TLB would check the virtual page against every entry in the TLB in parallel. Likewise, physical memory is a fully associative cache. Any page frame can hold any virtual page, and we can find where each virtual page is stored using a multi-level tree lookup. The set of page tables defines whether there is a match.

A problem with fully associative lookup is the cumulative impact of Moore's Law. As more memory can be packed on chip, caches become larger. We can use some of the added memory to make each table entry larger, but this has a limit depending on the amount of spatial locality in typical applications. Alternately, we can add more table entries, but this means more lookup hardware and comparators. As an example, a 2 MB on-chip cache with 64 byte blocks has 32K cache table entries! Checking each address against every table entry in parallel is not practical.

- **Direct mapped.** With a direct mapped cache, each address can only be stored in one location in the table. Lookup is easy: we hash the address to its entry, as shown in Figure 9.10. There is a cache hit if the address matches that entry and a cache miss otherwise.

    A direct mapped cache allows efficient lookup, but it loses much of that advantage in decreased flexibility. If a program happens to need two different addresses that both hash to the same entry, such as the program counter and the stack pointer, the system will thrash. We will first get the instruction; then, oops, we need the stack. Then, oops, we need the instruction again. Then oops, we need the stack again. The programmer will see the program running slowly, with no clue why, as it will depend on which addresses are assigned to which instructions

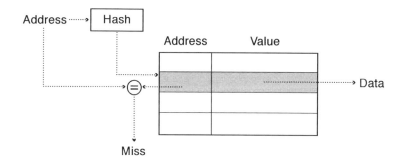

Figure 9.10: Direct mapped cache lookup. The cache hashes the address to determine which location in the table to check. The cache returns the value stored in the entry if it matches the address.

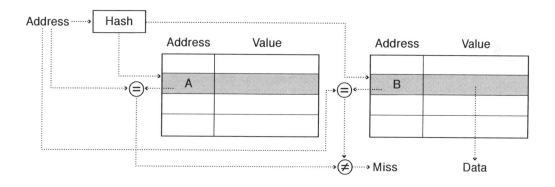

Figure 9.11: Set associative cache lookup. The cache hashes the address to determine which location to check. The cache checks the entry in each table in parallel. It returns the value if any of the entries match the address.

and data. If the programmer inserts a print statement to try to figure out what is going wrong, that might shift the instructions to a different cache block, making the problem disappear!

- **Set associative.** A set associative cache melds the two approaches, allowing a tradeoff of slightly slower lookup than a direct mapped cache in exchange for most of the flexibility of a fully associative cache. With a set associative cache, we replicate the direct mapped table and lookup in each replica in parallel. A k set associative cache has k replicas; a particular address block can be in any of the k replicas. (This is equivalent to a hash table with a bucket size of k.) There is a cache hit if the address matches any of the replicas.

  A set associative cache avoids the problem of thrashing with a direct mapped cache, provided the working set for a given bucket is larger

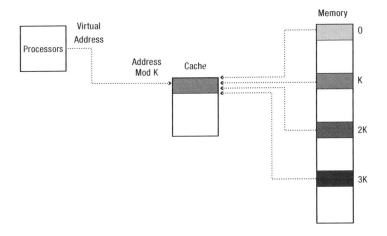

Figure 9.12: When caches are larger than the page size, multiple page frames can map to the same slice of the cache. A process assigned page frames that are separated by exactly the cache size will only use a small portion of the cache. This applies to both set associative and direct mapped caches; the figure assumes a direct mapped cache to simplify the illustration.

than k. Almost all hardware caches and TLBs today use set associative matching; an 8-way set associative cache structure is common.

Direct mapped and set associative caches pose a design challenge for the operating system. These caches are much more efficient if the working set of the program is spread across the different buckets in the cache. This is easy with a TLB or a virtually addressed cache, as each successive virtual page or cache block will be assigned to a cache bucket. A data structure that straddles a page or cache block boundary will be automatically assigned to two different buckets.

However, the assignment of physical page frames is up to the operating system, and this choice can have a large impact on the performance of a physically addressed cache. To make this concrete, suppose we have a 2 MB physically addressed cache with 8-way set associativity and 4 KB pages; this is typical for a high performance processor. Now suppose the operating system happens to assign page frames in a somewhat odd way, so that an application is given physical page frames that are separated by exactly 256 KB. Perhaps those were the only page frames that were free. What happens?

If the hardware uses the low order bits of the page frame to index the cache, then every page of the current process will map to the same buckets in the cache. We show this in Figure 9.12. Instead of the cache having 2 MB of useful space, the application will only be able to use 32 KB (4 KB pages times the 8-way set associativity). This makes it a lot more likely for the application to thrash.

Even worse, the application would have no way to know this had happened. If by random chance an application ended up with page frames that map to the same cache buckets, its performance will be poor. Then, when the user re-runs the application, the operating system might assign the application a completely different set of page frames, and performance returns to normal.

page coloring   To make cache behavior more predictable and more effective, operating systems use a concept called *page coloring*. With page coloring, physical page frames are partitioned into sets based on which cache buckets they will use. For example, with a 2 MB 8-way set associative cache and 4 KB pages, there will be 64 separate sets, or colors. The operating system can then assign page frames to spread each application's data across the various colors.

9.5 | Replacement Policies

Once we have looked up an address in the cache and found a cache miss, we have a new problem. Which memory block do we choose to replace? Assuming the reference pattern exhibits temporal locality, the new block is likely to be needed in the near future, so we need to choose some block of memory to evict from the cache to make room for the new data. Of course, with a direct mapped cache we do not have a choice: there is only one block that can be replaced. In general, however, we will have a choice, and this choice can have a significant impact on the cache hit rate.

As with processor scheduling, there are a number of options for the replacement policy. We caution that there is no single right answer! Many replacement policies are optimal for some workloads and pessimal for others, in terms of the cache hit rate; policies that are good for a working set model will not be good for Zipf workloads.

Policies also vary depending on the setting: hardware caches use a different replacement policy than operating system does in managing main memory as a cache for disk. A hardware cache will often have a limited number of replacement choices, constrained by the set associativity of the cache, and it must make its decisions very rapidly. In the operating system, there is often both more time to make a choice and a much larger number cached items to consider; e.g., with 4 GB of memory, a system will have a million separate 4 KB pages to choose from when deciding which to replace. Even within the operating system, the replacement policy for the file buffer cache is often different than the one used for demand paged virtual memory, depending on what information is easily available about the access pattern.

We first discuss several different replacement policies in the abstract, and then in the next two sections we consider how these concepts are applied to the setting of demand paging memory from disk.

9.5.1   Random

Although it may seem arbitrary, a practical replacement policy is to choose a random block to replace. Particularly for a first-level hardware cache, the

					FIFO									
Reference	A	B	C	D	E	A	B	C	D	E	A	B	C	D	E
1	A				E				D				C		
2		B				A				E				D	
3			C				B				A				E
4				D				C				B			

Figure 9.13: Cache behavior for FIFO for a repeated scan through memory, where the scan is slightly larger than the cache size. Each row represents the contents of a page frame or cache block; each new reference triggers a cache miss.

system may not have the time to make a more complex decision, and the cost of making the wrong choice can be small if the item is in the next level cache. The bookkeeping cost for more complex policies can be non-trivial: keeping more information about each block requires space that may be better spent on increasing the cache size.

Random's biggest weakness is also its biggest strength. Whatever the access pattern is, Random will not be pessimal — it will not make the worst possible choice, at least, not on average. However, it is also unpredictable, and so it might foil an application that was designed to carefully manage its use of different levels of the cache.

9.5.2 First-In-First-Out (FIFO)

A less arbitrary policy is to evict the cache block or page that has been in memory the longest, that is, First In First Out, or FIFO. Particularly for using memory as a cache for disk, this can seem fair — each program's pages spend a roughly equal amount of time in memory before being evicted.

Unfortunately, FIFO can be the worst possible replacement policy for workloads that happen quite often in practice. Consider a program that cycles through a memory array repeatedly, but where the array is too large to fit in the cache. Many scientific applications do an operation on every element in an array, and then repeat that operation until the data reaches a fixed point. Google's PageRank algorithm for determining which search results to display uses a similar approach. PageRank iterates repeatedly through all pages, estimating the popularity of a page based on the popularity of the pages that refer to it as computed in the previous iteration.

On a repeated scan through memory, FIFO does exactly the wrong thing: it always evicts the block or page that will be needed next. Figure 9.13 illustrates this effect. Note that in this figure, and other similar figures in this figures in this chapter, we show only a small number of cache slots; note that these policies also apply to systems with a very large number of slots.

Optimality of MIN

The proof that MIN is optimal is a bit involved. If MIN is not optimal, there must be some alternative optimal replacement policy, which we will call ALT, that has fewer cache misses than MIN on some specific sequence of references. There may be many such alternate policies, so let us focus on the one that differs from MIN at the latest possible point. Consider the first cache replacement where ALT differs from MIN — by definition, ALT must choose a block to replace that is used sooner than the block chosen by MIN.

We construct a new policy, ALT′, that is at least as good as ALT, but differs from MIN at a later point and so contradicts the assumption. We construct ALT′ to differ from ALT in only one respect: at the first point where ALT differs from MIN, ALT′ chooses to evict the block that MIN would have chosen. From that point, the contents of the cache differ between ALT and ALT′ only for that one block. ALT contains y, the block referenced farther in the future; ALT′ is the same, except it contains x, the block referenced sooner. On subsequent cache misses to other blocks, ALT′ mimics ALT, evicting exactly the same blocks that ALT would have evicted.

It is possible that ALT chooses to evict y before the next reference to x or y; in this case, if ALT′ chooses to evict x, the contents of the cache for ALT and ALT′ are identical. Further, ALT′ has the same number of cache misses as ALT, but it differs from MIN at a later point than ALT. This contradicts our assumption above, so we can exclude this case.

Eventually, the system will reference x, the block that ALT chose to evict; by construction, this occurs before the reference to y, the block that ALT′ chose to evict. Thus, ALT will have a cache miss, but ALT′ will not. ALT will evict some block, q, to make room for x; now ALT and ALT′ differ only in that ALT contains y and ALT′ contains q. (If ALT evicts y instead, then ALT and ALT′ have the same cache contents, but ALT′ has fewer misses than ALT, a contradiction.) Finally, when we reach the reference to y, ALT′ will take a cache miss. If ALT′ evicts q, then it will have the same number of cache misses as ALT, but it will differ from MIN at a point later than ALT, a contradiction.

9.5.3 Optimal Cache Replacement (MIN)

If FIFO can be pessimal for some workloads, that raises the question: what replacement policy is optimal for minimizing cache misses? The optimal policy, called MIN, is to replace whichever block is used farthest in the future. Equivalently, the worst possible strategy is to replace the block that is used soonest.

As with Shortest Job First, MIN requires knowledge of the future, and so we ca not implement it directly. Rather, we can use it as a goal: we want to come up with mechanisms which are effective at predicting which blocks will be used in the near future, so that we can keep those in the cache.

Reference	A	B	A	C	B	D	A	D	E	D	A	E	B	A	C
LRU															
1	A		+				+				+			+	
2		B			+								+		
3				C					E			+			
4						D		+		+					C
FIFO															
1	A		+				+		E						
2		B			+						A			+	
3				C								+	B		
4						D		+		+					C
MIN															
1	A		+				+				+			+	
2		B			+								+		C
3				C					E			+			
4						D		+		+					

Figure 9.14: Cache behavior for LRU (top), FIFO (middle), and MIN (bottom) for a reference pattern that exhibits temporal locality. Each row represents the contents of a page frame or cache block; + indicates a cache hit. On this reference pattern, LRU is the same as MIN up to the final reference, where MIN can choose to replace any block.

If we were able to predict the future, we could do even better than MIN by prefetching blocks so that they arrive "just in time" — exactly when they are needed. In the best case, this can reduce the number of cache misses to zero. For example, if we observe a program scanning through a file, we can prefetch the blocks of the file into memory. Provided we can read the file into memory fast enough to keep up with the program, the program will always find its data in memory and never have a cache miss.

9.5.4   Least Recently Used (LRU)

One way to predict the future is to look at the past. If programs exhibit temporal locality, the locations they reference in the future are likely to be the same as the ones they have referenced in the recent past.

A replacement policy that captures this effect is to evict the block that has not been used for the longest period of time, or the least recently used (LRU) block. In software, LRU is simple to implement: on every cache hit, you move the block to the front of the list, and on a cache miss, you evict the block at the end of the list. In hardware, keeping a linked list of cached blocks is too complex to implement at high speed; instead, we need to approximate LRU, and we will discuss exactly how in a bit.

In some cases, LRU can be optimal, as in the example in Figure 9.14. The

LRU															
Reference	A	B	C	D	E	A	B	C	D	E	A	B	C	D	E
1	A				E				D				C		
2		B				A				E				D	
3			C				B				A				E
4				D				C				B			

MIN															
1	A					+					+			+	
2		B					+					+	C		
3			C					+	D					+	
4				D	E					+					+

Figure 9.15: Cache behavior for LRU (top) and MIN (bottom) for a reference pattern that repeatedly scans through memory. Each row represents the contents of a page frame or cache block; + indicates a cache hit. On this reference pattern, LRU is the same as FIFO, with a cache miss on every reference; the optimal strategy is to replace the most recently used page, as that will be referenced farthest into the future.

table illustrates a reference pattern that exhibits a high degree of temporal locality; when recent references are more likely to be referenced in the near future, LRU can outperform FIFO.

On this particular sequence of references, LRU behaves similarly to the optimal strategy MIN, but that will not always be the case. In fact, LRU can sometimes be the worst possible cache replacement policy. This occurs whenever the least recently used block is the next one to be referenced. A common situation where LRU is pessimal is when the program makes repeated scans through memory, illustrated in Figure 9.15; we saw earlier that FIFO is also pessimal for this reference pattern. The best possible strategy is to replace the most recently referenced block, as this block will be used farthest into the future.

9.5.5 Least Frequently Used (LFU)

Consider again the case of a web proxy cache. Whenever a user accesses a page, it is more likely for that user to access other nearby pages (spatial locality); sometimes, as with a flash crowd, it can be more likely for other users to access the same page (temporal locality). On the surface, Least Recently Used seems like a good fit for this workload.

However, when a user visits a rarely used page, LRU will treat the page as important, even though it is probably just a one-off. When I do a Google search for a mountain hut for a stay in Western Iceland, the web pages I visit will not suddenly become more popular than the latest Facebook update from Katy Perry.

A better strategy for references that follow a Zipf distribution is Least Frequently Used (LFU). LFU discards the block that has been used least often;

Replacement policy and file size

Our discussion up to now has assumed that all cached items are equal, both in size and in cost to replace. When these assumptions do not hold, however, we may sometimes want to vary the policy from LFU or LFU, that is, to keep some items that are less frequently or less recently used ahead of others that are more frequently or more recently used.

For example, consider a web proxy that caches files to improve web responsiveness. These files may have vastly different sizes. When making room for a new file, we have a choice between evicting one very large web page object or a much larger number of smaller objects. Even if each small file is less frequently used than the large file, it may still make sense to keep the small files. In aggregate they may be more frequently used, and therefore they may have a larger benefit to overall system performance. Likewise, if a cached item is expensive to regenerate, it is more important to keep cached than one that is more easily replaced.

Parallel computing makes the calculus even more complex. The performance of a parallel program depends on its critical path — the minimum sequence of steps for the program to produce its result. Cache misses that occur on the critical path affect the response time while those that occur off the critical path do not. For example, a parallel MapReduce job forks a set of tasks onto processors; each task reads in a file and produces an output. Because MapReduce must wait until all tasks are complete before moving onto the next step, if any file is not cached it is as bad as if all of the needed files were not cached.

it therefore keeps popular pages, even when less popular pages have been touched more recently.

LRU and LFU both attempt to predict future behavior, and they have complementary strengths. Many systems meld the two approaches to gain the benefits of each. LRU is better at keeping the current working set in memory; once the working set is taken care of, however, LRU will yield diminishing returns. Instead, LFU may be better at predicting what files or memory blocks will be needed in the more distant future, e.g., after the next working set phase change.

9.5.6   Belady's Anomaly

Intuitively, it seems like it should always help to add space to a memory cache; being able to store more blocks should always either improve the cache hit rate, or at least, not make the cache hit rate any worse. For many cache replacement strategies, this intuition is true. However, in some cases, adding space to a cache can actually hurt the cache hit rate. This is called *Belady's anomaly*, after the person that discovered it.

Belady's anomaly

	FIFO (3 slots)											
Reference	A	B	C	D	A	B	E	A	B	C	D	E
1	A			D			E					+
2		B			A			+		C		
3			C			B			+		D	

	FIFO (4 slots)											
1	A				+		E				D	
2		B				+		A				E
3			C						B			
4				D						C		

Figure 9.16: Cache behavior for FIFO with two different cache sizes, illustrating Belady's anomaly. For this sequence of references, the larger cache suffers ten cache misses, while the smaller cache has one fewer.

First, we note that many of the schemes we have defined can be proven to yield no worse cache behavior with larger cache sizes. For example, with the optimal strategy MIN, if we have a cache of size k blocks, we will keep the next k blocks that will be referenced. If we have a cache of size $k + 1$ blocks, we will keep all of the same blocks as with a k sized cache, plus the additional block that will be the $k + 1$ next reference.

We can make a similar argument for LRU and LFU. For LRU, a cache of size $k + 1$ keeps all of the same blocks as a k sized cache, plus the block that is referenced farthest in the past. Even if LRU is a lousy replacement policy — if it rarely keeps the blocks that will be used in the near future — it will always do at least as well as a slightly smaller cache also using the same replacement policy. An equivalent argument can be used for LFU.

Some replacement policies, however, do not have this behavior. Instead, the contents of a cache with $k + 1$ blocks may be completely different than the contents of a cache with k blocks. As a result, there cache hit rates may diverge. Among the policies we have discussed, FIFO suffers from Belady's anomaly, and we illustrate that in Figure 9.16.

9.6 | Case Study: Memory-Mapped Files

demand paging

To illustrate the concepts presented in this chapter, we consider in detail how an operating system can implement *demand paging*. With demand paging, applications can access more memory than is physically present on the machine, by using memory pages as a cache for disk blocks. When the application accesses a missing memory page, it is transparently brought in from disk. We start with the simpler case of a demand paging for a single, memory-mapped file and then extend the discussion to managing multiple processes competing for space in main memory.

As we discussed in Chapter 3, most programs use explicit read/write system calls to perform file I/O. Read/write system calls allow the program to work on a *copy* of file data. The program opens a file and then invokes the system call read to copy chunks of file data into buffers in the program's address space. The program can then use and modify those chunks, without affecting the underlying file. For example, it can convert the file from the disk format into a more convenient in-memory format. To write changes back to the file, the program invokes the system call write to copy the data from the program buffers out to disk. Reading and writing files via system calls is simple to understand reasonably efficient for small files.

memory-mapped file

An alternative model for file I/O is to map the file contents into the program's virtual address space. For a *memory-mapped file*, the operating system provides the illusion that the file is a program segment; like any memory segment, the program can directly issue instructions to load and store values to the memory. Unlike file read/write, the load and store instructions do not operate on a copy; they directly access and modify the contents of the file, treating memory as a write-back cache for disk.

We saw an example of a memory-mapped file in the previous chapter: the program executable image. To start a process, the operating system brings the executable image into memory, and creates page table entries to point to the page frames allocated to the executable. The operating system can start the program executing as soon as the first page frame is initialized, without waiting for the other pages to be brought in from disk. For this, the other page table entries are set to invalid — if the process accesses a page that has not reached memory yet, the hardware traps to the operating system and then waits until the page is available so it can continue to execute. From the program's perspective, there is no difference (except for performance) between whether the executable image is entirely in memory or still mostly on disk.

We can generalize this concept to any file stored on disk, allowing applications to treat any file as part of its virtual address space. File blocks are brought in by the operating system when they are referenced, and modified blocks are copied back to disk, with the bookkeeping done entirely by the operating system.

9.6.1   Advantages

Memory-mapped files offer a number of advantages:

- **Transparency.** The program can operate on the bytes in the file as if they are part of memory; specifically, the program can use a pointer into the file without needing to check if that portion of the file is in memory or not.

- **Zero copy I/O.** The operating system does not need to copy file data from kernel buffers into user memory and back; rather, it just changes the program's page table entry to point to the physical page frame containing that portion of the file. The kernel is responsible for copying data back and forth to disk. We should note that it is possible to implement zero copy I/O for explicit read/write file system calls in certain restricted cases; we will explain how in the next chapter.

- **Pipelining.** The program can start operating on the data in the file as soon as the page tables have been set up; it does not need to wait for the entire file to be read into memory. With multiple threads, a program can use explicit read/write calls to pipeline disk I/O, but it needs to manage the pipeline itself.

- **Interprocess communication.** Two or more processes can share information instantaneously through a memory-mapped file without needing to shuffle data back and forth to the kernel or to disk. If the hardware architecture supports it, the page table for the shared segment can also be shared.

- **Large files.** As long as the page table for the file can fit in physical memory, the only limit on the size of a memory-mapped file is the size of the virtual address space. For example, an application may have a giant multi-level tree indexing data spread across a number of disks in a data center. With read/write system calls, the application needs to explicitly manage which parts of the tree are kept in memory and which are on disk; alternatively, with memory-mapped files, the application can leave that bookkeeping to the operating system.

9.6.2   Implementation

To implement memory-mapped files, the operating system provides a system call to map the file into a portion of the virtual address space. In the system call, the kernel initializes a set of page table entries for that region of the virtual address space, setting each entry to invalid. The kernel then returns to the user process.

When the process issues an instruction that touches an invalid mapped address, a sequence of events occurs, illustrated in Figures 9.17 and 9.18:

- **TLB miss.** The hardware looks the virtual page up in the TLB, and finds that there is not a valid entry. This triggers a full page table lookup in hardware.

page fault
- **Page table exception.** The hardware walks the multi-level page table and finds the page table entry is invalid. This causes a hardware *page fault* exception trap into the operating system kernel.

- **Convert virtual address to file offset.** In the exception handler, the kernel looks up in its segment table to find the file corresponding to the faulting virtual address and converts the address to a file offset.

Figure 9.17: Before a page fault, the page table has an invalid entry for the referenced page and the data for the page is stored on disk.

Figure 9.18: After the page fault, the page table has a valid entry for the referenced page with the page frame containing the data that had been stored on disk. The old contents of the page frame are stored on disk and the page table entry that previously pointed to the page frame is set to invalid.

- **Disk block read.** The kernel allocates an empty page frame and issues a disk operation to read the required file block into the allocated page frame. While the disk operation is in progress, the processor can be used for running other threads or processes.

- **Disk interrupt.** The disk interrupts the processor when the disk read finishes, and the scheduler resumes the kernel thread handling the page fault exception.

- **Page table update.** The kernel updates the page table entry to point to the page frame allocated for the block and sets the entry to valid.

- **Resume process.** The operating system resumes execution of the process at the instruction that caused the exception.

- **TLB miss.** The TLB still does not contain a valid entry for the page, triggering a full page table lookup.

- **Page table fetch.** The hardware walks the multi-level page table, finds the page table entry valid, and returns the page frame to the processor. The processor loads the TLB with the new translation, evicting a previous TLB entry, and then uses the translation to construct a physical address for the instruction.

To make this work, we need an empty page frame to hold the incoming page from disk. To create an empty page frame, the operating system must:

- **Select a page to evict.** Assuming there is not an empty page of memory already available, the operating system needs to select some page to be replaced. We discuss how to implement this selection in Section 9.6.3 below.

- **Find page table entries that point to the evicted page.** The operating system then locates the set of page table entries that point to the page to be
core map
    replaced. It can do this with a *core map* — an array of information about each physical page frame, including which page table entries contain pointers to that particular page frame.

- **Set each page table entry to invalid.** The operating system needs to prevent anyone from using the evicted page while the new page is being brought into memory. Because the processor can continue to execute while the disk read is in progress, the page frame may temporarily contain a mixture of bytes from the old and the new page. Therefore, because the TLB may cache a copy of the old page table entry, a TLB shootdown is needed to evict the old translation from the TLB.

- **Copy back any changes to the evicted page.** If the evicted page was modified, the contents of the page must be copied back to disk before the new page can be brought into memory. Likewise, the contents of modified pages must also be copied back when the application closes the memory-mapped file.

How does the operating system know which pages have been modified? A correct, but inefficient, solution is to simply assume that every page in a memory-mapped file has been modified; if the data has not been changed, the operating system will have wasted some work, but the contents of the file will not be affected.

A more efficient solution is for the hardware to keep track of which pages have been modified. Most processor architectures reserve a bit in each page
dirty bit
    table entry to record whether the page has been modified. This is called a *dirty*

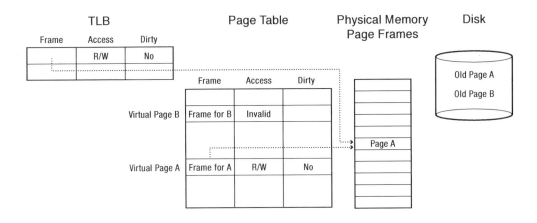

Figure 9.19: When a page is clean, its dirty bit is set to zero in both the TLB and the page table, and the data in memory is the same as the data stored on disk.

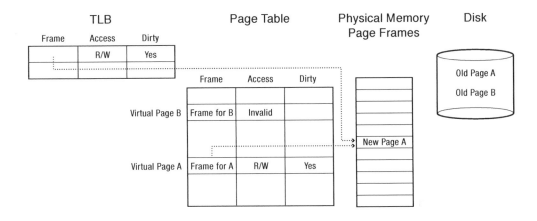

Figure 9.20: On the first store instruction to a clean page, the hardware sets the dirty bit for that page in the TLB and the page table. The contents of the page will differ from what is stored on disk.

bit. The operating system initializes the bit to zero, and the hardware sets the bit automatically when it executes a store instruction for that virtual page. Since the TLB can contain a copy of the page table entry, the TLB also needs a dirty bit per entry. The hardware can ignore the dirty bit if it is set in the TLB, but whenever it goes from zero to one, the hardware needs to copy the bit back to the corresponding page table entry. Figures 9.19 and 9.20 show the state of the TLB, page table, memory and disk before and after the first store instruction to a page.

If there are multiple page table entries pointing at the same physical page frame, the page is dirty (and must be copied back to disk) if *any* of the page

Emulating a hardware dirty bit in software

Interestingly, hardware support for a dirty bit is not strictly required. The operating system can emulate a hardware dirty bit using page table access permissions. An unmodified page is set to allow only read-only access, even though the program is logically allowed to write the page. The program can then execute normally. On a store instruction to the page, the hardware will trigger a memory exception. The operating system can then record the fact that the page is dirty, upgrade the page protection to read-write, and restart the process.

To clean a page in the background, the kernel resets the page protection to read-only and does a TLB shootdown. The shootdown removes any translation that allows for read-write access to the page, forcing subsequent store instructions to cause another memory exception.

---

tables have the dirty bit set. Normally, of course, a memory-mapped file will have a single page table shared between all of the processes mapping the file.

Because evicting a dirty page takes more time than evicting a clean page, the operating system can proactively clean pages in the background. A thread runs in the background, looking for pages that are likely candidates for being evicted if they were clean. If the hardware dirty bit is set in the page table entry, the kernel resets the bit in the page table entry and does a TLB shootdown to remove the entry from the TLB (with the old value of the dirty bit). It then copies the page to disk. Of course, the on-chip processor memory cache and write buffers can contain modifications to the page that have not reached main memory; the hardware ensures that the new data reaches main memory before those bytes are copied to the disk interface.

The kernel can then restart the application; it need not wait for the block to reach disk — if the process modifies the page again, the hardware will simply reset the dirty bit, signaling that the block cannot be reclaimed without saving the new set of changes to disk.

9.6.3 Approximating LRU

A further challenge to implementing demand paged memory-mapped files is that the hardware does not keep track of which pages are least recently or least frequently used. Doing so would require the hardware to keep a linked list of every page in memory, and to modify that list on every load and store instruction (and for memory-mapped executable images, every instruction fetch as well). This would be prohibitively expensive. Instead, the hardware maintains a minimal amount of access information per page to allow the operating system to approximate LRU or LFU if it wants to do so.

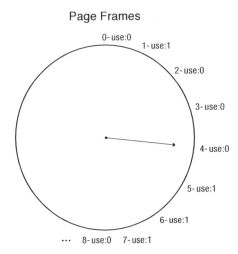

Page Frames

Figure 9.21: The clock algorithm sweeps through each page frame, collecting the current value of the use bit for that page and resetting the use bit to zero. The clock algorithm stops when it has reclaimed a sufficient number of unused page frames.

We should note that explicit read/write file system calls do not have this problem. Each time a process reads or writes a file block, the operating system can keep track of which blocks are used. The kernel can use this information to prioritize its cache of file blocks when the system needs to find space for a new block.

use bit   Most processor architectures keep a *use bit* in each page table entry, next to the hardware dirty bit we discussed above. The operating system clears the use bit when the page table entry is initialized; the bit is set in hardware whenever the page table entry is brought into the TLB. As with the dirty bit, a physical page is used if *any* of the page table entries have their use bit set.

The operating system can leverage the use bit in various ways, but **clock algorithm** commonly used approach is the *clock algorithm*, illustrated in Figure 9.21. Periodically, the operating system scans through the core map of physical memory pages. For each page frame, it records the value of the use bit in the page table entries that point to that frame, and then clears their use bits. Because the TLB can have a cached copy of the translation, the operating system also does a shootdown for any page table entry where the use bit is cleared. Note that if the use bit is already zero, the translation cannot be in the TLB. While it is scanning, the kernel can also look for dirty and recently unused pages and flush these out to disk.

Each sweep of the clock algorithm through memory collects one bit of information about page usage; by adjusting the frequency of the clock algorithm, we can collect increasingly fine-grained information about usage, at the cost of increased software overhead. On modern systems with hundreds of

Emulating a hardware use bit in software

Hardware support for a use bit is also not strictly required. The operating system kernel can emulate a use bit with page table permissions, in the same way that the kernel can emulate a hardware dirty bit. To collect usage information about a page, the kernel sets the page table entry to be invalid even though the page is in memory and the application has permission to access the page. When the page is accessed, the hardware will trigger an exception and the operating system can record the use of the page. The kernel then changes the permission on the page to allow access, before restarting the process. To collect usage information over time, the operating system can periodically reset the page table entry to invalid and shootdown any cached translations in the TLB.

Many systems use a hybrid approach. In addition to active pages where the hardware collects the use bit, the operating system maintains a pool of unused, clean page frames that are unmapped in any virtual address space, but still contain their old data. When a new page frame is needed, pages in this pool can be used without any further work. However, if the old data is referenced before the page frame is reused, the page can be pulled out of the pool and mapped back into the virtual address space.

Systems with a software-managed TLB have an even simpler time. Each time there is a TLB miss with a software-managed TLB, there is a trap to the kernel to look up the translation. During the trap, the kernel can update its list of frequently used pages.

---

thousands and sometimes millions of physical page frames, the overhead of the clock algorithm can be substantial.

not recently used

The policy for what to do with the usage information is up to the operating system kernel. A common policy is called *not recently used*, or k'th chance. If the operating system needs to evict a page, the kernel picks one that has not been used (has not had its use bit set) for the last k sweeps of the clock algorithm. The clock algorithm partitions pages based on how recently they have been used; among page frames in the same k'th chance partition, the operating system can evict pages in FIFO order.

Some systems trigger the clock algorithm only when a page is needed, rather than periodically in the background. Provided some pages have not been accessed since the last sweep, an on-demand clock algorithm will find a page to reclaim. If all pages have been accessed, e.g., if there is a storm of page faults due to phase change behavior, then the system will default to FIFO.

9.7 | Case Study: Virtual Memory

We can generalize on the concept of memory-mapped files, by backing *every* memory segment with a file on disk. This is called *virtual memory*. Program executables, individual libraries, data, stack and heap segments can all be demand paged to disk. Unlike memory-mapped files, though, process memory is ephemeral: when the process exits, there is no need to write modified data back to disk, and we can reclaim the disk space.

The advantage of virtual memory is flexibility. The system can continue to function even though the user has started more processes than can fit in main memory at the same time. The operating system simply makes room for the new processes by paging the memory of idle applications to disk. Without virtual memory, the user has to do memory management by hand, closing some applications to make room for others.

All of the mechanisms we have described for memory-mapped files apply when we generalize to virtual memory, with one additional twist. We need to balance the allocation of physical page frames between processes. Unfortunately, this balancing is quite tricky. If we add a few extra page faults to a system, no one will notice. However, a modern disk can handle at most 100 page faults per second, while a modern multi-core processor can execute 10 billion instructions per second. Thus, if page faults are anything but extremely rare, performance will suffer.

9.7.1 Self-Paging

One consideration is that the behavior of one process can significantly hurt the performance of other programs running at the same time. For example, suppose we have two processes. One is a normal program, with a working set equal to say, a quarter of physical memory. The other program is greedy; while it can run fine with less memory, it will run faster if it is given more memory. We gave an example of this earlier with the sort program.

Can you design a program to take advantage of the clock algorithm to acquire more than its fair share of memory pages?

We give an example in Figure 9.22, which we will dub "pig" for obvious reasons. It allocates an array in virtual memory equal in size to physical memory; it then uses multiple threads to cycle through memory, causing each page to be brought in while the other pages remain very recently used.

A normal program sharing memory with the pig will eventually be frozen out of memory and stop making progress. When the pig touches a new page, it triggers a page fault, but all of its pages are recently used because of the background thread. Meanwhile, the normal program will have recently touched many of its pages but there will be some that are less recently used. The clock algorithm will choose those for replacement.

As time goes on, more and more of the pages will be allocated to the pig. As the number of pages assigned to the normal program drops, it starts

```
static char *workingSet;        // The memory this program wants to acquire.
static int soFar;               // How many pages the program has so far.
static sthread_t refreshThread;

// This thread touches the pages we have in memory, to keep them recently used.
void refresh () {
    int i;

    while (1) {
        // Keep every page in memory recently used.
        for (i = 0; i < soFar; i += PAGESIZE)
            workingSet[i] = 0;
    }
}

int main (int argc, char **argv) {
    // Allocate a giant array.
    workingSet = malloc(ARRAYSIZE);
    soFar = 0;

    // Create a thread to keep our pages in memory, once they get there.
    thread_create(&refreshThread, refresh, 0);

    // Touch every page to bring it into memory.
    for (; soFar < ARRAYSIZE; soFar += PAGESIZE)
        workingSet[soFar] = 0;

    // Now that everything is in memory, run computation.
    // ...
}
```

Figure 9.22: The "pig" program to greedily acquire memory pages. The implementation assumes we are running on a multicore computer. When the pig triggers a page fault by touching a new memory page (soFar), the operating system will find all of the pig's pages up to soFar recently used. The operating system will keep these in memory and it will choose to evict a page from some other application.

experiencing page faults at an increasing frequency. Eventually, the number of pages drops below the working set, at which point the program stops making much progress. Its pages are even less frequently used, making them easier to evict.

Of course, a normal user would probably never run (or write!) a program like this, but a malicious attacker launching a computer virus might use this approach to freeze out the system administrator. Likewise, in a data center setting, a single server can be shared between multiple applications from different users, for example, running in different virtual machines. It is in the interest of any single application to acquire as many physical resources as possible, even if that hurts performance for other users.

self-paging   A widely adopted solution is *self-paging*. With self-paging, each process or user is assigned its fair share of page frames, using the max-min scheduling algorithm we described in Chapter 7. If all of the active processes can fit in memory at the same time, the system does not need to page. As the system starts to page, it evicts the page from whichever process has the most allocated to it. Thus, the pig would only be able to allocate its fair share of page frames, and beyond that any page faults it triggers would evict its own pages.

Unfortunately, self-paging comes at a cost in reduced resource utilization. Suppose we have two processes, both of which allocate large amounts of virtual address space. However, the working sets of the two programs can fit in memory at the same time, for example, if one working set takes up 2/3rds of memory and the other takes up 1/3rd. If they cooperate, both can run efficiently because the system has room for both working sets. However, if we need to bulletproof the operating system against malicious programs by self-paging, then each will be assigned half of memory and the larger program will thrash.

9.7.2 Swapping

Another issue is what happens as we increase the workload for a system with virtual memory. If we are running a data center, for example, we can share physical machines among a much larger number of applications each running in a separate virtual machine. To reduce costs, the data center needs to support the maximum number of applications on each server, within some performance constraint.

If the working sets of the applications easily fit in memory, then as page faults occur, the clock algorithm will find lightly used pages — that is, those outside of the working set of any process — to evict to make room for new pages. So far so good. As we keep adding active processes, however, their working sets may no longer fit, even if each process is given their fair share of memory. In this case, the performance of the system will degrade dramatically.

This can be illustrated by considering how system throughput is affected by the number of processes. As we add work to the system, throughput increases as long as there is enough processing capacity and I/O bandwidth. When we reach the point where there are too many tasks to fit entirely in memory, the system starts demand paging. Throughput can continue to improve if there are enough lightly used pages to make room for new tasks, but eventually throughput levels off and then falls off a cliff. In the limit, every instruction will trigger a page fault, meaning that the processor executes at 100 instructions per second, rather than 10 billion instructions per second. Needless to say, the user will think the system is dead even if it is in fact inching forward very slowly.

As we explained in the Chapter 7 discussion on overload control, the only way to achieve good performance in this case is to prevent the overload condition from occurring. Both response time and throughput will be better if we prevent additional tasks from starting or if we remove some existing tasks. It is better to completely starve some tasks of their resources, if the alternative, assigning each task their fair share, will drag the system to a halt.

swapping Evicting an entire process from memory is called *swapping*. When there is too much paging activity, the operating system can prevent a catastrophic degradation in performance by moving *all* of the page frames of a particular process to disk, preventing it from running at all. Although this may seem terribly unfair, the alternative is that *every* process, not just the swapped process, will run much more slowly. By distributing the swapped process's pages to other processes, we can reduce the number of page faults, allowing system performance to recover. Eventually the other tasks will finish, and we can bring the swapped process back into memory.

9.8 | Summary and Future Directions

Caching is central to many areas of computer science: caches are used in processor design, file systems, web browsers, web servers, compilers, and kernel memory management, to name a few. To understand these systems, it is important to understand how caches work, and even more importantly, when they fail.

The management of memory in operating systems is a particularly useful case study. Every major commercial operating system includes support for demand paging of memory, using memory as a cache for disk. Often, application memory pages and blocks in the file buffer are allocated from a common pool of memory, where the operating system attempts to keep blocks that are likely to be used in memory and evicting those blocks that are less likely to be used. However, on modern systems, the difference between finding a block in memory and needing to bring it in from disk can be as much as a factor of 100,000. This makes virtual memory paging fragile, acceptable only when used in small doses.

Moving forward, several trends are in progress:

- **Low latency backing store.** Due to the weight and power drain of magnetic disks, many portable devices have moved to solid state persistent storage, such as non-volatile RAM. Current solid state storage devices have significantly lower latency than disk, and even faster devices are likely in the future. Similarly, the move towards data center computing has added a new option to memory management: using DRAM on other nodes in the data center as a low-latency, very high capacity backing store for local memory. Both of these trends reduce the cost of paging, making it relatively more attractive.

- **Variable page sizes.** Many systems use a standard 4 KB page size, but there is nothing fundamental about that choice — it is a tradeoff chosen to balance internal fragmentation, page table overhead, disk latency, the overhead of collecting dirty and usage bits, and application spatial locality. On modern disks, it only takes twice as long to transfer 256 contiguous pages as it does to transfer one, so internally, most operating systems arrange disk transfers to include many blocks at a time. With new technologies such as low latency solid state storage and cluster memory, this balance may shift back towards smaller effective page sizes.

- **Memory aware applications.** The increasing depth and complexity of the memory hierarchy is both a boon and a curse. For many applications, the memory hierarchy delivers reasonable performance without any special effort. However, the wide gulf in performance between the first level cache and main memory, and between main memory and disk, implies that there is a significant performance benefit to tuning applications to the available memory. The poses a particular challenge for operating systems to adapt to applications that are adapting to their physical resources.

Exercises

1. A computer system has a 1 KB page size and keeps the page table for each process in main memory. Because the page table entries are usually cached on chip, the average overhead for doing a full page table lookup is 40 ns. To reduce this overhead, the computer has a 32-entry TLB. A TLB lookup requires 1 ns. What TLB hit rate is required to ensure an average virtual address translation time of 2 ns?

2. Most modern computer systems choose a page size of 4 KB.

    a) Give a set of reasons why doubling the page size might increase performance.

    b) Give a set of reasons why doubling the page size might decrease performance.

3. For each of the following statements, indicate whether the statement is true or false, and explain why.

    a) A direct mapped cache can sometimes have a higher hit rate than a fully associative cache (on the same reference pattern).

    b) Adding a cache never hurts performance.

4. Suppose an application is assigned 4 pages of physical memory and the memory is initially empty. It then references pages in the following sequence:

    ACBDBAEFBFAGEFA

    a) Show how the system would fault pages into the four frames of physical memory, using the LRU replacement policy.

    b) Show how the system would fault pages into the four frames of physical memory, using the MIN replacement policy.

    c) Show how the system would fault pages into the four frames of physical memory, using the clock replacement policy.

5. Is least recently used a good cache replacement algorithm to use for a workload following a zipf distribution? Briefly explain why or why not.

6. Briefly explain how to simulate a modify bit per page for the page replacement algorithm if the hardware does not provide one.

7. Suppose we have four programs:

    a) One exhibits both spatial and temporal locality.

    b) One touches each page sequentially, and then repeats the scan in a loop.

    c) One references pages according to a Zipf distribution (e.g., it is a web server and its memory consists of cached web pages).

    d) One generates memory references completely at random using a uniform random number generator.

    All four programs use the same total amount of virtual memory — that is, they both touch N distinct virtual pages, amongst a much larger number of total references.

    For each program, sketch a graph showing the rate of progress (instructions per unit time) of each program as a function of the physical memory available to the program, from 0 to N, assuming the page replacement algorithm approximates least recently used.

8. Suppose a program repeatedly scans linearly through a large array in virtual memory. In other words, if the array is four pages long, its page reference pattern is ABCDABCDABCD...

    For each of the following page replacement algorithms, sketch a graph showing the rate of progress (instructions per unit time) of each program as a function of the physical memory available to the program, from 0 to N, where N is sufficient to hold the entire array.

    a) FIFO

    b) Least recently used

    c) Clock algorithm

    d) Nth chance algorithm

    e) MIN

9. Consider a computer system running a general-purpose workload with demand paging. The system has two disks, one for demand paging and one for file system operations. Measured utilizations (in terms of time, not space) are given in Figure 9.23.

    For each of the following changes, say what its likely impact will be on processor utilization, and explain why. Is it likely to significantly increase, marginally increase, significantly decrease, marginally decrease, or have no effect on the processor utilization?

Processor utilization	20.0%
Paging Disk	99.7%
File Disk	10.0%
Network	5.0%

Figure 9.23: Measured utilizations for sample system under consideration.

a) Get a faster CPU

b) Get a faster paging disk

c) Increase the degree of multiprogramming

10. An operating system with a physically addressed cache uses page coloring to more

   a) How many page colors are needed to fully utilize a physically addressed cache, with 1 TB of main memory, an 8 MB cache with 4-way set associativity, and a 4 KB page size?

   b) Develop an algebraic formula to compute the number of page colors needed for an arbitrary configuration of cache size, set associativity, and page size.

11. The sequence of virtual pages referenced by a program has length p with n distinct page numbers occurring in it. Let m be the number of page frames that are allocated to the process (all the page frames are initially empty). Let $n > m$.

   a) What is the lower bound on the number of page faults?

   b) What is the upper bound on the number of page faults?

   The lower/upper bound should be for any page replacement policy.

12. You have decided to splurge on a low end netbook for doing your operating systems homework during lectures in your non-computer science classes. The netbook has a single-level TLB and a single-level, physically addressed cache. It also has two levels of page tables, and the operating system does demand paging to disk.

   The netbook comes in various configurations, and you want to make sure the configuration you purchase is fast enough to run your applications. To get a handle on this, you decide to measure its cache, TLB and paging performance running your applications in a virtual machine. Figure 9.24 lists what you discover for your workload.

   The TLB is refilled automatically by the hardware on a TLB miss. The page tables are kept in physical memory and are not cached, so looking up a page table entry incurs two memory accesses (one for each level of the page table). You may assume the operating system keeps a pool of

Measurement	Value
$P_{CacheMiss}$ = probability of a cache miss	0.01
$P_{TLBmiss}$ = probability of a TLB miss	0.01
P_{fault} = probability of a page fault, given a TLB miss occurs	0.00002
T_{cache} = time to access cache	$1\,ns = 0.001\,\mu s$
T_{TLB} = time to access TLB	$1\,ns = 0.001\,\mu s$
T_{DRAM} = time to access main memory	$100\,ns = 0.1\,\mu s$
T_{disk} = time to transfer a page to/from disk	$10^7\,ns = 10\,ms$

Figure 9.24: Sample measurements of cache behavior on the low-end netbook described in the exercises.

clean pages, so pages do not need to be written back to disk on a page fault.

a) What is the average memory access time (the time for an application program to do one memory reference) on the netbook? Express your answer algebraically and compute the result to two significant digits.

b) The netbook has a few optional performance enhancements:

Item	Specs	Price
Faster disk drive	Transfers a page in 7 ms	$100
500 MB more DRAM	Makes probability of a page fault 0.00001	$100
Faster network card	Allows paging to remote memory.	$100

With the faster network card, the time to access remote memory is 500 ms, and the probability of a remote memory miss (need to go to disk), given there is a page fault is 0.5.

Suppose you have $200. What options should you buy to maximize the performance of the netbook for this workload?

13. On a computer with virtual memory, suppose a program repeatedly scans through a very large array. In other words, if the array is four pages long, its page reference pattern is ABCDABCDABCD...

Sketch a graph showing the paging behavior, for each of the following page replacement algorithms. The y-axis of the graph is the number of page faults per referenced page, varying from 0 to 1; the x-axis is the size of the array being scanned, varying from smaller than physical memory to much larger than physical memory. Label any interesting points on the graph on both the x and y axes.

a) FIFO

b) LRU

      c) Clock

      d) MIN

14. Consider two programs, one that exhibits spatial and temporal locality, and the other that exhibits neither. To make the comparison fair, they both use the same total amount of virtual memory — that is, they both touch N distinct virtual pages, among a much larger number of total references.

    Sketch graphs showing the rate of progress (instructions per unit time) of each program as a function of the physical memory available to the program, from 0 to N, assuming the clock algorithm is used for page replacement.

    a) Program exhibiting locality, running by itself

    b) Program exhibiting no locality, running by itself

    c) Program exhibiting locality, running with the program exhibiting no locality (assume both have the same value for N).

    d) Program exhibiting no locality, running with the program exhibiting locality (assume both have the same N).

15. Suppose we are using the clock algorithm to decide page replacement, in its simplest form ("first-chance" replacement, where the clock is only advanced on a page fault and not in the background).

    A crucial issue in the clock algorithm is how many page frames must be considered in order to find a page to replace. Assuming we have a sequence of F page faults in a system with P page frames, let $C(F, P)$ be the number of pages considered for replacement in handling the F page faults (if the clock hand sweeps by a page frame multiple times, it is counted each time).

    a) Give an algebraic formula for the minimum possible value of $C(F, P)$.

    b) Give an algebraic formula for the maximum possible value of $C(F, P)$.

All problems in computer science can be solved by another level of indirection.

David Wheeler

10 Advanced Memory Management

At an abstract level, an operating system provides an execution context for application processes, consisting of limits on privileged instructions, the process's memory regions, a set of system calls, and some way for the operating system to periodically regain control of the processor. By interposing on that interface — most commonly, by catching and transforming system calls or memory references — the operating system can transparently insert new functionality to improve system performance, reliability, and security.

Interposing on system calls is straightforward. The kernel uses a table lookup to determine which routine to call for each system call invoked by the application program. The kernel can redirect a system call to a new enhanced routine by simply changing the table entry.

A more interesting case is the memory system. Address translation hardware provides an efficient way for the operating system to monitor and gain control on every memory reference to a specific region of memory, while allowing other memory references to continue unaffected. (Equivalently, software-based fault isolation provides many of the same hooks, with different tradeoffs between interposition and execution speed.) This makes address translation a powerful tool for operating systems to introduce new, advanced services to applications. We have already shown how to use address translation for:

- **Protection.** Operating systems use address translation hardware, along with segment and page table permissions, to restrict access by applications to privileged memory locations such as those in the kernel.

- **Fill-on-demand/zero-on-demand.** By setting some page table permissions to invalid, the kernel can start executing a process before all of its code

465

and data has been loaded into memory; the hardware will trap to the kernel if the process references data before it is ready. Similarly, the kernel can zero data and heap pages in the background, relying on page reference faults to catch the first time an application uses an empty page. The kernel can also allocate memory for kernel and user stacks only as needed. By marking unused stack pages as invalid, the kernel needs to allocate those pages only if the program executes a deep procedure call chain.

- **Copy-on-write.** Copy-on-write allows multiple processes to have logically separate copies of the same memory region, backed by a single physical copy in memory. Each page in the region is mapped read-only in each process; the operating system makes a physical copy only when (and if) a page is modified.

- **Memory-mapped files.** Disk files can be made part of a process's virtual address space, allowing the process to access the data in the file using normal processor instructions. When a page from a memory-mapped file is first accessed, a protection fault traps to the operating system so that it can bring the page into memory from disk. The first write to a file block can also be caught, marking the block as needing to be written back to disk.

- **Demand paged virtual memory.** The operating system can run programs that use more memory than is physically present on the computer, by catching references to pages that are not physically present and filling them from disk or cluster memory.

In this chapter, we explore how to construct a number of other advanced operating system services by catching and re-interpreting memory references and system calls.

Chapter roadmap:

- **Zero-Copy I/O.** How do we improve the performance of transferring blocks of data between user-level programs and hardware devices? (Section 10.1)

- **Virtual Machines.** How do we execute an operating system on top of another operating system, and how can we use that abstraction to introduce new operating system services? (Section 10.2)

- **Fault Tolerance.** How can we make applications resilient to machine crashes? (Section 10.3)

- **Security.** How can we contain malicious applications that can exploit unknown faults inside the operating system? (Section 10.4)

- **User-Level Memory Management.** How do we give applications control over how their memory is managed? (Section 10.5)

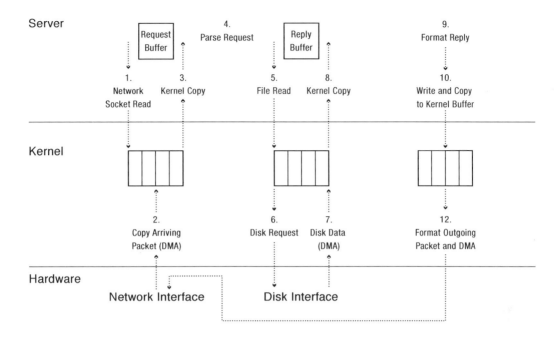

Figure 10.1: A web server gets a request from the network. The server first asks the kernel to copy the requested file from disk or its file buffer into the server's address space. The server then asks the kernel to copy the contents of the file back out to the network.

10.1 | Zero-Copy I/O

A common task for operating systems is to stream data between user-level programs and physical devices such as disks and network hardware. However, this streaming can be expensive in processing time if the data is copied as it moves across protection boundaries. A network packet needs to go from the network interface hardware, into kernel memory, and then to user-level; the response needs to go from user-level back into kernel memory and then from kernel memory to the network hardware.

Consider the operation of the web server, as pictured in Figure 10.1. Almost all web servers are implemented as user-level programs. This way, it is easy to reconfigure server behavior, and bugs in the server implementation do not necessarily compromise system security.

A number of steps need to happen for a web server to respond to a web request. For this example, assume that the connection between the client and server is already established, there is a server thread allocated to each client connection, and we use explicit read/write system calls rather than memory mapped files.

- **Server reads from network.** The server thread calls into the kernel to wait for an arriving request.

- **Packet arrival.** The web request arrives from the network; the network hardware uses DMA to copy the packet data into a kernel buffer.

- **Copy packet data to user-level.** The operating system parses the packet header to determine which user process is to receive the web request. The kernel copies the data into the user-level buffer provided by the server thread and returns to user-level.

- **Server reads file.** The server parses the data in the web request to determine which file is requested. It issues a file read system call back to the kernel, providing a user-level buffer to hold the file contents.

- **Data arrival.** The kernel issues the disk request, and the disk controller copies the data from the disk into a kernel buffer. If the file data is already in the file buffer cache, as will often be the case for popular web requests, this step is skipped.

- **Copy file data to user-level.** The kernel copies the data into the buffer provided by the user process and returns to user-level.

- **Server write to network.** The server turns around and hands the buffer containing the file data back to the kernel to send out to the network.

- **Copy data to kernel.** The kernel copies the data from the user-level buffer into a kernel buffer, formats the packet, and issues the request to the network hardware.

- **Data send.** The hardware uses DMA to copy the data from the kernel buffer out to the network.

Although we have illustrated this with a web server, a similar process occurs for any application that streams data in or out of a computer. Examples include a web client, online video or music service, BitTorrent, network file systems, and even a software download. For each of these, data is copied from hardware into the kernel and then into user-space, or vice versa.

We could eliminate the extra copy across the kernel-user boundary by moving each of these applications into the kernel. However, that would be impractical as it would require trusting the applications with the full power of the operating system. Alternately, we could modify the system call interface to allow applications to directly manipulate data stored in a kernel buffer, without first copying it to user memory. However, this is not a general-purpose solution; it would not work if the application needed to do any work on the buffer as opposed to only transferring it from one hardware device to another.

zero-copy I/O   Instead, two solutions to *zero-copy I/O* are used in practice. Both eliminate the copy across the kernel-user boundary for large blocks of data; for small chunks of data, the extra copy does not hurt performance.

The more widely used approach manipulates the process page table to simulate a copy. For this to work, the application must first align its user-level

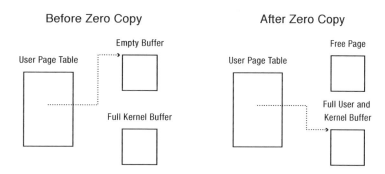

Figure 10.2: The contents of the page table before and after the kernel "copies" data to user-level by swapping the page table entry to point to the kernel buffer.

buffer to a page boundary. The user-level buffer is provided to the kernel on a read or write system call, and its alignment and size is up to the application.

The key idea is that a page-to-page copy from user to kernel space or vice versa can be simulated by changing page table pointers instead of physically copying memory.

For a copy from user-space to the kernel (e.g., on a network or file system write), the kernel changes the permissions on the page table entry for the user-level buffer to prevent it from being modified. The kernel must also *pin* the page to prevent it from being evicted by the virtual memory manager. In the common case, this is enough — the page will not normally be modified while the I/O request is in progress. If the user program does try to modify the page, the program will trap to the kernel and the kernel can make an explicit copy at that point.

In the other direction, once the data is in the kernel buffer, the operating system can simulate a copy up to user-space by switching the pointer in the page table, as shown in Figure 10.2. The process page table originally pointed to the page frame containing the (empty) user buffer; now it points to the page frame containing the (full) kernel buffer. To the user program, the data appears exactly where it was expected! The kernel can reclaim any physical memory behind the empty buffer.

More recently, some hardware I/O devices have been designed to be able to transfer data to and from virtual addresses, rather than only to and from physical addresses. The kernel hands the virtual address of the user-level buffer to the hardware device. The hardware device, rather than the kernel, walks the multi-level page table to determine which physical page frame to use for the device transfer. When the transfer completes, the data is automatically where it belongs, with no extra work by the kernel. This procedure is a bit more complicated for incoming network packets, as the decision as to which process should receive which packet is determined by the contents of the packet header. The network interface hardware therefore has to parse the incoming packet to deliver the data to the appropriate process.

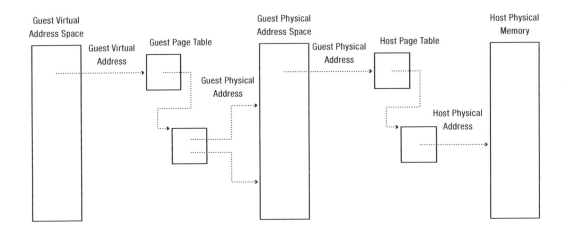

Figure 10.3: A virtual machine typically has two page tables: one to translate from guest process addresses to the guest physical memory, and one to translate from guest physical memory addresses to host physical memory addresses.

10.2 | Virtual Machines

A virtual machine is a way for a host operating system to run a guest operating system as an application process. The host simulates the behavior of a physical machine so that the guest system behaves as if it was running on real hardware. Virtual machines are widely used on client machines to run applications that are not native to the current version of the operating system. They are also widely used in data centers to allow a single physical machine to be shared between multiple independent uses, each of which can be written as if it has system administrator control over the entire (virtual) machine. For example, multiple web servers, representing different web sites, can be hosted on the same physical machine if they each run inside a separate virtual machine.

Address translation throws a wrinkle into the challenge of implementing a virtual machine, but it also opens up opportunities for efficiencies and new services.

10.2.1 Virtual Machine Page Tables

With virtual machines, we have two sets of page tables, instead of one, as shown in Figure 10.3:

- **Guest physical memory to host physical memory.** The host operating system provides a set of page tables to constrain the execution of the guest operating system kernel. The guest kernel thinks it is running on real, physical memory, but in fact its addresses are virtual. The hardware page table translates each guest operating system memory reference into a physical memory location, after checking that the guest has permission to read or write each location. This way the host operating system can prevent bugs in the guest operating system from overwriting memory in the host, exactly as if the guest were a normal user-level process.

- **Guest user memory to guest physical memory.** In turn, the guest operating system manages page tables for its guest processes, exactly as if the guest kernel was running on real hardware. Since the guest kernel does not know anything about the physical page frames it has been assigned by the host kernel, these page tables translate from the guest process addresses to the guest operating system kernel addresses.

First, consider what happens when the host operating system transfers control to the guest kernel. Everything works as expected. The guest operating system can read and write its memory, and the hardware page tables provide the illusion that the guest kernel is running directly on physical memory.

Now consider what happens when the guest operating system transfers control to the guest process. The guest kernel is running at user-level, so its attempt to transfer of control is a privileged instruction. Thus, the hardware processor will first trap back to the host. The host kernel can then simulate the transfer instruction, handing control to the user process.

However, what page table should we use in this case? We cannot use the page table as set up by the guest operating system, as the guest operating system thinks it is running in physical memory, but it is actually using virtual addresses. Nor can we use the page table as set up by the host operating system, as that would provide permission to the guest process to access and modify the guest kernel data structures. If we grant access to the guest kernel memory to the guest process, then the behavior of the virtual machine will be compromised.

shadow page table   Instead, we need to construct a composite page table, called a *shadow page table*, that represents the composition of the guest page table and the host page table, as shown in Figure 10.4. When the guest kernel transfers control to a guest process, the host kernel gains control and changes the page table to the shadow version.

To keep the shadow page table up to date, the host operating system needs to keep track of changes that either the guest or the host operating systems make to their page tables. This is easy in the case of the host OS — it can check to see if any shadow page tables need to be updated before it changes a page table entry.

To keep track of changes that the guest operating system makes to its page tables, however, we need to do a bit more work. The host operating system sets the memory of the guest page tables as read-only. This ensures that the guest OS traps to the host every time it attempts to change a page table entry. The host uses this trap to change the both the guest page table and the corresponding shadow page table, before resuming the guest operating system (with the page table still read-only).

The Intel architecture has recently added direct hardware support for the composition of page tables in virtual machines. Instead of a single page table,

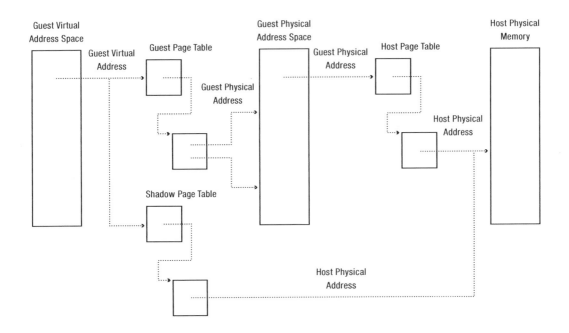

Figure 10.4: To run a guest process, the host operating system constructs a shadow page table consisting of the composition of the contents of the two page tables.

the hardware can be set up with two page tables, one for the host and one for the guest operating system. When running a guest process, on a TLB miss, the hardware translates the virtual address to a guest physical page frame using the guest page table, and the hardware then translates the guest physical page frame to the host physical page frame using the host page table. In other words, the TLB contains the composition of the two page tables, exactly as if the host maintained an explicit shadow page table. Of course, if the guest operating system itself hosts a virtual machine as a guest user process, then the guest kernel must construct a shadow page table.

Although this hardware support simplifies the construction of virtual machines, it is not clear if it improves performance. The handling of a TLB miss is slower since the host operating system must consult two page tables instead of one; changes to the guest page table are faster because the host does not need to maintain the shadow page table. It remains to be seen if this tradeoff is useful in practice.

10.2.2 Transparent Memory Compression

A theme running throughout this book is the difficulty of multiplexing multiplexors. With virtual machines, both the host operating system and the guest operating system are attempting to do the same task: to efficiently multiplex a set of tasks onto a limited amount of memory. Decisions the guest operat-

Paravirtualization

One way to enable virtual machines to run faster is to assume that the guest operating system is *ported* to the virtual machine. The hardware dependent layer, specific to the underlying hardware, is replaced with code that understands about the virtual machine. This is called paravirtualization, because the resulting guest operating system is almost, but not precisely, the same as if it were running on real, physical hardware.

Paravirtualization is helpful in several ways. Perhaps the most important is handling the idle loop. What should happen when the guest operating system has no threads to run? If the guest believes it is running on physical hardware, then nothing — the guest spins waiting for more work to do, perhaps putting itself in low power mode. Eventually the hardware will cause a timer interrupt, transferring control to the host operating system. The host can then decide whether to resume the virtual machine or run some other thread (or even some other virtual machine).

With paravirtualization, however, the idle loop can be more efficient. The hardware dependent software implementing the idle loop can trap into the host kernel, yielding the processor immediately to some other use.

Likewise, with paravirtualization, the hardware dependent code inside the guest operating system can make explicit calls to the host kernel to change its page tables, removing the need for the host to simulate guest page table management.

---

ing system takes to manage its memory may work at cross-purposes to the decisions that the host operating system takes to manage its memory.

Efficient use of memory can become especially important in data centers. Often, a single physical machine in a data center is configured to run many virtual machines at the same time. For example, one machine can host many different web sites, each of which is too small to merit a dedicated machine on its own.

To make this work, the system needs enough memory to be able to run many different operating systems at the same time. The host operating system can help by sharing memory between guest kernels, e.g., if it is running two guest kernels with the same executable kernel image. Likewise, the guest operating system can help by sharing memory between guest applications, e.g., if it is running two copies of the same program. However, if different guest kernels both run a copy of the same user process (e.g., both run the Apache web server), or use the same library, the host kernel has no (direct) way to share pages between those two instances.

Another example occurs when a guest process exits. The guest operating system places the page frames for the exiting process on the free list for reallocation to other processes. The contents of any data pages will never be

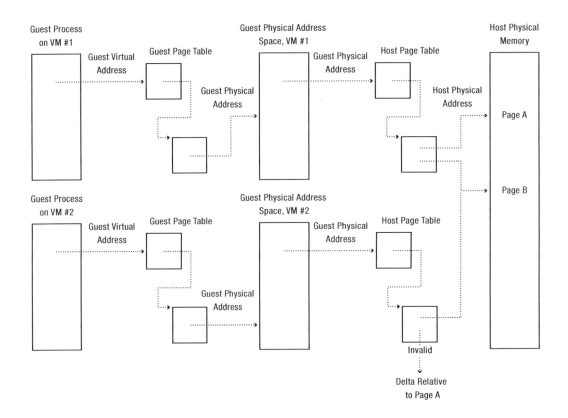

Figure 10.5: When a host kernel runs multiple virtual machines, it can save space by storing a delta to an existing page (page A) and by using the same physical page frame for multiple copies of the same page (page B).

used again; in fact, the guest kernel will need to zero those pages before they are reassigned. However, the host operating system has no (direct) way to know this. Eventually those pages will be evicted by the host, e.g., when they become least recently used. In the meantime, however, the host operating system might have evicted pages from the guest that are still active.

One solution is to more tightly coordinate the guest and host memory managers so that each knows what the other is doing. We discuss this in more detail later in this Chapter.

Commercial virtual machine implementations take a different approach, exploiting hardware address protection to manage the sharing of common pages between virtual machines. These systems run a scavenger in the background that looks for pages that can be shared across virtual machines. Once a common page is identified, the host kernel manipulates the page table pointers to provide the illusion that each guest has its own copy of the page, even though the physical representation is more compact.

There are two cases to consider, shown in Figure 10.5:

- **Multiple copies of the same page.** Two different virtual machines will often have pages with the same contents. An obvious case is zeroed pages: each kernel keeps a pool of pages that have been zeroed, ready to be allocated to a new process. If each guest operating system were running on its own machine, there would be little cost to keeping this pool at the ready; no one else but the kernel can use that memory. However, when the physical machine is shared between virtual machines, having each guest keep its own pool of zero pages is wasteful.

  Instead, the host can allocate a single zero page in physical memory for all of these instances. All pointers to the page will be set read-only, so that any attempt to modify the page will cause a trap to the host kernel; the kernel can then allocate a new (zeroed) physical page for that use, exactly as in copy-on-write. Of course, the guest kernels do not need to tell anyone when they create a zero page, so in the background, the host kernel runs a scavenger to look for zero pages in guest memory. When it finds one, it reclaims the physical page and changes the page table pointers to point at the shared zero page, with read-only permission.

  The scavenger can do the same for other shared page frames. The code and data segments for both applications and shared libraries will often be the same or quite similar, even across different operating systems. An application like the Apache web server will not be re-written from scratch for every separate operating system; rather, some OS-specific glue code will be added to match the portable portion of the application to its specific environment.

- **Compression of unused pages.** Even if a page is different, it may be close to some other page in a different virtual machine. For example, different versions of the operating system may differ in only some small respects. This provides an opportunity for the host kernel to introduce a new layer in the memory hierarchy to save space.

  Instead of evicting a relatively unused page, the operating system can compress it. If the page is a delta of an existing page, the compressed version may be quite small. The kernel manipulates page table permissions to maintain the illusion that the delta is a real page. The full copy of the page is marked read-only; the delta is marked invalid. If the delta is referenced, it can be re-constituted as a full page more quickly than if it was stored on disk. If the original page is modified, the delta can be re-compressed or evicted, as necessary.

10.3 | Fault Tolerance

All systems break. Despite our best efforts, application code can have bugs that cause the process to exit abruptly. Operating system code can have bugs that cause the machine to halt and reboot. Power failures and hardware errors can also cause a system to stop without warning.

Most applications are structured to periodically save user data to disk for just these types of events. When the operating system or application restarts, the program can read the saved data off disk to allow the user to resume their work.

In this section, we take this a step further, to see if we can manage memory to recover application data structures after a failure, and not just user file data.

10.3.1   Checkpoint and Restart

One reason we might want to recover application data is when a program takes a long time to run. If a simulation of the future global climate takes a week to compute, we do not want to have to start again from scratch every time there is a power glitch. If enough machines are involved and the computation takes long enough, it is likely that at least one of the machines will encounter a failure sometime during the computation.

Of course, the program could be written to treat its internal data as precious — to periodically save its partial results to a file. To make sure the data is internally consistent, the program would need some natural stopping point; for example, the program can save the predicted climate for 2050 before it moves onto computing the climate in 2051.

A more general approach is to have the operating system use the virtual memory system to provide application recovery as a service. If we can save the state of a process, we can transparently restart it whenever the power fails, exactly where it left off, with the user none the wiser.

To make this work, we first need to suspend each thread executing in the process and save its state — the program counter, stack pointer, and registers to application memory. Once all threads are suspended, we can then store a copy of the contents of the application memory on disk. This is called a
checkpoint   *checkpoint* or snapshot, illustrated in Figure 10.6. After a failure, we can resume the execution by restoring the contents of memory from the checkpoint and resuming each of the threads from from exactly the point we stopped them.
restart   This is called an application *restart*.

What would happen if we allow threads to continue to run while we are saving the contents of memory to disk? During the copy, we have a race condition: some pages could be saved before being modified by some thread, while others could be saved after being modified by that same thread. When we try to restart the application, its data structures could appear to be corrupted. The behavior of the program might be different from what would have happened if the failure had not occurred.

Fortunately, we can use address translation to minimize the amount of time we need to have the system stalled during a checkpoint. Instead of copying the contents of memory to disk, we can mark the application's pages as copy-on-write. At this point, we can restart the program's threads. As each page reaches disk, we can reset the protection on that page to read-write. When the

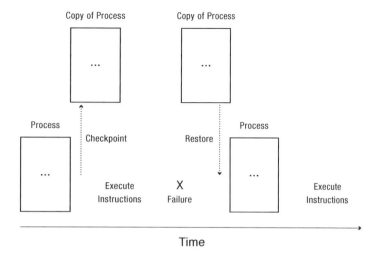

Figure 10.6: By checkpointing the state of a process, we can recover the saved state of the process after a failure by restoring the saved copy.

Checkpoints and system calls

An implementation challenge for checkpoint/restart is to correctly handle any system calls that are in process. The state of a program is not only its user-level memory; it also includes the state of any threads that are executing in the kernel and any per-process state maintained by the kernel, such as its open file descriptors. While some operating systems have been designed to allow the kernel state of a process to be captured as part of the checkpoint, it is more common for checkpointing to be supported only at the virtual machine layer. A virtual machine has no state in the kernel except for the contents of its memory and processor registers. If we need to take a checkpoint while a trap handler is in progress, the handler can simply be restarted.

program tries to modify a page before it reaches disk, the hardware will take an exception, and the kernel can make a copy of the page — one to be saved to disk and one to be used by the running program.

We can take checkpoints of the operating system itself in the same way. It is easiest to do this if the operating system is running in a virtual machine. The host can take a checkpoint by stopping the virtual machine, saving the processor state, and changing the page table protections (in the host page table) to read-only. The virtual machine is then safe to restart while the host writes the checkpoint to disk in the background.

process migration   *Process migration* is the ability to take a running program on one system, stop its execution, and resume it on a different machine. Checkpoint and restart provide a basis for transparent process migration. For example, it is now common practice to checkpoint and migrate entire virtual machines inside a data center, as one way to balance load. If one system is hosting two web servers, each of which becomes heavily loaded, we can stop one and move it to a different machine so that each can get better performance.

10.3.2   Recoverable Virtual Memory

Taking a complete checkpoint of a process or a virtual machine is a heavy-weight operation, and so it is only practical to do relatively rarely. We can use copy-on-write page protection to resume the process after starting the checkpoint, but completing the checkpoint will still take considerable time while we copy the contents of memory out to disk.

Can we provide an application the illusion of persistent memory, so that the contents of memory are restored to a point not long before the failure? The

recoverable virtual   ability to do this is called *recoverable virtual memory*. An example where we
memory   might like recoverable virtual memory is in an email client; as you read, reply, and delete email, you do not want your work to be lost if the system crashes.

If we put efficiency aside, recoverable virtual memory is possible. First, we take a checkpoint so that some consistent version of the application's data is
log   on disk. Next, we record an ordered sequence, or *log*, of every update that the application makes to memory. Once the log is written to disk we recover after a failure by reading the checkpoint and applying the changes from the log.

This is exactly how most text editors save their backups, to allow them to recover uncommitted user edits after a machine or application failure. A text editor could repeatedly write an entire copy of the file to a backup, but this would be slow, particularly for a large file. Instead, a text editor will write a version of the file, and then it will append a sequence of every change the user makes to that version. To avoid having to separately write every typed character to disk, the editor will batch changes, e.g., all of the changes the user made in the past 100 milliseconds, and write those to disk as a unit. Even if the very latest batch has not been written to disk, the user can usually recover the state of the file at almost the instant immediately before the machine crash.

A downside of this algorithm for text editors is that it can cause information to be leaked without it being visible in the current version of the file. Text editors sometimes use this same method when the user hits "save" — just append any changes from the previous version, rather than writing a fresh copy of the entire file. This means that the old version of a file can potentially still be recovered from a file. So if you write a memo insulting your boss, and then edit it to tone it down, it is best to save a completely new version of your file before you send it off!

Will this method work for persistent memory? Keeping a log of every change to every memory location in the process would be too slow. We would need to trap on every store instruction and save the value to disk. In other

Figure 10.7: The operating system can recover the state of a memory segment after a crash by saving a sequence of incremental checkpoints.

words, we would run at the speed of the trap handler, rather than the speed of the processor.

However, we can come close. When we take a checkpoint, we mark all pages as read-only to ensure that the checkpoint includes a consistent snapshot of the state of the process's memory. Then we trap to the kernel on the first store instruction to each page, to allow the kernel to make a copy-on-write. The kernel resets the page to be read-write so that successive store instructions to the same page can go at full speed, but it can also record the page as having been modified.

incremental checkpoint

We can take an *incremental checkpoint* by stopping the program and saving a copy of any pages that have been modified since the previous checkpoint. Once we change those pages back to read-only, we can restart the program, wait a bit, and take another incremental checkpoint. After a crash, we can recover the most recent memory by reading in the first checkpoint and then applying each of the incremental checkpoints in turn, as shown in Figure 10.7.

How much work we lose during a machine crash is a function of how quickly we can completely write an incremental checkpoint to disk. This is governed by the rate at which the application creates new data. To reduce the cost of an incremental checkpoint, applications needing recoverable virtual memory will designate a specific memory segment as persistent. After a crash, that memory will be restored to the latest incremental checkpoint, allowing the program to quickly resume its work.

10.3.3   Deterministic Debugging

A key to building reliable systems software is the ability to locate and fix problems when they do occur. Debugging a sequential program is comparatively easy: if you give it the same input, it will execute the same code in the same order, and produce the same output.

Debugging a concurrent program is much harder: the behavior of the program may change depending on the precise scheduling order chosen by the operating system. If the program is correct, the same output should be produced on the same input. If we are debugging a program, however, it is probably not correct. Instead, the precise behavior of the program may vary from run to run depending on which threads are scheduled first.

Debugging an operating system is even harder: not only does the operating system make widespread use of concurrency, but it is hard to tell sometimes what is its "input" and "output."

It turns out, however, that we can use a virtual machine abstraction to provide a repeatable debugging environment for an operating system, and we can in turn use that to provide a repeatable debugging environment for concurrent applications.

It is easiest to see this on a uniprocessor. The execution of an operating system running in a virtual machine can only be affected by three factors: its initial state, the input data provided by its I/O devices, and the precise timing of interrupts.

Because the host kernel mediates each of these for the virtual machine, it can record them and play them back during debugging. As long as the host exactly mimics what it did the first time, the behavior of the guest operating system will be the same and the behavior of all applications running on top of the guest operating system will be the same.

Replaying the input is easy, but how do we replay the precise timing of interrupts? Most modern computer architectures have a counter on the processor to measure the number of instructions executed. The host operating system can use this to measure how many instructions the guest operating system (or guest application) executed between the point where the host gave up control of the processor to the guest, and when control returned to the kernel due to an interrupt or trap.

To replay the precise timing of an asynchronous interrupt, the host kernel records the guest program counter and the instruction count at the point when the interrupt was delivered to the guest. On replay, the host kernel can set a trap on the page containing the program counter where the next interrupt will be taken. Since the guest might visit the same program counter multiple times, the host kernel uses the instruction count to determine which visit corresponds to the one where the interrupt was delivered. (Some systems make this even easier, by allowing the kernel to request a trap whenever the instruction count reaches a certain value.)

Moreover, if we want to skip ahead to some known good intermediate point, we can take a checkpoint, and play forward the sequence of interrupts and input data from there. This is important as sometimes bugs in operating systems can take weeks to manifest themselves; if we needed to replay everything from boot the debugging process would be much more cumbersome.

Matters are more complex on a multicore system, as the precise behavior of both the guest operating system and the guest applications will depend on the precise ordering of instructions across the different processors. It is an ongoing area of research how best to provide deterministic execution in this setting. Provided that the program being debugged has no race conditions — that is, no access to shared memory outside of a critical section — then its behavior will be deterministic with one more piece of information. In addition to the initial state, inputs, and asynchronous interrupts, we also need to record which thread acquires each critical section in which order. If we replay the threads in that order and deliver interrupts precisely and provide the same device input, the behavior will be the same. Whether this is a practical solution is still an open question.

10.4 | Security

Hardware or software address translation provides a basis for executing untrusted application code, to allow the operating system kernel to protect itself and other applications from malicious or buggy implementations.

A modern smartphone or tablet computer, however, has literally hundreds of thousands of applications that could be installed. Many or most are completely trustworthy, but others are specifically designed to steal or corrupt local data by exploiting weaknesses in the underlying operating system or the natural human tendency to trust technology. How is a user to know which is which? A similar situation exists for the web: even if most web sites are innocuous, some embed code that exploits known vulnerabilities in the browser defenses.

If we cannot limit our exposure to potentially malicious applications, what can we do? One important step is to keep your system software up to date. The malicious code authors recognize this: a recent survey showed that the most likely web sites to contain viruses are those targeted at the most novice users, e.g., screensavers and children's games.

In this section, we discuss whether there are additional ways to use virtual machines to limit the scope of malicious applications.

Suppose you want to download a new application, or visit a new web site. There is some chance it will work as advertised, and there is some chance it will contain a virus. Is there any way to limit the potential of the new software to exploit some unknown vulnerability in your operating system or browser?

virtual machine honeypot
One interesting approach is to clone your operating system into a new virtual machine, and run the application in the clone rather than on the native operating system. A virtual machine constructed for the purpose of executing suspect code is called a *virtual machine honeypot*. By using a virtual machine, if the code turns out to be malicious, we can delete the virtual machine and leave the underlying operating system as it was before we attempted to run the application.

Creating a virtual machine to execute a new application might seem extravagant. However, earlier in this chapter, we discussed various ways to make this more efficient: shadow page tables, memory compression, efficient checkpoint and restart, and copy-on-write. And of course, reinstalling your system after it has become infected with a virus is even slower!

Both researchers and vendors of commercial anti-virus software make extensive use of virtual machine honeypots to detect and understand viruses.

For example, a frequent technique is to create an array of virtual machines, each with a different version of the operating system. By loading a potential virus into each one, and then simulating user behavior, we can more easily determine which versions of software are vulnerable and which are not.

A limitation is that we need to be able to tell if the browser or operating system running in the virtual machine honeypot has been corrupted. Often, viruses operate instantly, by attempting to install logging software or scanning the disk for sensitive information such as credit card numbers. There is nothing to keep the virus from lying in wait; this has become more common recently, particularly those designed for military or business espionage.

Another limitation is that the virus might be designed to infect both the guest operating system running in the clone and the host kernel implementing the virtual machine. (In the case of the web, the virus must infect the browser, the guest operating system, and the host.) As long as the system software is kept up to date, the system is vulnerable only if the virus is able to exploit some unknown weakness in the guest operating system and a separate unknown weakness in the host implementation of the virtual machine. This provides **defense in depth**   *defense in depth*, improving security through multiple layers of protection.

10.5 | User-Level Memory Management

With the increasing sophistication of applications and their runtime systems, most widely used operating systems have introduced hooks for applications to manage their own memory. While the details of the interface differs from system to system, the hooks preserve the role of the kernel in allocating resources between processes and in preventing access to privileged memory. Once a page frame has been assigned to a process, however, the kernel can leave it up to the process to determine what to do with that resource.

Operating systems can provide applications the flexibility to decide:

- **Where to get missing pages.** As we noted in the previous chapter, a modern memory hierarchy is deep and complex: local disk, local non-volatile memory, remote memory inside a data center, or remote disk. By giving applications control, the kernel can keep its own memory hierarchy simple and local, while still allowing sophisticated applications to take advantage of network resources when they are available, even when those resources are on machines running completely different operating systems.

- **Which pages can be accessed.** Many applications such as browsers and databases need to set up their own application-level sandboxes for executing untrusted code. Today this is done with a combination of hardware and software techniques, as we described in Chapter 8. Finer-grained control over page fault handling allows more sophisticated models for managing sharing between regions of untrusted code.

- **Which pages should be evicted.** Often, an application will have better information than the operating system over which pages it will reference in the near future.

Many applications can adapt the size of their working set to the resources provided by the kernel but they will have worse performance whenever there is a mismatch.

- **Garbage collected programs.** Consider a program that does its own garbage collection. When it starts up, it allocates a block of memory in its virtual address space to serve as the heap. Periodically, the program scans through the heap to compact its data structures, freeing up room for additional data structures. This causes all pages to appear to be recently used, confounding the kernel's memory manager. By contrast, the application knows that the best page to replace is one that was recently cleaned of application data.

  It is equally confounding to the application. How does the garbage collector know how much memory it should allocate for the heap? Ideally, the garbage collector should use exactly as much memory as the kernel is able to provide, and no more. If the runtime heap is too small, the program must garbage collect, even though more page frames available. If the heap is too large, the kernel will page parts of the heap to disk instead of asking the application to pay the lower overhead of compacting its memory.

- **Databases.** Databases and other data processing systems often manipulate huge data sets that must be streamed from disk into memory. As we noted in Chapter CachingChNum, algorithms for large data sets will be more efficient if they are customized to the amount of available physical memory. If the operating system evicts a page that the database expects to be in memory, these algorithms will run much more slowly.

- **Virtual machines.** A similar issue arises with virtual machines. The guest operating system running inside of a virtual machine thinks it has a set of physical page frames, which it can assign to the virtual pages of applications running in the virtual machine. In reality, however, the page frames in the guest operating system are virtual and can be paged to disk by the host operating system. If the host operating system could tell the guest operating system when it needed to steal a page frame (or donate a page frame), then the guest would know exactly how many page frames were available to be allocated to its applications.

In each of these cases, the performance of a resource manager can be compromised if it runs on top of a virtualized, rather than a physical, resource. What is needed is for the operating system kernel to communicate how much memory is assigned to a process or virtual machine so that the application to do its own memory management. As processes start and complete, the amount

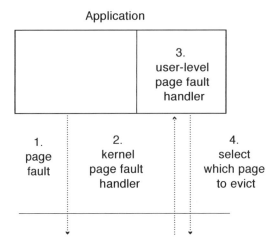

Figure 10.8: The operation of a user-level page handler. On a page fault, the hardware traps to the kernel; if the fault is for a segment with a user-level pager, the kernel passes the fault to the user-level handler to manage. The user-level handler is pinned in memory to avoid recursive faults.

of available physical memory will change, and therefore the assignment to each application will change.

To handle these needs, most operating systems provide some level of application control over memory. Two models have emerged:

pin

- **Pinned pages.** A simple and widely available model is to allow applications to *pin* virtual memory pages to physical page frames, preventing those pages from being evicted unless absolutely necessary. Once pinned, the application can manage its memory however it sees fit, for example, by explicitly shuffling data back and forth to disk.

user-level page
handler

- **User-level pagers.** A more general solution is for applications to specify a *user-level page handler* for a memory segment. On a page fault or protection violation, the kernel trap handler is invoked. Instead of handling the fault itself, the kernel passes control to user-level handler, as in a UNIX signal handler. The user-level handler can then decide how to manage the trap: where to fetch the missing page, what action to take if the application was sandbox, and which page to replace. To avoid infinite recursion, the user-level page handler must itself be stored in pinned memory.

10.6 | Summary and Future Directions

In this chapter, we have argued that address translation provides a powerful tool for operating systems to provide a set of advanced services to applications to improve system performance, reliability, and security. Services such as checkpointing, recoverable memory, deterministic debugging, and honeypots are now widely supported at the virtual machine layer, and we believe that they will come to be standard in most operating systems as well.

Moving forward, it is clear that the demands on the memory management system for advanced services will increase. Not only are memory hierarchies becoming increasingly complex, but the diversity of services provided by the memory management system has added even more complexity.

Operating systems often go through cycles of gradually increasing complexity followed by rapid shifts back towards simplicity. The recent commercial interest in virtual machines may yield a shift back towards simpler memory management, by reducing the need for the kernel to provide every service that any application might need. Processor architectures now directly support user-level page tables. This potentially opens up an entire realm for more sophisticated runtime systems, for those applications that are themselves miniature operating systems, and a concurrent simplification of the kernel. With the right operating system support, applications will be able to set up and manage their own page tables directly, implement their own user-level process abstractions, and provide their own transparent checkpointing and recovery on memory segments.

Exercises

1. This question concerns the operation of shadow page tables for virtual machines, where a guest process is running on top of a guest operating system on top of a host operating system. The architecture uses paged segmentation, with a 32-bit virtual address divided into fields as follows:

4 bit segment number	12 bit page number	16 bit offset

   The guest operating system creates and manages segment and page tables to map the guest virtual addresses to guest physical memory. These tables are as follows (all values in hexadecimal):

   The host operating system creates and manages segment and page tables to map the guest physical memory to host physical memory. These tables are as follows:

Segment Table		Page Table A		Page Table B	
0	Page Table A	0	0002	0	0001
1	Page Table B	1	0006	1	0004
x	(rest invalid)	2	0000	2	0003
		3	0005	x	(rest invalid)
		x	(rest invalid)		

Segment Table		Page Table K	
0	Page Table K	0	BEEF
x	(rest invalid)	1	F000
		2	CAFE
		3	3333
		4	(invalid)
		5	BA11
		6	DEAD
		7	5555
		x	(rest invalid)

a) Find the host physical address corresponding to each of the following guest virtual addresses. Answer "invalid guest virtual address" if the guest virtual address is invalid; answer "invalid guest physical address if the guest virtual address maps to a valid guest physical page frame, but the guest physical page has an invalid virtual address.

  i. 00000000

  ii. 20021111

  iii. 10012222

  iv. 00023333

  v. 10024444

b) Using the information in the tables above, fill in the contents of the shadow segment and page tables for direct execution of the guest process.

c) Assuming that the guest physical memory is contiguous, list three reasons why the host page table might have an invalid entry for a guest physical page frame, with valid entries on either side.

2. Suppose we doing incremental checkpoints on a system with 4 KB pages and a disk capable of transferring data at 10 MB/s.

a) What is the maximum rate of updates to new pages if every modified page is sent in its entirety to disk on every checkpoint and we require that each checkpoint reach disk before we start the next checkpoint?

b) Suppose that most pages saved during an incremental checkpoint are only partially modified. Describe how you would design a system to save only the modified portions of each page as part of the checkpoint.

Part IV

Persistent Storage

Memory is the treasury and guardian of all things.
                                    Marcus Tullius Cicero

11 File Systems: Introduction and Overview

Computers must be able to reliably store data. Individuals store family photos, music files, and email folders; programmers store design documents and source files; office workers store spreadsheets, text documents, and presentation slides; and businesses store inventory, orders, and billing records. In fact, for a computer to work at all, it needs to be able to store programs to run and the operating system, itself.

For all of these cases, users demand a lot from their storage systems:

- **Reliability.** A user's data should be safely stored even if a machine's power is turned off or its operating system crashes. In fact, much of this data is so important that users expect and need the data to survive even if the devices used to store it are damaged. For example, many modern storage systems continue to work even if one of the magnetic disks storing the data malfunctions or even if a data center housing some of the system's servers burns down!

- **Large capacity and low cost.** Users and companies store enormous amount of data, so they want to be able to buy high capacity storage for a low cost. For example, it takes about 350 MB to store an hour of CD-quality losslessly encoded music, 4 GB to store an hour-long high-definition home video, and about 1 GB to store 300 digital photos. As a result of these needs, many individuals own 1 TB or more of storage for their personal files. This is an enormous amount: if you printed 1 TB of data as text on paper, you would produce a stack about 20 miles high. In contrast, for less than $100 you can buy 1 TB of storage that fits in a shoebox.

Unit	Binary Bytes	Decimal Bytes
MB	2^{20}	10^{6}
GB	2^{30}	10^{9}
TB	2^{40}	10^{12}
PB	2^{50}	10^{15}
EB	2^{60}	10^{18}

- **High performance.** For programs to use data, they must be able to access it, and for programs to use large amounts of data, this access must be fast. For example, users want program start-up to be nearly instantaneous, a business may need to process hundreds or thousands of orders per second, or a server may need to stream a large number of video files to different users.

- **Named data.** Because users store a large amount of data, because some data must last longer than the process that creates it, and because data must be shared across programs, storage systems must provide ways to easily identify data of interest. For example, if you can name a file (e.g., /home/alice/assignments/hw1.txt) you can find the data you want out of the millions of blocks on your disk, you can still find it after you shut down your text editor, and you can use your email program to send the data produced by the text editor to another user.

- **Controlled sharing.** Users need to be able to share stored data, but this sharing needs to be controlled. As one example, you may want to create a design document that everyone in your group can read and write, that people in your department can read but not write, and that people outside of your department cannot access at all. As another example, it is useful for a system to be able to allow anyone to execute a program while only allowing the system administrator to change the program.

Nonvolatile storage and file systems.   The contents of a system's main DRAM memory can be lost if there is an operating system crash or power failure. In contrast, *non-volatile storage* is durable and retains its state across crashes and power outages; non-volatile storage is also called or *persistent storage* or *stable storage*. Nonvolatile storage can also have much higher capacity and lower cost than the volatile DRAM that forms the bulk of most system's "main memory."

non-volatile
storage

persistent storage

stable storage

However, non-volatile storage technologies have their own limitations. For example, current non-volatile storage technologies such as magnetic disks and high-density flash storage do not allow random access to individual words of storage; instead, access must be done in more coarse-grained units — 512, 2048, or more bytes at a time.

Furthermore, these accesses can be much slower than access to DRAM; for example, reading a sector from a magnetic disk may require activating a motor to move a disk arm to a desired track on disk and then waiting for the spinning disk to bring the desired data under the disk head. Because disk accesses involve motors and physical motion, the time to access a random sector on a disk can be around 10 milliseconds. In contrast, DRAM latencies are typically under 100 nanoseconds. This large difference — about five orders of magnitude in the case of spinning disks — drives the operating system to organize and use persistent storage devices differently than main memory.

File systems are a common operating system abstraction to allow applications to access non-volatile storage. File systems use a number of techniques

Goal	Physical Characteristic	Design Implication
High performance	Large cost to initiate IO access	Organize data placement with *files, directories, free space bitmap,* and *placement heuristics* so that storage is accessed in large sequential units
		Caching to avoid accessing persistent storage
Named data	Storage has large capacity, survives crashes, and is shared across programs	Support *files* and *directories* with meaningful names
Controlled sharing	Device stores many users' data	Include access-control *metadata* with files
Reliable storage	Crash can occur during update	Use *transactions* to make a set of updates atomic
	Storage devices can fail	Use *redundancy* to detect and correct failures
	Flash memory cells can wear out	Move data to different storage locations to even the wear

Figure 11.1: Characteristics of persistent storage devices affect the design of an operating system's storage abstractions.

to cope with the physical limitations of non-volatile storage devices and to provide better abstractions to users. For example, Figure 11.1 summarizes how physical characteristics motivate several key aspects of file system design.

- **Performance.** File systems amortize the cost of initiating expensive operations — such as moving a disk arm or erasing a block of solid state memory — by grouping where its placement of data so that such operations access large, sequential ranges of storage.

- **Naming.** File systems group related data together into directories and files and provide human-readable names for them (e.g., /home/alice/Pictures/summer-vacation/hiking.jpg.) These names for data remain meaningful even after the program that creates the data exits, they help users organize large amounts of storage, and they make it easy for users to use different different programs to create, read, and edit, their data.

- **Controlled sharing.** File systems include metadata about who owns which files and which other users are allowed to read, write, or execute data and program files.

- **Reliability.** File systems use transactions to atomically update multiple blocks of persistent storage, similar to how the operating system uses critical sections atomically update different data structures in memory.

  To further improve reliability, file systems store checksums with data to detect corrupted blocks, and they replicate data across multiple storage devices to recover from hardware failures.

Impact on application writers.   Understanding the reliability and performance properties of storage hardware and file systems is important even if you are not designing a file system from scratch. Because of the fundamental limitations of existing storage devices, the higher-level illusions of reliability and performance provided by the file system are imperfect. An application programmer needs to understand these limitations to avoid having inconsistent data stored on disk or having a program run orders of magnitude slower than expected.

For example, suppose you edit a large document with many embedded images and that your word processor periodically auto-saves the document so that you would not lose too many edits if the machine crashes. If the application uses the file system in a straightforward way, several of unexpected things may happen.

- **Poor performance.** First, although file systems allow existing bytes in a file to be overwritten with new values, they do not allow new bytes to be inserted into the middle of existing bytes. So, even a small update to the file may require rewriting the entire file either from beginning to end or at least from the point of the first insertion to the end. For a multi-megabyte file, each auto-save may end up taking as much as a second.

- **Corrupt file.** Second, if the application simply overwrites the existing file with updated data, an untimely crash can leave the file in an inconsistent state, containing a mishmash of the old and new versions. For example, if a section is cut from one location and pasted in another, after a crash the saved document may end up with copies of the section in both locations, one location, or neither location; or it may end up with a region that is a mix of the old and new text.

- **Lost file.** Third, if instead of overwriting the document file, the application writes updates to a new file, then deletes the original file, and finally moves the new file to the original file's location, an untimely crash can leave the system with no copies of the document at all.

Programs use a range of techniques to deal with these types of issues. For example, some structure their code to take advantage of the detailed semantics of some operating systems. For example, some operating systems guarantee that when a file is renamed and a file with the target name already exists, the target name will always refer to either the old or new file, even after a crash in the middle of the rename operation. In such a case, an implementation can create a new file with the new version of the data and use the rename command to atomically replace the old version with the new one.

Other programs essentially build a miniature file system over the top of the underlying one, structuring their data so that the underlying file system can better meet their performance and reliability requirements.

For example, a word processor might use a sophisticated document format, allowing it to, for example, add and remove embedded images and to always update a document by appending updates to the end of the file.

As another example, a data analysis program might improve its performance by organizing its accesses to input files in a way that ensures that each input file is read only once and that it is read sequentially from its start to its end.

Or, a browser with a 1 GB on-disk cache might create 100 files, each containing 10 MB of data, and group a given web site's objects in a sequential region of a randomly selected file. To do this, the browser would need to keep metadata that maps each cached web site to a region of a file, it would need to keep track of what regions of each file are used and which are free free, it would need to decide where to place a new web site's objects, and it would need to have a strategy for growing or moving a web site's objects as additional objects are fetched.

Roadmap. To get good performance and acceptable reliability, both application writers and operating systems designers must understand how storage devices and file systems work. This chapter and the next three discuss the key issues:

- **API and abstractions.** The rest of this chapter introduces file systems by describing a typical API and set of abstractions, and it provides an overview of the software layers that provide these abstractions.

- **Storage devices.** The characteristics of persistent storage devices strongly influence the design of storage system abstractions and higher level applications. Chapter 12 therefore explores the physical characteristics of common storage devices.

- **Implementing files and directories.** Chapter 13 describes how file systems keep track of data by describing several widely used approaches to implementing files and directories.

- **Reliable storage.** Although we would like storage to be perfectly reliable, physical devices fall short of that ideal. Chapter 14 describes how storage systems use transactional updates and redundancy to improve reliability.

11.1 | The File System Abstraction

Today, almost anyone who uses a computer is familiar with the high-level file system abstraction. File systems provide a way for users to organize their data and to store it for long periods of time. For example, Bob's computer might store a collection of applications such as /Applications/Calculator and /Program Files/Text Edit and a collection of data files such as /home/Bob/correspondence/letter-to-mom.txt, and /home/Bob/Classes/OS/hw1.txt.

More precisely, a *file system* is an operating system abstraction that provides persistent, named data. *Persistent data* is stored until it is explicitly deleted, even if the computer storing it crashes or loses power. *Named data* can be accessed via a human-readable identifier that the file system associates with the file. Having a name allows a file to be accessed even after the program that created it has exited, and allows it to be shared by multiple applications.

There are two key parts to the file system abstraction: files, which define sets of data, and directories, which define names for files.

File.   A *file* is a named collection of data in a file system. For example, the programs /Applications/Calculator or /Program Files/Text Edit are each files, as are the data /home/Bob/correspondence/letter-to-mom.txt or /home/Bob/Classes/OS/hw1.txt.

Files provide a higher-level abstraction than the underlying storage device: they let a single, meaningful name refer to an (almost) arbitrarily-sized amount of data. For example /home/Bob/Classes/OS/hw1.txt might be stored on disk in blocks 0x0A713F28, 0xB3CA349A, and 0x33A229B8, but it is much more convenient to refer to the data by its name than by this list of disk addresses.

A file's information has two parts, metadata and data. A *file's metadata* is information about the file that is understood and managed by the operating system. For example, a file's metadata typically includes the file's *size*, its *modification time*, its *owner*, and its *security information* such as whether it may be read, written, or executed by the owner or by other users.

A *file's data* can be whatever information a user or application puts in it. From the point of view of the file system, a file's data is just an array of untyped bytes. Applications can use these bytes to store whatever information they want in whatever format they choose. Some data have a simple structure. For example, an ASCII text file contains a sequence of bytes that are interpreted as letters in the English alphabet. Conversely, data structures stored by applications can be arbitrarily complex. For example, a .doc files can contain text, formatting information, and embedded objects and images, an ELF (Executable and Linkable File) files can contain compiled objects and executable code, or a database file can contain the information and indices managed by a relational database.

Directory.   Whereas a file contains system-defined metadata and arbitrary data, directories provide names for files. In particular, a *directory* is a list of human-readable names and a mapping from each name to a specific underlying file or directory. One common metaphor is that a directory is a folder that contains documents (files) and other folders (directories).

As Figure 11.2 illustrates, because directories can include names of other directories, they can be organized in a hierarchy so that different sets of associated files can be grouped in different directories. So, the directory /bin may include binary applications for your machine while /home/tom (Tom's "home directory") might include Tom's files. If Tom has many files, Tom's home directory may include additional directories to group them (e.g., /home/tom/

Executing "untyped" files

Usually, an operating system treats a file's data as an array of untyped bytes, leaving it up to applications to interpret a file's contents. Occasionally, however, the operating system needs to be able to parse a file's data.

For example, Linux supports a number of different executable file types such as the ELF and a.out binary files and tsch, csh, and perl scripts. You can run any of these files from the command line or using the exec() system call. E.g.,

```
> a.out
Hello world from hello.c compiled by gcc!
> hello.pl
Hello world from hello.pl, a perl script!
> echo "Hello world from /bin/echo, a system binary!"
Hello world from /bin/echo, a system binary!
```

To execute a file, the operating system must determine whether it is a binary file or a script. If it is the former, the operating system must parse the file to determine where in the target process's memory to load code and data from the file and which instruction to start with. If it is the latter, the operating system must determine which interpreter program it should launch to execute the script.

Linux does this by having executable files begin with a *magic number* that identifies the file's format. For example, ELF binary executables begin with the four bytes 0x7f, 0x45, 0x4c, and 0x46 (the ASCII characters DEL, E, L, and F); once an executable is known to be an ELF file, the ELF standard defines how the operating system should parse the rest of the file to extract and load the program's code and data. Similarly, script files begin with #! followed by the name of the interpreter that should be used to run the script (e.g., a script might begin with #! /bin/sh to be executed using the Bourne shell or #! /usr/bin/perl to be executed using the perl interpreter.

Alternative approaches include determining a file's type by its name *extension* — the characters after the last dot (.) in the file's name (e.g., .exe, .pl, or .sh) — or including information about a file's type in its metadata.

Music and /home/tom/Work.) Each of these directories may have subdirectories (e.g.,/home/tom/Work/Class and /home/tom/Work/Docs) and so on.

path The string that identifies a file or directory (e.g., /home/tom/Work/Class/OS/hw1.txt or /home/tom) is called a *path*. Here, the symbol / (pronounced *slash*) separates components of the path, and each component represents an entry in a directory. So, hw1.txt is a file in the directory OS; OS is a directory in the directory Work; and so on.

root directory If you think of the directory as a tree, then the root of the tree is a directory called, naturally enough, the *root directory*. Path names such as /bin/ls that begin

Multiple data streams

For traditional files, the file's data is a single logical sequence of bytes, and each byte can be identified by its offset from the start of the sequence (e.g., byte 0, byte 999, or byte 12481921 of a file.)

Some file systems support multiple sequences of bytes per file. For example, Apple's MacOS Extended file system supports multiple *forks* per file — a data fork for the file's basic data, a resource fork for storing additional attributes for the file, and multiple named forks for application-defined data. Similarly, Microsoft's NTFS supports *alternate data streams* that are similar to MacOS's named forks.

In these systems, when you open a file to read or write its data, you specify not only the file but also the fork or stream you want.

---

absolute path   with / define *absolute paths* that are interpreted relative to the root directory. So, /home refers to the directory called home in the root directory.

Path names such as Work/Class/OS that do not begin with / define *relative paths* that are interpreted by the operating system relative to a process's

relative path

current working directory *current working directory*. So, if a process's current working directory is /home-/tom, then the relative path Work/Class/OS is equivalent to the absolute path /home/tom/Work/Class/OS.

When you log in, your shell's current working directory is set to your

home directory *home directory*. Processes can change their current working directory with the chdir(path) system call. So, for example, if you log in and then type cd Work/Class/OS, your current working directory is changed from your home directory to the subdirectory Work/Class/OS in your home directory.

If each file or directory is identified by exactly one path, then the directory hierarchy forms a tree. Occasionally, it is useful to have several different names for the same file or directory. For example, if you are actively working on a project, you might find it convenient to have the project appear in both your "todo" directory and a more permanent location (e.g., /home/tom/todo/hw1.txt and /home/tom/Work/Class/OS/hw1.txt as illustrated in Figure 11.3.)

hard link   The mapping between a name and the underlying file is called a *hard link*. If a system system allows multiple hard links to the same file, then the directory hierarchy may no longer be a tree. Most file systems that allow multiple hard links to a file restrict these links to avoid cycles, ensuring that their directory structures form a directed acyclic graph (DAG.) Avoiding cycles can simplify management by, for example, ensuring that recursive traversals of a directory structure terminate or by making it straightforward to use reference counting to garbage collect a file when the last link to it is removed.

In addition to hard links, many systems provide other ways to use multiple names to refer to the same file. See the sidebar for a comparison of hard links, soft links, symbolic links, shortcuts, and aliases.

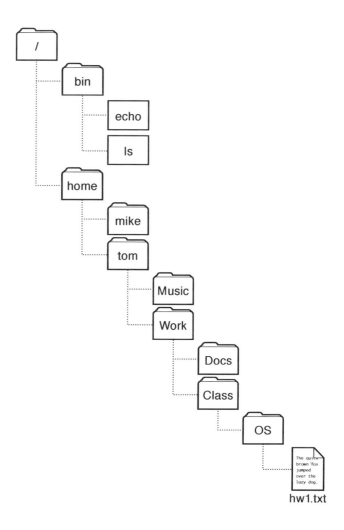

Figure 11.2: Example of a hierarchical organization of files using directories.

Volume. Each instance of a file system manages files and directories for a
volume. A *volume* is a collection of physical storage resources that form a
logical storage device.

volume

A volume is an abstraction that corresponds to a logical disk. In the simplest case, a volume corresponds to a single physical disk drive. Alternatively,
a single physical disk can be partitioned and store multiple volumes or several physical disks can be combined so that a single volume spans multiple
physical disks.

A single computer can make use of multiple file systems stored on multiple
volumes by mounting multiple volumes in a single logical hierarchy. *Mounting*
a volume on an existing file system creates a mapping from some path in the
existing file system to the root directory of the mounted volume's file system

mount

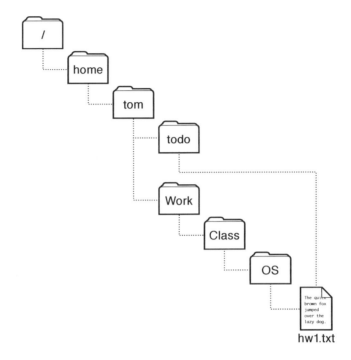

Figure 11.3: Example of a directed acyclic graph directory organization with multiple hard links to a file.

. and .. and ~

You may sometimes see path names in which directories are named ., .., or . For example,

```
> cd ~/Work/Class/OS
> cd ..
> ./a.out
```

., .., and   are special directory names in Unix. . refers to the *current directory,* .. refers to the *parent directory,*   refers to the *current user's home directory,* and *name* refers to the *home directory of user* name.

So, the first shell command changes the current working directory to be the Work/Class/OS directory in the user's home directory (e.g., /home/tom/Work/Class/OS). The second command changes the current working directory to be the Work/Class directory in the user's home directory (e.g., /Work/Class or /home/tom/Work/Class.) The third command executes the program a.out from the current working directory (e.g., /Work/Class/a.out or /home/tom/Work/Class/a.out.)

Hard links, soft links, symbolic links, shortcuts, and aliases

A hard link is a directory mapping from a file name directly to an underlying file. As we will see in Chapter 13, directories will be implemented by storing mappings from *file names* to *file numbers* that uniquely identify each file. When you first create a file (e.g., /a/b), the directory entry you create is a hard link the the new file. If you then use link() to add another hard link to the file (e.g., link("/a/b", "/c/d"),) then both names are equally valid, independent names for the same underlying file. You could, for example, unlink("/a/b"), and /c/d would remain a valid name for the file.

Many systems also support *symbolic links* also known as *soft links*. A symbolic link is a directory mappings from a file name to *another file name*. If a file is opened via a symbolic link, the file system first translates the name in the symbolic link to the target name and then uses the target name to open the file. So, if you create /a/b , create a symbolic link from /c/d/ to /a/b, and then unlink /a/b, the file is no longer accessible and open("/c/d") will fail.

Although the potential for such dangling links is a disadvantage, symbolic links have a number of advantages over hard links. First, systems usually allow symbolic links to directories, not just regular files. Second, a symbolic link can refer to a file stored in a different file system or volume.

Some operating systems such as Microsoft Windows also support *shortcuts*, which appear similar to symbolic links but which are interpreted by the windowing system rather than by the file system. From the file system's point of view, a shortcut is just a regular file. The windowing system, however, treats shortcut files specially: when the shortcut file is selected via the windowing system, the windowing system opens that file, identifies the target file referenced by the shortcut, and acts as if the target file had been selected.

A MacOS file *alias* is similar to a symbolic link but with an added feature: if the target file is moved to have a new path name, the alias can still be used to reference the file.

---

and lets the mounted file system control mappings for all extensions of that path.

For example, suppose a USB drive contains a file system with the directories /Movies and /Backup as shown in Figure 11.4. If Alice plugs that drive into her laptop, the laptop's operating system might mount the USB volume's file system with the path /Volumes/usb1/ as shown in Figure 11.5. Then, if Alice calls open("/Volumes/usb1/Movies/vacation.mov"), she will open the file /Movies/vacation.mov from the file system on the USB drive's volume. If, instead, Bob plugs that drive into his laptop, the laptop's operating system might mount the volume's file system with the path /media/disk-1, and Bob would access the same file using the path /media/disk-1/Movies/vacation.mov.

Figure 11.4: This USB disk holds a volume that is the physical storage for a file system.

11.2 | API

For concreteness, Figure 11.6 shows a simple file system API for accessing files and directories.

Creating and deleting files.   Processes create and destroy files with create() and unlink(). Create() does two things: it creates a new file that has initial metadata but no other data, and it creates a name for that file in a directory.

Link() creates a hard link—a new path name for an existing file. After a successful call to link(), there are multiple path names that refer to the same underlying file.

Unlink() removes a name for a file from its directory. If a file has multiple names or links, unlink() only removes the specified name, leaving the file accessible via other names. If the specified name is the last (or only) link to a file, then unlink() also deletes the underlying file and frees its resources.

Mkdir() and rmdir() create and delete directories.

EXAMPLE   **Linking to files vs. linking to directories.**
Systems such as Linux support a link() system call, but they do not allow new hard links to be created to a directory. E.g., existingPath must not be a directory. Why does Linux mandate this restriction?

ANSWER   Preventing multiple hard links to a directory prevents cycles, ensuring that the directory structure is always a directed acyclic graph (DAG).

Additionally, allowing hard links to a directory would muddle a directory's parent directory entry (e.g., ".." as discussed in the sidebar on page 500.)

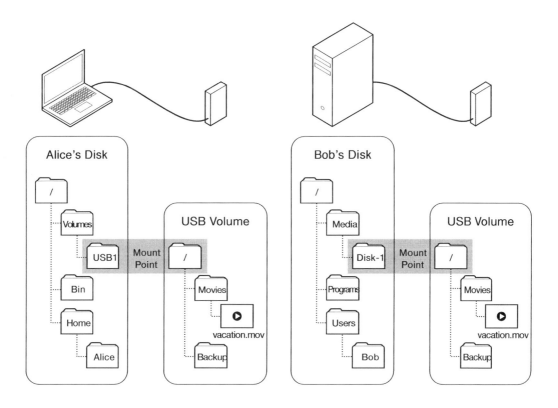

Figure 11.5: A volume can be mounted to another file system to join their directory hierarchies. For example, when the USB drive is connected to Alice's computer, she can access the vacation.mov movie using the path /Volumes/usb1/Movies/vacation.mov, and when the drive is connected to Bob's computer, he can access the movie using the path /media/disk-1/Movies/vacation.mov.

☐

file descriptor

file handle

file stream

Open and close.   To start accessing a file, a process calls open() to get a *file descriptor* it can use to refer to the open file. *File descriptor* is Unix terminology; in other systems and APIs objects playing similar roles may be called *file handles* or *file streams*.

Operating systems require processes to explicitly open() files and access them via file descriptors rather than simply passing the path name to read() and write() calls for two reasons. First, path parsing and permission checking can be done just when a file is opened and need not be repeated on each read or write. Second, when a process opens a file, the operating system creates a data structure that stores information about the process's open file such as the file's ID, whether the process can write or just read the file, and a pointer to the process's current position within the file. The file descriptor can thus be

Creating and deleting files	
create(pathName)	Create a new file with the specified name.
link(existingName, newName)	Create a hard link — a new path name that refers to the same underlying file as an existing path name.
unlink(pathName)	Remove the specified name for a file from its directory; if that was the only name for the underlying file, then remove the file and free its resources.
mkdir(pathName)	Create a new directory with the specified name.
rmdir(pathName)	Remove the directory with the specified name.
Open and close	
fileDescriptor open(pathName)	Prepare to access to the specified file (e.g., check access permissions and initialize kernel data structures for tracking per-process state of open files).
close(fileDescriptor)	Release resources associated with the specified open file.
File access	
read(fileDescriptor, buf, len)	Read len bytes from the process's current position in the open file fileDescriptor and copy the results to a buffer buf in the application's memory.
write(fileDescriptor, len, buf)	Write len bytes of data from a buffer buf in the process's memory to the process's current position in the open file fileDescriptor.
seek(fileDescriptor, offset)	Change the process's current position in the open file fileDescriptor to the specified offset.
dataPtr mmap(fileDescriptor, off, len)	Set up a mapping between the data in the file fileDescriptor from off to off + len and an area in the application's virtual memory from dataPtr to dataPtr + len.
munmap(dataPtr, len)	Remove the mapping between the application's virtual memory and a mapped file.
fsync(fileDescriptor)	Force to disk all buffered, dirty pages for the file associated with fileDescriptor.

Figure 11.6: A simple API for accessing files.

thought of as a reference to the operating system's per-open-file data structure that the operating system will use for managing the process's access to the file.

When an application is done using a file, it calls close(), which releases the open file record in the operating system.

File access.   While a file is open, an application can access the file's data in two ways. First, it can use the traditional procedural interface, making system calls to read() and write() on an open file. Calls to read() and write() start from the process's current file position, and they advance the current file position by the number of bytes successfully read or written. So, a sequence of read() or write() calls moves sequentially through a file. To support random access

Modern File Access APIs

The API shown in Figure 11.6 is similar to most widely used file access APIs, but it is somewhat simplified.

For example, each of the listed calls is similar to a call provided by the POSIX interface, but the API shown in Figure 11.6 omits some arguments and options found in POSIX. The POSIX open() call, for example, includes two additional arguments one to specify various flags such as whether the file should be opened in read-only or read-write mode and the other to specify the access control permissions that should be used if the open() call creates a new file.

In addition, real-world file access APIs are likely to have a number of additional calls. For example, the Microsoft Windows file access API includes dozens of calls including calls to lock and unlock a file, to encrypt and decrypt a file, or to find a file in a directory whose name matches a specific pattern.

---

within a file, the seek() call changes a process's current position for a specified open file.

Rather than using read() and write() to access a file's data, an application can use mmap() to establish a mapping between a region of the process's virtual memory and some region of the file. Once a file has been mapped, memory loads and stores to that virtual memory region will read and write the file's data either by accessing a shared page from the kernel's file cache, or by triggering a page fault exception that causes the kernel to fetch the desired page of data from the file system into memory. When an application is done with a file, it can call munmap() to remove the mappings.

Finally, the fsync() call is important for reliability. When an application updates a file via a write() or a memory store to a mapped file, the updates are buffered in memory and written back to stable storage at some future time. Fsync() ensures that all pending updates for a file are written to persistent storage before the call returns. Applications use this function for two purposes. First, calling fsync() ensures that updates are durable and will not be lost if there is a crash or power failure. Second, calling fsync() between two updates ensures that the first is written to persistent storage before the second. Note that calling fsync() is not always necessary; the operating system ensures that all updates are made durable by periodically flushing all dirty file blocks to stable storage.

11.3 Software Layers

As shown in Figure 11.7, operating systems implement the file system abstraction through a series of software layers. Broadly speaking, these layers have two sets of tasks:

Figure 11.7: Layered abstractions provide access to I/O systems such as storage systems.

- **API and performance.** The top levels of the software stack — user-level libraries, kernel-level file systems, and the kernel's block cache — provide a convenient API for accessing named files and also work to minimize slow storage accesses via caching, write buffering, and prefetching.

- **Device access.** Lower levels of the software stack provide ways for the operating system to access a wide range of I/O devices. Device drivers hide the details of specific I/O hardware by providing hardware-specific code for each device, and placing that code behind a simpler, more general interfaces that the rest of the operating system can use such as a block device interface. The device drivers execute as normal kernel-level code, using the systems' main processors and memory, but they must interact with the I/O devices. A system's processors and memory communicate with its I/O devices using Memory-Mapped I/O, DMA, and Interrupts.

In the rest of this section, we first talk about the file system API and performance layers. We then discuss device access.

11.3.1   API and Performance

The top levels of the file system software stack — divided between application libraries and operating system kernel code — provide the file system API and also provide caching and write buffering to improve performance.

System calls and libraries.   The file system abstraction such as the API shown in Figure 11.6 can be provided by directly by system calls. Alternatively, application libraries can wrap the system calls to add additional functionality such as buffering.

For example, in Linux, applications can access files directly using system calls (e.g., open(), read(), write(), and close().) Alternatively, applications can use the stdio library calls (e.g., fopen(), fread(), fwrite(), and fclose()). The advantage of the latter is that the library includes buffers to aggregate a program's small reads and writes into system calls that access larger blocks, which can reduce overheads. For example, if a program uses the library function fread() to read 1 byte of data, the fread() implementation may use the read() system call to read a larger block of data (e.g., 4 KB) into a buffer maintained by the library in the application's address space. Then, if the process calls fread() again to read another byte, the library just returns the byte from the buffer without needing to do a system call.

Block cache.   Typical storage devices are much slower than a computer's main memory. The operating system's block cache therefore caches recently read blocks, and it buffers recently written blocks so that they can be written back to the storage device at a later time.

In addition to improving performance by caching and write buffering, the block cache serves as a synchronization point: because all requests for a given block go through the block cache, the operating system includes information with each buffer cache entry to, for example, prevent one process from reading a block while another process writes it or to ensure that a given block is only fetched from the storage device once, even if it is simultaneously read by many processes.

Prefetching.   Operating systems use prefetching to improve I/O performance. For example, if a process reads the first two blocks of a file, the operating system may prefetch the next ten blocks.

Such prefetching can have several beneficial effects:

- **Reduced latency.** When predictions are accurate, prefetching can help the latency of future requests because reads can be serviced from main memory rather than from slower storage devices.

- **Reduced device overhead.** Prefetching can help reduce storage device overheads by replacing a large number of small requests with one large one.

- **Improved parallelism.** Some storage devices such as Redundant Arrays of Inexpensive Disks (RAIDs) and Flash drives are able to process multiple requests at once, in parallel. Prefetching provides a way for operating systems to take advantage of available hardware parallelism.

Prefetching, however, must be used with care. Too-aggressive prefetching can cause problems:

- **Cache pressure.** Each prefetched block is stored in the block cache, and it may displace another block from the cache. If the evicted block is needed before the prefetched one is used, prefetching is likely to hurt overall performance.

- **I/O contention.** Prefetch requests consume I/O resources. If other requests have to wait behind prefetch requests, prefetching may hurt overall performance.

- **Wasted effort.** Prefetching is speculative. If the prefetched blocks end up being needed, then prefetching can help performance; otherwise, prefetching may hurt overall performance by wasting memory space, I/O device bandwidth, and CPU cycles.

11.3.2   Device Drivers: Common Abstractions

device driver   *Device drivers* translate between the high level abstractions implemented by the operating system and the hardware-specific details of I/O devices.

An operating system may have to deal with many different I/O devices. For example, a laptop on a desk might be connected to two keyboards (one internal and one external), a trackpad, a mouse, a wired ethernet, a wireless 802.11 network, a wireless bluetooth network, two disk drives (one internal and one external), a microphone, a speaker, a camera, a printer, a scanner, and a USB thumb drive. And that is just a handful of the literally thousands of devices that could be attached to a computer today. Building an operating system that treats each case separately would be impossibly complex.

Layering helps simplify operating systems by providing common ways to access various classes of devices. For example, for any given operating system, **block device**   storage device drivers typically implement a standard *block device* interface that allows data to be read or written in fixed-sized blocks (e.g., 512, 2048, or 4096 bytes).

Such a standard interface lets an operating system easily use a wide range of similar devices. A file system implemented to run on top of the standard block device interface can store files on any storage device whose driver implements that interface, be it a Seagate spinning disk drive, an Intel solid state drive, a Western Digital RAID, or an Amazon Elastic Block Store volume. These devices all have different internal organizations and control registers, but if each manufacturer provides a device driver that exports the standard interface, the rest of the operating system does not need to be concerned with these per-device details.

11.3.3   Device Access

How should an operating system's device drivers communicate with and control a storage device? At first blush, a storage device seems very different from the memory and CPU resources we have discussed so far. For example, a disk drive includes several motors, a sensor for reading data, and an electromagnet for writing data.

Challenge: Device Driver Reliability

Because device drivers are hardware-specific, they are often written and updated by the hardware manufacturer rather than the operating system's main authors. Furthermore, because there are large numbers of devices — some operating systems support tens of thousands of devices — device driver code may represent a large fraction of an operating system's code.

Unfortunately, bugs in device drivers have the potential to affect more than the device. A device driver usually runs as part of the operating system kernel since kernel routines depend on it and because it needs to access the hardware of its device. However, if the device driver is part of the kernel, then a device driver's bugs have the potential to affect the overall reliability of a system. For example, in 2003 it was reported that drivers caused about 85% of failures in the Windows XP operating system.

To improve reliability, operating systems are increasingly using protection techniques similar to those used to isolate user-level programs to isolate device drivers from the kernel and from each other.

Memory mapped I/O.   As Figure 11.8 illustrates, I/O devices are typically connected to an I/O bus that is connected to the system's memory bus. Each I/O device has controller with a set of registers that can be written and read to transmit commands and data to and from the device. For example, a simple keyboard controller might have one register that can be read to learn the most recent key pressed and another register than can be written to turn the caps-lock light on or off.

Memory mapped I/O

To allow I/O control registers to be read and written, systems implement memory mapped I/O. *Memory mapped I/O* maps each device's control registers to a range of physical addresses on the memory bus. Reads and writes by the CPU to this physical address range do not go to main memory. Instead, they go to registers on the I/O devices's controllers. Thus, the operating system's keyboard device driver might learn the value of the last key pressed by reading from physical address, say, 0xC00002000.

The hardware maps different devices to different physical address ranges. Figure 11.9 shows the physical address map for a hypothetical system with a 32 bit physical address space capable of addressing 4 GB of physical memory. This system has 2 GB of DRAM in it, consuming physical addresses 0x00000000 (0) to 0x7FFFFFFF (2^{31} - 1). Controllers for each of its three I/O devices are mapped to ranges of addresses in the first few kilobytes above 3 GB. For example, physical addresses from 0xC0001000 to 0xC0001FFF access registers in the disk controller.

DMA.   Many I/O devices, including most storage devices, transfer data in bulk. For example, operating systems don't read a word or two from disk, they

Figure 11.8: I/O devices are attached to the I/O bus, which is attached to the memory bus.

usually do transfers of at least a few kilobytes at a time. Rather than requiring the CPU to read or write each word of a large transfer, I/O devices can use direct memory access. When using *direct memory access (DMA)*, the I/O device copies a block of data between its own internal memory and the system's main memory.

direct memory access (DMA)

To set up a DMA transfer, a simple operating system could use memory mapped I/O to provide a target physical address, transfer length, and operation code to the device. Then, the device copies data to or from the target address without requiring additional processor involvement.

After setting up a DMA transfer, the operating system must not use the target physical pages for any other purpose until the DMA transfer is done. The operating system therefore "pins" the target pages in memory so that they cannot be reused until they are unpinned. For example, a pinned physical page cannot be swapped out to disk and then remapped to some other virtual address.

Interrupts. The operating system needs to know when I/O devices have completed handling a request or when new external input arrives. One option is *polling*, repeatedly using memory mapped I/O to read a status register on the device. Because I/O devices are often much slower than CPUs and because inputs received by I/O devices may arrive at irregular rates, it us

polling

Figure 11.9: Physical address map for a system with 2 GB of DRAM and 3 memory mapped I/O devices.

usually better for I/O devices to use interrupts to notify the operating system of important events.

11.3.4 Putting It All Together: A Simple Disk Request

When a process issues a system call like read() to read data from disk into the process's memory, the operating system moves the calling thread to a wait queue. Then, the operating system uses memory mapped I/O both to tell the disk to read the requested data and to set up DMA so that the disk can place that data in the kernel's memory. The disk then reads the data and DMAs it into main memory; once that is done, the disk triggers an interrupt. The operating system's interrupt handler then copies the data from the kernel's buffer into the process's address space. Finally, the operating system moves the thread the ready list. When the thread next runs, it will returns from the system call with the data now present in the specified buffer.

11.4 | Summary and Future Directions

The file system interface is a stable one, and small variations of interface described here can be found in many operating systems and for many storage devices.

Port mapped I/O

Today, memory mapped I/O is the dominant paradigm for accessing I/O device's control registers. However an older style, *port mapped I/O*, is still sometimes used. Notably, the x86 architecture supports both memory mapped I/O and port mapped I/O.

Port mapped I/O is similar to memory mapped I/O in that instructions read from and write to specified addresses to control I/O devices. There are two differences. First, where memory mapped I/O uses standard memory-access instructions (e.g., load and store) to communicate with devices, port mapped I/O uses distinct I/O instructions. For example, the x86 architecture uses the in and out instructions for port mapped I/O. Second, whereas memory mapped I/O uses the same physical address space as is used for the system's main memory, the address space for port mapped I/O is distinct from the main memory address space.

For example, in x86 I/O can be done using either memory mapped or port mapped I/O, and the low-level assembly code is similar for both cases:

Memory mapped I/O	**Port mapped I/O**

```
MOV register , memAddr // To read      IN register , portAddr  // To read
MOV memAddr, register // To write      OUT portAddr , register // To write
```

Port mapped I/O can be useful in architectures with constrained physical memory addresses since I/O devices do not need to consume ranges of physical memory addresses. On the other hand, for systems with sufficiently large physical address spaces, memory mapped I/O can be simpler since no new instructions or address ranges need to be defined and since device drivers can use any standard memory access instructions to access devices. Also, memory mapped I/O provides a more unified model for supporting DMA — direct transfers between I/O devices and main memory.

Yet, the file system abstraction is imperfect, and application writers need to use it carefully to get acceptable performance and reliability. For example, if an application write()s a file, the update may not be durable when the write() call returns; application writers often call fsync() to ensure durability of data.

Could better file system APIs simplify programming? For example, if file systems allowed users to update multiple objects atomically, that might simplify many applications that currently must carefully constrain the order that their updates are stored using crude techniques such as using fsync as a barrier between one set of updates and the next.

Could better file system APIs improve performance? For example, one proposed interface allows an application to direct the operating system to transfer a range of bytes from a file to a network connection. Such an interface

Advanced DMA

Although a setting up a device's DMA can be as simple as providing a target physical address and length and then saying "go!", more sophisticated interfaces are increasingly used.

For example rather than giving devices direct access to the machine's physical address space, some systems include an *I/O memory management unit (IOMMU)* that translates device virtual addresses to main memory physical addresses similar to how a processor's TLB translates processor virtual addresses to main memory physical addresses. An IOMMU can provide both protection (e.g., preventing a buggy IO device from overwriting arbitrary memory) and simpler abstractions (e.g., allowing devices to use virtual addresses so that, for example, a long transfer can be made to a range of consecutive virtual pages rather than a collection of physical pages scattered across memory.)

Also, some devices add a level of indirection so that they can interrupt the CPU less often. For example, rather than using memory mapped I/O to set up each DMA request, the CPU and I/O device could share two lists in memory: one list of pending I/O requests and another of completed I/O requests. Then, the CPU could set up dozens of disk requests and only be interrupted when all of them are done.

Sophisticated I/O devices can even be configured to take different actions depending the data they receive. For example, some high performance network interfaces parse incoming packets and direct interrupts to different processors based on the network connection to which a received packet belongs.

---

might, for example, reduce overheads for a movie server that streams movies across a network to clients.

Exercises

1. **Discussion** Suppose a process successfully opens an existing file that has a single hard link to it, but while the process is reading that file, another process unlinks that file. What should happen to subsequent reads by the first process? Should they succeed? Should they fail? Why?

2. In Linux, suppose a process successfully opens an existing file that has a single hard link to it, but while the process is reading that file, another process unlinks that file? What happens to subsequent reads by the first process? Do they succeed? Do they fail? (Answer this problem by consulting documentation or by writing a program to test the behavior of the system in this case.)

3. Write a program that creates a new file, writes 100KB to it, flushes the writes, and deletes it. Time how long each of these steps takes.

Hint You may find the POSIX system calls creat(), write(), fflush(), close(), and gettimeofday() useful. See the manual pages for details on how to use these.

4. Consider a text editor that saves a file whenever you click a save button. Suppose that when you press the button, the editor simply (1) animates the button "down" event (e.g., by coloring the button grey), (2) uses the write() system call to write your text to your file, and then (3) animates the button "up" event (e.g., by coloring the button white). What bad thing could happen if a user edits a file, saves it, and then turns off her machine by flipping the power switch (rather than shutting the machine down cleanly)?

5. Write a program that times how long it takes to issue 100,000 one-byte writes in each of two ways. First, time how long it takes to use the POSIX system calls creat(), write(), and close() directly. Then see how long these writes take if the program uses the stdio library calls (e.g., fopen(), fwrite(), and fclose()) instead. Explain your results.

Treat disks like tape.

John Ousterhout

12 | Storage Devices

Although today's persistent storage devices have large capacity and low cost, they have drastically worse performance than volatile DRAM memory.

Not only that, but the characteristics are different and are peculiar to specific persistent storage devices. For example, although programs can access random individual words of DRAM with good performance, programs can only access today's disk and flash storage devices hundreds or thousands of bytes at a time. Furthermore, even if an application restricts itself to supported access sizes (e.g., 2 KB per read or write), if the application access pattern is random, the application may be slower by a factor of several hundred than if the application accessed the same amount of data sequentially.

To cope with the limitations and to maximize the performance of storage devices, both file system designers and application writers need to understand the physical characteristics of persistent storage devices.

Roadmap.   This chapter discusses two types of persistent storage: *magnetic disks* and *flash memory*. Both are widely used. Magnetic disks provide persistent storage for most servers, workstations, and laptops. Flash memory provides persistent storage for most smart phones, tablets, and cameras and for an increasing fraction of laptops.

12.1 | Magnetic Disk

Magnetic disk is a non-volatile storage technology that is widely used in laptops, desktops, and servers. Disk drives work by magnetically storing data

Figure 12.1: A partially-disassembled magnetic disk drive.

on a thin metallic film bonded to a glass, ceramic, or aluminum disk that rotates rapidly. Figure 12.1 shows a disk drive without its protective cover, and Figure 12.2 shows a schematic of a disk drive, identifying key components.

platters   Each drive holds one or more *platters*, thin cylinders that hold the magnetic material. Each platter has two *surfaces*, one on each side. When the drive powers up, the platters are constantly spinning on a *spindle* powered by a *motor*. In 2011, disks commonly spin at 4200–15000 RPM (70–250 revolutions per second.)

surfaces

spindle

head   A disk *head* is the component that reads and writes data by sensing or introducing a magnetic field on a surface. There is one head per surface, and as a surface spins underneath a head, the head reads or writes a sequence of bits along a circle centered on the disk's spindle. As a disk platters spins, it creates a layer of rapidly spinning air, and the disk head floats on that layer, allowing the head to get extremely close to the platter without contacting it. A *head crash* occurs when the disk head breaks through this layer with enough force to damage the magnetic surface below; head crashes can be caused by excessive shock such as dropping a running drive.

head crash

arm   To reach the full surface, each disk head attaches to an *arm*, and all of a disk's arms attach to a single *arm assembly* that includes a motor that can move the arms across the surfaces of the platters. Note that an assembly has just one motor, and all of its arms move together.

arm assembly

sectors   Data bits are stored in fixed-size *sectors*; typically, sectors are 512 bytes. The disk hardware cannot read or write individual bytes or words; instead, it must always read or write at least an entire sector. This means that to change one byte in a sector, the operating system must read the old sector, update the byte in memory, and rewrite the entire sector to disk. One reason for this restriction

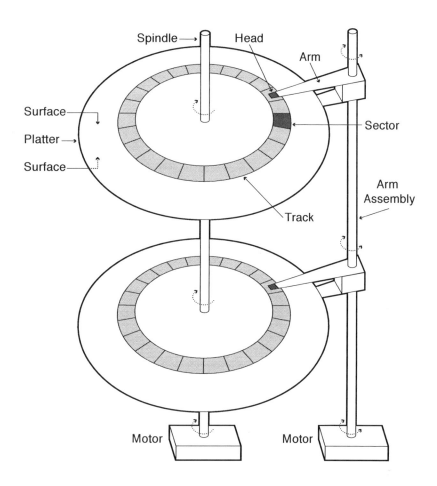

Figure 12.2: Key components of a magnetic disk drive.

is that the disk encodes each sector with additional error correction code data, allowing it to fix (or at least detect) imperfectly read or written data, which, in turn allows higher density storage and higher bandwidth operation.

track   A circle of sectors on a surface is called a *track*. The disk can read or write all of the data on a track without having to move the disk arm, so reading or writing a sequence of sectors on the same track is much faster than reading or writing sectors on different tracks.

To maximize sequential access speed, logical sector zero on each track is staggered from sector zero on the previous track by an amount corresponding to time it takes the disk to move the head from one track to another or to switch from the head on one surface to the head on another one. This staggering is track skewing   called *track skewing*.

To increase storage density and disk capacity, disk manufacturers make tracks and sectors as thin and small as possible. If there are imperfections in

a sector, then that sector may be unable to reliably store data. Manufacturers therefore include spare sectors distributed across each surface. The disk
firmware or the file system's low-level formatting can then use *sector sparing* to
remap sectors to use spare sectors instead of faulty sectors. *Slip sparing* helps
retain good sequential access performance by remapping all sectors from the
bad sector to the next spare, advancing each logical sector in that range by one
physical sector on disk.

sector sparing

slip sparing

Disk drives often include a few MB of *buffer memory*, memory that the
disk's controller uses to buffer data being read from or written to the disk, for
track buffering, and for write acceleration.

buffer memory

Track buffering improves performance by storing sectors that have been
read by the disk head but have not yet been requested by the operating system.
In particular, when a disk head moves to a track, it may have to wait for
the sector it needs to access to rotate under the disk head. While the disk is
waiting, it reads unrequested sectors to its rack buffer so that if the operating
system requests those sectors later, they can be returned immediately.

track buffer

Write acceleration stores data to be written to disk in the disk's buffer
memory and acknowledges the writes to the operating system before the data
is actually written to the platter; the disk firmware flushes the writes from the
track buffer to the platter at some later time. This technique can significantly
increase the apparent speed of the disk, but it carries risks — if power is lost
before buffered data is safely stored, then data might be lost.

write acceleration

Server drives implementing the SCSI or Fibre Channel interfaces and
increasing numbers of commodity drives with the Serial ATA (SATA) interface
implement a safer form of write acceleration with *tag command queueing* (TCQ)
(also called *native command queueing* (NCQ) for SATA drives.) TCQ allows an
operating system to issue multiple concurrent requests to the disk and for the
disk to process those requests out of order to optimize scheduling, and it can
be configured to only acknowledge write requests when the blocks are safely
on the platter.

**tag command
queueing**

**native command
queueing**

12.1.1   Disk Access and Performance

Operating systems send commands to a disk to read or write one or more
consecutive sectors. A disk's sectors are identified with *logical block addresses*
(LBAs) that specify the surface, track, and sector to be accessed.

**logical block
addresses**

To service a request for a sequence of blocks starting at some sector, the
disk must first seek to the right track, wait for the first desired sector to rotate
to the head, and then transfer the blocks. Therefore, the time for a disk access
is:

$$\text{disk access time} = \text{seek time} + \text{rotation time} + \text{transfer time}$$

seek

- **Seek.** The disk must first *seek* — move its arm over the desired track. To
  seek, the disk first activates a motor that moves the arm assembly to
  approximately the right place on disk. Then, as arm stops vibrating from

Beware of "average seek time"

Although the name *average seek time* makes it tempting to use this metric when estimating the time it will take a disk to complete a particular workload, it is often the wrong metric to use. Average seek time — the average across seeks between each possible pair of tracks on disk — was defined this way to make it a well-defined, standard metric, not because it is representative of common workloads.

The definition of average seek time essentially assumes no locality in a workload, so it is very nearly a worst-case scenario. Many workloads access sectors that are likely to be near one another; for example, most operating systems attempt to place files sequentially on disk and to place different files in a directory on the same track or on tracks near one another. For these (common) workloads, the seek times observed may be closer to the disk's minimum seek time than its "average" seek time.

---

settle   the motion of the seek, the disk begins reading positioning information embedded in the sectors to determine exactly where it is and to make fine-grained positioning corrections to *settle* on the desired track. Once the head has settled on the right track, the disk uses signal strength and positioning information to make minute corrections in the arm position to keep the head over the desired track.

A request's seek time depends on how far the disk arm has to move.

minimum seek time   A disk's *minimum seek time* is the time it takes for the head to move from one track to an adjacent one. For short seeks, disks typically just "resettle" the head on the new track by updating the target track number in the track-following circuitry. Minimum seek times of 0.3–1.5 ms are typical.

head switch time   If a disk is reading the tth track on one surface, its *head switch time* is the time it would take to begin reading the tth track on a different surface. Tracks can be less than a micron wide and tracks on different surfaces are not perfectly aligned. So, a head switch between the same tracks on different surfaces has a cost similar to a minimum seek: the disk begins using the sensor on a different head and then resettles the disk on the desired track for that surface.

maximum seek time   A disk's *maximum seek time* is the time it takes the head to move from the innermost track to the outermost one or vice versa. Maximum seek times are typically over 10 ms and can be over 20 ms.

average seek time   A disk's *average seek time* is the average across seeks between each possible pair of tracks on a disk. This value is often approximated as the time to seek one third of the way across the disk.

- **Rotate.** Once the disk head has settled on the right track, it must wait

The demise of the cylinder

A *cylinder* on a disk is a set of tracks on different surfaces with the same track index. For example, on a 2-platter drive, the 8th tracks on surfaces 0, 1, 2, and 3 would form the 8th cylinder of the drive.

Some early file systems put related data on different surfaces but in the same cylinder. The idea was that data from the different tracks in the cylinder could be read without a requiring a seek. Once a cylinder was full, the file system would start placing data in one of the adjacent cylinders.

As disk densities have increased, the importance of the cylinder has declined. Today, a disk's tracks can be less than a micron wide. To follow a track at these densities, a controller monitors the signals from a disk's head to control the disk arm assembly's motor to keep the head centered on a track. Furthermore, at these densities, the tracks of a cylinder may not be perfectly aligned. As a result, when a disk switches disk heads, the new head must center itself over the desired track. So, switching heads within a cylinder ends up being similar to a short 1-track seek: the controller chooses the new cylinder/track and the disk head settles over the target track. Today, accessing different tracks within the same cylinder costs about the same as accessing adjoining tracks on the same platter.

---

rotational latency

for the target sector to rotate under it. This waiting time is called the *rotational latency*. Today, most disks rotate at 4200 RPM to 15,000 RPM (15 ms to 4 ms per rotation), and for many workloads a reasonable estimate of rotational latency is one-half the time for a full rotation — 7.5 ms–2 ms.

Once a disk head has settled on a new track, most disks immediately begin reading sectors into their buffer memory, regardless of which sectors have been requested. This way, if there is a request for one of the sectors that have already passed under the disk head, the data can be transferred immediately, rather than having to delay the request for nearly a full rotation to reread the data.

- **Transfer.** Once the disk head reaches a desired sector, the disk must transfer the data from the sector to its buffer memory (for reads) or vice versa (for writes) as the sectors rotate underneath the head. Then, for reads, it must transfer the data from its buffer memory to the host's main memory. For writes, the order of the transfers is reversed.

  surface transfer time

  To amortize seek and rotation time, disk requests are often for multiple sequential sectors. The time to transfer one or more sequential sectors from (or to) a surface once the disk head begins reading (or writing) the first sector is the *surface transfer time*.

On a modern disk, the surface transfer time for a single sector is much smaller than the seek time or rotational latency. For example, disk bandwidths often exceed 100 MB/s, so the surface transfer time for a 512-byte sector is often under 5 microseconds (0.005 ms).

Because a disk's outer tracks have room for more sectors than its inner tracks and because a given disk spins at a constant rate, the surface transfer bandwidth is often higher for the outer tracks than the inner tracks.

host transfer time

For a disk read, once sectors have been transferred to the disk's buffer memory, they must be transferred to the host's memory over some connection such as SATA (serial ATA), SAS (serial attached SCSI), Fibre Channel, or USB (universal serial bus). For writes, the transfer goes in the other direction. The time to transfer data between the host's memory and the disk's buffer is the *host transfer time*. Typical bandwidths range from 60 MB/s for USB 2.0 to 2500 MB/s for Fibre Channel-20GFC.

For multi-sector reads, disks pipeline transfers between the surface and disk buffer memory and between buffer memory and host memory; so for large transfers, the total transfer time will be dominated by whichever of these is the bottleneck. Similarly, for writes, disks overlap the host transfer with the seek, rotation, and surface transfer; again, the total transfer time will be dominated by whichever is the bottleneck.

12.1.2 Case Study: Toshiba MK3254GSY

Figure 12.3 shows some key parameters for a recent 2.5-inch disk drive for laptop computers.

This disk stores 320 GB of data on two platters, so it stores 80 GB per surface. The platters spin at 7200 revolutions per minute, which is 8.3 ms per revolution; since each platter's diameter is about 6.3 cm, the outer edge of each platter is moving at about 85 km/hour!

The disk's data sheet indicates an average seek time for the drive of 10.5 ms for reads and 12.0 ms for writes. The seek time for reads and writes differs because the disk starts attempting to read data before the disk arm has completely settled, but it must wait a bit longer before it is safe to write.

When transferring long runs of contiguous sectors, the disk's bandwidth is 54-128 MB/s. The bandwidth is expressed as a range because the disk's outer tracks have more sectors than its inner tracks, so when the disk is accessing data on its outer tracks, sectors sweep past the disk head at a higher rate.

Once the data is transferred off the platter, the disk can send it to the main memory of the computer at up to 375 MB/s via a SATA (Serial ATA) interface.

Random vs. sequential performance. Given seek and rotational times measured in milliseconds, small accesses to random sectors on disk are much slower than large, sequential accesses.

Size	
Platters/Heads	2/4
Capacity	320 GB
Performance	
Spindle speed	7200 RPM
Average seek time read/write	10.5 ms/ 12.0 ms
Maximum seek time	19 ms
Track-to-track seek time	1 ms
Transfer rate (surface to buffer)	54–128 MB/s
Transfer rate (buffer to host)	375 MB/s
Buffer memory	16 MB
Power	
Typical	16.35 W
Idle	11.68 W

Figure 12.3: Hardware specifications for a laptop disk (Toshiba MK3254GSY) manufactured in 2008.

EXAMPLE **Random access workload.** For the disk described in Figure 12.3, consider a workload consisting of 500 read requests, each of a randomly chosen sector on disk, assuming requests are serviced in FIFO order. How long will servicing these requests take?

ANSWER Disk access time is seek time + rotation time + transfer time.

Seek time. Each request requires a seek from a random starting track to a random ending track, so the disk's average seek time of 10.5 ms is a good estimate of the cost of each seek.

Rotation time. Once the disk head settles on the right track, it must wait for the desired sector to rotate under it. Since there is no reason to expect the desired sector to be particularly near or far from the disk head when it settles, a reasonable estimate for rotation time is 4.15 ms, one half of the time that it takes a 7200 RPM disk to rotate once.

Transfer time. The disk's surface bandwidth is at least 54 MB/s, so transferring 512 bytes takes at most 9.5 μS (0.0095 ms).

Total time. 10.5 + 4.15 + .0095 = 14.66 ms per request, so **500 requests will take about 7.33 seconds**.

□

EXAMPLE **Sequential access workload.** For the disk described in Figure 12.3, consider a workload consisting of a read request for 500 sequential sectors on the same track. How long will servicing these requests take?

ANSWER Disk access time is seek time + rotation time + transfer time.

Seek time. Since we do not know which track we are starting with or which track we are reading from, we use the average seek time, 10.5 ms, as an estimate for the seek time.

Rotation time. Since we don't know the position of the disk when the request is issued, a simple and reasonable estimate for the time for the first desired block to rotate to the disk head is 4.15 ms, one half of the time that it takes a 7200 RPM disk to rotate once.

Transfer time. A simple estimate is that 500 sectors can be transferred in 4.8 to 2.0 ms, depending on whether they are on the inner or outer tracks.

$$500 \text{ sectors} * 512\frac{\text{bytes}}{\text{sector}} * \frac{\text{second}}{54 * 10^6 \text{bytes}} = 4.8 \text{ ms}$$

$$500 \text{ sectors} * 512\frac{\text{bytes}}{\text{sector}} * \frac{\text{second}}{128 * 10^6 \text{bytes}} = 2 \text{ ms}$$

(Too) simple answer. These three estimates give us a range from

$$10.5 + 4.15 + 2 = 16.7 \text{ ms}$$

to

$$10.5 + 4.15 + 4.8 = 19.5 \text{ ms}$$

More precise answer. However, this simple answer ignores the track buffer. Since the transfer time is a large fraction of the rotation time (about 1/4 to 1/2 of the time for a full rotation), we know that the request covers a significant fraction of a track. This means that there is a good chance that after the seek and settle time, the disk head will be in the middle of the region to be read. In this case, the disk will immediately read some of the track into the track buffer; then it will wait for the first track to rotate around; then it will read the remainder of the desired data.

We can estimate that for the outer track, there is a one in four chance that the initial seek and settle will finish while the head is within the desired range of sectors, and that when that happens, we read an average of $\frac{1}{8}$th of the desired data before we arrive at the first desired sector. So, for the outer track, this overlap will save us $\frac{1}{4} * \frac{1}{8} = \frac{1}{32}$ of a rotation for the average transfer. This effect slightly reduces the average access time: $16.7 \text{ ms} - \frac{1}{32} * 8.3 \text{ ms} = 16.4 \text{ ms}$.

Similarly, for the inner tracks, there is about a one in two chance that the initial seek will settle in the middle of the desired data, saving on average $\frac{1}{2} * \frac{1}{4} = \frac{1}{8}$. This reduces the average access time: $19.5 \text{ ms} - \frac{1}{8} * 8.3 \text{ ms} = 18.5 \text{ ms}$.

So, we estimate that **such an access would take between 16.4 ms and 18.5 ms**.

$\square$

Notice that the sequential workload takes vastly less time than the random workload (less than 20 milliseconds vs. 5.5 seconds). This orders of magnitude disparity between sequential and random access performance influences many aspects of file system design and use.

Still, even for a 500 sector request, a non-trivial amount of the access time is spent seeking and rotating rather than transferring.

EXAMPLE   **Effective bandwidth.** For the transfer of 500 sequential sectors examined in the previous example, what fraction of the disk's surface bandwidth is realized?

ANSWER   The effective bandwidth ranges from

$$(500\,\text{sectors})(512\,\frac{\text{bytes}}{\text{sector}})(\frac{1}{18.5\,\text{ms}})(\frac{1\,\text{MB}}{1000000\,\text{bytes}})(\frac{1000\,\text{ms}}{\text{s}}) = 13.8\,\text{MB/s}$$

$$(500\,\text{sectors})(512\,\frac{\text{bytes}}{\text{sector}})(\frac{1}{16.4\,\text{ms}})(\frac{1\,\text{MB}}{1000000\,\text{bytes}})(\frac{1000\,\text{ms}}{\text{s}}) = 15.6\,\text{MB/s}$$

This gives us a range of $\frac{13.8\,\text{MB/s}}{54\,\text{MB/s}} = $ **26% to** $\frac{15.6\,\text{MB/s}}{128\,\text{MB/s}} = $ **12%** of the maximum bandwidth from the inner to the outer tracks.   □

So, even a fairly large request (500 sectors or 250 KB in this case) can incur significant overheads from seek and rotational latency.

EXAMPLE   **Efficient access.** For the disk described in Figure 12.3, how large must a request that begins on a random disk sector be to ensure that the disk gets at least 80% of its advertised maximum surface transfer bandwidth?

ANSWER   When reading a long sequence of logically sequential blocks, the disk will read an entire track, then do a 1 track seek (or a head switch and resettle, which amounts to the same thing) and then read the next track. Notice that track buffering allows the disk to read an entire track in one rotation regardless of which sector the head is over when it settles on the track and starts successfully reading. So, for the outer tracks, it reads for one rotation (8.4 ms) and then does a minimum seek (1 ms).

Thus, to achieve 80% of peak bandwidth after a random seek (10.5 ms), we need to read enough rotations worth of data to ensure that we spend 80% of the total time reading. If x is the number of rotations we will read, then we have:

$$0.8\,\text{totalTime} = x\,\text{rotationTime}$$
$$0.8(10.5\,\text{ms} + (1 + 8.4)x\,\text{ms}) = 8.4x\,\text{ms}$$
$$x = 9.09$$

We therefore need to read at least 9.09 rotations worth of data to reach an efficiency of 80%. Since each rotation takes 8.4 ms and transfers data at 128 MB/s, 9.09 rotations transfers **9.77 MB** of data, **or about 19,089 sectors**.
          □

12.1.3 Disk Scheduling

Because moving the disk arm and waiting for the platter to rotate is so expensive, performance can be significantly improved by optimizing the order in which pending requests are serviced. Disk scheduling can be done by the operating system, by the disk's firmware, or both.

FIFO. The simplest thing to do is to process requests in first-in-first-out (FIFO) order. Unfortunately, a FIFO scheduler can yield poor performance. For example, a sequence of requests that alternate between the outer and inner tracks of a disk will result in many long seeks.

SPTF/SSTF. An initially appealing option is to use a greedy scheduler that, given the current position of the disk head and platter, always services the pending request that can be handled in the minimum amount of time. This approach is called *shortest positioning time first* (SPTF) (or *shortest seek time first* (SSTF) if rotational positioning is not considered.)

shortest positioning time first

shortest seek time first

SPTF and SSTF have two significant limitations. First, because moving the disk arm and waiting for some rotation time affects the cost of serving subsequent requests, these greedy approaches are not guaranteed to optimize disk performance. Second, these greedy approaches can cause starvation when, for example, a continuous stream of requests to inner tracks prevents requests to outer tracks from ever being serviced.

EXAMPLE

SPTF is not optimal. Suppose a disk's head is just inside the middle track of a disk so that seeking to the inside track would cost 9.9 ms while seeking to the outside track would cost 10.1 ms. Assume that for the disk in question, seeking between the outer and inner track costs 15 ms and that a rotation takes 10 ms.

Also suppose that the disk has two sets of pending requests. The first set is 1000 requests to read each of the 1000 sectors on the inner track of the disk; the second set is 2000 requests to read each of the 2000 sectors on the outer track of the disk.

Compare the average response time per request for the SPTF schedule (first read the "nearby" inner track and then read the outer track) and the alternative of reading the outer track first and then the inner track.

ANSWER

The total amount of time taken to complete all requests is slightly shorter by seeking first to the inside track and then to the outside. However, the *average* response time per request is less in the opposite order.

To service either set of requests, the disk must seek to the appropriate track and then wait for one full rotation while all of the track's data sweeps under the arm. For either set, the average response time for a request in that set will be the delay until the seek completes plus one half the disk's rotation time. Notice that the set handled second must wait until the first one is completely done before it can start, adding to the response time observed for requests in that set.

If we follow SPTF and read the sectors on the inner track first, the response time of the average request is the weighted average of the response time of the inner requests and the outer requests:

$$(1000(9.9 + 5) + 2000(9.9 + 10 + 15 + 5))/3000 \quad = 31.6 \, \text{ms}$$

If, instead, we read the outer tracks first, the weighted average is:

$$(2000(10.1 + 5) + 1000(10.1 + 10 + 15 + 5))/3000 \quad = 23.3 \, \text{ms}$$

In this case, seeking to the nearest sector moves the disk head away from the majority of the requests, **increasing the overall average response time by 8.3 ms**. □

Elevator, SCAN, and CSCAN. Elevator-based algorithms like SCAN and CSCAN have good performance and also ensure fairness in that no request is forced to wait for an inordinately long time. The basic approach is similar to how an elevator works: when an elevator is going up, it keeps going up until all pending requests to go to floors above it have been satisfied; then, when an elevator is going down, it keeps going down until all pending requests to go to floors below it have been satisfied.

SCAN   The *SCAN* scheduler works in the same way. The disk arm first sweeps from the inner to the outer tracks, servicing all requests that are between the arm's current position and the outer edge of the disk. Then, the arm sweeps from the outer to the inner tracks. Then the process is repeated. Figure 12.4-(left) illustrates the SCAN algorithm travelling from outer-to-inner tracks to service four pending requests and then travelling from inner-to-outer tracks to service three additional requests.

CSCAN   The *CSCAN* (circular SCAN) scheduler is a slight variation on SCAN in which the disk only services requests when the head is traveling in one direction (e.g., from inner tracks to outer ones). When the last request in the direction of travel is reached, the disk immediately seeks to where it started (e.g., the most inner track or the most inner track with a pending request) and services pending requests by moving the head *in the same direction* as the original pass (e.g., from inner tracks to outer ones again.) Figure 12.4-(center) illustrates the CSCAN algorithm travelling from outer-to-inner tracks to service four pending requests and then skipping to the outer track and travelling from outer-to-inner tracks to service three additional requests.

     The advantage of CSCAN over SCAN is that if after a pass in one direction, the disk head were to just switch directions (as in SCAN), it will encounter a region of the disk where pending requests are sparse (since this region of the disk was just serviced). Seeking to the opposite side of the disk (as in CSCAN) moves the disk head to an area where pending requests are likely to be denser. In addition, CSCAN is more fair than SCAN in that seeking to the

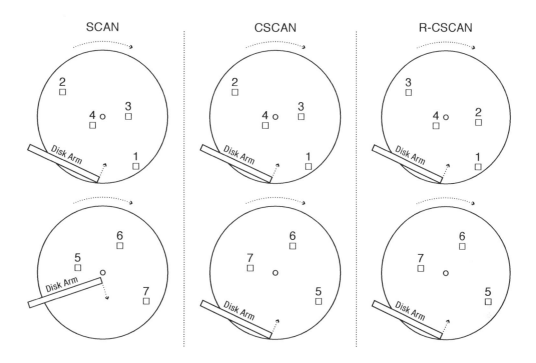

Figure 12.4: Elevator-based scheduling algorithms: (left) SCAN, (center) CSCAN, and (right) R-CSCAN. The numbering represents the order that each algorithm services requests 1-4 and then 5-7.

opposite side of the disk allows it to begin servicing the requests that likely been waiting longer than requests near but "just behind" the head.

Rather than pure seek-minimizing SCAN or CSCAN, schedulers also take into account rotation time and allow small seeks "in the wrong direction" **R-SCAN** to avoid extra rotational delays using the rotationally-aware *R-SCAN* or *R-* **R-CSCAN** *CSCAN* variations. For example, if the disk head is currently over sector 0 of track 0 and there are pending requests at sector 1000 of track 0, sector 500 of track 1, and sector 0 of track 10,000, a R-CSCAN scheduler might service the second request, then the first, and then the third. Figure 12.4-(right) illustrates the R-CSCAN algorithm handling a request on the outer track, then one a few tracks in, then another request on the outer track, and a request near the center on the arm's first sweep. The arm's second sweep is the same as for CSCAN.

EXAMPLE   **Effect of disk scheduling.** For the disk described in Figure 12.3, consider a workload consisting of 500 read requests, each to a randomly chosen sector on disk, assuming that the disk head is on the outside track and that requests are serviced in CSCAN order from outside to inside. How long will servicing these requests take?

ANSWER   Answering a question like this requires making some educated guesses; different people may come up with different reasonable estimates here.

Seek time. We first note that with 500 pending requests spread randomly across the disk, the average seek from one request to the next will seek 0.2% of the way across the disk. With four surfaces, most of these seeks will also require a head switch. We don't know the exact time for a seek 0.2% of the way across the disk, but we can estimate it by interpolating between the time for a 1 track seek (1 ms) and the time for a 33.3% seek (10.5 ms for reads.) (Disk seek time is not actually linear in distance, but as we will see in a moment, the exact seek time seems unlikely to affect our answer much.)

$$\text{estimated .2\% seek time} \quad = \left(1 + \tfrac{.2}{33.3}10.5\right)\text{ms}$$
$$= 1.06\text{ ms}$$

Rotation time. Since we don't know the position of the disk when the seek finishes and since sectors are scattered randomly, a simple and reasonable estimate for the time after the seek finishes for the desired block to rotate to the disk head is 4.15 ms, one half of the time that it takes a 7200 RPM disk to rotate once.

Transfer time. Similar to the example on page 524, the transfer time for each sector is at most 0.0095 ms

Total time. 1.06 + 4.15 + .0095 = 5.22 ms per request, so **500 requests will take about 2.6 s.** Notice that the time for the SCAN scheduled time is less than half the 7.8 s time for the FIFO-scheduled time for the example on page 524

□

12.2 | Flash Storage

What is flash storage and how does it work?

Over the past decade, flash storage has become a widely used storage medium. Flash storage is the dominant storage technology for handheld devices from phones to cameras to thumb drives, and it is used in an increasing fraction of laptop computers and machine room servers.

solid state storage

Flash storage is a type of *solid state storage*: it has no moving parts and stores data using electrical circuits. Because it has no moving parts, flash storage can have much better random IO performance than disks, and it can use less power and be less vulnerable to physical damage. On the other hand, flash storage remains significantly more expensive per byte of storage than disks.

Each flash storage element is a floating gate transistor. As Figure 12.5 illustrates, an extra gate in such a transistor "floats"—it is not connected to any circuit. Since the floating gate is entirely surrounded by an insulator, it will hold an electrical charge for months or years without requiring any power. Even though the floating gate is not electrically connected to anything, it can be charged or discharged via electron tunneling by running a sufficiently high-voltage current near it. The floating gate's state of charge affects the transistor's threshold voltage for activation. Thus, the floating gate's state can be detected by applying an intermediate voltage to the transistor's control

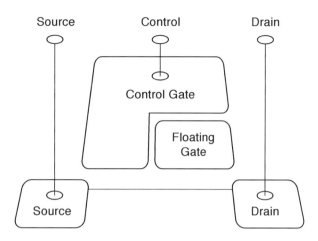

Figure 12.5: A floating gate transistor.

gate that will only be sufficient to activate the transistor if the floating gate is changed.

In single-level flash storage, the floating gate stores one bit (charge or not charged); in multi-level flash storage, the floating gate stores multiple bits by storing one of several different charge levels.

NOR flash storage is wired to allow individual words to be written and read. NOR flash storage is useful for storing device firmware since it can be executed in place. NAND flash storage is wired to allow reads and writes of a page at a time, where a page is typically 2 KB to 4 KB. NAND flash is denser than NOR flash, so NAND is used in the storage systems we will consider.

Flash storage access and performance   Flash storage is accessed using three operations.

- **Erase erasure block.** Before flash memory can be written, it must be erased by setting each cell to a logical "1". Flash memory can only be erased in large units called *erasure blocks*. Today, erasure blocks are often 128 KB to 512 KB. Erasure is a slow operation, usually taking several milliseconds.

erasure blocks

  Erasing an erasure block is what gives flash memory its name for its resemblance to the flash of a camera.

- **Write page.** Once erased, NAND flash memory can be written on a page-by-page basis, where each page is typically 2048-4096 bytes. Writing a page typically takes tens of microseconds.

- **Read page.** NAND flash memory can be read on a page by page basis. Reading a page typically takes tens of microseconds.

flash translation layer

Notice that to write a page, its entire erasure block must first be erased. This is a challenge both because erasure is slow and because erasure affects a large number of pages. Flash drives implement a *flash translation layer* (FTL) that maps logical flash pages to different physical pages on the flash device. Then, when a single logical page is overwritten, the FTL writes the new version to some free, already-erased physical page and remaps the logical page to that physical page.

Write remapping significantly improves flash performance.

EXAMPLE

Remapping flash writes. Consider a flash drive with a 4 KB pages, 512 KB erasure blocks, 3 ms flash times, and 50 μs read-page and write-page times. Suppose writing a page is done with a naive algorithm that reads an entire erasure block, erases it, and writes the modified erasure block. How long would each page write take?

ANSWER

This naive approach would require:

$$\frac{512 \text{ KB/erasure block}}{4 \text{ KB/page}} * (\text{page read time} + \text{page write time}) + \text{block erase time}$$

$$= 128 * (50 + 50)\mu s + 3 \text{ ms}$$

$$= \textbf{15.8 ms per write}$$

□

Suppose remapping is used and that a flash device always has at least one unused erasure block available for a target workload. How long does an average write take now?

ANSWER

With remapping, the cost of flashing an erasure block is amortized over 512/4 = 128 page writes. This scenario gives a cost of $\frac{3 \text{ ms}}{128} + 50 \mu s = \textbf{73.4} \mu \textbf{s}$ per write.

□

In practice, there is likely to be some additional cost per write under the remapping scheme because in order to flash an erasure block to free it for new writes, the firmware may need to garbage collect live pages from that erasure block and copy those live pages to a different erasure block.

Internally, a flash device may have multiple independent data paths that can be accessed in parallel. Therefore, to maximize sustained bandwidth when accessing a flash device, operating systems issue multiple concurrent requests to the device.

Durability. Normally, flash memory can retain its state for months or years without power. However, over time the high current loads from flashing and writing memory causes the circuits to degrade. Eventually, after a few thousand to a few million program-erase cycles (depending on the type of flash), a given cell may *wear out* and no longer reliably store a bit.

wear out

In addition, reading a flash memory cell a large number of times can cause the surrounding cells' charges to be disturbed. A *read disturb error* can occur

read disturb error

if a location in flash memory is read to many times without the surrounding memory being written.

To improve durability in the face of wear from writes and disturbs from reads, flash devices make use of a number of techniques:

- **Error correcting codes.** Each page has some extra bytes that are used for error correcting codes to protect against bit errors in the page.

- **Bad page and bad erasure block management.** If a page or erasure block has a manufacturing defect or wears out, firmware on the device marks it as bad and stops storing data on it.

- **Wear leveling.** As noted above, rather than overwrite a page in place, the flash translation layer remaps the logical page to a new physical page that has already been erased. This remapping ensures that a hot page that is overwritten repeatedly does not prematurely wear out a particular physical page on the flash device.

wear leveling

  Wear leveling moves a flash device's logical pages to different physical pages to ensure that no physical page gets an inordinate number of writes and wears out prematurely. Some wear leveling algorithms also migrate unmodified pages to protect against read disturb errors.

- **Spare pages and erasure blocks.** Flash devices can be manufactured with spare pages and spare erasure blocks in the device. This spare capacity serves two purposes.

  First, it provides extra space for wear leveling: even if the device is logically "full" the wear leveling firmware can copy live pages out of some existing erasure blocks into a spare erasure block, allowing it to flash those existing erasure blocks.

  Second, it allows bad page and bad erasure block management to function without causing the logical size of the device to shrink.

In addition to affecting reliability, wear out affects a flash device's performance over time.

First, as a device wears out, accesses may require additional retries, slowing them. Second, as spare pages and erasure blocks are consumed by bad ones, the wear leveling algorithms have less spare space and have to garbage collect live pages — copying them out of their existing erasure blocks — more frequently.

Example: Intel 710 Series Solid-State Drive Figure 12.6 shows some key parameters for an Intel 710 Series solid state drive manufactured in 2011. This drive uses multi-level NAND flash to get high storage densities. Normally, multi-level flash is less durable than single-level, but this Intel drive uses sophisticated wear leveling algorithms and a large amount of spare space to provide high durability.

The sequential performance of this drive is very good, with peak sustained read and write bandwidths of 270 MB/s and 210 MB/s respectively. In

Size	
Capacity	300 GB
Page Size	4 KB
Performance	
Bandwidth (Sequential Reads)	270 MB/s
Bandwidth (Sequential Writes)	210 MB/s
Read/Write Latency	75 μs
Random Reads Per Second	38,500
Random Writes Per Second	2,000
	2,400 with 20% space reserve
Interface	SATA 3 Gb/s
Endurance	
Endurance	1.1 PB
	1.5 PB with 20% space reserve
Power	
Power Consumption Active/Idle	3.7 W / 0.7 W

Figure 12.6: Key parameters for an Intel 710 Series Solid State Drive manufactured in 2011.

comparison, a high-end Seagate Cheetah 15K.7 drive manufactured in 2010 spins at 15,000 revolutions per minute and provides 122 MB/s to 204 MB/s of sustained bandwidth.

Random read performance is excellent. The latency for a single random 4 KB read is just 75 μs, and when multiple concurrent requests are in flight, the drive can process 38,500 random reads per second — one every 26 μs. This is orders of magnitude better than the random read performance of a spinning disk drive.

Random write performance is also very good, but not as good as random read performance. The latency for a single random 4 KB write is 75 μs; the drive reduces write latency by buffering writes in volatile memory, and it has capacitors that store enough charge to write all buffered updates to flash storage if a power loss occurs.

When multiple concurrent writes are in flight, the drive can process 2,000 random writes per second when it is full; if it is less than 80% full, that number rises to 2,400. Random write throughput increases when the drive has more free space because the drive has to garbage collect live pages from erasure blocks less often and because when the drive eventually does do that garbage collection, the erasure blocks are less full.

The drive's is rated for 1.1 PB ($1.1 * 10^{15}$ bytes) of endurance (1.5 PB if it is less than 80% full.) For many workloads, this endurance suffices for years or decades of use. However, solid state drives may not always be a good match for high-bandwidth write streaming. In the extreme, an application constantly streaming writes at 200 MB/s could wear this drive out in 64 days.

Technology Affects Interfaces—the TRIM Command

Historically, when a file system deleted a file stored on a spinning disk, all it needed to do was to update the file's metadata and the file system's free space bitmap. It did not need to erase or overwrite the file's data blocks on disk—once the metadata was updated, these blocks could never be referenced, so there was no need to do anything with them.

When such file systems were used with flash drives, users observed that their drives got slower over time. As the amount of free space fell, the drives' flash translation layer was forced to garbage collect erasure blocks more frequently; additionally, each garbage collection pass became more expensive because there were more live pages to copy from old erasure blocks to the new ones.

Notice that this slowing could occur even if the file system appeared to have a large amount of free space. For example, if a file system moves a large file from one range of blocks to another, the storage hardware has no way to know that the pages in the old range are no longer needed unless the file system can tell it so.

The TRIM command was introduced into many popular operating systems between 2009 and 2011 to allow file systems to inform the underlying storage when the file system has stopped using a page of storage. The TRIM command makes the free space known to the file system visible to the underlying storage layer, which can significantly reduce garbage collection overheads and help flash drives retain good performance as they age.

EXAMPLE **Random read workload.** For the solid state disk described in Figure 12.6, consider a workload consisting of 500 read requests, each of a randomly chosen page. How long will servicing these requests take?

ANSWER The disk can service random read requests at a rate of 38,500 per second, so 500 requests will take 500/38500 = **13 ms**. In contrast, for the spinning disk example on page 12.1.2, the same 500 requests would take 7.33 seconds. □

EXAMPLE **Random vs. sequential reads.** How does this drive's random read performance compare to its sequential read performance?

ANSWER The effective bandwidth in this case is 500 requests * 4 $\frac{KB}{request}$ / 13 milliseconds = 158 MB/s. The random read bandwidth is thus 158/270 = **59% of the sequential read bandwidth**. □

EXAMPLE **Random write workload.** For the solid state disk described in Figure 12.6, consider a workload consisting of 500 write requests, each of a randomly chosen page. How long will servicing these requests take?

ANSWER   The disk can service random write requests at a rate of 2000 per second (assuming the disk is nearly full), so 500 requests will take $500/2000 = $ **250 ms**.
                                                                                          □

EXAMPLE   **Random vs. sequential writes.** How does this random write performance compare to the drive's sequential write performance?

ANSWER   The effective bandwidth in this case is 500 requests $* 4 \frac{KB}{request}$ / 250 ms = 8.2 MB/s. The random write bandwidth is thus $8.2/210 = $ **3.9% of the sequential write bandwidth**.
                                                                                          □

12.3 | Summary and Future Directions

Today, spinning disk and flash memory dominate storage technologies, and each has sufficient advantages to beat the other for some workloads and environments.

Spinning disk vs. flash storage.   Spinning disks are often used when capacity is the primary goal. For example, spinning disk is often used for storing media files and home directories. For workloads limited by storage capacity, spinning disks can often provide much better capacity per dollar than flash storage. For example, in October 2011, a 2 TB Seagate Barracuda disk targeted at workstations cost about $80 and a 300 GB Intel 320 Series solid state drive targeted at laptops cost about $600, giving the spinning disk about a 50:1 advantage in GB per dollar.

Both spinning disks and flash storage are viable when sequential bandwidth is the goal. In October 2011, flash drives typically have modestly higher per-drive sequential bandwidths than spinning drives, but the spinning drives typically have better sequential bandwidth per dollar spent than flash drives. For example, the same Seagate disk has a sustained bandwidth of 120 MB/s (1.5 MB/s per dollar) while the same Intel SSD has a read/write bandwidth of 270/205 MB/s (about 0.4 MB/s per dollar.)

Flash storage is often used when good random access performance or low power consumption is the goal. For example, flash storage is frequently used in database transaction processing servers, in smart phones, and in laptops. For example, the Seagate drive described above rotates at 5900 RPM, so it takes about 5 ms for a half rotation. Even with good scheduling and even if data is confined to a subset of tracks, it would be hard to get more than 200 random I/Os per second from this drive (about 2.5 random I/Os per second per dollar.) Conversely, the Intel SSD can sustain 23,000 random writes and 39,500 random reads per second (about 38 or 66 random writes or reads per second per dollar.)

With respect to power, spinning disks typically consume 10-20W depending on whether it is just spinning or actively reading and writing data, while a

Figure 12.7: In 2011, flash storage "keys" such as this one can store as much as 256 GB in a device that is a few centimeters long, and 1-2 cm wide and tall.

Metric	Spinning Disk	Flash
Capacity/Cost	Excellent	Good
Sequential BW/Cost	Good	Good
Random I/O per Second/Cost	Poor	Good
Power Consumption	Fair	Good
Physical Size	Good	Excellent

Figure 12.8: Relative advantages and disadvantages of spinning disk and flash storage.

flash drive might consume 0.5W-1W when idle and 3-5W when being accessed. Flash drives' power advantage makes them attractive for portable applications such as laptop and smartphone storage.

Flash memory can also have a significant form factor advantage with respect to physical size and weight. Although some flash drives are designed as drop-in replacements for spinning disks and so are similar in size, flash storage can be much smaller than a typical spinning disk. For example, in 2011, a USB flash storage "key" such as the one in Figure 12.7 can store as much as 256 GB in a device that is not much larger than a house key.

Figure 12.8 summarizes these advantages and disadvantages; of course, many systems need to do well on multiple metrics, so system designers may need to compromise on some metrics or use combinations of technologies.

Technology trends. Over the past decades, the cost of storage capacity has fallen rapidly for both spinning disks and solid state storage. Compare the 2 TB disk drive for $80 in 2011 to a 15 MB drive costing $113 in 1984 (or about $246 in 2011 dollars): the cost per byte has improved by a factor of about 400,000 over 27 years — over 50% per year for nearly 3 decades.

Recent rates of improvement for flash storage have been even faster. For example, in 2001, the Adtron S35PC 14 GB flash drive cost $42,000. Today's Intel 320 costs 70 times less for 21 times more capacity, an improvement of about 2x per year over the past decade.

The first disk drive

Prior to the invention of magnetic disks, magnetic cylinders, called drums, were used for on-line storage. These drums spun on their axes and typically had one head per track. So, there was no seek time to access a block of data; one merely waited for a block to rotate underneath its head.

By using spinning disks instead of drums, the magnetic surface area, and hence the storage capacity, could be increased.

Photo by U. S. Army Red River Arsenal.

The first disk drive, the IBM 350 Disk System (two are shown in the foreground of this photograph), was introduced in 1956 as part of the IBM RAMAC ("Random Access Method of Accounting and Control") 305 computer system. The 350 Disk system stored about 3.3 MB on 50 platters, rotated its platters at 1200 RPM, had an average seek time of 600 ms, and weighed about a ton. The RAMAC 305 computer system with its 350 disk system could be leased for $3,200 per month. Assuming a useful life of 5 years and converting to 2011 dollars, the cost was approximately $1.3 million for the system — about $400,000 per megabyte.

Similar capacity improvements for spinning disk and flash are expected for at least the next few years. Beyond that, there is concern that we will be approaching the physical limits of both magnetic disk and flash storage, so the longer-term future is less certain. (That said, people have worried that disks were approaching their limits several times in the past, and we will not be surprised if the magnetic disk and flash industries continue rapid improvements for quite a few more years.)

In contrast to capacity, performance is likely to improve more slowly for both technologies. For example, a mid-range spinning disk in 1991 might have had a maximum bandwidth of 1.3 MB/s and an average seek time of 17 ms. Bandwidths have improved by about a factor of 90 in two decades (about 25% per year) while seek times and rotational latencies have only improved by about a factor of two (less than 4% per year.) Bandwidths have improved more quickly than rotational latency and seek times because bandwidth benefits from increasing storage densities, not just increasing rotational rates.

For SSDs, the story is similar, though recent increases in volumes have helped speed the pace of improvements. For example, in 2006 a BitMicro E-Disk flash drive could provide 9,500 to 11,700 random reads per second and 34-44 MB/s sustained bandwidth. Compared to the Intel 320 SSD from 2011, bandwidths have improved by about 40% per year and random access throughput has improved by about 25% per year over the past 5 years.

New technologies. This is an exciting time for persistent storage. After decades of undisputed reign as the dominant technology for on-line persistent storage, spinning magnetic disks are being displaced by flash storage in many application domains, giving both operating system designers and application writers an opportunity to reexamine how to best use storage. Looking forward, many researchers speculate that new technologies may soon be nipping at the heels and even surpassing flash storage.

phase change memory   For example, *phase change memory* (PCM) uses a current to alter the state of chalcogenide glass between amorphous and crystalline forms, which have significantly different electrical resistance and can therefore be used to represent data bits. Although PCM does not yet match the density of flash, researchers speculate that the technology is fundamentally more scalable and will ultimately be able to provide higher storage densities at lower costs. Furthermore, PCM is expected to have much better write performance and endurance than flash.

memristors   As another example, *memristors* are circuit elements whose resistance depends on the amounts and directions of currents that have flowed through them in the past. A number of different memristor constructions are being pursued, and some have quite promising properties. For example, in 2010 Hewlett Packard labs described a prototype memristor constructed of a thin titanium dioxide film with 3 nm by 3 nm storage elements that can switch states in 1 ns. These densities are similar to contemporary flash memory devices and these switching times are similar to contemporary DRAM chips. The devices also have write endurance similar to flash, and extremely long (theoretically unlimited) storage lifetimes. Furthermore, researchers believe that these and others memristors' densities will scale well in the future. For example, in 2009 a design for 3-D stacking of memristors was published in the *Proceedings of National Academy of Sciences* by Dmitri Strukov and R. Stanley Williams of HP Labs.

If technologies such as these pan out as hoped, operating system designers will have opportunities to rethink our abstractions for both volatile and

Size	
Form factor	2.5 inch
Capacity	320 GB
Performance	
Spindle speed	5400 RPM
Average seek time	12.0 ms
Maximum seek time	21 ms
Track-to-track seek time	2 ms
Transfer rate (surface to buffer)	850 Mbit/s (maximum)
Transfer rate (buffer to host)	3 Gbit/s
Buffer memory	8 MB

Figure 12.9: Hardware specifications for a 320 GB SATA disk drive.

nonvolatile storage: how should we make use of word-addressable, persistent memory with densities exceeding current flash storage devices and with memory access times approaching those of DRAM? What could we do if each core on a 32 core processor chip had access to a few gigabytes of stacked memristor memory?

Exercises

1. **Discussion.** Some high-end disks in the 1980s had multiple disk arm assemblies per disk enclosure in order to allow them to achieve higher performance. Today, high-performance server disks have a single arm assembly per disk enclosure. Why do you think disks so seldom have multiple disk arm assemblies today?

2. For the disk described in Figure 12.3 on page 524:

    a) What is the range of the number of sectors per track on the disk?

    b) Estimate the number of tracks on the disk.

    c) Estimate the distance from the center of one track to the center of the next track.

3. A disk may have multiple surfaces, arms, and heads, but when you issue a read or write, only one head is active at a time. It seems like one could greatly increase disk bandwidth for large requests by reading or writing with all of the heads at the same time. Given the physical characteristics of disks, can you figure out why no one does this?

4. For the disk described in Figure 12.3 on page 524, consider a workload consisting of 500 read requests, each of a randomly chosen sector on disk, assuming that the disk head is on the outside track and that requests

are serviced in P-CSCAN order from outside to inside. How long will servicing these requests take?

Note: Answering this question will require making some estimates.

5. Suppose I have a disk such as the 320 GB SATA drive described in Figure 12.9 on page 540 and I have a workload consisting of 10000 reads to sectors randomly scattered across the disk. How long will these 10000 requests take (total) assuming the disk services requests in FIFO order?

6. Suppose I have a disk such as the 320 GB SATA drive described in Figure 12.9 on page 540 and I have a workload consisting of 10000 reads to 10000 sequential sectors on the outer-most tracks of the disk. How long will these 10000 requests take (total) assuming the disk services requests in FIFO order?

7. Suppose I have a disk such as the 320 GB SATA drive described in Figure 12.9 on page 540 and I have a workload consisting of 10000 reads to sectors randomly scattered across the disk. How long will these 10000 requests take (total) assuming the disk services requests using the SCAN/Elevator algorithm.

8. Suppose I have a disk such as the 320 GB SATA drive described in Figure 12.9 on page 540 and I have a workload consisting of 10000 reads to sectors randomly scattered across a 100 MB file, where the 100 MB file is laid out sequentially on the disk. How long will these 10000 requests take (total) assuming the disk services requests using the SCAN/Elevator algorithm?

9. Write a program that creates a 100 MB file on your local disk and then measures the time to do each of four things:

   a) **Sequential overwrite.** Overwrite the file with 100 MB of new data by writing the file from beginning to end and then calling fsync() (or the equivalent on your platform).

   b) **Random buffered overwrite.** Do the following 50,000 times: choose a 2 KB-aligned offset in the file uniformly at random, seek to that location in the file, and write 2 KB of data at that position. Then, once all 50,000 writes have been issued, call fsync() (or the equivalent on your platform).

   c) **Random buffered overwrite.** Do the following 50,000 times: choose a 2 KB-aligned offset in the file uniformly at random, seek to that location in the file, write 2 KB of data at that position, and call fsync() (or the equivalent on your platform) after each individual write.

   d) **Random read.** Do the following 50,000 times: choose a 2 KB-aligned offset in the file uniformly at random, seek to that location in the file, and read 2 KB of data at that position.

Size	
Usable capacity	2 TB (SLC flash)
Cache Size	64 GB (Battery-backed RAM)
Page Size	4 KB
Performance	
Bandwidth (Sequential Reads from flash)	2048 MB/s
Bandwidth (Sequential Writes to flash)	2048 MB/s
Read Latency (cache hit)	15 μs
Read Latency (cache miss)	200 μs
Write Latency	15 μs
Random Reads (sustained from flash)	100,000 per second
Random Writes (sustained to flash)	100,000 per second
Interface	8 Fibre Channel ports with 4 Gbit/s per port
Power	
Power Consumption	300 W

Figure 12.10: Key parameters for a hypothetical high-end flash drive in 2011.

Explain your results.

10. Write a program that creates three files, each of 100 MB, and then measures the time to do each of three things:

   a) **fopen()/fwrite().** Open the first file using fopen() and issue 256,000 sequential four-byte writes using fwrite().

   b) **open()/write().** Open the second file using open() and issue 256,000 sequential four-byte writes using write().

   c) **mmap()/store.** Map the third file into your program's memory using mmap() and issue 256,000 sequential four-byte writes by iterating through memory and writing to each successive word of the mapped file.

Explain your results.

11. Suppose that you have a 256 GB solid state drive that the operating system and drive both support the TRIM command. To evaluate the drive, you do an experiment where you time the system's write performance for random page-sized when the file system is empty compared to its performance when the file system holds 255 GB of data, and you find that write performance is significantly worse in the latter case.

What is the likely reason for this worse performance as the disk fills despite its support for TRIM?

What can be done to mitigate this slowdown?

12. Suppose you have a flash drive such as the one described in Figure 12.10 on page 542 and you have a workload consisting of 10000 4 KB reads to pages randomly scattered across the drive. Assuming that you wait for request i to finish before you issue request $i + 1$, how long will these 10000 requests take (total)?

13. Suppose you have a flash drive such as the one described in Figure 12.10 on page 542 and you have a workload consisting of 10000 4 KB reads to pages randomly scattered across the drive. Assuming that you issue requests concurrently, using many threads, how long will these 10000 requests take (total)?

14. Suppose you have a flash drive such as the one described in Figure 12.10 on page 542 and you have a workload consisting of 10000 4 KB writes to pages randomly scattered across the drive. Assuming that you wait for request i to finish before you issue request $i + 1$, how long will these 10000 requests take (total)?

15. Suppose you have a flash drive such as the one described in Figure 12.10 on page 542 and you have a workload consisting of 10000 4 KB writes to pages randomly scattered across the drive. Assuming that use a large number of threads to issue many writes concurrently, how long will these 10000 requests take (total)?

16. Suppose you have a flash drive such as the one described in Figure 12.10 on page 542 and you have a workload consisting of 10000 4 KB reads to 10000 sequential pages. How long will these 10000 request take (total)?

What's in a name? That which we call a rose
By any other name would smell as sweet.

Juliet
Romeo and Juliet (II, ii, 1-2)
(Shakespeare)

13 Files and Directories

Recall from Chapter 11 that file systems use directories to provide hierarchically named files, and that each file contains metadata and a sequence of data bytes. However, as Chapter 12 discussed, storage devices provide a much lower-level abstraction — large arrays of data blocks. Thus, to implement a file system, we must solve a translation problem: How do we go from a file name and offset to a block number?

A simple answer is that file systems implement a dictionary that maps keys (file name and offset) to values (block number on a device). We already have many data structures for implementing dictionaries, including hash tables, trees, and skip lists, so perhaps we can just use one of them?

Unfortunately, the answer is not so simple. File system designers face four major challenges:

- **Performance.** File systems need to provide good performance while coping with the limitations of the underlying storage devices. In practice, this means that file systems strive to ensure good *spatial locality*, where blocks that are accessed together are stored near one another, ideally in sequential storage blocks.

    spatial locality

- **Flexibility.** One major purpose of file systems is allowing applications to share data, so file systems must be jacks-of-all-trades. They would be less useful if we had to use one file system for large sequentially-read files, another for small seldom-written files, another for large random-access files, another for short-lived files, and so on.

- **Persistence.** File systems must maintain and update both user data and their internal data structures on persistent storage devices so that

File Name   Directory   File Number   Index Structure   Storage
Offset   ·······················>   Offset   ·······················>   Block

Figure 13.1: File systems map file names and file offsets to storage blocks in two steps. First, they use directories to map names to file numbers. Then they use an index structure such as a persistently stored tree to find the block that holds the data at any specific offset in that file.

everything survives operating system crashes and power failures.

- **Reliability.** File systems must be able to store important data for long periods of time, even if machines crash during updates or some of the system's storage hardware malfunctions.

This chapter discusses how file systems are organized to meet the first three challenges. Chapter 14 addresses reliability.

13.1 | Implementation Overview

What four key ideas are the core of file system design?

File systems must map file names and offsets to physical storage blocks in a way that allows efficient access. Although there are many different file systems, most implementations are based on four key ideas: directories, index structures, free space maps, and locality heuristics.

Directories and index structures.   As Figure 13.1 illustrates, file systems map file names and file offsets to specific storage blocks in two steps.

directory

First, they use *directories* to map human-readable file names to file numbers. Directories are often just special files that contain lists of *file name → file number* mappings.

index structure

Second, once a file name has been translated to a file number, file systems use a persistently stored *index structure* to locate the blocks of the file. The index structure can be any persistent data structure that maps a file number and offset to a storage block. Often, to efficiently support a wide range of file sizes and access patterns, the index structure is some form of tree.

free space map

Free space maps.   File systems implement *free space maps* to track which storage blocks are free and which are in use as files grow and shrink. At a minimum, a file system's free space map must allow the file system to find a free block when a file needs to grow, but because spatial locality is important, most modern file systems implement free space maps that allow them to find free blocks near a desired location. For example, many file systems implement free space maps as bitmaps in persistent storage.

```
music   320
work    219
foo.txt 871
```

Figure 13.2: A directory is a file that contains a collection of *file name → file number* mappings.

Locality heuristics. Directories and index structures allow file systems to locate desired file data and metadata no matter where they are stored, and free space maps allow them to locate free the space near any location on the persistent storage device. These *mechanisms* allow file systems to employ various *policies* to decide where a given block of a given file should be stored.

locality heuristics

These policies are embodied in *locality heuristics* for grouping data to optimize performance. For example, some file systems group each directory's files together but spread different directories to different parts of the storage device. Others periodically *defragment* their storage, rewriting existing files so that each file is stored in sequential storage blocks and so that the storage device has long runs of sequential free space so that new files can be written sequentially. Still others optimize writes over reads and write all data sequentially, whether a given set of writes contains updates to one file or to many different ones.

defragment

Implementation details. In this chapter, we first discuss how directories are implemented. Then, we look at the details of how specific file systems handle the details of placing and finding data in persistent storage by implementing different index structures, free space maps, and locality heuristics.

13.2 | Directories: Naming Data

How do file systems group related files and translate from file names to file numbers?

As Figure 13.1indicates, to access a file, the file system first translates the file's name to its number. For example, the file called /home/tom/foo.txt might internally known as file 66212871. File systems use directories to store their mappings from human-readable names to internal file numbers, and they organize these directories hierarchically so that users can group related files and directories.

Implementing directories in a way that provides hierarchical, name-to-number mappings turns out to be simple: use files to store directories. So, if the system needs to determine a file's number, it can just open up the appropriate directory file and scan through the file name/file number pairs until it finds the right one.

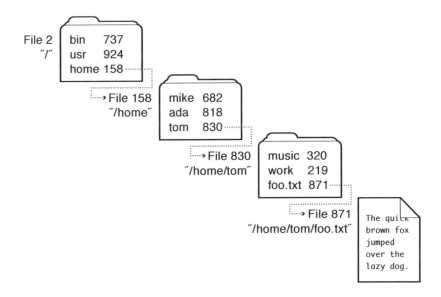

Figure 13.3: Directories can be arranged hierarchically by having one directory contain the *file name* → *file number* mapping for another directory.

For example, illustrates Figure 13.2 the contents of a single directory file. To open file foo.txt, the file system would scan this directory file, find the foo.txt entry, and see that file foo.txt has file number 66212871.

Of course, if we use files to store the contents of directories such as /home-/tom, we still have the problem of finding the directory files, themselves. As Figure 13.3 illustrates, the file number for directory /home/tom can be found by looking up the name tom in the directory /home, and the file number for directory /home can be found by looking up the name home in the root directory /.

Recursive algorithms need a base case—we cannot discover the root directories file number by looking in some other directory. The solution is to agree on the root directory's file number ahead of time. For example, the Unix Fast File System (FFS) and many other Unix and Linux file systems use two as the predefined file number for the root directory of a file system.

So, to read file /home/tom/foo.txt in Figure 13.3, we first read the root directory by reading the file with the well-known root number two. In that file, we search for the name home and find that directory /home is stored in file 88026158. By reading file 88026158 and searching for the name tom, we learn that directory /home/tom is stored in file 5268830. Finally, by reading file 5268830 and searching for the name foo.txt, we learn that /home/tom/foo.txt is file number 66212871.

Although looking up a file's number can take several steps, we expect there to be locality (e.g., when one file in a directory is accessed, other files in the directory are often likely to be accessed soon), so we expect that caching will reduce the number of disk accesses needed for most lookups.

Directory API. If file systems use files to store directory information, can we just use the standard open/close/read/write API to access them?

No. Directories use a specialized API because they must control the contents of these files. For example, file systems must prevent applications from corrupting the list of *name → file number* mappings, which could prevent the operating system from performing lookups or updates. As another example, the file system should enforce the invariant that each file number in a valid directory entry refers to a file that actually exists.

File systems therefore provide special system calls for modifying directory files. For example, rather than using the standard write system call to add a new file's entry to a directory, applications use the create call. By restricting updates, these calls ensure that directory files can always be parsed by the operating system. These calls also bind together the creation or removal of a file and the file's directory entry, so that directory entries always refer to actual files and that all files have at least one directory entry.

In the API described in Figure Overview in Chapter 11, the other calls that modify directory files are mkdir, link, unlink, and rmdir.

So, for example, for the file system illustrated in Figure 13.3, Tom could rename foo.txt to hw1.txt in his home directory by running a process that makes the following two system calls

```
link(''foo.txt'', ''hw1.txt'');
unlink(''foo.txt'');
```

Processes can simply read directory files with the standard read call.

EXAMPLE **Reading directories.** It is useful for programs to be able to get a list of all file names in a directory to, for example, recursively traverse a hierarchy from some point. However, the file system API described in Figure Overview in Chapter 11 does not have call specifically for reading directories.

Given just the system call API in that figure, how could a process learn the names of files in the process's current working directory?

ANSWER **Processes can read the contents of directory files using the standard file read system call used to read the contents of "normal" files.**

Although operating systems must restrict writes to directory files to ensure invariants on directory structure, they need not restrict applications from reading the contents of directory files (that they have permission to read). For simplicity, applications would access this function via a standard library that also includes routines for parsing directory files. □

Although it is not fundamentally necessary to have dedicated system calls for reading directories, it can be convenient. For example, Linux includes a getdents ("get directory entries") system call that reads a specified number of directory entries from an open file.

Figure 13.4: A linked list implementation of a directory. This example shows a directory file containing five entries: Music, Work, and foo.txt, along with . (the current directory) and .. (the parent directory).

Directory internals.   Many early implementations simply stored linear lists of *file name, file number* pairs in directory files. For example, in the original version of the Linux ext2 file system, each directory file stored a linked list of directory entries as illustrated in Figure 13.4.

Simple lists work fine when the number of directory entries is small, and that was the expected case for many early file systems, but systems occasionally encounter workloads that generate thousands of files in a directory. Once a directory has a few thousand entries, simple list-based directories become sluggish.

To efficiently support directories with many entries, many recent file systems including Linux XFS, Microsoft NTFS, and Oracle ZFS organize a directory's contents as a tree. Similarly, newer versions of ext2 augment the underlying linked list with an additional hash-based structure to speed searches.

For example, Figure 13.5-(a) illustrates a tree-based directory structure similar to the one used in Linux XFS, and Figure 13.5-(b) illustrates how these records are physically arranged in a directory file.

In this example, directory records mapping file names to file numbers are stored in a B+tree that is indexed by the hash of each file's name. To find the file number for a given file name (e.g., out2), the file system first computes a hash of the name (e.g., 0x0000c194). It then uses that hash as a key to search for the directory entry in the tree: starting at the B+tree root at a well-known offset in the file (BTREE_ROOT_PTR), and proceeding through the B+tree's internal nodes to the B+tree's leaf nodes. At each level, a tree node contains an array of *(hash key, file offset)* pairs that each represent a pointer to the child node containing entries with keys smaller than *hash key* but larger than the previous entry's *hash key*. The file system searches the node for the first entry with a *hash key* value that exceeds the target key, and then it follows the corresponding *file offset* pointer to the correct child node. The *file offset* pointer in the record at the leaf nodes points to the target directory entry.

In the XFS implementation, directory entries are stored in the first part of the directory file. The B+tree's root is at a well-known offset within file (e.g., BTREE_ROOT_PTR). The fixed-size internal and leaf nodes are stored after the root node, and the variable-size directory entries are stored at the start of

(a) Logical view

(b) Physical storage

Figure 13.5: Tree-based directory structure similar to the one used in Linux's XFS file system.

the file. Starting from the root, each tree node includes pointers to where in the file its children are stored.

Hard and soft links. Many file systems allow a given file to have multiple names. For example, /home/tom/Work/Classes/OS/hw1.txt and /home/tom/todo/hw1.txt may refer to the same file, as Figure 13.6 illustrates.

hard link   *Hard links* are multiple file directory entries that map different path names to the same file number. Because a file number can appear in multiple directo-

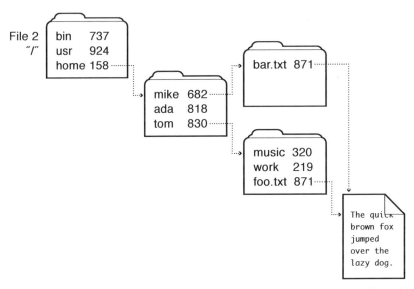

Figure 13.6: Example of a directed acyclic graph directory organization with multiple hard links to a file (figure repeated from Chapter 11)

Figure 13.7: In this directory, the hard links foo.txt and bar.txt and the soft link baz.txt all refer to the same file.

ries, file systems must ensure that a file is only deleted when the last hard link to it has been removed.

To properly implement garbage collection, file systems use reference counts by storing with each file the number of hard links to it. When a file is created, it has a reference count of one, and each additional hard link made to the file (e.g., link(existingName, newName)) increments its reference count. Conversely, each call to unlink(name) decrements the file's reference count, and when the reference count falls to zero, the underlying file is removed and its resources marked as free.

soft link   Rather than mapping a file name to a file number, *soft links* or *symbolic links* are directory entries that map one name to another name.

symbolic link

For example, Figure 13.7 shows a directory that contains three names that all refer to the same file. The entries foo.txt and bar.txt are hard links to the same file — number 66212871; baz.txt is a soft link to foo.txt.

Notice that if we remove entry foo.txt from this directory using the unlink system call, the file can still be opened using the name bar.txt, but if we try to open it with the name baz.txt, the attempt will fail.

EXAMPLE **File metadata.** Most file systems store a file's metadata (e.g., a file's access time, owner ID, permissions, and size) in a file header that can be found with the file number. One could imagine storing that metadata in a file's directory entry instead. Why is this seldom done?

ANSWER **In file systems that support hard links, storing file metadata in directory entries would be problematic.** For example, whenever a file's attribute like its size changed, all of a file's directory entries would have to be located and updated. As another example, if file metadata were stored in directory entries, it would be hard to maintain a file reference count so that the file's resources are freed when and only when the last hard link to the file is removed.

The venerable Microsoft FAT file system stores file metadata in directory entries, but it does not support hard links. □

13.3 | Files: Finding Data

How do file systems organize and find a file's blocks?

Once a file system has translated a file name into a file number using a directory, the file system must be able to find the blocks that belong to that file. In addition to this functional requirement, implementations of files typically target five other goals:

- Support sequential data placement to maximize sequential file access

- Provide efficient random access to any file block

- Limit overheads to be efficient for small files

- Be scalable to support large files

- Provide a place to store per-file metadata such as the file's reference count, owner, access control list, size, and access time

File system designers have a great deal of flexibility to meet these goals. Recall from Section 13.1 that

- A file's *index structure* provides a way to locate each block of the file. Index structures are usually some sort of tree for scalability and to support locality.

- A file system's *free space map* provides a way to allocate free blocks to grow a file. When files grow, choosing which free blocks to use is important for providing good locality. A file system's free space map is therefore often implemented as a bitmap so that it is easy to find a desired number of sequential free blocks near a desired location.

	FAT	FFS	NTFS	ZFS
Index structure	linked list	tree (fixed, asymmetric)	tree (dynamic)	tree (COW, dynamic)
Index structure granularity	block	block	extent	block
Free space management	FAT array	bitmap (fixed)	bitmap in file (file)	space map (log-structured)
Locality heuristics	defragmentation	block groups reserve space	best fit defragmentation	write-anywhere block groups

Figure 13.8: Summary of key ideas discussed for four common file systems approaches.

- A file system's *locality heuristics* define how a file system groups data in storage to maximize access performance.

Within this framework, the design space for file systems is large. To understand the trade-offs and to understand the workings of common file systems, we will examine four case study designs that illustrate important implementation techniques and that represent approaches that are in wide use today.

- **FAT.** The Microsoft File Allocation Table (FAT) file system traces its roots to the late 1970s.

  Techniques: The FAT file system uses an extremely simple index structure — a *linked list* — so it is a good place to discuss our discussion of implementation techniques.

  Today: The FAT file system is still widely used in devices like flash memory sticks and digital cameras where simplicity and interoperability are paramount.

- **FFS.** The Unix Fast File System (FFS) was released in the mid 1980s, and it retained many of the data structures in Ritchie and Thompson's original Unix file system from the early 1970s.

  Techniques: FFS uses a *tree-based multilevel index* for its index structure to improve random access efficiency, and it uses a collection of *locality heuristics* to get good spatial locality for a wide range of workloads.

  Today: In Linux, the popular ext2 and ext3 file systems are based on the FFS design.

- **NTFS.** The Microsoft New Technology File System (NTFS) was introduced in the early 1990s as a replacement for the FAT file system.

  Techniques: Like FFS, NTFS uses a tree-based index structure, but the tree is *more flexible than FFS's fixed tree*. Additionally, NTFS optimizes its index structure for sequential file layout by indexing variable-sized *extents* rather than individual blocks.

  Today: NTFS remains the primary file system for Microsoft operating systems such as Windows 7. In addition, the flexible tree and extent techniques are representative of several widely used file systems such as

Sectors vs. pages; blocks vs. clusters; extents vs. runs

Although storage hardware arranges data in *sectors* (for magnetic disk) or *pages* (for flash), file systems often group together a fixed number of disk sectors or flash pages into a larger allocation unit called a *block*. For example, we might format a file system running on a disk with 512 byte sectors to use 4 KB blocks. Aggregating multiple sectors into a block can reduce the overheads of allocating, tracking, and de-allocating blocks, but it may increase space overheads slightly.

FAT and NTFS refer to blocks as *clusters*, but for consistency we will use the term *block* in our discussions.

Finally, some file systems like NTFS, ext4, and btrfs store data in variable-length arrays of contiguous tracks called *extents* in most file systems and *runs* in NTFS. For consistency, we will use the term *extent* in our discussions.

---

the Linux ext4, XFS, and Reiser4 file systems, the AIX/Linux Journaled File System (JFS), and the Apple Hierarchical File Systems (HFS and HFS+).

- **COW/ZFS.** Copy-on-write (COW) file systems update existing data and metadata blocks by writing new versions to free disk blocks. This approach optimizes write performance: because any data or metadata can be written to any free space on disk, the file system can group otherwise random writes into large, sequential group writes.

  To see how these ideas are implemented, we will examine the open-source ZFS, a prominent copy-on-write file system that was introduced in the early 2000's by Sun Microsystems. ZFS is designed to scale to file systems spanning large numbers of disks, to provide strong data integrity guarantees, and to optimize write performance.

Figure 13.8 summarizes key ideas in these systems that we will detail in the sections that follow.

13.3.1 FAT: Linked List

The Microsoft File Allocation Table (FAT) file system was first implemented in the late 1970s and was the main file system for MS-DOS and early versions of Microsoft Windows. The FAT file system has been enhanced in many ways over the years. Our discussion will focus on the most recent version, FAT-32, which supports volumes with up to 2^{28} blocks and files with up to $2^{32} - 1$ bytes.

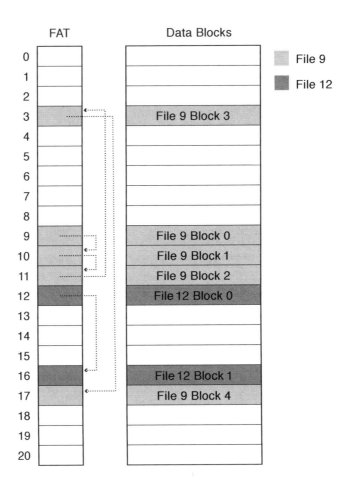

Figure 13.9: A FAT file system with one 5-block file and one 2-block file.

file allocation table   **Index structures.**   The FAT file system is named for its *file allocation table*, an array of 32-bit entries in a reserved area of the volume. Each file in the system corresponds to a linked list of FAT entries, with each FAT entry containing a pointer to the next FAT entry of the file (or a special "end of file" value). The FAT has one entry for each block in the volume, and the file's blocks are the blocks that correspond to the file's FAT entries: if FAT entry i is the jth FAT entry of a file, then storage block i is the jth data block of the file.

Figure 13.9 illustrates a FAT file system with two files. The first begins at block 9 and contains five blocks. The second begins at block 12 and contains two blocks.

Directories map file names to file numbers, and in the FAT file system, a file's number is the index of the file's first entry in the FAT. Thus, given a file's number, we can find the first FAT entry and block of a file, and given the first FAT entry, we can find the rest of the file's FAT entries and blocks.

Free space tracking.   The FAT is also used for free space tracking. If data block i is free, then FAT[i] contains 0. Thus, the file system can find a free block by scanning through the FAT to find a zeroed entry.

Locality heuristics.   Different implementations of FAT may use different allocation strategies, but FAT implementations' allocation strategies are usually simple. For example, some implementations use a *next fit* algorithm that scans sequentially through the FAT starting from the last entry that was allocated and that returns the next free entry found.

defragment
Simple allocation strategies like this may fragment a file, spreading the file's blocks across the volume rather than achieving the desired sequential layout. To improve performance, users can run a *defragmentation* tool that reads files from their existing locations and rewrites them to new locations with better spatial locality. The FAT defragmenter in Windows XP, for example, attempts to copy the blocks of each file that is spread across multiple extents to a single, sequential extent that holds all the blocks of a file.

Discussion   The FAT file system is widely used because it is simple and supported by many operating systems. For example, many flash storage USB keys and camera storage cards use the FAT file system, allowing them to be read and written by almost any computer running almost any modern operating system.

Variations of the FAT file system are even used by applications for organizing data within individual files. For example, Microsoft .doc files produced by versions of Microsoft Word from 1997 to 2007 are actually compound documents with many internal pieces. The .doc format creates a FAT-like file system within the .doc file to manage the objects in the .doc file.

The FAT file system, however, is limited in many ways. For example,

- **Poor locality.** FAT implementations typically use simple allocation strategies such as next fit. These can lead to badly fragmented files.

- **Poor random access.** Random access within a file requires sequentially traversing the file's FAT entries until the desired block is reached.

- **Limited file metadata and access control.** The metadata for each file includes information like the file's name, size, and creation time, but it does not include access control information like the file's owner or group ID, so any user can read or write any file stored in a FAT file system.

- **No support for hard links.** FAT represents each file as a linked list of 32-bit entries in the file allocation table. This representation does not include room for any other file metadata, file metadata in stored with directory entries with the file's name. This approach demands that each file be accessed via exactly one directory entry, ruling out multiple hard links to a file.

- **Limitations on volume and file size.** FAT table entries are 32 bits, but the top four bits are reserved. Thus, a FAT volume can have at most 2^{28} blocks. With 4 KB blocks, the maximum volume size is limited (e.g., 2^{28} blocks/volume * 2^{12} bytes/block = 2^{40} bytes/volume = 1 TB). Block sizes up to 256 KB are supported, but they risk wasting large amounts of disk space due to internal fragmentation.

    Similarly, file sizes are encoded in 32 bits, so no file can be larger than $2^{32} - 1$ bytes (just under 4 GB).

- **Lack of support for modern reliability techniques.** Although we will not discuss reliability until Chapter 14, we note here that FAT does not support the transactional update techniques that modern file systems use to avoid corrupting critical data structures if the computer crashes while writing to storage.

13.3.2   FFS: Fixed Tree

The Unix Fast File System (FFS) illustrates important ideas for both indexing a file's blocks so they can be located quickly and for placing data on disk to get good locality.

In particular, FFS's index structure, called a *multilevel index*, is a carefully structured tree that allows FFS to locate any block of a file and that is efficient for both large and small files.

Given the flexibility provided by FFS's multilevel index, FFS employs two locality heuristics — *block group placement* and *reserve space* — that together usually provide good on-disk layout.

Index structures.   To keep track of the data blocks that belong to each file, FFS uses a fixed, asymmetric tree called a *multilevel index*, as illustrated in Figure 13.10.

multilevel index

Each file is a tree with fixed-sized data blocks (e.g., 4 KB) as its leaves. Each file's tree is rooted at an *inode* that contains the file's metadata (e.g., the file's owner, access control permissions, creation time, last modified time, and whether the file is a directory or not).

inode

A file's inode (root) also contains array of pointers for locating the file's data blocks (leaves). Some of these pointers point directly to the tree's data leaves and some of them point to internal nodes in the tree. Typically, an inode contains 15 pointers. The first 12 pointers are *direct pointers* that point directly to the first 12 data blocks of a file.

The 13th pointer is an *indirect pointer*, which points to an internal node of the tree called an *indirect block*; an indirect block is a regular block of storage that contains an array of direct pointers. To read the 13th block of a file, you first read the inode to get the indirect pointer, then the indirect block to get the direct pointer, then the data block. With 4 KB blocks and 4-byte block pointers,

indirect block

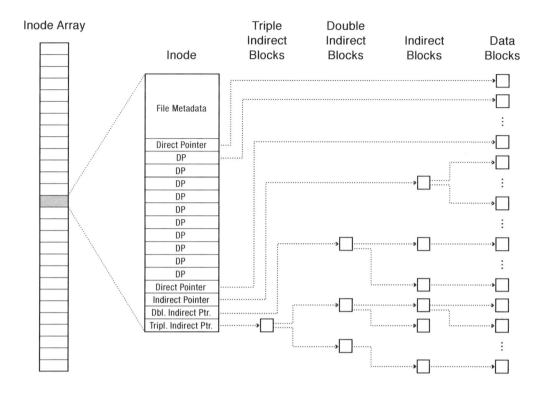

Figure 13.10: An FFS inode is the root of an asymmetric tree whose leaves are the data blocks of a file.

an indirect block can contain as many as 1024 direct pointers, which allows for files up to a little over 4 MB.

The 14th pointer is a *double indirect pointer*, which points to an internal node of the tree called a *double indirect block*; a double indirect block is an array of indirect pointers, each of which points to an indirect block. With 4 KB blocks and 4-byte block pointers, a double indirect block can contain as many as 1024 indirect pointers. Thus, a double indirect pointer can index as many as $(1024)^2$ data blocks.

double indirect block

Finally, the 15th pointer is a *triple indirect pointer* that points to a *triple indirect block* that contains an array of double indirect pointers. With 4 KB blocks and 4-byte block pointers, a triple indirect pointer can index as many as $(1024)^3$ data blocks containing $4\,\text{KB} * 1024^3 = 2^{12} * 2^{30} = 2^{42}$ bytes (4 TB).

triple indirect block

All of a file system's inodes are located in an *inode array* that is stored in a fixed location on disk. A file's file number, called an *inumber* in FFS, is an index into the inode array: to open file (e.g., foo.txt), we look in the file's directory to find its inumber (e.g., 91854), and then look in the appropriate entry of the inode array (e.g., entry 91854) to find its metadata.

inode array

inumber

FFS's multilevel index has four important characteristics:

FFS Access Control

The FFS inode contains information for controlling access to a file. Access control can be specified for three sets of people:

- **User (owner).** The user that owns the file.

- **Group.** The set of people belonging to a specified Unix group. Each Unix group is specified elsewhere as a group name and list of users in that group.

- **Other.** All other users.

Access control is specified in terms of three types of activities:

- **Read.** Read the regular file or directory.

- **Write.** Modify the regular file or directory.

- **Execute.** Execute the regular file or traverse the directory to access files or subdirectories in it.

Each file's inode stores the identities of the file's user (owner) and group as well as 9 basic access control bits to specify read/write/execute permission for the file's user (owner)/group/other. For example, the command ls -ld / shows the access control information for the root directory:

```
> ls -ld /
drwxr-xr-x  40 root  wheel  1428 Feb  2 13:39 /
```

This means that the file is a directory (d), owned by the user root the group wheel. The root directory can be read, written, and executed (traversed) by the owner (rwx), and it can be read and executed (traversed) but not written by members of group wheel (r-x) and all other users (r-x).

---

1. **Tree structure.** Each file is represented as a tree, which allows the file system to efficiently find any block of a file.

2. **High degree.** The FFS tree uses internal nodes with many children compared to the binary trees often used for in-memory data structures (i.e., internal nodes have high *degree* or *fan out*). For example, if a file block is 4 KB and a blockID is 4 bytes, then each indirect block can contain pointers to 1024 blocks.

   High degree nodes make sense for on-disk data structures where (1) we want to minimize the number of seeks, (2) the cost of reading several kilobytes of sequential data is not much higher than the cost of reading

Setuid and setgid programs

In addition to the 9 basic access control bits, the FFS inode stores two important additional bits:

- **Setuid.** When this file is executed by any user (with execute permission) it will be executed with the file owner's (rather than the user's) permission. For example, the lprm program allows a user to remove a job from a printer queue. The print queue is implemented as a directory containing files to be printed, and because we do not want users to be able to remove other users' jobs, this directory is owned by and may only be modified by the root user. So, the lprm program is owned by the root user with the setuid bit set. It can be executed by anyone, but when it runs, it executes with root permissions, allowing it to modify the print queue directory.

  E.g.,

  ```
  -rwsr-xr-x 1 root root 507674 2010-07-05 12:39 /lusr/bin/lprm*
  ```

  Of course, making a program setuid is potentially dangerous. Here, for example, we rely on the lprm program to verify that actual user is deleting his own print jobs, not someone else's. A bug in the lprm program could let one user remove another's printer jobs. Worse, if the bug allows the attacker to execute malicious code (e.g., via a buffer overflow attack), a bug in lprm could give an attacker total control of the machine.

- **Setgid.** The setguid bit is similar to the setuid bit, execept that the file is executed with the file's group permission. For example, on some machines, sendmail executes as a member of group smmsp so that it can access a mail queue file accessible to group smmsp.

  E.g.,

  ```
  -r-xr-sr-x  1   root  smmsp  2264923  2011-06-23  14:51  /lusr/opt/sendmail-8.14.4/lib/mail/sendmail*
  ```

the first byte, and (3) data must be read and written at least a sector at a time.

High degree nodes also improve efficiency for sequential reads and writes — once in indirect block is read, hundreds of data blocks can be read before the next indirect block is needed. Runs between reads of double indirect blocks are even larger.

3. **Fixed structure.** The FFS tree has a fixed structure. For a given configura-

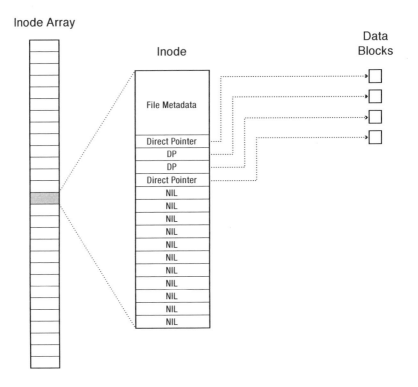

Figure 13.11: A small FFS file whose blocks are all reachable via direct pointers in the inode.

tion of FFS, the first set of d pointers always point to the first d blocks of a file; the next pointer is an indirect pointer that points to an indirect block; etc.

Compared to a dynamic tree that can add layers of indirection above a block as a file grows, the main advantage of the fixed structure is implementation simplicity.

4. **Asymmetric.** To efficiently support both large and small files with a fixed tree structure, FFS's tree structure is asymmetric. Rather than putting each data block at the same depth, FFS stores successive groups of blocks at increasing depth so that small files are stored in a small-depth tree, the bulk of medium files are stored in a medium-depth tree, and the bulk of large files are stored in a larger-depth tree. For example, Figure 13.11 shows a small, 4-block file whose inode includes direct pointers to all of its blocks. Conversely, for the large file shown in Figure 13.10, most of the blocks must be accessed via the triple indirect pointer.

In contrast, if we use a fixed-depth tree and want to support reasonably large files, small files would pay high overheads. With triple indirect pointers and 4 KB blocks, storing a 4 KB file would consume over 16 KB (the 4 KB of data, the small inode, and 3 levels of 4 KB indirect blocks), and reading the file would require reading five blocks to traverse the tree.

The FFS principles are general; many file systems have adopted variations on its basic approach.

EXAMPLE **FFS variation.** Suppose BigFS is a variation of FFS that includes in each inode 12 direct, 1 indirect, 1 double indirect, 1 triple indirect, and 1 *quadruple indirect* pointers. Assuming 4 KB blocks and 8-byte pointers, what is the maximum file size this index structure can support?

ANSWER 12 direct pointers can index $12 * 4\,\mathrm{KB} = 48\,\mathrm{KB}$

When used as an internal node, each storage block can contain as many as $4\,\mathrm{KB}/\mathrm{block}/8\,\mathrm{bytes}/\mathrm{pointer} = 512\,\mathrm{pointers}/\mathrm{block} = 2^9\,\mathrm{pointers}/\mathrm{block}$ pointers.

So, the indirect pointer points to an indirect block with 2^9 pointers, referencing as much as $2^9\,\mathrm{blocks} * 2^{12}\,\mathrm{bytes}/\mathrm{block} = 2^{21}\,\mathrm{bytes} = 2\,\mathrm{MB}$.

Similarly, the double indirect pointer references as much as $2^9 * 2^9 * 2^{12} = 2^{30}\,\mathrm{bytes} = 1\,\mathrm{GB}$, the triple indirect pointer references as much as $2^9 * 2^9 * 2^9 * 2^{12} = 2^{39}\,\mathrm{bytes} = 512\,\mathrm{GB}$, and the quadruple indirect pointer references as much as $2^9 * 2^9 * 2^9 * 2^9 * 2^{12} = 2^{48}\,\mathrm{bytes} = 256\,\mathrm{TB}$.

So, **BigFS can support files a bit larger than 256.5 TB.** □

Sparse files.   Tree-based index structures like FFS's can support *sparse files* in which one or more ranges of empty space are surrounded by file data. The ranges of empty space consume no disk space.

For example, if we create a new file, write 4 KB at offset 0, seek to offset 2^{30}, and write another 4 KB, as Figure 13.12 illustrates, an FFS system with 4 KB blocks will only consume 16 KB—two data blocks, a double indirect block, and a single indirect block.

In this case, if we list the *size of the file* using the ls command, we see that the file's size is 1.1 GB. But, if we check the *space consumed by the file*, using the du command, we see that it consumes just 16 KB of storage space.

```
>ls -lgGh sparse.dat
-rwx------ 1 1.1G 2012-01-31 08:45 sparse.dat*
>du -hs sparse.dat
16K sparse.dat
```

If we read from a hole, the file system produces a zero-filled buffer. If we write to a hole, the file system allocates storage blocks for the data and any required indirect blocks.

Similar to efficient support for sparse virtual memory address spaces, efficient support of sparse files is useful for giving applications maximum flexibility in placing data in a file. For example, a database could store its

Figure 13.12: A sparse FFS file with two 4 KB bocks, one at offset 0 and one at offset 2^{30}.

tables at the start of its file, its indices at 1 GB into the file, its log at 2 GB, and additional metadata at 4 GB.

Sparse files have two important limitations. First, not all file systems support them, so an application that relies on sparse file support may not be portable. Second, not all utilities correctly handle sparse files, which can lead to unexpected consequences. For example, if I read a sparse file from beginning to end and write each byte to a different file, I will observe runs of zero-filled buffers corresponding to holes and write those zero-filled regions to the new file. The result is a new non-sparse file whose space consumption matches its size.

```
>cat sparse.dat > /tmp/notSparse.dat
>ls -lgGh /tmp/notSparse.dat
-rw-r--r-- 1 1.1G 2012-01-31 08:54 /tmp/notSparse.dat
 >
>du -hs /tmp/notSparse.dat
1.1G /tmp/notSparse.dat
```

Free space management.   FFS's free space management is simple. FFS allocates a *bitmap* with one bit per storage block. The ith bit in the bitmap indicates whether the ith block is free or in use. The position of FFS's bitmap is fixed when the file system is formatted, so it is easy to find the part of the bitmap that identifies free blocks near any location of interest.

bitmap

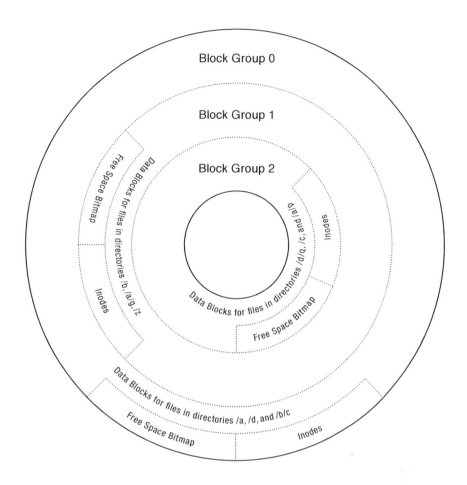

Figure 13.13: FFS divides a disk into block groups, splits free space and inode metadata across block groups, and puts data blocks for the files in a directory in the same block group.

Locality heuristics. FFS uses two important locality heuristics to get good performance for many workloads: *block group placement* and *reserved space*.

Block group placement. FFS places data to optimize for the common case where a file's data blocks, a file's data and metadata, and different files from the same directory are accessed together.

Conversely, because everything cannot be near everything, FFS lets different directories' files be far from each other.

This placement heuristic has four parts:

block group

- **Divide disk into block groups.** As Figure 13.13 illustrates, FFS divides a disk in to sets of nearby tracks called *block groups*. The seek time between any blocks in a block group will be small.

- **Distribute metadata.** Earlier multilevel index file systems put the inode array and free space bitmap in a contiguous region of the disk. In such a centralized metadata arrangement, the disk head must often make seeks between a file's data and its metadata.

  In FFS, the inode array and free space bitmap are still conceptually arrays of records, and FFS still stores each array entry at a well-known, easily calculable location, but the array is now split into pieces distributed across the disk. In particular, each block group holds a portion of these metadata structures as Figure 13.13 illustrates,

  For example, if a disk has 100 block groups, each block group would store 1% of the file system's inodes and the 1% portion of the bitmap that tracks the status of the data blocks in the block group.

- **Place file in block group.** FFS puts a directory and its files in the same block group: when a new file is created, FFS knows the inumber of the new file's directory, and from that it can determine the range of inumbers in the same block group. FFS chooses an inode from that group if one is free; otherwise, FFS gives up locality and selects an inumber from a different block group.

  In contrast with regular files, when FFS creates a new directory, it chooses an inumber from a different block group. Even though we might expect a subdirectory to have some locality with its parent, putting all subdirectories in the same block group would quickly fill it, thwarting our efforts to get locality within a directory.

  Figure 13.13 illustrates how FFS might groups files from different directories into different block groups.

- **Place data blocks.** Within a block group, FFS uses a first-free heuristic. When a new block of a file is written, FFS writes the block to the first free block in the file's block group.

  Although this heuristic may give up locality in the short term, it does so to improve locality in the long term. In the short term, this heuristic might spread a sequence of writes into small holes near the start of a block group rather than concentrating them to a sequence of contiguous free blocks somewhere else. This short term sacrifice brings long term benefits, however: fragmentation is reduced, the block will tend to have a long run of free space at its end, subsequent writes are more likely to be sequential.

  The intuition is that a given block group will usually have a handful of holes scattered through blocks near the start of the group and a long run of free space at the end of the group. Then, if a new, small file is created, its blocks will likely go to a few of the small holes, which is not ideal, but which is acceptable for a small file. Conversely, if a large file is created and written from beginning to end, it will tend to have the first few blocks scattered through the holes in the early part of the block, but

Figure 13.14: FFS's block placement heuristic is to put each new file block in the first free block in that file's block group

then have the bulk of its data written sequentially at the end of the block group.

If a block group runs out of free blocks, FFS selects another block group and allocates blocks there using the same heuristic.

Reserved space. Although the block group heuristic can be effective, it relies on there being a significant amount of free space on disk. In particular, when a disk is nearly full, there is little opportunity for the file system to optimize locality. For example, if a disk has only a few kilobytes of free sectors, most block groups will be full, and others will have only a few free blocks; new writes will have to be scattered more or less randomly around the disk.

FFS therefore reserves some fraction of the disk's space (e.g., 10%) and presents a slightly reduced disk size to applications. If the actual free space on the disk falls below the reserve fraction, FFS treats the disk as full. For example, if a user's application attempts to write a new block in a file when all but the reserve space is consumed, that write will fail. When all but the reserve space is full, the super user's processes will still be able to allocate new blocks, which is useful for allowing an administrator to log in and clean things up.

The reserved space approach works well given disk technology trends. It sacrifices a small amount of disk capacity, a hardware resource that has been improving rapidly over recent decades, to reduce seek times, a hardware property that is improving only slowly.

13.3.3   NTFS: Flexible Tree With Extents

The Microsoft New Technology File System (NTFS), released in 1993, improved on Microsoft's FAT file system with many new features including new index structures to improve performance, more flexible file metadata, improved security, and improved reliability.

We will discuss some of NTFS's reliability features in Chapter 14. Here, we will focus on how NTFS stores data and metadata.

Index structures.   Whereas FFS tracks file blocks with a fixed tree, NTFS and many other recent file systems such as Linux ext4 and btrfs track *extents* with *flexible trees*.

extent

- **Extents.** Rather than tracking individual file blocks, NTFS tracks *extents*, variable-sized regions of files that are each stored in a contiguous region on the storage device.

- **Flexible tree and master file table.** Each file in NTFS is represented by a variable-depth tree. The extent pointers for a file with a small number of extents can be stored in a shallow tree, even if the file, itself, is large. Deeper trees are only needed if the file becomes badly fragmented.

master file table (MFT)

attribute record

The roots of these trees are stored in a master file table that is similar to FFS's inode array. NTFS's *master file table (MFT)* stores an array of 1 KB MFT records, each of which stores a sequence of variable-size *attribute records*. NTFS uses attribute records to store both data and metadata — both are just considered attributes of a file.

resident attribute

nonresident attribute

Some attributes can be too large to fit in an MFT record (e.g., a data extent) while some can be small enough to fit (e.g., a file's last modified time). An attribute can therefore be *resident* or *nonresident*. A *resident attribute* stores its contents directly in the MFT record while a *nonresident attribute* stores extent pointers in its MFT record and stores its contents in those extents.

Figure 13.15 illustrates the index structures for a basic NTFS file. Here, the file's MFT record includes a *nonresident data* attribute, which is a sequence of extent pointers, each of which specifies the starting block and length in blocks of an extent of data. Because extents can hold variable numbers of blocks, even a multi-gigabyte file can be represented by one or a few extent pointers in an MFT record, assuming file system fragmentation is kept under control.

If a file is small, the data attribute may be used to store the file's actual contents right in its MFT record as a resident attribute as Figure 13.16 illustrates.

An MFT record has a flexible format that can include range of different attributes. In addition to data attributes, three common metadata attribute types include

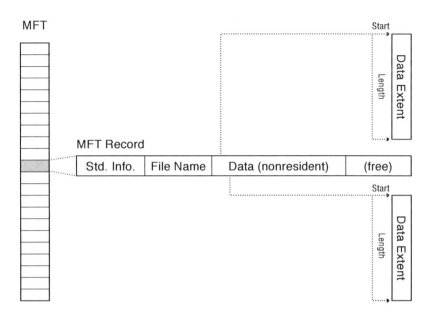

Figure 13.15: NTFS index structures and data for a basic file with two data extents.

Figure 13.16: A small file's data can be *resident*, meaning that the file's data is stored in its MFT record.

Figure 13.17: Most NTFS files store their attributes in a single MFT record, but a file's attributes can grow to span multiple MFT records. In those cases, the first MFT record includes an *attribute list* attribute that indicates where to find each attribute record.

- **Standard information.** This attribute holds standard information needed for all files. Fields include the file's creation time, modification time, access time, owner ID, and security specifier. Also included is a set of flags indicating basic information like whether the file is a read only file, a hidden file, or a system file.

- **File name.** This attribute holds the file's name and the file number of its parent directory. Because a file can have multiple names (e.g., if there are multiple hard links to the file), it may have multiple file name attributes in its MFT record.

- **Attribute list.** Because a file's metadata may include a variable number of variable sized attributes, a file's metadata may be larger than a single MFT record can hold. When this case occurs, NTFS stores the attributes in multiple MFT records and includes an attribute list in the first record. When present, the attribute list indicates which attributes are stored in which MFT records. For example, Figure 13.17 shows MFT records for two files, one whose attributes are contained in a single MFT record and one of whose attributes spans two MFT records.

As Figure 13.18 illustrates, a file can go through four stages of growth, depending on its size and fragmentation. First, a small file may have its contents included in the MFT record as a resident data attribute. Second, more typically, a file's data lies in a small number of extents tracked by a single nonresident data attribute. Third, occasionally if a file is large and the file system fragmented, a file can have so many extents that the extent pointers will not fit in a single MFT record. In this case, as a file can have multiple nonresident data attributes in multiple MFT records, with the attribute list in the first MFT record indicating which MFT records track which ranges of extents. Fourth and finally, if a file is huge or the file system fragmentation is extreme, a file's attribute list can be made nonresident, allowing almost arbitrarily large numbers of MFT records.

Metadata files Rather than doing ad-hoc allocation of special regions of disk for file system metadata like free space bitmaps, NTFS stores almost all of its metadata in about a dozen ordinary files with well-known low-numbered file numbers. For example, file number 5 is the root directory, file number 6 is the free space bitmap, and file number 8 contains a list of the volume's bad blocks.

File number 9, called $Secure, contains security and access control information. NTFS has a flexible security model in which a file can be associated with a list of users and groups, with specific access control settings for each listed principal. In early versions of NTFS, such an access control list was stored with each file, but these lists consumed a nontrivial amount of space and many lists had identical contents. So, current implementations of NTFS store each unique access control list once in the special $Secure file, indexed by a fixed-length unique key. Each individual file just stores the appropriate fixed-length key in its MFT record, and NTFS uses a file's security key to find the appropriate access control list in the $Secure file.

Even the master file table, itself, is stored as a file, file number 0, called $MFT. So, we need to find the first entry of the MFT in order to read the MFT! To locate the MFT, the first sector of an NTFS volume includes a pointer to the first entry of the MFT.

Storing the MFT in a file avoids the need to statically allocate all MFT entries as a fixed array in a predetermined location. Instead, NTFS starts with a small MFT and grows it as new files are created and new entries are needed.

best fit   **Locality heuristics.** Most implementations of NTFS use a variation of *best fit*, where the system tries to place a newly allocated file in the smallest free region that is large enough to hold it. In NTFS's variation, rather than trying to keep the allocation bitmap for the entire disk in memory, the system caches the allocation status for a smaller region of the disk and searches that region first. If the bitmap cache holds information for areas where writes recently occurred, then writes that occur together in time will tend to be clustered together.

An important NTFS feature for optimizing its best fit placement is the SetEndOfFile() interface, which allows an application to specify the expected

Figure 13.18: An NTFS file's data attribute can be in: (i) a *resident data attribute*, (ii) extents tracked by a *single nonresident data attribute*, (iii) extents tracked by *multiple nonresident data attributes* in multiple MFT entries tracked by a *resident attribute list attribute*, or (iv) extents tracked by *multiple nonresident data attributes* stored in multiple MFT entries tracked by a *nonresident attribute list attribute*.

size of a file at creation time. In contrast, FFS allocates file blocks as they are written, without knowing how large the file will eventually grow.

To avoid having the master file table file ($MFT) become fragmented, NTFS reserves part of the start of the volume (e.g., the first 12.5% of the volume) for MFT expansion. NTFS does not place file blocks in the MFT reserve area until the non-reserved area is full, at which point it halves the size of the MFT reserve area and continues. As the volume continues to fill, NTFS continues to halve the reserve area until it reaches the point where the remaining reserve area is more than half full.

Finally, Microsoft operating systems with NTFS include a defragmentation

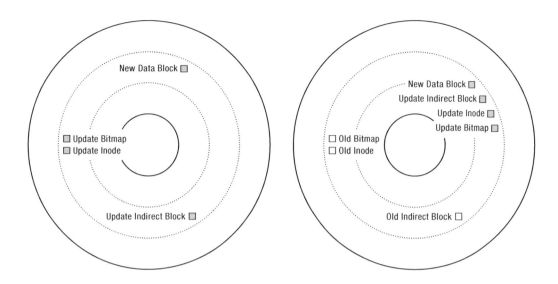

Figure 13.19: An update-in-place file system (left) updates data and metadata in their existing locations, while a copy-on-write file system (right) makes new copies of data and metadata whenever they are updated.

utility that takes fragmented files and rewrites them to contiguous regions of disk.

13.3.4   Copy-On-Write File Systems

copy-on-write (COW) file system

When updating an existing file, *copy-on-write (COW) file systems* do not overwrite the existing data or metadata; instead, they write new versions to new locations.

COW file systems do this to optimize writes by transforming random I/O updates to sequential ones. For example, when appending a block to a file, a traditional, update-in-place file system might seek to and update its free space bitmap, the file's inode in the inode array, the file's indirect block, and the file's data block. In contrast, a COW file system might just find a sequential run of free space and write the new bitmap, inode, indirect block, and data block there as illustrated in Figure 13.19.

Several technology trends are driving widespread adoption of COW file systems:

- **Small writes are expensive.** Disk performance for large sequential writes is much better than for small random writes. This gap is likely to continue to grow because bandwidth generally improves faster than seek time or rotational latency: increasing storage density can increase bandwidth even if the rotational speed does not increase.

As a result the benefits of converting small random writes to large sequential ones is large and getting larger.

- **Small writes are especially expensive on RAID.** Redundant arrays of inexpensive disks (RAIDs) are often used to improve storage reliability. However, as we will discuss in the next chapter, updating a single block stored with parity on a RAID requires four disk I/Os: we must read the old data, read the old parity, write the new data, and write the new parity. In contrast, RAIDs are efficient when an entire stripe—all of the blocks sharing the same parity block—are updated at once. In that case, no reads are needed, each new data block is written, and the parity update is amortized across the data blocks in the stripe.

  Widespread use of RAIDs magnifies the benefits of converting random writes to sequential ones.

- **Caches filter reads.**

  For many workloads, large DRAM caches can handle essentially all file system reads. But our ability to use DRAM to buffer writes is limited by the need to durably store data soon after it is written.

  Thus, the cost of writes often dominates performance, so techniques that optimize write performance are appealing.

- **Widespread adoption of flash storage.**

  Flash storage has two properties that make the COW techniques important. First, in order to write a small (e.g., 4 KB) flash page, one must first clear the large (e.g., 512 KB) erasure block on which it resides. Second, each flash storage element can handle a limited number of write-erase cycles before wearing out, so *wear leveling*—spreading writes evenly across all cells—is important for maximizing flash endurance.

  wear leveling

  A flash drive's flash translation layer uses COW techniques to virtualize block addresses, allowing it to present a standard interface to read and write specific logical pages while internally redirecting writes to pages on already-cleared erasure blocks and while moving existing data to new physical pages so that their current erasure blocks can be cleared for future writes.

  Note that a flash drive's flash translation layer operates below the file system—standard update in place or COW file systems are still used over that layer. But, flash translation layers are constructed using the same basic principles as the COW file systems discussed here.

- **Growing capacity enables versioning.** Large storage capacities make it attractive for file systems to provide interfaces by which users can access old versions of their files.

  Since updates in COW systems do not overwrite old data with new, supporting versioning is relatively straightforward, as we discuss below.

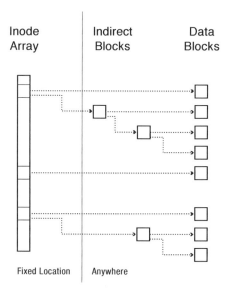

Figure 13.20: A traditional, update-in-place file system, such as FFS.

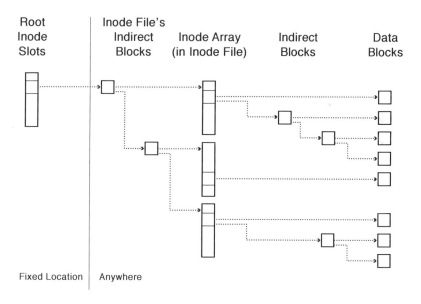

Figure 13.21: A simple copy-on-write (COW) file system.

Implementation principles.   Figures 13.20 and 13.21 illustrate the core idea of COW file systems by comparing a traditional file system (FFS in this case) with a COW implementation that uses the same basic index structures.

In the traditional system (Figure 13.20), a file's indirect nodes and data

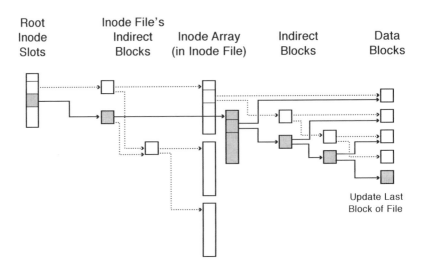

Figure 13.22: In a COW file system, writing a data block causes the system to allocate new blocks for and to write the data block and all nodes on the path from that data block to the root inode.

blocks can be located anywhere on disk, and given a file's inumber, we can find its inode in a fixed location on disk.

In the COW version (Figure 13.21), we do not want to overwrite inodes in place, so we must make them mobile. A simple way to do that is to store them in a file rather than in a fixed array. Of course, that is not quite the end of the story — we still need to be able to find the inode file's inode, called the *root inode*.

root inode

The simplest thing to do would be to store the root inode in a fixed location. If we did that, then we could find any file's inode by using the root inode to read from a computed offset in the inode file, and from that we could find its blocks.

However, it is useful to make even the root inode copy-on-write. For example, we do not want to risk losing the root inode if there is a crash while it is being written. A solution is to include a monotonically increasing version number and a checksum in the root inode and to keep a small array of slots for the current and recent root inodes, updating the oldest one when a write occurs. After a crash, we scan all of the slots to identify the newest root inode that has a correct checksum.

In this design, all the file system's contents are stored in a tree rooted in the root inode, when we update a block, we write it — and all of the blocks on the path from it to the root — to new locations. For example, Figure 13.22 shows what happens when one block of a file is updated in our simple COW system.

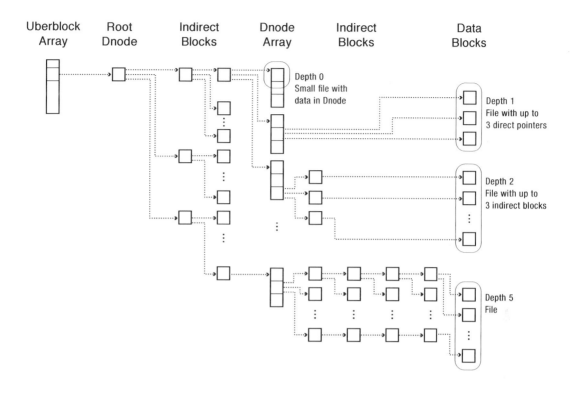

Figure 13.23: ZFS index structures. Note that this diagram is slightly simplified. In reality, there are a few more levels of indirection between the uberblock and a file system's root dnode.

ZFS index structures.   To better understand how copy-on-write file systems are implemented, we will look at the open source ZFS file system.

As Figure 13.23 illustrates, the root of a ZFS storage system is called the **uberblock**   *uberblock*. ZFS keeps an array of 256 uberblocks in a fixed storage location and rotates successive versions among them. When restarting, ZFS scans the uberblock array and uses the one with a valid checksum that has the highest sequence number.

The current uberblock conceptually includes a pointer to the current root dnode, which holds the dnode array for a ZFS file system. (We say "conceptually" because we are simplifying things a bit here. Once you have read this description, see the sidebar if you want the gory details.)

dnode   The basic metadata object in ZFS is called a *dnode*, and it plays a role similar to an inode in FFS or an MFT entry in NTFS: a file is represented by variable-depth tree whose root is a dnode and whose leaves are its data blocks. A dnode has space for three block pointers, and it has a field that specifies the tree's depth: zero indicates that the dnode stores the file's data; one means that the pointers are direct pointers to data blocks; two means that the dnode's pointers point to indirect blocks, which point to data blocks; three means that

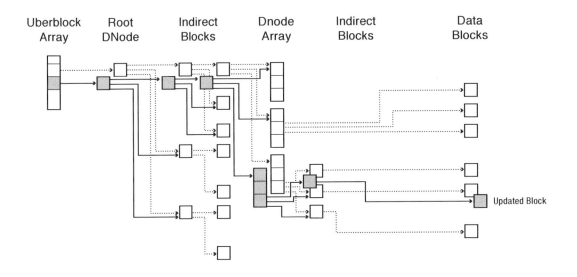

Figure 13.24: Updating a block of a ZFS file

the dnode's pointers point to double indirect blocks; and so on, up to six levels of indirection.

Data block and indirect block sizes are variable from 512 bytes to 128KB and specified in a file's dnode. Note, however, that even a 128 KB indirect node holds fewer block pointers than you might expect because each block pointer is a 128 byte structure.

ZFS's block pointers are relatively large structures because they include fields to support advanced features like large storage devices, block compression, placing copies of the same block on different storage devices, file system snapshots, and block checksums. Fortunately, we can ignore these details and just treat each block pointer structure as a (rather large) pointer.

Figure 13.24 shows what happens when we update the last block in a 2-level ZFS file. We allocate a new data block and store the new data in it, but that means that we need to update the indirect block that points to it. So, we allocate a new indirect block and store the version with the updated pointer there, but that means we need to update the indirect pointer that points to it. And so on, up through the file's dnode, the indirect blocks that track the dnode array, the root dnode, and the uberblock.

ZFS space map.   ZFS's space maps track free space in a way designed to scale to extremely large storage systems.

One concern the ZFS designers had with bitmaps was that the size of a bitmap grows linearly with storage capacity and can become quite large for large-scale systems. For example, with 4 KB block size, a file server with 1 PB of disk space would have 32 GB of bitmaps.

ZFS uberblock, meta-root dnode, and root dnodes

For simplicity, the body of the text describes the uberblock as pointing directly to the file system's root dnode.

In reality, there are a few additional levels of indirection to allow multiple file systems and snapshots to share a ZFS storage pool under a single uberblock. The uberblock has a pointer to a meta-root dnode (called the Meta Object Store dnode in ZFS terminology). The meta-root dnode tracks the meta-root dnode array. The meta-root dnode array is used by what is essentially a little file system with hierarchical directories that provide mappings from the names of file systems to "files" that store the metadata for each file system, including a pointer to the block where the file system's root dnode is (currently) stored.

So, a more complete picture looks like this:

Large bitmaps affect both a server's memory requirements and the time needed to read the bitmaps on startup. Although one might attempt to cache a subset of the bitmap in memory and only allocate from the currently cached subset, we cannot control when blocks are freed. For workloads in which frees have poor locality, caching will be ineffective.

ZFS's space maps use three key ideas to scale to large storage systems:

- **Per block group space maps.** ZFS maintains a space map for each block group, it restricts allocation of new blocks to a subset of block groups at any given time, and it keeps those block groups' space maps in memory.

- **Tree of extents.** Each block group's free space is represented as an AVL tree of extents. The tree allows ZFS to efficiently find a free extent of a desired size, and its search performance does not degrade as the block group becomes full.

- **Log-structured updates.** As noted above, caching a portion of a space map works for allocations but it may not help frees. Therefore, rather than directly updating the on-disk spacemap, ZFS simply appends spacemap updates to a log. When a block group is activated for allocation, ZFS reads in the most recently stored spacemap and then it reads all subsequently logged updates to bring the space map up to date. After applying updates to the in-memory spacemap, ZFS can store the new spacemap to limit the length of its update log.

ZFS locality heuristics. We started the discussion of COW file systems by saying that they are designed to optimize write performance, but the example in Figure 13.24 make it sound like ZFS does a lot of work just to update a block. ZFS does two important things to optimize write behavior:

- **Sequential writes.** Because almost everything in ZFS is mobile, almost all of these updates can be grouped into a single write to a free range of sequential blocks on disk. Only the uberblock needs to go elsewhere. Because sequential writes are much faster than random ones, ZFS and other COW file systems can have excellent write performance even though they write more metadata than update-in-place file systems.

- **Batched updates.** Figure 13.24 shows what happens when we update a single block of a single file, but ZFS does not typically write one update at a time. Instead, ZFS updates several seconds of updates and writes them to disk as a batch. So, updates to a file's dnode and indirect nodes may be amortized over many writes to the file, and updates to the uberblock, root dnode, and the dnode array's indirect blocks may be amortized over writes to many files.

When it is time to write a batch of writes, ZFS needs to decide where to write the new block versions. It proceeds in three steps:

- **Choose a device.** A ZFS storage pool may span multiple devices, so the first step is to choose which device to use. To maximize throughput by spreading load across devices, ZFS uses a variation of round robin with two tweaks. First, to even out space utilization, ZFS biases selection towards devices with large amounts of free space. Second, to maintain good locality for future reads, ZFS places about 512 KB on one device before moving on to the next one.

- **Choose a block group.** ZFS divides each device into several hundred groups of sequential blocks. ZFS's first choice for is to continue to use the block group it used most recently. However, if that group is so full or fragmented that its largest free region is smaller than 128 KB, ZFS selects a new block group.

    New block group selection is biased towards groups that have more free space, that are nearer the outer edge of a disk (to improve bandwidth), and that have recently been used to store some data (to limit the range of tracks across which the disk head must seek).

- **Choose a block within the group.** To maximize opportunities to group writes together, ZFS uses first fit allocation within a block group until the group is nearly full. At that point, it falls back on best fit to maximize space utilization.

13.4 | Putting It All Together: File and Directory Access

In Section 13.2 we saw that directories are implemented as files, containing file name to file number mappings, and in Section 13.3 we saw that files are implemented using an index structure—typically a tree of some sort—to track the file's blocks.

In this section, we walk through the steps FFS takes to read a file, given that file's name. The steps for the other file systems we have discussed are similar.

Suppose we want to read the file /foo/bar/baz.

First, we must read the root directory / to determine /foo's inumber. Since we already know the root directory's inumber (it is a pre-agreed number compiled into the kernel, e.g., 2), we open and read file 2's inode in step 1 in Figure 13.25. Recall that FFS stores pieces of the inode array at fixed locations on disk, so given a file's inumber it is easy to find and read the file's inode.

From the root directory's inode, we extract the direct and indirect block pointers to determine which block stores the contents of the root directory (e.g., block 48912 in this example). We can then read that block of data to get the list of name to inumber mappings in the root directory and discover that directory file /foo has inumber 231 (step 2).

Now that we know /foo's inumber, in step 3 we can read inode 231 to find where /foo's data blocks are stored—block 1094 in the example. We can then read those blocks of data to get the list of name to inumber mappings in the /foo directory and discover that directory file /foo/bar has inumber 731 (step 4).

We follow similar steps to read /foo/bar's inode (step 5) and data block 30991 (step 6) to determine /foo/bar/baz inumber 402.

Finally, in step 7, we read /foo/bar/baz's inode (402), and in step 8, we read its data blocks (89310, 14919, and 23301): "I hear and I forget. I see and I remember. I do and I understand."

Partitioning, Formatting, and Superblocks

How does an operating system know where to find FFS's inode array, NTFS's MFT, or ZFS's uberblock? How does it know how large these structures are? How does it even know what type of file system is on a disk?

A disk device's space can be divided into multiple *partitions*, each of which appears a separate (smaller) virtual storage device that can be formatted as a separate file system. To partition a disk, an operating system writes a special record (e.g., a master boot record (MBR) or GUID partition table (GPT)) in the first blocks of the disk. This record includes the disk's unique ID, size, and the list of the disk's partitions. Each partition record stores the partition's type (e.g., general file system partition, swap partition, RAID partition, bootable partition), partition ID, partition name, and the partition's starting and ending blocks.

To improve reliability, operating systems store multiple copies of a disk's partition table — often in the first few and last few of a disk's blocks.

Once a disk has been partitioned, the operating system can *format* some or all of the partitions by initializing the partition's blocks according to the requirements of the type of file system being created.

Formatting a file system includes writing a *superblock* that identifies the file system's type and its key parameters such as its type, block size, and inode array or MBR location and size. Again, for reliability, a file system typically stores multiple copies of its superblock at several predefined locations.

Then, when an operating system boots, it can examine a disk to find its partitions, and it can examine each partition to identify and configure its file systems.

This may seem like a lot of steps just to read a file. Most of the time, we expect much of this information to be cached so that some steps can be avoided. For example, if the inodes and blocks for / and /foo are cached, then we would skip steps 1 to 4. Also, once file /foo/bar/baz has been opened, the open file data structure in the operating system will include the file's inumber so that individual reads and writes of the file can skip steps 1 to 6 (and step 7 while the inode is cached).

EXAMPLE   **Reading a file.** What would you get if you read the file /foo/fie in the FFS file system illustrated in Figure 13.25?

ANSWER   First we read the root inode (inode 2) and file (block 48912), then /foo's inode (inode 231) and file (block 1094), and then /foo/fie's inode (inode 402 again) and file (blocks 89310, 14919, and 23301 again) — /foo/bar/baz and /foo/fie are hard links to the same file.   □

Figure 13.25: The circled numbers identify the steps required to read /foo/bar/baz in the FFS file system.

13.5 | Summary and Future Directions

We are seeing significant shifts in the technologies and workloads that drive file system design.

Practical solid state storage technologies like flash memory change the constraints around which file systems can be designed. Random access performance that is good both in relative terms compared to sequential access performance and in absolute terms provide opportunities to reconsider many aspects of file system design — directories, file metadata structures, block placement — that have been shaped by the limitations of magnetic disks. Promising future solid state storage technologies like phase change memory or memristors may allow even more dramatic restructuring of file systems to take advantage of their even better performance and their support for fine-grained writes of a few bytes or words.

On the other hand, the limited lifetime and capacity of many solid state technologies may impose new constraints on file system designs. Perhaps we should consider hybrid file systems that, for example, store metadata and the content of small files in solid state storage and the contents of large files on magnetic disks.

Even the venerable spinning disk continues to evolve rapidly, with capacity increases continuing to significantly outpace performance improvements, making it more and more essential to organize file systems to maximize sequential transfers to and from disk.

Workloads are also evolving rapidly, which changes demands on file systems. In servers, the rising popularity of virtual machines and cloud computing pressure operating systems designers to provide better ways to share storage devices with fair and predictable performance despite variable and mixed workloads. At clients, the increasing popularity of apps and specialized compute appliances are providing new ways for organizing storage: rather than having users organize files into directories, apps and appliances often manage their own storage, providing users with a perhaps very different way of identifying stored objects. For example, rather than requiring users to create different directories for different, related sets of photos into different directories, many photo organizing applications provide an interface that groups related photos into events that may or may not reflect where in the file system the events are stored. Perhaps our reliance on directories for naming and locality will need to be rethought in the coming years.

Exercises

1. Why do we many file systems have separate system calls for removing a regular file (e.g., unlink) and removing a directory (e.g., rmdir)?

2. In Figure 13.4, suppose we create a new file z.txt and then unlink Work, removing that entry. Draw a figure similar to Figure 13.4 that shows the new contents of the directory.

3. What effect will doubling the block size in the UNIX Fast File System have on the maximum file size?

4. Is there a limit on the maximum size of a file in an extent-based file system? Why or why not?

5. Suppose a variation of FFS includes in each inode 12 direct, 1 indirect, 1 double indirect, 2 triple indirect, and 1 quadruple indirect pointers. Assuming 6 KB blocks and 6-byte pointers

    (a) What is the largest file that can be accessed via direct pointers only?

(b) To within 1%, what is the maximum file size this index structure can support?

6. On a Unix or Linux system, use the ls -l command to examine various directories. After the first ten characters that define each file's access permissions, there is a field that indicates the number of hard links to the file. For example, here we have two files, bar with two links and foo with just one.

drwxr-sr-x 2 dahlin prof 4096 2012-02-03 08:37 bar/
-rw-r--r-- 1 dahlin prof   0 2012-02-03 08:36 foo

For directories, what is the smallest number of links you can observe? Why?

For directories, even though regular users cannot make hard links to directories, you may observe some directories with high link counts. Why?

7. In NTFS, a master file table entry maximizes the number of extent pointers it can store by storing extent pointers as a sequence of variable-length records: the first four bits encode the size used to store pointer to the start of the extent and the next four bits encode the size used to store the extent length. To further reduce record size, the extent-start pointer is stored as an offset from the previous extent's pointer. Thus, if we have a 10 block extent starting at block 0x20000 and then a 5 block extent starting at block 0x20050, then the first (absolute) starting address (0x200000) will be stored in three bytes while the second (relative) starting address will be stored in one byte (0x20050 - 0x20000 = 0x50).

An apparent disadvantage of this approach is that seeking to a random offset in a file requires sequentially scanning all of the extent pointers. Given your understanding of NTFS and disk technology trends, explain why this apparent disadvantage may not be a problem in practice.

8. When user tries to write a file, the file system needs to detect if that file is a directory so that it can restrict writes to maintain the directory's internal consistency.

Given a file's name, how would you design each file system listed below to keep track of whether each file is a regular file or a directory?

a) The FAT file system

b) FFS

c) NTFS

9. Why would it be difficult to add hard links to the FAT file system?

10. For the FFS file system illustrated in Figure 13.25, what reads and writes of inodes and blocks would occur to create a new file /foo/sparse and write blocks 1 and 2,000,000 of that file. Assume that inodes have pointers for 11 direct blocks, 1 indirect block, 1 double-indirect block, and 1 triple indirect block, and assume 4KB blocks with 4-byte block pointers.

11. Give a formula for the minimum and maximum number of disk blocks that must be read in the UNIX Fast File System to fetch the first block of a file, as a function of the number of "/" characters in the file name (in other words, the depth of the file in the directory tree). Assume that nothing is in the file cache.

12. A web client and web server are running on the same uniprocessor computer. They have an open connection and are ready to send/receive web requests. List a possible sequence of user-mode/kernel-mode boundary crossings (counting one for each direction, and including interrupts) needed for the client to issue a simple web request, the server to receive the request and fetch the data from the file system, and for the server to send the data to the client.

Assume that there is a low priority background task running on the processor, the current directory is cached, but the requested file is not in the server cache or the file system cache. Also assume that both the request and the requested file data are small (e.g., they fit inside a single disk block). You may assume any of the file systems described in this chapter, provided you label which one you are assuming.

A stitch in time saves nine

English Proverb

14 Reliable Storage

Highly reliable storage is vitally important across a wide range of applications from businesses that need to know that that their billing records are safe to families that have photo albums they would like to last for generations.

So far, we have treated disk and flash as ideal non-volatile storage: stored data will remain forever or until it is overwritten. Physical devices cannot achieve such perfection — they may be defective, they may wear out, or they may be damaged so they may lose some or all of their data.

Unfortunately, the limits of physical devices are not merely abstract concerns. For example, some large organizations have observed annual disk failure rates of 2% to 4%, meaning that an organization with 10,000 disks might expect to see hundreds of failures per year and that important data stored on a single disk by a naive storage system might have more than a 30% chance of disappearing within a decade.

The central question of this chapter is: How can we make a storage system more reliable than the physical devices out of which it is built?

reliable
available

A system is *reliable* if it performs its intended function. Reliability is related to, but different from, availability. A system is *available* if it currently can respond to a request.

system reliability

In the case of storage, a storage system is reliable as long as it continues to store a given piece of data and as long as its components are capable of reading or overwriting that data. We define a storage system's *reliability* as the probability that it will continue to be reliable for some specified period of time. A storage system is available at some moment if a read or write operation could be completed at that time, and we define a storage system's *availability* as the probability that the system will be available at any given time.

system availability

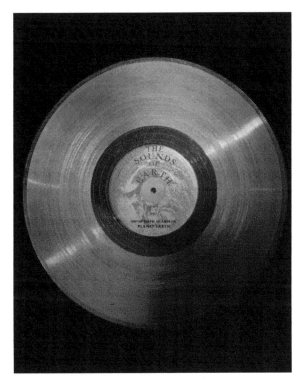

Figure 14.1: The Voyager "Golden Record," a highly reliable but highly unavailable storage device. Photo Credit: NASA.

To see the difference between reliability and availability, consider the highly reliable but highly unavailable storage device shown in Figure 14.1. In the 1970's, the two Voyager spacecraft sent out of our solar system each included a golden record on which various greetings, diagrams, pictures, natural sounds, and music were encoded, as stated on each record by President Carter, as "a present from a small, distant world, a token of our sounds, our science, our images, our music, our thoughts and our feelings." To protect against erosion, the record is encased in an aluminum and uranium cover. This storage device is highly reliable — it is expected to last for many tens of thousands of years in interstellar space — but it is not highly available (at least, not to us).

To take a more pedestrian example, suppose a storage system required each data block to be written to a disk on each of 100 different machines physically distributed across 100 different machine rooms spread across the world. Such a system would be highly reliable, since it would take a spectacular catastrophe to wipe out all of the copies of any data that is stored. It would be highly available for reads, since there are 100 different locations to read from. But it would not be highly available for writes, since new writes cannot complete if any one of 100 machines is unavailable.

Two problems.   Broadly speaking, storage systems must deal with two threats to reliability.

- **Operation interruption.** A crash or power failure in the middle of a series of related updates may leave the stored data in an inconsistent state.

  For example, suppose that a user has asked an operating system to move a file from one directory to another:

  > mv drafts/really-important.doc final/really-important.doc

  As we discussed in Chapter 13, such a move may entail many low-level operations: writing the drafts directory file to remove really-important.doc, updating the last-modified time of the drafts directory, growing the final directory's file to include another block of storage to accommodate a new directory entry for really-important.doc, writing the new directory entry to the directory file, updating the file system's free space bitmap to note that the newly allocated block is now in use, and updating the size and last-modified time of the final directory.

  Suppose that the system's power fails when the updates to the drafts directory are stored in non-volatile storage but when the updates to the final directory are not; in that case, the file really-important.doc may be lost. Or, suppose that the operating system crashes after updating the drafts and final directories but before updating the file system's free space bitmap; in that case, the file system will still regard the new block in the final directory as free, and it may allocate that block to be part of some other file. The storage device then ends up with a block that belongs to two files, and updates intended for one file may corrupt the contents of the other file.

- **Loss of stored data.** Failures of non-volatile storage media can cause previously stored data to disappear or be corrupted. Such failures can affect individual blocks, entire storage devices, or even groups of storage devices.

  For example, a disk sector may be lost if it is scratched by a particle contaminating the drive enclosure; a flash memory cell might lose its contents when large numbers of reads of nearby cells disturb its charge; a disk drive can fail completely because bearing wear causes the platters to vibrate too much to be successfully read or written; or a set of drives might be lost when a fire in a data center destroys a rack of storage servers.

Two solutions.   Fortunately, system designers have developed two sets of powerful solutions to these problems, and the rest of the chapter discusses them.

- **Transactions for atomic updates.** When a system needs to make several related updates to non-volatile storage, it may want to ensure that the state is modified atomically: even if a crash occurs the state reflects either all of the updates or none of them. Transactions are a fundamental technique to provide atomic updates of non-volatile storage

  Transactions are simple to implement and to use, and they often have as good or better performance than ad-hoc approaches. The vast majority of widely used file systems developed over the past two decades have used transactions internally, and many applications implement transactions of their own to keep their persistent state consistent.

- **Redundancy for media failures.** To cope with data loss and corruption, storage systems use several forms of redundancy such as checksums to detect corrupted storage and replicated storage to recover from lost or corrupted sectors or disks.

  Implementing sufficient redundancy at acceptably low cost can be complex. For example, a widely used, simple model of RAID (Redundant Array of Inexpensive Disks) paints an optimistic picture of reliability that can be off by orders of magnitude. Modern storage systems often make use of multiple levels of checksums (e.g., both in storage device hardware and file system software), include sufficient redundancy to survive two or more hardware failures (e.g., keeping three copies of a file or two parity disks with a RAID), and rely on software that to detect failures soon after they occur and to repair failures quickly (e.g., background processes that regularly attempt to read all stored data and algorithms that parallelize recovery when a device fails). Systems that fail to properly use these techniques may be significantly less reliable than expected.

14.1 | Transactions: Atomic Updates

How can we update multiple persistent data structures at once?

When a system makes several updates to non-volatile storage and a crash occurs, some of those updates may be stored and survive the crash and others may not. Because a crash may occur without warning, storage systems and applications need to be constructed so that no matter when the crash occurs, the system's non-volatile storage is left in some sensible state.

This problem occurs in many contexts. For example, if a crash occurs while you are installing an update for a suite of applications, upon recovery you would like to be able to use either the old version or the new version, not be confronted with a mishmash of incompatible programs. For example, if you are moving a subdirectory from one location to another when a crash occurs, when you recover you want to see the data in one location or the other; if the subdirectory disappears because of an untimely crash, you will be (justifiably) upset with the operating system designer. Finally, if a bank is moving $100 from Alice's account to Bob's account when a crash occurs, it wants to be certain that upon recovery either the funds are in Alice's account and records show that the transfer is still to be done or that the funds are in Bob's account and the records show that the transfer has occurred.

This problem is quite similar to the critical section problem in concurrency. In both cases, we have several updates to make and we want to avoid having anyone observe the state in an intermediate, inconsistent state. In addition, we have no control when other threads might try to access the state in the first case or when a crash might occur in the second — we must develop a structured solution that works for any possible execution. The solution is similar, too; we want to make the set of updates atomic. However, because we are dealing with non-volatile storage rather than main memory, the techniques for achieving atomicity differ in significant ways.

Transactions extend the concept of atomic updates from memory to stable storage, allowing systems to atomically update multiple persistent data structures.

14.1.1   Ad Hoc Approaches

Until the mid-1990's, many file systems used ad hoc approaches to solving the problem of consistently updating multiple on-disk data structures.

For example, the Unix fast file system (FFS) would carefully control the order that its updates were sent to disk so that if a crash occurred in the middle of a group of updates, a scan of the disk during recovery could identify and repair inconsistent data structures. When creating a new file, for example, FFS would first update the free-inode bitmap to indicate that the previously free inode was now in use. After making sure this update was on disk, it would initialize the new file's inode, clear all of the direct, indirect, double-indirect, and other pointers, set the file length to 0, and set the file's ownership and access control list. Finally, once the inode update was safely on disk, the file system would update the directory to contain an entry for the newly created file, mapping the file's name to its inode.

If a system running FFS crashed, then when it rebooted it would use a program called fsck (file system check) to scan all of the file system's metadata (e.g., all inodes, all directories, and all free space bitmaps) to make sure that all metadata items were consistent. If, for example, fsck discovered an inode that was marked as *allocated* in the free-inode bitmap but that did not appear in any directory entry, it could infer that the inode was part of a file in the process of being created (or deleted) when the crash occurred. Since the create had not finished or the delete had started, fsck could mark the inode as free, undoing the partially completed create (or completing the partially completed delete).

Similar logic was used for other file system operations.

This approach of careful ordering of operations with scanning and repair of on-disk data structures was widespread until the 1990's, when it was largely abandoned. In particular, this approach has three significant problems:

fsck Lives

Although few file systems today rely on scanning disks when recovering from a crash, fsck and other similar programs are often still used as an "emergency fix" when on-disk data structures are corrupted for other reasons (e.g., due to software bug or storage device failure).

1. **Complex reasoning.** Similar to trying to solve the multi-threaded synchronization problem with just atomic loads and stores, this approach requires reasoning carefully about all possible operations and all possible failure scenarios to make sure that it is always possible to recover the system to a consistent state.

2. **Slow updates.** To ensure that updates are stored in an order that allowed the system's state to be analyzed, file systems are forced to insert sync operations or barriers between dependent operations, reducing the amount of pipelining or parallelism in the stream of requests to storage devices.

   For example, in the file creation example above to ensure that the individual updates hit disk in the required order, the system might suffer three full rotations of the disk to update three on-disk data structures even though those data structures may be quite near each other.

3. **Extremely slow recovery.** When a machine reboots after a crash, it has to scan all of its disks for inconsistent metadata structures.

   In the 1970's and 1980s, it was possible to scan the data structures on most servers' disks in a few seconds or minutes. However, by the 1990's this scanning could take tens of minutes to a few hours for large servers with many disks, and technology trends indicated that scan times would rapidly grow worse.

Although the first two were significant disadvantages of the approach, it was the third that finally made depending on careful ordering and fsck untenable for most file systems. New file systems created since the late 1980's almost invariably use other techniques—primarily various forms of transactions that we discuss in the rest of this section.

Application-level approaches.   Although modern file systems often use transactions internally, some standard file system APIs such as the POSIX API provide only weaker abstractions, forcing applications to take their own measures if they want to atomically apply a set of updates. Many use application-level transactions, but some continue to use ad hoc approaches.

For example, suppose that a user has edited several parts of a text file and then wants to save the updated document. The edits may have inserted text at various points in the document, removed text at others, and shifted the remaining text forwards or backwards — even a small insertion or deletion early in the document could ripple through the rest of the file.

If the text editor application were simply to use the updated file in its memory to overwrite the existing file, an untimely crash could leave the file in an incomprehensible state. The operating system and disk schedulers may choose any order to send the updated blocks to non-volatile storage, so after the crash the file may be an arbitrary mix of old and new blocks, sometimes repeating sections of text, sometimes omitting them entirely.

To avoid this problem, the text editor may take advantage of the semantics of the POSIX rename operation, which renames the file called sourceName to be called targetName instead. POSIX promises that if a file named targetName already exists, rename's shift from having targetName refer to the old file to having it refer to the new one will be atomic. (This atomicity guarantee may be provided by transactions within the file system or by ad hoc means.)

Therefore, to update an existing file design.txt, the text editor first writes the updates to a new, temporary file such as #design.txt#. Then it renames the temporary file to atomically replace the previously stored file.

14.1.2   The Transaction Abstraction

Transactions provide a way to atomically update multiple pieces of persistent state.

For example, suppose you are updating a web site and you want to replace the current collection of documents in /server/live with a new collection of documents you have created in /development/ready. You don't want users to see intermediate steps when some of the documents have been updated and others have not — they might encounter broken links or encounter new descriptions referencing old pages or vice versa. Transactional file systems like Windows Vista's TxF (Transactional NTFS) provide an API that lets applications apply all of these updates atomically, allowing the programmer to write something like the pseudo-code in Figure 14.2.

commit

roll back

Notice that a transaction can finish in one of two ways: it can *commit*, meaning all of its updates occur, or it can *roll back* meaning that none of its updates occur.

Here, if the transaction commits, we are guaranteed that all of the updates will be seen by all subsequent reads, but if it encounters and error and rolls back or crashes without committing or rolling back, no reads outside of the transaction will see any of the updates.

transaction

ACID properties

More precisely, a *transaction* is a way to perform a set of updates while providing the following *ACID properties*:

- **Atomicity.** Updates are "all or nothing." If the transaction *commits*, all updates in the transaction take effect. If the transaction *rolls back*, then none of the updates in the transaction have any effect.

```
ResultCode publish () {
    transactionID = beginTransaction ();
    foreach file f in /development/ready that is not in /server/live {
        error = move f from /development/ready to /server/live ;
        if (error) {
            rollbackTransaction (transactionID);
            return ROLLED_BACK;
        }
    }

    foreach file f in /server/live that is not in /development/ready {
        error = delete f;
        if (error) {
            rollbackTransaction (transactionID);
            return ROLLED_BACK;
        }
    }

    foreach file f in /development/ready that differs from /server/live {
        error = move f from /development/ready to /server/live ;
        if (error) {
            rollbackTransaction (transactionID);
            return ROLLED_BACK;
        }
    }
    commitTransaction (transactionID);
    return COMMITTED;
}
```

Figure 14.2: Pseudo-code for using a transactional file system.

In the website update example above, doing the updates within a transaction guarantees that each of the update is only stored or readable if all of the updates are stored and readable.

- **Consistency.** The transaction moves the system from one legal state to another. A system's invariants on its state can be assumed to hold at the start of a transaction and must hold when the transaction commits.

  In the example above, by using a transaction we can maintain the invariant that every link from one document to another on the server references a valid file.

- **Isolation.** Each transaction appears to execute on its own, and is not affected by other in-progress transactions. Even if multiple transactions execute concurrently, for each pair of transactions T and T', it either appears that T executed entirely before T' or vice versa.

  By executing the web site update in a transaction, we guarantee that each transaction to read from the web site occurs against either the old set of web pages or the new set, not some mix of the two.

  Of course, if each individual read of an object is in its own transaction, then a series of reads to assemble a web page and its included elements could see the old web page and a mix of old and new elements. If

In operating systems, we use the term *consistency* in two ways. In the context of critical sections and transactions, we use "consistency" to refer to the idea of a system's invariants being maintained (e.g., "are my data structures consistent?") In the context of distributed memory machines and distributed systems, we use "consistency" to refer to the memory model — the order in which updates can become visible to reads (e.g., "are my system's reads at different caches sequentially consistent?").

Where there is potential confusion, we will use the terms *transaction consistency* or *memory model consistency*.

web protocols were changed to allow a browser to fetch a page and its elements in a single transaction, then we could guarantee that the user would see either the old page and elements or the new ones.

- **Durability.** A committed transaction's changes to state must survive crashes. Once a transaction is committed, the only way to change the state it produces is with another transaction.

  In our web update example, the system must not return from the commit-Transaction() call until all of the transaction's updates have been safely stored in persistent storage.

Transactions vs. Critical Sections.   The ACID properties are closely related to the properties of critical sections. Critical sections provide a way to update state that is atomic, consistent, and isolated but not durable. Adding the durability requirement significantly changes how we implement atomic updates.

14.1.3   Implementing Transactions

The challenge with implementing transaction is that we want a group of related writes to be atomic, but for persistent storage hardware like disks and flash, the atomic operation is a single-sector or single-page write. Therefore, we must devise a way for a group of related writes to take effect when a single-sector write occurs.

If a system simply starts updating data structures in place, then it is vulnerable to a crash in the middle of a set of updates: the system has neither the complete set of old items (to roll back) nor a complete set of new items (to commit), so an untimely crash can force the system to violate atomicity.

Instead, a transactional system can persistently store all of a transaction's
intentions   *intentions*, the updates that will be made if the transaction commits, in some separate location of persistent storage. Only when all intentions are stored and

the transaction commits should the system begin overwriting the target data structures; if the overwrites are interrupted in the middle, then on recovery the system can complete the transaction's updates using the persistently stored intentions.

Redo Logging

redo logging

A common and very general way to implement transactions is redo logging. *Redo logging* uses a persistent log for recording intentions and executes a transaction in four stages:

1. **Prepare.** Append all planned updates to the log.

   This step can happen all at once, when the transaction begins to commit, or it can happen over time, appending new updates to the log as the transaction executes. What is essential is that all updates are safely stored in the log before proceeding to the next step.

2. **Commit.** Append a commit record to the log, indicating that the transaction has committed.

   Of course, a transaction may roll back rather than commit. In this case, a roll-back record may be placed in the log to indicate that the transaction was abandoned. Writing a roll-back record is optional, however, because a transaction will only be regarded as committed if a commit record appears in the log.

3. **Write-back.** Once the commit record is persistent in the log, all of a transaction's updates may be written to their target locations, replacing old values with new ones.

4. **Garbage collect.** Once a transaction's write-back completes, its records in the log may be garbage collected.

atomic commit

The moment in step 2 when the sector containing the commit record is successfully stored is the *atomic commit*: before that moment, the transaction may safely be rolled back; after that moment, the transaction must take effect.

Recovery.   If a system crashes in the middle of a transaction, it must execute a recovery routine before processing new requests. For redo logging, the recovery routine is simple: scan sequentially through the log, taking the following actions for each type of record:

1. **Update record for a transaction.** Add this record to a list of updates planned for the specified transaction.

2. **Commit record for a transaction.** Write-back all of the transaction's logged updates to their target locations.

3. **Roll-back record for a transaction.** Discard the list of updates planned for the specified transaction.

a) Original state

b) Updates appended to log

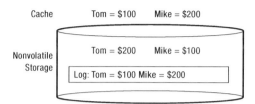

c) Commit appended to log

d) Updates applied

e) Garbage collect completed transactions from log

Figure 14.3: Example transaction with redo logging.

When the end of the log is reached, the recovery process discards any update records for transactions that do not have commit records in the log.

Example. Consider, for example, a transaction that transfers $100 from Tom's account to Mike's account. Initially, as Figure 14.3-(a) shows, data stored on disk and in the volatile memory cache indicates that Tom's account has $200 and Mike's account has $100.

Then, the cached values are updated and the updates are appended to the non-volatile log (b). At this point, if the system were to crash, the updates in cache would be lost, the updates for the uncommitted transaction in the log would be discarded, and the system would return to its original state.

Once the updates are safely in the log, the commit record is appended to the log (c). This commit record should be written atomically based on the properties of the underlying hardware (e.g., by making sure it fits on a single disk sector and putting a strong checksum on it). This step is the atomic commit: prior to the successful storage of the commit record, a crash would cause the transaction to roll back; the instant the commit record is persistently stored, the transaction has committed and is guaranteed to be visible to all reads in the future. Even if a crash occurs, the recovery process will see the committed transaction in the log and apply the updates.

Now, the records in persistent storage for Tom and Mike's accounts can be updated (d).

Finally, once Tom and Mike's accounts are updated, the transaction's records in the log may be garbage collected (e).

Implementation details.   A few specific techniques and observations are important for providing good performance and reliability for transactions with redo logs.

- **Logging concurrent transactions.** Although the previous example shows a single transaction, multiple transactions may be executing at once. In these cases, each record in the log must identify the transaction to which it belongs.

- **Asynchronous write-back.** Step 3 of a transaction (*write-back*) can be asynchronous — once the updates and commit are in the log, the write-back can be delayed until it is convenient or efficient to perform it.

  This flexibility yields two advantages. First, it minimizes the latency from when a transaction calls commit to when the call returns. As soon as the commit is appended to the sequential log, the call can return. Second, the throughput for write-back is higher because the disk scheduler can operate on large batches of updates.

  Two things limit the maximum write-back delay, but both are relatively loose constraints. First, larger write-back delays mean that crash recovery may take longer because there may be more updates to read and apply from the log. Second, the log takes space in persistent storage, which may in some cases be constrained.

- **Repeated write-backs are OK.** Some of the updates written back during recovery may already have been written back before the crash occurred. For example, in Figure 14.4 all of the records from the persistent log-head pointer to the volatile one have already been written back, and some of the records between the volatile log-head pointer may have been written back.

  It is OK to reapply an update from a redo log multiple times because these updates are (and must be) *idempotent* — they have the same effect whether executed once or multiple times. For example, if a log record says "write 42 to each byte of sector 74" then it doesn't matter whether that value is written once, twice, or a hundred times to sector 74.

  Conversely, redo log systems cannot permit non-idempotent records such as "add 42 to each byte in sector 74."

idempotent

Volatile Memory

Figure 14.4: Volatile and persistent data structures for a transactional system based on a replay log.

- **Restarting recovery is OK.** What happens if another crash occurs during recovery? When the system restarts, it simply begins recovery again. The same sequence of updates to committed transactions will be discovered in the log, and the same write-backs will be issued. Some of the write-backs may already have finished before the first crash or during some previous, but repeating them causes no problems.

- **Garbage collection constraints.** Once write-back completes and is persistently stored for a committed transaction, its space in the log can be reclaimed.

  For concreteness, Figure 14.4 illustrates a transaction log with an area of the log that is in use, an area that is no longer needed because it contains only records for transactions whose write-backs have completed, and an area that is free.

  In this example, the system's volatile memory maintains pointers to the head and tail of the log; new transaction records are appended to the log's tail and cached in volatile memory; a write-back process asynchronously writes pending write-backs for committed transactions to their final locations in persistent storage; and a garbage collection process periodically advances a persistent log-head pointer so that recovery can skip at least some of the transactions whose write-backs are complete.

EXAMPLE   **New writes vs. garbage collection.** Suppose we have a circular log or-
                 ganized like the one in Figure 14.4. We must ensure that new records
                 do not overwrite records that we may read during recovery, so we must
                 ensure that the log-tail does not catch the log-head. But there are two
                 log-heads, one in volatile memory and another in persistent storage.
                 Which log-head represents the barrier that the log-tail must not cross?

ANSWER   **The log-tail must not catch the persistent log-head pointer.** Even
                 though the records between the persistent and volatile log-heads have
                 already been written back, during crash recovery, the recovery process
                 will begin reading the log from the location indicated by the persistent
                 log-head pointer. As long as the records are intact, recovering from the
                 persistent log-head pointer rather than the volatile one may waste some
                 work, but it will not affect correctness.   □

- **Ordering is essential.** It is vital to make sure that all of a transaction's
  updates are on disk in the log before the commit is, that the commit is
  on disk before any of the write-backs are, and that all of the write-backs
  are on disk before a transaction's log records are garbage collected.

  In Linux, an application can call sync() or fsync() to tell the operating
  system to force buffered writes to disk. These calls return only once
  the updated blocks are safely stored. Within the operating system, a
  request can be tagged with a BIO_RW_BARRIER tag, which tells the
  device driver and storage hardware to ensure that all preceding writes
  and no subsequent ones are stored before the tagged request is.

Isolation and concurrency revisited.   Redo logging provides a mechanism
for atomically making multiple updates durable, but if there are concurrent
transactions operating on shared state, we must also ensure isolation—each
transaction must appear to execute alone, without interference from other
transactions.

two-phase locking   A common way to enforce isolation among transactions is *two-phase locking*,
which divides a transaction into two phases. During the *expanding* phase, locks
may be acquired but not released. Then, in the *contracting* phase, locks may
be released but not acquired. In the case of transactions, because we want
isolation and durability, the second phase must wait until after the transaction
commits or rolls back so that no other transaction sees updates that later
disappear.

serializability   As we discussed in Chapter 6, two phase locking ensures a strong form of
isolation called serializability. *Serializability* across transactions ensures that
the result of any execution of the program is equivalent to an execution in
which transactions are processed one at a time in some sequential order. So,
even if multiple transactions are executed concurrently, they can only produce

Undo logging

Although transactions are often implemented with redo logging in which updates and the commit are written to the log and then the updates are copied to their final locations, transactions can also be implemented with *undo logging*.

To update an object, a transaction first writes the *old* version of the object to the log. It then writes the new version to its final storage location. When the transaction completes, it simply appends *commit* to the log. Conversely, if the transaction rolls back, the updates are undone by writing the old object versions to their storage locations.

The recovery process takes no action for committed transactions it finds in the log, but it undoes uncommitted transactions by rewriting the original object versions stored in the log.

Undo logging allows writes to objects to be sent to their final storage locations when they are generated and requires them to be persistently stored before a transaction is committed. This pattern is similar to update-in-place approaches, so in some cases it may be easier to add undo logging than redo logging to legacy systems. On the other hand, for storage systems like disks whose sequential bandwidth dominates their random I/O performance, undo logging may require more random I/Os before a transaction is committed (hurting latency) and by writing each transaction's updates immediately, it gives up chances to improve disk-head scheduling by writing large numbers of transaction updates as a batch.

Undo/redo logging stores both the old and new versions of an object in the log. This combination allows updated objects to be written to their final storage locations whenever convenient, whether before or after the transaction is committed. If the transaction rolls back, any modified objects can be restored to the proper state, and if the system crashes, any committed transactions can have their updates redone and any uncommitted transactions can have their updates undone.

---

results that they could have produced had they been executed one at a time in some order.

Although acquiring multiple locks in arbitrary orders normally risks deadlock, transactions provide a simple solution. If a set of transactions deadlocks, one or more of the transactions can be forced to roll back, release their locks, and restart at some later time.

Performance of redo logging.   It might sound like redo logging will impose a significant performance penalty compared to simply updating data in place: redo logging writes each update twice — first to the log and then to its final storage location.

Things are not as bad as they initially seem. Redo logging can have excel-

Multiversion Concurrency Control

An alternative to enforcing transaction isolation with locks is to enforce it with multiversion concurrency control. In *multiversion concurrency control* each write of an object x creates new version of x, the system keeps multiple versions of x and directs each read to a specific version of x. By keeping multiple versions of objects, the system can allow transaction A to read a version of x that has been overwritten by transaction B even if B needs to be serialized after A.

Several multiversion concurrency control algorithms ensure serializability. A simple one is multiversion timestamp ordering (MVTO). MVTO processes concurrent transactions, enforces serializability, never blocks a transaction's reads or writes, but may cause a transaction to roll back if it detects that a read of a later transaction (based on the serializable schedule MVTO is enforcing) was executed before — and therefore did not observe — the write of an earlier transaction (in serialization order).

MVTO assigns each transaction T a logical timestamp. Then, when T writes an object x, MVTO creates a new version of x labeled with T's timestamp t_T, and when T reads an object y, MVTO returns the version of y, y_v with the highest timestamp that is at most T's timestamp; MVTO also makes note that y_v was read by transaction t_T. Finally, when T attempts to commit, MVTO blocks the commit until all transactions with smaller timestamps have committed or aborted.

MVTO rolls back a transaction rather than allowing it to commit in three situations. First, if MVTO aborts any transaction, it removes the object versions written by that transaction and rolls back any transactions that read those versions. Notice that a transaction that reads a version must have a higher timestamp than the one that wrote it, so no committed transactions need to be rolled back.

Second, if a transaction T writes an object that has already been read by a later transaction T' that observed the version immediately prior to T's write, T MVTO rolls back T. It does this because if T were to commit, T''s read must return T's write, but that did not occur.

Third, if MVTO garbage collects old versions and transaction T reads an object for which the last write by an earlier transaction has been garbage collected, then MVTO rolls back T.

---

lent performance — often better than update in place — especially for small writes. Four factors allow efficient implementations of redo logging:

- **Log updates are sequential.** Because log updates are sequential, appending to the log is fast. With spinning disks, large numbers of updates can be written as a sequential stream without seeks or rotational delay once the write begins. Many high-performance systems dedicate a sepa-

Relaxing Isolation

In this book we focus on the strong and relatively simple isolation requirement of serializability: no matter how much concurrency there is, the system must ensure that the results of any execution of the program is equivalent to an execution in which transactions are processed one at a time in some sequence. However, strong isolation requirements sometimes force transactions to block (e.g., when waiting to acquire locks) or roll back (e.g., when fixing a deadlock or encountering a "late write" under multiversion concurrency control).

Relaxing the isolation requirement can allow effectively higher levels of concurrency by reducing the number of cases in which transactions must block or roll back. The cost, of course, is potentially increased complexity in reasoning about concurrent programs, but several relaxed isolation semantics have proven to be sufficiently strong to be widely used.

For example, *snapshot isolation* requires each transaction's reads appear to come from a snapshot of the system's committed data taken when the transaction starts. Each transaction is buffered until the transaction commits, at which point the system checks all of the transaction's updates for *write-write conflicts*. A write-write conflict occurs if transaction T reads an object o from a snapshot at time t_{start} and tries to commit at time t_{commit} but some other transaction T' commits an update to o between T's read at t_{start} and T's attempted commit at t_{commit}. If a write-write conflict is detected for any object being committed by T, T is rolled back.

Snapshot isolation is weaker than serializability because each transaction's reads logically happen at one time and its writes logically happen at another time. This split allows, for example, *write skew anomalies* where one transaction reads object x and updates object y and a concurrent transaction reads object y and updates object x. If there is some constraint between x and y, it may now be violated. For example, if x and y represent the number of hours two managers have assigned you to work on each of two tasks with a constraint that $x + y \leq 40$. Manager 1 could read $x = 15$ and $y = 15$, attempt to assign 10 more hours of work on task x, and verify that $x + y = 25 + 15 \leq 40$. In the mean time manager 2 could read $x = 15$ and $y = 15$, attempt to assign 10 more hours of work on task y, verify that that $x + y = 15 + 25 \leq 40$, and successfully commit the update, setting $y = 25$. Finally, manager 1 could successfully commit its update, set $x = 25$, and ruin your weekend.

---

rate disk for logging so that log appends never require seeks. For flash storage, sequential updates are often significantly faster than random updates, though the advantage is not as pronounced.

- **Write-back is asynchronous.** Because write-back can be delayed until some time after a transaction has been committed, transactions using redo logs can have good response time (because the transaction commit only requires appending a commit record to the log) and can have good throughput (because batched write-backs can be scheduled more efficiently than individual or small groups of writes that must occur immediately).

- **Fewer barriers or synchronous writes are required.** Some systems avoid using transactions by carefully ordering updates to data structures so that they can ensure that if a crash occurs, a recovery process will be able to scan, identify, and repair inconsistent data structures. However, these techniques often require large number of barrier or synchronous write operations, which reduce opportunities to pipeline or efficiently schedule updates.

  In contrast, transactions need a relatively small number of barriers: one after the updates are logged and before the commit is logged, another after the commit is logged but before the transaction is reported as successful (and before write-backs begin), and one after a transaction's write-backs complete but before the transaction's log entries are garbage collected.

group commit
- **Group commit.** *Group commit* can further improve transaction performance. Group commit techniques combine a set of transaction commits into one log write to amortize the cost of initiating the write (e.g., seek and rotational delays). Group commit techniques can also be used to reduce the number of barrier or sync operations needed to perform a group of transactions.

EXAMPLE   **Performance of small-write transactions.** Suppose you have a 1 TB disk that rotates once every 10 ms, that has a maximum sustained platter transfer rate of 50 MB/s for inner tracks and 100 MB/s for outer tracks, and that has a 5 ms average seek time, a 0.5 ms minimum seek time, and a 10 ms maximum seek time.

Consider updating 100 randomly selected 512-byte sectors; assume that the updates must be ordered for safety (e.g., update i must be on disk before update $i + 1$ is applied).

Compare the total time to complete these updates using a simple update in place approach with the cost when using transactions implemented with a redo log.

ANSWER   Using a simple update in place approach, we need to use FIFO scheduling to ensure updates hit the disk in order, so the time for each update is approximately:

$$
\begin{aligned}
\text{time per update} \;&=\; \text{average seek time} + 0.5 \text{ rotation time} + \text{transfer time} \\
&=\; 5\,\text{ms} + 5\,\text{ms} + \text{transfer time}
\end{aligned}
$$

Transfer time will be at most $\frac{512}{50*10^6}$ seconds, which will be negligible compared to the other terms. Thus, we have **10 ms per request** or **1 s for 100 requests** for update in place.

For transactions, we first append the 100 writes to the log. We will conservatively assume that each update consumes 2 sectors (one for the data and the other for metadata indicating the transaction number and the target sector on disk). So, assuming that the disk head is at a random location when the request arrives, our time to log the requests is:

$$
\begin{aligned}
\text{time to write log} &= \text{average seek time} + 0.5 \text{ rotation time} + \text{transfer time} \\
&= 5\,\text{ms} + 5\,\text{ms} + \text{transfer time} \\
&= 5\,\text{ms} + 5\,\text{ms} + \text{transfer time} \\
&= 5\,\text{ms} + 5\,\text{ms} + \frac{200 * 512}{100 * 10^6}\,\text{s} \\
&= 11.0\,\text{ms}
\end{aligned}
$$

Next, we need to append the commit record to the transaction. If the disk hardware supports a barrier instruction to enforce ordering of multiple in-progress requests, the operating system can issue this request along with the 100 writes. Here, we will be conservative and assume that the system does not issue the commit's write until after the 100 writes in the body of the transaction are in the log. Thus, we will likely have to wait one full revolution of the disk to finish the commit: *10 ms.*

Finally, we need to write the 100 writes to their target locations on disk. Unlike the case for update in place, ordering does not matter here, so we can schedule them and write them more efficiently. Estimating this time takes engineering judgment, and different people are likely to make different estimates. For this example, we will assume that the disk uses a variant of shortest service time first (SSTF) scheduling in which the scheduler looks at the four requests on the next nearest tracks and picks the one with the shortest predicted seek time + rotational latency from the disk head's current position. Because the scheduler gets to choose from four requests, we will estimate that the average rotational latency will be one fourth of a rotation, 2.5 ms. This may be conservative since it ignores the fact that request i will always remove from the four requests being considered the one that would have been rotationally farthest away if it were an option for request $i + 1$. Because we initially have 100 requests and because we are considering the four requests on the nearest tracks, the farthest seek should be around 4% of the way across the disk, and the average one to a member of the group being considered should be around 2%. We will estimate that seeking 2-4% of the way across disk costs twice the minimum seek time: 1 ms.

Putting these estimates for write-back time together, the write-backs of the 100 sectors should take about:

$$per\text{-}request\ write\text{-}back\ time = seek\ time + rotational\ latency$$
$$= 1.0\,ms + 2.5\,ms$$
$$= 3.5\,ms$$

giving us a total of 350 ms for 100 requests.

Adding the logging, commit, and write-back times, we have:

$$total\ write\ time = log\ time + commit\ time + write\text{-}back\ time$$
$$= 11.0\,ms + 10\,ms + 350\,ms$$
$$= \mathbf{371\,ms}$$

The transactional approach is almost three times faster even though it writes the data twice and even though it provides the stronger atomic-update semantics.   □

EXAMPLE   For the same two approaches, compare the response time latency from when a call issuing these requests is issued until that call can safely return because all of the updates are durable.

ANSWER   The time for **update in place** is the same as above: **1 s**. The time for the **transactional approach** is the time for the first two steps: logging the updates and then logging the commit: *10.24 ms + 10 ms = **20.24 ms**.*   □

Although small writes using redo logging may actually see performance benefits compared to update in place approaches, large writes may see significant penalties.

EXAMPLE   **Performance of large-write transactions.** Considering the same disk and approaches as in the example above, compare the total time to for 100 writes, but now assume that each of the 100 writes updates a randomly selected 1 MB range of sequential sectors.

ANSWER   For the update in place approach, the time for each update is approximately *average seek time + 0.5 rotation time + transfer time = 5 ms + 5 ms + transfer time.* We will assume that the bandwidth for an average transfer is 75 MB/s — between the 50 MB/s and 100 MB/s inner and out tracks' transfer rates. Thus, we estimate the average transfer time to be 100 MB/75 MB/s = 1.333 s, giving a total time of *.005 s + .005 s + 1.333 s = 1.343 s* per request and *134.3 s* for 100 requests.

For the transactional approach, our time will be *time to log updates + time to commit + time to write back.*

For logging the updates, we assume a reasonably efficient encoding of metadata that makes the size of the metadata for a 100 MB sequential update negligible compared to the data. Thus, logging the data will take *seek time +*

rotational latency + transfer time = 5 ms + 5 ms + 100 * 100 MB/100 MB/s = .005 s + .005 s + 100 s ≈ 100 s.

Writing the commit adds another 10 ms as in the above example.

Finally, as above, doing the write-backs *estimated scheduled seek time + estimated scheduled latency + transfer time = 1.0 ms + 2.5 ms + 100 MB/75 MB/s,* giving a total of *1.337 s* per request and **133.7 s** for 100 requests.

Adding the data logging, commit, and write-back times together, the **transactional approach takes about 233 s** while the **update in place approach takes about 134 s**. In this case, transactions do impose a significant cost, nearly doubling the total time to process these updates.   □

EXAMPLE   Now compare the latency from when the call making the 100 writes is issued until it may safely return.

ANSWER   Under the update in place approach, we can only return when everything is written, while under the transactional approach, we can return once the commit is complete. Thus, we have comparable times: **134 s for update in place** and **100 s for transactions**.   □

One way to reduce transaction overheads for large writes is to add a level of indirection: write the large data objects to a free area of the disk, but not in the circular log. Then, the update in the log just needs to be a reference to that data rather than the data itself. Finally, after the transaction commits, perform the write-back by updating a pointer in the original data structure to point to the new data.

14.1.4   Transactions and File Systems

File systems must maintain internal consistency when updating multiple data structures. For example, when a file system like FFS creates a new file, it may need to update the file's inode, the free inode bitmap, the parent directory, the parent directory's inode, and the free space bitmap. If a crash occurs in the middle of such a group of updates, the file system could be left in an inconsistent state with, say, the new file's inode allocated and initialized but without an entry in the parent directory.

As discussed in Section 14.1.1, some early file systems used ad-hoc solutions such as carefully ordering sequences of writes and scanning the disk to detect and repair inconsistencies when restarting after a crash. However, these approaches suffered from complexity, slow updates, and — as disk capacity grew — unacceptably slow crash recovery.

To address these problems, most modern file systems use transactions.

Traditional file systems.   Transactions are added to traditional, update-in-place file systems like FFS and NTFS using either *journaling* or *logging* .

- **Journaling.** Journaling file systems apply updates to the system's meta-data via transactions, but they update the contents of users' files in place.

  By protecting metadata updates, these systems ensure consistency of their persistent data structures (e.g., updates to inodes, bitmaps, directories, and indirect blocks). Journaling file systems first write metadata updates to a redo log, then commit them, and finally write them back to their final storage locations.

  Updates to the contents of regular (non-directory) files are not logged, they are applied in place. This avoids writing file updates twice, which can be expensive for large updates. On the other hand, updating file contents in place means that journaling file systems provide few guarantees when a program updates a file: if a crash occurs in the middle of the update, the file may end up in an inconsistent state with some blocks but not others updated. If a program using a journaling file system requires atomic multi-block updates, it needs to provide them itself.

- **Logging.** Logging file systems simply include all updates to disk — both metadata and data — in transactions.

Today, journaling file systems are common: Microsoft's NTFS, Apple's HFS+, and Linux's XFS, JFS, and ReiserFS all use journaling; and Linux's ext3 and ext4 use journaling in their default configurations.

Logging file systems are also widely available, at least for Linux. In particular, Linux's ext3 and ext4 file systems can be configured to use either journaling or logging.

Copy-on-write file systems. Copy-on-write file systems like the open source ZFS are designed from the ground up to be transactional. They do not over-write data in place; updating the root inode or ZFS uberblock is an atomic action that commits a set of updates.

For example, suppose we update just a file's data block or just its indirect blocks, its inode, and the indirect blocks for the inode file, leaving the state as shown in Figure 14.5(a) or (b). If the system were to crash in such an intermediate state, before the root inode is updated, none of these changes would be included in the file system's tree, and they would have no effect. Only when the root inode is updated as in Figure 14.5(c) do all of these changes take effect at once.

The implementations of ZFS and other copy-on-write file systems often add two performance optimizations.

- **Batch updates.** Rather than applying each update individually, ZFS buffers several seconds worth of updates before writing them to stable storage as a single atomic group.

  Batching yields two advantages.

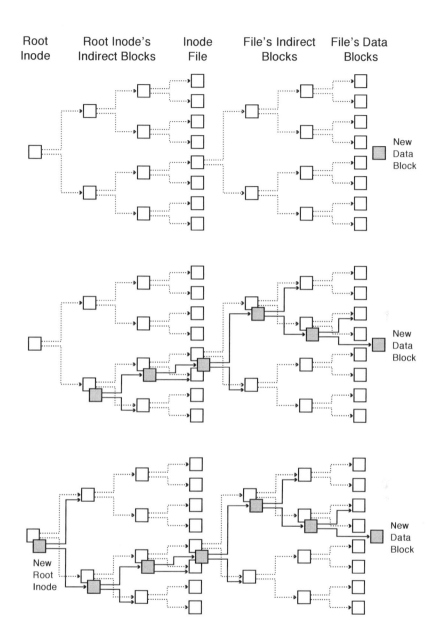

Root   Root Inode's   Inode   File's Indirect   File's Data
Inode   Indirect Blocks   File   Blocks   Blocks

Figure 14.5: In a copy-on-write file system, intermediate states of an update such as (top) and (center) are not observable; they atomically take effect when the root inode is updated (bottom).

First, it allows the system to transform many small, random writes into a few large, sequential writes, which improves performance for most storage devices including individual magnetic disks, RAIDs (Redundant Arrays of Inexpensive Disks), and even some flash storage devices.

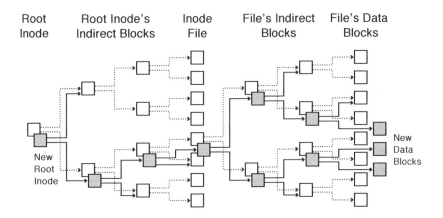

Figure 14.6: With batch updates in a COW file system, updates of inodes and indirect blocks are amortized across updates of multiple data blocks.

Second, not only does batching make writing each block more efficient, it actually reduces how many blocks must be written by coalescing multiple updates of the same indirect blocks and inodes. For example, Figure 14.6 illustrates how updates of inodes and indirect blocks are amortized across updates of multiple data blocks.

- **Intent log.** ZFS typically accumulates several seconds of writes before performing a large batch update, but some applications need immediate assurance that their updates are safely stored on non-volatile media. For example, when a word processor's user saves a file, the program might call fsync() to tell the file system to make sure the updates are stored on disk. Forcing the user to wait several seconds to save a file is not acceptable.

  ZFS's solution is the ZFS Intent Log (ZIL), which is essentially a redo log. The ZIL is a linked list of ZFS blocks that contain updates that have been forced to disk but whose batch update may not yet have been stored. The ZIL is replayed when the file system is mounted.

  ZFS includes several optimizations in the ZIL implementation. First, by default writes are buffered and committed in their batch update without being written to the ZIL; only writes that are explicitly forced to disk are written to the ZIL. Second, the ZIL may reside on a separate, dedicated logging device; this allows us to use a fast device (e.g., flash) for the ZIL and slower, high-capacity devices (e.g., disks) for the main pool; if no separate ZIL device is provided, ZFS uses the main block pool for the ZIL. Finally, the contents of small data writes are included in the ZIL's blocks directly, but the contents of larger writes are written to separate blocks that are referenced by the ZIL; then, the subsequent batch commit can avoid rewriting those large blocks by updating metadata to point to the copies already on disk.

14.2 | Error Detection and Correction

Because data storage hardware is imperfect, storage systems must be designed to detect and correct errors. Storage systems take a layered approach:

- Storage hardware detects many failures with checksums and device-level checks, and it corrects small corruptions with error correcting codes

- Storage systems include redundancy using RAID architectures to reconstruct data lost by individual devices

- Many recent file systems include additional end-to-end correctness checks

These techniques are essential. Essentially all persistent storage devices include internal redundancy to achieve high storage densities with acceptable error rates. This internal redundancy is insufficient on its own. Storage systems for important data add additional redundancy for error correction, and it is hard to think of a significant file system developed in the last decade that does not include higher-level checksums.

Though essential and widespread, there are significant pitfalls in designing and using these techniques. In our discussions, we will point out issues that, if not handled carefully, can drastically reduce reliability.

The rest of this section examines error detection and correction for persistent storage, starting with the individual storage devices, then examining how RAID replication helps tolerate failures by individual storage devices, and finally looking at the end-to-end error detection in many recent file systems.

14.2.1   Storage Device Failures and Mitigation

Storage hardware pushes the limits of physics, material sciences, and manufacturing processes to maximize storage capacity and performance. These aggressive designs leave little margin for error, so manufacturing defects, contamination, or wear can cause stored bits to be lost.

Individual spinning disks and flash storage devices exhibit two types of failure. First, isolated disk sectors or flash pages can lose existing data or degrade to the point where they cannot store new data. Second, an entire device can fail, preventing access to all of its sectors or pages. We discuss each of these in turn to understand the problems higher-level techniques need to deal with.

What causes sector or page failures?

For spinning disks, permanent sector failures can be caused by a range of faults such as pits in the magnetic coating where a contaminant flaked off the surface, scratches in the coating where a contaminant was dragged across the surface by the head, or smears of machine oil across some sectors of a disk surface.

Transient sector faults occur when a sector's stored data is corrupted but new data can still be successfully written to and read from the sector. These can be caused by factors such as write interference where writes to one track disturb bits stored on nearby tracks and "high fly writes" where the disk head gets too far from the surface, producing magnetic fields too weak to be accurately read.

For flash storage, permanent page failures can be caused by manufacturing defects or by wear-out when a page experience a large number of write/erase cycles.

Transient flash storage failures can be caused by: (i) write disturb errors where charging one bit also causes a nearby bit to be charged; (ii) read disturb errors where repeatedly reading one page changes values stored on a nearby page; (iii) over-programming errors where too high a voltage is used to write a cell, which may cause incorrect reads or writes; and (iv) data retention errors where charge may leak out of or into a flash cell over time, changing its value. Wear-out from repeated write/erase cycles can make devices more susceptible to data retention errors.

Sector and Page Failures

sector failure

page failure

Disk *sector failures* occur when data on one or more individual sectors of a disk are lost, but the rest of the disk continues to operate correctly. Flash *page failures* are the equivalent for flash pages.

Storage devices use two techniques to mitigate sector or page failures: error correcting codes and remapping.

error correcting codes

Mitigation: Error correcting codes. *Error correcting codes* deal with failures when some of the bits in a sector or page are corrupted. When the device stores data, it encodes the data with additional redundancy. Then, if a small number of bits are corrupted in a sector or page being read, the hardware automatically corrects the error, and the read successfully completes. If the damage is more extensive, then with high likelihood the read fails and returns an error code. Being told that the device has lost data is not a perfect solution, but it is better than having the device silently return the wrong data.

Manufacturers balance storage space overheads against error correction capabilities to achieve acceptable advertised sector or page failure rate, typically expressed as the expected number of bits that can be read before encountering

non-recoverable
read error

bit error rate

an unreadable sector or page. In 2011, advertised disk and flash *non-recoverable read error* rates typically range between one sector/page per 10^{14} to 10^{16} bits read. The non-recoverable read error rate is sometimes called the *bit error rate*.

Mitigation: Remapping   Disks and flash are manufactured with some number of spare sectors or pages so that they can continue to function despite some number of permanent sector or page failures by remapping failed sectors or pages to good ones. Before shipping hardware to users, manufacturers scan devices to remap bad sectors or pages caused by manufacturing defects. Later, if additional permanent failures are detected, the operating system or device firmware can remap the failed sectors or pages to good ones.

Pitfalls.   Although devices' non-recoverable read rate specifications are helpful, designers must avoid a number of common pitfalls:

- **Assuming that non-recoverable read error rates are negligible.** Storage devices' advertised error rates sound impressive, but with the large capacities of today's storage, these error rates are non-negligible. For example, if you completely read a 2 TB disk with a bit error rate of one sector per 10^{14} bits, there may be more than a 10% chance of encountering at least one error.

- **Assuming non-recoverable read error rates are constant.** Although a device may specify a single number as its unrecoverable read error rate, many factors can affect the rate at which such errors manifest. A given device's actual bit error rate may depend on its load (e.g., some faults may be caused by device activity), its age (e.g., some faults may become more likely as a device ages), or even its specific workload (e.g., faults in some sectors or pages may be caused by reads or writes to nearby sectors or pages).

- **Assuming independent failures.** Errors may be correlated in time or space: finding an error in one sector may make it more likely that you will find one in a nearby sector or that you will to find a fault in another sector soon.

- **Assuming uniform error rates.** The relative contributions of different causes of non-recoverable read errors can vary across models and different generations or production runs of the same model. For example, one model of disk drive might have many of its sector read errors caused by contaminants damaging its recording surfaces while another model might have most of its errors caused by write interference where writes to one track perturb data stored on nearby tracks. The first might see its error rate rise over time, while the second might have an error rate that increases as its write/read ratio increases.

Failure rates can even vary across different individual devices. If you deploy several outwardly identical disks, some may exhibit tens of non-recoverable read errors in a year, while others operate flawlessly.

EXAMPLE

Unrecoverable read errors. Suppose that the nearly-full 500 GB disk on your laptop has just stopped working. Fortunately, you have a recent, full backup on a 500 GB USB drive with an unrecoverable read error rate of one sector per 10^{14} bits read. Estimate the probability of successfully reading the entire USB backup disk when restoring your data to a replacement laptop disk.

ANSWER

We need to read 500 GB, so the expected number of failures is $500\,\text{GB} * 8 * 10^9 \frac{\text{bits}}{\text{GB}} * 10^{-14} \frac{\text{errors}}{\text{bit}} = 0.04$. The probability of encountering at least one failure might be a bit lower than that (since we may encounter multiple failures as we scan the entire disk), but there appears to be a chance of at least a few percent that the restoration will not be fully successful.

We can approach the problem in a slightly different way by interpreting the unrecoverable read rate as meaning that each bit has a 10^{-14} chance of being wrong and that failures are independent (both somewhat dubious assumptions, but probably OK for a ballpark estimate). Then each bit has a $1 - 10^{-14}$ chance of being correct, and the chance of reading all bits successfully is $P_S = (1 - 10^{-14})^{8*500*10^9} = 0.9608$. Under this calculation, we estimate that there is slightly less than a 4% chance of encountering a failure during the full-disk read of the backup disk.

As noted in the sidebar, these calculations ignore some important factors, so the results may not be precise. But, even if they are off by as much as an order of magnitude, then it is still reasonable to conclude that the rate of non-recoverable read errors is likely to be non-negligible.   □

Note that the impact of a small number of lost sectors may be modest (e.g., the backup software succeeds in restoring all but a file or two) or it may be severe (e.g., no data is restored). For example, if the sector failure corrupts the root directory, a significant fraction of the data may be lost.

Device Failures

disk device failure,
flash device failure

Full disk or flash drive failures are when a device stops being able to service reads or writes to all sectors.

When a whole device fails, the host computer's device driver will detect the failure, and reads and writes to the device will return error codes rather than, for example, returning incorrect data. This explicit failure notification is important because it reduces the amount of cross-device redundancy needed to correct failures.

annual failure rate

mean time before
failure (MTTF)

Full device failure rates are typically characterized by an *annual failure rate*, the fraction of disks expected to fail each year, or by a *mean time before failure (MTTF)*, which is the inverse of the specified constant annual failure rate. In 2011, specified annual failure rates (or MTTFs) for spinning disks typically

What causes whole-device failures?

Disk failures can be caused by a range of faults such as a disk head being damaged, a capacitor failure or power surge that damages the electronics, or mechanical wear-out that makes it difficult for the head to stay centered over a track.

Common causes of flash device failures include wear-out, when enough individual pages fail that the device runs out of spare pages to use for remapping, and failures of the device's electronics such as having a capacitor fail.

---

range from 0.5% ($1.7 * 10^6$ hours) to 0.9% ($1 * 10^6$ hours); specified failure rates for flash solid state drives are similar.

Pitfalls. Storage system designers must consider several pitfalls when considering advertised device failure rates.

- **Relying on advertised failure rates.** Studies across several large collections of spinning disks have found significantly variability in failure rates. In these studies, many systems experienced failure rates of 2%, 4%, or higher, despite advertised failure rates of less than 1%.

  Some of the discrepancy may be due to different definitions of "failure" by manufacturers and users, some may be due to challenging field conditions, and some may be due to the limitations of the accelerated-aging and predictive techniques used by manufacturers to estimate MTTF.

- **Assuming uncorrelated failures.** Evidence from deployed systems suggests that when one fault occurs, other nearby devices are more likely to fail soon. Many factors can cause such correlation. For example, manufacturing irregularities can cause a batch of disks to be substandard, and an organization that purchases disks in bulk may find an entire batch of disks failing at the same time. As another example, disks in the same machine or rack may be of a similar age, may experience similar environmental stress and workloads, and may wear out at a similar time.

- **Confusing a device's MTTF with its useful life.** If a device has an MTTF of one million or more hours, it does not mean that it is expected to last for 100 years or more. Disks are designed to be operated for some finite lifetime, perhaps 5 years. A disk's advertised annual failure rate (i.e., 1/MTTF) applies during the disk's intended service life. As that lifetime is approached, failure rates may rise as the device wears out.

- **Assuming constant failure rates.** A device may have different failure rates over its lifetime. Some devices exhibit *infant mortality*, where their

infant mortality

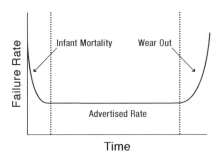

Figure 14.7: Bathtub model of device lifetimes.

wear out

failure rate may be higher than normal during their first few weeks of use as latent manufacturing defects are exposed. Others exhibit *wear out*, where their failure rate begins to rise after some years.

bathtub model

A simple model for understanding infant mortality and wear out is the *bathtub model* illustrated in Figure 14.7.

SMART
(Self-Monitoring,
Analysis, and
Reporting
Technology)

- **Ignoring warning signs.** Some device failures happen without warning, but others are preceded by increasing rates of non-fatal anomalies. Many storage devices implement the *SMART (Self-Monitoring, Analysis, and Reporting Technology)* interface, which provides a way for the operating system to monitor events that may be useful in predicting failures such as read errors, sector remappings, inaccurate seek attempts, or failures to spin up to the target speed.

- **Assuming devices behave identically.** Different device models or even different generations of the same model may have significantly different failure behaviors. One generation might exhibit significantly higher failure rates than expected and the next might exhibit significantly lower rates.

EXAMPLE

Disk failures in large systems. Suppose you have a departmental file server with 100 disks, each with an estimated MTTF of $1.5 * 10^6$ hours. Estimate the expected time until one of those disks fails. For simplicity, assume that each disk has a constant failure rate and that disks fail independently.

ANSWER

If each disk has a MTTF of $1.5 * 10^6$ hours, then 100 disks fail at a 100 times greater rate, giving us a MTTF of $1.5 * 10^4$ hours. So, although the annual failure rate of a single disk is $\frac{1 \text{ failure}}{1.5 * 10^6 \text{ hours}} * 24 \frac{\text{hours}}{\text{day}} * 365 \frac{\text{days}}{\text{year}} = 0.00585 \frac{\text{failures}}{\text{year}}$, the annual failure rate of the 100 disk system is $0.585 = 58.5\%$.

☐

EXAMPLE

Pitfalls. Given the pitfalls discussed above, is this calculation above likely to overestimate or underestimate the failure rate of the system?

ANSWER   Of the factors listed above, the pitfall of *relying on advertised failure rates* seems most significant, and it could lead us to significantly *underestimate* the failure rate of the system.

This solution does *assume constant failure rates*. If the disks are very new or very old, they may suffer higher failure rates than expected, which might cause us to *underestimate* the failure rate of the system.

Because we are only interested in the average rate, the *correlation* pitfall is probably not particularly relevant to our analysis.

□

14.2.2   RAID: Multi-Disk Redundancy for Error Correction

Given the limits of physical storage devices, storage systems use additional techniques to get acceptable end-to-end reliability. In particular, rather than trying to engineer perfectly reliable (and extremely expensive) storage devices, storage systems use Redundant Arrays of Inexpensive Disks (RAIDs) so that a partial or total failure of one device will not cause data to be lost.

Basic RAIDs

RAID   A *Redundant Array of Inexpensive Disks (RAID)* is a system that spreads data redundantly across multiple disks in order to tolerate individual disk failures. Note that the term RAID traditionally refers to redundant *disks*, and for simplicity, we will discuss RAID in the context of disks. The principles, however, apply equally well to other storage devices like flash drives.

Figures 14.8 and 14.9 illustrate two common RAID architectures: mirroring and rotating parity.

mirroring   • **Mirroring.** In RAIDs with *mirroring* (also called *RAID 1*), the system writes
RAID 1   each block of data to two disks and can read any block of data from either disk as Figure 14.8 illustrates. If one of the disks suffers a sector or whole-disk failure, no data is lost because the data can still be read from the other disk.

rotating parity   • **Rotating parity.** In RAIDs with *rotating parity* (also called *RAID 5*), the
RAID 5   system reduces replication overheads by storing several blocks of data on several disks and protecting those blocks with one redundant block stored on yet another disk as Figure 14.9 illustrates.

In particular, this approach uses groups of G disks, and writes each of $G - 1$ blocks of data to a different disk and 1 block of parity to the remaining disk. Each bit of the parity block is produced by computing the exclusive-or of the corresponding bits of the data blocks:

$$parity = data_0 \oplus data_1 \oplus \ldots \oplus data_{G-1}$$

The exponential distribution

When—as in the example—device failures occur at a constant rate, the number of failure events in a fixed time period can be mathematically modeled as a Poisson process, and the interarrival time between failure events follows an exponential distribution.

The exponential distribution is *memoryless*—since the rate of failure events is constant across time, then the expected time to the next failure event is the same—no matter what the current time and no matter how long it has been since the last failure. Thus, if a device has an annual failure rate of 0.5 and thus a mean time to failure of 2 years, and we have been operating the device without a failure for a year, the expected time from the current time to the next failure is still 2 years.

If random variable T represents the time between failures and has an exponential distribution with λ representing the average number of failure events per unit of time, then the probability density function $f_T t$ is:

$$f_T(t) = \begin{cases} \lambda e^{-\lambda t} & \text{if } t \geq 0 \\ 0 & \text{if } t < 0 \end{cases}$$

The mean time to failure is $MTTF = \frac{1}{\lambda}$.

Exponential distributions have a number of convenient mathematical properties. For example, because the failure rate is constant, the mean time to failure is the inverse of the failure rate; this is why it is easy to convert between MTTF and annual failure rates in storage specifications. Also, if the expected number of failures is given for one duration (e.g., 0.1 failures per year), it can easily be converted to the expected number for a different duration (e.g., 0.0003 failures per day). Finally, if we have k independent failure processes with rates of $\lambda_1, \lambda_2, \ldots, \lambda_k$, then the aggregate failure function—the rate at which failures of any of the k kinds occurs—is

$$\lambda_{tot} = \lambda_1 + \lambda_2 + \ldots + \lambda_k$$

and the mean time to the next failure of any kind is $MTTF_{tot} = \frac{1}{\lambda_{tot}}$. For example, if we have 100 disks, each with a $MTTF_{disk} = 1.5 * 10^6$ hours or, equivalently, each failing at a rate of 0.00585 failures per year, then the overall 100-disk system suffers failures at a rate of $100 * 0.00585 = 0.585$ failures per year or, equivalently, the 100-disk system has $MTTF_{100disks} = 1.5 * 10^4$ hours.

Warning. Because the exponential distribution is so mathematically convenient, is tempting to use it even when it is not appropriate. Remember that failures in real systems may be correlated (i.e., they are not independent) and may vary over time (i.e., they are not constant).

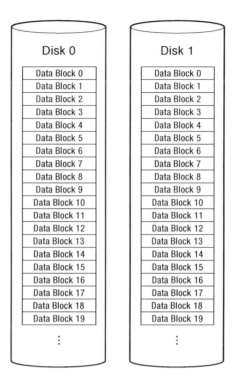

Figure 14.8: RAID 1 with mirroring.

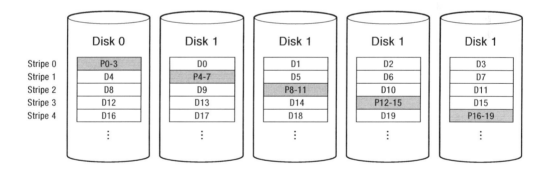

Figure 14.9: RAID 5 with rotating parity.

If one of the disks suffers a sector or whole-disk failure, lost data blocks can be reconstructed using the corresponding data and parity blocks from the other disks. Note that because the system already knows which disk has failed, parity is sufficient for error correction, not just error detection. For example, if the disk containing block $data_0$ fails, the block can be reconstructed by computing the exclusive-or of the parity block and the remaining data blocks:

$$data_0 = parity \oplus data_1 \oplus \ldots \oplus data_{G-1}$$

To maximize performance, rotating parity RAIDs carefully organize their data layout by rotating parity and striping data to balance parallelism and sequential access:

- **Rotating parity.** Because the parity for a given set of blocks must be updated each time any of the data blocks are updated, the average parity block tends to be accessed more often than the average data block. To balance load, rather than having $G - 1$ disks store only data blocks and 1 disk store only parity blocks, each disk dedicates $\frac{1}{G}$th of its space to parity and is responsible for storing $\frac{1}{G}$th of the parity blocks and $\frac{G-1}{G}$ of the data blocks.

- **Striping data.** To balance parallelism versus sequential-access efficiency, a *strip* of several sequential blocks is placed on one disk before shifting to another disk for the next strip. A set of $G - 1$ data strips and their parity strip is called a *stripe*.

      strip

      stripe

  By striping data, requests larger than a block but smaller than a strip require just one disk to seek and then read or write the full sequential run of data rather than requiring multiple disks to seek and then read smaller sequential runs. Conversely, the RAID can service more widely spaced requests in parallel.

Combining rotating parity and striping, we have the arrangement shown in Figure 14.9.

EXAMPLE   **Updating a RAID with rotating parity.** For the rotating parity RAID in Figure 14.9, suppose you update data block 21. What disk I/O operations must occur?

ANSWER   The challenge is that we must not only update data block 21, we must also update the corresponding parity block. Since data block 21 is block 1 of its strip and the strip is part of stripe 1, we need to update parity block 1 of the parity strip for stripe 1 (*Parity (1,1,1)* in the figure).

     It takes 4 I/O operations to update both the data and parity. First we read the old data D_{21} **and parity** $P_{1,1,1}$ and "remove" the old data from the parity calculation $P_{tmp} = P_{1,1,1} \oplus D_{21}$. Then we can compute the new parity from the new data $P'_{1,1,1} = P_{tmp} \oplus D'_{21}$. **Finally, we can write the new data** D'_{21} **and parity** $P'_{1,1,1}$ to disks 2 and 1, respectively.

□

RAIDs with rotating parity have high overheads for small writes. Their overheads are far smaller for reads and for full-stripe writes.

Atomic update of data and parity

A challenge in implementing RAID is atomically updating both the data and the parity (or both data blocks in a RAID with mirroring).

Consider what would happen if the RAID system in Figure 14.9 crashes in the middle updating block 21, after updating the data block on disk 2 but before updating the parity block on disk 1. Now, if disk 2 fails, the system will reconstruct the wrong (old) data for block 21.

The situation may be even worse if a write to a mirrored RAID is interrupted. Because reads can be serviced by either disk, reads of the inconsistent block may sometimes return the new value and sometimes return the old one.

Solutions. Three solutions and one non-solution are commonly used to solve (or not) the atomic update problem.

- **Non-volatile write buffer.** Hardware RAID systems often include a battery-backed write buffer. An update is removed from the write buffer only once it is safely on disk. The RAID's startup procedures ensure that any data in the write buffer is written to disk after a crash or power outage.

- **Transactional update.** RAID systems can use transactions to atomically update both the data block and the parity block. For example, Oracle's RAID-Z integrates RAID striping with the ZFS file system to avoid overwriting data in place and to atomically update data and parity.

- **Recovery scan.** After a crash, the system can scan all of the blocks in the system and update any inconsistent parity blocks. Note that until that scan is complete, some parity blocks may be inconsistent, and incorrect data may be reconstructed if a disk fails. The Linux md (multiple device) software RAID driver uses this approach.

- **Cross your fingers.** Some software and hardware RAID implementations do not ensure that the data and parity blocks are in sync after a crash. *Caveat emptor.*

Recovery.   In either RAID arrangement, if a disk suffers a sector failure, the disk reports an error when there is an attempt to read the sector and, if necessary, remaps the damaged sector to a spare one. Then, the RAID system reconstructs the lost sector from the other disk(s) and rewrites it to the original disk.

If a disk suffers a whole-disk failure, an operator replaces the failed disk, and the RAID system reconstructs all of the disk's data from the other disk(s) and rewrites the data to the replacement disk. The average time from when a disk fails until it has been replaced and rewritten is called the *meantime to repair (MTTR)*.

mean time to repair/MTTR

RAID Levels

An early paper on RAIDs, http://dl.acm.org/citation.cfm?id=50214"A Case for Redundant Arrays of Inexpensive Disks (RAID)," by David Patterson, Garth Gibson, and Randy Katz described a range of possible RAID organizations and named them RAID 0, RAID 1, RAID 2, RAID 3, RAID 4, and RAID 5. Several of these RAID levels were intended to illustrate key concepts rather than for real-world deployment.

Today, three of these variants are in wide use:

- **RAID 0: JBOD.** RAID level 0 spreads data across multiple disks without redundancy. Any disk failure results in data loss. For this reason, the term RAID is somewhat misleading, and this organization is often referred to as JBOD (Just a Bunch Of Disks).

- **RAID 1: Mirroring.** RAID level 1 mirrors identical data to two disks.

- **RAID 5: Rotating Parity.** RAID level 5 stripes data across G disks. $G-1$ of the disks in a stripe store $G-1$ different blocks of data and the remaining disk stores a parity block. The role of storing the parity block for different data blocks is rotated among the disks to balance load.

Subsequent to the "Case for RAID" paper, new organizations emerged, and many of them were named in the same spirit. Some of these names have become standard.

- **RAID 6: Dual Redundancy.** RAID level 6 is similar to RAID level 5, but instead of one parity block per group, two redundant blocks are stored. These blocks are generated using erasure codes such as Reed-Solomon codes that allow reconstruction of all of the original data as long as at most two disks fail.

- **RAID 10 and RAID 50: Nested RAID.** RAID 10 and RAID 50 were originally called RAID 1+0 and RAID 5+0. They simply combine RAID 0 with RAID 1 or RAID 5. For example, a RAID 10 system mirrors pairs of disks for redundancy (RAID 1), treats each pair of mirrored disks as a single reliable logical disk, and then stripes data non-redundantly across these logical disks (RAID 0).

Many other RAID levels have been proposed. In some cases, these new "levels" have more to do with marketing than technology. ("Our company's RAID 99+ is much better than your company's puny RAID 14.") In any event, we regard the particular nomenclature used to describe exotic RAID organizations as relatively unimportant; our discussion focuses on mirroring (RAID 1), rotating parity (RAID 5), and dual redundancy (RAID 6). Other organizations can be analyzed using principles from these approaches.

RAID Reliability

A RAID with one redundant disk per group (e.g., mirroring or rotating parity RAIDs) can lose data in three ways: two full disk failures, a full disk failure and one or more sector failures on other disks, and overlapping sector failures on multiple disks. The expected time until one of these events occurs is called the *mean time to data loss (MTTDL)*.

mean time to data loss

MTTDL **Two full-disk failures.** If two disks fail, the system will be unable to reconstruct the missing data.

To get a sense of how serious a problem this might be, suppose that a system has N disks with one parity block per G blocks, and suppose that disks fail independently with a mean time to failure of $MTTF$ and a mean time to replace a failed disk and recover its data of $MTTR$.

Then, when the system is operating properly, the expected time until the first failure is $MTTF/N$. Assuming $MTTR << MTTF$, there is essentially a race to replace the disk and reconstruct its data before a second disk fails. We lose this race and hit the second failure before the repair is done with probability $\frac{MTTF/(G-1)}{MTTR}$, giving us a mean time to data loss from multiple full-disk failures of

$$MTTDL_{two-full-disk} = \frac{MTTF^2}{N(G-1)MTTR}$$

EXAMPLE **Mean time to double-disk failure.** Suppose you have 100 disks organized into groups of 10, with one disk storing a parity block per nine disks storing data blocks. Assuming that disk failures are independent and the per-disk mean time to failure is 10^6 hours and assuming that the mean time to repair a failed disk is 10 hours, estimate the expected mean time to data loss due to a double-disk failure.

ANSWER Because failures are assumed to occur independently and at a constant rate, we can use the equation above:

$$
\begin{aligned}
MTTDL_{two-full-disk} &= \frac{MTTF^2}{N(G-1)MTTR} \\
&= \frac{(10^6 \text{ hours})^2}{(10^2)(9)(10 \text{ hours})} \\
&\approx \mathbf{10^8 \text{ hours}}
\end{aligned}
$$

Thus, assuming independent failures at the expected rate and assuming no other sources of data loss, this organization appears to have raised the mean time to data loss from about 100 years (for a single disk) to about 10,000 years (for 90 disks worth of data and 10 disks worth of parity). □

One full-disk failure and a sector failure. If one or more disks suffer sector failures and another disk suffers a full-disk failure, the RAID system cannot recover all of its data. Assuming independent failures that arrive at a constant rate, we can estimate probability of data loss over some interval as the probability of suffering a disk failure times the probability that we will fail to read all data needed to reconstruct the lost disk's data:

$$P_{lostDataFromDiskAndSector} = P_{DiskFailure} \cdot P_{RecoveryError}$$
$$P_{lostDataFromDiskAndSector} = \frac{N}{MTTF} \cdot P_{fail\_recovery\_read}$$

If this gives us the probability of losing data over some period of time or equivalently the rate of data-loss failures, then inverting this equation gives us the mean time to data loss (MTTDL). Thus, we can estimate the mean time to data loss from this failure mode based on the expected time between full disk failures divided by the odds of failing to read all data needed to reconstruct the lost disk's data.

$$MTTDL_{disk+sector} = \frac{MTTF}{N} \cdot \frac{1}{P_{fail\_recovery\_read}}$$

EXAMPLE   **Mean time to failed disk and failed sector.** Assuming that during recovery, latent sector errors are discovered at a rate of 1 per 10^{15} bits read and assuming that the mean time to failure for each of 100 1 TB disks organized into groups of 10 is 10^6 hours, what is the expected mean time to data loss due to full-disk failure combined with a sector failure?

ANSWER

$$MTTDL_{disk+sector} = \frac{MTTF}{N} \cdot \frac{1}{P_{fail\_recovery\_read}}$$
$$= \frac{10^6}{100} \cdot \frac{1}{P_{fail\_recovery\_read}}$$

To estimate $P_{fail\_recovery\_read}$ we will assume that each bit fails independently and is successfully read with probability $(1/(1 - 10^{-15}))$. Then the probability of reading 1 TB from each of 9 disks is:

$$P_{succeed\_recovery\_read} = P_{succeed\_bit\_read}^{numberofbits}$$
$$= \left(1 - 10^{-15})\right)^{9 \, disks \cdot 10^{12} \frac{bytes}{disk} * 8 \frac{bits}{byte}}$$
$$\approx 0.93$$

So, there is roughly a 93% chance that recovery will succeed and a 7% chance that recovery will fail. We then have

$$MTTDL_{disk+sector} = \frac{10^6}{100} \cdot \frac{1}{.07} = \mathbf{1.4 \cdot 10^5\ hours}$$

Notice that this rate of data loss is much higher than the rate from double disk failures calculated above. Of course, the relative contributions of each failure mode will depend on disks' MTTF, size, and bit error rates as well as the system's MTTR. □

Failure of two sectors sharing a redundant sector. In principle, it is also possible to lose data because the corresponding sectors fail on different disks. However, with billions of distinct sectors on each disk and small numbers of latent failures per disk, this failure mode is likely to be a negligible risk for most systems.

Overall data loss rate. If we assume independent failures and constant failure rates, then we can add the failure rates from the two significant failure modes to estimate the combined failure rate:

$$
\begin{aligned}
FailureRate_{indep+const} &= FailureRate_{two-full-disk} + FailureRate_{disk+sector} \\
&= \frac{1}{MTTDL_{two-full-disk}} + \frac{1}{MTTDL_{disk+sector}} \\
&= \frac{N(G-1)MTTR}{MTTF^2} + \frac{N \cdot P_{fail\_recovery\_read}}{MTTF} \\
&= \frac{N}{MTTF}\left(\frac{MTTR(G-1)}{MTTF} + P_{fail\_recovery\_read}\right)
\end{aligned}
$$

The total failure rate is thus the rate that the first disk fails times the rate that either a second disk in the group fails before the repair is completed or a sector error is encountered when the disks are being read to rebuild the lost disk.

We label the above $FailureRate_{indep+const}$ to emphasize the strong assumptions of independent failures and constant failure rates. As noted above, failures are likely to be correlated in many environments and failure rates of some devices may increase over time. Both of these factors may result significantly higher failure rates than expected.

EXAMPLE   **Combined failure rate.** For the system described in the previous examples (100 disks, rotating parity with a group size of 10, mean time to failure of 10^6 hours, mean time to repair of 10 hours, and non-recoverable read error rate of one sector per 10^{15} bits) assuming that all failures are independent, estimate the MTTDL when both double-disk and single-disk-and-sector failures are considered.

ANSWER

$$FailureRate_{indep+const} = \frac{N}{MTTF}\left(\frac{MTTR(G-1)}{MTTF} + P_{fail\_recovery\_read}\right)$$

$$= \frac{100 \text{ disks}}{10^6} \text{ hours}\left(\frac{10 \text{ hours}}{10^6 \text{ hours}} + 0.0694\right)$$

$$= \frac{1}{10^4 \text{ hours}}\left(\frac{1}{10^4} + 0.0694\right)$$

$$= \frac{1}{10^4 \text{ hours}}(0.0695)$$

$$= 6.95 \cdot 10^{-6} \frac{\text{failures}}{\text{hour}}$$

Inverting the failure rate gives the mean time to data loss:

$$MTTDL_{const+indep} = \frac{1}{FailureRate_{indep+const}}$$

$$= 1.44 \cdot 10^5 \frac{\text{hours}}{\text{failure}}$$

$$= \mathbf{16.4} \frac{\textbf{years}}{\textbf{failure}}$$

□

Two things in the example above are worth special note. First, for these parameters, the dominant cause of data loss is likely to be a single disk failure combined with a non-recoverable read error during recovery. Second, for these parameters and this configuration, the resulting 6% chance of losing data per year may be unacceptable for many environments. As a result, systems use various techniques to improve the MTTDL in RAID systems.

Improving RAID Reliability

What can be done to further improve reliability? Broadly speaking, we can do three things: (1) increase redundancy, (2) reduce non-recoverable read error rates, and (3) reduce mean time to repair. All of these approaches, in various combinations, are used in practice.

Here are some common approaches:

Increasing redundancy with more redundant disks.   Rather than having a single redundant block per group (e.g., using two mirrored disks or using one parity disk for each stripe) systems can use double redundancy (e.g., three disk replicas or two error correction disks for each stripe). In some cases, systems may use even more redundancy. For example, the Google File System (GFS) is designed to provide highly reliable and available storage across thousands of disks; by default, GFS stores each data block on three different disks.

dual redundancy array   A *dual redundancy array* ensures that data can be reconstructed despite any

RAID 6

two failures in a stripe by generating two redundant blocks using erasure codes such as Reed-Solomon codes. This approach is sometimes called *RAID 6.*

A system with dual redundancy can be much more reliable than a simple single redundancy RAID. With dual redundancy, the most likely data loss scenarios are (a) three full-disk failures or (b) a double-disk failure combined with one or more non-recoverable read errors.

If we optimistically assume that failures are independent and occur at a constant rate, a system with two redundant disks per stripe has a potentially low combined data loss rate:

$$FailureRate_{dual+indep+const} = \frac{N}{MTTF} \\ \times \frac{MTTR(G-1)}{MTTF} \\ \times (\frac{MTTR(G-2)}{MTTF} + P_{fail\_recovery\_read})$$

This data loss rate is nearly $\frac{MTTF}{MTTR(G-1)}$ times better than the single-parity data loss rate; for disks with MTTFs of over one million hours, MTTRs of less than 10 hours, and group sizes of ten or fewer disks, double parity improves the estimated rate by about a factor of 10,000.

We emphasize, however, that the above equation almost certainly underestimates the likely data loss rate for real systems, which may suffer correlated failures, varying failure rates, higher failure rates than advertised, and so on.

Reducing non-recoverable read errors with scrubbing.   A storage device's sector-level error rate is typically expressed as a single *non-recoverable read rate*, suggesting that the rate is constant. The reality is more complex. Depending on the device, errors may accumulate over time and heavier workloads may increase the rate at which errors accumulate.

scrubbing

An important technique for reducing a disk's non-recoverable read rate is *scrubbing*: periodically reading the entire contents of a disk, detecting sectors with unrecoverable read errors, reconstructing the lost data from the remaining disks in the RAID array, and attempting to write and read the reconstructed data to and from the suspect sector. If writes and reads succeed, then the error was caused by a transient fault, and the disk continues to use the sector, but if the sector cannot be successfully accessed, the error is permanent, and the system remaps that sector to a spare and writes the reconstructed data there.

Reducing non-recoverable read error rates with more reliable disks.   Different disk models promise significantly different non-recoverable read error rates. In particular, in 2011, many disks aimed at laptops and personal computers claim unrecoverable read error rates of one per 10^{14} bits read, while disks aimed at enterprise servers often have lower storage densities but can promise unrecoverable read error rates of one per 10^{16} bits read. This two order of magnitude improvement greatly reduces the probability that a RAID system loses data from a combination of a full disk failure and a non-recoverable read error during recovery.

Reducing mean time to repair with hot spares.   Some systems include "hot spare" disk drives that are idle, but plugged into a server so that if one of the server's disks fails, the hot spare can be automatically activated to replace the lost disk.

Note that even with hot spares, the mean time to repair a disk is limited by the time it takes to write the reconstructed data to it, and this time is often measured in hours. For example, if we have a 1 TB disk and can write at 100 MB/s, the mean time to repair for the disk will be at least 10^4 seconds — about 3 hours. In practice, repair time may be even larger if the bandwidth achieved is less than assumed here.

Reducing mean time to repair with declustering.   Disks with hundreds of giga-bytes to a few terabytes can take hours to fully write with reconstructed data. *Declustering* splits reconstruction of a failed disk across multiple disks. Declus-tering thus allows parallel reconstruction, thus speeding up reconstruction and reducing MTTR.

declustering

For example, the Hadoop File System (HDFS) is a cluster file system that writes each data block to three out of potentially hundreds or thousands of disks. It chooses the three disks for each block more or less randomly. If one disk fails, it re-replicates the lost blocks approximately randomly across the remaining disks. If we have N disks each with a bandwidth of B, total reconstruction bandwidth can approach $\frac{N}{2}B$; for example, if there are 1000 disks with 100 MB/s bandwidths, reconstruction bandwidth can theoretically approach 500 GB/s, allowing re-replication of a 1 TB disk's data in a few seconds.

In practice, re-replication will be slower than this for at least three reasons. First, resources other than the disk (e.g., the network) may bottleneck recovery. Second, the system may throttle recovery speed to avoid starving user requests. Third, if a server crashes and its disks become inaccessible, the system may delay starting recovery — hoping that the server will soon recover — to avoid imposing extra load on the system.

Pitfalls

When constructing a reliable storage system, it is not enough to plug provide enough redundancy to tolerate a target number of failures. We also need to consider how failures are likely to occur (e.g., they may be correlated) and what it takes to correct them (e.g., successfully reading a lot of other data). More specifically, be aware of the following pitfalls:

- **Assuming uncorrelated failures..** It is easy to get gaudy MTTDL numbers by adding a redundant device or two and multiplying the devices' MT-

TFs. But the simple equation on page 625 only applies when failures are uncorrelated. Even a 1% chance of correlated failures dramatically changes the estimate. Unfortunately, it is often difficult to estimate correlation rates *a priori*, so designers must sometimes just add a significant safety margin and hope that it is enough.

- **Ignoring the risk from latent errors..** It is not uncommon to see analyses of RAID reliability that considers full device failures but not non-recoverable read failures. As we have seen above, non-recoverable read errors can dramatically reduce the probability of successfully recovering data after a disk failure.

- **Not implementing scrubbing..** Periodically scrubbing disks to detect and correct latent errors can significantly reduce the risk of data loss. Although it can be difficult to predict the appropriate scrubbing frequency *a priori*, a system that uses scrubbing can monitor the rate at which non-correctable read errors are found and corrected and use the measured rate to adjust the scrubbing frequency.

- **Not having a backup..** The techniques discussed in this section can protect a system against many, but not all, faults. For example, a widespread correlated failure (e.g., a building burning down), an operator error (e.g., "rm -r *"), or a software bug could corrupt or delete data stored across any number of redundant devices.

backup

A *backup* system provides storage that is separate from a system's main storage. Ideally, the separation is both physical and logical.

physical separation

Physical separation means that backup storage devices are in different locations than the primary storage devices. For example, some systems achieve physical separation by copying data to tape and storing the tapes in a different building than the main storage servers. Other systems achieve physical separation by storing data to remote disk arrays such as those provided by cloud backup and disaster recovery services.

logical separation

Logical separation means that the interface to the backup system is restricted to prevent premature deletion of data. For example, some backup systems provide an interface that allows a user to read *but not write* old versions of a file (e.g., the file as it existed one hour, two hours, four hours, one day, one week, one month, and one year ago).

14.2.3 Software Integrity Checks

Although storage devices include sector- or page-level checksums to detect data corruption, many recent file systems have included additional, higher-level, checksums and other integrity checks on their data.

These checks can catch a range of errors that hardware-level checksums can miss. For example, they can detect *wild writes* or *lost writes* where a bug

Modeling Real Systems

The equations in the main text for estimating a system's mean time to data loss are only applicable if failure rates are constant and if failures are uncorrelated. Unfortunately, empirical studies often observe correlation among full-disk failures, among sector-level failures, and between sector-level and full-disk failures, and they frequently find failure rates that vary significantly with disks' ages. Unfortunately, if failure rates vary over time or failures are correlated, the failure arrival distribution is no longer described by an exponential distribution, and the math quickly gets difficult.

One solution is to use randomized simulation to estimate the probability of data loss over some duration of interest. For example, we might want to estimate the probability of losing data over 10 years for a 1000-disk system organized in groups of 10 disks with rotating parity.

To do this, our simulation would track which disks are functioning normally, which have latent sector errors, and which have suffered full disk failures. The transitions between states could be based on measurement studies or field data on key factors: (a) the rate that disks suffer full disk failures (possibly dependent on the disks' ages, the number of recent full disk failures, or the number of individual sector failures a disk has had); (b) the rate at which sector failures arise (possibly dependent on the age of the disk, workload of the disk, and recent frequency of sector failures); (c) the repair time when a disk fails; and (d) the expected time for scrubbing to detect and repair a sector error.

To estimate the probability of data loss, we would repeatedly simulate the system for a decade and count the number of times the system enters a state in which data is lost (i.e., a group has two full disk failures or has both a full disk failure and a sector failure on another disk).

---

in the operating system software, device driver software, or device firmware misdirects a write to the wrong block or page or fails to complete an intended write. They can also detect rare *ECC false negatives* when the hardware-level error correcting codes fail to detect a multi-bit corruption.

When a software integrity check fails on a block read or during latent-error scrubbing, the system reconstructs the lost or corrupted block using the redundant storage in the RAID.

Two examples of software integrity checks used today are *block integrity metadata* and *file system fingerprints*.

Block integrity metadata.   Some file systems, like Network Appliance's WAFL file system, include *block integrity metadata* that allows the software to validate the results of each block it reads.

block integrity metadata

As Figure 14.10 illustrates, WAFL stores a 64 byte *data integrity segment*

Data Block

Data Integrity
Segment (DIS)

4096	64	448 Unused

512	512	512	512	512	512	512	512	512

Figure 14.10: To improve reliability Network Appliance's WAFL file system stores a 64 byte data integrity segment (DIS) with each 4 KB data block.

(DIS) with each 4 KB data block. The DIS contains a checksum of the data block, the identity of the data block (e.g., the ID of the file to which it belongs and the block's offset in that file), and a checksum of the DIS, itself.

Then, when a block is read, the system performs three checks. First, it checks the DIS's checksum. Second, it verifies that the data in the block corresponds to the checksum in the block's data integrity segment. Third, it verifies that the identity in the block's DIS corresponds to the file block it was intending to read. If all of these checks pass, the file system can be confident it is returning the correct data; if not, the file system can reconstruct the necessary data from redundant disks in the RAID.

File system fingerprints. Some file systems, like Oracle's ZFS, include *file system fingerprints* that provide a checksum across the entire file system in a way that allows efficient checks and updates when individual blocks are read and written.

file system fingerprint

As illustrated in Figure 14.11(top), all of ZFS's data structures are arranged in a tree of blocks with a root node called the uberblock. At each internal node of the tree, each reference to a child node includes both a pointer to and a checksum of the child. Thus, the reference to any subtree includes a checksum that covers all of that subtree's contents, and the uberblock holds a checksum that covers the entire file system.

When ZFS reads data (i.e., leaves of the tree) or metadata (i.e., internal nodes of the tree), it follows the pointers down the tree to find the right block to read, computing a checksum of each internal or leaf block and comparing it to the checksum stored with the block reference. Similarly, as Figure 14.11(bottom) illustrates, when ZFS writes a block, it updates the references from the updated block to the uberblock so that each includes both the new checksum and (since ZFS never updates data structures in place) new block pointer.

14.3 | Summary and Future Directions

Although individual storage devices include internal error correcting codes, additional redundancy for error detection and correction is often needed to

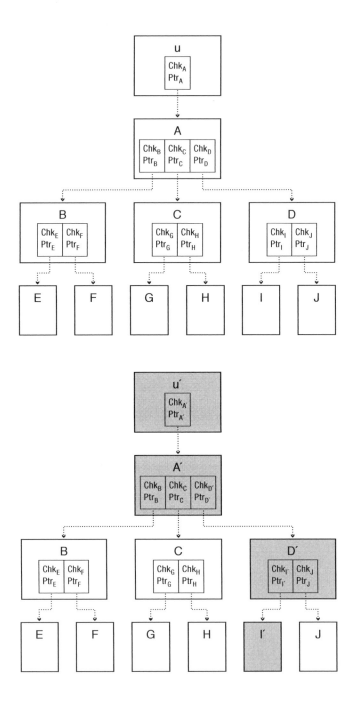

Figure 14.11: (top) ZFS stores all data in a Merkle tree so that each node of the tree includes both a pointer to and a checksum of each of its children (Chk and Ptr in the figure). On an update (bottom), all nodes from the updated block (I′) to the root (u′) are changed to reflect the new pointer and checksum values.

Layers Upon Layers Upon Layers

In this chapter we focus on error detection and correction at three levels: the individual storage devices (e.g., disks and flash), storage architectures (e.g., RAID), and file systems.

Today, storage systems with important data often include not just these layers, but additional ones. Enterprise and cloud storage systems distribute data across several geographically distributed sites and may include high-level checksums on that geographically replicated data. Within a site, they may replicate data across multiple servers using what is effectively a distributed file system. At each server, the distributed file system may store data using a local file system that includes file-system-level checksums on the locally stored data. And, invariably, the local server will use storage devices that detect and sometimes correct low-level errors.

Although we do not discuss cross-machine and geographic replication in any detail, the principles described in this chapter also apply to these systems.

provide acceptably reliable storage. In fact, today, it is seldom acceptable to store valuable data on a single device without some form of RAID-style redundancy. By the same token, many if not most file systems designed over the past decade have included software error checking to catch data corruption and loss occurrences that are not detectable by device-level hardware checks.

Increasingly now and in the future, systems go beyond just replicating data across multiple disks on a single server to distributed replication across multiple servers. Sometimes these replicas are configured to protect data even if significant physical disasters occur.

For example, Amazon's Simple Storage Service (S3) allows customers to pay a monthly fee to store data on servers run by Amazon. Amazon states that the system is "designed to provide 99.999999999% durability of objects over a given year." To provide such high reliability, S3 stores data at multiple data centers, quickly detects and repairs lost redundancy, and validates checksums of stored data.

Exercises

1. Suppose that a text editor application uses the rename technique discussed on page 594 for safely saving updates by saving the updated file to a new filed (e.g., #doc.txt# and then calling rename("#doc.txt#", "doc.txt") to change the name of the updated file from #doc.txt# to doc.txt. POSIX rename promises that the update to doc.txt will be atomic—even if a crash occurs, doc.txt will refer to either the old file or the new one. However, POSIX does not guarantee that the entire rename operation will be atomic. In particular, POSIX allows implementations in which there is a

window in which a crash could result in a state where both doc.txt and #doc.txt# refer to the same, new document.

a) How should a text-editing application react if, on startup, it sees both doc.txt and doc.txt and (i) both refer the same file or (ii) each refers to a file with different contents?

b) Why might POSIX permit this corner case (where we may end up with two names that refer to the same file) to exist?

c) Explain how an FFS-based file system without transactions could use the "ad hoc" approach discussed in Section 14.1.1 to ensure that (i) doc.txt always refers to either the old or new file, (ii) the new file is never lost – it is always available as at least one of doc.txt or #doc.txt#, and (iii) there is some window where the new file may be accessed as both doc.txt and #doc.txt#.

d) Section 14.1.1 discusses three reasons that few modern file systems use the "ad-hoc" approach. However, many text editors still do something like this. Why have the three issues had less effect on applications like text editors than on file systems?

2. Above, we defined two-phase locking for basic mutual exclusion locks. Extend the definition of two-phase locking for systems that use readers-writers locks.

3. Suppose that x and y represent the number of hours two managers have assigned you to work on each of two tasks with a constraint that $x + y \le 40$. On page 605, we showed that snapshot isolation could allow one transaction to update x and another concurrent transaction to update y in a way that would violate the constraint $x + y \le 40$. Is such an anomaly possible under serializability? Why or why not?

4. Suppose you have transactional storage system tStore that allows you to read and write fixed-sized 2048-byte blocks of data within transactions, and you run the code in Figure 14.12.

The system crashes at the point indicated above.

Assume that ALL_ONES, ALL_TWOS, etc. are each arrays of 2048 bytes with the indicated value. Assume that when the program is started, all blocks in the tStore have the value ALL_ZEROS.

Just before the system crashes, what is the value of b1 and what is the value of b2?

a) In the program above, just before the system crashes, what is the value of b3 and what is the value of b4?

b) Suppose that after the program above runs and crashes at the indicated point. After the system restarts and completes recovery and all write-backs, what are the values stored in each of blocks 1, 2, 3, 4, and 5 of the tStore?

```
...
byte b1[2048];   byte b2[2048];
byte b3[2048];   byte b4[2048];

TransID t1 = tStore.beginTransaction();
TransID t2 = tStore.beginTransaction();
TransID t3 = tStore.beginTransaction();
TransID t4 = tStore.beginTransaction();

// Interface is
//    writeBlock(TransID tid, int blockNum, byte buffer[]);
tStore.writeBlock(t1, 1, ALL_ONES);
tStore.writeBlock(t1, 2, ALL_TWOS);
tStore.writeBlock(t2, 3, ALL_THREES);
tStore.writeBlock(t1, 3, ALL_FOURS);
tStore.writeBlock(t1, 2, ALL_FIVES);
tStore.writeBlock(t3, 2, ALL_SIXES);
tStore.writeBlock(t4, 4, ALL_SEVENS);
tStore.readBlock(t2, 1, b1);
tStore.commit(t3);
tStore.readBlock(t2, 3, b2);
tStore.commit(t2);
tStore.readBlock(t1, 3, b3);
tStore.readBlock(t4, 3, b4);
tStore.commit(t1);

// At this point, the system crashes
```

Figure 14.12: Sample code for a transactional storage system.

5. Go to an on-line site that sells hard disk drives, and find the largest capacity disk you can buy for less than $200. Now, track down the spec sheet for the disk and, given the disk's specified bit error rate (or unrecoverable read rate), estimate the probability of encountering an error if you read every sector on the disk once.

6. Suppose we define a RAID's *access cost* as the number disk accesses divided by the number of data blocks read or written. For each of following configurations and workloads, what is the access cost?

   a) Workload: a series of random 1-block writes
   Configuration: mirroring

   b) Workload: a series of random 1-block writes
   Configuration: distributed parity

   c) Workload: a series of random 1-block reads
   Configuration: mirroring

   d) Workload: a series of random 1-block reads
   Configuration: distributed parity

   e) Workload: a series of random 1-block reads
   Configuration: distributed parity with group size G and one failed disk

Figure 14.13: Example of a poor design choice for the content of redundant blocks.

f) Workload: a long sequential write
Configuration: mirroring

g) Workload: a long sequential write
Configuration: distributed parity with a group size of G

7. Suppose that an engineer who has not taken this class tries to create a disk array with dual-redundancy but instead of using an appropriate error correcting code such as Reed-Solomon, the engineer simply stores a copy of each parity block on two disks, as in Figure 14.13.

Give an example of how a two-disk failure can cause a stripe to lose data in such a system. Explain why data cannot be reconstructed in that case.

8. Some RAID systems improve reliability with intra-disk redundancy to protect against non-recoverable read failures. For example, each individual disk on such a system might reserve one 4KB parity block in every 32 KB extent and then store 28KB (7 4KB blocks) of data and 4 KB (1 4KB block) of parity in each extent.

In this arrangement, each data block is protected by two parity blocks: one interdisk parity block on a different disk and on intradisk parity block on the same disk.

This approach may reduce a disk's effective non-recoverable read error rate because if one block in an extent is lost, it can be recovered from the remaining sectors and parity on the disk. Of course, if multiple blocks in the same extent are lost, the system must rely on redundancy from other disks.

a) Assuming that a disk's non-recoverable read errors are independent and occur at a rate of one lost 512 byte sector per 10^{15} bits read, what is the effective non-recoverable read error rate if the operating system stores one parity block per seven data blocks on the disk?

Hint: You may find the bc or dc arbitrary-precision calculators useful. These programs are standard in many Unix, Linux, and OSX distributions. See the man pages for instructions.

b) Why is the above likely to significantly overstate the impact of intra-disk redundancy?

Size	
Platters/Heads	2/4
Capacity	320 GB
Performance	
Spindle speed	7200 RPM
Average seek time read/write	10.5 ms / 12.0 ms
Maximum seek time	19 ms
Track-to-track seek time	1 ms
Transfer rate (surface to buffer)	54–128 MB/s
Transfer rate (buffer to host)	375 MB/s
Buffer memory	16 MB
Reliability	
Nonrecoverable read errors per sectors read	1 sector per 10^{14}
MTBF	600,000 hours
Product life	5 years or 20,000 power-on hours
Power	
Typical	16.35 W
Idle	11.68 W

Figure 14.14: Disk specification

9. Many RAID implementations allow on-line repair in which the system continues to operate after a disk failure, while a new empty disk is inserted to replace the failed disk, and while regenerating and copying data to the new disk.

   Sketch a design for a 2-disk, mirrored RAID that allows the system to remain on-line during reconstruction, while still ensuring that when the data copying is done, the new disk is properly reconstructed (i.e., it is an exact copy of other disk.)

   In particular, specify (1) what is done by a recovery thread, (2) what is done on a read during recovery, and (3) what is done on a write during recovery. Also explain why your system will operate correctly even if a crash occurs in the middle of reconstruction.

10. Suppose you are willing to sacrifice no more than 1% of a disk's bandwidth to scrubbing. What is maximum frequency at which you could scrub a 1 TB disk with 100 MB/s bandwidth?

11. Suppose a 3 TB disk in a mirrored RAID system crashes. Assuming the disks used in the system can sustain 100MB/s sequential bandwidth, what is the minimum mean time to repair that can be achieved? Why might a system be configured to perform recovery slower than this?

12. Suppose I have a disk such as the one described in Figure 14.14 and a workload consisting of a continuous stream of updates to random blocks of the disk.

Assume that the disk scheduler uses the SCAN/Elevator algorithm.

a) What is the throughput in number of requests per second if the application issues one request at a time and waits until the block is safely stored on disk before issuing the next request?

b) What is the throughput in number of requests per second if the application buffers 100 MB of writes, issues those 100 MB worth of writes to disk as a batch, and waits until those writes are safely on disk before issuing the next 100 MB batch of requests?

Suppose that we must ensure that – even in the event of a crash – the ith update can be observed by a read after crash recovery only if all updates that preceded the ith update can be read after the crash. That is, we have a FIFO property for updates – the i+1'st update cannot "finish" until the ith update finishes. (1) Design an approach to get good performance for this workload. (2) Explain why your design ensures FIFO even if crashes occur. (3) Estimate your approach's throughput in number of requests per second. (For comparison with the previous part of the problem, your solution should not require significantly more than 100MB of main-memory buffer space.)

c) Design an approach to get good performance for this workload. (Be sure to explain how writes, reads, and crash recovery work.)

d) Explain why your design ensures FIFO even if crashes occur.

e) Estimate your approach's throughput in number of requests per second.

References

[1]   Keith Adams and Ole Agesen. A comparison of software and hardware techniques for x86
        virtualization. In *Proceedings of the 12th International conference on Architectural Support for
        Programming Languages and Operating Systems*, ASPLOS-XII, pages 2–13, 2006.

[2]   Thomas E. Anderson, Brian N. Bershad, Edward D. Lazowska, and Henry M. Levy.
        Scheduler activations: effective kernel support for the user-level management of
        parallelism. *ACM Trans. Comput. Syst.*, 10(1):53–79, February 1992.

[3]   Thomas E. Anderson, Henry M. Levy, Brian N. Bershad, and Edward D. Lazowska. The
        interaction of architecture and operating system design. In *Proceedings of the fourth
        International conference on Architectural Support for Programming Languages and Operating
        Systems*, ASPLOS-IV, pages 108–120, 1991.

[4]   Andrew W. Appel and Kai Li. Virtual memory primitives for user programs. In *Proceedings
        of the fourth International conference on Architectural Support for Programming Languages and
        Operating Systems*, ASPLOS-IV, pages 96–107, 1991.

[5]   Amittai Aviram, Shu-Chun Weng, Sen Hu, and Bryan Ford. Efficient system-enforced
        deterministic parallelism. In *Proceedings of the 9th USENIX conference on Operating Systems
        Design and Implementation*, OSDI'10, pages 1–16, 2010.

[6]   Özalp Babaoglu and William Joy. Converting a swap-based system to do paging in an
        architecture lacking page-referenced bits. In *Proceedings of the eighth ACM Symposium on
        Operating Systems Principles*, SOSP '81, pages 78–86, 1981.

[7]   David Bacon, Joshua Bloch, Jeff Bogda, Cliff Click, Paul Haahr, Doug Lea, Tom May,
        Jan-Willem Maessen, Jeremy Manson, John D. Mitchell, Kelvin Nilsen, Bill Pugh, and
        Emin Gun Sirer. The "double-checked locking is broken" declaration.
        http://www.cs.umd.edu/$\sim$pugh/java/memoryModel/DoubleCheckedLocking.html.

[8]   Gaurav Banga, Peter Druschel, and Jeffrey C. Mogul. Resource containers: a new facility
        for resource management in server systems. In *Proceedings of the third USENIX symposium
        on Operating Systems Design and Implementation*, OSDI '99, pages 45–58, 1999.

[9]   Paul Barham, Boris Dragovic, Keir Fraser, Steven Hand, Tim Harris, Alex Ho, Rolf
        Neugebauer, Ian Pratt, and Andrew Warfield. Xen and the art of virtualization. In
        Proceedings of the nineteenth ACM Symposium on Operating Systems Principles, SOSP '03,
        pages 164–177, 2003.

[10]   Blaise Barney. POSIX threads programming. *http://computing.llnl.gov/tutorials/pthreads/*,
        2013.

[11]   Joel F. Bartlett. A nonstop kernel. In *Proceedings of the eighth ACM Symposium on Operating
        Systems Principles*, SOSP '81, pages 22–29, 1981.

[12]   Andrew Baumann, Paul Barham, Pierre-Evariste Dagand, Tim Harris, Rebecca Isaacs,
        Simon Peter, Timothy Roscoe, Adrian Schüpbach, and Akhilesh Singhania. The
        multikernel: a new OS architecture for scalable multicore systems. In *Proceedings of the 22nd
        ACM Symposium on Operating Systems Principles*, SOSP '09, pages 29–44, 2009.

[13]   A. Bensoussan, C. T. Clingen, and R. C. Daley. The multics virtual memory: concepts and
        design. *Commun. ACM*, 15(5):308–318, May 1972.

[14] Tom Bergan, Nicholas Hunt, Luis Ceze, and Steven D. Gribble. Deterministic process groups in dOS. In *Proceedings of the 9th USENIX conference on Operating Systems Design and Implementation*, OSDI'10, pages 1–16, 2010.

[15] B. N. Bershad, S. Savage, P. Pardyak, E. G. Sirer, M. E. Fiuczynski, D. Becker, C. Chambers, and S. Eggers. Extensibility safety and performance in the SPIN operating system. In *Proceedings of the fifteenth ACM Symposium on Operating Systems Principles*, SOSP '95, pages 267–283, 1995.

[16] Brian N. Bershad, Thomas E. Anderson, Edward D. Lazowska, and Henry M. Levy. Lightweight remote procedure call. *ACM Trans. Comput. Syst.*, 8(1):37–55, February 1990.

[17] Brian N. Bershad, Thomas E. Anderson, Edward D. Lazowska, and Henry M. Levy. User-level interprocess communication for shared memory multiprocessors. *ACM Trans. Comput. Syst.*, 9(2):175–198, May 1991.

[18] Andrew Birrell. An introduction to programming with threads. Technical Report 35, Digital Equipment Corporation Systems Research Center, 1991.

[19] Andrew D. Birrell and Bruce Jay Nelson. Implementing remote procedure calls. *ACM Trans. Comput. Syst.*, 2(1):39–59, February 1984.

[20] Silas Boyd-Wickizer, Austin T. Clements, Yandong Mao, Aleksey Pesterev, M. Frans Kaashoek, Robert Morris, and Nickolai Zeldovich. An analysis of Linux scalability to many cores. In *Proceedings of the 9th USENIX conference on Operating Systems Design and Implementation*, OSDI'10, pages 1–8, 2010.

[21] Lee Breslau, Pei Cao, Li Fan, Graham Phillips, and Scott Shenker. Web caching and Zipf-like distributions: evidence and implications. In *INFOCOM*, pages 126–134, 1999.

[22] Thomas C. Bressoud and Fred B. Schneider. Hypervisor-based fault tolerance. *ACM Trans. Comput. Syst.*, 14(1):80–107, February 1996.

[23] Sergey Brin and Lawrence Page. The anatomy of a large-scale hypertextual web search engine. In *Proceedings of the seventh International conference on the World Wide Web*, WWW7, pages 107–117, 1998.

[24] Max Bruning. ZFS on-disk data walk (or: Where's my data?). In *OpenSolaris Developer Conference*, 2008.

[25] Edouard Bugnion, Scott Devine, Kinshuk Govil, and Mendel Rosenblum. Disco: running commodity operating systems on scalable multiprocessors. *ACM Trans. Comput. Syst.*, 15(4):412–447, November 1997.

[26] Brian Carrier. *File System Forensic Analysis*. Addison Wesley Professional, 2005.

[27] Miguel Castro, Manuel Costa, Jean-Philippe Martin, Marcus Peinado, Periklis Akritidis, Austin Donnelly, Paul Barham, and Richard Black. Fast byte-granularity software fault isolation. In *Proceedings of the 22nd ACM Symposium on Operating Systems Principles*, SOSP '09, pages 45–58, 2009.

[28] J. Chapin, M. Rosenblum, S. Devine, T. Lahiri, D. Teodosiu, and A. Gupta. Hive: fault containment for shared-memory multiprocessors. In *Proceedings of the fifteenth ACM Symposium on Operating Systems Principles*, SOSP '95, pages 12–25, 1995.

[29] Jeffrey S. Chase, Henry M. Levy, Michael J. Feeley, and Edward D. Lazowska. Sharing and protection in a single-address-space operating system. *ACM Trans. Comput. Syst.*, 12(4):271–307, November 1994.

[30] J. Bradley Chen and Brian N. Bershad. The impact of operating system structure on memory system performance. In *Proceedings of the fourteenth ACM Symposium on Operating Systems Principles*, SOSP '93, pages 120–133, 1993.

[31] Peter M. Chen and Brian D. Noble. When virtual is better than real. In *Proceedings of the Eighth Workshop on Hot Topics in Operating Systems*, HOTOS '01, 2001.

[32] David Cheriton. The V distributed system. *Commun. ACM*, 31(3):314–333, March 1988.

[33] David R. Cheriton and Kenneth J. Duda. A caching model of operating system kernel functionality. In *Proceedings of the 1st USENIX conference on Operating Systems Design and Implementation*, OSDI '94, 1994.

[34] David D. Clark. The structuring of systems using upcalls. In *Proceedings of the tenth ACM Symposium on Operating Systems Principles*, SOSP '85, pages 171–180, 1985.

[35] Jeremy Condit, Edmund B. Nightingale, Christopher Frost, Engin Ipek, Benjamin Lee, Doug Burger, and Derrick Coetzee. Better I/O through byte-addressable, persistent memory. In *Proceedings of the 22nd ACM Symposium on Operating Systems Principles*, SOSP '09, pages 133–146, 2009.

[36] Fernando J. Corbató. On building systems that will fail. *Commun. ACM*, 34(9):72–81, September 1991.

[37] Fernando J. Corbató and Victor A. Vyssotsky. Introduction and overview of the Multics system. *AFIPS Fall Joint Computer Conference*, 27(1):185–196, 1965.

[38] R. J. Creasy. The origin of the VM/370 time-sharing system. *IBM J. Res. Dev.*, 25(5):483–490, September 1981.

[39] Michael D. Dahlin, Randolph Y. Wang, Thomas E. Anderson, and David A. Patterson. Cooperative caching: using remote client memory to improve file system performance. In *Proceedings of the 1st USENIX conference on Operating Systems Design and Implementation*, OSDI '94, 1994.

[40] Robert C. Daley and Jack B. Dennis. Virtual memory, processes, and sharing in Multics. *Commun. ACM*, 11(5):306–312, May 1968.

[41] Wiebren de Jonge, M. Frans Kaashoek, and Wilson C. Hsieh. The logical disk: a new approach to improving file systems. In *Proceedings of the fourteenth ACM Symposium on Operating Systems Principles*, SOSP '93, pages 15–28, 1993.

[42] Jeffrey Dean and Sanjay Ghemawat. MapReduce: simplified data processing on large clusters. In *Proceedings of the 6th USENIX Symposium on Operating Systems Design & Implementation*, OSDI'04, 2004.

[43] Peter J. Denning. The working set model for program behavior. *Commun. ACM*, 11(5):323–333, May 1968.

[44] P.J. Denning. Working sets past and present. *Software Engineering, IEEE Transactions on*, SE-6(1):64 – 84, jan. 1980.

[45] Jack B. Dennis. Segmentation and the design of multiprogrammed computer systems. *J. ACM*, 12(4):589–602, October 1965.

[46] Jack B. Dennis and Earl C. Van Horn. Programming semantics for multiprogrammed computations. *Commun. ACM*, 9(3):143–155, March 1966.

[47] E. W. Dijkstra. Solution of a problem in concurrent programming control. *Commun. ACM*, 8(9):569–, September 1965.

[48] Edsger W. Dijkstra. The structure of the "THE"-multiprogramming system. *Commun. ACM*, 11(5):341–346, May 1968.

[49] Mihai Dobrescu, Norbert Egi, Katerina Argyraki, Byung-Gon Chun, Kevin Fall, Gianluca Iannaccone, Allan Knies, Maziar Manesh, and Sylvia Ratnasamy. Routebricks: exploiting parallelism to scale software routers. In *Proceedings of the 22nd ACM Symposium on Operating Systems Principles*, SOSP '09, pages 15–28, 2009.

[50] Alan Donovan, Robert Muth, Brad Chen, and David Sehr. Portable Native Client executables. Technical report, Google, 2012.

[51] Fred Douglis and John Ousterhout. Transparent process migration: design alternatives and the Sprite implementation. *Softw. Pract. Exper.*, 21(8):757–785, July 1991.

[52] Richard P. Draves, Brian N. Bershad, Richard F. Rashid, and Randall W. Dean. Using continuations to implement thread management and communication in operating systems. In *Proceedings of the thirteenth ACM Symposium on Operating Systems Principles*, SOSP '91, pages 122–136, 1991.

[53] Peter Druschel and Larry L. Peterson. Fbufs: a high-bandwidth cross-domain transfer facility. *SIGOPS Oper. Syst. Rev.*, 27(5):189–202, December 1993.

[54] George W. Dunlap, Samuel T. King, Sukru Cinar, Murtaza A. Basrai, and Peter M. Chen. ReVirt: enabling intrusion analysis through virtual-machine logging and replay. *SIGOPS Oper. Syst. Rev.*, 36(SI):211–224, December 2002.

[55] Petros Efstathopoulos, Maxwell Krohn, Steve VanDeBogart, Cliff Frey, David Ziegler, Eddie Kohler, David Mazières, Frans Kaashoek, and Robert Morris. Labels and event processes in the Asbestos operating system. In *Proceedings of the twentieth ACM Symposium on Operating Systems Principles*, SOSP '05, pages 17–30, 2005.

[56] D. R. Engler, M. F. Kaashoek, and J. O'Toole, Jr. Exokernel: an operating system architecture for application-level resource management. In *Proceedings of the fifteenth ACM Symposium on Operating Systems Principles*, SOSP '95, pages 251–266, 1995.

[57] Dawson Engler, David Yu Chen, Seth Hallem, Andy Chou, and Benjamin Chelf. Bugs as deviant behavior: a general approach to inferring errors in systems code. In *Proceedings of the eighteenth ACM Symposium on Operating Systems Principles*, SOSP '01, pages 57–72, 2001.

[58] R. S. Fabry. Capability-based addressing. *Commun. ACM*, 17(7):403–412, July 1974.

[59] Jason Flinn and M. Satyanarayanan. Energy-aware adaptation for mobile applications. In *Proceedings of the seventeenth ACM Symposium on Operating Systems Principles*, SOSP '99, pages 48–63, 1999.

[60] Christopher Frost, Mike Mammarella, Eddie Kohler, Andrew de los Reyes, Shant Hovsepian, Andrew Matsuoka, and Lei Zhang. Generalized file system dependencies. In *Proceedings of twenty-first ACM Symposium on Operating Systems Principles*, SOSP '07, pages 307–320, 2007.

[61] Gregory R. Ganger, Marshall Kirk McKusick, Craig A. N. Soules, and Yale N. Patt. Soft updates: a solution to the metadata update problem in file systems. *ACM Trans. Comput. Syst.*, 18(2):127–153, May 2000.

[62] Simson Garfinkel and Gene Spafford. *Practical Unix and Internet security (2nd ed.)*. O'Reilly & Associates, Inc., 1996.

[63] Tal Garfinkel, Ben Pfaff, Jim Chow, Mendel Rosenblum, and Dan Boneh. Terra: a virtual machine-based platform for trusted computing. In *Proceedings of the nineteenth ACM Symposium on Operating Systems Principles*, SOSP '03, pages 193–206, 2003.

[64] Kirk Glerum, Kinshuman Kinshumann, Steve Greenberg, Gabriel Aul, Vince Orgovan, Greg Nichols, David Grant, Gretchen Loihle, and Galen Hunt. Debugging in the (very) large: ten years of implementation and experience. In *Proceedings of the 22nd ACM Symposium on Operating Systems Principles*, SOSP '09, pages 103–116, 2009.

[65] R.P. Goldberg. Survey of virtual machine research. *IEEE Computer*, 7(6):34–45, June 1974.

[66] Kinshuk Govil, Dan Teodosiu, Yongqiang Huang, and Mendel Rosenblum. Cellular Disco: resource management using virtual clusters on shared-memory multiprocessors. In *Proceedings of the seventeenth ACM Symposium on Operating Systems Principles*, SOSP '99, pages 154–169, 1999.

[67] Jim Gray. The transaction concept: virtues and limitations (invited paper). In *Proceedings of the seventh International conference on Very Large Data Bases*, VLDB '81, pages 144–154, 1981.

[68] Jim Gray. Why do computers stop and what can be done about it? Technical Report TR-85.7, HP Labs, 1985.

[69] Jim Gray, Paul McJones, Mike Blasgen, Bruce Lindsay, Raymond Lorie, Tom Price, Franco Putzolu, and Irving Traiger. The recovery manager of the System R database manager. *ACM Comput. Surv.*, 13(2):223–242, June 1981.

[70] Jim Gray and Andreas Reuter. *Transaction Processing: Concepts and Techniques*. Morgan Kaufmann, 1993.

[71] Jim Gray and Daniel P. Siewiorek. High-availability computer systems. *Computer*, 24(9):39–48, September 1991.

[72] Diwaker Gupta, Sangmin Lee, Michael Vrable, Stefan Savage, Alex C. Snoeren, George Varghese, Geoffrey M. Voelker, and Amin Vahdat. Difference engine: harnessing memory redundancy in virtual machines. In *Proceedings of the 8th USENIX conference on Operating Systems Design and Implementation*, OSDI'08, pages 309–322, 2008.

[73] Hadoop. *http://hadoop.apache.org*.

[74] Steven M. Hand. Self-paging in the Nemesis operating system. In *Proceedings of the third USENIX Symposium on Operating Systems Design and Implementation*, OSDI '99, pages 73–86, 1999.

[75] Per Brinch Hansen. The nucleus of a multiprogramming system. *Commun. ACM*, 13(4):238–241, April 1970.

[76] Mor Harchol-Balter and Allen B. Downey. Exploiting process lifetime distributions for dynamic load balancing. In *Proceedings of the fifteenth ACM Symposium on Operating Systems Principles*, SOSP '95, pages 236–, 1995.

[77] Kieran Harty and David R. Cheriton. Application-controlled physical memory using external page-cache management. In *Proceedings of the fifth International conference on Architectural Support for Programming Languages and Operating Systems*, ASPLOS-V, pages 187–197, 1992.

[78] Rober Haskin, Yoni Malachi, and Gregory Chan. Recovery management in QuickSilver. *ACM Trans. Comput. Syst.*, 6(1):82–108, February 1988.

[79] John L. Hennessy and David A. Patterson. *Computer Architecture - A Quantitative Approach (5. ed.)*. Morgan Kaufmann, 2012.

[80] Maurice Herlihy. Wait-free synchronization. *ACM Trans. Program. Lang. Syst.*, 13(1):124–149, January 1991.

[81] Maurice Herlihy and Nir Shavit. *The Art of Multiprocessor Programming*. Morgan Kaufmann, 2008.

[82] Dave Hitz, James Lau, and Michael Malcolm. File system design for an NFS file server appliance. Technical Report 3002, Network Appliance, 1995.

[83] C. A. R. Hoare. Monitors: An operating system structuring concept. *Communications of the ACM*, 17:549–557, 1974.

[84] C. A. R. Hoare. Communicating sequential processes. *Commun. ACM*, 21(8):666–677, August 1978.

[85] C. A. R. Hoare. The emperor's old clothes. *Commun. ACM*, 24(2):75–83, February 1981.

[86] Thomas R. Horsley and William C. Lynch. Pilot: A software engineering case study. In *Proceedings of the 4th International conference on Software engineering*, ICSE '79, pages 94–99, 1979.

[87] Raj Jain. *The Art of Computer Systems Performance Analysis*. John Wiley & Sons, 1991.

[88] Asim Kadav and Michael M. Swift. Understanding modern device drivers. In *Proceedings of the seventeenth international conference on Architectural Support for Programming Languages and Operating Systems*, ASPLOS '12, pages 87–98, New York, NY, USA, 2012. ACM.

[89] Paul A. Karger, Mary Ellen Zurko, Douglas W. Bonin, Andrew H. Mason, and Clifford E. Kahn. A retrospective on the VAX VMM security kernel. *IEEE Trans. Softw. Eng.*, 17(11):1147–1165, November 1991.

[90] Yousef A. Khalidi and Michael N. Nelson. Extensible file systems in Spring. In *Proceedings of the fourteenth ACM Symposium on Operating Systems Principles*, SOSP '93, pages 1–14, 1993.

[91] Gerwin Klein, Kevin Elphinstone, Gernot Heiser, June Andronick, David Cock, Philip Derrin, Dhammika Elkaduwe, Kai Engelhardt, Rafal Kolanski, Michael Norrish, Thomas Sewell, Harvey Tuch, and Simon Winwood. sel4: formal verification of an OS kernel. In *Proceedings of the ACM SIGOPS 22nd Symposium on Operating Systems Principles*, SOSP '09, pages 207–220, 2009.

[92] L. Kleinrock and R. R. Muntz. Processor sharing queueing models of mixed scheduling disciplines for time shared system. *J. ACM*, 19(3):464–482, July 1972.

[93] Leonard Kleinrock. *Queueing Systems, Volume II: Computer Applications*. Wiley Interscience, 1976.

[94] H. T. Kung and John T. Robinson. On optimistic methods for concurrency control. *ACM Trans. Database Syst.*, 6(2):213–226, June 1981.

[95] Leslie Lamport. A fast mutual exclusion algorithm. *ACM Trans. Comput. Syst.*, 5(1):1–11, January 1987.

[96] B. W. Lampson. Hints for computer system design. *IEEE Softw.*, 1(1):11–28, January 1984.

[97] Butler Lampson and Howard Sturgis. Crash recovery in a distributed data storage system. Technical report, Xerox Palo Alto Research Center, 1979.

[98] Butler W. Lampson and David D. Redell. Experience with processes and monitors in Mesa. *Commun. ACM*, 23(2):105–117, February 1980.

[99] Butler W. Lampson and Howard E. Sturgis. Reflections on an operating system design. *Commun. ACM*, 19(5):251–265, May 1976.

[100] James Larus and Galen Hunt. The Singularity system. *Commun. ACM*, 53(8):72–79, August 2010.

[101] Hugh C. Lauer and Roger M. Needham. On the duality of operating system structures. In *Operating Systems Review*, pages 3–19, 1979.

[102] Edward D. Lazowska, John Zahorjan, G. Scott Graham, and Kenneth C. Sevcik. *Quantitative system performance: computer system analysis using queueing network models*. Prentice-Hall, Inc., 1984.

[103] Will E. Leland, Murad S. Taqqu, Walter Willinger, and Daniel V. Wilson. On the self-similar nature of Ethernet traffic (extended version). *IEEE/ACM Trans. Netw.*, 2(1):1–15, February 1994.

[104] N. G. Leveson and C. S. Turner. An investigation of the Therac-25 accidents. *Computer*, 26(7):18–41, July 1993.

[105] H. M. Levy and P. H. Lipman. Virtual memory management in the VAX/VMS operating system. *Computer*, 15(3):35–41, March 1982.

[106] J. Liedtke. On micro-kernel construction. In *Proceedings of the fifteenth ACM Symposium on Operating Systems Principles*, SOSP '95, pages 237–250, 1995.

[107] John Lions. *Lions' Commentary on UNIX 6th Edition, with Source Code*. Peer-to-Peer Communications, 1996.

[108] J. S. Liptay. Structural aspects of the System/360 model 85: ii the cache. *IBM Syst. J.*, 7(1):15–21, March 1968.

[109] David E. Lowell, Subhachandra Chandra, and Peter M. Chen. Exploring failure transparency and the limits of generic recovery. In *Proceedings of the 4th conference on Symposium on Operating Systems Design and Implementation*, OSDI'00, pages 20–20, 2000.

[110] David E. Lowell and Peter M. Chen. Free transactions with Rio Vista. In *Proceedings of the sixteenth ACM Symposium on Operating Systems Principles*, SOSP '97, pages 92–101, 1997.

[111] P. McKenney. Is parallel programming hard, and, if so, what can be done about it? *http://kernel.org/pub/linux/kernel/people/paulmck/perfbook/perfbook.2011.05.30a.pdf*.

[112] Paul E. McKenney, Dipankar Sarma, Andrea Arcangeli, Andi Kleen, Orran Krieger, and Rusty Russell. Read-copy update. In *Ottawa Linux Symposium*, pages 338–367, June 2002.

[113] Marshall K. McKusick, William N. Joy, Samuel J. Leffler, and Robert S. Fabry. A fast file system for UNIX. *ACM Trans. Comput. Syst.*, 2(3):181–197, August 1984.

[114] Marshall Kirk McKusick, Keith Bostic, Michael J. Karels, and John S. Quarterman. *The design and implementation of the 4.4BSD operating system*. Addison Wesley Longman Publishing Co., Inc., 1996.

[115] John M. Mellor-Crummey and Michael L. Scott. Algorithms for scalable synchronization on shared-memory multiprocessors. *ACM Trans. Comput. Syst.*, 9(1):21–65, February 1991.

[116] Scott Meyers and Andrei Alexandrescu. C++ and the perils of double-checked locking. *Dr. Dobbs Journal*, 2004.

[117] Jeffrey C. Mogul and K. K. Ramakrishnan. Eliminating receive livelock in an interrupt-driven kernel. *ACM Trans. Comput. Syst.*, 15(3):217–252, August 1997.

[118] Jeffrey C. Mogul, Richard F. Rashid, and Michael J. Accetta. The packet filter: An efficient mechanism for user-level network code. In *In the Proceedings of the eleventh ACM Symposium on Operating Systems Principles*, pages 39–51, 1987.

[119] C. Mohan, Don Haderle, Bruce Lindsay, Hamid Pirahesh, and Peter Schwarz. ARIES: a transaction recovery method supporting fine-granularity locking and partial rollbacks using write-ahead logging. *ACM Trans. Database Syst.*, 17(1):94–162, March 1992.

[120] Gordon E. Moore. Cramming more components onto integrated circuits. *Electronics*, 38(8):114–117, 1965.

[121] Madanlal Musuvathi, Shaz Qadeer, Thomas Ball, Gerard Basler, Piramanayagam Arumuga Nainar, and Iulian Neamtiu. Finding and reproducing Heisenbugs in concurrent programs. In *Proceedings of the 8th USENIX conference on Operating Systems Design and Implementation*, OSDI'08, pages 267–280, 2008.

[122] Kai Nagel and Michael Schreckenberg. A cellular automaton model for freeway traffic. *J. Phys. I France*, 1992.

[123] George C. Necula and Peter Lee. Safe kernel extensions without run-time checking. In *Proceedings of the second USENIX Symposium on Operating Systems Design and Implementation*, OSDI '96, pages 229–243, 1996.

[124] Edmund B. Nightingale, Kaushik Veeraraghavan, Peter M. Chen, and Jason Flinn. Rethink the sync. *ACM Trans. Comput. Syst.*, 26(3):6:1–6:26, September 2008.

[125] Elliott I. Organick. *The Multics system: an examination of its structure*. MIT Press, 1972.

[126] Steven Osman, Dinesh Subhraveti, Gong Su, and Jason Nieh. The design and implementation of Zap: a system for migrating computing environments. In *Proceedings of the fifth USENIX Symposium on Operating Systems Design and Implementation*, OSDI '02, pages 361–376, 2002.

[127] John Ousterhout. Scheduling techniques for concurrent systems. In *Proceedings of Third International Conference on Distributed Computing Systems*, pages 22–30, 1982.

[128] John Ousterhout. Why aren't operating systems getting faster as fast as hardware? In *Proceedings USENIX Conference*, pages 247–256, 1990.

[129] John Ousterhout. Why threads are a bad idea (for most purposes). In *USENIX Winter Technical Conference*, 1996.

[130] Vivek S. Pai, Peter Druschel, and Willy Zwaenepoel. Flash: an efficient and portable web server. In *Proceedings of the annual conference on USENIX Annual Technical Conference*, ATEC '99, 1999.

[131] Vivek S. Pai, Peter Druschel, and Willy Zwaenepoel. IO-lite: a unified I/O buffering and caching system. In *Proceedings of the third USENIX Symposium on Operating Systems Design and Implementation*, OSDI '99, pages 15–28, 1999.

[132] David A. Patterson, Garth Gibson, and Randy H. Katz. A case for redundant arrays of inexpensive disks (RAID). In *Proceedings of the 1988 ACM SIGMOD International conference on Management of Data*, SIGMOD '88, pages 109–116, 1988.

[133] L. Peterson, N. Hutchinson, S. O'Malley, and M. Abbott. RPC in the x-Kernel: evaluating new design techniques. In *Proceedings of the twelfth ACM Symposium on Operating Systems Principles*, SOSP '89, pages 91–101, 1989.

[134] Jonathan Pincus and Brandon Baker. Beyond stack smashing: recent advances in exploiting buffer overruns. *IEEE Security and Privacy*, 2(4):20–27, July 2004.

[135] Eduardo Pinheiro, Wolf-Dietrich Weber, and Luiz André Barroso. Failure trends in a large disk drive population. In *Proceedings of the 5th USENIX conference on File and Storage Technologies*, FAST '07, pages 2–2, 2007.

[136] Vijayan Prabhakaran, Lakshmi N. Bairavasundaram, Nitin Agrawal, Haryadi S. Gunawi, Andrea C. Arpaci-Dusseau, and Remzi H. Arpaci-Dusseau. IRON file systems. In *Proceedings of the twentieth ACM Symposium on Operating Systems Principles*, SOSP '05, pages 206–220, 2005.

[137] Richard Rashid, Robert Baron, Alessandro Forin, David Golub, Michael Jones, Daniel Julin, Douglas Orr, and Richard Sanzi. Mach: A foundation for open systems. In *Proceedings of the Second Workshop on Workstation Operating Systems(WWOS2)*, 1989.

[138] Richard F. Rashid, Avadis Tevanian, Michael Young, David B. Golub, Robert V. Baron, David L. Black, William J. Bolosky, and Jonathan Chew. Machine-independent virtual memory management for paged uniprocessor and multiprocessor architectures. *IEEE Trans. Computers*, 37(8):896–907, 1988.

[139] E.S. Raymond. *The Cathedral and the Bazaar: Musings On Linux And Open Source By An Accidental Revolutionary*. O'Reilly Series. O'Reilly, 2001.

[140] David D. Redell, Yogen K. Dalal, Thomas R. Horsley, Hugh C. Lauer, William C. Lynch, Paul R. McJones, Hal G. Murray, and Stephen C. Purcell. Pilot: an operating system for a personal computer. *Commun. ACM*, 23(2):81–92, February 1980.

[141] Dennis M. Ritchie and Ken Thompson. The UNIX time-sharing system. *Commun. ACM*, 17(7):365–375, July 1974.

[142] Mendel Rosenblum and John K. Ousterhout. The design and implementation of a log-structured file system. *ACM Trans. Comput. Syst.*, 10(1):26–52, February 1992.

[143] Chris Ruemmler and John Wilkes. An introduction to disk drive modeling. *Computer*, 27(3):17–28, March 1994.

[144] J. H. Saltzer, D. P. Reed, and D. D. Clark. End-to-end arguments in system design. *ACM Trans. Comput. Syst.*, 2(4):277–288, November 1984.

[145] Jerome H. Saltzer. Protection and the control of information sharing in Multics. *Commun. ACM*, 17(7):388–402, July 1974.

[146] M. Satyanarayanan, Henry H. Mashburn, Puneet Kumar, David C. Steere, and James J. Kistler. Lightweight recoverable virtual memory. *ACM Trans. Comput. Syst.*, 12(1):33–57, February 1994.

[147] Stefan Savage, Michael Burrows, Greg Nelson, Patrick Sobalvarro, and Thomas Anderson. Eraser: a dynamic data race detector for multithreaded programs. *ACM Trans. Comput. Syst.*, 15(4):391–411, November 1997.

[148] Bianca Schroeder and Garth A. Gibson. Disk failures in the real world: what does an MTTF of 1,000,000 hours mean to you? In *Proceedings of the 5th USENIX conference on File and Storage Technologies*, FAST '07, 2007.

[149] Bianca Schroeder and Mor Harchol-Balter. Web servers under overload: How scheduling can help. *ACM Trans. Internet Technol.*, 6(1):20–52, February 2006.

[150] Michael D. Schroeder, David D. Clark, and Jerome H. Saltzer. The Multics kernel design project. In *Proceedings of the sixth ACM Symposium on Operating Systems Principles*, SOSP '77, pages 43–56, 1977.

[151] Michael D. Schroeder and Jerome H. Saltzer. A hardware architecture for implementing protection rings. *Commun. ACM*, 15(3):157–170, March 1972.

[152] D. P. Siewiorek. Architecture of fault-tolerant computers. *Computer*, 17(8):9–18, August 1984.

[153] E. H. Spafford. Crisis and aftermath. *Commun. ACM*, 32(6):678–687, June 1989.

[154] Structured Query Language (SQL). *http://en.wikipedia.org/wiki/SQL*.

[155] Michael Stonebraker. Operating system support for database management. *Commun. ACM*, 24(7):412–418, July 1981.

[156] Michael M. Swift, Muthukaruppan Annamalai, Brian N. Bershad, and Henry M. Levy. Recovering device drivers. *ACM Trans. Comput. Syst.*, 24(4):333–360, November 2006.

[157] K. Thompson. Unix implementation. *Bell System Technical Journal*, 57:1931–1946, 1978.

[158] Ken Thompson. Reflections on trusting trust. *Commun. ACM*, 27(8):761–763, August 1984.

[159] Paul Tyma. Thousands of threads and blocking i/o. *http://www.mailinator.com/tymaPaulMultithreaded.pdf*, 2008.

[160] Robbert van Renesse. Goal-oriented programming, or composition using events, or threads considered harmful. In *ACM SIGOPS European Workshop on Support for Composing Distributed Applications*, pages 82–87, 1998.

[161] Joost S. M. Verhofstad. Recovery techniques for database systems. *ACM Comput. Surv.*, 10(2):167–195, June 1978.

[162] Michael Vrable, Justin Ma, Jay Chen, David Moore, Erik Vandekieft, Alex C. Snoeren, Geoffrey M. Voelker, and Stefan Savage. Scalability, fidelity, and containment in the Potemkin virtual honeyfarm. In *Proceedings of the twentieth ACM Symposium on Operating Systems Principles*, SOSP '05, pages 148–162, 2005.

[163] Robert Wahbe, Steven Lucco, Thomas E. Anderson, and Susan L. Graham. Efficient software-based fault isolation. In *Proceedings of the fourteenth ACM Symposium on Operating Systems Principles*, SOSP '93, pages 203–216, 1993.

[164] Carl A. Waldspurger. Memory resource management in VMware ESX server. *SIGOPS Oper. Syst. Rev.*, 36(SI):181–194, December 2002.

[165] Andrew Whitaker, Marianne Shaw, and Steven D. Gribble. Scale and performance in the Denali isolation kernel. In *Proceedings of the fifth USENIX Symposium on Operating Systems Design and Implementation*, OSDI '02, pages 195–209, 2002.

[166] J. Wilkes, R. Golding, C. Staelin, and T. Sullivan. The HP AutoRAID hierarchical storage system. In *Proceedings of the fifteenth ACM Symposium on Operating Systems Principles*, SOSP '95, pages 96–108, 1995.

[167] Alec Wolman, M. Voelker, Nitin Sharma, Neal Cardwell, Anna Karlin, and Henry M. Levy. On the scale and performance of cooperative web proxy caching. In *Proceedings of the seventeenth ACM Symposium on Operating Systems Principles*, SOSP '99, pages 16–31, 1999.

[168] W. Wulf, E. Cohen, W. Corwin, A. Jones, R. Levin, C. Pierson, and F. Pollack. Hydra: the kernel of a multiprocessor operating system. *Commun. ACM*, 17(6):337–345, June 1974.

[169] Bennet Yee, David Sehr, Gregory Dardyk, J. Bradley Chen, Robert Muth, Tavis Ormandy, Shiki Okasaka, Neha Narula, and Nicholas Fullagar. Native Client: a sandbox for portable, untrusted x86 native code. In *Proceedings of the 2009 30th IEEE Symposium on Security and Privacy*, SP '09, pages 79–93, 2009.

[170] Nickolai Zeldovich, Silas Boyd-Wickizer, Eddie Kohler, and David Mazières. Making information flow explicit in HiStar. *Commun. ACM*, 54(11):93–101, November 2011.

Glossary

abstract virtual machine The interface provided by an operating system to its applications, including the system call interface, the memory abstraction, exceptions, and signals.

acquire-all/release-all A design pattern to provide atomicity of a request consisting of multiple operations. A thread acquires all of the locks it might need before starting to process a request; it releases the locks once the request is done.

address translation The conversion from the memory address the program thinks it is referencing to the physical location of the memory.

affinity scheduling A scheduling policy where tasks are preferentially scheduled onto the same processor they had previously been assigned, to improve cache reuse.

API See: application programming interface.

application programming interface The system call interface provided by an operating system to applications.

arrival rate The rate at which tasks arrive for service.

asynchronous I/O A design pattern for system calls to allow a single-threaded process to make multiple concurrent I/O requests. When the process issues an I/O request, the system call returns immediately. The process later on receives a notification when the I/O completes.

asynchronous procedure call A procedure call where the caller starts the function, continues execution concurrently with the called function, and later waits for the function to complete.

atomic operations Indivisible operations that cannot be interleaved with or split by other operations.

atomic read-modify-write instruction A processor-specific instruction that lets one thread temporarily have exclusive and atomic access to a memory location while the instruction executes. Typically, the instruction (atomically) reads a memory location, does

some simple arithmetic operation to the value, and stores the result.

availability The percentage of time that a system is usable.

AVM See: abstract virtual machine.

base and bound An early system for memory protection where each process is limited to a specific range of physical memory.

batch operating system An early type of operating system that efficiently ran a queue of tasks. While one program was running, another was being loaded into memory.

Belady's anomaly For some cache replacement policies and some reference patterns, adding space to a cache can hurt the cache hit rate.

BIOS The initial code run when an Intel x86 computer boots; acronym for Basic Input/Output System. See also: Boot ROM.

blocking bounded queue A bounded queue where a thread trying to remove an item from an empty queue will wait until an item is available, and a thread trying to put an item into a full queue will wait until there is room.

Bohrbugs Bugs that are deterministic and reproducible, given the same program input. See also: Heisenbugs.

Boot ROM Special read-only memory containing the initial instructions for booting a computer.

bootloader Program stored at a fixed position on disk (or flash RAM) to load the operating system into memory and start it executing.

bounded queue A queue with a fixed size limit on the number of items stored in the queue.

bounded resources A necessary condition for deadlock: there are a finite number of resources that threads can simultaneously use.

buffer overflow attack An attack that exploits a bug where input can overflow the buffer allocated to hold it, overwriting other important program data structures with data provided by the attacker. One common variation overflows a buffer allocated on the stack (e.g., a local, automatic variable) and replaces the function's return address with a return address specified by the attacker, possibly to code "pushed" onto the stack with the overflowing input.

bulk synchronous A type of parallel application where work is split into independent tasks and where each task completes before the results of any of the tasks can be used.

bulk synchronous parallel programming See: data parallel programming.

bursty distribution A probability distribution that is less evenly distributed around the mean value than an exponential distribution. See: exponential distribution. Compare: heavy-tailed distribution.

busy-waiting A thread spins in a loop waiting for a concurrent event to occur, consuming CPU cycles while it is waiting.

cache A copy of data that can be accessed more quickly than the original.

cache hit The cache contains the requested item.

cache miss The cache does not contain the requested item.

checkpoint A consistent snapshot of the entire state of a process, including the contents of memory and processor registers.

circular waiting A necessary condition for deadlock to occur: there is a set of threads such that each thread is waiting for a resource held by another.

client-server communication Two-way communication between processes, where the client sends requests to the server to do some task, and when the operation is complete, the server replies back to the client.

clock algorithm An method for identifying a not recently used page to evict. The algorithm sweeps through each page frame: if the page use bit is set, it is cleared; if the use bit is not set, the page is reclaimed.

cloud computing A model of computing where large-scale applications run on shared computing and storage infrastructure in data centers instead of on the user's own computer.

compare-and-swap An atomic read-modify-write instruction that firsts tests the value of a memory location, and if the value has not been changed, sets it to a new value.

compute-bound task A task that primarily uses the processor and does little I/O.

computer virus A computer program that modifies an operating system or application to copy itself from computer to computer without the computer owner's permission or knowledge. Once installed on a computer, a virus often provides the attacker control over the system's resources or data.

concurrency Multiple activities that can happen at the same time.

condition variable A synchronization variable that enables a thread to efficiently wait for a change to shared state protected by a lock.

continuation A data structure used in event-driven programming that keeps track of a task's current state and its next step.

cooperative caching Using the memory of nearby nodes over a network as a cache to avoid the latency of going to disk.

cooperative multi-threading Each thread runs without interruption until it explicitly relinquishes control of the processor, e.g., by exiting or calling thread_yield.

copy-on-write A method of sharing physical memory between two logically distinct copies (e.g., in different processes). Each shared page is marked as read-only so that the operating system kernel is invoked and can make a copy of the page if either process tries to write it. The process can then modify the copy and resume normal execution.

core map A data structure used by the memory management system to keep track of the state of physical page frames, such as which processes reference the page frame.

critical path The minimum sequence of steps for a parallel application to compute its result, even with infinite resources.

critical section A sequence of code that operates on shared state.

cross-site scripting An attack against a client computer that works by compromising a server visited by the client. The compromised server then provides scripting code to the client that accesses and downloads the client's sensitive data.

cryptographic signature A specially designed function of a data block and a private cryptographic key that allows someone with the corresponding public key to verify that an authorized entity produced the data block. It is computationally intractable for an attacker without the private key to create a different data block with a valid signature.

data breakpoint A request to stop the execution of a program when it references or modifies a particular memory location.

data parallel programming A programming model where the computation is performed in parallel across all items in a data set.

deadlock A cycle of waiting among a set of threads, where each thread waits for some other thread in the cycle to take some action.

deadlocked state The system has at least one deadlock.

defense in depth Improving security through multiple layers of protection.

defragment Coalesce scattered disk blocks to improve spatial locality, by reading data from its present storage location and rewriting it to a new, more compact, location.

demand paging Using address translation hardware to run a process without all of its memory physically present. When the process references a missing page, the hardware traps to the kernel, which brings the page into memory from disk.

deterministic debugging The ability to re-execute a concurrent process with the same schedule and sequence of internal and external events.

direct mapped cache Only one entry in the cache can hold a specific memory location, so on a lookup, the system must check the address against only that entry to determine if there is a cache hit.

direct memory access Hardware I/O devices transfer data directly into/out of main memory at a location specified by the operating system.

dirty bit A status bit in a page table entry recording whether the contents of the page have been modified relative to what is stored on disk.

disable and enable interrupts Privileged hardware instructions to temporarily defer any hardware interrupts, to allow the kernel to complete a critical task.

DMA See: direct memory access.

double-checked locking A pitfall in concurrent code where a data structure is lazily initialized by first, checking without a lock if it has been set, and if not, acquiring a lock and checking again, before calling the initialization function. With instruction re-ordering, double-checked locking can fail unexpectedly.

dual-mode operation Hardware processor that has (at least) two privilege levels: one for executing the kernel with complete access to the capabilities of the hardware and a second for executing user code with restricted rights. See also: kernel-mode operation, user-mode operation.

earliest deadline first A scheduling policy that performs the task that needs to be completed first, but only if it can be finished in time.

EDF See: earliest deadline first.

efficiency The lack of overhead in implementing an abstraction.

event-driven programming A coding design pattern where a thread spins in a loop; each iteration gets and processes the next I/O event.

exception See: processor exception.

executable image File containing a sequence of machine instructions and initial data values for a program.

execution stack Space to store the state of local variables during procedure calls.

exponential distribution A convenient probability distribution for use in queueing theory because it has the property of being memoryless. For a continuous random variable with a mean of $\frac{1}{\lambda}$, the probability density function is $f(x) = \lambda e^{-\lambda x}$.

external fragmentation In a system that allocates memory in contiguous regions, the unusable memory between valid contiguous allocations. A new request for memory may find no single free region that is both contiguous and large enough, even though there is enough free memory in aggregate.

fairness Partitioning of shared resources between users or applications either equally or balanced according to some desired priorities.

false sharing Extra inter-processor communication required because a single cache entry contains portions of two different data structures with different sharing patterns.

fate sharing When a crash in one module implies a crash in another. For example, a library shares fate with the application it is linked with; if either crashes, the process exits.

fault isolation An error in one application should not disrupt other applications, or even the operating system itself.

fill-on-demand A method for starting a process before all of its memory is brought in from disk. If the first access to the missing memory triggers a trap to the kernel, the kernel can fill the memory and then resume.

fine-grained locking A way to increase concurrency by partitioning an object's state into different subsets each protected by a different lock.

finished list The set of threads that are complete but not yet de-allocated, e.g., because a join may read the return value from the thread control block.

first-in-first-out A scheduling policy that performs each task in the order in which it arrives.

fork-join parallelism A type of parallel programming where threads can be created (forked) to do work in parallel with a parent thread; a parent may asynchronously wait for a child thread to finish (join).

fully associative cache Any entry in the cache can hold any memory location, so on a lookup, the system must check the address against all of the entries in the cache to determine if there is a cache hit.

gang scheduling A scheduling policy for multiprocessors that performs all of the runnable tasks for a particular process at the same time.

Global Descriptor Table The x86 terminology for a segment table for shared segments. A Local Descriptor Table is used for segments that are private to the process.

grace period (RCU) For a shared object protected by a read-copy-update lock, the time from when a new version of a shared object is published until the last reader of the old version is finished.

green threads A thread system implemented entirely at user-level without any reliance on operating system kernel services, other than those designed for single-threaded processes.

guest operating system An operating system running in a virtual machine.

hardware abstraction layer A module in the operating system that hides the specifics of different hardware implementations. Above this layer, the operating system is portable.

hardware timer A hardware device that can cause a processor interrupt after some delay, either in time or in instructions executed.

heap Space to store dynamically allocated data structures.

heavy-tailed distribution A probability distribution such that events far from the mean value (in aggregate) occur with significant probability. When used for the distribution of time between events, the remaining time to the next event is positively related to the time already spent waiting — you expect to wait longer the longer you have already waited.

Heisenbugs Bugs in concurrent programs that disappear or change behavior when you try to examine them. See also: Bohrbugs.

hint A result of some computation whose results may no longer be valid, but where using an invalid hint will trigger an exception.

host operating system An operating system that provides the abstraction of a virtual machine, to run another operating system as an application.

hyperthreading See: simultaneous multi-threading.

I/O-bound task A task that primarily does I/O, and does little processing.

incremental checkpoint A consistent snapshot of the portion of process memory that has been modified since the previous checkpoint.

independent threads Threads that operate on completely separate subsets of process memory.

inode In the Unix Fast File System (FFS) and related file systems, an inode stores a file's metadata and an array of pointers that can be used to find all of the file's blocks. The term inode is sometimes used more generally to refer to any file system's per-file metadata data structure.

internal fragmentation With paged allocation of memory, the unusable memory at the end of a page because a process can only be allocated memory in page-sized chunks.

interrupt An asynchronous signal to the processor that some external event has occurred that may require its attention.

interrupt handler A kernel procedure invoked when an interrupt occurs.

interrupt stack A region of memory for holding the stack of the kernel's interrupt handler. When an interrupt, processor exception, or system call trap causes a context switch into the kernel, the hardware changes the stack pointer to point to the base of the kernel's interrupt stack.

interrupt vector table A table of pointers in the operating system kernel, indexed by the type of interrupt, with each entry pointing to the first instruction of a handler procedure for that interrupt.

inverted page table A hash table used for translation between virtual page numbers and physical page frames.

kernel thread A thread that is implemented inside the operating system kernel.

kernel-mode operation The processor executes in an unrestricted mode that gives the operating system full control over the hardware. Compare: user-mode operation.

least frequently used A cache replacement policy that evicts whichever block has been used the least often, over some period of time.

least recently used A cache replacement policy that evicts whichever block has not been used for the longest period of time.

LFU See: least frequently used.

Little's Law In a stable system where the arrival rate matches the departure rate, the number of tasks in the system equals the system's throughput multiplied by the average time a task spends in the system: $N = XR$.

liveness property A constraint on program behavior such that it always produces a result. Compare: safety property.

lock A type of synchronization variable used for enforcing atomic, mutually exclusive access to shared data.

lock ordering A widely used approach to prevent deadlock, where locks are acquired in a pre-determined order.

lock-free data structures Concurrent data structure that guarantees progress for some thread: some method will finish in a finite number of steps, regardless of the state of other threads executing in the data structure.

log An ordered sequence of steps saved to persistent storage.

LRU See: least recently used.

max-min fairness A scheduling objective to maximizes the minimum resource allocation given to each task.

MCS lock An efficient spinlock implementation where each waiting thread spins on a separate memory location.

mean time to failure The average time that a system runs without failing.

mean time to repair The average time that it takes to repair a system once it has failed.

memory address alias Two or more virtual addresses that refer to the same physical memory location.

memory barrier An instruction that prevents the compiler and hardware from reordering memory accesses across the barrier — no accesses before the barrier are moved after the barrier and no accesses after the barrier are moved before the barrier.

memory protection Hardware or software-enforced limits so that each application process can read and write only its own memory and not the memory of the operating system or any other process.

memoryless property For a probability distribution for the time between events, the remaining time to the next event does not depend on the amount of time already spent waiting. See also: heavy-tailed distribution.

memory-mapped file A file whose contents appear to be a memory segment in a process's virtual address space.

microkernel An operating system design where the kernel itself is kept small, and instead most of the functionality of a traditional operating system kernel is put into a set of user-level processes, or servers, accessed from user applications via interprocess communication.

MIN cache replacement See: optimal cache replacement.

MIPS An early measure of processor performance: millions of instructions per second.

model A simplification that tries to capture the most important aspects of a more complex system's behavior.

monolithic kernel An operating system design where most of the operating system functionality is linked together inside the kernel.

Moore's Law Transistor density increases exponentially over time. Similar exponential improvements have occurred in many other component technologies; in the popular press, these often go by the same term.

MTTF See: mean time to failure.

MTTR See: mean time to repair.

multi-level feedback A scheduling policy with multiple priority levels managed using round robin queues, where a task is moved between priority levels based on how much processing time it has used.

multi-level paged segmentation A virtual memory mechanism where physical memory is allocated in page frames, virtual addresses are segmented, and each segment is translated to physical addresses through multiple levels of page tables.

multi-level paging A virtual memory mechanism where physical memory is allocated in page frames, and virtual addresses are translated to physical addresses through multiple levels of page tables.

multiple independent requests A necessary condition for deadlock to occur: a thread first acquires one resource and then tries to acquire another.

multiprogramming See: multitasking.

multitasking The ability of an operating system to run multiple applications at the same time, also called multiprogramming.

multi-threaded process A process with multiple threads.

multi-threaded program A generalization of a single-threaded program. Instead of only one logical sequence of steps, the program has multiple sequences, or threads, executing at the same time.

mutual exclusion When one thread uses a lock to prevent concurrent access to a shared data structure.

mutually recursive locking A deadlock condition where two shared objects call into each other while still holding their locks. Deadlock occurs if one thread holds the lock on the first object and calls into the second, while the other thread holds the lock on the second object and calls into the first.

nested waiting A deadlock condition where one shared object calls into another shared object while holding the first object's lock, and then waits on a condition variable. Deadlock results if the thread that can signal the condition variable needs the first lock to make progress.

network effect The increase in value of a product or service based on the number of other people who have adopted that technology and not just its intrinsic capabilities.

no preemption A necessary condition for deadlock to occur: once a thread acquires a resource, its ownership cannot be revoked until the thread acts to release it.

non-blocking data structures Concurrent data structure where a thread is never required to wait for another thread to complete its operation.

not recently used A cache replacement policy that evicts some block that has not been referenced recently, rather than the least recently used block.

oblivious scheduling A scheduling policy where the operating system assigns threads to processors without knowledge of the intent of the parallel application.

open system A system whose source code is available to the public for modification and reuse, or a system whose interfaces are defined by a public standards process.

operating system A layer of software that manages a computer's resources for its users and their applications.

operating system kernel The kernel is the lowest level of software running on the system, with full access to all of the capabilities of the hardware.

optimal cache replacement Replace whichever block is used farthest in the future.

overhead The added resource cost of implementing an abstraction versus using the underlying hardware resources directly.

ownership design pattern A technique for managing concurrent access to shared objects in which at most one thread owns an object at any time, and therefore the thread can access the shared data without a lock.

page coloring The assignment of physical page frames to virtual addresses by partitioning frames based on which portions of the cache they will use.

page fault A hardware trap to the operating system kernel when a process references a virtual address with an invalid page table entry.

page frame An aligned, fixed-size chunk of physical memory that can hold a virtual page.

paged memory A hardware address translation mechanism where memory is allocated in aligned, fixed-sized chunks, called pages. Any virtual page can be assigned to any physical page frame.

paged segmentation A hardware mechanism where physical memory is allocated in page frames, but virtual addresses are segmented.

pair of stubs A pair of short procedures that mediate between two execution contexts.

paravirtualization A virtual machine abstraction that allows the guest operating system to make system calls into the host operating system to perform hardware-specific operations, such as changing a page table entry.

PCB See: process control block.

performance predictability Whether a system's response time or other performance metric is consistent over time.

phase change behavior Abrupt changes in a program's working set, causing bursty cache miss rates: periods of low cache misses interspersed with periods of high cache misses.

physical address An address in physical memory.

physically addressed cache A processor cache that is accessed using physical memory addresses.

pin To bind a virtual resource to a physical resource, such as a thread to a processor or a virtual page to a physical page.

policy-mechanism separation A system design principle where the implementation of an abstraction is independent of the resource allocation policy of how the abstraction is used.

poll A strategy for waiting for an asynchronous event to occur, by looping, or busy-waiting, until the event occurs.

polling An alternative to hardware interrupts, where the processor loops checking an input/output device to see if an event that requires handling has occurred.

portability The ability of software to work across multiple hardware platforms.

precise interrupts All instructions that occur before the interrupt or exception, according to the program execution, are completed by the hardware before the interrupt handler is invoked.

preemption When a scheduler takes the processor away from one task and gives it to another.

preemptive multi-threading The operating system scheduler may switch out a running thread, e.g., on a timer interrupt, without any explicit action by the thread to relinquish control at that point.

prefetch To bring data into a cache before it is needed.

principle of least privilege System security and reliability are enhanced if each part of the system has exactly the privileges it needs to do its job and no more.

priority donation A solution to priority inversion: when a thread waits for a lock held by a lower priority thread, the lock holder is temporarily increased to the waiter's priority until the lock is released.

priority inversion A scheduling anomaly that occurs when a high priority task waits indefinitely for a resource (such as a lock) held by a low priority task, because the low priority task is waiting in turn for a resource (such as the processor) held by a medium priority task.

privacy Data stored on a computer is only accessible to authorized users.

privileged instruction Instruction available in kernel mode but not in user mode.

process The execution of an application program with restricted rights — the abstraction for protection provided by the operating system kernel.

process control block A data structure that stores all the information the operating system needs about a particular process: e.g., where it is stored in memory, where its executable image is on disk, which user asked it to start executing, and what privileges the process has.

process migration The ability to take a running program on one system, stop its execution, and resume it on a different machine.

processor exception An hardware event caused by user program behavior that causes a transfer of control to a kernel handler. For example, attempting to divide by zero causes a processor exception in many architectures.

processor scheduling policy When there are more runnable threads than processors, the policy that determines which threads to run first.

processor status register A hardware register containing flags that control the operation of the processor, including the privilege level.

producer-consumer communication Interprocess communication where the output of one process is the input of another.

proprietary system A system that is under the control of a single company; it can be changed at any time by its provider to meet the needs of its customers.

protection The isolation of potentially misbehaving applications and users so that they do not corrupt other applications or the operating system itself.

publish (RCU) A single, atomic memory write that updates a shared object protected by a read-copy-update lock. The write allows new reader threads to observe the new version of the object.

queueing delay The time a task waits in line without receiving service.

quiescent (RCU) No reader thread that was active at the time of the last modification is still active.

race condition When the behavior of a program relies on the interleaving of operations of different threads.

RCU See: read-copy-update.

read-copy-update (RCU) A synchronization abstraction that allows concurrent access to a data structure by multiple readers and a single writer at a time.

readers/writers lock A lock which allows multiple "reader" threads to access shared data concurrently provided they never modify the shared data, but still provides mutual exclusion whenever a "writer" thread is reading or modifying the shared data.

ready list The set of threads that are ready to be run but which are not currently running.

real-time constraint A constraint that computation that must be completed by a deadline if it is to have value.

recoverable virtual memory The abstraction of persistent memory, so that the contents of a memory segment can be restored after a failure.

reliability A property of a system that does exactly what it is designed to do.

request parallelism Parallel execution on a server that arises from multiple concurrent requests.

response time The time for a task to complete, from when it starts until it is done.

restart The resumption of a process from a checkpoint, e.g., after a failure or for debugging.

round robin A scheduling policy that takes turns running each ready task for a limited period before switching to the next task.

safe state (deadlock) A state of an execution such that regardless of the sequence of future resource requests, there is at least one safe sequence of decisions as to when to satisfy requests such that all pending and future requests are met.

safety property A constraint on program behavior such that it never computes the wrong result. Compare: liveness property.

sample bias A measurement error that occurs when some members of a group are less likely to be included than others, and where those members differ in the property being measured.

sandbox A context for executing untrusted code, where protection for the rest of the system is provided in software.

scheduler activations A multiprocessor scheduling policy where each application is informed of how many processors it has been assigned and whenever the assignment changes.

secondary bottleneck A resource with relatively low contention, due to a large amount of queueing at the primary bottleneck. If the primary bottleneck is improved, the secondary bottleneck will have much higher queueing delay.

security A computer's operation cannot be compromised by a malicious attacker.

security enforcement The mechanism the operating system uses to ensure that only permitted actions are allowed.

security policy What operations are permitted — who is allowed to access what data, and who can perform what operations.

segmentation A virtual memory mechanism where addresses are translated by table lookup, where each entry in the table is to a variable-size memory region.

segmentation fault An error caused when a process attempts to access memory outside of one of its valid memory regions.

segment-local address An address that is relative to the current memory segment.

self-paging A resource allocation policy for allocating page frames among processes; each page replacement is taken from a page frame already assigned to the process causing the page fault.

semaphore A type of synchronization variable with only two atomic operations, P() and V(). P waits for the value of the semaphore to be positive, and then atomically decrements it. V atomically increments the value, and if any threads are waiting in P, triggers the completion of the P operation.

serializability The result of any program execution is equivalent to an execution in which requests are processed one at a time in some sequential order.

service time The time it takes to complete a task at a resource, assuming no waiting.

set associate cache The cache is partitioned into sets of entries. Each memory location can only be stored in its assigned set, by it can be stored in any cache entry in that set. On a lookup, the system needs to check the address against all the entries in its set to determine if there is a cache hit.

shadow page table A page table for a process inside a virtual machine, formed by constructing the composition of the page table maintained by the guest operating system and the page table maintained by the host operating system.

shared object An object (a data structure and its associated code) that can be accessed safely by multiple concurrent threads.

shell A job control system implemented as a user-level process. When a user types a command to the shell, it creates a process to run the command.

shortest job first A scheduling policy that performs the task with the least remaining time left to finish.

simultaneous multi-threading A hardware technique where each processor simulates two (or more) virtual processors, alternating between them on a cycle-by-cycle basis.

single-threaded program A program written in a traditional way, with one logical sequence of steps as each instruction follows the previous one. Compare: multi-threaded program.

software transactional memory (STM) A system for general-purpose transactions for in-memory data structures.

software-loaded TLB A hardware TLB whose entries are installed by software, rather than hardware, on a TLB miss.

spatial locality Programs tend to reference instructions and data near those that have been recently accessed.

spinlock A lock where a thread waiting for a BUSY lock "spins" in a tight loop until some other thread makes it FREE.

stable property A property of a program, such that once the property becomes true in some execution of the program, it will stay true for the remainder of the execution.

stack frame A data structure stored on the stack with storage for one invocation of a procedure: the local variables used by the procedure, the parameters the procedure was called with, and the return address to jump to when the procedure completes.

staged architecture A staged architecture divides a system into multiple subsystems or stages, where each stage includes some state private to the stage and a set of one or more worker threads that operate on that state.

starvation The lack of progress for one task, due to resources given to higher priority tasks.

state variable Member variable of a shared object.

STM See: software transactional memory.

structured synchronization A design pattern for writing correct concurrent programs, where concurrent code uses a set of standard synchronization primitives to control access to shared state, and where all routines to access the same shared state are localized to the same logical module.

superpage A set of contiguous pages in physical memory that map a contiguous region of virtual memory, where the pages are aligned so that they share the same high-order (superpage) address.

swapping Evicting an entire process from physical memory.

synchronization barrier A synchronization primitive where n threads operating in parallel check in to the barrier when their work is completed. No thread returns from the barrier until all n check in.

synchronization variable A data structure used for coordinating concurrent access to shared state.

system call A procedure provided by the kernel that can be called from user level.

tagged TLB A translation lookaside buffer whose entries contain a process ID; only entries for the currently running process are used during translation. This allows TLB entries for a process to remain in the TLB when the process is switched out.

task A user request.

TCB See: thread control block.

temporal locality Programs tend to reference the same instructions and data that they had recently accessed.

test and test-and-set An implementation of a spinlock where the waiting processor waits until the lock is FREE before attempting to acquire it.

thrashing When a cache is too small to hold its working set. In this case, most references are cache misses, yet those misses evict data that will be used in the near future.

thread context switch Suspend execution of a currently running thread and resume execution of some other thread.

thread control block The operating system data structure containing the current state of a thread.

thread scheduler Software that maps threads to processors by switching between running threads and threads that are ready but not running.

thread-safe bounded queue A bounded queue that is safe to call from multiple concurrent threads.

throughput The rate at which a group of tasks are completed.

time of check vs. time of use attack A security vulnerability arising when an application can modify the user memory holding a system call parameter (such as a file name), *after* the kernel checks the validity of the parameter, but *before* the parameter is used in the actual implementation of the routine. Often abbreviated TOCTOU.

time quantum The length of time that a task is scheduled before being preempted.

timer interrupt A hardware processor interrupt that signifies a period of elapsed real time.

time-sharing operating system An operating system designed to support interactive use of the computer.

TLB See translation lookaside buffer.

TLB hit A TLB lookup that succeeds at finding a valid address translation.

TLB miss A TLB lookup that fails because the TLB does not contain a valid translation for that virtual address.

TLB shootdown A request to another processor to remove a newly invalid TLB entry.

TOCTOU See: time of check vs. time of use attack.

translation lookaside buffer A small hardware table containing the results of recent address translations.

trap A synchronous transfer of control from a user-level process to a kernel-mode handler. Traps can be caused by processor exceptions, memory protection errors, or system calls.

two-phase locking A strategy for acquiring locks needed by a multi-operation request, where no lock can be released before all required locks have been acquired.

unsafe state (deadlock) A state of an execution such that there is at least one sequence of future resource requests that leads to deadlock no matter what processing order is tried.

upcall An event, interrupt, or exception delivered by the kernel to a user-level process.

use bit A status bit in a page table entry recording whether the page has been recently referenced.

user-level memory management The kernel assigns each process a set of page frames, but how the process uses its assigned memory is left up to the application.

user-level page handler An application-specific upcall routine invoked by the kernel on a page fault.

user-level thread A type of application thread where the thread is created, runs, and finishes without calls into the operating system kernel.

user-mode operation The processor operates in a restricted mode that limits the capabilities of the executing process. Compare: kernel-mode operation.

utilization The fraction of time a resource is busy.

virtual address An address that must be translated to produce an address in physical memory.

virtual machine An execution context provided by an operating system that mimics a physical machine, e.g., to run an operating system as an application on top of another operating system.

virtual machine honeypot A virtual machine constructed for the purpose of executing suspect code in a safe environment.

virtual machine monitor See: host operating system.

virtual memory The illusion of a nearly infinite amount of physical memory, provided by demand paging of virtual addresses.

virtualization Provide an application with the illusion of resources that are not physically present.

virtually addressed cache A processor cache which is accessed using virtual, rather than physical, memory addresses.

wait while holding A necessary condition for deadlock to occur: a thread holds one resource while waiting for another.

wait-free data structures Concurrent data structure that guarantees progress for every thread: every method finishes in a finite number of steps, regardless of the state of other threads executing in the data structure.

waiting list The set of threads that are waiting for a synchronization event or timer expiration to occur before becoming eligible to be run.

web proxy cache A cache of frequently accessed web pages to speed web access and reduce network traffic.

work-conserving scheduling policy A policy that never leaves the processor idle if there is work to do.

working set The set of memory locations that a program has referenced in the recent past.

workload A set of tasks for some system to perform, along with when each task arrives and how long each task takes to complete.

wound wait An approach to deadlock recovery that ensures progress by aborting the most recent transaction in any deadlock.

write-back cache A cache where updates can be stored in the cache and only sent to memory when the cache runs out of space.

write-through cache A cache where updates are sent immediately to memory.

zero-copy I/O A technique for transferring data across the kernel-user boundary without a memory-to-memory copy, e.g., by manipulating page table entries.

zero-on-reference A method for clearing memory only if the memory is used, rather than in advance. If the first access to memory triggers a trap to the kernel, the kernel can zero the memory and then resume.

Zipf distribution The relative frequency of an event is inversely proportional to its position in a rank order of popularity.

Index

About The Authors

Thomas Anderson is the Robert E. Dinning Professor of Computer Science and Engineering at the University of Washington, where he has been teaching computer science since 1997.

Professor Anderson has been widely recognized for his work, receiving the Diane S. McEntyre Award for Excellence in Teaching, the USENIX Lifetime Achievement Award, the the IEEE Koji Kobayashi Computers and Communications Award, the ACM SIGOPS Mark Weiser Award, the USENIX Software Tools User Group Award, the IEEE Communications Society William R. Bennett Prize, the NSF Presidential Faculty Fellowship, and the Alfred P. Sloan Research Fellowship. He is an ACM Fellow. He has served as program co-chair of the ACM SIGCOMM Conference and program chair of the ACM Symposium on Operating Systems Principles (SOSP). In 2003, he helped co-found the USENIX/ACM Symposium on Networked Systems Design and Implementation (NSDI).

Professor Anderson's research interests span all aspects of building practical, robust, and efficient computer systems, including operating systems, distributed systems, computer networks, multiprocessors, and computer security. Over his career, he has authored or co-authored over one hundred peer-reviewed papers; eighteen of his papers have won best paper awards.

Michael Dahlin is a Principal Engineer at Google. Prior to that, from 1996 to 2014, he was a Professor of Computer Science at the University of Texas in Austin, where he taught operating systems and other subjects as and where he was awarded the College of Natural Sciences Teaching Excellence Award.

Professor Dahlin's research interests include Internet- and large-scale services, fault tolerance, security, operating systems, distributed systems, and storage systems.

Professor Dahlin's work has been widely recognized. Over his career, he has authored over seventy peer reviewed papers; ten of which have won best paper awards. He is both an ACM Fellow and an IEEE Fellow, and he has received an Alfred P. Sloan Research Fellowship and an NSF CAREER award. He has served as the program chair of the ACM Symposium on Operating Systems Principles (SOSP), co-chair of the USENIX/ACM Symposium on Networked Systems Design and Implementation (NSDI), and co-chair of the International World Wide Web conference (WWW).

36380186R00385

Made in the USA
San Bernardino, CA
22 July 2016